Mary Pride's
Complete
Guide to
Getting Started in
Homeschooling

Mary Pride's Complete Guide to Getting Started in Homeschooling

MARY PRIDE

A PRACTICAL HOMESCHOOLING® BOOK

HARVEST HOUSE PUBLISHERS
EUGENE, OREGON

Mary Pride's Complete Guide to Getting Started in Homeschooling
Copyright ©2004 by Home Life, Inc.
Published by Harvest House Publishers
Eugene, Oregon 97402

Library of Congress Cataloging-in-Publication Data:
Pride, Mary
   Mary Pride's complete guide to getting started in homeschooling / Mary Pride.
     p. cm.
   Includes bibliographical references and indexes.
   ISBN 0-7369-0918-4 (v. 1)—ISBN 0-7369-0919-2 (v. 2)—
ISBN 0-7369-0920-6 (v. 3)
     1. Home schooling—United States. 2. Home schooling—Curricula—United States.
3. Education—Parent participation—United States. 4. Child rearing—United States.
I. Title: Complete guide to getting started in homeschooling. II. Title.
   LC40.P75 2002
   371.04'2—dc21   2001051579

Cover by Terry Dugan Design, Minneapolis, MN.

Clip art image page 55 provided by ©1990 Dynamic Graphics, Inc.

Quotes from *Phyllis Schlafly Report* are reprinted by permission from the Phyllis Schlafly Report, PO Box 618, Alton, IL 62002 www.eagleforum.org/psr. This is an indispensable source of cut-to-the-chase, thoroughly documented information on the major threats arising to our freedoms of education, family life, and citizenship. Well worth the $20 annual subscription fee.

Quotes from the *Education Advocate* are used by permission of The Commonwealth Education Organization (CEO), a nonprofit, nonpartisan organization that disseminates information on a broad array of school issues to parents, taxpayers, educators and political leaders. For more information, contact CEO at 90 Beta Drive, Pittsburgh, PA 15238. 412.967.9691, info@ceopa.org, www.ceopa.org. Fax: 412.967.9694. Email: ceo@telerama.com. An annual subscription to their excellent and informative newsletter is $10.

Liability Disclaimer

We trust our readers to be intelligent human beings who can benefit from our information in the spirit in which it is offered—as a help to making your own decisions, not as a replacement for them. We have made every effort to ensure that the information contained in this book is reliable. However, since products change and companies come and go, neither the editor, the reviewers, nor the publisher can warrant or guarantee this information.

It is the reader's responsibility to check out current prices, product availability, and so forth before making a final purchasing decision regarding any product or company mentioned in this book. You are also responsible to check out the company from which you intend to purchase the product, to make sure it is capable of delivering the product and offering the kind of customer service and support you expect. Although we have done what we can to check out the bona fides of companies mentioned in this book, we cannot be responsible for any problems customers may encounter with them in the future. We shall not assume any liability for any loss or damage caused or alleged to be caused directly or indirectly by suggestions found in this book or by products reviewed in it.

Trademarks

In this book we review or mention hundreds of trademarked products and company names. Rather than clutter up the book with trademark symbols, we state we are using each trademarked name only for editorial purposes and to the benefit of the trademark owner with no intent to infringe any trademark.

Printed in the United States of America

04 05 06 07 08 09 10 11 12 13 / RDW/ 10 9 8 7 6 5 4 3 2 1

Contents

MICHAEL FARRIS

Foreword

The power of Mary Pride's writing cannot be overestimated. She has been one of the truly exceptional voices throughout the revitalization of American home education for the past two decades. She has helped change homeschooling. She has helped to change my family in a very big way.

Vickie and I were happily raising our three daughters and had been introduced to the concept of homeschooling in spring of 1982. It sounded like a good idea so we thought we would try it. In September of that year we began homeschooling Christy, our oldest, who was then in the second grade.

It wasn't very many years later when a friend handed us a volume that became known in our family as "the pink book"—aka *The Way Home* by Mary Pride. Vickie had become convinced that we should let God plan the size of our family after reading this book. She wanted me to read it. I didn't want to. I didn't want to even think about the possibility of changing my mind, but eventually I succumbed and read it. While I didn't agree with everything, there was a central argument I couldn't shake. God says that children are a blessing. My decisions were saying that God was wrong. I changed my mind.

Jessica, Angie, Michael, Jr., Emily, Jonathan, Joseph, and Peter have all been added to our family since we began homeschooling. Even though we probably would have had four or five children without changing our fundamental convictions, God used Mary's writing to change our mind and change our lives. (Vickie has chronicled all of this in more detail in her mom-encouraging book, *A Mom Just Like You,* now published by Broadman & Holman.)

I have recommended earlier versions of *Mary Pride's Complete Guide* to thousands of people. It remains one of the classic works of home education—even though because of the nature of the content it must be a constantly updated classic. But Mary continues to do all the things that made her book a classic in the first place. She researches. She makes good analyses. She writes her analysis in clear, crisp, and often funny prose.

Homeschooling is a challenging task for any mother, regardless of your family size. And Mary helps moms with what I consider the number one rule for curriculum choice—it had better be user-friendly for Mom. If it isn't user friendly for Mom, don't buy it.

Michael Farris is the founder of Home School Legal Defense Association, where he now serves as Chairman and General Counsel. In recognition for his work in home education, *Education Week* magazine

named Farris one of the top "100 Faces of the 20th Century" in the field of education. In September 2000, Farris was inaugurated as the first President of Patrick Henry College, the first college in America with a homeschooled majority in the student body. PHC is a Christian college blending classical instruction with apprenticeship methodology. He is the author of nine books, including three novels. The latest, *Forbid Them Not,* a legal thriller portraying life under the UN Convention on the Rights of the Child, was released in January 2002. Mike and his wife, Vickie, are the parents of 10 homeschooled children and have six grandchildren.

The truth is, however, what is user-friendly for one mom is quite cumbersome for other moms. Just as children have learning styles, moms have their own styles and strengths as well. *Mary Pride's Complete Guide* gives moms (and dads who want to be helpful) the ability to assess materials in light of their own strengths and their own style. Mary recognizes that one size doesn't fit all and helps you make your own choices with good analyses, not coercive directives.

The materials available to homeschoolers are getting better and more numerous. Mary and her staff of experienced homeschool reviewers and writers make the whole world of homeschool curriculum user-friendly for moms and dads by their diligent, creative, and comprehensive work.

Preface to This New Edition

Hi! I'm Mary Pride, and this is where you can find out the history of the book you are now holding in your hands.

It Used to Be Called the "Big Book"

Way back when dinosaurs roamed the earth, or at least as far back as 1985, homeschoolers didn't have very much in the way of how-to books and curriculum resources. Most of us didn't even know where to find the resources that were available. So I thought it would be a good idea if "someone" came out with a resource guide for homeschoolers.

"Someone" turned out to be me, as I managed to obtain the entire curriculum of a dozen and a half major publishers and reviewed them all in detail. That slim spiral-bound booklet was called *The Curriculum Buyer's Guide*.

Meanwhile, I had the bright idea of including a chapter about homeschooling in a book I was writing. That chapter became an entire book: *The Big Book of Home Learning*. Then came a second edition, which was two oversized books in size, and the third edition, which was four large volumes. For the fourth edition, we scaled back to three books, but we made them each bigger.

Now I have a new publisher, and the new edition of my book has a new name: *Mary Pride's Complete Guide to Getting Started in Homeschooling*. Although like most folks I like the sound of my own name, I did not decide to name the book after myself. This was one of those decisions made by the marketing people, who figured:

(a) I was pretty well known by now after writing all those books, starting our website, and publishing my magazine.
(b) Most people could see for themselves they were getting a "big" book.
(c) "Pride" rhymes with "Guide," which is a good thing in book titles.

This is the way I looked when I was putting together the last edition. Check out the back cover to see how the years, and a really bad haircut, have taken their toll.

What's New in the Format

We have added *lots* more photos! We have also changed the format of the contact information. Since companies' addresses change more frequently than their toll-free numbers or websites, we have decided to just provide the state, rather than the entire street address. This lets you know which time zone you're calling without cluttering up the margins with soon-to-be-outdated information. So "Focus on the Family Publishing, CO," means that Focus on the Family is in Colorado. If you need a company's street address, it is almost always readily available via their website address (which we do provide) under the "Contact Us" or "About Us" menu.

Also please note that all *unsigned* reviews are by me, Mary Pride. I don't love my name so much that I want to see it everywhere, and I thought you'd get pretty tired of it too.

What's New in This Edition

Those of you dear, wonderful people who have faithfully purchased edition after edition of *The Big Book of Home Learning* will notice we've added many new chapters and several entire new sections to this edition. In particular, most of the "Education 101" section is new, as is most of the "Unit Studies" section and all of the "Homeschooling with a School or Group" and "Homeschooling Away from Home" section. New chapters include "How Has Homeschooling Changed?" "Seven New Reasons to Homeschool," "Laptop Homeschooling," "The Maloney Method," and "The WholeHearted Method." You'll also find new appendixes, a new resource guide, and of course updated information, statistics, and resources all through this entire book.

Why So Informal?

Many of the bad things in our education system have come about because of an overreliance on "experts" who have flashy academic *credentials* but no real *expertise* or *results* they can point to. Such "experts" tend to mask their incompetence by authoritarian jargon and bureaucratic speech patterns. We old-time homeschoolers are allergic to this kind of verbal arrogance, and I, for one, have no intention of inflicting it on you. (Besides, it's *really* boring to read.)

What's Coming

This book will eventually be joined by its sister volumes, *Mary Pride's Complete Guide to Homeschooling from Birth to Grade 6* and *Mary Pride's Complete Guide to Homeschooling Grades 7–12*. Don't pester me if they aren't out yet by the time you read this; I'm doing the best I can, considering I still have seven children at home engaged at some level in homeschooling (our second-oldest son, Joseph, is at the Coast Guard Academy, and our oldest daughter, Sarah, is attending Patrick Henry College). Plus there's always another issue of *Practical Homeschooling* magazine to put out and more good stuff to add to our website, Homeschool World at www.home-school.com, where our oldest son, Ted, is the webmaster—be sure to drop in and visit us!

PART 1

What's It All About?

In 2000, homeschoolers swept the field in the Scripps Howard National Spelling Bee. Shown here is first-place winner George Thampy, grade 7, from Maryland Heights, MO, receiving the winner's trophy from Scripps-Howard News Service Chief Operating Officer Ken Lowe. This win was George's third appearance in the Spelling Bee. In 1998 he tied for fourth place and in 1999 he took third. Before that, as our family knows from personal experience, he had many years of winning in local and regional spelling bees here in Missouri.

Mark Bowen © Scripps Howard News Service

Second place 2000 Spelling Bee winner Sean Conley was also homeschooled. Sean represented the San Francisco Examiner. We see him here spelling "mackinaw" correctly in the fourth round. The year before, Sean placed ninth. In 2000, he hung on for 14 rounds, finally missing the unlikely word "apotropaic."

Homeschooler Alison Miller captured third place in 2000. Here we see her in Round 1, at the beginning of the national Spelling Bee. Alison woke herself up two hours early every morning for two months to study her spelling words, and it paid off!

CHAPTER 1

What's So Great About Homeschooling?

Are you one of those people who was not in the 99th percentile on every test? Have you learned to think of yourself as an "average" person, or perhaps even "slow"? Are you one of the millions who entered kindergarten with bright-eyed enthusiasm but who lost their love of learning along the way? If you are, then this book is for you.

Or perhaps you *were* in the 99th percentile. You soared gracefully through school while others waddled. This book is for you too.

Has your child been labeled "learning disabled" or "dyslexic" or "retarded" (or even "gifted")? Have you have gone around and around with the school, trying to find out what the label means and what the school plans to do about it? Are you looking for a sensible way to help your child, one that doesn't depend on federal funding or special programs? Would you like to see *dramatic* improvement in your child's academic progress? The sources that can help you are right here.

Maybe you have already decided to teach your children at home. You look at the schools near you and are not thrilled at the prospect of incarcerating your children in them for 13 years. You have precious values that you want to pass on, and you are determined to fight for your children's souls and minds. This book is *especially* for you!

Learning at home is the magic key that millions of people have used to unlock the educational treasure-chest. No longer must you or your children climb the academic beanstalk in competition with a hundred other Jacks, each of whom can only succeed by knocking his fellows off into the depths. No longer must you spend a fortune on college credits for knowledge offered elsewhere for a pittance. No longer must you watch your child shrivel up under the burden of a label that some trendy educrat has stuck on him or her. In the comfort and privacy of your own home you can learn whatever you want to, whenever you want to—and so can your children.

> "When 40 percent of our eight-year-olds cannot read as well as they should, we have to do something."
> —*Former President Bill Clinton*

Current estimates now place the number of homeschooled children at over two million. That's a lot of practical, one-on-one teaching experience homeschoolers have gained over the past decade, since the movement changed from a tiny trickle into a full-grown flood.

While homeschoolers cover the entire political and lifestyle spectrum, we do have one thing in common:

> ## We believe that parents can do a great job of teaching their children at home.

No, let me put that more strongly:

> ## We know from experience that you can do a great job of teaching your children at home!

Homeschooled children consistently test academically ahead of public-schooled children. (See the detailed research summary in Appendix 1.) In most categories, they even surpass the test scores of children from the finest private schools. The one exception? Math computation speed. Moral: homeschool moms don't like math drills!

Generally, homeschooled children are at least one year ahead academically. When it comes to reasoning skills, homeschooled children test an unbelievable *seven years* ahead of public-school children!

The academic rocket boost homeschooling provides often translates into homeschooled children winning competitions. Although homeschooled kids are just a fraction of the schooled population, and most homeschoolers don't enter competitions (a situation I expect to change as information about contests become more accessible—see the chapter and appendix devoted to contests in this book), it's becoming more and more common for homeschoolers to win, place, or show in academic competitions of all kinds. A few prominent examples of some of these pioneering contestants:

- In 1997, a delighted Rebecca Sealfon was the first homeschooler to win the Scripps Howard National Spelling Bee. Three short years later, homeschoolers swept the Spelling Bee, winning first, second, *and* third places!
- In 1999, homeschooler Rio Bennin won the Intel Science Talent Search, the USA's most prestigious science competition for high schoolers. Accepted at Harvard, Berkeley, and Cambridge University in England, he chose to go to Harvard.
- Also in 1999, homeschooler David Biehl won the National Geography Bee.

Homeschooled kids are performing brilliantly in everything from music competitions, to science fairs, to writing competitions, to Latin and mythology competitions, to sports and martial arts. They have won essay contents, chess contests, and math contests. They have received community service awards and been recognized by members of Congress.

Homeschool graduates have been accepted into Ivy League universities such as Harvard and Yale. They have served with distinction in the military. They have joined apprenticeship programs, served as missionaries, and started their own businesses.

Often, they have done this at younger ages than their schooled counterparts. While nobody in the homeschool movement advocates whizzing through school for its own sake, thousands of homeschoolers have been mature enough and well enough prepared academically to start taking community-college or Advanced Placement courses at age 16 or earlier. Both are favored options for these younger children, because they save money, allow students of high-school age to accumulate credits toward a college degree in a more prominent institution, and allow kids to live at home when they might be too young to go away to college.

Freed by homeschooling from the necessity of following rigorous school schedules or attending class in one physical location, some families have shared adventures that range from sailing trips around the world to professional and semiprofessional careers in theatre, dance, circus, and other performing arts. Still others have become expert cyberspace "netizens," creating their own websites, writing their own programs, publishing their own electronic newsletters, or attending online academies.

Take a look at the homeschooled kids featured on the section pages throughout this book for just a small taste of the success homeschoolers are enjoying. Truly, homeschooling has more than proved itself as a road to success in education . . . and in life.

But man does not live by test scores alone; most parents choose homeschooling for reasons beyond academics. The list of public school deficiencies is familiar and depressing:

The 15 Habits of Highly Defective Schooling

- drugs
- violence
- gangs
- morally and theologically questionable curriculum
- peer pressure
- an alarming number of teachers who can't pass basic competency tests
- censorship of traditional religion
- plummeting test scores
- dumbed-down curriculum

- age segregation (the notion that people learn best in the company of dozens of people exactly their own age)
- isolation from community life
- busywork
- little to no one-to-one interaction with the teacher
- lockstep learning (your child has to learn at the same speed as everyone else)
- lack of opportunities to pursue special projects and interests

In all these areas where public schools fall short, homeschools excel.

Ten Ways Homeschool Beats "Regular" School

1. **"Isolation from community life."** Not a chance! For most homeschool families, Friday is Field Trip Day. Everyone piles in the car to visit local businesses and educational attractions. Many homeschool children volunteer or work in the community on a regular basis. And *all* of us hang out at the library!

Unusual Homeschool Fact: According to *Library Journal*, homeschoolers now account for a staggering 20 percent of all library checkouts!

A SENATOR SPEAKS OUT ON VIOLENCE IN THE SCHOOLS

"Mr. President . . . I was reading just the other day a prominent survey of the condition in elementary schools. It is fairly alarming. It suggested that 4 out of 10 students in elementary school today are frightened by some aspect or fearful of violence in the school. Mr. President, the survey concluded that 3 out of 10 students in elementary school will have property stolen from them in the schools. It suggested that 1 out of 10 will be confronted with a deadly weapon while they are in school.

"So, 4 in 10 are fearful; 3 in 10 are going to be robbed; 1 in 10 is going to face a weapon; and all of them will tell you the nature of drugs and the availability of drugs. . . ."

—*Senator Paul Coverdell, Remarks before the Senate of the United States, Sept. 22, 1997*

LIBRARIANS LOVE US . . . AND WE LOVE THEM!

Since 1995, librarians everywhere have been making serious efforts to cater to homeschoolers. In February of that year, *Library Journal* ran a lengthy article reviewing dozens of homeschool books and magazines.

Now there even is a book for librarians on the sole subject of how to serve homeschool families!

2. **"Drugs, violence, and gangs."** Not in my backyard! It's extremely rare for a homeschooled child to be charged with any crime. In the few instances we're aware of, the child had until recently been educated in a school situation. Jails are not packed with homeschooled kids; they are packed with people who have had the benefit of ten or more years of being "socialized" in public schools. Added benefit: homeschooled children don't have to cope with increasingly unsafe school environments.

3. **"Little to no interaction with teacher."** You wish! As opposed to regular school classes, where the teacher asks all the questions, homeschool provides children with the chance to ask *their* questions without fear of other children calling them names for doing so. This means you answer a *lot* of questions!

4. **"Lockstep learning."** Not a problem at home. If your child doesn't "get it," you can always come back to that lesson in a day, a week, a month, or even a year. If, on the other hand, he wants to zoom ahead, you can feed him the advanced courses he craves without the social problems he would face in public school.

5. **"Censorship of traditional religion."** At home we are free to move beyond the Easter bunny and Santa Claus. We are also not forced to endure having our children subjected to one-sided propaganda for religious and philosophical points of view that we disagree with.

6. **"Peer pressure."** Did you know that the number one predictor of whether your child will be a genius or not is how much time he spends with adults? It's true! As the Bible says, "He who walks with the wise becomes wise, but a companion of fools suffers harm."

7. **"Lack of opportunities to pursue special projects and interests."** We have a section in our magazine, *Practical Homeschooling*, where we print photos of homeschooled kids who have won various contests or done special projects. Over the years these have ranged from model rocketry to designing stamps for the Post Office. It's a lot easier to talk Mom and Dad into letting you do these things than to get a classroom teacher to redesign the year's curriculum to accommodate your child's special interest!

8, 9, and 10. **"Dumbed-down curriculum . . . busywork . . . morally questionable curriculum."** Not a problem if you own this book!

Three Big Advantages of Homeschooling

Three advantages of learning at home that you'll notice right away are *price*, *freedom*, and *options*. Home educational products come wrapped in Kraft paper and delivered by the mailman. Classroom products come wrapped in classrooms (very expensive) and delivered by the school administration (likewise, very expensive). Home learning can be done at your convenience, and in most cases there are no deadlines at all.

At home, you have thousands of choices at your fingertips. Away from home, you either are limited to whatever options are offered in your geographical area—or forced to pay exorbitant sums for transportation in order to get to that great seminar in San Diego or that workshop in Bangor, Maine. At home nobody nags you or grades you unless you want them to. Schools, however, *run* on grades, and you must do the work *they* require when *they* want you to do it and in the way *they* want you to do it, or you come away empty-handed.

Let's look at how you can reap the advantages of price, freedom, and options by learning at home.

PRICE

What do you think you'd pay for private guitar lessons from guitar legend Doc Watson? $100 per hour? $200? More? Homespun Tapes will sell you 90 minutes of this Grammy Award winner on video, teaching you all his tricks for just $39.95. This amounts to actually ten or more hours' worth of lessons, as in person you would be taking a considerable amount of lesson time practicing the techniques. Further, you can rewind the tapes and hear Doc Watson over and over again. No real-life teacher is *that* patient! When you count these latter factors in, the price of a lesson from a musical master comes to less than the price your next-door neighbor would charge.

What would it cost for you to send your child to one of the top private schools in the country? The going rate is now over $7,000 per year for these elite schools, and even those who have money are often turned away because there are fewer places than would-be students. You can, however, get one year of the Calvert School program, including teacher grading and counseling, for between $850 and $900. Calvert's home-taught graduates consistently demonstrate the same achievement as its classroom students. You have thus purchased virtually all the benefits of one of the nation's most exclusive schools at a fraction of the in-person price.

FREEDOM

School, like time and Amtrak, waits for no man. The oldest grandfather in graduate school has no more freedom than the youngest preschooler when it comes to deciding *when* he wants to learn. The whole class must lurch forward at once, and laggards are left holding a lonely "F."

Under our present inefficient "credentialing" system, which focuses more on classroom attendance than actual knowledge and experience, education becomes a form of involuntary servitude. You give up control of your own life in order to (you hope) gain that coveted credential. You are not allowed to proceed at your own pace or select the educational content or method you prefer. This applies equally to children and adults, with the major difference being that adults can switch from one institution to another or walk away from the whole thing if they are totally disgusted, whereas children usually have no choices at all.

At home, you are in control. You can pick and choose from a variety of sources instead of being tied down to whatever is physically available in your area. You can do the work when it is convenient for you. If you are looking for knowledge, not credentials, you can skip the whole stupefying mass of busywork and tests and concentrate only on what interests you. Learning becomes a pleasant adventure rather than a burden.

OPTIONS

Lovers of the offbeat and unusual are sure to be delighted with the educational offerings available at home. From talking globes to authentic pioneer stories to science riddles, the homeschool market is popping with surprises! Buy a bridge-building construction kit for your granddaughter! Find out how to teach decimals with colorful "french fries"! Dance about the room to grammar songs! Cut out and assemble a Viking village! Play a grammar card game!

Some items you need are available *only* at home. You can't just bop down to the local Wal-Mart and pick up the organizers reviewed in this volume, for example. And I am seeing an increasing number of products

THE ROLE OF PARENTS IN EDUCATION

My son, hear the instruction of thy father, and forsake not the law of thy mother;

For they shall be an ornament of grace unto thy head, and chains about thy neck.

—King Solomon (Proverbs 1:8,9)

specifically designed for families learning at home, from complete curriculum to clever games and teaching devices.

On reading instruction, are you stuck with whatever method the local school uses, no matter how poorly your children respond? Not at all! There are dozens of excellent programs, and although most public schools and even a goodly number of private schools pass them by (witness our national illiteracy), that doesn't mean *you* can't rescue *your* children by reaching for *Alpha-Phonics* or *Sing, Spell, Read and Write*.

And, thanks to community organizations, co-ops, and innovative new schooling options (all covered later in this book), your children can also enjoy group learning activities. In fact, homeschooled kids on the average participate in *more* such activities than schooled kids!

Change Your Child, Change the World

In the long run, any positive transformation of our culture has to begin at home. If everyone lived the way most homeschool families live, there wouldn't be any crime, broken families, or wars.

You're in the right place to make a real difference in the lives of your children and everyone whose lives they touch. At home you can give your children a safe, happy childhood . . . a superior, caring education . . . and help them grow into people who will care for their own children and reach out to make a difference in the lives of others.

There is no more important task.

CHAPTER 2

How Has Homeschooling Changed?

A lot has changed for homeschoolers over the past few years.

- The homeschooling movement has continued to grow, now exceeding 2 million children by conservative estimates.
- A flood of homeschool curriculum has been released, both from companies that have always supported homeschooling and more recently from companies that traditionally only sold to teachers and schools.
- Homeschoolers' shopping habits have changed: Curriculum fair sales are down and Internet shopping is way, way up.
- The media have finally begun to notice homeschooling in a big way. They often get the story wrong, but more on that later.

The type of parents looking at homeschooling has also changed. Rob Shearer, founder of Greenleaf Press, has been known to describe the changing face of homeschooling something like this:

- The original homeschoolers were the **pioneers**. Starting from scratch, with no support networks or readily available curriculum, these families broke new ground for those who followed, including fighting the initial legal battles.
- The next wave of homeschoolers was the **settlers**. Building on the work of the pioneers, they expanded the homeschool community to include many more resources, organizations, and activities.
- Next came the **refugees**. Fleeing what they saw as intolerable conditions in the schools, this group arrived with less research and organization-building experience under their belts. They were happy to find that a well-organized homeschool community already existed, and more than willing to make use of its many offerings.
- Now that homeschooling has become so well established, there are even **tourists**—people who aren't extremely sold on homeschooling but are willing to "check it out" because they've heard good things about it.

Old Definition of Homeschooling: You Do All the Work

You, the parent, pick all the books, workbooks, and other resources, and do all the teaching. (It never actually worked exactly this way, but this is what the media and the public have always thought of as "homeschooling"—i.e., school at home.)

New Definition of Homeschooling: You Do the Research and You're In Charge

You and your children work together to pick the resources—including outside-the-home classes and learning adventures—that will become your homeschool curriculum. You, the parent, teach some courses and supervise the rest.

Key to this definition is that the parents, not school authorities, are in charge, and you have the authority and ability to change the homeschool curriculum and schedule at any time. Surrendering authority and oversight to any school, tutor, organization, or individual is not homeschooling.

How Far Will You Go?

Another big change in the last few years is in the length of time families plan to homeschool. In the past, the majority of families homeschooled through elementary school, with some putting their kids back into school at the junior-high level, and most putting their kids back in by the end of high school.

However, according to *The Home School Court Report* of July/August 2001, a survey of 1,800 Home School Legal Defense Association family members revealed that only 1 percent plan to end homeschooling after elementary school. Seven percent plan to homeschool through middle school, **83 percent plan to homeschool all the way through the end of high school**, and a surprising **9 percent plan to homeschool through college!**

This change is partly due to the increasingly unsafe conditions and morally unpleasant environment in the schools. It's also been caused by the vastly improved availability of resources for homeschooling high-school-age students, from tutorial videos and DVDs to online academies and correspondence programs. The outstanding success of so many homeschool graduates doesn't hurt, either!

The Charter School Option

Also new on the homeschool landscape: charter schools. Supposedly a great way to homeschool with little effort at government expense, the charter school option comes with a hidden price tag. See the chapter on that subject later in this book.

Are you a tourist . . . refugee . . . settler . . . or grizzled old pioneer? Who cares! The important thing is that you're *here.*

While the pioneers and settlers rightly deserve honor for what they have built, there's no reason for the next generations of homeschoolers to feel bad because they didn't have to reinvent the wheel. There's no particular virtue in suffering for its own sake. Heaven knows I wouldn't have struggled through all those books on education and spent years comparing curricula if someone else had done it for me!

Everyone who even considers homeschooling is thinking about *what is best for their children,* and you can't beat that for a starting point!

It is my sincere hope that if you fit into the "refugee" or "tourist" category, you'll find the help in this book that encourages you to become a permanent part of the homeschool community.

How Your Job Has Changed

Originally, homeschooling operated like this:

1. You picked a textbook-and-workbook curriculum.
2. You learned how to teach it to your children. This second step could be tough, as the curricula in question were all written for classroom use, replete with educational jargon and loaded with activities that were way too time-consuming for home use.

Today, most of the "how to" has been done for you. The vast majority of popular homeschool materials are written just for homeschoolers from the get-go, meaning they are very easy for the average parent to use. You no longer need to become Super Teacher (although of course, knowing a lot about teaching never hurts). Instead, you are Super Shopper, Super Organizer, and Teacher-in-Progress.

Your new job is to design a curriculum ideally suited to your children, using the vast menu of options available and the vast number of community resources available. Organization and follow-through have become more important than the ability to teach every single subject all by yourself

You might not even have to teach some subjects, as you can draw upon:

- School classes and activities (take one here and one there without signing up your child as a full-time student)
- Tutoring centers, such as Sylvan and Kumon
- Sports and recreational activities sponsored by your local support group
- Classes at community organizations, such as the Jewish Community Center or YMCA
- Groups with educational programs, such as 4-H and Civil Air Patrol
- Tutors and mentors of all kinds, from older siblings and relatives to neighbors, friends, and other trusted adults
- Online academies, homework help centers, and tutoring sites
- Educational software that actually teaches—it's not all "drill and kill" nowadays!
- Educational videos and DVDs
- Educational audiocassettes and CDs
- Self-instructional materials for your older children

In short, you are called on to be more of a conductor of the educational orchestra than a one-man band.

This book's section on Homeschooling Away from Home will help you find and take advantage of these many additional learning opportunities.

Who Are These Wacky Homeschoolers, Anyway?

Aside from the plethora of new curricula and support options, a lot about homeschooling remains the same. The very same organizations that built the present homeschool movement are still around, run by the very same types of people and offering the same annual conferences, newsletters, support groups, lobbying services, and so forth.

However, you've probably seen at least one magazine or newspaper article about homeschooling that goes like this:

> *"Years ago, homeschooling was the province of right-wing Christian fanatics and hippie kooks, but now it's become mainstream. Yes, normal people can homeschool today."*

The funny thing is, I was there when the modern homeschooling movement started, and I distinctly remember it including people from the following groups:

- Catholics
- Protestants
- Jews
- Mormons
- Seventh-Day Adventists
- Agnostics
- Atheists
- Baha'is
- Buddhists
- New Agers
- Amish
- Mennonites
- Etc.

and also . . .

- Poor folks
- Rich folks
- In-between folks
- Moms in jeans
- Moms in long dresses
- Moms in jumpers
- Dads with beards
- Dads without beards
- People with PhDs
- High school dropouts
- Voters
- Nonvoters
- Pacifists
- Members of the military
- People on houseboats
- City dwellers
- Farm folk
- Suburbanites
- Doctors and lawyers
- Housewives
- Blue-collar workers
- Etc.

From the beginning, homeschooling was a diverse movement in terms of the wide range of people who were homeschooling. Yes, there was a majority of Bible-believing Christians and a smaller, but noticeable, segment of hippies and ex-hippies. In some cases the same people were in both groups. And yes, in fact, unschoolers led the way, and Bible-believing Christians developed most of the existing organizations and curriculum. But there was never a *requirement* that you had to own goats or be a Bible scholar in order to homeschool.

What such media writers and commentators are really saying is, "Now that it's undeniable that homeschooling is a strong, vibrant movement that produces academic excellence, we are loath to give credit for its success to despised groups such as ex-hippies and Bible-believing Christians. We would

Straight from the Fox's Mouth

Legal in all 50 states since the 1980s, homeschooling has often been criticized as a paranoid practice of right-wing religious fanatics that stunts children's emotional growth.

But as that first generation of homeschoolers settles into young adulthood, the criticism is proving unfounded. If anything, some experts say, the homeschoolers are proving to be better prepared for adulthood than their traditionally schooled peers.

—*Robin Wallace, "First Wave of Homeschoolers Comes of Age," Fox News, April 5, 2002*

HOMESCHOOL NATION

If you're interested in the history of homeschooling from the perspective of a highly qualified outsider, see the write-up of **Kingdom of Children** by Mitchell L. Stevens in chapter 10.

prefer to believe that the reason the homeschool movement is so strong is that folks like us are finally homeschooling. Also, our biases against Bible-believing Christians make it impossible for us to believe that new homeschoolers who aren't Christian can be welcomed except by other non-Christians."

Sorry, folks. Very little of the heavy lifting that started the homeschool movement was done by Hollywood, Madison Avenue, or the mainstream press. It was done by the parents who were most concerned about their children's education, from both sides of the political spectrum.

Thanks to the power of their belief that it's OK and even good for moms to raise their own children at home, Bible-believing Christians are the majority of homeschoolers to this day. Thanks to their comfort with organization and chain-of-command authority, most of the homeschool organizations are also run by Bible-believing Christians or Catholics, according to Christian principles. Those who find this situation uncomfortable have founded their own homeschool groups, but these new groups are by no means the driving force behind modern homeschooling.

Think of it like this. Most of the original 13 American colonies were founded by Christians, according to Christian principles. Yet non-Christians were always welcome as immigrants. Those who had trouble getting along under the existing Christian governments went off and founded their own colonies. And finally, all the colonies, overtly Christian or not, banded together against the might of the British Empire and won their freedom.

Yet none of the states that grew out of the original colonies are Christian today. With the lessons of history in mind, the leaders of Christian homeschool organizations want to preserve their freedom to have Christian prayers at meetings, Christian speakers, and other religious freedoms. This means that, when challenged years ago to merge with all other state groups into one larger secular organization, the Christian groups said no.

The individual states were able to retain their identity while working together for their political freedom. That's why the country they formed is called the *United* States of America. Similarly, today's homeschool movement consists of all kinds of parents, a majority of them Christian, who care fervently about their children's education, all standing together for academic freedom—as it has from the very beginning.

Everyone Is Welcome!

The "Show & Tell" feature in *Practical Homeschooling* is where we spotlight the special achievements of homeschooled students. The section pages of this book you are now holding are adorned with some of these kids and their successes.

When I first started the magazine, most of the kids whose photos I printed were white Anglos, because most homeschoolers were white Anglos. Lately I've been seeing more photos of kids from other groups, which is a good thing!

Up to this point, the major division among homeschool groups has been between Christian ("believers") and secular ("inclusive," meaning everyone is welcome but no religious point of view may be promoted). There has been absolutely no exclusion on racial or ethnic lines, and I don't expect there ever will be.

Heightened parental involvement is the greatest indicator of future educational success. By homeschooling, you are automatically entering the upper zone of parental involvement and can expect success *whatever* curriculum and method you choose.

Don't let anyone scare you off because "homeschooling isn't a thing people in our group do." You just take the lead, and sooner or later your skeptical friends will be asking you how *they* can homeschool!

The Homeschool Way

One thing that hasn't changed: Homeschooling, by its nature, is extremely personal. We are doing this out of love for our families, and that carries over into interest about other people's families.

In fact, the homeschooling movement itself resembles an enormous family! I have seen numerous instances where homeschoolers who only knew each other through an online message board have prayed for each other's needs and sent gifts of various sorts to help when times were tough. At homeschool events, you can really feel this sense of "family," as all the kids make friends so easily and all the parents seem to share an instant rapport. It's not uncommon to see a fashion-model-thin mom in a designer dress, high heels, jewelry, and makeup talking earnestly with a makeup-free mom wearing an old denim jumper and sneakers, or a 14-year-old patiently showing an eight-year-old how to fold a piece of origami. The "in" crowd, such as it is, are the families that work the hardest providing services for the others, and becoming part of it is as easy as volunteering to help put away the chairs after a meeting. In the homeschool world, a person is known by their character, not the color of their skin, the number of their PhDs, or the size of their bank account.

Whoever you are, if you love your kids, you've found a home.

CHAPTER 3

Answers to Your Questions About Homeschooling

I f you're considering homeschooling, you have lots of questions. If you've been homeschooling for any length of time, you've been *asked* lots of questions.

Here are some of the biggies:

- "What about socialization?"

- "Can homeschooled children get into college?"

- "Is it true that all homeschoolers have to bake their own bread and raise goats?"

"FAQ" stands for Frequently Asked Questions. On the Internet, an FAQ list is where "newbies" (new users) find the answers to their questions so veteran users don't have to answer them again and again.

Homeschoolers definitely need an FAQ list.

And here it is!

"Is it legal?"

Homeschooling is legal, under varying conditions, in every state and territory of the USA, every province of Canada, and in England, Scotland, Ireland,

The one and only question *not* to ask about homeschooling is,

"Where can I find someone to homeschool my child?"

You can:

- Join a homeschool co-op (in which you will have to do some work)
- Enroll your child in a parent-run school
- Hire a private tutor or tutors to teach *some* subjects

But a homeschool family can't "take in" your child unless they are willing to register as a private school and abide by the many private-school regulations, including building safety regs.

Wales, Australia, and New Zealand. Dependents of the US military are right now being homeschooled around the world, and the Home School Legal Defense Association (HSLDA) is working with parent groups and the authorities in several non-English-speaking countries to make it legal there as well.

In the United States, some states require you to register with the authorities. This is the most restrictive situation. Most allow you a range of options by which to show you are making a good faith effort to homeschool. Standardized testing, keeping a portfolio of the children's work, using a recognized curriculum, and keeping a log of the hours each child spends on school subjects are some common options. Some states also require certain subjects to be taught. These are most likely the subjects you plan to teach anyway.

One important piece of advice you *must* follow:

Very important: Check with your state homeschool group for their recommendations on compliance.

For example, if a state law *allows* you to register your homeschool but does not *require* it, the state group will probably recommend you *not* register, so as to discourage any attempts to build up a state database of all known homeschoolers.

The state leaders know the ins and outs of the law—after all, they probably helped draft parts of it!—and they are well aware of the battles that have been fought over how the law is to be interpreted, so my advice is to follow *their* advice.

See Appendix 2 to locate information about the laws in your state.

"Where do I sign up?"

Get ready for a shock. It's called "academic freedom," and it means that in many states you don't have to tell anyone or ask anyone's permission to homeschool. See Appendix 2 to locate information on the rules in your state.

Even in the more restrictive states, you generally only have to fill out a form telling the authorities you plan to homeschool, or at the very most listing your planned curriculum. For American parents, pleading with school authorities for permission to teach your own son or daughter is a thing of the past except in the People's Republic of Massachusetts.

There certainly is no official group you must join to be a bone fide homeschooler, though it is always smart to join your state group and the Home School Legal Defense Association (HSLDA). I'll explain how to do this in the chapter on "What to Join."

"Is there a required curriculum?"

Shock follows shock, as again we discover that in most states, you can use any curriculum you please. In some others, your curriculum must meet some fairly flexible minimum standards—e.g., it must teach subjects sequentially and progressively. Just don't plan to teach calculus before addition and composition before reading—as if you would!

Your state may require that you spend a certain number of hours on certain subjects, but not exactly what materials or methods you may use to teach those subjects. So put on your shopping shoes, limber up your computer mouse, and get your phone handy, because you're going to get to do some serious curriculum browsing!

"Where can I find homeschool curriculum?"

As soon as the other two volumes in this edition come out, you'll be all set. They'll each have hundreds of reviews, by grade level and subject, of all the curriculum you could possibly need, plus prices and full information on where to get it, so you'll be able to comparison shop from your easy chair.

In the meantime, at the back of this book you'll find a Quick Resource Guide with addresses, telephone numbers, and websites for plenty of homeschool curriculum publishers.

And be sure to send for the catalogs mentioned in Chapter 11!

"What does the research show about homeschooling?"

Turn to Appendix 1 for an easy-to-follow illustrated overview of research about homeschooling. I've also strewn nuggets of information in the margins throughout this book—look for them!

"Do I need a teaching certificate to homeschool?"

Not unless you're a nonmilitary family living in American Samoa. Nowhere else do you need a teaching certificate to homeschool, and for very good reason. Research has shown that whether or not a homeschool parent is a certified teacher makes absolutely no difference to their children's academic success. See Appendix 1 for more details.

"How can I get my GED at home?"

For some reason, this is one of the most-asked questions on our "Getting Started" online forum. The answer: You can't. The GED is only offered in authorized testing locations.

If you're a prospective homeschool parent whose state requires homeschooling parents to have a high-school diploma or pass the GED, your local bookstore has plenty of books on how to prepare for the GED.

For homeschool students, we *do not recommend* the GED as your proof of high-school completion. Colleges and the military look down (unfairly) on GED holders. Rather, you should put together a high-school transcript, just like any other school. I'll show you how to do this in *Mary Pride's Complete Guide to Homeschooling Grades 7–12*.

Since the GED test is owned by its producer, not by the government, they can and have made rules about how old a student must be before taking it. This varies from state to state, but never goes below 16 years of age, thus lessening its value as a way to show social-service and school authorities that your teenager is actually a high-school graduate who should not fall under the compulsory attendance laws. In such cases, your teen is better off taking the SAT and enrolling at least part-time in a local community college.

"What about socialization?"

SERIOUS ANSWER #1. A person who is well socialized is able to relate to people from a wide variety of age groups and lifestyles. Homeschooling is the ideal option for this type of training, as it affords the opportunity to relate to people in the real world rather than a fabricated world that is limited in scope to those who are within one or two years of being the same age of the student. Study after study has shown that homeschooled children excel in every area of "socialization."

**ACTIVITIES GALORE. . .
AND NOT JUST IN WICHITA!**

. . .In the [last] decade and a half, Wichita's home schoolers have hit adolescence. And with the legality of home schooling firmly established, homeschoolers have been joined by an exodus from the city's troubled public schools.

The result is a metropolitan area that today boasts 1,500 home-school families, many with teenage children demanding basketball teams, theater productions and science labs. So the home-school movement in Wichita has literally outgrown the home. Wichita's home schoolers boast three bands, a choir, a bowling group, a math club, a 4-H Club, boy- and girl-scout troops, a debate team, a yearly musical, two libraries and a cap-and-gown graduation. In donated rooms across Wichita, home schoolers attend classes in algebra, English, science, swimming, accounting, sewing, public speaking and Tae Kwan Do.

Parental support groups with names like BEST (Believing, Encouraging and Studying Together) and HOPE (Helping Other Parents Educate) crisscross the city, organizing field trips and swapping lesson plans. This year the Wichita Home School Warriors hosted two basketball tournaments, attended by 54 teams from around the U.S. and scouts from half a dozen colleges.

—TIME, *October 26, 1998*

NOT-QUITE-SERIOUS ANSWER #2. The jails are full of the products of public school socialization. Are homeschoolers likely to do worse?

SERIOUS ANSWER #3. There are two types of socialization: peer-group socialization ("babies teaching babies") and adult-child socialization (otherwise known as "mentoring," "walking with the wise," or "training"). In public schools, the adults are outnumbered as much as 30 to 1, so the main form of socialization is peer-group socialization. If the peers are paragons of virtue and fountains of wisdom, this is not a problem. Unfortunately, in real life, peer groups tend to fall to the level of the worst influences among them, which is why you hear so much about "peer pressure" today and why public school children even have to worry about just saying no.

SERIOUS ANSWER #4. Homeschooled kids actually participate in *more* social activities than schooled kids! See Appendix 1 for details.

THOUGHT FOR THE DAY. Did you know that the greatest predictor of genius is the amount of time a child spends with adults? In other words, the more time your child spends with you and other adults, the more likely he or she is to exhibit advanced intellectual abilities.

SERIOUS ANSWER #5. I thought children went to school to *learn!*

"What about college?"

THOUGHTFUL ANSWER #1. Many, many colleges currently accept homeschoolers. Some even court them, giving preference to homeschoolers! And those few who haven't yet just haven't realized what a gold mine we are!

As your student gets closer to college age (say, ninth grade), start looking at colleges that he or she would like to attend. Then write the colleges, tell them you're interested, and ask what kind of records, tests, and so forth they like to see from homeschoolers.

If your *student* writes the initial letter to the college (and it sounds good), and continues a correspondence up through the time he actually applies, he will have a valuable contact there.

Some colleges only require a standardized test, like the SAT or the ACT. Most like to see a sample of the student's writing. They look very closely at this to see how well the prospective student expresses himself. Sometimes they want a reading list (all the impressive books read during the high-school years). Homeschooled students have been accepted on the basis of their impressive portfolios and also on the basis of their impressive transcripts. The best applications include both. You can create the transcript yourself—but you have to have some kind of justification for why you gave which grade and how you decided when a credit was earned.

THOUGHTFUL ANSWER #2. Going to college *at home*—in other words, homeschooling right up to the (hopefully not bitter) end—is becoming more of a real option these days. Just about every state college offers some correspondence courses, and a growing number of colleges have full degree programs. Also available are several legitimate programs that allow you to cobble a potpourri of distance education courses, plus credit for "passing" courses via tests, plus credit for life experience, into genuine accredited degrees. For more details, see *Mary Pride's Complete Guide to Homeschooling Grades 7–12.*

THOUGHTFUL ANSWER #3. Don't neglect to investigate other options for post-high-school education: video courses, tutorial software, library books, magazines, TV and satellite courses, seminars, apprenticeships, and starting your own business! For young graduates, a year "off" to explore the world, and the world of work, can be a big help in preparing for college . . . and for life.

COLLEGE? NO PROBLEM!

Perhaps three-quarters of universities now have policies for dealing with home-schooled applicants, according to Cafi Cohen, author of *The Homeschoolers' College Admissions Handbook* [Prima Publishing, 2000]. Today Harvard admissions officers attend home-schooling conferences looking for applicants, and Rice and Stanford admit home schoolers at rates equal to or higher than those for public schoolers. These schools compete for students like L.J. Decker, 17, from Katy, Texas, who scored 1560 on the SAT and was part of a team of home schoolers who won the Toshiba ExploraVision contest for their idea of a futuristic scuba device that would use artificial hemoglobin to convert the oxygen in water into air.

Some colleges, like Kennesaw State University in Georgia, aggressively recruit home schoolers. . . .

—*John Cloud and Jodie Morse,*
"Home Sweet School,"
TIME, *August 27, 2001*

"What do I tell my in-laws?"

FOOLISH ANSWER #1. "Hi! We've gone insane and decided to ruin our children's future by homeschooling them!"

FOOLISH ANSWER #2. (To your parents:) "I am so upset at the job you did raising me, Mom and Dad, that I refuse to follow in your footsteps by sending *my* kids to the public school!"

BETTER ANSWER #1. It's common for in-laws, especially parents, to "read" your choice of homeschooling as a rejection of them and the way they were raised or the way they raised you. Also, in spite of all the bad publicity public schools have garnered over the past few decades, many older people still have sentimental memories of public school days, and fear you will be depriving your children if they can't be on the football team or go to the prom. (NOTE: By the time you read this, homeschooled children in your town *may* be able to play public school sports and join after-school clubs such as the theater club or chess club. But your parents don't know this!) So don't panic if their first reaction is negative. What counts is the long run!

We've found that the best approach is a gradual one devoid of any defensiveness on your part. Find common ground from which you can build. Are your in-laws concerned or alarmed about the state of the public schools? Have your in-laws ever mentioned the negative effects of peer pressure? Do they want your children to be taught a biblical worldview? Do they in any way share some of your vision for your family? If so, you can discuss these areas of common ground and share how you believe homeschooling is the best solution for your family.

Most in-laws will probably be initially skeptical and will have a lot of questions. Some will accept your answers; others will need "hard facts" from "experts." The hard facts, including numerous studies showing that homeschooling really works, are readily available from sources such as your state homeschool group, Home School Legal Defense Association (HSLDA), homeschool books found in your public library, and this very book you now hold in your hands!

When your in-laws respond to this onslaught of well-researched information with pursed lips and dire pronouncements of doom, calmly reply, "We are sorry if you don't agree with our decision to homeschool, but we are convinced this is what we should be doing. We really don't want to argue about it." Families we know who have faced strong opposition from relatives have found that a calm, no-nonsense statement of this sort will prevent many disagreements and nasty scenes.

BETTER ANSWER #2. After you have been homeschooling a while, invite your in-laws to a "Show and Tell" day. Let the children give oral presentations of their work, complete with visual aids (flip charts, projects they have made, etc.). Make this a formal occasion, with the guests seated nicely and served refreshments. Some really anti-home-school relatives have been won over when they saw how well-behaved and informed the children were. (Of course, it helps if you have been training your children to be well-behaved and informed!)

BETTER ANSWER #3. Head off trouble at the pass by inviting your in-laws to help you teach! The same Grandma and Grandpa, or Aunt Joan and Uncle Fred, who have been disparaging your homeschool will often become its biggest boosters once they have a part in it. Grandparents are great at teaching hands-on skills such as cooking and woodworking. Or if your skeptical family members have any special skills, such as piano proficiency or math, ask them to come over a few times and help teach in these areas.

> Ten years ago, the first thing people used to say when you said you planned to homeschool was, "What about socialization?" Five years ago, they'd ask, "What about college?" Today, the most common reaction is, "I don't blame you. The schools aren't safe anymore."

To find your state and local homeschool support groups, go to **www.home-school.com** and click on "Groups." Or check out Appendix 3!

These "in-law classes" don't have to be daily, or even weekly, to be effective at the socialization that really counts—socializing your in-laws to the benefits of homeschooling!

BETTER ANSWER #4. Frequently in-laws are *thrilled* to find out you'll be homeschooling!

"How can I meet other homeschoolers?"

THE TRADITIONAL ANSWER. The best way to meet other home schoolers is through your local support group. Many states have a statewide group that will give the phone numbers of groups in your area. If you hear of a church that has lots of homeschoolers, contact them. Homeschoolers are generally very helpful to new families. Most support groups have experienced leaders who can steer you in the right direction to find information, encouragement, and support. Get involved in your local homeschool group by volunteering to help in even a little job, and you will be amazed at the friends you make. Just as a Christian needs fellow Christians, so homeschoolers need others for fellowship and support.

THE WIRED ANSWER. Visit online forums! One place to start: the forums on Homeschool World at www.home-school.com. We have forums on Getting Started, Special Needs, Homeschooling Overseas, and Military Homeschooling (homeschooling for military families, not how to run your home like a military academy!). We also have expert-led forums on Art, Math, Science, Preschool, and Unit Studies. Make some online friends and meet some mentors!

THE OVERWHELMING ANSWER. Attend your state homeschool convention. There you'll have a chance to meet between 200 and 10,000 homeschool families—all at once!

"How do I know we're covering everything we need to?"

Public schools use a tool called a "scope and sequence." This chart or list tells you, for each subject in each grade level, what skills are supposed to be covered.

Big-time homeschool curriculum publishers such as A Beka Book, Alpha Omega Publications, Bob Jones University Press, and Christian Light Education also have scope and sequences. You can request them to send you one, usually for a very small sum or even free.

Smaller curriculum publishers sometimes include a scope and sequence in their catalogs.

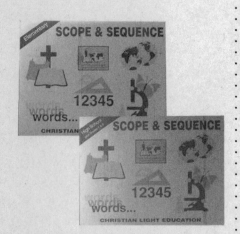

A publisher's scope and sequence, of course, just tells you what the publisher's materials cover, not necessarily what they *should* cover.

So here's an important fact to remember:

There is nothing sacred about the particular subjects taught in school or the order in which they are taught!

With the exception of math, phonics, and some math-based science topics, which really do need to be taught in a step-by-step sequence, almost everything taught in school can be taught in just about any order. Someone somewhere just sat down and *decreed* "this shall be taught in second grade." But they could just as easily have decreed it should be taught in fourth grade, or eighth grade, or not at all!

Who says Earth Science should be taught before Chemistry, anyway? And why? Why do college-bound high school graduates have to spend three years (at least) in Science class but not one single term learning CPR and basic nursing care? (Unless they live in Massachusetts, which since the last edition of this book has added first aid and CPR to its required high-school curriculum.)

Why should American History be taught before European History? Or vice versa? And what American History do we study—the newly fashionable "multicultural" kind, which ignores George Washington, or the old-fashioned kind where you had to memorize "The Midnight Ride of Paul Revere"?

Is there any good reason for teaching nouns before verbs? (The most popular homeschool grammar program teaches *prepositions* first!)

In public school, a subject is educational because the teacher (or more likely, some Curriculum Facilitator somewhere) says it is. This means public schools waste lots of time doing things they *don't* need to—such as spending a week building Valentine's Day villages out of shoeboxes. (I am not making this up. *Instructor* magazine actually ran a how-to article suggesting that elementary schoolteachers do this project.)

At home, *you* are the teacher. You can decide *which* subjects to cover and *when* to cover them. This book you are now reading tells you which subjects other homeschoolers are teaching and where to find resources to teach them. You will be covering "everything we need to" when:

- Your children have learned to read.
- Your children have learned to write and type.
- Your children have adequate grammar and spelling.
- Your children have learned to cipher (do basic math).
- Your children have read a lot of books (both fiction and non-fiction).
- You have determined what your goals are for your children and what their goals are for themselves, and picked out the materials that will help them meet those goals.

"What age should I begin homeschooling?"

THE LONG ANSWER. You already have! If your child has learned to speak, or play "Peek a Boo," or is toilet trained, you are a home educator!

What you mean is, "What age should I begin *formal academic* homeschooling?" The obvious answer is, "When your child is ready for it."

Boys tend to be about a year behind girls in seatwork and reading skills, for example. In public school, the boys are pushed before they are ready, and then many of them are labeled "hyperactive" or "ADD" (Attention Deficit Disorder) and put on brain-changing drugs such as Ritalin. At home, you can afford to offer a subject every so often until the child appears able to handle it, and use exercise and diet to curb any excess of energy instead of powerful and addictive brain-altering drugs.

Famous people throughout history have learned to read any time between age 2 and age 10. Sir Isaac Newton, the great scientist and mathematician, was slow in math until he became motivated to outshine a fellow student. While we would not use these examples to encourage homeschool "slacking"—letting kids goof off—we encourage you to observe your student's progress and be flexible enough to accommodate his maturity and skill level.

While public schools are set up for steady progress and everyone working at the same rate, in real life children grow in spurts. The same child

You've Got Company!
Even the largest estimates still put the home schooled at only 4% of the total K–12 population—but that would mean more kids learn at home than attend all the public schools in Alaska, Delaware, Hawaii, Montana, New Hampshire, North Dakota, Rhode Island, South Dakota, Vermont and Wyoming combined.
—TIME, *August 27, 2001*

SHORTER HOURS, BUT MORE GETS DONE

In response to what to say when your children or you are questioned by others about why your children are not doing school while other children are still in school:

In Germany, during the first four grades school is usually over by 12 PM or earlier. For the later grades, school is normally over by 1:30 PM. Sometimes they stay longer for extra-curricular activities or extra classes or tutoring. Sometimes they are even out earlier. And that is in all three school systems (*Hauptschule, Realschule,* and *Gymnasium*).

They don't get warm lunches: you bring your own or you can buy something from a kiosk, and they don't have all these long breaks. And even though they are much earlier at home, I don't hear about children graduating without knowing how to read, write and do math.

I know the standards are getting lower in Germany as well as in the US, but I believe they still learn more in the few hours they are in school compared to the US kids.

Knowing this may provide an example of a method of schooling which does not have long days, yet provides efficient, productive schooling with measurable results.

If a public school system proves effective with these principles, then it is reasonable to expect the same or better results from a homeschool which has much more flexibility and can form the teaching to the individual student much better than a public school system.

—*Martina Kilburn, Mons, Belgium*

who just doesn't "get" his phonics flashcards will suddenly surprise you by knowing them all perfectly! And his little brother or sister may be ready for the same lessons a year sooner than he was—or a year later.

Remember also that you don't have to do the same grade level of every subject. Quite often a child will be ready for fourth-grade work in math but only second-grade in language arts, or vice versa. A customized education is just one of the benefits of homeschooling!

"What kind of schedule should I follow?"

THE FBI-WARNING ANSWER. Figure it out fast, because the federal agencies are hanging around outside your house ready to nail you if you pick the wrong scheduling option. (We're just kidding. Actually, they're sitting in your bushes trying to catch you copying a videotape.)

THE AVERAGE ANSWER. Devotions and breakfast first, chores second, then school lessons. Most families wrap this up by early afternoon, and spend the afternoons on outside activities, fun projects, recreational reading, community service, or whatever. And don't forget, Friday is for field trips!

THE DAD WORKS NIGHT SHIFT ANSWER. Switch morning and afternoons, and you can spend mornings with Dad!

THE WE-LIVE-ON-A-BOAT ANSWER. Do whatever you want. Everything you do on a boat counts for something educational and can lead to a valuable future career, assuming you're silly enough to ever leave home and get a job. Even so, you probably use the Calvert curriculum, judging by the number of you who write in to their newsletter. Just don't forget the sunblock.

THE YEAR-ROUND ANSWER. Why stop homeschooling in the summer? The kids will just forget a lot of what they've learned. (Mary's advice: take it a little easy on this philosophy if it's really beautiful outside. Unless you live on a boat, in which case the rest of us will feel better if we know you're inside slaving over work pages.)

THE SIX-ON, TWO-OFF ANSWER. Six weeks of homeschool followed by two weeks of vacation. Lather, then repeat.

THE REGULAR SCHOOL YEAR ANSWER. You have less to explain to the neighbors when your children are on vacation during regular vacation time. This also helps if your curriculum publisher still has lesson plans that assume Christmas seasonal activities should happen in Month 4. But it really tweaks the curriculum companies when everyone tries to order at once . . . in the third week in August. So if you follow the regular school year, order early, and maybe you'll even get a special discount!

THE SPONTANEOUS ANSWER. You provide lots of great resources, make yourself available to answer questions, and never "schedule homeschool" as such. This works best if your children learn to read *early,* or if your lifestyle involves lots of hands-on, real-world activities, or both. Prepare to take a deep breath and get more organized when high school rolls around.

"How much does it cost?"

TAMMY'S ANSWER. The best analogy we have seen in reference to the cost of homeschooling is the "birthday cake" analogy (thank you, Robin Sampson). The mom who spends time to make her child's birthday cake from scratch will spend almost no money. The mom who spends less time and uses packaged mixes and purchased decorations will spend a little more money on the cake. The mom who spends no more time than what it takes to run to the bakery to pick up a purchased cake will spend a much larger amount of money.

The same holds true in your child's education. If you choose to pursue the unit study approach and use the public library as your primary source, you can spend an absolute minimum amount of money. Between unit studies and (relatively expensive) prepackaged curricula there are many options. Your cost will be determined by which option you choose.

PEGGY'S ANSWER. In a survey I did, I found that some people spent under $100 per year, and there were others who spent well over $750 per year. The cost often depends upon the approach. If you use a textbook, you may have some higher initial costs, but you may also be able to find the book used. The Textbook Exchange company here in Oklahoma offers used textbooks (Christian ones also) for $7.50 per inch. They pile up your textbooks and measure the stack. I bought five levels of Saxon math for about $40! Of course, I don't have the teacher's manuals; they were out of them at the time. But since my husband has gone through calculus and loves math, that should not be a problem.

I guess that the cost will depend upon what you feel is necessary and what you feel would be "nice." We spend a *lot* of money on homeschooling, but we feel that we are building a library, and our approach requires lots of books. Others that I know spend money for math and English and use the library for the rest.

I wouldn't look at cost till I knew how I wanted to homeschool— whether I wanted to use textbooks, workbooks, unit studies, or other materials. Then I would look to buy as many of them as was possible from another homeschooler.

JOHN'S ANSWER. It depends on materials. We spend from $100 to $700 per year per child. It sure beats private school tuition, though. One family I know who budgeted to send their kids to a private Christian school ($3,000–$5,000/year tuition per kid) kept the same budget when they started homeschooling. Imagine all the materials you could get!

MARY'S ANSWER. I would encourage you not to take a bargain-basement approach to your child's education if you can possibly help it. Dads particularly get into this mode of thought: "Here's $20 to buy all the kids' school materials, dear. Don't spend it all in one place!" This is a mistake. Homeschooling is not "cheap private school." It is an investment in your child's future and his immortal soul.

Trying to save money by letting the government foot the bill is a *terrible* idea. Public school is public school, even if it takes place in your home. Do you want to have your home life controlled by the same bureaucrats whose schools and social policies you're trying to escape? See the chapter on Charter Schools for how government funding brings government control.

"What do I need to buy?"

What you *don't* need: School desks. Pull-down maps. Slide projectors. Filmstrips. A bell for ringing to indicate the end of class periods. School uniforms. Television. Workbooks full of "busywork."

What is *nice* to have, but not *necessary:* Whiteboard or chalkboard (also available in student sizes, and even as wallcovering—a neat idea!). Bulletin board. Maps. Videocamera. Videocassette player. DVD player. Puzzles. Home computer with modem, Internet hookup, and adult-quality word processing software. Educational software.

What is *essential:* Curriculum. Pencils with good erasers. Pens (and a bottle of Liquid Paper). Paper (including different kinds of art paper). Envelopes (for writing to relatives and pen pals). Homeschool books and

> To find used curriculum online, visit the "Curriculum Trades" forum at **www.home-school.com**. To locate other used-curriculum venues online, go to **yahoo.com** and type in "used homeschool curriculum" just like that. Don't forget the quote marks!

magazines. Camera. Cassette player. Good encyclopedia. Globe. Atlas. Dictionary. Library card. Art supplies. Some method of record keeping. A stopwatch or timing device.

RENEE'S ADVICE. Don't buy a formal science or history textbook for second grade or less. In fact, don't buy one at all, unless it's for reference. Use real books instead.

"Will my children respect me as their teacher?"

RESPECTFUL ANSWER #1. Do they respect you as their parent? If they don't, you need to earn their respect anyway.

RESPECTFUL ANSWER #2. Respect them as a student, and teach them to respect you. They will see more of you and more of your mistakes, but also more of your good points and more of your love. They will learn to like you and the rest of their family even more.

RESPECTFUL ANSWER #3. If your children have been in school, they may seriously doubt that you, a lowly Mom or Dad, could possibly know as much as a Real Teacher. However, don't let that deter you. The wonderful thing about homeschooling is that it will foster respect. Initially, there might be a bit of a struggle, some testing of the boundaries, some poor attitudes. This is not so much a homeschooling problem as it is a child-rearing problem. Many parents have found it best not to make a formal distinction between their mothering and teaching roles. Thus, instead of saying things like "Would you talk to a teacher at school this way?" or "Pay attention to me; I am your teacher, after all!" it is best to appeal to your God-given authoritative role as their mother: "I can't allow you to talk to me this way." "When your mother is talking, you need to listen." Don't allow any sort of poor behavior during school time that you wouldn't allow the rest of the day, and vice versa. Be natural, be yourself, and give everybody room to make the adjustment. Most important, express your love and affection for your children during school times; don't get too serious! Eventually, you will be surprised to discover how homeschooling has melted away all sorts of bad attitudes and replaced them with a loving respect for one another.

"How can I teach many children at once?"

DANA'S ANSWER. It seems funny that we can expect a teacher to teach 30 kids she hardly knows at the same time, but a parent can't teach when they have a large family!

First, as much as possible I teach science and history to everyone together. We do a lot of reading together, and then I am able to give individual assignments according to ability. As our children have gotten older they are able to do quite a bit of their work on their own.

Each day I spend a set amount of time working with each child. The amount of time depends on how much attention that child needs at that time. During the rest of the school day they work on their assignments on their own. I make myself available for any questions and help they may need while they are working on their own. If they need help while I am helping someone else, they lightly tap me on the arm and wait until I can stop to answer their questions.

This year a few times I have had my oldest child teach a lesson to the other children. It worked well, and I plan to continue doing it.

MARY'S ANSWER. Part of a child's education ought to be learning how to teach. When older children help with the younger ones, they reinforce their own old lessons and learn what they'll need to someday homeschool their own children!

"Help! I have a preschooler! How can I teach the older children with him around?"

CONNIE'S ANSWER. I have a four-year-old, plus children aged 11,10, and 9. My four-year-old isn't really ready for formal schooling. He likes to color, so I just picked up some beginning shape and color workbooks and we informally do things while the other kids are working. Remember that their attention span isn't very long at this age. Right now, it might be best to just lay the foundation for later, reading lots of books to him, coloring, letting her help in the kitchen, etc. There are lots of good suggestions on all the online homeschooling message boards for curricula for later use. It's not as hard as you might fear.

LYNDA'S ANSWER. Let him/her play, play, play. Provide new play materials . . . not necessarily toys. For example, use scraps of fabric, shells, twigs, or milk jug tops and a big bottle of glue for sculpture. Go bowling with an orange and toilet paper tubes. . . . And most of all, *relax!* Have fun.

MARY'S ANSWER. Crowd control is important. I like to have the little one in the middle of the room, with the older ones on couches and chairs around the edges. I know some of you are anti-playpen, but when they are at the age of no common sense and great speed, I find it saves me lots of grey hairs if a crawling baby is trained to be good in the playpen.

Of course, if a preschooler wants to scrunch up next to the others with a book, that's great! He doesn't have to be able to read, either. For all of our nine children, books were their favorite toys . . . probably because they saw all of us spending so much time with them.

Important rule: Spend time with the little one *first*. This fills up his "love bucket" and keeps him from being restless and overly demanding when you have to spend time with the older children. Have a variety of toys handy, and keep switching the toys week by week. Take some away and put others out. Let a preschooler "do school" with simple activities, five minutes here and there, with flashcards, simple crafts, etc.

Speaking of the older children, they can also help by taking turns spending time with the baby or toddler.

Another rule: Take him with you when you do chores. Then you know where he is, plus if he is old enough he can learn to help!

"Do I have to do ALL the teaching?"

Here's a little secret: We *call* it "homeschooling," but it's really "real-world schooling." For once, the whole village actually gets to teach the child—*if*, and this is a big "if," you, the parents, feel any particular village member is trustworthy and a good mentor for your child.

So, where do you find these mentors? Here are some answers.

- **First, the homegrown mentors.** Older children can help a lot with the younger ones. Reading books aloud to the little kids is a favorite activity. So is playing educational games with them. Do you have an older relative living with you? A family member living nearby? Does this person have any valuable knowledge and enjoy your children's company? Well, then!
- **Kids can drill kids.** Even better, educational software can do the drilling. Lots more fun than flashcards!
- **Charles Dickens** makes a great history and literature tutor. For writing style, you can't beat C.S. Lewis. David Macaulay knows a thing or two about science and engineering too. Do you see where I'm going with this? Yup, right to the bookstore and library!

Including Very Young Learners in Your Homeschool

Ages 2–5. Available from (800) 745-8212, www.joyceherzog.com

Including Very Young Learners in Your Homeschool is packed with ideas for simple-to-make activities and games that you can prepare ahead of time. Have these ready to go and available when you need to teach your toddler/preschooler one of the most important lessons of all: How to pay attention, follow directions, and stick with it. Not formal, just fun! 12 pages. *Renee Mathis*

Expecting outside teachers to do the whole job is part of what's killing the schools, as teachers themselves agree. Every good parent gets involved in their children's education, whether or not the family homeschools.

Even if you use online courses or correspondence courses, it's vital that you stay in close touch with your student's assignments and grades, and be ready to help if snags arrive. This may require talking to the teacher, researching answers on your own, or just knowing where to point your student. "Go look it up in the dictionary/encyclopedia/atlas/online," is always good advice, plus it builds valuable research skills!

"WILL HOMESCHOOLING MAKE ME CRAZY?"

After Houston wife and mother Andrea Pia Yates drowned her five children, ages 6 months to 7 years, several articles appeared blaming this tragedy on homeschooling. This is, of course, ridiculous. Millions of stay-at-home moms, and hundreds of thousands of homeschool moms, have managed to deal with the stresses of raising young children without killing them.

What you may not have heard, because the mass media seemed reluctant to report it, is that for years Mrs. Yates had been prescribed overly potent doses of psychoactive drugs in strange and dangerous combinations. According to *Insight* magazine of July 2001, these included:

- "Haldol, an antipsychotic most often used to treat schizophrenia . . ." Psychologist Peter Breggin, cited in the article, calls Haldol "blunting" and "a drug that produces what can only be referred to as a chemical lobotomy that tends to make a person more docile and robotic" (shades of the *Stepford Wives*!).
- "Effexor, an antidepressant very similar to selective serotonin reuptake inhibitors (SSRIs)"
- "Wellbutrin, a unique antidepressant that has amphetaminelike effects . . ."
- Finally, she was prescribed a "pharmapsychological cocktail" that "contained Effexor and, at the end, Remeron. . . . Yates' husband has said that his wife was given Effexor at a dosage nearly twice the recommended maximum limit. Just days before the murders, the Effexor was for some reason reduced to just slightly more than the recommended maximum dosage of 225 mg per day and the Remeron was added."

- **Volunteering** is a great way for teens to gain all sorts of useful skills. Every community has dozens, if not hundreds, of organizations that can use a helping hand. See the chapter on Volunteering in Volume 3.
- **Your church or house of worship** likely offers classes in a variety of topics—at times that don't conflict with your regular school hours too!
- **Seminars and camps** are available year-round for all ages. Some popular options: short-term missions assignments, space camp, computer camp, leadership conferences for youth, and worldview training institutes. You will want to make sure the staff is trustworthy and supports your spiritual and moral outlook.
- **Homeschool co-ops** are increasingly popular, especially for those using unit-study curricula. In this scenario, several families get together and share the major teaching chores. One mom might teach piano, while another does math and science. Or one might arrange to purchase all the supplies (with costs shared evenly), while another supervises the creative activities. The options are endless!
- **Your local homeschool support group** likely offers social events, and some of its members teach classes. Art, music, and creative-writing classes seem especially popular.
- **Online academies** provide trained teachers, usually for the upper grades.
- **Local private schools** might offer classes just for homeschoolers or welcome homeschool enrollment in just a class or two, such as lab science.
- **To be used with caution:** In some locations, the public schools allow homeschoolers to enroll in extracurricular activities. Be sure they respect your right to control the rest of your curriculum if you select this option.
- **Can you spell Y-M-C-A, A-W-A-N-A, and 4-H?** Local children's clubs of all sorts offer educational opportunities and welcome homeschoolers. Our local Y even has special classes during school hours just for homeschoolers!
- **If a student has a job**, often the company will teach a motivated teen as many skills as the teen is willing to learn.
- **Don't forget videos, software, and the Internet!**

For more details, see the entire section in this book on "Homeschooling Away from Home."

One cautionary note: There should still be *some* "home" in "homeschooling." It's possible to get so excited about all the great educational opportunities out in the big beautiful world that you miss out on one of the greatest beauties of homeschooling: family togetherness. When in doubt, go for more time to think and to be together.

"What if my child REALLY wants to go to school?"

THE INSIGHTFUL ANSWER. Before you even think about this question, you need to find out *why* your child is so anxious to attend school. Usually the reason is "friends." Less often, it's some special activity, such as cheerleading or sports. I have yet to encounter a child who wants to attend school because he or she believes the school will provide a better education.

If you are firmly convinced that homeschooling is best for your child, but you are meeting resistance over the "friends" issue, you can handle this two ways. First, you can arrange for your child to get together with his existing friends outside school hours. Invite them over. Take them to the mall. Arrange skating parties. Whatever works. Second, you can help your child make some new homeschooled friends. If the group offers "Homeschool Skating Hour" at the local rink, be there. Sign up for the art fair. Enroll in the YMCA classes scheduled during school hours just for homeschoolers (they do this in our area!). Invite the new friends over. Maybe even start a co-op class.

If your child craves involvement in some special activity, perhaps he can still be involved as a homeschooler. Or maybe the homeschoolers in your area have their own marching band or basketball team. Ask! But the bottom line has to be that your child's spiritual development, character, and academics come before social activities.

THE WORLDVIEW ANSWER. The more your child knows about what education *should* be like, and what's wrong with the schools, the more likely he is to support the homeschooling solution. So share your reading with him.

THE LITTLE KID ANSWER. If your child has never been to school, but is sure he wants to, a few facts of life regarding time on the bus, hours in the classroom, needing to ask permission to go to the bathroom, school bullies, and homework should quell any romantic fantasies. As an alternative, let him read "Calvin and Hobbes."

THE HOLLYWOOD ANSWER. If you're willing to break your family rule against letting the preteens and teens watch "R"-rated movies, then a viewing of *187, The Substitute, Stand and Deliver,* or *Lean on Me* will reveal that all is not roses in big-city high schools. Even the TV show *Buffy the Vampire Slayer* shows the general meanness and put-downs of the less-than-perfectly-fashionable-and-beautiful that are daily fare in the best-groomed suburban middle and high schools. Who knows? Your child may decide to homeschool *and* choose teaching as a career (because those schooled kids really need help) all in one night!

"What if my child has ADD or needs special help?"

THE ACRONYM ANSWER. What you really mean is, "What if my child has been *labeled* as having ADD, ADHD, or one of those other vague-yet-scary acronyms?" See the chapter on "How Real Are Learning Disabilities?"

THE PROFESSIONAL ANSWER. First, breathe a sigh of relief. There is no law saying you have to be the expert in every area just because you are taking on the responsibility of your child's education. Instead, think of yourself as choosing from a vast array of other professionals and their expertise when necessary. Speech therapy? Vision problems? Auditory difficulties? All these are areas that you may need to seek outside assistance with if needed. The good news is that you as a loving, concerned parent are in the best place to make those decisions on behalf of your child.

THE NEIGHBORLY ANSWER. Check with state and local support groups for more info, or post your questions online in the Special Needs Homeschooling forum at www.home-school.com. You'll probably find someone who has been there or has been in a worse situation. Homeschoolers really do like to help each other!

THE AUTHOR'S ANSWER. Check out the chapters on "Help for Distractible Learners" and "Help for the Challenged." Relax—thousands of other families have successfully traveled this road before you!

"What if my child is gifted?"

Amazingly, we have three chapters on this topic, too!

Other people have had similar psychotic episodes when their powerful brain-altering drug prescriptions were changed or reduced. As *Insight* put it, "It's well-documented that when doses are increased or decreased, patients experience negative reactions. A great many of the court cases [involving prescription drug users acting psychotically and harming themselves or others], but certainly not all of them, are a result of the drastic change in the medication."

Case in point: in June 2001 "a jury in Cheyenne, Wyoming, found that the antidepressant Paxil, one of the newer SSRIs distributed by GlaxoSmithKline PLC [remember, one of Andrea Yates' many drugs was similar to an SSRI], 'can cause some individuals to commit suicide and/or homicide.' The jury said Paxil caused Donald Schell, a retired oil-rig worker, to shoot and kill his wife, daughter and granddaughter before turning the gun on himself. Schell had been on the mind-altering drug only two days."

So, does it sound to you like homeschooling drove Andrea Yates over the edge? Or did she just happen to be homeschooling at the time something else took over her life?

As those of us who have experienced it know, homeschooling a young child is a delightfully warm and emotionally rewarding experience. Little in the way of results is expected from a 7-year-old, so the pressure on both parent and student is minimal, while the fun factor is high.

I always feel *better* after spending homeschool time with my little ones . . . and I have way more kids than Andrea Yates . . . but then, I am not loaded down with prescription drugs that from the sound of it were both blunting her natural affections and making her feel like she was crawling out of her skin.

My conclusion: Something indeed may have been driving Andrea Yates crazy, just as something apparently drove Donald Schell crazy. But it wasn't homeschooling.

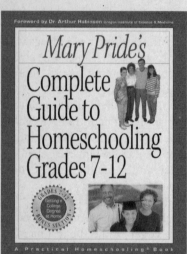

"Where can I find more information about homeschooling?"

MARY'S ANSWER. With this huge book in your hand, you need *more* information? But seriously . . .

Don't forget the upcoming volumes of *Mary Pride's Complete Guide to Homeschooling from Birth to Grade 6* and *Mary Pride's Complete Guide to Homeschooling Grades 7–12*. They provide detailed subject-by-subject reviews and information for preschool through elementary, and junior high through college, respectively.

Also, there are state support groups, local support groups, conventions and seminars, online services, homeschool websites, homeschool magazines, homeschool books, and your friends that homeschool, to name a few sources!

Where *not* to start: your local school or state Board of Education. Although homeschooling is legal everywhere, sometimes local and state officials are not aware of this. Although many school and state officials are wonderful, friendly people, those who are less enlightened may try to bully you out of exercising your rights or act unpleasantly towards you in other ways.

If you have a computer with online access, the quickest way to pick up information is by surfing over to Homeschool World (www.home-school.com). This site, sponsored by *Practical Homeschooling* magazine, will put you in touch with more free information about homeschooling than you know what to do with!

If you're not sure where to start, check your library. They most likely have a good selection of homeschool books and may know about or sponsor events for homeschoolers. See also Chapter 10, "What to Read," and the chapters on homeschool methods for leads to books in your particular subjects of interest.

All set? Great! Now on to the next chapter, where we'll see why so many other parents have decided to homeschool . . . and why you might want to, also!

CHAPTER 4

Why Do So Many Families Homeschool?

Once you finally make the decision to homeschool, people will start asking you why you decided to do it. All sorts of folks, from the supermarket checkout clerk to large polling organizations, want to know *why* you're homeschooling.

So, what are you going to tell them?

It helps to be sure of your reasons, not only for the sake of all those curious questioners, but for your own sake. When the tough days come . . . and they will . . . it really helps to remember just why you decided to do this. When you're under the weather, and the house is a mess because the kids are in the middle of some really creative projects, and Jimmie swears he didn't do any math all morning because he couldn't find his pencil, and the other kids are arguing over who gets to use the glue gun, and the doorbell rings to announce your grumpy old aunt, who thinks you were nuts to even think of homeschooling, you'll feel inclined to agree with her. *Unless* you remember you have good reasons, *serious* reasons, that outweigh your need for:

- A perfectly clean house at all times
- The immediate respect and support of those around you
- Large amounts of personal time and space
- Peace and quiet
- Perfect confidence in your ability to do this job (it will come with time, trust me, but every homeschool mom and dad experiences periods of panic)

In this chapter, we'll look first at the six classic reasons families homeschool. Then we'll briefly touch on 12 *new*—and extremely serious—reasons more and more informed families are choosing the homeschool option.

What to Say When You're Put on the Spot

"I love my children. I want the best for them. After investigating all the alternatives, I believe that homeschooling is their best educational option."

It's Good to be Bad?

TIME magazine, in its August 27, 2001, homeschool feature, revealed:

"In 1992 psychotherapist Larry Shyers did a study while at the University of Florida in which he closely examined the behavior of 35 home schoolers and 35 public schoolers. He found that home schoolers were generally more patient and less competitive. They tended to introduce themselves to one another more; they didn't fight as much. And the home schoolers were much more prone to exchange addresses and phone numbers. In short, they behaved like miniature adults."

Kids with good character and nice manners. Homeschool parents deserve a pat on the back, right? Not according to TIME, who went on to say,

"Which is great, unless you believe that kids should be kids before they are adults. . . . consider Rachel Ahern, 21, of Grand Junction, Colo., who never set foot in a classroom until she went to Harvard at 18. As a child, she socialized with older kids and adults at church and in music classes at a nearby college. 'I never once experienced peer pressure,' she says. But is that a good thing? Megan Wallace of Atlanta says if she had gone to high school, 'I would have gotten into so much trouble.' One could argue that kids need to get into a certain amount of trouble to learn how to handle temptations and their consequences."

Or one could argue that unwed pregnancy, drug addiction, date rape, drunken car crashes, bullying, joining a gang, and other common ways today's teens get into trouble are almost impossible to recover from. Many of us as adults bear lasting emotional and physical scars from the far less dangerous "trouble" we got into as youths.

Hopefully, the next time TIME does an article on homeschooling, the view that "it's good for kids to be bad" will seem as archaic as the view often expressed in the past that it's normal and OK for kids to encounter physical and verbal bullying at school.

Classic Reason #1: Family Unity

Those raised on a steady diet of TV families might believe that family unity is a pipe dream, but homeschoolers know it isn't so. Just like the vast majority of families throughout time and around the world, homeschoolers have found the secret of truly normal family life:

- Training the older kids to love and help the younger kids instead of looking down on them
- Parents spending time with their kids doing real-world activities (not just academics!)

Without the negative and time-consuming outside influences of public-school peer groups and courses that actively encourage kids to reject their parents' beliefs and morality and to pick *anyone* other than their parents as a confidante and role model, families have the chance to build strong, lasting bonds.

Classic Reason #2: Judeo-Christian Beliefs

Those with traditional Christian religious beliefs are getting warier these days about announcing them to total strangers. For several decades we have seen "religious" coupled with "fanatics" in magazine article after magazine article, and the term "fundamentalist," which was invented by American Bible-believers, used for Muslim terrorists, thus lumping all fundamentalists in the "crazy and dangerous" semantic category.

Given the fact that we homeschoolers are defending our right to raise our children in a way that many people still find offensive ("If the public schools are good enough for *my* kids, why aren't they good enough for *your* kids?"), I think there's a general feeling that it's not wise to wave any red flags in front of those who demand our reasons for homeschooling.

Having said all that, it's even more true today than it was 20 years ago, when the modern homeschooling movement started, that the public

The More Involved You Are with Your Kids, the Better

The National Center on Addiction and Substance Abuse (CASA) at Columbia University recently released a six-year study identifying factors that most influence teens relative to substance abuse. Consistent with their previous studies, these CASA findings indicate that the family is fundamental to keeping children away from tobacco, alcohol, and illegal drugs. More specifically, this ongoing study is researching the impact of parental conduct on teen substance abuse.

What did the study conclude?

Parents count!

The message is very clear. Parents who behave as parents, not pals, greatly reduce the risk that their child will use harmful substances. The study further indicates that whether the family structure is a two-parent home or headed by a single mom or dad, **hands-on parents can counter the negative influences of a teen's world.**

Who are these hands-on parents?

Hands-on parents who establish a household culture of rules and expectations tend to practice common behaviors. They include:

- imposing a curfew
- eating dinner with their teens almost every night
- expecting to be told the truth
- knowing where their teens are after school and on weekends
- having households where an adult is present when teens return from school
- making it very clear that they would be "extremely upset" if their teens used pot

- being "very aware" of their teen's academic performance [who's more aware than a home-schooling parent?]
- turning off the TV at dinner time
- monitoring the TV
- monitoring the Internet
- putting restrictions on CD purchases
- assigning regular chores

Who are the hands-off parents?

In contrast, "hands-off" parents fail to:

- give a clear message about drug use
- know where their teens are
- have dinner with their teens almost every night
- monitor TV and Internet viewing
- restrict CD purchases

Both teens and parents benefit from a strong family environment. Forty-seven percent of teens living in "hands-on" households report an excellent relationship with their father. Only 13% living in "hands-off" households do. The same is true for mothers and teens, with 57% of teens living in "hands-on" households reporting an excellent relationship with their mother. Only 24% in "hands-off" households do.

Unfortunately, only about 25% of American teens live in "hands-on" households. This statistic is significant because the present social climate looks to teachers, administrators, guidance personnel, and expensive government programs to address teen substance abuse issues. The most important factor is being overlooked: **engaged parents offer the best and most powerful prevention.**

To download the report, go to **www.casacolumbia.org**

—Education Advocate, *May/June 2001*

schools are not a Christian environment. This does not mean they are a religiously neutral environment. Consider these two bizarre examples:

Pagan Worship in Public School. Parents in the Bedford Central School District of New York State had to go to court to stop their children from being forced to participate in religious rituals such as:

- Creating paper images of a Hindu god
- Making toothpick-and-yarn "worry dolls" to ward off anxiety
- What the federal district judge called "truly bizarre" Earth Day celebrations

About those Earth Day rituals: According to the judge's ruling, these events "take on [many] of the attributes of the ceremonies of worship by organized religions."

In the words of the lawsuit, "Students and senior citizens, who have also become part of earth worship services, sit in concentric circles around a giant inflated globe placed atop a bamboo tripod. The elderly people form the inside circle, symbolizing that they are closer to the earth and will return to it to nourish it."

> **75% of all children raised in Christian homes who attend public schools will reject the Christian faith by their first year of college.**
>
> —*Caryl Matrisciana,*
> *VP Jeremiah Films*
> *Let My Children Go video*

To the beat of a chorus of tom-tom drums, teachers and school officials read speeches. The ceremony pretends that the earth is deified, and students were urged to "do something to make Mother Earth smile."

According to the story in the October 1999 *Phyllis Schlafly Report*:

Evidence submitted in this case included an audiotape (Exhibit 62) entitled "Listening to Nature," which intersperses prayers and invocations sonorously uttered along with background sounds of forest and ocean. The plaintiff parents particularly objected to the fact that the tape, which they characterized as "nature worship and guided imagery," was played in science classes.

The accompanying book contains this creed: "This is what we believe. The Mother of us all is the Earth. The Father is the Sun. The Grandfather is the Creator who bathed us with his mind and gave life to all things. The Brother is the beasts and trees. The Sister is that with wings. . . .

Page 65 of the book instructs children that, when they need to cut down a tree or remove a plant from their garden, they should pray to Mother Earth. The children are supposed to "ask your permission, your consent for this killing." . . .

The school district is expected to appeal the decision in this case, Altman et al. v. Bedford Central School District. . . .

This is by no means the only school district where Earth Day celebrations are used to promote pantheism, or where children are required to make idols of various sorts for class assignments. In art class, they may be required to make African tribal masks, which were used originally in animistic ceremonies. They may construct Native American totems, worry dolls, raincallers, or other relics of American Indian religions. Hindu gods are a bit more uncommon, but Wiccan projects are on the rise in schools, as an offshoot of the Harry Potter books.

You don't see anything wrong with this? Then imagine how a school administrator would react if a teacher wanted to require students to make crucifixes and pray the Lord's Prayer, or draw the Stations of the Cross and explain each one as a class assignment, or make illuminated Bible verses in art class, or gather the whole school together for a Ten Commandments rally, or put on a class Purim celebration, or invite a cantor and rabbi to help stage a Yom Kippur assembly.

It seems that "religious neutrality" means "anything goes except Christianity or orthodox Judaism."

Islam in the Public Schools. And I mean, *anything.* Unbelievably, the Byron Union School District in California has instituted a mandatory course in Islam for the 125 seventh graders in its Excelsior School, in which the children are required to participate in Muslim worship right in their classroom. According to a fund-raising letter I received from the American Center for Law and Justice, dated February 5, 2002, the children in this school must:

- Pray "in the name of Allah the Compassionate, the Merciful"
- Chant "Praise to Allah, Lord of Creation"
- "Pretend" they are Muslims and wear Muslim clothing to school
- Choose a Muslim name to replace their own
- Write six Islamic phrases in Arabic and organize a make-believe "hajj," or journey, to Mecca

- And unbelievably in the aftermath of 9/11, these public school children are required to stage their own mock "jihad," or "holy war" . . . by way of a dice game!

"From the beginning, you and your classmates will become Muslims." That's what the course handout says, according to an article in the *Washington Times.*

It's hard to see how Christian schoolkids can have their independent art projects ripped off the walls (because they feature Christian symbols), or how a Christian kindergartner can be asked to leave the lunch room because he prayed before eating, and yet something like this can "slip" by.

Huge numbers of Christian parents, children, and teachers have put up for almost 40 years with the humiliating removal of every vestige of Christianity from the public schools founded by once-Christian communities, because they were convinced that this was necessary in order to protect religious freedom. The arguments start looking pretty thin when other major religions get this kind of red-carpet treatment.

Relativism in the Public Schools. Perhaps the worst religious teaching in the public schools, that each and every schoolchild soaks up and to which the vast majority pledge allegiance by the time they graduate, is the notion that there *is no such thing* as absolute truth . . . what's "true" for me may not be "true" for you . . . and that it's the height of arrogance for anyone to proclaim they actually know truth. Thanks to years of public-school indoctrination, truth has been mutated into "what works," not "what is."

Students functioning with this view of reality are unable to oppose *any* evil or love any good. So college kids today know Hitler was evil, but when pressed can't defend even that position. For anyone other than Hitler, they're convinced that there are two sides to every story. And if not for the efforts of Jewish educators who are determined that we shall never forget the Holocaust, these kids wouldn't even be sure Hitler was that bad.

Most of you reading this have yourselves received your main religious instruction in public school. You know it did nothing to prepare you to know God, love God, or serve God. If you want more than this for your children, the choice is obvious.

Classic Reason #3: Meeting Your Child's Special Needs

One size does not fit all. If your child

- Learns more slowly than others his age
- Learns much faster than others her age
- Is extremely antsy in a classroom environment
- Gets sick a lot
- Requires specialized medical equipment
- Has trouble fitting in socially
- Is extremely bored in school
- Is trapped with an incompetent or emotionally abusive teacher

or for any other reason does not fit into the lockstep age-segregated model of education, you can either spend the next 13 years battling the system, with no results guaranteed, or put that same energy into meeting your child's needs right now.

While there might be some nobility in leading a crusade for changes that benefit a group of children, there's no point in letting your child suffer year after year because the system doesn't fit him.

RELATIVE INDOCTRINATION

There is one thing a professor can be absolutely certain of: Almost every student entering the university believes, or says he believes, that truth is relative. If this belief is put to the test, one can count on the students' reaction: They will be uncomprehending. That anyone would regard the proposition as not self-evident astonishes them, as though he were calling into question 2 + 2 = 4. . . .

Openness—and the relativism that makes it the only plausible stance in the face of various claims to truth and various ways of life and kinds of human beings—is the great insight of our times. . . .

The study of history and of culture [according to this view] teaches that all the world was mad in the past; men always thought they were right, and that led to wars, persecutions, slavery, xenophobia, racism, and chauvinism.

The point is not to correct the mistakes and really be right; rather it is not to think you are right at all.

The students, of course, cannot defend their opinion. It is something with which they have been indoctrinated.

—*Allan Bloom*
The Closing of the American Mind,
(New York: Simon and Schuster, 1987)

WHAT IS EDUCATION?

This, then, is what we are concerned with: adventures in human self-understanding. Not the bare protestation that a human being is a self-conscious, reflective intelligence and that he does not live by bread alone, but the actual enquiries, utterances, and actions in which human beings have expressed their understanding of the human condition. This is the stuff of what has come to be called a "liberal" education—"liberal" because it is liberated from the distracting business of satisfying contingent wants.

—*Michael Oakeshott,* The Voice of Liberal Learning (*Liberty Fund, 2001*)

Four Years Ahead

In one of the most extensive studies to date, the Iowa Test of Basic Skills was administered to over twenty thousand home schooled students, representing all grades and all fifty states. The results are consistent with virtually every other study that has compared the academic success of home schooled children with their public school counterparts. This study reported that on average home school students in the first four grades perform one grade level above their public and private school peers. Further, by the time the home schoolers reach grade eight, on average they are four years ahead of public school students.

—*William Eckenwiler,* A+ Education: Choosing the Best School Option for Your Child (*2002, Baker Book House*). *Referring to the study by Lawrence M. Rudner, "Scholastic Achievement and Demographic Characteristics of Home School Students in 1998,"* Education Policy Analysis Archives (*23 March 1999*), *available online at epaa.asu.edu/epaa/v7n8*

Classic Reason #4: Special Interests & Careers

Here are some more reasons for homeschooling. Your child:

- Is a serious competitor in individual sports (e.g., figure skating)
- Has a deep interest in subjects not covered in school (e.g., veterinary work)
- Wants the time to pursue an interest in depth (e.g., community theatre)
- Wants to volunteer for activities normally offered during the school day

Or maybe it's the whole family that has a special interest or situation. Your family:

- Lives on a houseboat and cruises all over
- Goes into showbiz, like the juggling Boehmer family or the Hanson singing group
- Moves around a lot (military and diplomatic families)
- Lives in an inaccessible area (Alaska or the mission field)

This might be the oldest classic reason for homeschooling. Calvert School started selling its correspondence curriculum over 100 years ago to families just like these!

Classic Reason #5: Better Academics

Although this isn't my personal #1 reason, this is the reason I usually give first in radio interviews because it leads so nicely into discussing all the good news about how well homeschoolers do academically.

"I want to give my kids a better education than they'll get in school"

might have sounded arrogant a few decades ago, when people still believed in the schools. Today it just sounds like you're a concerned parent who is willing to work extra hard to make sure your child succeeds.

One extremely important point here: We're not just talking about standardized test scores and the ability to land a job, important as those are. The very definition of education is at stake. The public school is redefining its mission as preparing a preponderance of low-level workers to be tracked into the jobs central planners have projected will be needed when they graduate. This is the infamous "School-to-Work" program you may have heard people arguing about on the radio.

Do you want your children to be taught a handful of "useful" skills for menial jobs that may vanish in a few years? Or do you want them:

- To be excellent at the basic skills of reading and writing
- To learn how to learn anything they ever need to learn in the future
- To be exposed to the great and beautiful in as many areas as possible

If that's what you want, it's a good reason to teach your children at home.

Instead of an Education, Learn to Flip a Burger

The following graphic, distributed by the Minnesota Department of Children, Families and Learning (DCFL), explains how School-to-Work is a government plan to interlock public school "reform" of curriculum with workforce preparation (job training) and economic development (national economic planning). This official state publication states that the School-to-Work mission is "to create a seamless system of education and workforce preparation for all learners, tied to the needs of a competitive economic marketplace."

School-to-Work means that the mission of the public schools is no longer to educate children to be all they can be, but instead to train students to take entry-level jobs as needed by the global economy. The different motivations of several special interests perfectly mesh in School-to-Work: the Clinton Administration economic gurus (Marc Tucker, Ira Magaziner and Robert Reich) who say they want America to imitate the German school-workforce sys-

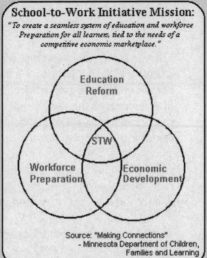

School-to-Work Initiative Mission:
"To create a seamless system of education and workforce Preparation for all learners, tied to the needs of a competitive economic marketplace."

Education Reform

STW

Workforce Preparation

Economic Development

Source: "Making Connections"
- Minnesota Department of Children, Families and Learning

tem, the Clinton Administration education activists (particularly the teachers unions and Education Department bureaucrats) who want to control the school system, and the multinational corporations that seek a poorly-educated but well-trained labor force willing to work for low wages to compete with low-paid workers in the Third World.

The master plan to federalize education and tie it into the workforce originated with the now infamous "Dear Hillary" letter written on November 11, 1992 by Marc Tucker, president of the National Center on Education and the Economy (NCEE). It lays out a plan "to remold the entire American system" into "a seamless web that literally extends from cradle to grave and is the same system for everyone," coordinated by "labor market boards at the local, state and federal levels" where curriculum and "job matching" will be handled by counselors "accessing the integrated computer-based program."

—Phyllis Schlafly Report, *April 2000*

Classic Reason #6: Get a Job

Nothing worries parents today as much as the possibility that their child will grow up to be unemployed—and unemployable. As a close second, there's the worry that they will end up in a dead-end menial job, like so many other GenX'ers. On a survival level, you might feel that great academics are nice, but you'd settle for just being sure your son or daughter can always get a decent job.

Homeschoolers have two advantages here:

1. Homeschool culture lends itself to starting your own business. You can't get fired if you're the boss!
2. The word is out: Homeschoolers make excellent workers. They're energetic, enthusiastic, comfortable with adults and authority figures, more polite than other kids, and good team players, thanks to years of helping Mom and Dad with the chores.

As *HR Magazine* of December 4, 2001, reported:

At Chick-fil-A headquarters in Atlanta, Andy Lorenzen helps recruit the 30,000 front-line workers at the company's 1,000 restaurants across the country. It's a daunting task in the fast-food industry's revolving-door environment. It's especially challenging at Chick-fil-A, where the goal is to hire young counter workers and kitchen aides—average age 17—for the long run. As of last year, more than half of Chick-fil-A restaurant operators had come up through the ranks.

THE SHIFT FROM ACADEMICS TO ATTITUDES

Elementary and secondary school education used to be organized around subjects such as reading, math, history, geography, language, and science. While smatterings of those subjects are still taught, the focus has been shifted from academic subject matter to teaching attitudes, beliefs, values, themes, behaviors, and job skills. This is indoctrination, not education. Left wing professors write the textbooks and the teachers unions control the public schools, so the ideology is what those groups deem politically correct.

—Phyllis Schlafly Report, *March 2002*

HOMESCHOOLERS ARE THRIVING IN THE BUSINESS WORLD

The number of homeschooled children has tripled over the past decade. Those in the first wave have graduated, gone to college and entered the workforce, and now employers are getting their first glimpse of what homeschoolers can do. Anecdotal reports show that homeschoolers are thriving. Long before they get their first full-time jobs, many have accrued years of experience through apprenticeships, part-time employment or work in their own enterprises or in their families' businesses.

"They're well-versed in basic business principles," says Gary Knowles, professor of adult education at the Ontario Institute of Studies in Education at the University of Toronto. Knowles, who has studied home educated adults, says, "There's a sense that if they want to do something, they can. They have discipline to either run their own business or become quite focused employees."

—HR Magazine, *December 4, 2001*

Employers will always pick a worker who has a good attitude and decent skills over one with a borderline attitude and excellent skills. With homeschooling, you can turn out a kid who has both the excellent attitude *and* the excellent skills ... and the savvy and confidence to get where he's going.

To find reliable employees, Chick-fil-A prefers to tap what it believes is a unique source of talent—high school- and college-age homeschoolers—young people who have been educated at home rather than sent to public or private schools.

"They're smart, ambitious and very driven," Lorenzen says of his homeschool employees. "They have a high level of loyalty to the business, are diligent and have a good work ethic." A nine-year HR veteran at Chick-fil-A, Lorenzen's success depends on the quality of his hires. "When it comes to homeschoolers, I've only heard good things from our restaurant operators who employ them."

Chick-fil-A may be on to something. Homeschoolers are popping up everywhere, moving seamlessly into college and the workplace, thriving in internships and in entry- and professional-level jobs.

They're also making a mark as entrepreneurs. . . .

In the final analysis, if you're hiring, homeschoolers may be a good investment. Cutting through the stereotypes, [Patricia] Lines, [a former U.S. Department of Education researcher and now a senior fellow at the Discovery Institute, a Seattle based public policy organization] who has studied the movement for many years, perhaps says it best. "If I didn't know anything about someone other than their education background, I'd rather hop into a foxhole with a homeschool kid than one from public school. The homeschool kid will be a little better educated and dependable. It's just the law of averages."

We've looked at the six classic reasons for homeschooling. Now, here are 12 more, some of which have only emerged in the last few years.

- "I don't want my child shot at, stabbed, or scared by school bomb threats."
- "I don't want my child to be bullied at school."
- "I don't want my kid to get addicted to illegal drugs or alcohol."
- "I don't want my medically frail or young child to be exposed to unnecessary infectious diseases . . . or my child, who has an infectious disease, to put other children at risk."
- "I don't want my child to be a junk-food junkie."
- "I worry about mandated vaccinations for schoolchildren."
- "I don't want my child on Ritalin."
- "I don't want my child fingerprinted like a crook."
- "I don't want my child exposed to invasive and manipulative classroom surveys."
- "I want my child to gain real self-confidence based on achievement, not phony self-esteem based on inflated grades."
- "I want my son to have confidence in his masculinity, instead of being made to feel guilty for being a boy."
- "I don't want my sons and daughters exposed to the idea that sexual promiscuity is OK and inevitable, or sexual how-tos that now start as early as kindergarten."

If you're nodding your head in agreement, you're ready to find out what nobody ever tells new homeschoolers . . . important things you need to know . . . in the very next chapter!

CHAPTER 5

Ten Things You Need to Know Before You Get Started

I n this chapter, we're looking at the Frequently *Un*-asked Questions. These are all the questions you don't know enough to ask, but that will save your life when you find the answers! We asked veteran home-schoolers to share their most valuable piece of advice—in a nutshell. And here's what we got.

Protect Your Time

YOUR UNASKED QUESTION: "How do I say no when well-meaning people ask me to take the time I should be spending on homeschooling and put it into various other worthy projects instead?"

TAMMY SAYS: If the word *no* is not in your vocabulary, add it now. Friends, your church, your son's scout troop . . . These people and more will see you as a stay-at-home parent with time on your hands. You're not.

So practice saying, "I'm sorry, Sue, but NO, I can't talk right now. We're in the middle of school." "I would love to help with the church social, but NO, I really won't have enough free time." "I know you're in a bind, Bill, but NO, I don't believe I could take over the scout troop right now."

Now, obviously, you won't be telling *everyone* no. There are many enriching things you can do and will make time for if necessary. I can almost guarantee, however, that you will have many opportunities to use this new addition to your vocabulary.

ANOTHER MOM SAYS: I never could say no easily. So I would say, "Let me check my schedule and get back to you." This made it easier to determine if I really wanted to do something extra and allowed me to consult with my spouse and others involved.

WHAT WE WISH WE'D KNOWN

Dear Friends,

You ask whether there is anything we wish we had known before we started homeschooling. First, we expected we could make school completely fun for our child....

Second ... we expected our child to naturally love learning. The advertisements for curriculum materials all show happy and motivated students, don't they?

Third, we got the idea that if our child was having difficulties, it must be the curriculum's fault.

A fourth part of faulty thinking on our part was that it wouldn't take that much of our time to homeschool. Even with an "independent study" type of curriculum like Christian Light Education, some time must still be taken for preparation.

Then, we somehow got the notion that it would not take our child long to do his work. This did not prove to be true either.

Also, we expected our little pupil to be able to work quite independently without a lot of supervision. While this picture may have some validity in the upper grades, plan on spending several hours each day working with very young children, especially those who are just learning to read.

Finally, we expected things to go smoothly.

When we actually began homeschooling, however, we were in for a bit of a shock.

We spent much time and effort trying to make up games and exciting ways of presenting the material, but our little pupil was not nearly as enthralled ... as we thought he would be. We finally realized that no matter how well the material is presented, it still takes a certain amount of effort to learn it. Our little pupil simply did not want to work. When we finally realized this, we stopped expending so much effort on making things fun

_____ Check calendar

_____ Check money

_____ Check babysitter

_____ Check feelings

If these feel uncomfortable in any way, the answer is always NO!

RICK SAYS: My/our bit of advice is this: When homeschooling, make sure *that* time is only for homeschooling. Put the phone on auto-answer, make no appointments during that time because it is "convenient," and dedicate your attention to your children and their learning. This teaches prioritization, gives structure, and lets the kids know that their learning is very important to you. They will respond with a much more serious attitude about their own learning, knowing that both parents are also committed to it (and that you walk the talk).

PAM SAYS: You are pouring your life into the next generation of leaders. That is a very time-consuming and worthwhile investment. Give it your all, not your leftovers. God bless you as you persist. May you not take any comments or reactions from others personally, but may you bless them. Our esteem comes from the Lord—being true to His Word, not our peers. Isn't that what we are teaching our young ones?

Don't Expect Amazing Results Overnight (It Takes a Few Years)

YOUR UNASKED QUESTION: "How do I know when I'm doing enough? Shouldn't my child be discovering nuclear fusion or at least building perfect scale models of the Eiffel Tower by our second week of homeschooling?"

REBECCA SAYS: Often, even as a veteran homeschooler, I wonder if I'm doing OK by my child. Remember, the only frame of reference we have is the institutional setting—it's what we grew up with. Don't judge what you are doing by what the schools are doing. Relax, your kids are learning more than you may realize.

MARY SAYS: I used to wonder the same thing. Then, as my children got older, they began doing the exciting things that they were too young to attempt for the first years we homeschooled. What made the biggest difference to this overanxious momma was when they started entering contests. Even when they didn't win, their skills improved measurably, and they made some great-looking projects. So I'd say, "Give time a chance, and try a few contests." The spelling bee, local homeschool science fair, and local homeschool art competition are great places to start.

Build Lots of Bookshelves

YOUR UNASKED QUESTION: "Where am I going to put all of the books I will eventually end up buying?

KEN SAYS: We started in one room we naturally call the library, then added two walls in our daughter's room. Now we are in the process of putting two walls of shelves in the older boys' bedroom. After that we will go over the doorways in the library and possibly into the living room, but just up high. It seems like all the children have the same habit of collecting good books, so their rooms seem like the appropriate place. I just keep wondering who in the world would buy this house if we decided to move!

ANOTHER PARENT SAYS: We built bookshelves down our long narrow hallway using cinder blocks and eight-foot boards. Now all our encyclopedias and etc. are available to us. There are no nail holes in the wall. And it keeps the hallway from being wasted space.

MARY SAYS: If I had it all to do over again, when we bought our house I'd have lobbied for a relatively inexpensive wall of bookshelves in our living room instead of the expensive fireplace, which actually makes our house *colder* on the few occasions we've used it. We've lined half the walls in our basement with bookshelves, plus most of our bedrooms, and *still* it's not enough shelf space!

Update Your Insurance

YOUR UNASKED QUESTION: "What disaster am I forgetting to prevent?"

"D LADY BUG" SAYS: Go get your home owner's or renter's insurance updated. We had a fire that wiped out everything from the stairs up. Sit and think about the replacement cost of all those books you buy, and shudder. Don't think it can't happen; you just never know. Educational materials are very expensive. Update the insurance value frequently, especially after a large purchase.

MARY SAYS: When you hear on the news that an entire community is devastated by floods, a hurricane, or an earthquake, this means that the homeschooling families in that community suffer the loss of their curriculum. We've seen the homeschool community pull together to help such families, but prevention is better than cure! If your home and possessions aren't insured, or aren't insured sufficiently, now is the time to get up to date. And that goes double for life insurance. Sufficient life insurance means the surviving spouse will be able to continue homeschooling—and providing that continuity in your children's lives—when those children need it most.

Don't Buy It Until You Need It

YOUR UNASKED QUESTION: "Should I stock up on curriculum for future years?"

TAMMY SAYS: I was given this advice in my first year of homeschooling (ignored it, of course) and ended up with a houseful of junk that I later had to get rid of because it took up more space than it was worth, tied up more money than it was worth, etc. I've found that, no matter how much I think I might need something in the future, when the future gets here I generally have plenty of time to go out and buy it. I suppose the only exception to this would be if a generous set of grandparents were to say, "Buy whatever you need to get started, and I'll foot the bill." I'd still try to be realistic, though, because you later find yourself feeling guilty about the things you're not using.

Don't Be Scared to Buy It If You Think You Need It

YOUR UNASKED QUESTION: "Do I dare to buy *anything?* I'm panicked thinking I might end up with a product I don't like or can't use."

MARY SAYS: You are going to spend money on products you will never use. This happens to all of us (see Tammy's advice above!). Even if you're careful to wait until you need it *right now,* you may find you don't enjoy it, it doesn't work, you find something better, and so on. Don't let this worry you. First, you usually can find another homeschooler who'll buy it from you at a discount. Second, every time you buy a homeschool product, you're not just buying "stuff for the kids," you're buying an education for *yourself.* When you start saying, "I could do better than that packaged curriculum," or "I

and concentrated on the discipline of learning. Now when we do have games, they are more appreciated!

We tried several highly touted (and rather expensive!) reading and math packages with indifferent results. After these experiments, we finally came to the conclusion that there is no "perfect" curriculum. . . . In the end we decided to pick a curriculum that lines up with our Christian convictions as closely as possible and just stick with it. . . . Now, we may add or subtract a few things, but we are not constantly looking for something bigger and better.

What we discovered is that homeschooling tends to show up our own character flaws. It can be hard to admit our own weaknesses, but as we do so we have a chance both to grow ourselves and to teach our children. It's been encouraging to discover that one does not have to be perfect to get the job done. Remember, we trust in our wise heavenly Father for grace to persevere and for wisdom to learn the lessons He has for us. We have found that He is indeed faithful!

—Letter from "a Virginia homeschool family," Christian Light Education LightLines, *Homeschool Edition*

disagree with the way this grammar course works," you're *really* saying, "This product has taught me something important about what works and what does not work." Think of it this way: It would cost you tens of thousands of dollars, and years of time, to get an education degree. If you end up spending even hundreds of "wasted" dollars to become an expert homeschooler, that's a tremendous savings in comparison!

Learn to Do At Least Some of Your Own Research

YOUR UNASKED QUESTION: "If I need help, shouldn't I just ask?"
MARY SAYS: Sure, go ahead and ask, but *first* do a few simple things:

1. **If you're thinking of posting a question on an online forum, first read the previous posts in that forum.** Recently one of our forum contributors started a message thread entitled, "Doesn't anyone ever read the posts?" remarking on this very tendency. The favorite oft-repeated questions: "How do I start?" and "Where can I find out how to take the GED at home?" (Answer: You can't, because it isn't offered at home.) Homeschool veterans are happy to help . . . but not anxious to keep repeating themselves again and again when they have already made the effort to share the requested information.

2. **Try to be specific.** Every homeschool veteran knows what it's like to get a call from an eager newbie wanting to hear "all about" homeschooling. (If this is you, read this *whole* book first before you call your friend!) If you need help getting a rebellious child to study, or motivating a daydreamer, or preparing a unit study on Alaska, say so. And if you don't know *what* you're looking for, describe your situation in detail, so others have some hope of spotting what kind of help is needed.

3. **Put yourself in the position of the homeschool veteran or leader you're talking to or emailing.** Recognize this individual is taking time from his or her busy life to answer your questions—time he or she could be spending with his or her own family—and try to keep it brief.

4. **Don't take it personally** if the person you ask for help redirects you to a book or online source. Your questions may very well need the longer and more detailed answers found in such resources.

5. **If the people you ask say they'd like to help, but just don't have the time to answer your questions, believe them.** We all get swamped from time to time.

6. And here's one from me personally: ***Please* don't ask homeschool magazines to email you articles from back issues!** Big-time magazines and newspapers maintain articles databases and charge you for every article you read. Small-time magazines, like all homeschool magazines, often need to make a few dollars from selling their back issues. They may have put some of their back issues online for free, but that doesn't mean they have the staff to put everything they ever printed online for free, or that they can afford to do so. If you don't find it online, realize you'd be asking someone to spend a couple of hours processing this article just for you, while not paying them a dime.

How to Use Search Engines

People email me all the time with questions like, "How can I find out information on homeschooling children with special needs?" or "Where can I find statistics about homeschooling?" If they had gone to **www.yahoo.com** and typed in

homeschooling and "special needs"

or

homeschooling and research

respectively, they would have found the sites they were looking for on their own.

The rule is, "Put quotes around phrases you want to appear in the site." If you type

homeschooling and special needs

(notice the lack of quote marks) you could bring up a story on how a *homeschooling* child named Suzy has a *special* doll and her mom thinks homeschooling does the best job of meeting Suzy's *needs*. This would not be what you're looking for, so be sure to use those quote marks!

To find more advanced searching techniques, just click on the "Advanced Search Techniques" link on the Yahoo search page.

The best thing about doing your own online searching is that so often it leads you to unexpected treasures—sites you would otherwise never have known were there. Plus, you'll feel much more independent and expert, which is always a good thing!

Aletheia's Guide to Homeschool Slang
by Aletheia Price, homeschool graduate

In general, I abhor modern slang. This is not due to any extraordinary prudishness about perversions of the English language, but rather to aesthetics; modern slang sounds ugly when spoken, idiotic when written. For quite some time, I rather prided myself on the fact that most homeschoolers refrain from cultivating slang. However, I was proved wrong; as one public schooled friend pointed out, "You homeschoolers all sound alike!" Unlike traditionally schooled folk, who pick up their day-to-day vocabulary primarily from social interaction with their peers, homeschoolers are more likely to acquire the bulk of their vocabulary from the literature they read. Consequently, homeschoolers tend to, as the same friend put it, "talk like a book." Homeschoolers across the country are likely to have vocabularies and means of expressing themselves that differ markedly from the language patterns of any high schooled group; in short, homeschoolers have their own sort of slang.

I am admittedly biased towards homeschooling slang, finding it much more flavorful than the public schooled variety; however, for the benefit of those who might want to learn both sets of slang, I offer a Public School/Homeschool Slang Translation Guide. [Editor's note: Additional "translations" in brackets were submitted by homeschool graduates Joseph and Sarah Pride.]

Public School	Homeschool
Cool!	Frabjous! [or, Fascinating!]
Yo!	Forsooth! [or, What ho!]
'Sup?	How fare thee?
Bite me!	Go and boil your bottom, you son of a silly person!
Right on!	Indubitably! [or, Precisely!]
Hang out.	Languidly converse.
Baaaaad.	Exquisite.
Hottie.	Magnificent chap/resplendent maid.
Keep it real.	To thine own self be true.
My bad!	Mea culpa!
Wuss.	Lily-livered poltroon.
Cash.	Lucre.
Lame.	Putrid.
Airhead.	Capital nincompoop.
Totally.	Exceedingly.
Hip.	Cognizant.
Tight!	Superlative!
Bro.	Crony.
Chill!	Don't get yourself in such a tizzy! [or, Just take a deep breath and look around.]
Dude.	Earthling.
Bail out.	Make an ignominious retreat.
Phat.	Peachy keen.
Scrub.	Sub optimal.
And he was all, like…	**No translation available.**
Stoked.	Euphorious.
Wack.	Noisome.

Men, we're the heads of our households. That means I have authority over everything that happens in mine. Right? That *also* means that I'm *responsible* for everything.

If I want the dishes done after every meal, I can

- Assign the task to someone appropriate and make sure they do it
- Delegate the assigning and checking up to my wife
- Do it myself

Have you ever seen the manager of your local grocery store manning a cash register when a worker called in sick, or the manager of your local Denny's acting as a host or bussing tables? They do what they have to do so the job can get done.

Bosses pitch in and help when it's needed.

When your wife starts homeschooling, your house may not be as sparkly clean all the time, the laundry might pile up, and your meals may not be as fancy or as prompt. Take it like a man. Pitch in or hold your peace. The mission of raising your kids to be honorable, righteous, well-educated people comes first.

Here are some Bible verses on how a Christian man should treat his family:

- **"Encourage one another daily"**
- **[Jesus speaking] "Whoever welcomes one of these little ones in my name, welcomes me"**
- **"Husbands, love your wives, as Christ loved the church and gave himself for her"**
- **"Whoever would be greatest among you shall be servant of all"**

How to Help Your Wife

YOUR UNASKED QUESTION: "How can I help my wife, who will be doing most of the homeschooling?"

MARY SAYS: This is a really great question, and thanks for asking. You are a sweetie pie!

If you are extremely wealthy, you could:

- Hire a maid
- Buy individual laptop computers for each child
- Hire a live-in mother's helper so you can take your wife out to dinner whenever she wants and so she can go to the health club or go shopping during school hours without having to bring along all the kids

Since you're not that wealthy, you can:

- Mentally reset your clock so your working day doesn't end until one hour *after* you get home. Use that extra hour to give your wife a break, deal with any discipline matters that have cropped up, and let your wife and kids tell and show you what they accomplished today.
- Encourage your wife a *lot*. Especially after she's had a baby, when she may be physically feeling rather low.
- Insist that the children respect their mother, and *always* back her up.
- Insist that the children treat each other kindly and support each other in public. Remember, you're homeschooling to create a *positive* peer environment.
- Act proud of your wife in public. Homeschooling is a major accomplishment, and she deserves accolades for it.
- Open your wallet when it comes to curriculum. To do the school, you need the tools.

Above is the *minimal* support any homeschooling mom needs. In addition, it would be great if you could:

- Include the kids in your real-world work or hobbies. Show them how to change a tire, make a birdhouse, solder circuit boards, fix the plumbing, catch a fish, and mow the grass. (I'm sure you can think of some extra reasons for teaching them that last one!)
- Could you maybe teach one subject in the evening, such as math or science? Or at least grade the children's work in one subject?

If she's sinking under the strain, be prepared to jump in and help out. God loves a man with dishpan hands.

Say Thank You to Your Leaders

YOUR UNASKED QUESTION: "How can I be a blessing to other homeschoolers right from the start?"

REBECCA SAYS: I hesitate to put this in, lest someone think I'm asking for a pat on the back . . . but here goes. Say, "THANK YOU!" to your support group leaders! One simple card can go a *long* way to encouraging him or her. And a card or note is better than a phone call—they can pull it out and refresh themselves when the going is bumpy. Believe me, I know, and the times I have gotten one are the best!

TAMMY SAYS: You've actually gotten a thank you? Golly. . . . All kidding aside, folks. I wouldn't have thought to say it myself, but I've been a leader since before we started homeschooling our sons five years ago (the word "drafted" comes to mind). I did consider giving it up last year and a large part of it was that I didn't feel like I was getting anywhere. Ah . . . I won't go into it. . . . but, yeah, a "thank you" is a wonderful idea.

RENEE SAYS: Me too! And I read those notes over and over! Actually, let's get real here: What we'd really like is an offer to babysit our kids and a gift certificate to an adult restaurant (one where they don't give you crayons when you are seated). Did you ever wonder why leaders always get nice gifts upon quitting? Seems like we should give them gifts to encourage them to stay on.

MARY SAYS: Believe it or not, even curriculum publishers and book writers appreciate a bit of encouragement now and then. If a writer, speaker, webmaster, tutor, neighbor, or relative has helped you be a better homeschooler, spread the sunshine around a little. After all, someday *you'll* be the one helping others!

Abraham Lincoln's Stepmom Was a Homeschooler

YOUR UNASKED QUESTION: "Make me feel better about this. Hasn't public schooling been around forever? I'm afraid I'll be doing something really new, untested, and radical."

MARY SAYS: Actually . . . you won't. There's nothing new or radical about homeschooling.

Most people are unaware what a recent invention modern schooling is. From the dawn of human history until the mid-1800s, it was understood worldwide that young children belonged at home with their mothers. If they lived in a literate culture, when they were ready to learn to read—at around age eight, or later—they would be either taught by their parents or sent to a "dame school" to learn the basics. Apprenticeship and mentoring were the way children learned the skills to become adults, with formal schooling a very small part of a very few people's lives.

Even after the public school system was set up and compulsory attendance laws were passed, some parents still managed to give their children their special, personal kind of education.

To the right, you'll see a list of some famous people who have been homeschooled, both in "olden times" and more recently. As you can see, this is an educational method with proven results. And the parents of all these famous people weren't superstars. Abraham Lincoln's stepmother, Sarah, didn't even have a high-school diploma!

Still, is homeschooling the right educational method for *you?* Are you up to the job?

In the next chapter, you'll see why homeschooling, although it does take time and effort, is not as overwhelming or complex as you may have thought it was.

FAMOUS HOMESCHOOLERS

While this book would not be big enough to list *all* the famous people in history who have been homeschooled, here is a small sampling, in no particular order:

- The four faces on Mount Rushmore: Abraham Lincoln, Franklin Delano Roosevelt, George Washington, and Thomas Jefferson
- Hans Christian Anderson, author of *The Little Mermaid* (the original story, not the movie!) and many other beloved fairy-tale classics
- Alexander Graham Bell, inventor of the telephone and phonograph
- Irving Berlin, composer
- Noel Coward, playwright
- Charlie Chaplin, actor
- George Washington Carver, African-American savior of the agriculture of the South
- Winston Churchill, British Prime Minister
- Thomas Edison (his teacher said he was "addled" and impossible to educate, so his mom pulled him out of school and the rest, as they say, is history!)
- Albert Einstein, inventor of the Theory of Special Relativity
- Benjamin Franklin, Founding Father, author, publisher, and inventor
- C.S. Lewis, author of the tales of Narnia and much more
- The Wright Brothers, inventors of the airplane
- Wolfgang Amadeus Mozart, pianist, composer, and child prodigy
- Patrick Henry, Founding Father
- John Wesley, founder of Methodism
- Jonathan Edwards, preacher and first president of Princeton
- John Newton, hymnist
- John Marshall, the first Chief Justice of the Supreme Court
- Supreme Court Justice Sandra Day O'Connor, who used Calvert curriculum in kindergarten

CHAPTER 6

You Can Do It!

L ife is what happens while you're making other plans. Homeschool is what happens while you're living your life.

You don't need a special, ideal set of circumstances in order to successfully homeschool. You just have to start. Read this chapter and you'll see that if there's a will, there's always a way to homeschool!

You Don't Have to Be Home All Day Doing Nothing but Homeschooling

The ideal homeschool situation is for Mom and Dad to be home all day and relatively free to supervise and instruct the children. That's why many homeschool families start home businesses.

Many of you reading this are not blessed with this ideal situation. You might be the primary homeschool parent and be

- raising your children alone, due to death, divorce, or desertion of a spouse
- working outside the home part-time
- working outside the home full-time
- working at home part- or full-time
- working odd shifts

Families can and do homeschool in all these situations. It just takes more creativity—and a curriculum that doesn't exhaust you, preferably one where the children can do most of the work on their own. A lot depends on how reliable the children are, so character training *must* come first. In practical terms, this is best accomplished by teaching your children to do the household chores. This will uncover any areas that need character education more quickly than you could imagine! It also accomplishes another essential goal—freeing up enough of your time to actually teach them.

If a child is highly motivated, you can use any method compatible with his and your goals. If a child is less motivated, you'd be wise to consider "back to basics" textbooks (assign X pages a day, and you can immediately see if the work for each day is done), educational software (in this case, your child needs non-educational computer games to be *inaccessible* during homeschool hours), Robinson Method, and online academies. Contests can be highly motivating, but success often requires extra help from parents (e.g., drilling spelling words), so use sparingly.

You Don't Have to Have a Small Family

A large family is a blessing, and homeschoolers tend to have families larger than the national average. With more kids, it works well to "cluster" them in groups of two or even three, doing the same projects and contests and studying the same books. Older students can amplify their studies with additional reading.

Money is a factor in two ways: You probably have less of it per child, but on the other hand a reusable resource also costs less per kid. So a $159.95 Odyssey Atlasphere III costs almost $160 per child in a family with one child, but under $17 per child for my nine kids!

As a mother of nine, I would definitely urge other large families to go for reusable quality. Hardbound textbooks. Laminated wipe-off maps. Sturdy construction kits with storage cases (so the parts don't get lost and you end up having to rebuy the kit for another child). I can't think of a single time I've been sorry that I paid more for quality. But if you fall in love with a workbook series (such as Key Curriculum Press's wonderful Key to Geometry series), don't beat yourself up over having to buy it again and again for each child. Kids like to have *something* that wasn't passed down from an older sibling!

Use any homeschool method that fits your available time and goals. As you teach the same curriculum year after year, you'll just get better and better!

You Don't Have to Be Rich

Interested in advice on "frugal" homeschooling? See the review of *Home Schooling on a Shoestring* in Chapter 10.

In spite of the fact that one in twenty Americans is a millionaire (true fact: I did *not* make that up), in 48 years I have yet to meet anyone who describes himself or herself as "rich." Let me help you figure out where you stand as a homeschool shopper—and show you that *anyone* can homeschool, no matter how much or little they have to spend.

- **If you want something and are able to buy it immediately**, you are rich. But you don't have to admit it. Such families typically spend $900 and up per child per year for homeschool curriculum and supplies. This is great for the highschool years especially, when online academies can make advanced studies so much easier.
- **If you can buy *most* things you want right away** and only have to budget and save for *some* things, you are well off. This type of family typically spends $600–$900 per child per year for homeschool curriculum and supplies. This puts you in the market for an online course or two per child, plus more ordinary curriculum for other subjects.
- **If you have to budget and save for *most* things**, you are average. Expect to spend $300–$600 per child per year. This will get you a full year of most packaged curriculum, plus some extras.

- **If you are losing ground each month and don't know why**, you probably don't *have* a budget and need to contact Christian Financial Concepts immediately (800-722-1976, *www.cfministry.org*). Founded by noted Christian financial author and speaker Larry Burkett, their books, tapes, and free phone advice have helped tens of thousands of families get out of the debt trap. Trust me. Call them. And plan your curriculum around a lot of trips to the free public library.
- **If you are out of work, on welfare, or some combination of the above**, this would qualify as "poor" in America—which still is "rich" compared to three-fourths of the present world and 99 percent of those who lived in the past. I say this as someone who lived for many years on *less* than people on welfare were getting, so I'm not unsympathetic to your plight. Here are some things you can do: (1) Get together with others in the same situation to pool your resources. (2) Buy used curriculum. You can find advertisements for companies that sell used curriculum in the *Practical Homeschooling* classifieds. (3) And here's a special tip. **Libraries often buy materials recommended by their patrons.** If you'd like to see homeschooling books, magazines, videos, and reference materials in your library, *just ask for them.* It doesn't cost a dime to ask!

You Can Learn Along with Your Kids

Rule of thumb:

The better the parent's education, the less the child's curriculum has to cost.

I don't mean just *school* education, mind you. If you are a voracious reader, you probably know a *lot* more than you did when you completed your school education. Your life experiences have also taught you a lot, which you can and should share with your children for valuable character education.

A highly educated person *who has learned how to teach* can take a student up to college level in all subjects using only library books, pencils, and paper. A less highly educated person or one who has not yet learned how to teach will need some help. That where all the thousands of curriculum products reviewed in this and the other volumes of the *Mary Pride's Complete Guide* series come in.

The most cost-effective education is the one you give yourself. But if you lack the energy, time, or motivation to stay a year or two ahead of your student, then learning along with him or her works just fine. Most homeschool curriculum is designed to be used this way. High-school curriculum may not even require you to know *or* learn the subject, just grade the homework with the grading key. Online academies provide teachers, too!

A good homeschool curriculum will teach you how to teach. As you follow the lesson plans and teaching instructions, you'll automatically pick up teaching techniques and learn how teaching works. That's why I recommend new homeschoolers *use a packaged curriculum* from among those found in the Quick Resource Guide *for at least one full school year.* The day-after-day practice of doing it "their way" will eventually lead you either to decide you *love* "their way" . . . or to rebel and start getting your own ideas. Either response is great. If you have found the perfect curriculum for your

HOMESCHOOLING NEAR AND FAR

Every issue of *Practical Homeschooling* features "Day at Our House" diaries from homeschool families. So far, we've had diaries from city families, missionary families, and travelling families from across the USA and Canada and around the world!

EXACTLY!

I regularly teach classes at a local university that are full of students well on their way to becoming public school teachers. In a recent class, I was sharing the research that seems to support the strong achievement of home schoolers. In an attempt to stimulate their thinking, I was lobbying rather forcefully for the virtues of this educational choice.

After listening patiently, one student raised her hand and rather heatedly stated, "If I had one or two children, instead of thirty, I could produce the same results. That mom is getting those results not because she is a brilliant teacher but because she has a huge numerical advantage over me."

—*William Eckenwiler,*
A+ Education: Choosing the Best
School Option for Your Child

family, why change? You'll just get better each year you teach it. If, on the other hand, this curriculum has taught you what you do and don't want to do, it has made you independent. You can't help but win!

Of course, I do not recommend picking a curriculum you are bound to eventually hate. About half of this book was written to help you avoid this ugly fate!

You Can Homeschool Anywhere

The country is definitely the place for unit studies and projects of all kinds. You have the room, the land, and the animals. You can roam around outdoors without worrying unduly about muggers or "bad air days."

The city is the place for field trips. Museum. Orchestra. Planetarium. Botanical garden. Stage shows. You name it, a large city will have it, as well as chess clubs, amateur dramatic societies, martial arts academies, and on and on.

Suburbs are usually close enough to a city for *some* field trips. They also tend to have good libraries with no spooky characters hanging around in them. Sadly, suburbs universally forbid you to own useful animals (goats, sheep, chickens) while allowing all those who are so inclined to own loud, menacing dogs. I have never been able to grasp the logic behind this, except that if you had some useful animals it might seem you *needed* them to help make ends meet and thus were *poor* (how awful!). In my suburban neighborhood, you can't put up so much as a tiny shed in your backyard with special permission (which will likely not be forthcoming). This can severely crimp the style of a would-be 4-H'er or State Fair competitor.

You can use any curriculum in any of these environments, but if you live in the city or the country, you might want to give some thought to taking advantage of the unique opportunities in your present area.

You Don't Have to Be a Certified Teacher

Classroom teachers need to know many things that homeschool parents don't need at all. It's like what lion tamers need to know, compared to what cat owners need to know.

Let's put this in the form of one of those analogies students are faced with on the SAT:

CERTIFIED TEACHERS:HOMESCHOOL PARENTS::
LION TAMERS:CAT OWNERS

A lion tamer needs to know how to control groups of large, dangerous beasts, armed only with a chair and (maybe) a whip. He also needs to know how to teach these animals to do difficult tricks successfully even when they are distracted by loud music and cheering crowds. This requires years of training.

A cat owner, on the other hand, only needs to know where to buy "Kibbles," how to clean a litter box, and how to tell if their one particular cat is in good health or ill.

Similarly, a classroom teacher needs to know how to control large groups of strange children, armed only with her voice and personality, plus (maybe) some backup from the school administration. Most of the useful part of teacher training is about how to do this.

But you will not be managing large groups of children unrelated to you in your homeschool, will you?

The other side of the coin is that certified teachers are actually among the least academically successful college graduates. While not to impugn the abilities of the many fine teachers out there, the fact is that the average certified teacher did *less* well in high school and college than the average college graduate. This is not a group of specially selected academic whizzes, in other words.

Most people still don't know that certified math teachers do not have to be math majors or even take special math courses, science teachers don't have to be science majors, and so on. What they require is a certain number of credit hours in math *education* and science *education,* which is a very different subject. The actual facts and skills of math and science are not taught in these education courses. This explains how large numbers of schoolteachers each year fail basic tests of competence that require only an eighth-grade level of competence to pass.

Based on the first federal study to follow college graduates into the workplace, *Education Week* made the following statement in 2000:

- "Both those who prepared to teach as undergraduates and those who went on to do so were less likely to have scored in the top 25% on such tests (college entrance exams) than their peers who chose other professions."
- "The brightest novice teachers, as measured by the college-entrance exams, were the most likely to leave (teaching)."

Dr. Joseph M. Horn of the University of Texas at Austin, agrees. In his *Critical Look at Texas Colleges of Education* released in February 1999, he concludes, "Across Texas and the U.S., SAT's for education majors and education graduates are consistently the lowest of all college majors—from 100 to 200 points lower in most cases."

I'm not telling you to look down on classroom teachers. They have a much harder job than you do. Just realize that a teaching certificate doesn't necessarily prove the bearer is any smarter than you, and that your job as a homeschool parent is more like taking care of one little cuddly kitten that you know really well than maintaining order in a cage of wildcats.

You Can Manage Three Minutes a Day

One area you won't have to worry about beating the schools in: personal time spent with the student.

Robert Doman, head of the National Academy of Child Development, has said that the average child gets only *three minutes* of individualized instruction daily in school. Three minutes!

I don't know where Mr. Doman gets his figures, but my own school experience sure validates them.

Do you think you can beat this at home? Even fifteen minutes a day is five times more personal instruction than your children get in school!

You Can Answer Questions or Look Up the Answers

Most of the time teachers spend in class is *not* spent answering questions. In fact, a survey in *Instructor* magazine several years ago showed that in the average class the teacher answered between 0 and 1 questions per hour *from the entire class*. In most cases, the teacher didn't answer *any* questions. In fact, teachers are reduced to begging the class to even answer *their* questions ("Can anyone tell us when the Declaration of Independence was signed? Anyone? Anyone?")

So What ARE They Teaching Certified Teachers?

A recent report on the education schools in Colorado sheds a great deal of light on the content of teacher education. The Colorado Council of Higher Education commissioned education professor David Saxe of Penn State to study the ed schools there to determine whether they were meeting the standards set by the state for such institutions. Saxe's report is a real eye-opener.

Colorado's "flagship" university is the University of Colorado at Boulder. Saxe's analysis of UC's education program was devastating. The school is accredited by the National Council for Accreditation of Teacher Education (NCATE), which may sound nice, but in fact requires an institution to embrace the "progressive" faddishness that Professor Saxe and other believers in traditional pedagogy decry. He wrote that the program at UC was "systematically shaped by progressive theories of social justice" and that most of the courses were characterized by "excessive proselytizing" and "strident indoctrination of students."

Proselytizing for what? NCATE is a bastion of educationists committed to the view that the main goal of schools is to right the wrongs of society (from a collectivist perspective) rather than to teach children fundamental skills and knowledge. Saxe quotes one prominent educationist who writes that "teaching and teacher education are fundamentally political activities and it is impossible to teach in ways that are not political and value-laden." Schools should "help students understand and prepare to take action against social and institutional inequities that are embedded in our society." Forget the three Rs; saturate the kids with collectivist ideology.

—George C. Leef, "The Trouble with Teacher Training," Ideas on Liberty, *November 2001.* Ideas on Liberty *is a publication of the Foundation for Economic Education (800-452-3518, www.fee.org)*

50 Weeks to Educate a Legend

"An American," Francis Grund remarked in 1837, "is almost from his cradle brought up to reflect on his condition and from the time he is able to act, employed with the means of improving it."

Lincoln, hardly a slouch as writer, speaker, or thinker, packed 50 weeks of formal schooling into his entire life over the 12-year period 1814 to 1826. Even that little seemed a waste to his relatives. Unless you want to argue that those few weeks made a decisive difference to Abe, we need to look elsewhere for his education. Clifton Johnson thinks it happened this way:

He acquired much of his early education at home. In the evening he would pile sticks of dry wood into the brick fireplace. These would blaze up brightly and shed a strong light over the room, and the boy would lie down flat on the floor before the hearth with his book in front of him. He used to write his arithmetic sums on a large wooden shovel with a piece of charcoal. After covering it all over with examples, he would take his jackknife and whittle and scrape the surface clean, ready for more ciphering. Paper was expensive and he could not afford a slate. Sometimes when the shovel was not at hand he did his figuring on the logs of the house walls and on the doorposts, and other woodwork that afforded a surface he could mark on with his charcoal.

—*John Taylor Gatto*, The Underground History of American Education

Since children learn best when *they* are asking the questions, right here is one of the reasons American education isn't working. For whatever reason, kids in school learn it isn't "cool" to show any enthusiasm in class. Any child who willingly answers a teacher's question without having to be drafted is labeled a "teacher's pet," "brownnoser," or "nerd." (And those are the *nice* names!) To actually *ask a question* in class is like putting on a flashing sign that says, "I am a dork. Kick me."

At home, it's just the opposite. Homeschooled kids never learn it's uncool to ask questions, so they do what comes naturally and ask you questions all day! The beauty of this is that you don't even have to know the answers. Showing kids that adults find answers by looking them up—and teaching the kids to look up answers by themselves—is an important part of a quality education.

You Can Teach Skills More Quickly Than You Expected

Here is one simple thought that can greatly reduce stress in learning. *You can master any new skill in a reasonable amount of time.*

This idea does not sound earthshaking. But when you compare it to the way schools usually teach, you'll see how revolutionary it is.

Say Johnny wants to learn to read. Does his teacher say, "OK, Johnny, I'll teach you to read. It should take about 20 hours total, and then with practice you will be able to read anything you want"? No way! Johnny is facing up to *eight years* of reading instruction. No matter how well he can read, every year he will be reviewing his sight words, writing out spelling lists, filling out endless "reading comprehension" tests, and on and on and on. Would this discourage *you*? Of course it would! And it discourages Johnny too. The task seems endless. Nothing he does will make it shorter.

> For dramatic results in your home program, just make it clear to the student that this task will *not* go on forever.

If he applies himself, he *can* finish it more quickly. Promise *not* to review him constantly on his skills. Instead, immediately put those skills to work.

How do you do this? Well, let's say you are teaching your daughter arithmetic. Once she has learned addition, throw a party. Buy her a present. Treat her to a yogurt popsicle. Do *something* to celebrate. Any ceremony you come up with will help cement the fact that an era is over. Addition study is over. (Celebrating will also make her more anxious to finish the *next* step!) Now you are not going to study addition any more. Rather, you are going to *use* addition. Let her help you tally up the checks when you balance your checkbook. Have her keep running tabs on the cost of your shopping trip. Addition is used in multiplication and division, which she will be studying next, so if you don't do anything special at all she will still be using it.

If you are trying to teach your child something that he never gets any practice using in daily life, you probably didn't need to teach it in the first place.

You Can Teach the Basics Very Quickly

Another reason school seems like such a hopeless burden to many children is that it goes on so long. Thirteen years is a longer sentence than most murderers get nowadays. Yet we toss kids into school and lock the door on them for 13 years and expect them to be enthusiastic about it!

> ## Nobody needs 13 years to learn what most schools have to teach. At the most, you need three or four.

Let me explain why I said that. It's really pretty obvious when you see how our forebears handled education. In those olden golden days, kids didn't start school until age eight or nine. They attended classes for, at the most, three six-week sessions a year, six hours a day, and by the time they were 16 they could read, write, and cipher rings around modern children. Nor was their instruction confined to the Three R's. American children of the 1700s through the early 1900s learned history, theology, geography, practical science, and hundreds of practical skills that are now only tackled in college, if at all.

When you add up the total time in school, it comes out to eight years of 18 weeks each. Modern children go to school 36 weeks a year; so by simple arithmetic four years of old-time instruction should be all it takes for similar results.

In actual fact, it has been shown again and again that 20 hours of phonics instruction is all that children need in order to read.

As for math, I had a personal experience that might shed some light on how long it should take to learn basic math up through algebra. My father, a college professor, taught me eight years of math in the summer I turned seven. For three months, he made me do nothing but math for two hours per weekday. That amounted to 120 hours for *all* basic math, as opposed to the 1,440 hours the schools now spend. Surely I am not 12 times smarter than everyone else!

Similar reasoning applies to the other subjects: history, geography, handwriting, composition, and so forth.

WHAT THIS MEANS: *Every* child who attends school, public or private, is retarded. "Retarded" means "held back." Schools are in the business of keeping children off the street and out of the job market for 12 years. So they drag out learning needlessly for years and fill up the time with mindless, boring exercises.

You may wonder what to do with a child who flashes through the standard school subjects. Don't worry. *He'll* know what to do! The whole point of learning the basics is to get to the good stuff—other languages, literature, serious writing, theological studies, designing and inventing, art, music, and on and on. By the time your children finish their basic education, it should be clear what subjects interest them enough to qualify for further study. Let Junior start a business. Send his articles to magazines. Patent his amazing arcade game. Give him a one-man show and invite the artistic community in to admire his work and suggest improvements. With the whole wide world out there, who wants to spend eight years with reading comprehension worksheets!

Independence Day

John Holt became famous for suggesting that kids can teach themselves *without* adult interference. Although this idea can be carried to extremes, it is undoubtedly easier to learn without someone hovering over you and babbling in your ear while you are trying to work.

Anyone who has a fine crop of youngsters to teach at home quickly discovers the importance of letting students do as much as they possibly can by themselves. One of my favorite lines is, "Try it. If you have trouble, come and ask for help."

Independence Motivates

Young people in [early] America were expected to make something of themselves, not to prepare themselves to fit into a pre-established hierarchy. Every foreign commentator notes the early training in independence, the remarkable precocity of American young, their assumption of adult responsibility. Tom Nichols, a New Hampshire schoolboy in the 1820s, recalls in his memoir how electrifying the air of expectation was in early American schools.

Our teachers constantly stimulated us by the glittering prizes of wealth, honors, offices, which were certainly within our reach—there were a hundred avenues to wealth and fame opening fair before us if we only chose to learn our lessons.
—*John Taylor Gatto*, The Underground History of American Education

Is There Anyone Who Shouldn't Homeschool?

There are only four classes of parents who in my opinion shouldn't consider homeschooling:

- The illiterate
- The deranged
- The criminal
- The totally selfish (but this group won't read my book anyway!)

So if you are reading and understanding this book, and you didn't steal it, you're a good candidate for homeschooling.

If you have an illiterate friend who'd like to homeschool, let them know there is hope. The desire to teach one's own children has caused many parents to pick up the threads of their own neglected educations. Once your friend has mastered the skills that will allow them to pass the GED, they're good to go!

What It Really Takes to Homeschool

These parents [from a variety of backgrounds who decided to homeschool] got fed up in different ways, but what they have in common is a willingness to sacrifice—money, career opportunities, watching soap operas—for their children's education.

—TIME, *August 27, 2001*

Sooner or later, your child will have an Independence Day. He will discover that it's actually *more* fun to tackle a tough problem and figure out the answer on his own. At this point, he may head into areas of study that *you* never learned (e.g., website design).

When that day comes, your job as a home teacher is basically over. All you'll have to do from that point on is act as a sounding board, help him find the resources he needs, and revel in your new role as the voice of experience and wisdom. You'll be amazed that it all went so fast.

You see, it's a small job after all.

PART 2

Steps to a Successful Homeschool

You don't need a laptop, a graphing calculator, or even a chair to have a successful home-school—just one motivated student and a good curriculum. Not that the electronic gizmos hurt. Judicial use of advanced technology helped our son Joseph Pride, pictured here, become a National Merit Finalist and a United States Coast Guard Academy cadet.

Homeschooling can yield financial dividends! Daniel Story earned more than $9,700 in scholarship money as a National Merit Finalist. He decided to attend Christian-based Taylor University for its computer department, even through he was offered a $34,000 scholarship to Calvin College as a merit finalist. Daniel is pictured here with his family.

CHAPTER 7

Finding Your Goals

New homeschoolers often tell me that they feel "overwhelmed." I point out that every new teacher feels this way. At least you don't have to face a class of 20 strange kids!

The good news is that you don't need to teach everything at once. You don't even need to teach everything over time.

It's doubtful, for example, that your child will need to learn model rocketry, nuclear chemistry, automotive engine repair, weaving, how to storyboard a movie, gourmet cooking, the names of all the emperors of China, advanced calculus, acrobatics, oil painting, website design, *and* Latin. Most schools only touch on a few of these skills. Some don't teach any!

The world is full of things to learn and teach. But not all are of equal importance, at least to *you*.

Figuring out your goals for your child will help determine your curriculum content and your educational method, greatly simplifying your task.

This section will help you see

- How to discover your educational goals and use them to create a short list of homeschool methods that will help you meet them
- How to make a plan based on your true priorities and resources

After you've figured out your goals and plan, I'll reveal the 12 simple steps that lead to a successful homeschool. These include:

- Four ways to connect with other homeschoolers
- Three ways to begin your own lifelong learning of the noble profession of teacher
- Four places to find homeschooling curriculum
- What to expect in your first homeschool day, week, month, and year

Go for the Goal!

The state's reasoning that children need to "learn skills for a possible goal" does not motivate learning. Students are told to learn algebra without ever being told when they may use algebra in real life. If the child doesn't know what the goal is, or if he will ever even be interested in such a goal, learning the skills is boring to the child. Adults learn the other way around —we choose a goal, then find out what skills are needed. When our eyes are on the goal, we are automatically motivated to learn the necessary skills.—*Robin Sampson*, What Your Child Needs to Know When

The Many Goals of Homeschooling

The goal of homeschooling, oddly enough, is not to give your child a quality education.

It is *to meet your goals for your children and family*—including, but by no means limited to, your goals for your children's education.

The first step in choosing a curriculum that fits is to become aware of what your true goals really are. The same applies to choosing a homeschool method. Choose the one that best meets your goals, the deep-down wishes you may not even have dared express, and you're home free.

So what *are* your goals?

Here's how we're going to try to figure this out. I'll start by listing seven major goals. These, or a combination of them, probably include your own true goals. I'm then going to explain which types of curriculum and which methods are best suited to each goal. Finally, we will take a look together at which "seasons" of life are best for each goal. This process of thinking through each goal can be applied to any additional goals you might come up with.

The goals we will be looking at fall into four categories:

- Emotional
- Spiritual
- Vocational/success
- Academic

These categories sound pretty bloodless, so let's start fleshing them out right now.

Possible Goal One—A Happy Childhood

Giving your child a happy childhood is probably the most common, and least mentioned, homeschooling goal. People who have had miserable childhoods want to give their kids the childhood they never had. People who had wonderful childhoods want to share the best of their experiences with their children. This "emotional" goal feeds into the very heart of fatherhood and motherhood—the desire to protect and nurture.

Homeschooling is a powerful way—in fact, in our world, the *only* way—to control the emotional quality of your children's life. As many of us have found, schools are cold places where children do not learn to love each other and show kindness to others on a daily basis. At worst, a child can spend 13 years being persecuted for his appearance, brightness or dullness, race, ethnic background, social class, or even for something as foolish as a funny-sounding first or last name. (Sidenote: I remember reading that an extremely large percentage of chronic criminals have odd names.) At best, schoolchildren can form small protective circles of like-minded friends. In either case, they will spend the bulk of their school years sitting still and listening to someone else talk. They will have their young shoulders loaded down with politically correct doom-and-gloom about endangered species, racism, sexism, overpopulation, pollution, world hunger, and the like, all the time being told that it's up to *them* to solve these problems *immediately*. They will be forced to engage in mindless group activities that actively assault their personal dignity. (I still vividly remember my kindergarten experience where the whole class was told, "Pretend you are a little tree waving its leaves in the breeze." Even as a five-year-old, I felt insulted.) They will be made to fear AIDS and nuclear holocaust. They will be expected to fixate on drugs, with (at best) whistle-in-the-dark campaigns with T-shirts and speeches against drug use and (at worst) curriculum that promotes the idea they should learn all about why drugs are so popular and then make their own decisions about whether to use them or not. If they are black, Native American, or any other significant racial minority, their textbooks will teach them to hate and fear whites. If they are girls, the stories they read and their history texts will teach them to resent men and boys. If they are white boys, they will be subtly taught to hate and fear themselves. Boy or girl, black or white, they will be warned that the end of the world is coming by ecological catastrophe—again, unless they *personally* take *immediate political action as children*.

Consider how you feel about the above paragraph. If you had a strong feeling of agreement with what I said, and a visceral desire to protect your children against all such negative influences, a "happy childhood" is likely one of your major, perhaps unstated, goals. If you feel neutral, or disagree, thinking perhaps that "we can't bury our heads in the sand" and therefore that even young children should be taught all about such things, I submit to you that, while you wouldn't want your children to have an *un-*happy childhood, you have other goals much higher on the list than a "happy childhood."

Please understand, I am not condemning anyone here. If close relatives of yours were Holocaust victims, for example, you might feel it is more important for your children to understand that such things can happen and to know their family history than for them to have a childhood untroubled by such thoughts. Arguments can be made on both sides: the "happy" side and the "tell them all about it" side. What I'm trying to do here is to get you to think *seriously* about your *real* goals. A knee-jerk reaction of, "Of course I want my children to have a happy childhood," defeats the purpose.

Assuming you have come down strongly on the "happy" side, here are the kinds of curriculum and resources that will most motivate and appeal to you:

- Educational and just-for-fun games of all kinds
- Shared experiences, such as field trips
- Shared projects, such as baking cookies or making a bird-house
- Reading favorite books aloud to the children and having them read to you
- Family pets
- Gardening and other outdoors activities
- Noncompetitive, or at least not wildly competitive, sports
- Co-oping with other homeschool families so the kids can make like-minded friends
- Hands-on activities of all kinds (e.g., science kits)

Methods most suitable to a happy childhood:

- Unit studies
- One of the really good correspondence programs (these employ enough mental stimulation and hands-on work to keep kids interested, and many do grow up to look upon their childhood lessons very fondly)
- Charlotte Mason Method
- Montessori Method
- WholeHearted Method
- Unschooling

What will realistically not appeal even if your friends talk you into it:

- Textbooks and workbooks for young kids. (Exception: the kind of workbooks that are full of cut-n-paste, coloring, and other hands-on activities.)
- Early formal education
- The Principle Approach
- Accelerated Education (unless your child is exceptionally brilliant and loves seatwork)
- Anything that involves forcing a reluctant writer to write a lot. It won't be a happy childhood if you spend all your time fighting over schoolwork!

Safety First Is Every Parent's Goal

Civilization began with the family, with children protected by mothers and fathers willing to sacrifice and even die for them.

If the family wasn't safe any more, if the government couldn't or wouldn't protect the family from the depredations of rapists and child molesters and killers, if homicidal sociopaths were released from prison after serving less time than fraudulent evangelists who embezzled from their churches and greedy hotel-rich millionairesses who underpaid their taxes, then civilization had ceased to exist. If children were fair game—as any issue of a daily paper would confirm they were—then the world had devolved into savagery. Civilization existed only in tiny units, within the walls of those houses where the members of a family shared a love strong enough to make them willing to put their lives on the line in the defense of one another.

—*Dean Koontz*, Mr. Murder
(*G. P. Putnam's Sons, 1993*)

Possible Goal Two—A Loving Family

In today's world of fractured families, the goal of a loving, together family is a deep "emotional" motivator. This differs from the "happy childhood" goal in that its main focus is on the child's bond with his parents and siblings, not on a medley of happy memories for the child to enjoy in later life.

It is important to note here that the "loving family" may not be present when homeschooling begins. You may have decided to homeschool because your children were turning into angry or cold strangers before your very eyes. You may be conscious of not having "been there" for them in the past, and be determined to rectify that error. You may have an unsupportive or missing spouse, and want desperately to give your children whatever family life you can in spite of it. Thus, you may not be sure you'll be able to provide a happy environment, but you're committed to forging the strong family links that will someday *result* in a happy home environment.

On the other hand, you may already have a great family life, and just not want to bust it up by sending the children off to an institution that believes peer group dependency is the pinnacle of socialization.

Either way, you plan to take positive action to make sure *your* family doesn't just drift away on the tide.

That being said, it's clear that *togetherness* is important to you. All forms of education that involve kids learning with minimal parental or sibling input will not work well for you. This means you should at first avoid:

- Traditional textbooks and workbooks (each kid is in a different grade, and while Mom can work with each kid individually, they are each isolated from their siblings by their studies. Exception: if the older children have already gone through the exact same books as the younger ones and if the older ones actively help the younger ones with their work.)
- Correspondence programs (same objections and exceptions as above)
- Video school (unless you all watch the videos together—not possible if you're using A Beka Video School for more than one grade at once)
- Early formal education
- Robinson Method and other forms of independent study
- Accelerated Education (unless all the kids are accelerated at once)

All the "happy childhood" activities will work for you. The list of most suitable methods, however, differs from the "happy childhood" list because now the essential question is whether or not several children, or the whole family, can participate in a given method. Consider choosing from:

- Unit studies (what could be more fun than making all kinds of projects and having Mom and Dad read lots of books with you?)
- Charlotte Mason Method (it's gentle and sweet)
- Great Books (if you all read them together or read them aloud to the whole family)
- Classical Education (again, learning what few people know today is a bonding experience of its own! Mom and Dad need to be willing to learn Latin, though.)
- Montessori Method (it's also gentle and sweet)
- Principle Approach is somewhat dubious, due to the large amount of time spend individually researching and writing. If American history and government is a passion with you, though, this too can be a bonding experience.
- Unschooling

One last thought to consider: While our society is fixated on the idea that each young adult should "start from scratch" and pick his own career without giving a thought to his father's vocation, carrying on the family business, or the family tradition of being involved in the military, or medicine, or teaching, forms a bond of its own. So does a daughter choosing to be a stay-at-home homeschooling mom like her mother. If a child is willing to follow in Dad or Mom's footsteps, then try hard to pick a method that lends itself to picking up that vocation in the teen and adult years. See Possible Goals Four, Five, and Six below.

Possible Goal Three—The Young Graduate

You may have good reasons for wanting your kids to be ahead of others their own age. You may have been a whiz kid yourself and enjoyed the experience. You may have relatives and neighbors breathing down your neck and need some easy way to prove to them that your homeschool is not a stupid, irresponsible idea. You may just see no reason for wasting 13 years to cover what should only take six to nine years, if you leave out all the twaddle. Or like Frank Gilbreth, Sr., the father in *Cheaper by the Dozen,* you may have a serious medical condition and be anxious to get as many of your children as possible through college before you die.

Sometimes it's the kids who are anxious to get through school as quickly as possible. I was such a child myself. Some kids are just born wanting to go places and do things—in short, to *grow up*—in a hurry. The adult world may well appeal to such a child more than the "child's world" of school, where he or she doesn't fit in.

I say all this because some of us have the ingrained idea that accelerated education is the Little League of homeschool. Instead of parents screaming at their kids on the baseball field, we now have parents pushing their poor widdle kids to perform academically.

This may in fact be the case in some situations. There's nothing preventing a "Little League Mom" type from homeschooling! But homeschooling tends to balance itself out. If children are really miserable, the homeschool parent can't avoid suffering the results of their misery right along with them. There is no coach, no teacher, no principal to take the heat off of you. All the complaints will go directly into your own ear.

On the other hand, it would take an awful lot of acceleration to really "push" a kid, in most cases. Without even trying, homeschooled kids are

For more on early graduation, see Chapter 50, "What About Acceleration?"

usually one or two years ahead of schooled kids academically. You'd have to be trying to rush a kid through all 12 grades in four years or so to really exceed most kids' ability to learn, assuming you were using streamlined curriculum.

Did I mention the word "streamlined"? This is *the* word to remember if you're thinking acceleration may be one of your primary goals. You won't have time for fooling around with silly, time-wasting projects or endless worksheets that simply test and retest what the student already knows. You need to cut to the chase.

That being so, you'll want to avoid:

- Video school—it moves too slowly.
- Delayed formal education
- Classical education—while British prep schools were able to cover this material by age 14 or 16, it's a lot harder at home unless you already know Greek, Latin, rhetoric, formal logic, and philosophy. Besides, classical education requires lots of time for reflection, and rushing through school diminishes that time.
- Great Books—too much reading (save it for college)
- Principal Approach
- Unit studies

You'll want to consider:

- Traditional textbooks and workbooks. These are condensed, quantifiable, and it's easy to tell when you're done.
- Worktexts, for the same reasons
- Correspondence programs. The world's best-known advocate of accelerated education, Joyce Swann, has always used the Calvert School program, doing two lessons per child per day. It gets easier with each successive child, too.
- Early formal education—just for the reading, writing, and math. For this, the Maloney Method works great!
- The Robinson Method
- Online classes—for the more difficult or unique subjects, freeing the home teacher to concentrate on the basics
- Unschooling—I know for a fact that many unschooled children have entered college at relatively young ages. If done right, it breeds a habit of independent thinking and research that equips kids to move into the adult world well ahead of their peers.

Possible Goal Four—My Son, the Scholar

Although I refer for the sake of the famous phrase to "my *son*" in this headline, and the next three, we could also be talking about "my daughter, the scholar or whatever." The pertinent questions here are (1) whether you consider yourself to be an intellectual, (2) whether you want your child to move in the world of ideas, and (3) whether your child seems to have any aptitude or desire for this.

If you answered a resounding, "Yes!" to all three questions, this has got to be one of your major goals. You don't just want to teach your child at home—you want him or her to achieve academic *excellence*. You don't just want your children to outshine public-school students—you want them to be able to hold their own in the society of educated people anywhere in the world.

If you are not an intellectual yourself, this becomes a more difficult goal. But who can tell if you're an intellectual? I'll make it easy, with a one-minute test.

Answer these three questions and then ask your kids the same questions:

(1) How many nonfiction books did you read in the past year?
(2) How many substantive magazines do you subscribe to or regularly read? ("Substantive" in this context means "not focused on celebrities, fashion, sex, or ephemeral trends.")
(3) How many fiction books, aside from romance novels, did you read in the past year?

Score your answers thusly:

If your answer is, "Zero," you are not an intellectual.
If your answer is, "I'm just too busy," you're not an intellectual.
If your answer is, "I can't give an exact number because I read all the time," you are definitely an intellectual.

We are not all intellectuals, so don't be embarrassed if you like to buy books and magazines with Fabio on the cover. The point of this exercise is to find out the truth about what your homeschool goals really are, remember? So why waste time struggling with Latin if you're honestly not interested?

It is, of course, possible for a non-intellectual parent to have a highly intellectual child. And there's even a way for this homeschooling situation to work out:

- Laptop homeschooling. Since the actual teacher is not the parent, all the parent has to know is how to make sure the student is getting his homework in on time.

For the more common situation where an intellectual parent is homeschooling an intellectual child, here are the methods that make most sense:

- Great Books
- Classical education
- The Robinson Method
- Unschooling, if the child is good at locating scholarly mentors

In this case, I won't bother listing the methods that won't work as well. Where A is the universe of all the methods mentioned in this book, and A' is the set of methods listed above, consider A'' to be the set that results from subtracting A' from A, and you'll find that A'' yields the set of indifferent or unsuccessful methods when it comes to the task of raising a young scholar. Proof: trivial.

Possible Goal Five—My Son, the President

The goal we're talking about here is "leadership." Many talk about it, but few think about what it really means. The Bible says, "He who would be greatest among you shall be servant of all." This has several implications for homeschoolers:

Advice from a College Professor

My father, Dr. Stuart Martin, a professor of philosophy at Boston College, has been advising college students for many years.

His advice for students who want to pursue a scholarly career is as follows:

- Take Latin, Greek, German or the *most* difficult modern language in your field while still in high school, or even earlier. See if an ethnic organization in your city offers evening courses that teach that language. The Goethe Institute, for example, offers low-cost German courses in many cities.
- Spend your junior year abroad if at all possible. When choosing a college, make sure they offer this option and that the country you'll be living in is well-suited to your future specialty. Study the language *before* going.
- High scores on the SAT and ACT are essential—plan to spend extra time preparing for them.
- High scores on several AP exams are also important. See *Mary Pride's Complete Guide to Homeschooling Grades 7–12* for several online academies with AP courses, and for test-preparation resources.

Patrick Henry College

PO Box 1776, Purcellville, VA 20134-1776. (540) 338-1776, www.phc.edu.

Perhaps the ideal college for a homeschooled student whose goal is to work in a political office as an aide or a representative is the new Patrick Henry College, founded with the blessing of several people at Home School Legal Defense Association.

PHC is adding more majors. Originally their only major was government. They have since added a Classical Liberal Arts major with two concentrations—writing and education. Future majors are planned in film, TV production, drama, music, and art. If all goes well, a law school will be added next, for which the undergraduate courses will be a fine preparation.

Second, **PHC is affordable.** Tuition, room, and board is currently $18,000 per year. Compare that to $29,000 for a year at St. John's, a well-regarded classical liberal arts college. Work opportunities around campus are available to defray part of that expense. Private scholarships are encouraged. This is good, because as a matter of principle and conviction, PHC won't take any kind of government funding at all.

Third, **PHC is rigorous.** Freshman and sophomore year feature a very intensive classical liberal arts curriculum: American history and Western civilization, a lot of composition and literature, a little bit of math and science, and some foreign language, possibly Latin. This is all delivered at a much higher level than you'll find in most colleges because they're expecting their mostly homeschool students to have a stronger liberal-arts background than most high-school graduates.

Fourth, **PHC provides an unusual amount of real-world experience**, with the specific goal of providing "the nation's best training for young men and women to serve as legislative aides for the U.S. Congress or state legislative bodies, or in staff positions in executive or administrative agencies of federal, state, or local government." For instance, in the junior and senior year, government majors study how government works, major issues in economics/social policy/foreign policy, research techniques, writing, and speech (including debate). They also prepare actual legislative analysis for members of Congress, other government offices, or (as the opportunity arises) public policy organizations and think tanks. This "directed research" work is monitored and supervised by college faculty. Since the campus is based near Washington, D.C., students have opportunities to meet and get to know personnel in government agencies and Congressional staffs, all of which spells e-m-p-l-o-y-a-b-i-l-i-t-y.

- We should not raise our kids to boss others around, but to try to find ways to help them. Highfalutin rhetoric about how homeschooled kids will be leaders someday needs to yield to a conscious desire to benefit others *whether our own contributions are ever recognized and rewarded or not.*
- You can't serve others without being around others.
- Kids imitate what their parents *do,* not what they *say.*
- The best way to learn to serve others is to do it, starting as young as possible.

So if you see your child as a future senator or church elder, start by involving your whole family now in church ministries and community service. For starters, you could volunteer to help out in your local food pantry or missionary clothes closet. For the bold, street evangelism is wonderful practice in public speaking. For the timid, bringing friendship baskets to the sick might be more your style. Older children can volunteer to help at the library or the museum. Little kids can "help" bake cookies for a church dinner or wrap presents for the needy at Christmas time.

Some homeschool methods lend themselves better than others to the skills needed for service to others. These include:

- Montessori Method—the kids learn responsibility and chores starting in preschool!
- Unit studies—you can almost always integrate your ministry into your academic program.
- Unschooling—learning from real life is a natural fit with serving in real life.
- WholeHearted Method—the fifth "D" in this method is "Discretionary Studies," which includes community involvement and life skills.

In the higher grades, kids can gain the knowledge needed by statesmen and church leaders through:

- Classical education—with its emphasis on knowing and learning from the past, as well as the entrance it provides into the society of the similarly educated upper class
- Great Books—ditto
- Principle Approach—for a detailed analysis of how government ought to work and what the real issues are

Possible Goal Six—My Son, the Doctor

Or the plumber, or the farmer, or the graphics artist. Here we are looking at the "vocational" goal of a particular trade. You may not have the precise trade in mind, but you do know that it is extremely important to you that your child successfully hold a decent job. But the job you have in mind does not involve being a scholar steeped in the classics or a political or church leader.

What is needed here is:

- A good basic education, followed by
- A further education in the particular trade.

The winning methods here are:

- Traditional textbooks and workbooks. These are great in preparing you for the all-important standardized tests on which your high-school graduation and entrance into college or a vocation depend.
- Worktexts, ditto.
- Correspondence programs, ditto, with the additional advantage that in the high-school years you get a transcript signed by someone other than dear old Mom.
- Unit studies can be a natural way to discover and prepare for your vocation.
- Unschooled kids have frequently shown great ingenuity in obtaining "adult" jobs while still quite young. This is a particularly good option if you are considering a traditional trade, such as auto mechanic or Hollywood cameraman. If your sights are set on the doctor/lawyer/dentist type of trade, you will be forced to interrupt your unschooling with a stint in college and graduate school. Impressive projects and experiences you have undertaken while unschooling will work in your favor when seeking admittance to a high-quality college, and if you read voraciously like most unschooled kids, the standardized college-entrance tests should pose no problem.

Possible Goal Seven—A Man After God's Own Heart

I saved this one for last, so you would have a chance to consider the other goals before getting all guilty over this one!

If you're a pious parent, you will be saying right now, "Of course this has to be our family's main educational goal!" But it's not quite that simple. The fact is that you can use *any* method and end up with a pious child, or use *any* method and end up with an irreligious child. It's not the method that counts now—it's how you live with your children and the books and resources you choose for your home school.

You can:

- Choose a curriculum that explicitly teaches religious history and doctrine
- Choose secular curriculum (because you believe this particular curriculum is academically or in some other way superior to the religious curriculum, or because you find the available religious curriculum lacking in truthfulness or depth) and teach religion "on the side"

Sincere Christian parents are bringing up pious kids with both options. So, I assume, are sincere Jewish parents, Muslim parents, and so on.

I would beware of anyone who insists there is only one "Christian" (or Jewish, or Muslim . . .) way to homeschool. "One-size-fits-all" education does not fit a universe in which God has made every snowflake and every child different.

There are universal facts and truths we can all agree on, such as the law of gravity and that two plus two equals four in base ten. There are also important universal facts and truths on which many of us disagree, such as the nature of God and whether there is a God. (The fact of disagreement doesn't mean there is no truth to be found; nor does it mean all religions are "true"; to believe this is to abandon all logic, even ultimately the logic that lets us know the law of gravity or that two plus two equals four in base

The Purpose of Education

The purpose of education is not to enable the student to earn a good income.

The purpose of education is not to preserve our American system of government and political freedom.

The purpose of education is not world unification.

The purpose of education is not to teach young people a trade.

The purpose of education is not to encourage the never-ending search for truth.

The purpose of education is not to put the student in harmony with the cosmos.

The purpose of education is not to raise the consciousness of students and train them for world revolution.

The purpose of education is not to prepare students for productive careers.

The purpose of education is not to integrate the races.

The purpose of education is not social adjustment of the child.

The purpose of education is not to stay ahead of the Russians (or the Japanese) in technology.

The purpose of education is not to create good citizens.

No, the purpose of education is far different, far more noble than any of these things. The purpose of education is to make Christian men [people], men transformed by the renewing of their minds after the image of Him who created them.

—John Robbins,
from the preface to Gordon Clark's
A Christian Philosophy of Education

King Solomon on the Purpose of Education

To know wisdom and instruction; to perceive the words of understanding;

To receive the instruction of wisdom, justice, and judgment, and equity;

To give subtlety to the simple, to the young man knowledge and discretion.

A wise man will hear, and will increase learning; and a man of understanding shall attain unto wise counsels;

To understand a proverb, and the interpretation; the words of the wise, and their dark sayings.

The fear of the Lord is the beginning of knowledge; but fools despise wisdom and instruction.

—*Proverbs 1:2-7*

ten.) But the *way* we teach and learn the facts and truths we know can differ from child to child, even within the same family, or be the same for two families that follow different religions.

Ultimately, godliness is knowing God and obeying Him out of love. If this is your goal for your children, you need to watch over your other goals. Happiness can turn into self-indulgence. A loving family can become clannish and selfish. Accelerated academics can lead to toplofty pride. So can scholarly studies. The desire for leadership roles can result in cutthroat ambition. An obsession with getting the kids a good job may reflect underlying materialism and lack of faith. Even the pursuit of godliness itself could be a mask for a spiritual form of showing off. That's one reason why we should all stop periodically and reevaluate our homeschooling goals. Another reason is that your goals will naturally change, over time, as your children get older and reveal new talents and interests. Make certain your curriculum and methods fit your present goals—and that those goals are worthy ones.

CHAPTER 8

Making Your Plan

S uccess in any endeavor can be approached step-by-step in this way:

- Step One: Identify your goals.
- Step Two: Make a plan.
- Step Three: Get started.

After reading the last chapter, you should have some idea of what your most important goals are for your children's education. This chapter is about how to develop a very simple "scope and sequence"—a list of the topics you hope to cover and when exactly you plan to do each one.

Let me emphasize the words "very simple." We're just getting you started here! For planning a college-application-worthy high-school transcript, you'll need the more detailed instructions in a book dedicated to that subject, such as my *Guide to Homeschooling Grades 7–12*.

No Pain, Much Gain

Let me hasten to reassure you that learning to plan your homeschool program will be a painless process. You don't need to cringe in dread of dozens of worksheets to fill out. (If you *want* dozens of worksheets and planning forms, see the chapter on "How to Keep Great Records," where planners and organizers are reviewed.) At the moment, let's just concentrate on a kinder, gentler plan . . . what you'll plan to do first each day, and which subjects and activities you will plan to spend most effort on.

The Preschool Plan

This is the one age at which One Size truly Fits All. No matter what homeschool method you have chosen, or are about to choose, and no matter what your goals are, everyone agrees that your preschool priorities should be the following:

A strategy is a specific way of organizing your resources in order to consistently produce a specific result.
—*Anthony Robbins*,
Unleash the Power Within
(1999, Nightingale-Conant)

(NOTE: The "power within" referred to on this CD seminar is not some New Age force but your own native abilities.)

If Your Plan Isn't Working

If your child does not respond well to a particular learning opportunity, it's probably because you're pushing something for which he is not ready. Back off and try again in another week, month, or year. If he doesn't respond well to *any* learning opportunity, he either has a physical problem or a character problem. If he is uncooperative with chores you know he can do, it's likely a character problem, and your best way to overcome it is to work on getting him doing his chores with cheerful obedience rather than also battling him over supposedly "fun" learning experiences. Just one more reason for *always* doing chores *first!*

For help in recognizing and dealing with genuine physical problems (e.g., allergies, eye-tracking problems, slower brain speed), see Section 9, "Homeschooling Your Special-Needs Child."

- **Chores.** More about this later. Just remember, "For a homeschool that soars, always start with the chores!" Even a preschooler can carry trash to the wastebasket or put the spoons on the table. And if they're old enough to play with toys, they're old enough to put them *neatly* away.
- **Religious instruction.** This can be as simple as answering all the many questions your little one asks, or as elaborate as memorizing a catechism.
- **Prereading.** Read aloud to the munchkin . . . a *lot*. Tell stories. Help the little one develop the ability to "see" the story in his or her head and to retell it in his or her own words.
- **Prewriting.** Making shapes with large arm motions, finger-plays, writing with your finger in the sand, and gripping and molding motions of all kinds help develop the fine motor skills needed for handwriting.
- **Hands-on activities of all kinds.** Preschools spend a fortune trying to duplicate your kitchen with its pots and pans to nest inside each other, your laundry room with its socks to sort and its laundry to fold, and your living room with its comfy rug to lie on. To this add puzzles (to teach spatial skills and logic), age-appropriate construction toys such as Duplo bricks and Dr. Drew's Blocks, washable paint and paintbrushes, modeling clay, and whatever other craft activities move you. These don't have to be expensive; whole books have been written about crafts you can do with paper plates!
- **The great outdoors.** Nature walks, chasing fireflies, and even lying with your nose in the grass watching all the bugs scurry around are all invaluable experiences for the young child.
- **Science.** I heard this from Jane Hoffman, the Backyard Scientist, so it must be true. A study was done comparing two kindergarten classes. One class did nothing but science experiences and experiments all year. The other had a normal language-arts and math curriculum. By fourth grade, the all-science class averaged one grade level ahead of the other class in *every* subject area! I heartily recommend Jane's books and kits. Janice VanCleave has written some excellent science experiment and experience books for young children as well. Her books will be reviewed in my upcoming volume on homeschooling from birth through grade 6.
- **Love of learning.** Most of all, every homeschool should start off with a sense of wonder and fun. A kid who loves to learn is a kid you'll love to teach!

So, for your preschooler, your plan should be to do as much as possible of all of the above. This may involve scheduling biweekly library trips, or daily jaunts to the park, or supervised "backyard time" every morning. You may need to purchase some curriculum (such as the Jane Hoffman books) and supplies (arts and crafts goodies). You will know if you are meeting your plan if you can "tick" off many of the activities you planned to do, either on a list or in your head.

Remember, you can plan to *introduce* a skill, and give your child the *opportunity* to try it out, but it's not possible to force a child to be developmentally ready. With a preschooler, it is much better to plan to teach him a skill (let's call it X) than to plan to teach him X *by date Y.* Feel free to ignore the element of time; this is still the period when you are getting to know your child and his abilities.

The Kindergarten Plan

At this age, some methods advise early formal academics, while others say you should still concentrate on real-world experiences. Be certain of what you're aiming for and then work out a schedule that lets it happen.

Even if you are using a formal kindergarten curriculum, these usually take only an hour or two of your time per day. The main thing to remember is

Back off from *any* academic activity for which your child is not ready!

Some signs your child is not yet ready for a particular academic activity (e.g., formal phonics instruction):

- Yawning a lot during lessons (a sure sign of comprehension overload)
- Fidgeting a lot during lessons (this may also be a kinesthetic learner who needs less seatwork and more ACTION!)
- Crying or seeming otherwise emotionally stressed by the work

Plan in advance to *drop* any activity that causes this kind of frustration until the child seems readier to face it . . . or until you locate a more appropriate curriculum directed at your child's emerging learning style.

The Early Reader Plan

You may also think of this as the "Grade 1 and 2 Plan" if you like. My suggestion for this group is, "Focus on character training, religious instruction, learning to read and write, and basic arithmetic."

While your child is learning to read, how much sense does it make to also load him down with history, geography, spelling, grammar, and on and on? Unless you want to read every instruction in the workbook to him, he can't even do most of those subjects in any traditional way.

So I say, "Plan to teach reading along with verbal counting, number identification, skip counting, simple addition and subtraction, and whatever additional *verbal* math you feel up to. Consider everything else a bonus." This avoids early burnout and gives you extra time to pick the curriculum you will be using when your child is ready for more. Too, keep in mind that most instruction in these other subjects at these grade levels is, to be kind, rinky-dink.

The Good Reader Plan (Grade 3 and Up)

Now you're ready to really get serious! You're also ready to overload and burn out if you don't plan to leave some things *out* of your homeschool program.

Your plan for this point on is to meet the educational priorities dictated by

- Your goals
- Your energy
- Your available time
- Your child's talents and interests
- Your child's learning style

First determine your goals. (See the previous chapter if you haven't done that yet). Then select your ingredients (nature walks, books, etc.) and prioritize them. (This chapter is designed to help with that step.) Finally, pick the exact resources you'll use from the other two *Mary Pride's Complete Guide* volumes and make a schedule. It's a plan!

Obviously, this will differ from family to family, which is why we need all those different homeschool methods!

Let me suggest the following plan of attack for all those courses, subjects, and skills you want your child to learn.

First, list them. You'll find a suggested starting list in the sidebar. Then sort them into

- Necessary
- Essential
- Desirable
- Bonus

Necessary refers to topics and skills the child *must* learn, but that generally give neither you nor the child any bragging rights. Chief on the Necessary list are *chores* and *character training*. Necessary skills come first; never feel ashamed to say, "All we got done today was the chores." Days spent teaching your children lessons in meeting deadlines and getting work done before play are the most important teaching days you'll have.

Essential refers to the skills that make you feel comfortable about your homeschool. If your child is not learning these skills, you feel anxious and unsettled.

For most people, *reading* tops the Essential list because it's what concerned relatives, friends, and neighbors want to see your child doing. It validates your homeschool in their eyes. If this is the first child you've homeschooled, it also validates your homeschool in *your* eyes. But beyond that, family priorities determine the Essential list. For a circus family, basic trapeze work may be on the Essential list, while for another it may be math, and for yet another it could be cooking, or Latin, or music, or art.

The key is to ruthlessly prune this list until it only contains the skills and subjects you can't live without for your child *at his current age*. Let me stress that *your* expectations are key here: You're not trying to keep up with the Joneses, and if you do, you'll end up overloading. You then prioritize your schedule so that these are the first academic subjects covered each day.

Desirable includes all those subjects and skills you want your children to learn before they leave home. "If we never get around to this subject or skill, I won't feel comfortable, but I can live with postponing it for a while until everything else is under control." Some typical subjects on this list might include French or Spanish, art, and music appreciation. While for some families these subjects are essential or even necessary (picture a concert violinist whose family travels around Europe), for other families they are not.

Bonus skills and subjects are what you'd like to teach if you had the time, but your child could graduate from homeschool without them and you wouldn't go jump off a tall building. Good subjects to put on this list are those picked up in college and the working world, or that adults can teach themselves. An overview of classical music is important for general cultural literacy, for example, but a detailed study of opera can easily wait until the student decides to tackle it on his own in later life.

Now, sit down and make your own list of which subjects and skills fall into each area. Have your spouse and children do the same. Compare lists. It will be enlightening!

Don't Stagnate—Re-evaluate

You don't just plan out your homeschool all at once and then stick to that plan for 13 years. At least, most of us don't! The most important part of your plan is remembering to re-evaluate your priorities on a regular basis. Beyond giving your children the basic tools of learning, don't let anyone shame or bully you into making *their* priorities *your* priorities. If learning to fly a kite or make a compost pile is more important to you than learning to diagram a sentence, go fly your kite. It's possible that next week or next year diagramming may loom larger on your mental horizon. Far better to share your passion for learning and life with your children than to waste years spooning instantly forgotten facts into their heads.

It's About Time

Recognize the time-wasters in your home and plan how you're going to eliminate or control them. These include

- Lengthy phone calls with friends during the homeschool day (get CallNotes or an answering machine)
- The radio
- The TV
- The VCR
- The computer

One simple suggestion: No entertainment media whatever before 5:00, or until the day's work is done, whichever comes first. If a child is obsessive about a particular entertainment medium, lying and sneaking behind your back to use it constantly or during unapproved times, break the addiction by placing them on a "diet" where they are not allowed *any* access to that medium for a while. You may find out you can live without TV or rented videos altogether!

It's About You

Just as it's true that the best gift a man can give his family is to love his wife . . .

The best gift a homeschool parent can give his or her child is to love learning.

If you don't feel like you love learning now, I have good news for you; you were *born* loving to learn. School may have taught you to associate learning with various unpleasant experiences, but homeschool is going to reverse all that. You will learn that your instincts were correct; most "school" activities are a boring waste of time. You will learn to eliminate the "twaddle" and concentrate on what is fun, exciting, and effective. You will learn subjects and skills that totally eluded you in school. You will end up smarter and more confident than you started! (This applies even to those of you who went to M.I.T. or Harvard.)

So now it's time to plan what you're going to do to further *your* education. You need time to think and study, too. The best teacher is the one who knows the subject best and has learned to share his or her passion with others. Plan to go to the library and bookstore. Plan to read books and magazines on subjects that interest *you*. Plan to have or pick up a hobby and try to get good at it. Then share your new enthusiasms with your kids. They'll love it!

CHAPTER 9

What to Join

Y ou've decided you have sound reasons for homeschooling. You've selected your homeschool goals. You have a basic plan.
Now what?
In these next three chapters, you'll find twelve steps that will set you on your road to a successful homeschool.

Step One: Join HSLDA

Joining the **Home School Legal Defense Association**, otherwise known as **HSLDA** (PO Box 3000, Purcellville, VA 20134, (540) 338-5600, www. hslda.org), is a two-step process. Normally you have to send away for an application form, but we feel so strongly that every homeschool family should join HSLDA that we've included the form in the very last pages of this book. Fill out the form, including information on what curriculum you plan to use for each child, and send it in along with a $100 check. If you are accepted (which you most likely will be), you will receive one year's worth of protection for covered legal expenses. In most cases, HSLDA can stop overbearing social workers and uninformed truant officers right at the door. In those few other cases, won't you be glad you have protection?

In addition to legal protection, benefits offered to HSLDA members include the following:

- The ability to call and speak with a legal assistant or attorney for your state about homeschooling matters or other issues ranging from social service contacts to promoting family-friendly legislation.
- A year's subscription to *The Home School Court Report*, HSLDA's newsletter.
- Eligibility to subscribe to "Fax Alert" ($10 per year) or "E-Mail Alert" services that provide timely information on federal legislation that might affect homeschoolers.
- Counseling and helpful materials from the Special Needs Coordinator for those whose children face special challenges.
- A whole range of services to military homeschoolers worldwide
- Special member benefits including discounts on *Practical Homeschooling* subscriptions, computer hardware, and educational products from several vendors.

The Truth About HSLDA

Some homeschoolers have made a crusade out of dissing HSLDA, claiming that it's a waste of money now that state laws are so lenient, that you can always do the legal research yourself, and that HSLDA leadership is promoting its political ambitions and agenda at the movement's expense. The truth is:

(1) It's only a waste of money if you object to defending other's rights as long as you yourself are not personally threatened.

(2) If you ever are personally threatened it's a terrific deal, especially considering that HSLDA usually manages to resolve the situation before it ever ends up in a courtroom.

(3) Yes, you can do the legal research yourself, just like you can do your own plumbing, make your own clothes, and cut your own hair. But do you really feel unempowered unless you're spending weeks in a law library?

(4) HSLDA's political agenda is consistent with its claimed mission of more rights for responsible

s and children. To protect
educators, they have been
forced to take up "side issues."
But these often turn out not to
be such side issues after all.
HSLDA has fought for the right
of homeschooled kids to have
driver's licenses, for example.
When a state, trying to combat
the phenomenon of public-
school dropouts, passes a law
forbidding anyone under the age
of 18 who is not enrolled in a
school to drive, HSLDA is there
to remind them that home-
schoolers are not dropouts and
the law should accommodate
them. Similarly, HSLDA's response to issues ranging from
the U.N. Convention on the
Rights of the Child (which all
but requires governments to
control all aspects of a child's
education and makes all children essentially wards of the
state), to the free practice of religion, to how military recruits
are classified, all turn out to be
pertinent to homeschoolers.

(5) Mike Farris, founder and president of HSLDA, once ran for political office—vice governor of
Virginia, to be exact—and made
a creditable showing. That was
years ago, and he has not sought
political office since. HSLDA
funds were not used to support
his candidacy, and I am aware of
no law yet making it a political
crime for homeschoolers, even
homeschool leaders, to run for
office. In fact, one of our best
friends is a homeschool dad
who is currently serving in
Congress, and I personally wish
more homeschoolers were in
political offices! So I'm not sure
exactly what the issue is supposed to be here, but I present
the facts for your consideration
all the same.

The purpose of the Home School Legal Defense Association is to establish the fact that responsible homeschooling is legally permissible in every
state. They will provide experienced legal counsel and representation by
qualified attorneys to every member family who is challenged in the area of
home schooling. The attorney's fees will be paid in full by the Association.

Run by Concerned Women for America's former legal counsel, Michael
Farris, this is a reputable organization with over 80,000 member families.
Knowing you can obtain quality legal counsel is enough to dissuade potential persecutors in some cases. So is knowing what the law says, if your
state law is favorable to homeschooling. Ask your local homeschool group
for a copy of the law (someone should have it on file). Then, if you feel you
need more protection, or if you just want to contribute to the defense of
those families that are on the hot seat, join the Association.

HSLDA also provides a slew of valuable services to the homeschooling
community, such as their monthly packets for state leaders with summaries
of bills submitted to state and federal legislatures. They personally contact
government officials when some new policy impinges on our freedoms.
Example: HSLDA recently persuaded the military to upgrade homeschoolers who wish to enlist from "correspondence school graduate" rank (the
lowest possible) to a higher rank over a test period of five years. If the en-
listed homeschoolers perform well, the change will be made permanent.

Most people never need HSLDA's services, but the dues from those of us
who never get hassled support the legal firepower to keep the whole movement strong. Think of it as a charitable contribution or think of it as insurance: Either way it's a great investment. Total cost: $100 per family per year.

For those whose children have grown up and graduated, or those who
have no children, or whose children haven't yet reached school age,
HSLDA has launched their "Friends and Alumni Program." For $85 per
year, "Friends and Alumni" members can receive the same benefits offered
to homeschooling families.

WHY YOU NEED THIS STEP Because living in fear of the social worker, your
nosy neighbor, and your irate in-laws is no fun. Because even if *you* have
great neighbors, a friendly school district, supportive in-laws, and enlightened social workers, that doesn't mean everyone else does. Because $100 a
year just isn't that much for peace of mind.

Step Two: Join Your State Homeschool Group

You can get your state group's name, address, phone, and web address
from the appendix in the back of this book or from the listings on our
website at www.home-school.com. Join your group and *pay the dues!* These
pay the overhead for the sacrificial folks who have spent years struggling to
make homeschooling safe and legal. They also usually entitle you to the
state newsletter, which includes info on the local support groups and their
activities, and may garner you other goodies as well, such as a discount on
the cost of attending the state convention or an invitation to attend your local Six Flags Homeschool Day. If you have a state group membership card,
you also can request the "educator's discount" at teacher's stores and bookstores. Tell them you're a home educator, show them your membership
card, and most establishments that offer educator's discounts will grant you
one. This discount is usually worth somewhere between 5 percent and 20
percent off the goods you purchase in that store. Total cost of state group
dues: around $20 or so.

WHY YOU NEED THIS STEP Because without state homeschool groups,
there would *be* no homeschool movement. Because homeschooling operates under state laws, and your state group has spent years working with

the legislators on your behalf. Because the annual state convention is really great. Because you might be able to get an educator's discount at the bookstore. Because it's the right thing to do.

Step Three: Join Your Local Support Group

While your state group provides major events, such as annual conferences and "Days at the Capitol" for meeting with legislators, your *local* group is a place to make friends, ask your questions, and be a part of ongoing activities with like-minded people.

Here is a partial list of opportunities available through support groups in my area. Please note that this is *not* an especially amazing list of opportunities. I get dozens of homeschool newsletters from different states and can honestly say that the following list is pretty typical of the kinds of social and academic opportunities creative homeschool parents everywhere are making available to their groups:

- Bible Quiz teams
- Graduation ceremony for homeschooled high-school and eighth-grade graduates
- Speech and Theatre Club
- Marching band
- Fine Art competition
- Tutoring in forensics, public speaking, creative dramatics, create writing, beginning Latin, literature, speech, drama, English, reading, math, and physics
- Standardized testing
- Art classes
- Roller skating
- Bowling
- Swimming
- Special classes at the YMCA for homeschooled kids during regular school hours
- Choir
- Scouts
- Math Olympics
- Field trips (I still remember our group's field trip to an Amish farm! We had to ride a rented school bus two hours each way. Bounce, bounce, bounce. Talk about spinal pain! I wonder how kids can stand to ride a bus like that every day.)
- Spelling Bee
- Lending Library and Resource Center

Let's take another look at that last option. Many support groups now have lending libraries of popular homeschool resources and of other items that are hard for individual families to afford. A set of travel videos or college counseling books might be too expensive for an individual family but very affordable when a group clubs together to buy them.

But most of all, a support group makes it possible for new homeschoolers to find friends and mentors who have "been there" and can help you put your fears—and overoptimistic hopes—in perspective. You can find out how others who have tried a new resource *really* liked it, or get answers on how to deal with learning obstacles from experienced homeschoolers.

The best groups are those where everyone helps. Even if you're a neophyte homeschooler, you may be a math whiz or a terrific organizer. Try to find some way to be useful, and show your appreciation a *lot*. It's the best

---

No Local Support Group? (It's Unlikely, but Anyway Here's How to Start Your Own)

The Leader's Manual
$16 plus $4 shipping.
Christian Home Educators of Cincinnati, 9810 Sparrow Pl., Mason OH 45040-9325. www.chechome.org/lmordfm.htm

If the thought of starting your own support group fills you with fear and trembling, take heart. **The Leader's Manual: A Guide for Christian Home School Support Groups** will take you by the hand and walk you step-by-step through the entire process. Even if you are involved in an established group, you'll find ideas here for events and activities guaranteed to please your members. (Hint: if you want to please your support group leaders, why not buy this book and offer to coordinate one of the activities yourself?)

Meeting ideas, leadership helps, burnout prevention, basic group structure, and more are all included. Most helpful are the 25 reproducible forms: field trip planners, new member forms, schedules for planning special events, detailed instructions for science fairs, certificates, and more.

Most of these ideas can be implemented by any size group, but be prepared! Using this book will probably make your group so successful that you will experience some rapid growth. On this point I share a philosophical difference with the authors. While they include a chapter on how to split your group when it gets too large, I would prefer to see some discussion on how a larger group can operate effectively in its own right. All support groups don't have to be small; there are valid reasons for embracing growth and learning to take advantages of the resources offered by a larger group.

Regardless of the age or stage of your particular group, you'll find *The Leader's Manual* a valuable help. *Renee Mathis*

Help! I've Gotta Organize This Group!

Parents. $14.95.
Valerie Royce Coughlin, 13428 Cedar St., Hesperia, CA 92345
Phone/fax: (760) 947-3982
famfare1@earthlink.net

Help! I've Gotta Organize This Group is (no surprise) for use by homeschool support groups. It's smaller (80 pages) than Valerie Royce Coughlin's other book, *Help! I've Gotta Organize This Stuff*, and contains a few of the forms in the first book: calendars, group activities, awards, certificates, posters, even greeting cards. *Renee Mathis*

Online Message Boards

Our site, "Homeschool World," offers a variety of message boards. Some center around school subjects, such as math and science. Others focus on a particular homeschool method, such as classical education or unit studies. Each board has a guest expert who visits frequently to answer questions and share hot new ideas. To participate in a board, or just to "lurk" (online speak for reading everyone else's messages without posting any of your own) go to **www.home-school.com** and click on "Experts."

way to make sure those incredible people who plan all those fun activities keep energized and happy to do more for you!

WHY YOU NEED THIS STEP Because you're a brand-new homeschooler. Because you have no idea what you'll be missing if you *don't* join. Because you bake great cookies. Because your kids need friends. Because *you* need friends who understand what your life is really like now that you're homeschooling.

Step Four: Join Other Homeschoolers Online

Join your friendly international online support group. For no more than the cost of monthly online service—currently as little as $9.95—you can be part of a support group that is open 24 hours a day, every day of the week, and that numbers thousands of members from every state and province in America, Canada, and every English-speaking country in the world.

Online, you can:

- **Ask questions anonymously** that would embarrass you to blurt out in front of your neighbors. If your older child still wets his bed, or is having real problems with reading; if a non-custodial spouse is trying to make trouble for your homeschool; if your in-laws are being less than supportive of your decision to homeschool; you can ask for help and suggestions online without violating any of your near-and-dear's privacy or getting yourself in trouble. Just pick a "screen name" that's not identical to your real name, and ask away!
- **Find advice** for all kinds of homeschooling situations, from the rare to the common. "My child has been diagnosed with ADD. What do I do?" "I am blind and homeschooling a sighted child. Suggestions appreciated." "We are moving next week to Okinawa—can anyone tell me about the homeschooling situation there? Is there a group we can join?" If you can ask it, someone out there can and will answer it.
- **Locate and ask advice about resources** of all kinds, from the unusual to the popular. Whatever you want to know about, *someone* out there has already tried.
- **Share your opinions and concerns** (politely), tell jokes (clean ones), make friends (almost guaranteed)! Online is great!

WHY YOU NEED THIS STEP Because it's one of the few great reasons for having bought a computer in the first place. So you can "let it all hang out" when things *aren't* going great. So you can tell the world when things *are* going great. So you can have people around the country praying for you. So you can find answers to difficult questions. So your kids can make on-line pen pals, thus vastly improving their typing, spelling, and vocabulary. So you can really *feel* part of a million-person movement. As the first confidence-building step to maybe someday signing the kids up for an online course.

Even if you are a family of hermits living in the wilds on an island off the coast of Alaska, you can still join HSLDA and your state homeschool group. Most everyone else is within shouting distance of a hungry Internet Service Provider and a local homeschool support group. We're all anxious to meet you and get to know you. So don't be a stranger; drop in now, you hear?

CHAPTER 10

What to Read

O K. So you're a joiner, and you've rushed out to sign up with your state and local homeschool groups. Or so you're *not* a joiner, and you're ignoring all the wonderful advice in the last chapter.
   Either way, here are three more steps to homeschool success—both your success as a teacher and your children's success as learners.

DID YOU KNOW . . .
The average college graduate reads only one book a year? It's time to blow that average away!

INSIDER NOTE: The man and girl on the cover of the middle issue are my husband Bill and daughter Lillian. Bill lost 50 pounds and gained bunches of muscle using the fitness program we described in that issue.

Step Five: Magazines

   Subscribe to my magazine, **Practical Homeschooling**, also known as **PHS**. If you're a "newbie," you'd be smart to also snap up any back issue sets that are still available. Just call 1-800-346-6322 with your credit card handy or sign up online at www.home-school.com/catalog. For the price of a couple of pizzas, PHS will bring you up-to-date on all the latest educational trends and resources. Regular PHS features include columns by some of the best-known names in homeschooling, oodles of reviews of the latest new curriculum products and educational software (many from the people who brought you this book!), special research articles that take a complex topic such as special education and "open it up" to make it understandable, "Day at Our House" diaries from homeschool families around the world, story contests for the kids (with prizes!), a gallery of envelope art from our kid readers, "Show and Tell" highlights about homeschooled kids who do something special, cartoons and jokes, a lengthy letters section, and lots more. The magazine's tone is friendly; we don't care if you have a messy house, and we don't expect your kids to be perfect. PHS's viewpoint is Christian, but meekly so—this is a practical "how to" magazine, not an evangelistic treatise.

Other homeschool magazines are, of course, available. You'll likely be presented with a chance to subscribe when you visit your local curriculum fair or read your state newsletter.

So why do you need a homeschool magazine? Here are some possible reasons:

- To stimulate your thinking, or . . .
- To confirm your already-set opinions, or . . .
- To tell you what the publishers consider the "one best way" to homeschool. (You *won't* find this one in PHS!)
- To increase your confidence and give you a "lift"
- To keep you up with the latest resources—including those nobody in your support group has heard of or been brave enough to buy
- To provide answers to questions that involve a lot of research, such as how to get your homeschooled child into college and which colleges to consider
- To keep you up with current political news that affects homeschooling
- To keep you up with current educational news that affects homeschooling
- To find out what major homeschool thinkers think about an issue or subject
- To give you a number of ways to teach a subject, so you can pick the one that fits best

I'm sure you can think of other reasons, but these will do for now. As you can see, reasons *for* reading one magazine might be reasons *against* reading another! It depends what you're looking for. However, no matter which magazine(s) you choose, a magazine has an "immediacy," a feeling of belonging to an ongoing dialog, that a book lacks. A magazine also has a sense of permanence that a support group or online discussion lacks. Finally, a magazine can tackle issues and questions that are too short for an entire book but require too much research for you to spend the time yourself.

As a magazine publisher myself, I'm acutely aware of what a bargain a good magazine can be. We publish around 380 pages of *Practical Homeschooling* in a year, most in color and adorned with fancy graphics. A book with this much color and detail would run you at least $49, and more likely closer to $99. But a year's subscription will get you the finest minds in home education, the latest educational news, and reviews of the hottest new products, all for $19.95. Plus it comes in handy doses, is delivered directly to your mailbox, and you can enter one of our contests and win a prize worth more than the entire cost of your subscription. Even if you don't win a prize, it's a good—and inexpensive—way to quickly catch up on what homeschooling is all about.

WHY YOU NEED THIS STEP To get "connected" to what's going on right *now*. So you won't feel left out or like you're missing something. Because it's fun. Because there's a lot to learn, and magazine articles are more approachable than entire books. Because you like the cover. Because you're curious.

Step Six: Books!

Read a bunch of books about education, about public school, and about homeschooling. If you do this right, you'll end up knowing everything worth knowing about education that an education student pays tens of thousands of dollars to learn. Plus you'll know what the hopeful future teacher *doesn't* learn—what went wrong with public education and how to do a better job.

Your first step, of course, is reading *this* book. You paid for it, or at least borrowed it from the library or a friend, so why not go for the gusto and get your money's worth? We've tried to do a good job of distilling down for you what it would take thousands of hours to learn on your own. If we've succeeded, we hope to get the kinds of letters we received from readers of the previous editions. Typical example: "I used to be so confused about homeschooling, but after reading your book I feel like an expert!"

One book can't do it all, though. Even all three volumes of *Mary Pride's Complete Guide to Homeschooling* can't tell you everything there is to know about home education. Luckily for us, hundreds of books are now in print explaining the fine points of everything from how to write your own unit study to the real history of how public education got a foothold in the Land of the Free and the Home of the Brave. The books reviewed in this chapter are a good place to start.

WHY YOU NEED THIS STEP To be smart. To increase your confidence. Because learning all this stuff that you never knew before is fun. Because you love your kids and want to do a great job.

Top Ten Books Every New Homeschooler Should Read

Half of you just read that subtitle and can't wait to get your hand on all these books. The other half are screaming, "Help! I don't have time to read *ten books* on homeschooling!"

Relax. You don't have to read all ten, or all at once. Some may not even apply to your particular situation.

This list is not an assignment: it is my personal attempt to narrow down the dozens of homeschooling and education books into a handy number you can start with.

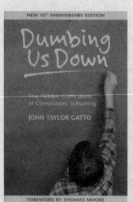

The author of **Dumbing Us Down**, New York State Teacher of the Year John Taylor Gatto, has become a legend in homeschool circles, invited to speak at dozens of homeschool conferences. His undeniable accomplishments as a "guerrilla" teacher in the public school system—smuggling *real* educational experiences into his classroom and smuggling his students *out* of the classroom to try their wings in the real world—are an inspiration to every homeschooler to break away from the mindset of imitating the public schools. But much more than this, his critique of *why* the public schools "fail" is essential reading for everyone the slightest bit interested in education.

Gatto's basic premise is that schools don't fail. They do exactly what they were designed to do, which is to dumb kids down. The "hidden curricu-

Dumbing Us Down, 10th Anniversary edition.
Parents. $11.95.
New Society Publishers, BC, CANADA.
250-247-9737, www.newsociety.com.

The 10th Anniversary edition has a new foreword by Thomas Moore, a new introduction by David Albert (with one speck of strong language), a new "About the Author" by the author, and a new "10 Years Later" afterword.

lum of compulsory schooling," as the book's subtitle reads, is to produce a not-too-well-educated, compliant force of workers, consumers, and voters who will continue to support the mass society. How and why this plan was set into motion can be found another of his books, *The Underground History of American Education,* which is also reviewed in this chapter. How it works in schoolkids' daily lives is the burden of *Dumbing Us Down.*

The heart of the book is a speech Mr. Gatto made in 1991, on the occasion of accepting the title of "New York State Teacher of the Year." I am informed that the Regents granting the award sat there with looks of blank astonishment as Gatto informed them about the seven lessons school *really* teaches: confusion, class position, indifference, emotional dependency, intellectual dependency, provisional self-esteem, and your inability to hide from government surveillance. Other essays included in this mind-blowing book are "The Psychopathic School," "The Green Monongahela" (experiences that shaped Gatto's views on education and life), "We Need Less School, Not More," and "The Congregational Principle" (in which using historical examples Gatto shows how local control beats federal social engineering). You'll have a whole new batch of reasons for homeschooling after reading this book!

Home Schooling on a Shoestring: A Jam-Packed Guide

Adult. $12.99
Shaw Books, CO. (719) 590-4999,
www.randomhouse.com/waterbrook/
shaw.

Homeschooling: The Right Choice

Parents. $14.99
Lifeway Christian Resources, Customer
Service Center (MSN108), TN.
(800) 458-2772, www.lifeway.com.

Home Schooling on a Shoestring: A Jam-Packed Guide is the most original homeschool book I've seen in *years.* The book maintains its "frugal" theme throughout, from running you through the calculations that show your family may actually not be much worse off without that second income, to money-saving and budgeting tips, to home business suggestions, to ways to save on your curriculum purchases. But it goes way beyond the crop of "tightwad" tomes in its 250 oversized pages, not only in what it covers—curriculum from low-tech to high-tech, homeschooling in the teen years, art, physical education, and more—but in the depth and practicality of its advice and resources. Authors Melissa Morgan (who runs a mini-farm and two home businesses as well as homeschooling her two children!) and Judith Waite Allen (who began homeschooling to help a foster child) have obviously done their own research and tried out their own ideas—all of which make sense!

Veteran homeschoolers will smile in recognition at many of their stories and suggestions, while pulling out a pad to take notes on the many fresh new hints. Novice homeschoolers will avoid many pitfalls and grab many opportunities by studying these pages. In fact, I feel like a more accurate title would have been *Practical Homeschooling* (but sorry, that's taken! <grin>). Even those with *huge* budgets will get a lot out of this book!

If you have been a *Practical Homeschooling* reader for any amount of time, you are well aware of the insightful, well-researched columns written by Chris Klicka. A homeschooling father of seven and Senior Counsel for Home School Legal Defense Association (HSLDA) who has worked full-time as an attorney to protect homeschoolers since 1985, Chris has served his time in the trenches.

This new edition of his classic **Homeschooling: The Right Choice** has more than 25 percent brand-new material to help homeschoolers face this new millennium. Like the previous edition, this book is a comprehensive indictment of public schooling and a rousing defense of homeschooling. The academic, moral, and spiritual benefits of homeschooling are fully explored, as is the history of homeschooling and anecdotal information on many famous homeschoolers of the past, including 10 US presidents. The section on your constitutional right to homeschool and the present legal atmosphere is quite complete and up-to-date, dealing with not only the well-known threat of overzealous truant officers and the like, but also official groups such as the NEA, "children's rights" advocates, and even the United Nations Convention on the Rights of the Child. A chapter every homeschool family should read discusses how to handle social workers and how to deal with a child welfare investigation. Since many homeschool legal contacts involve social workers who have been sicced on the family by disapproving relatives or neighbors, Chris has also included an appendix, "The Social Worker Skit: How to Handle a Visit from a Social Worker." For those who think the best defense is a good offense, several chapters and appendices explain at length how to influence state legislation, how to recruit local media support for homeschooling, and the benefits of a combined legal defense through HSLDA.

New material in this edition: an entire chapter on seven steps to successful homeschooling, another chapter on how homeschoolers can be admitted to college and how well they are doing there, many true stories demonstrating the major influence homeschoolers have earned in shaping legislation, the upcoming issue of vouchers, legal issues for families with special-needs children, and how homeschool grads can now be admitted into the military on the same footing as any other high-school graduate. Many new facts and figures demonstrating the success of homeschooling have also been added to this thoroughly researched and footnoted book. I only wish it also had an index—maybe next edition!

Kingdom of Children: Culture and Controversy in the Homeschooling Movement is an extremely important new book that every homeschool leader should consider buying. Since 1991, author Mitchell L. Stevens, Assistant Professor of Sociology at Hamilton College, has been interviewing homeschoolers, attending homeschool meetings, and researching homeschooling as a social trend. During this research, he found that homeschooling represents a distinct culture with two wings, which he dubbed the "believers" and the "inclusives." In the words of the book jacket, the bulk of the book "reveals that home schooling is not a random collection of individuals but an elaborate social movement with its own celebrities, networks, and characteristic lifeways."

Of course, we all knew that! What we may not have understood was the political and social dynamic underlying the inevitable conflict between the "believers" and the "inclusives," and why so far the believers have prevailed. Conservative Christians who believe in authority and leadership, the believers naturally have an advantage when trying to get things done, while the inclusives, who rose out of the liberal alternative schools movement of the '60s, are ideologically opposed to picking leaders, let alone following them. Politically, this parallels the difference between representative government and pure democracy. The believers also have an advantage in that large numbers of conservative Christian women are drawn to full-time motherhood, while, in the book's words, "women nearer to the cultural mainstream are more likely to see home education as incompatible with, or even threatening to, a gender identity scripted in large part by modern feminism." Hence, the relatively larger number of believers and the relatively larger strength of believers' organizations and resources is no accident.

However, believers should not relax quite yet, since the inclusives have "become masters at talking across difference" and their view that "human diversity is positive" (which in their case means serious diversity of belief, not just cultural diversity) "is an appropriate organizational philosophy for an increasingly heterogeneous American society." In other words, Christian homeschoolers, look out, since your groups' very existence denies the "diversity" so cherished by the mainstream media. You may have the larger numbers and the organizational skills, but your right to speak on behalf of

Kingdom of Children
Adult. $24.95
Princeton University Press.
800-777-4726, pup.princeton.edu.

your fellow homeschoolers is and has been under attack as long as you don't allow people who totally disagree with your most sacred beliefs to lead you. Which is what this has been all about, and why you need to read this book.

Kingdom of Children names names and provides dates, giving a deeper history of homeschooling as a movement with its own important events and players than we have seen before. It also celebrates the cultural achievements of homeschoolers in once again placing children at the center of family life in an age that seeks to relegate them to the fringe, and is not shy about noting our academic and social success as well. While the author is by no means a fan of conservative theology, he is fair in his treatment of all sides and objective in his views.

The copious footnotes are very helpful. However, a more thorough index would be a help, since I noted numerous instances where people and topics appeared in the book, but much less frequently (or not at all) in the index.

Published by a major university press, this book is bound to be influential, so we can be glad it has been so well researched.

The NEA: Trojan Horse in American Education

Parents. NEA, $19.95.
The Paradigm Company, ID.
(208) 322-4440, www.howtotutor.com.

The NEA: Trojan Horse in American Education shows how the schools have been turned into a political football and why our declining national intellectualism is no accident. Written in a lively, intelligent style, this is undoubtedly Sam Blumenfeld's most important book, and essential reading for anyone concerned about curing America's educational inferiority. (The solutions are surprisingly simple.)

While you're at it, check your public library or used bookstore for Sam's other classic **Is Public Education Necessary?** which is sadly now out of print. This is the first book to thoroughly document why we even have public education and who put it there. Did you know America survived just fine for over 200 years, from colonial times into the 1800s, without compulsory attendance laws, and that we had *greater* literacy *before* public education? Or that undercover socialists and Unitarians were the main forces pushing public education on us in the first place? (Hint: both the socialists and the Unitarians wanted to get children away from their parents' influence to mold them into the ideal citizen and the ideal human being, respectively.) Or that Protestant pastors went along, believing compulsory government schools could be used to transform the waves of Catholic immigrants into good mainstream Protestants? (It didn't work: the Catholics started their own schools.) Or that every single prediction the public-school promoters made, to persuade the public to accept government control of education, failed to come true? (I especially like their promise that government schooling would put an end to crime.) This, and much more that you never knew or suspected, is laid out for you, all amply documented.

Out of Control

Parents and mature teens. $10.99.
Huntington House Publishers, LA.
(800) 749-4009,
www.huntingtonhousebooks.com.
Reviewed by *Renee Mathis*

As could be expected from the subject matter at hand, **Out of Control: Who's Watching Our Child Protection Agencies?** is not enjoyable to read. No one at all is watching, according to this thoroughly researched and well-documented book by Brenda Scott. What with questionable statistics, denial of due process, under-educated social workers, sociological theories that scapegoat intact families as hotbeds of abuse (when research actually shows the vast majority of abuse occurs in non-biologically-related "families"—can you spell "live-in boyfriend?"—and where drugs and alcohol are involved), and medical abuse perpetrated in the name of "therapy," it all adds up to a social nightmare of enormous proportions. Sensitive readers beware: When the back cover proclaims, "This book of horror stories is true," it isn't exaggerating!

While we don't all have a calling to fight this particular set of injustices, we should be informed of what changes are necessary and what actions we can take on behalf of our families to maintain our safety and security. These topics are covered in the last two chapters of the book. For coverage of this subject as it specifically relates to homeschoolers, who social workers have been known to label "educational truants" and who sometimes fall afoul of anonymous calls from neighbors who disapprove of their educational choices, I'd recommend Chris Klicka's *Homeschooling: The Right Choice.*

From the introduction of **Schoolproof**: "Schoolproofing means making sure your children get a great education, no matter what political or educational theory happens to be in vogue. It means having children who learn to read in an age of illiteracy; who learn to obey legitimate authority in an age of sullen rebellion; who learn to stand against injustice in an age of craven conformity. . . . Schoolproofing means learning how to educate, so you can recognize good and bad education. It means learning your options: different ways of presenting a lesson, different educational philosophies, different types of teaching setups."

Some of what this handy-sized 200-page book covers:

- How today's popular educational philosophies treat children (as cogs, dogs, snobs, or gods) and how children *should* be treated (as unique, imperfect individuals who even so are made in the image of God)
- Organizing your learning area
- Twenty ways to present a lesson
- Twenty ways children can show you what they know (expand your horizons beyond "testing"!)
- Simple ways to multiply your teaching efforts
- How to recognize and ditch twaddle
- Learning styles and why even the same child learns at different rates at different times
- A vision of what education could look like *with* free enterprise and *without* government coercion

Schoolproof is probably the easiest-to-follow book on educational philosophies and methods you can find. I wrote it for exactly that purpose—to introduce parents in general, and homeschoolers in particular, to the *whys* and *hows* that books written for teachers shroud in impenetrable prose. As such, it's a good "first" book on these topics that also goes further and deeper than I could in this book.

A Survivor's Guide to Home Schooling is an absolutely delightful book. Written by two experienced home-school moms who have also run a *very* large extension program/support group, it answers the nitty-gritty questions other books ignore, such as "How am I ever going to get my laundry done?" The book has great stuff on subjects like Making Them Do It, reasons why *not* to hastily volunteer to teach other people's kids, ways to *realistically* schedule your days, and bushels more!

Schoolproof

Parents. $12.99.
Home Life, Inc., PO Box 1190, Fenton, MO 63026. (800) 346-6322, www.home-school.com/catalog.

An audiotape edition of *Schoolproof* is available for purchase ($17.96) or 30-day rental ($6.26) from Blackstone Audiobooks, Box 969, Ashland, OR 97520 (800) 729-2665 www.blackstoneaudio.com

A Survivor's Guide to Home Schooling

Parents. $12.99.
Home Life, Inc., PO Box 1190, Fenton, MO 63026. (800) 346-6322 www.home-school.com/catalog

As the name implies, *A Survivor's Guide to Home Schooling* is not so much designed to enchant people with the idea of homeschooling as to help them make it work. The authors deal with questions like

- What about the father who works outside the home and is unavailable for extended help in homeschooling?
- What if your child is a slow learner or has difficulties?
- How to avoid being suckered into loading up on expensive curriculum you will never, ever use
- What experienced homeschoolers' schedules *really* look like
- How to realistically cope with teaching many children of different ages at once

On top of this are valuable sections with information you won't find elsewhere:

- Plain Talk About Teaching Other People's Kids (the authors' advice is, "Don't, except in very unusual, limited circumstances")
- Serving Other Home Schoolers (how to start a support group and make it run)
- Mom, Will You Read Us a Story? (some fantastic insights into why and how reading aloud to your children is *the* essential preparation for their successful reading)
- Making Them Do It (in Luanne's immortal words, "School doesn't have to be fun, it just has to be done!")

Luanne Shackelford has been called the Erma Bombeck of homeschooling, giving you an idea of the book's sense of humor. She and Susan White have lots of experience and lots of children. A very warm book, salted with humor and peppered with vivid real-life examples. When you see the cover, you'll want to buy it!

The Underground History of American Education

High school and up. $30.
Home Life, Inc., PO Box 1190, Fenton, MO 63026
(800) 346-6322
www.home-school.com/catalog

The second book you should read from the author of *Dumbing Us Down*, New York State Teacher of the Year John Taylor Gatto, is his brand-new **The Underground History of American Education**.

An oversized 412 pages, this is nonetheless a hard book to put down. *Underground History* combines the thrill of a detective story—how did traditional excellent American education turn into the morass of modern schooling, and who is responsible?—with numerous memorable stories from Gatto's life. From his youth running free along the banks of the Monongahela River, to his miserable (but intellectually valuable) year in a Catholic boarding school, to his 26 years as a greatly beloved "guerrilla" classroom teacher, Gatto was always one of those special people who not only live life, or even observe life, but squeeze the juice out of life into a container they can pass on to others.

Underground History is not just a book you should read because it is informative, fun, dramatic, or even challenging, though it is all the above. This is a book you *must* read because Gatto has done what nobody else ever did—track down the roots of the centrally controlled mass society as it has taken shape in the USA, through the means of public schooling. This book names names. It explains how the great inventions based on coal and oil led to an elite group of empire-builders who feared that readily available energy would lead to an overproductive society, and who took steps to stop the American Experiment of genuine political and educational freedom in its tracks. We're not talking conspiracy theories here but well-documented historical facts that nobody ever put together in this way before. I guarantee you'll never look at prep schools, the bell curve, and the Daughters of the American Revolution the same way again!

Among Gatto's many eye-opening assertions:

- Kids can do a lot more at a younger age than we have been trained to expect.
- People will go to outrageous lengths for the privilege of working; how to nurture rather than kill this inbuilt motivation in your students.
- Everyday people can be trusted to live their own lives well, absent compelling government intervention and mass society manipulations.
- In Gatto's own words: "Spare yourself the anxiety of thinking of this school thing as a conspiracy, even though the project is indeed riddled with petty conspirators. It was and is a fully rational transaction in which all of us play a part. We trade the liberty of our kids and our free will for a secure social order and a very prosperous economy. It's a bargain in which most of us agree to become as children ourselves, under the same tutelage which holds the young, in exchange for food, entertainment, and safety. The difficulty is that the contract fixes the goal of human life so low that students go mad trying to escape it."

For the best results, I recommend you read Sam Blumenfeld's *Is Public Education Necessary?* before tackling *Underground History*. Blumenfeld has put together a good bit of the puzzle, and with his book under your belt, Gatto will fill in the whole picture. And, as a bonus, you will find out how the educational world really *ought* to work—a good thing to know before setting up your own little educational world!

Any reader of *Underground History* will get an amazing education in how the world really works and who the famous people are who made it this way. That's why I'm giving a copy to each of my teen children, with instructions to read a biography, or at least an encyclopedia entry, about each of the historical figures it names. Studying the book this way will make them better educated people than most college graduates.

NOTE: The edition I reviewed is the "Author's Edition." This is a limited-edition private printing by Gatto. He eventually plans to have the book published by a major publisher (many of them want it), and realizing that a mass publisher will most likely *not* want the book to name names, he wanted to make sure the full story was available for people like you and me. I bought a good supply of the Author's Edition, so if you want to be sure this edition is the one you're getting, order from my company, Home Life, Inc.

Step 7: Attend a Homeschool Seminar

I will tell you what to expect at your first homeschool conference or curriculum fair in Chapter 12. Right now we are talking about a homeschool *seminar:* an event designed for no other purpose than to teach you how to homeschool and inspire you to tackle homeschooling with gusto.

WHY YOU NEED THIS STEP Every new homeschooler ought to attend a homeschool seminar if at all possible. Here's why:

- Get your specific questions answered in person.
- Meet other new homeschoolers.
- Get all charged up!

You can find upcoming homeschool events by checking the "Events" box on the home page of www.home-school.com. For a more comprehensive listing, click on the "Homeschool Events" link.

Now here's the seminar I've been recommending for years.

The Home Schooling Workshop

The Basic Home Schooling Workshop: 8-tape set, $39.95. The Advanced Home Schooling Workshop: 8-tape set, $39.95. *Noble Publishing Associates, OR.* (800) 225-5259, *www.noblepublishing.com*

The Top Seminar for New Homeschoolers

The Home Schooling Workshop by Gregg Harris is great on tape, even better in person. This is probably the best-attended homeschool workshop of all time, with hundreds of thousands of alumni.

Attending Gregg Harris's workshop in St. Louis was the high point of that year for us. Gregg Harris tells how to help our children develop an enduring taste for righteousness by giving them a taste of it, "touching their young palates" with the best of our own experience and study. He shares practical principles of child discipline and instruction that help our children in the long run rather than just providing temporary relief. He explains how to use casual family storytelling to pass on our values and national heritage to our children without even having to take time out from our household work. Find out how to achieve financial independence and give children needed work experience through a home business and how to develop a ministry of hospitality (Gregg calls this "the original Bed and Breakfast plan"!). An extra: The tapes include insights on home evangelism, one of the modern church's most neglected areas.

The Home Schooling Workshop tape sets include all this, plus the info you'd expect on the advantages of home schooling, the dangers of age-segregated peer dependency, how to begin a home-study program, how to choose a curriculum, legal considerations, and instructional methods.

Gregg has cut down down on his live workshop schedule in order to concentrate more on his local church work. He has now produced a video version of his Friday evening introductory sessions, which presents strong arguments for keeping children out of conventional schools and teaching them at home. Also covered in this video is the educational strategy of secular humanism, clinical research in schooling readiness, and the biblical answer to "What about socialization?" Gregg is not given to cliches; I promise you will get some startling new insights from this presentation!

The sets each include eight cassettes. **The Basic Home Schooling Workshop** includes Why Home School, The Battle for Your Child, Child Training God's Way, How to Do a Great Job Home Schooling, Delight-Directed Studies, The Battle for Your Legal Rights, Teaching History in the Home, and Home Schooling Hazards (passive dads, active toddlers, and teacher burnout). **The Advanced Home Schooling Workshop** covers Home School & "The New World Order," The Seasons of Life for Your Family, How to Establish an Orderly Home, How to Keep Doing a Great Job, Leading the Lost to Christ, Sunday Schools & Youth Groups, Stewardship & Family Business, Courtship for Lasting Marriages.

You also have a choice of some fascinating (and inexpensive) special-purpose workshops, thanks to Gregg's habit of leaving a session in each live workshop open to address a special topic of current interest to home schoolers. The series now includes Age-Integrated Sunday Schools & Bible Studies, Learning Disabilities or Learning Differences?, Christian Home School Support Groups, Home Schooling Teenagers, and Learning Styles.

These are *the* home-schooling tapes to buy. And if your Christian home-school support group or co-op is considering hosting a homeschooling seminar, and by some amazing miracle hasn't already hosted Gregg's basic seminar, this is the one.

Where to Shop

For homeschoolers, shopping doesn't mean just dropping in at the mall. So far, there are no national chains of homeschool shops. This means you have to be more resourceful when hunting down homeschool goodies.

Step 8: Get These Catalogs

For your shopping pleasure, below are descriptions for a baker's dozen of what I consider the most essential homeschool catalogs. Send away for them!

WHY YOU NEED THIS STEP Because bookstores and teacher's stores don't carry everything (or even close to everything) that homeschoolers need. And one-stop-shopping beats buying products one at a time from individual vendors.

The full color **Christian Book Distributors** catalog is 64 pages of popular homeschool items, many discounted. Relatively few full curriculum items: most are fact books, fiction and fiction series, games, music, videos, and stand-alone items designed to teach a single subject. I don't have space here to list the dozens of entries in this catalog's table of contents, but I can tell you that "Harris Family," "VeggieTales," and "What Would Jesus Do?" each have a page of their own. Over 2,000 items in all.

Christian Book Distributors Homeschool Resources Catalog
Parents. Free catalog.
Christian Book Distributors (CBD), MA. (978) 977-4500, www.christianbook.com.

This is a big one! **The Elijah Company Catalog** is almost 145 oversized full-color pages. Started about 15 years ago, this is a "native" homeschool company run by a family that has always homeschooled their children. Their motto: "More Than a Catalog! Teaching Tips, Helpful Hints, The Best Books & Teaching Materials." The catalog includes cover photos of many items, detailed descriptions, and page after page of homeschooling advice from owners Chris and Ellyn Davis.

The Elijah Company Catalog
Parents. Catalog free online in .pdf format. Print catalog was $2; check for latest price.
Elijah Company, TN. (888) 2ELIJAH, www.elijahcompany.com.

The materials they cover have all been tested in homeschool use and include most popular items. Items are not discounted, and the reason for this is spelled out in detail in the back. About 75,000 copies of this catalog are distributed annually.

Farm Country General Store Catalog

Parents. Free catalog.
Farm Country General Store, IL.
(800) 551-FARM,
www.homeschoolfcgs.com.

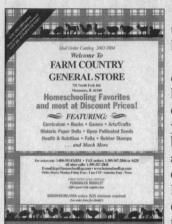

Farm Country General Store is hard to categorize. Established in 1991 by a homeschooling family, the current edition is 188 black-and-white pages with a two-color cover. It includes over 5,000 entries, about half with small accompanying photos. The entries are mostly not reviews, such as you'd find in the Elijah Company catalog, but sales copy that often includes a decent amount of product description. With the exception of Educational Insights, Kingfisher, and Betty Lukens, products are divided by topic. The index in the back makes finding any particular product easy. Most items are discounted. About 50,000 copies of this catalog are distributed annually.

Greenleaf Press Catalog

Parents. Free catalog.
Greenleaf Press, TN.
(800) 311-1508,
www.greenleafpress.com

The 96-page, full-color, oversized **Greenleaf Press** catalog is "guaranteed 100% Twaddle-Free." This must-have catalog is loaded with carefully picked, gorgeous, fun, and useful products to enhance your homeschooling, especially in the areas of history and science.

Catalog co-founders Rob and Cyndy Shearer are also authors of the popular "Greenleaf Guides" to various historical periods, and their research into the best "real" books and fact books to accompany their history studies has led to a great, well-organized group of products.

I know the products are great because I spent my entire speaking fee, plus some, on the items at Rob and Cyndy's table when we first met them at a conference in Tennessee. (Luckily, they threw in a couple of boxes for us to carry it all in!) I know they are well-organized because I am looking at their color-coded, topic-arranged catalog as I write this.

The catalog includes a section on Science (with a focus on Creation Science) and nature study resources. Greenleaf is about more than history and science, of course. Other catalog topics include art, Bible, phonics and reading, language arts, and music.

Individual catalog items, of which there are thousands, range from a few dollars (for a book or workbook) to $150 for a gorgeous over-sized book on Renaissance art. Catalog descriptions are detailed and accompanied with color photos, and the catalog also includes pages of advice and insight from the Shearers.

Thousands of Greenleaf catalogs are distributed each year, so you can see I'm not the only one who goes ga-ga over Greenleaf. Greenleaf also has a well-organized website and online catalog that includes all of the write-ups, reviews, and articles.

The Godzilla of "review" style catalogs was the **Lifetime Books & Gifts' Always Incomplete Resource Guide & Catalog**. This perfect-bound tome was as much of a book as a catalog. The "Always Incomplete" part came from the fact that it's hard to keep something this size current, which is why it is now available only online and on CD-ROM.

A "native" homeschool business, established in 1987 by a Christian family, this catalog includes a hefty 3,000-plus items—all locatable by category or index. You won't find photos, but that just leaves room for longer product descriptions and chatty articles. Items are divided by subject areas, including an interesting arrangement of Science and Nature items by the seven days of Creation, and sold at retail price. Thousands of homeschoolers swear by this catalog.

"Shekinah" is an Old Testament Hebrew word referring to the glory of the Lord. Established in 1983, this is a "native" homeschooling business, run by homeschool moms.

Shekinah Curriculum Cellar claims, like Elijah Company, to be "More Than a Catalog!" In their case, they promise you "A Commentary on Quality Books and Teaching Aids for Home Educators—By Home Educators." However, what you get is 36 pulp pages with no photos and short product descriptions. The longer descriptions are mainly on the website. A little picture of a cross also appears next to items from Christian publishers. They "strive to only include materials that do not promote secular humanism."

The first hook here is discounting. Shekinah will match any low price from another catalog.

The second hook: same-day shipping. If your order is received by 2 P.M. Central Standard Time, it will be shipped that day.

Most orders are now generated by Shekinah's complete online catalog, which features detailed descriptions and parents' reviews of many products. Contribute your own product review and get an automatic 5 percent off your order!

Shekinah's catalog contains over 1,000 products. About 70,000 copies of this catalog are distributed annually.

You need the **Sonlight Curriculum Catalog**. The vast majority of this catalog is a treasury of children's fiction and nonfiction, divided by grade level and topic, with many titles not available elsewhere. Many of the most popular homeschool curriculum products are here, too, as well as Sonlight's own unique instructor's guides. Since very few items in the catalog overall are published by Sonlight, it qualifies as a general-purpose catalog, not just a "Sonlight Curriculum" catalog.

Established in 1990 by two missionary homeschooling families, this catalog's specialty is international history and Christian worldview. By far the most multicultural catalog among those listed here, it includes award-winning books about all other historical periods and cultures around the world,

Lifetime Book
Always Incom
Guide & Catal
Parents. Online and on
Windows CD-ROM, $3 plus
shipping and handling.
Lifetime Books & Gifts, FL.
(800) 377-0390,
www.lifetimebooksandgifts.com

Shekinah Curriculum Cellar
Parents. Free catalog.
Shekinah Curriculum Cellar, TX.
(903) 643-2760, www.shekinahcc.com.

Sonlight Curriculum Catalog
Parents. Free, one per family.
Sonlight Curriculum, Ltd., CO. (303)
730-6292 or catalog@sonlight.com to
request catalog. No phone orders.
All orders via online or fax.
Fax: (303) 795-8668,
www.sonlight.com.

some of which are officially out of print and available only in these Sonlight editions. The index (hooray!) lists over 700 titles. Within each grade level, these are divided into Bible, History, Read-Alouds (in younger grades), and Readers (books children can read on their own). Within these sub-topics the books are listed alphabetically at last! This was not true in previous editions, and I'm very glad they changed to alphabetized listings.

The Sonlight catalog is a terrific resource for finding uplifting, thoughtful, and amusing books to enrich your homeschool program. You can also use it as a guide when you go to the library, but be prepared to discover that a large number of the books you're looking for are already checked out by other Sonlight users!

They distribute "thousands of catalogs" (they're not telling how many thousands), and many more people do all their Sonlight shopping online.

The Sycamore Tree Educational Services Catalog

Parents. Free catalog.
Sycamore Tree, CA.
(800) 779-6750,
www.sycamoretree.com.

Established in 1982 by Seventh-Day Adventists Bill and Sandy Gogel, **The Sycamore Tree** is one of the older homeschool catalog companies. They also offer curriculum services: see description in the Quick Resource Guide section of this book.

The Sycamore Tree catalog is 66 pages listing over 3,000 items. Item descriptions are short sales copy; a few photos are included. Products are divided by subject and also by type of product—e.g., games or school supplies. SDA influence is minor; most products listed are broadly popular among Christian and secular homeschoolers. About 40,000 copies of this catalog are distributed annually. A good one-stop shopping source if you already know what you're looking for.

Timberdoodle

Parents. Free catalog.
Timberdoodle Company, WA.
(360) 426-0672,
www.timberdoodle.com.

The **Timberdoodle** catalog started as a production of Dan and Deb Deffinbaugh and their family way back in 1985. They picked the word "timberdoodle" in honor of the elusive game bird. Still based in a rural setting, their family business has grown to employ over a dozen people.

As you might expect, the Timberdoodle catalog exudes wholesome family values. This 106-page handy-sized catalog is printed on paper one step up from newsprint and decorated with color photos and line art. Catalog descriptions are lengthy, folksy, and personal; catalog selection reflects the Deffinbaugh family's own tastes and interests. These are particularly strong in the areas of math, hands-on learning, and engineering, but many other topics are covered too: Bible tools, courtship, creationism, foreign languages, geography, handwriting, history, Keepers of the Faith, language arts, math, music, parent helps, phonics, piano, preschool, readers/reading, science, sewing, sign language, stickers, testing, thinking skills, and typing. The engineering emphasis shows in topics such as drafting skills, electronics, and Fischertechnik (Timberdoodle is one of the few US importers of this German construction kit system). I didn't have time to count them, but I estimate the catalog offers between 500 and 1,000 items. They distribute over 200,000 catalogs per year, making the unpretentious Timberdoodle Company one of the largest homeschool catalog companies.

Step 9: Go to the Teacher's Store

Did you know there are entire stores devoted just to educational goodies? It's true! Formerly called "teacher's stores" or "school supplies stores," many of these shops are now renaming themselves "parent and teacher stores." You can find them in the Yellow Pages under "School Supplies."

What you need to know about these stores:

To find your local Teacher's Store, go to **www.teacherstores.com**

- Nobody will ask you if you are a classroom teacher or demand to see your union card. These are not "teachers only" stores!
- Expect to see a terrific assortment of arts and crafts materials, writing implements, pencil toppers, posters, and bulletin-board materials. (That's why they're listed under "School Supplies.")
- You'll also find lots of fun workbooks, especially for younger grades. (If you don't think workbooks can be fun, you've never seen Frank Schaeffer workbooks!)
- Plus educational games, kits, and hands-on material of all kinds.
- Homeschoolers are welcome! In fact, many of these stores are putting in special sections just for homeschoolers.

For several years, my company has belonged to the National School Supply and Equipment Association. Their conferences are a great way for me to preview the neatest new educational products—and these are exactly the products your local teacher's store will be carrying. You will not be able to find all these goodies at Wal-Mart or Sears, or in homeschool catalogs either, for that matter. So head on down to your local teacher's store and tell them Mary Pride sent you!

WHY YOU NEED THIS STEP Because it's fun. Because your kids will love the store. Because you may never need to shop anywhere else for birthday presents again.

Step 10: Attend Your First Curriculum Fair

A curriculum fair is like a homeschooling bazaar. It doesn't have the speakers and workshops you will find at a seminar or convention. What it does have: tons of STUFF!

The typical curriculum fair will have some tables manned by exhibitors who paid to be there. These are usually gracious people who are willing to explain and demonstrate their products. In return, they hope you will at least seriously consider buying something from them. You may also find tables with used curriculum, which you can purchase for considerably less than a comparable new product. To make the most of used-curriculum shopping, it would help to have read all three *Mary Pride's Complete Guides* before attending the fair. This will give you an idea of the products you know you want to look out for.

WHY YOU NEED THIS STEP Because otherwise you'll hate yourself when your friends tell you about the great bargains and incredible products they found at the curriculum fair.

Step 11: Bookmark This Site!

Prefer to do your shopping online? No problem. Just bookmark this site: www.home-school.com. This is my website, Homeschool World. Click the "Homeschool Mall" button on the main page. This will take you to a page

where links to providers of homeschool products are listed by categories (e.g., "Art," "Math," etc.). Many of these linked sites have online shopping available. And don't forget to visit our Home Life Catalog while you're at it! We offer many educational books, kits, and games not available on other sites. (Again, just click the link to our catalog on the main page of Homeschool World.) When you've done your shopping, you can relax with the huge number of helpful articles of homeschooling and family life and other fun features found only on our site.

WHY YOU NEED THIS STEP Because there's a reason Yahoo lists Homeschool World as the most popular homeschool website in the world!

Step 12: Relax!

Take a breath. Put up your feet. Have a cup of tea or some other beverage you find relaxing. Think about how much you love your children and what a blessing it is to have them. Ask God to help you with any areas that worry you and thank Him for everything that's gone right so far.

If you're even thinking about tackling the 11 steps I outlined so far, your mind has been very active. Now it's time to realize:

It does not all depend on you and your efforts.

God wants you to succeed and is very willing to help if you ask!

When one of my small children can't lift something and starts complaining about it, my husband Bill asks, "Why aren't you using all the strength available to you?" His point is that, if the child only asks, Bill will gladly lift the burden that's too heavy for them.

In the same way, God will lift your burdens if you will trust Him enough to ask Him for help and to do what He says. In the final analysis, this may be the most important homeschool lesson of all.

CHAPTER 12

What to Expect

Congratulations! You have now completed all 12 steps to homeschool success, or at least *thought* about completing them. You now know that, for less than the cost of one college course, you can come up to speed with what's happening in the homeschool movement. If you complete the steps outlined in the previous three chapters, you will have the connections you need to feel safe and successful. Someone will be sure to hand you a list of answers to homeschool FAQ's (Frequently Asked Questions); someone else will answer your specific questions that books and magazines can't answer. In turn, you will have less of those questions, since you have been reading the books and magazines. In less time than you think, you'll feel like an old pro, and people will be asking *you* questions!

But before you can taste the heady elixir of becoming a homeschool expert, you have to face your first homeschool month. You might also have the chance to attend:

- Your first homeschool seminar
- Your first homeschool convention

These will all go a lot better if you know what to expect. So, away we go!

Your First Homeschool Seminar

A homeschool *seminar* differs from a homeschool *convention* in these important ways:

- **A seminar usually features only one speaker.** A major seminar presenter, such as Gregg Harris, may have a guest speaker or two, but this is the exception. A convention may have only one *keynote* speaker, but you can usually count on dozens of workshops presented by dozens of people.
- **A seminar will have a single theme**, such as "How to Get Started in Homeschooling" or "Why Unit Studies are My Favorite Method, Why I Think They Should Be Yours, and How to Do Them." The seminar title typically reflects the theme. A convention's theme, if there is one, is usually something like "Homeschooling Is Great!" This provides ample room to cover whatever the workshop leaders and keynote speakers might wish to talk about.

In the exciting new world of homeschooling . . .

- Experience and results count, not credentials
- Babies are a blessing!
- Moms are respected as professionals
- Kids are not "age" snobs. Big kids will play with and help little kids without fear of losing their "cool" image
- Kids and parents are huge book lovers
- Families are wired, with many having more than one computer in their homes and a fast Internet connection
- It's OK to have a messy house
- It's OK to be yourself: geek, jock, Beanie Baby collector, whatever
- Both kids and parents are eager to learn
- A strong do-it-yourself ethic spills over into parents becoming more "hands on" in other areas of their lives, such as cooking, home repairs, building, forming organizations, etc.
- Discovering that the real world is not congruent with the textbook world often leads to a more skeptical view of what the media and politicians are telling us, along with a strong desire to make things better.

The Future of Homeschooling

With Michael Farris

As a founder of both Home School Legal Defense Association and the National Center for Home Education, and the homeschooling dad of a *large* family, Michael Farris is one of the most influential—and knowledgeable—leaders in the homeschool movement today. He is also the author of a book entitled *The Future of Home Schooling,* making him the ideal person to ask about what likely lies ahead for the homeschool movement. Christopher Thorne, then the editor of *Practical Homeschooling,* interviewed Mr. Farris:

Practical Homeschooling: We're going to take a look at where homeschooling is and the future of homeschooling. Since you literally wrote the book on the subject, we'd love to talk with you and have you share your insights.

To go ahead and get started, I was wondering what you see as the major trends in homeschooling right now.

Michael Farris: Well, on the academic side, I see a trend in Classical Curriculum as being very hot. And also high-tech educational delivery systems are starting to reach some of their potential, although there's a long

way to go yet. There's still much more potential ahead. So there are two almost contrary trends, one of them going back to the past substance but the methodology of delivery of some of the extra help is very cutting edge.

PHS: So you see the trend toward Classical Education and Internet- or computer-assisted education as being complementary?

MF: Yeah. For example Fritz Hinrichs, who is the one who introduced me to the capability of high-tech delivery systems—and I would include in that DBS satellite and other broadcast forms of delivery, not just computers—he teaches classical education, world literature and history, Euclidean Geometry, and so on, over the Internet. He's the one who introduced me to both. So it can be combined; one is all about content and the other's all about how you get content into the home. So they're not at all incompatible in reality, though there's a surface incongruence.

PHS: It certainly seems that many homeschooling families are going that way. Can you explain a little bit more as to why you think Classical Education has caught on and is catching on? Why more people are moving toward that methodology?

MF: Well, I think that the reason they're moving there is that . . . if I can back up just a little . . . I think that basically in the first 15 years of the modern homeschool movement, it was a big enough thing to simply break away from the methodology and to make sure we had a better version of similar content. Those are the two things that the first 15 years accomplished. And what's happening now is an examination of whether we should have different content—not just better, but different. And so I see a desire to emulate not only the methodologies of the founding fathers but a lot of their substance as well, and recognizing that if we're going to be the leaders of Western

Civilization, we'd better understand the roots of Western Civilization. The way you get that is through Classical Education.

PHS: As a sidenote, you mentioned the modern homeschool movement. When would you say that the modern homeschool movement began?

MF: I would pick a particular date. Though I don't know the day, I know the event. It was April of 1982. That's when Focus on the Family and Dr. Dobson broadcast an interview with Raymond Moore. I view that as the date that really launched the modern homeschooling movement.

PHS: I know in your book you chronicle the history of homeschooling over the last decade or two. Do you think homeschooling will continue to grow, and along with that, how do you see the legal climate and attitude toward homeschooling changing and developing?

MF: The movement is continuing to grow. I'll break it into two components: the academic, or just the numerical growth, and then the legal growth. On the legal side of things, we have almost, but not completely, eradicated the idea that homeschooling is illegal. And so other than a handful of school districts out of 16,000 school districts in the country, everybody pretty well has conceded the fact that it's legal. There are some significant exceptions; for example, the chief attorney for the department of education in California thinks homeschooling is illegal. And that's not an insignificant exception. She's a politically weighty person.

But the biggest trend legally has been the harassment of homeschoolers through social workers, where they don't need to come after us with objective issues about education, but can come after us with subjective "concerns" about our family styles. All it takes is an anonymous hotline tip and you're in a bunch of trouble. So we spend more of our time dealing with social workers these days than with truant officers. Far more of our time.

PHS: Do you see that getting any better in the near future?

MF: No, I don't see any immediate change there. Fifteen years from now, I expect to sit here and tell you we've made real progress. But, if you look at the basic legal development of homeschooling, we're at the equivalent period of about 1984 for the development of the social services law in the right direction. It's going the right direction, but we're a year, year-and-a-half into it. I think it'll take about the same amount of time, about 15 years, before we see significant improvement.

PHS: Recent research has shown that homeschooling is growing at about 10–15 percent in the United States each year . . .

MF: Yeah, I think that's probably a good conservative number.

PHS: What is your impression of the growth of homeschooling in other countries?

MF: One of the trends that I see happening is that there's a real opportunity for ministry to people in other countries. Last week I visited with the ambassador to Switzerland about the homeschooling problems in his country. I went to the Czech republic earlier this year to speak to the first meeting of the brand-new homeschool association, and it was really interesting, kind of a flashback for me. Being there felt just like 1982 in the United States. There were literally two homeschool families in the Czech republic, and now there are about 30. We helped them to open the law for a five-year experiment, and HSLDA gave them a small grant to get their organization going. So we had the ability to give them a hand and to observe closely what's going on there.

Chris Klicka made a similar trip to South Africa last summer, and we continue to get many requests. It's going to catch on worldwide.

PHS: That's exciting.

MF: One of the things HSLDA is doing is sponsoring a conference with American missions organizations in January, with the goal of hopefully opening the eyes of these missions groups. If they sent people to other nations where their job assignment was to help homeschoolers in that nation, they'd have a tremendous tent-making missions approach. That's one of the things I see coming.

PHS: With the growth and overall positive outlook for homeschooling, do you think there's anything that could potentially hinder the growth of homeschooling, or anything that homeschoolers should watch for or be on guard for?

MF: I think that our movement will continue to grow both in numbers and in political freedom, until and unless there are significant numbers of irresponsible homeschoolers.

PHS: Ah. That's certainly a call to parents as well to continue the high standards.

MF: One thing that bothers me, that we see happening here, is superintendents don't like to have dropouts from their schools. So if they know a student is about to drop out, they say, "No, no, you're not a dropout; you're going to be a homeschooler." So they're not listing them as dropouts, but as homeschoolers. So we're kind of getting the dregs of society thrown into our camp, even though they're not actually homeschooling. If that ruse catches hold, and we get blamed for that kind of nonsense, then our freedoms could be put in jeopardy. It's really an unscrupulous act by a superintendent. That has been rare so far and hopefully won't be repeated too much. But it's a dangerous development.

The other thing I think that could significantly hurt the homeschooling movement would be to buy us off with public funds. A lot of school districts could realize, "These kids are worth about $5,000 a head to us; if we can get them enrolled in our homeschool program and we give them $500–$1,000 worth of money, books, and services, we make about a $4,000 a year profit." And the homeschoolers will be thinking,

"There's $500–$1,000 I don't have now." I think that arrangement is a recipe for losing our freedom, losing our spark, losing all the things that have made homeschooling a success. I hope we avoid the subsidization trap.

PHS: Doesn't New Zealand have an arrangement like that now?

MF: Could be. And frankly, in the Czech republic's experiment, there's going to be a little bit of subsidization in there. Certainly HSLDA didn't ask for it, and I don't think the homeschoolers even asked for it, but it's happening. But it's a different culture. And between what goes on in a former Communist country and what goes on in America, there are different cultural expectations, and I think there are different consequences. In our culture and in our legal system, I think the consequences of subsidization would be pretty bad.

PHS: Especially because it would open the door to more government control.

MF: Exactly.

PHS: To make it personal, what kind of differences has homeschooling made to your family? How are the lives of your children and grandchildren different because of it?

MF: I'm about a year away from the grandchildren business, but getting close. We have two children getting married this summer and fall. One in August and one in October. And given our philosophy about childbearing and our kids agreeing with it, about a year later we can expect to have grandkids!

The best way to answer the question is to compare my kids to myself at their age. My kids have been homeschooled for 16 years, and there's not any significant comparison. Christy was in a Christian school for kindergarten and first grade, and that's that. Nobody else has ever been in an institutional school. She's the oldest, she just graduated from college, and she's 23. I was raised in a Christian home, went to a good Bible-teaching church, was a good student, and by the world's standards I was always a good kid. By godly standards I didn't live up to everything I knew I should do, but judging by the world, I would have been one of the kids they would point to from the school and say, "Now here's an example of the way public schools work well." And I can just tell you that my kids are far more mature than I was, both in human terms and more importantly in spiritual terms.

They are at least as well-prepared academically and in some areas better. In their writing abilities, especially, they're much better prepared than I was. I graduated magna cum laude from college and was in the National Honor Society, and was in a school where two of my classmates got double-800 on the SATs, so I was in a very high-end academic program. Those of us who were in the honors program for six years—meaning 60 kids out of 600—we got great stuff. So I believe that a fair comparison is that my kids, and homeschool kids in general, get the same kind of education that those 60 of us did in this high-end program of academic excellence. But their moral life . . . the biggest thing is, they don't date, I did. And that change is a huge factor in things being better.

It's a night and day difference between where I was at their age and where they are, and I wouldn't trade it for anything in the world.

PHS: That's looking back a little bit. Now looking forward, what is the main difference that you see that the homeschooling movement will have made when history looks back from, say, 50 or even 100 years in the future? What impact will homeschoolers have had?

MF: We have been raising and will continue to raise a disproportionate number of the leaders in most of the fields of endeavor in our country. I don't think we're going to be all the leaders, but I think you'll see 15 to 20 percent of the political leaders, the business leaders, the church leaders, will have been homeschooled kids. And that's five to six times our numbers in society.

PHS: That's a significant impact.

MF: Right. We're seeing it already

in the national spelling bee, geography bees, and so on. When 20 percent of the people in Congress have been homeschooled, Congress is going to be a different place.

PHS: That's for sure.

MF: But I think we're probably 15 years from there.

PHS: In the present, how would you describe the effect that homeschooling is having on business, on the church, and on higher education here in America?

MF: I think it's had the most impact so far on the church. That churches have had to rethink their family policies and their youth group policies as a result of the dissatisfaction of homeschooling with the status quo as it was practiced for the last 15–20 years. So churches are starting to change and become more family-friendly. They used to be family-friendly in the sense that they had a room to stick every kid in when you went to church. Now they're actually becoming concerned about how the family operates as a family. There's a whole wide variety of approaches to that, and there's a lot of variance of desires among homeschoolers how they want it to be approached. Some want their kids with them at all times, others don't, but the common thread is that they want the family unit honored and supported and not ripped apart. I see churches changing that way. And I believe that 15 percent of the evangelical fundamental church in this country will homeschool their kids for at least a couple years in the very near future.

PHS: I know in my church it's certainly a growing phenomenon, with more and more families homeschooling.

MF: Turning back to my own family for a second, we've completed our sixteenth year of homeschooling, and we will have at least 17 more years of homeschooling by the time our youngest finishes. So I'll get to see at least the first 30 years of the modern homeschooling movement. My wife will really deserve the gold watch at the end of that time!

PHS: Are there any future plans for HSLDA?

MF: We're starting an apprentice-

ship-based college in September of 2000, called Patrick Henry College (www.phc.edu) [My daughter is going there now—Mary], where students would spend half the time in the classroom and half the time in an on-the-job kind of situation. The first degree will be in government. We hope to offer degrees in journalism and computer science, and eventually an accredited law school.

In the college, I think that homeschoolers will do for college education what they're done for K–12 education; and that is we're going to figure out an interesting and successful alternative to the status quo. I don't know exactly what that's going to be. What we've done is succeed remarkably at the status quo. But I think that people are looking for a change there as well.

One of the things we could do and be very successful is offer an education that's consistent with what was given in this country in the 50s and 60s in colleges, when it wasn't a crime to study the literature of dead white males. If we just did that, it would be significant. But I think it's going to be bigger and better than that. HSLDA wants to play a role as a spark—we don't want to fulfill it, but we would like to be a spark for some changes.

PHS: That is exciting. You mentioned classrooms. Will there be any way for students who can't move to its location to be enrolled perhaps through some distance learning program?

MF: Once we get the campus up and going, we are going to be looking into distance learning as well.

PHS: Do you have any personal plans for the future you would like to share with our readers, any special projects you're working on?

MF: Getting the college going, that's kind of my new project for the next few years. I'm not running for anything, and as Ollie North said, I'm not running from anything.

PHS: That's great. I want to thank you so much for your time, and for sharing your vision about the future of homeschooling with our readers.

MF: Thanks so much, and tell all your readers hello for me.

- **Conventions typically host curriculum vendors.** Lots of them. Seminars typically have a few tables where you can buy the speaker's books. One new trend—local Christian bookstores setting up table after table of homeschool curriculum, which is also available in the "Homeschool Corner" section of their store.

So here is what you can expect at a homeschool seminar:

- A number of sit-down sessions, where you listen to the speaker talk about his or her area of expertise. Expect an affable presentation laced with humor, "show 'n' tell" examples, personal anecdotes, and backed up with quotes and statistics. The whole deal might last one evening, or part of a Saturday.
- Time to browse the speaker's table and talk to him or her personally.
- I've never heard of a homeschool speaker who charges for his or her autograph, so if you're buying a book at the speaker's table, go for it!

You might also want to keep in mind that each speaker has a favorite homeschool method, so if the speaker tells you with great authority that theirs is the One Best Way to homeschool, take notes but reserve judgment. Homeschooling is a movement based on common sense; if anything you're hearing sounds implausible, use your common sense and check it out with your fellow homeschoolers before inflicting it on your family. I know one gal, for example, who used to rave about how all homeschool moms should set up "learning centers" in their homes. A "learning center" is a table with books and materials for studying a particular topic, such as birds. Schools and museums set them up for the convenience of the large crowds of kids who use these institutions. The speaker, an ex-schoolteacher, had spent years building creative learning centers in her classrooms and didn't have a clue that turning your home into a mini museum is educational overkill.

Which brings me to my last point about homeschool seminars—these are supposed to be *home*school seminars. Beware of seminar speakers whose main claim to fame is the years they spent teaching special ed in the schools, or math, or whatever. With rare exceptions, what's going on in today's classrooms *isn't working,* which is why we're homeschooling in the first place. Demand to see *results.* If Ms. So-and-So was such a great special ed teacher, what percent of her students did so well under her tutelage that they were ever graduated out of the special ed program? If Mr. So-and-So is such a great math teacher, how many of his students passed the AP Calculus exam or got 800s on the math portion of the SAT I? Did he coach a math team that year after year won the Math Olympics? Did this art teacher's students become Disney animators? Teachers like this do exist, and sometimes "cross over" into the homeschool movement, but there are also opportunists out there trying to hawk their education degrees whose "years of experience" are really years of failure. That's why most homeschool seminar speakers turn out to be homeschool moms and dads, with years of *homeschool* experience.

Your First Homeschool Convention

A homeschool convention is a horse of a different color. We're talking *big.* Lots of speakers. Lots of workshops. A huge curriculum fair. Between 500 (North Dakota) and 20,000 (California) people milling around. Whole hotels reserved for homeschool guests. The biggest convention center in town rented for the show.

Your best bet is to preregister, thereby saving about $10. You and your spouse, and possibly a few of your older children, can also register at the door. Little kids are, oddly enough, not allowed at many homeschool conventions, with the exception of nursing babies. The ostensible reason is the lack of available seating. The other reason is that the convention organizers fear many new or wannabe homeschoolers have not yet trained their little darlings to behave, and the organizers don't want to spend all day chasing after misbehaving kids.

The way I've gotten around the "no little kids" rule is to be the conference speaker. Vendors also often bring their kids of all ages, for the simple reason that they can't leave them all day in the hotel room. If you're not a speaker or a vendor, make *sure* young children are allowed before you show up at the convention in your minibus with seven children of all ages.

Now it is true that little kids would be bored at most homeschool conventions. The program usually runs on Friday night and all day Saturday. Friday night, which is often open to the public, starts off with announcements, sometimes music, and a keynote address by the big-name speaker. Saturday there are workshops, and maybe some more keynote addresses or workshops by the big-name speaker. Speeches and workshops run from 45 minutes to 75 minutes long. The curriculum hall is sometimes open all the time, and sometimes closed during keynote speeches. It depends on the convention.

Your experience will go like this:

- **Show up at the door.** Either pay for or pick up your prepaid ID badge. This will have your name, so you can fraternize with other attendees. So don't take it personally when you find other people staring at your chest, or collarbone, or whatever body part you pinned your badge over.
- **You likely will also be given a "goodie bag"** of homeschool catalogs, brochures, special offers, and the like. Your best move is to immediately march out to the car and unload all the heavy material in your bag that is not directly related to the convention. If you're really smart, you will have brought along a tote, bag, or box of your own for these goodies and others you will pick up at the curriculum tables. The key to preventing aching feet is to periodically empty the heavy purchases and goodies out into your car instead of lugging them around all weekend. Keep the workshop schedule and floor map in your goodie bag, add a pencil and a few sheets of blank paper if you like to take notes, and return to the convention.
- **If you're timid**, sit several rows back. Some speakers have been known to select "volunteers" from the first rows for various onstage antics.
- **If you're nursing**, sit way in the back and pick an aisle seat. I warned you about how jumpy some people (not me) get about crying babies.
- **Sit** through the announcements, music, and first speech. Then **wander outside** on the break and chat with everyone else about how good or bad the speaker is. Or sit in your seat and circle the workshops you want to attend and the booths you want to visit. Or take the kiddies to the rest room—an even more private place to chat with the other ladies about how the convention is going so far. (I know for a fact the women all chat in the bathroom in front of the mirrors; according to Dilbert's laws of male behavior, presumably the men don't do this.)
- **Pride's Law of Workshop Scheduling:** You discover all the workshops you most want to attend are scheduled at the same time. Being

clever, you and your spouse split up to cover at least two of them, or you decide to order tapes of the workshops you missed (if available).

- **If you're smart, you'll budget twice as much time** as you think you need to visit the curriculum hall. There's always at least one booth with products so fascinating you end up spending half your time there.

- **Unless you're especially fashion-conscious**, sneakers or sandals are the way to go. If you decide to cover every table in the curriculum hall, you'll be doing a *lot* of walking.

- **Lunch is usually available on-site.** If it is, pay the extra few bucks and eat right there. It's a great way to meet a few people, and the food is usually pretty good, too. (That's because the homeschooled teens made most of it!)

- **Bring lots of cash**, although credit cards and checks are accepted by most vendors. The kids will all want homeschool T-shirts and caps, and you will find some unusual curriculum and bargain opportunities as well.

- **It is not considered good manners** to roam the curriculum hall with a bargain catalog in your back pocket. It is considered even worse manners to blatantly compare prices on the table with prices in the bargain catalog. The worst of all is to make the poor curriculum vendor explain his product, demonstrate it, practically wrap it up for you, and *then* drag out the bargain catalog and tell him you're going to buy it mail-order instead. If the vendor spent a lot of time with you, consider his time as worth the few bucks extra it may cost to pick up the product right there as opposed to ordering it from a discount catalog.

- **If you want to make a lot of good friends** among the local homeschool leadership, plan to stay late and volunteer to help clean up. Older kids are also very good at this, and it's a way for them to make friends with the other responsible kids who are cleaning up too.

Other Major Homeschool Events

I've had the pleasure of speaking at a couple of Six Flags Homeschool Days. Park attendance for homeschool days, and other special events, is lower than the 40,000 or so that can and often do jam in at other times—a mere 7,500 to 15,000. This means you don't have to stand in line for most rides, everyone in the park is a potential friend, and the tickets cost less. You can even go listen to the homeschool speaker and check out the curriculum tables if you want to.

Six Flags theme parks also host "educational" days that until now have been only marketed to school groups. In St. Louis, for example, there is Physics Day (with handouts about the physics involved in doing loop-the-loops on the roller coaster!), Science Day (with special exhibits), and St. Louis History Day (with reenactments of important historical events that occurred in St. Louis). Other Six Flags parks have similar educational days. You might want to check them out.

Also, the "homeschool vacation" is coming into its own. The idea of such events is that you can bring the whole family (including the little kids this time) and for a single package price get room, board, homeschool speakers, a curriculum fair, and lot of fun outdoors and indoors activities. I spoke at one of the first of these vacation events, at Glorieta Conference Center in New Mexico. They received twice as many registrations as they expected, leading to talk of setting up other state-by-state homeschool vacations. My hope is that such events will be coordinated with the state groups. If there is enough demand, who knows? Homeschool educational cruises, anyone? ◄- -

BELIEVE IT OR NOT
Since I wrote this, several cruise companies have put together cruises just for homeschoolers!

You Might Be Homeschooled/Unschooled If:

by Aletheia Price, homeschool graduate

Aletheia kindly gave us permission to reprint this list we found on her website, www.eatbug.com. I present it to you now to give you an idea of what homeschooling is really like from a student's-eye view . . . so your children will also know what to expect!

- You don't own a television
- You are firmly convinced that high school causes brain damage
- You sleep in till 9 A.M. on weekdays but get up at 7 A.M. on Sundays
- You have more siblings than sweaters
- You know what a "Park Day" is
- Your favorite author is Jane Austen, G.K. Chesterton, or P.G. Wodehouse
- You have ever suffered through Saxon Math
- All birthdays are school holidays
- You have ever finished your schoolwork before breakfast
- You taunt high schooled friends during finals week
- People compliment you on your polka-dot suspenders and mismatched socks
- You spend more than two hours each day reading and writing . . . voluntarily
- You are 16 years of age or older and have never been on a date
- You know what "Unit Studies" are
- You have more than two science experiments going on in your room
- You know more than one Latin paradigm
- You have ever spent the entire school day in pajamas
- You regularly utilize words such as *malingering*, *tedious*, and *indubitably*
- You consider sled riding phys ed
- Your IQ is greater than your weight
- You check out more than ten books each time you visit the library
- You have ever attempted to teach yourself physics
- When asked about your GPA, you say: "Oh, probably 4.0"
- You have no idea as to what rock bands are currently popular . . . but you can recite all of the stages of cellular mitosis (in order)
- You believe that you are the most intelligent human in your age bracket within a ten-mile radius
- You actually *want* to receive books on your birthday
- You are on a first-name basis with your local librarians
- You have ever vented for more than five minutes on the evils of standardized testing
- Every time your dad wants to encourage you to do yard work he calls it "extra credit"!
- You memorize Latin roots to impress your friends
- You have the Dewey Decimal system memorized
- You've tried memorizing the laws of thermodynamics for fun
- You believe that learning is best accomplished in a tree, while eating a peanut butter sandwich
- You can quote lines from Shakespeare, but not from *South Park*
- You read the dictionary for fun
- Textbooks seem handy for starting fires, and that's about it
- Your idea of an awesome weekend is Plato, hot tea, and a microscope
- You've ever had nightmares about attending public school
- You have a standard four-minute speech to give to teachers, aunts, mothers-in-law, and school officials about why you are homeschooled
- You've ever laughed out loud when someone asked you "What about socialization?"

Your First Homeschool Month

You've read the books (or at least this one), subscribed to a magazine, attended a seminar, pre-registered for the state convention. So far so good, but now it's showtime—your first day of homeschool.

You are very excited. Either that, or you are feeling desperate. Your child, or children, are also feeling excited. Or not. We can list these alternatives thusly:

- **The Excited Homeschool Parent** Your child is about to be homeschooled for the first time, friends have homeschooled successfully, and you can't wait to start.
- **The Desperate Homeschool Parent** Your child used to be in school, but for a variety of excellent reasons this turned out to be a bad idea, so now you feel you *have* to homeschool him or her, but you're not feeling very confident.

- **The Excited Homeschool Child** Your child is about to start homeschool for the first time, or has been begging you to let him or her be homeschooled.
- **The Unexcited Homeschool Child** Mom and/or Dad has developed convictions about homeschooling, but this previously schooled child really would rather be in school with friends.

If you're excited, and your children are excited, your first month will probably go great. You have clever and creative activities planned, and they will love them.

If you're excited, and they're unexcited, you'd better resolve from the first not to take a lot of guff. Whining, moaning, and complaining can take the edge off the most prepared parent. Your best tactic is probably to demand that they "give it a chance." This is obviously reasonable. If the problem is perceived lack of friends, invite their friends over after school and on weekends, and take part in support group activities designed for kids of their age. If the problem is that they simply hate schoolwork, be patient. Hatred of learning is not natural; it was acquired in school and will take some time to evaporate.

If you're desperate, but they're excited, not to worry. Just provide library books, math workbooks, and some fun hands-on materials to start with. This will build up your confidence and keep their excitement high. In the meantime, add to your confidence by repeating Steps 1 through 12. Later on you can add more "serious" resources, once you're hitting your homeschooling stride.

If you're desperate, and they're unexcited, *rush* to the nearest support group meeting. Join an online homeschooling forum. Buy homeschooling books and magazines galore. Visit the library, the zoo, the museum, the seashore, the mountains . . . whatever new environments you can find. Your job is to jolt this child out of an acquired hatred of learning, as well as remove him from the previously corrupting or intimidating influences which caused him to withdraw emotionally in the first place. Once he gets "hooked" on *any* positive interest, you're on your way . . . because one thing homeschoolers have discovered is that *any* interest, if pursued far enough, will lead to a need to learn the academic basics.

No matter how prepared you think you are, you will encounter surprises during your first month of homeschool. The project you thought they'd love the most will turn out to be a tedious waste of time. On the other hand, simply reading aloud may be a big hit. You'll discover more about your child in this month than you did in years before. You'll also discover your personality flaws mirrored in your child. The house will not stay spotlessly clean. Nor will it clean itself. The phone will ring just when you finally got all the materials together, and when you get off it, the children will have wandered away. You will spend half a hour searching for a pencil, only to sit down on the couch and hear it go "Crack!" under the cushion. A formerly distant child will start to become affectionate. A child who has been convinced he is "dumb" will spend hours building elaborate creations with his Lego bricks. Someone will call and ask you to volunteer for a church or community function "because you don't work and have the time for it." The UPS man will start to consider your house a regular stop. The librarian will call you by name. Some art supplies will get spilled and make a mess. You will start wondering which walls of your house are big enough to tack up a timeline on. You will sleep late by accident, and realize it doesn't matter—there's no schoolbus to catch!

Surprises aside, here are the four main things to remember if you want your first homeschool month to be a success:

TV Guardian

Principal Solutions, AR. (888) 799-4884, www.tvguardian.com

Clean up any movie on video!

You've probably seen ads for ten or twenty programs to block out filth on the Internet, each claiming it's the best. Have you ever seen the same for TV or movies? Why not? You may have heard of the "V-Chip," which will block out entire programs with offensive material. But you've probably seen movies which had a great story, a compelling plot, lovable characters . . . and language too filthy to ever let you show them to the kids. Rather than reject the entire program, the **TV Guardian** uses the closed-captioning to block out lines with "colorful" language. We've used it, and it cuts the sound for a line with any recognizable swear word and can be set to display a cleaned-up version of the text. It can display entire cleaned-up dialogue, for the benefit of the hearing-impaired. On top of all that, you can lock the cables and the setting switches inside, so curious kids can't turn it off even if they want to!

The TV Guardian isn't perfect. If the screenwriters are inventive with their sexual allusions, some may slip by around the edges. Also, in cases where the captioning isn't timed quite right, or where there is no captioning at all, a rented video may still surprise you with some unwanted vocabulary. Nevertheless, the TV Guardian does a good job. It doesn't leave a single bad word in *Men In Black,* for example— quite an accomplishment.

This product can't shut down the audio on a DVD unless your DVD player requires a separate sound system. E.g., it might work with an inexpensive modular DVD player, but not a fancy integrated system. *Review by Joseph Pride*

(1) **No TV.** Oh, the agony! Try renting videos instead, to be played only after the school day is over. It's only for a month. See what happens.

(2) **Do the chores first.** This is the Iron Law of Homeschooling. Even if doing the chores takes all day, and *no* academic work gets done, your children must do their chores first. Trust me. This habit will do more for your homeschool success than any other. The habit of being responsible, doing a job well, and doing it completely is best learned hands-on, with chores. Without these habits, your children will become the dreaded Homeschool Slackers.

(3) **It's only the first month.** Really, it's OK if your child doesn't make it through the entire Suzuki violin book series, doesn't win a blue ribbon at the state fair for his home-bred gerbils, and doesn't invent nuclear fusion. Never mind what the kids in the homeschool magazines are doing. He has *years* to do all this. Relax.

(4) **Keep your accomplishments**, or what you may be thinking of as your *lack* of accomplishment, **in perspective.** If your child didn't do drugs, didn't get drunk, didn't stab or shoot anyone or get stabbed or shot by anyone, didn't become an unwed father or mother, didn't form a clique to reject the less-attractive kids, didn't get rejected by a clique of "in" kids, didn't swear or get sworn at, didn't engage in occult religious rituals, and didn't abandon the faith, your homeschool month was lots better than the months lots of kids were having in school. You say they learned something, as well as avoiding all that bad stuff? Then congratulate yourself—you're off to a great start!

PART 3

How Kids Really Learn

James Hill, an 18-year-old from Hutto, TX, is yet another homeschooled National Merit Scholar and the winner of a $2,500 National Merit Scholarship, one of only 2,500 students in the nation to receive this honor each year. James plans to use his scholarship to study computer engineering at Harding University in Searcy, Arkansas, where he will be a member of the honors scholars program. During his high-school years, he enjoyed pursuing his interest in computers by participating in an apprenticeship program offered in Austin, becoming licensed as a Microsoft Certified Professional, working as a programmer for Dell Computer Corporation, and successfully designing and marketing Bible study software.

James' mom, Becky Hill, sent the above photo because she says it typifies the spirit of homeschooling to her. I personally am intrigued by the rope attached to his knee. My theory is he is using it to rock himself while he studies. Just more proof not everyone learns best at a desk!

Melissa Anne Murata, a 12-year-old homeschooler
from San Antonio, TX, won the M.S. Poster Contest for
San Antonio—A Great Place to Visit. This contest was
sponsored by the Tourism Council and Fiesta Magazine
to promote National Tourism Week and the Alamo City.
   Melissa is pictured here with San Antonio Mayor
Howard Peak, who was on hand for the awards presentation at the Tower of Americas. In addition to the
recognition, Melissa received $100. Her poster was
auctioned off at the Annual Tourism Banquet and now
hangs in the River City Mall at the Imax theater.

CHAPTER 13

The Five Steps of Learning

In this section, you will learn how children *really* learn. First, we will look at the five steps of learning—not *what* children need to know, but *how* they learn it. Next, you will discover your child's preferred discovery channel—what used to be called "learning styles." Finally, you will learn what type of thinking style your child has. Even the class clown and the daydreamer can learn rapidly and well once their individual learning needs are met.

As a no-extra-cost bonus, you can also use this section to discover *your* discovery channel and thinking style. Be careful: This could change your life!

Along the way, you'll discover why the schools, as presently conceived, cannot possibly meet the learning needs of the majority of children; why the kids the schools have the most trouble with may in fact have the gifts our society needs the most; and how you, at home, can give your children exactly the kind of education that each of them really needs.

How You Use Your Brain

Take a look at the brain. It's that roundish mass inside your skull that looks like the Green Giant's left-over chewing gum. Understand how the brain operates and you will know why some educational methods work and others don't.

Oversimplifying grossly, we see that thinking involves two main operations: storage and retrieval. You store everything that comes in through your senses in infinitesimal brain cells. If you could remember all of this, you'd probably go crazy; but you can't remember it, since you quite easily lose track of what is stored there.

> **Learning is the art of connecting your memories in a way that makes enough sense for you to be able to retrieve them rapidly.**

> **Thinking is the act of making new connections between your memories.**

> A journey of a thousand miles must begin with a single step.
> —*Lao-tsu, an ancient Chinese philosopher*

> All men by nature desire knowledge.
> —*Aristotle*

In the brain, thinking causes physical connections to grow between the brain cells. The more connections you have, the better your thinking powers. The brains of geniuses are convoluted and heavy with all the connections they have made. Newborn babies, on the other hand, have smooth brains with almost no connections.

Let us, then, develop a very simple theory of education based on these two observable truths:

(1) You can't connect what isn't there.
(2) You can't find what is there without a logical connection.

> **Thus, it is vital to expose the student, whatever his age, to a lot of raw data *before* trying to "teach" him anything concerning that data. After he has soaked up hundreds of facts and experiences, it is equally vital to supply him with a means of connecting them all.**

You could call this the "Data-Connection Theory," but since there is actually nothing original about it, call it anything you like. It works like this:

Say you want to teach a child to read. You do not shove a book in front of his face and start teaching. First, you expose him to a lot of print. Big print, little print. Newsprint. Books. Cereal boxes. Meanwhile, you read to him. Snuggled in your lap, he is both cozy and unafraid—ideal conditions for learning. Slowly he will get the idea: Those black marks are letters, letters make words, and words are what Mommy is reading to me. Once he understands what reading is all about, he will probably ask you to teach him to read. Your task, then, is to provide the logical patterns (phonics) which translate all those letters into sounds.

True, reading is a complex subject, and we haven't discussed the idea of physical readiness (i.e., brain maturation) or methods of teaching yet. But I want you to understand that there are really only four basic approaches to teaching, three of which are wrong.

> ✘ **Wrong: Framework Without Data** Number One is to begin laying a logical framework *without* first supplying any individual data. You can actually feel the strain on your brain of trying to learn this way. You see, you are not only trying to connect your brain cells, but to fill them at the same time! It's easy to see that a lot gets lost in the shuffle this way. Much of higher math, from algebra on up, is commonly taught this way. Which is why most kids avoid it like the plague.
>
> ✘ **Wrong: Data Without Framework** Number Two is to supply the original data, but fail to show how the individual facts hang together. This is what the schools do when they load a kid up with "Readiness" activities and then spring sight-word reading on him. He is stuck trying to memorize zillions of seemingly unconnected facts. Some kids do manage to invent their own phonics patterns and survive, but it's in spite of, not because of, the way they are taught. This rote memorization approach is used all over: in history, in math, in spelling, in my college engineering courses. Learners are handed hundreds of little "rules" or "facts" without any reasonable way of hanging them all in order. The brain does not want to work

this way, and so although individual students can stuff the facts down for a test, they promptly forget it all in a week. This is not real learning.

✘ **Wrong: Erratic Data and Incomprehensible Framework** Number Three is to provide *neither* initial experiences *nor* a framework. Fluffhead professors with no communication abilities are the chief perpetrators of this style of "teaching." Others are deluded into thinking the profs are brilliant because nobody understands them. But flunking all your students is *not* a sign of genius. If a teacher gets garbage out, it's probably because he put garbage in.

✔ **Right: Data First, Framework Second** The only way that works consistently, because it is based on the way the brain operates, is Number Four: providing the learner with raw data and, after he's had time to digest it, with a permanent framework for storing the data. New data can then be connected to the old with minimal effort.

In history, the framework would be a time line. In geography, the framework is a globe. The learner must have some way of getting a panoramic view of the field he is studying or he will be, as he puts it, "lost." Once he has that panoramic view, he can fill in the details as long as he lives.

Some educational products provide data (which, as you remember, includes experiences). Others provide a learning framework, such as a good phonics program. Some provide both. As we learn to discern which product does what, we can educate ourselves and our children much more efficiently.

What I am going to say now is even less original. Since the beginning of time, mothers and fathers have mastered these five simple steps of learning. Only in our science-worshiping age have we tried to bypass the wisdom of our grandparents—with the dismal results you now see. *Their* generation was 99 percent literate, remember?

Step 1: Playing

Let kids be kids. That's step one. *Play* is the first step of learning. Earthshaking, isn't it? Any kindergarten teacher could tell you that!

Ah, but do we *act* on this knowledge? How many times do we or Johnny's teachers try to rush him into "mastering" some new skill without giving him any chance to play around with it first?

Everyone gets ready to learn by playing.

Play is the stage where you fool around with something before settling down to get serious about it. When your husband picks up his hammer and hefts it experimentally, he is playing. When your wife tries on a new dress that she doesn't intend to actually wear anywhere today, she is playing.

Play turns the strange into the comfortable, the unknown into the familiar. Dad hefts his new hammer because he wants to know how heavy it feels before he risks his fingers using it on a piece of wood. Mom tries on her dress because she needs to feel comfortable about how she looks in it before appearing in public.

In the very same way, children need to get comfortable with new words, new objects, and new ideas before they can be reasonably expected to do anything serious with them.

Who Is a Genius?

Some people have taken me to task for a what they consider a too-egalitarian view of human ability. They, quite rightly, point out that a genius, by definition, is different from other people. According to them, most children can't possibly be geniuses.

I do recognize that we are all born with a different amount of native quickness. But genius is not only, or primarily, quickness. Ask Thomas Edison. He said that genius was one percent inspiration and ninety-nine percent perspiration. And Thomas Edison should know. He invented the electric light and the phonograph, to name just a few of his contributions. Nobody has ever questioned whether Edison was a genius!

The real question, then, is why do some people perspire and sweat after knowledge, while others don't? The answer is simple—and explains why our present school system produces such an amazing shortfall of genius.

A genius is a person to whom learning is a game.

And we can help our children and students discover the game of learning.

—Schoolproof

Hold Me, Touch Me

Several writers on education have noticed that children who are allowed to play with learning equipment before being put through any exercises with the equipment do much better than those who are immediately forced to use the equipment for its "proper" use.

In his book *How Children Learn* (Dell Publishing Company, 1983, revised edition) John Holt tells about his friend Bill Hull's experience with the attribute blocks he invented:

"They found a very interesting thing about the way children reacted to these materials. If, when a child came in for the first time, they tried to get him 'to work' right away, to play some of their games and solve some of their puzzles, they got nowhere. . . . But if at first they let the child alone for a while, let him play with the materials in his own way, they got very different results. . . . When, through such play and fantasy, the children had taken those materials into their minds, mentally swallowed and digested them, so to speak, they were then ready and willing to play very complicated games that in the more organized and businesslike situation had left other children completely baffled. This proved to be so consistently true that the experimenters made it a rule always to let children have a period of completely free play with the materials before asking them to do directed work with them."

If you're going to open up unfamiliar new territory in your brain, your best move is to send out some scouts. Survey the terrain. Get to know what it looks like. Then you'll feel confident about building a town out there. Play is the brain's scouting expedition.

How does this apply in real life? Here are some examples:

- **Children should *see* print and *hear* it read before trying to learn to read.** If possible, they should also *manipulate* letters (like alphabet puzzle pieces) and *write* letters before beginning their reading lessons.
- **Children should be allowed to scribble freely** before you try to help them make specific marks on the paper. Allow them to use any color they want, and to color outside the lines in the coloring book. So far, all nine of my children have gone through the scribble stage and the color-it-any-color-but-the-right-one stage, and *without any help from me* all nine have gone on to neat, accurate coloring.
- **Words like *noun* and *verb* should be used well in advance of any grammar lessons.** Ditto for all terminology and every subject. Making a student of any age learn both unfamiliar words *and* unfamiliar concepts at the same time is cruel and unusual punishment.
- **Grabbiness is part of learning.** See how quickly a baby explores the box his Christmas present came in! He is not satisfied until he has gone thoroughly over it with eyes, ears, nose, fingers, and mouth. Babies, more than the rest of us, are determined to make the unfamiliar familiar. They know they don't know, and are trying to catch up. (Incidentally, knowing we don't know and un-self-consciously humbling ourselves to learn may be part of what Jesus had in mind when He said we must become like little children.)

Step 2:
Setting Up Your Framework

A child learning to read and an adult studying aeronautical engineering both need the same thing: a framework to help them organize their data. This framework is like a filing cabinet loaded with files. It provides slots in which to fit the ever-accumulating new data. In history, the time line; in geography, the globe; in reading, the alphabet; in language, the web of grammar; these are frameworks under which myriads of new facts can be filed.

A good framework answers the question, "What in all tarnation is *this?*"

History is about people and movements and dates; hence the time line. Geography is about where things are; hence the globe. Engineering is about putting little pieces together to make a building (or airplane, or circuit board). Grammar is about putting words together to make a sentence. Handwriting is about making marks on paper that people can read.

A framework is the big picture, the panoramic view of your subject.

Your framework is what's going to glue together all the thousands of facts and ideas you are going to learn.

One big reason kids flounder in school is because the teachers are so wrapped up in skills and subskills and testing and grades that their students forget what they are trying to accomplish. If a student can't see the relationship between filling out 14 workbook pages on beginning consonants and beginning to read (and believe me, the connection is pretty tenuous), his mind will not be storing the new information under the right headings. Reading will seem a succession of unrelated hoops the teacher is trying to make him jump through, and it won't "come together" for him. This is also why students shy away from those fuzzy graduate courses where the teacher wanders all over the landscape without ever making it clear what the course is *about*.

It's not hard to set up a learning framework. All classical instruction included frameworks. Just giving a subject a *name*, like Oceanography or Weaving or Renaissance Art, is the beginning of a framework. If you know what you're trying to learn—whether TV repairing or gourmet cookery or the story of Ethelred the Unready—you're on your way!

Step 3: Categories

Think of your filing cabinet, if you have one. Can you easily find papers you have filed away, or do you have to grumble your way through umpteen folders every time you need a paper?

Those of us who have expanded into several filing cabinets quickly find that we need a system to keep it all straight. Some use colored folders, some use colored dots, some use each drawer for a special purpose—it doesn't matter. The main thing is that without organization our bulging files are as useless as if they were in Timbuktu.

You see, a framework is only half the story. You can have a filing cabinet (framework) without an organized arrangement of files. Without organization, though you can happily file new facts by the ton, you can't find them except by accident.

Efficient learners make it their practice to break every new subject down into manageable categories.

They don't study the American Revolution all at once, for instance. They study Famous Loyalists, Famous Generals, Spies and Traitors, Naval Battles, the Continental Congress, or whatever categories give them most insight into what they are trying to learn.

It invariably happens that, as you go deeper into a subject, your original categories become too broad and you have to make subcategories. In our example above, the Continental Congress quickly becomes too wide a field for the serious student. So he might break it down further into Congressional Leaders, Congressional Committees, Southern Congressmen, or other subcategories, each of which in turn can be further divided.

Let's take another example: reading. Why do phonics courses always spend so much time talking about Vowels and Consonants and Short Vowels and Long Vowels and Blends and Digraphs and Diphthongs? Those are *categories*, that's why! Anyone can remember five Short Vowels and twenty-one Consonants. These little boxes make the data much more findable. Contrast this with the sight-word method used in 85 percent of public schools, where Junior is trying to memorize the individual shapes of all the words in the English language, and you'll have a clue as to why we have a national reading problem.

The difference in learning efficiency between a product or course that organizes the data for you into categories, and one that doesn't, is immense. Although the latter may contain gobs of useful knowledge, you'll have a real struggle walking away with any of it. Keep this in mind as you shop.

Step 4: Putting Your Data in Order

Once you've become comfortable with your object of study, the next step is to pick up more information about it. You can do this by memorizing categories of facts, but your task will be much easier if you can sort the information into patterns.

> **Patterns are your method for filing new facts into a category.**

Going back to our example of the file cabinet, let's say you have organized your file cabinet by categories. The top drawer is for family records and the bottom one is for your home business. Within each drawer you have file folders (subcategories), also organized by topic. You have, for example, one file folder exclusively for Personal Correspondence. All is well and good so far. But if you want to quickly find the letter your Aunt Theresa wrote you six months ago, you'd better have a method for filing letters inside that folder.

You could have filed your letters with the most recent to the front of the folder and the oldest correspondence to the back. You could have filed letters by the names of the people writing to you, or by the topics on which they wrote. Although some of these schemes would be more efficient than others, *any* of them would be more efficient than simply shoving each letter helter-skelter into the folder.

In the same way, you will hold onto new facts much better if you can arrange them in order using a systematic pattern.

What do I mean by a "pattern"? As I said, *patterns are your organizing method.*

> **When you have a category of related facts (such as, in phonics, words ending with "at"), the systematic way you file them (in this case, alphabetic order) is your pattern.**

Let's look at the pattern for our example of "at" words (alphabetically, by digraphs, by diphthongs):

at	pat	plat
bat	rat	slat
cat	sat	spat
fat	vat	sprat
hat	brat	splat
mat	flat	that

Once a child gets used to writing out families of words in alphabetic order, he has a tool for generating dozens of new words from *every* word ending or category he learns.

Some facts need to be sorted alphabetically, as in our example above. Others have a natural chronological pattern (as when studying the battles in a war). Still others sort out numerically, starting with the smallest and ascending to the largest. Arithmetic is full of these kinds of patterns, e.g.:

$$1 + 1 = 2$$
$$2 + 1 = 3$$
$$3 + 1 = 4$$
$$\cdots\cdots\cdots$$
$$10 + 1 = 11$$

Learning the "one-pluses" by this pattern is much easier than trying to memorize individual "math facts" out of order.

Matter can be organized by its physical layout. You will notice that this series you are now reading follows a definite pattern. Each chapter begins with text that discusses the issues in an educational field. The text is followed by reviews, sorted in alphabetical order. Each review has contact information next to it in the margin. This makes the book easier to use than if all the information were jumbled together.

Why are we spending so much time talking about patterns? Because patterns are what make or break many educational products. If data is not patterned, or is ordered according to the wrong pattern, it becomes much harder to use. Try this simple example. Which of the following foreign language programs would be easier to use? The first categorizes phrases together that deal with, say, table manners, and leaves it at that (this one has categories, but no patterns). The second categorizes the phrases and lists them in alphabetical order (category plus pattern). The third categorizes phrases, and lists them in *grammatical* order (e.g., "I like the meal. You like the meal. He likes the meal. She likes the meal . . ."). The third program sorts the data into *the form in which you need it*, since you talk in terms of I or he or she, not in alphabet lists.

Similarly, it is easy to learn the days of the week in chronological order, which is the way we use them, whereas if you memorized them in random order, or alphabetical order, it would be extremely difficult to use them quickly.

Not every individual fact can be sorted into a pattern. You've just got to memorize the value of pi, for instance. But the vast majority of useful data does follow systematic patterns. It's the scientist's job to find these patterns, and the teacher's job to use them.

If you want to learn effortlessly, and remember what you learn, insist on products that provide both categories and patterns.

Step 5: Fusion

Have you ever had a brainstorm? Suddenly you could almost hear the clicking as light turned on inside your head. Misty ideas suddenly coalesced. Hundreds of previously unrelated facts joined arms and marched along singing.

That marvelous experience is what some writers call "synthesis," "flow," or "the genius state," and I prefer to call "fusion." Fusion is when frameworks link. All at once electrical impulses can take the express from Point A to Point B when they used to have to make detours and swim muddy streams of consciousness to make the trip.

Go with the Flow

Flow states are critical to the development of talent. When in a flow state, one is mastering challenges that are neither too easy nor too difficult. Mastery of each challenge leads to mastery of a higher level of challenge. According to Csikszentmihalyi, the kind of person who is able to achieve flow is characterized by high curiosity, achievement and endurance, openness to experience, and strong attunement to sensory information.

—*Ellen Winner,*
Gifted Children: Myths & Realities
(1996, Basic Books)

When you're experiencing fusion, you're concentrating intensely, enjoying it, and losing track of your own physical state and the outside world. Inventors, composers, and other gifted people may experience fusion states that last for hours or days at a time. But even the rest of us have all had times when we were so immersed in a creative activity we lost all track of time. The "pieces came together" of whatever we were trying to do, and our brains made sense of it all.

Fusion *feels* good. It lets you spend the energy that used to be wasted hacking through jungles of confusion on more edifying pursuits.

Fusion is the opposite of *con*fusion, which is what happens when our carefully built frameworks turn out to be all wrong and we have to start rebuilding them from scratch. This confusion is the eternal lot of those who are heedless about looking for answers to the deep questions of life.

We live in an age when people are being taught that there *are* no answers, so one might as well not bother asking the questions. The only consistent responses if this is true are despair or ruthless hedonism. And these are the lifestyles we are seeing today.

Although the antiphilosophy of relativism—that there is no right and wrong—has had great success, it is not correct. The human brain was not constructed to be open to *everything*. People have a built-in need for right and wrong, for security, for an integrating philosophy of life. Perhaps the best books ever written on this subject, that describe our present confusion and the timeless solution, are *Escape from Reason* by Dr. Francis Schaeffer (published by InterVarsity Press) and *L'Abri* by Edith Schaeffer (published by Tyndale House). Look for them at your favorite bookstore or library.

We don't need to understand the meaning of our lives in order to eat, sleep, and park the car. But human beings are not worms in the mud; the more we learn about the world and the joys and injustices of life, the more every thinking person asks, "What is this all for?" How tragic if we, and our children, have been taught to strangle these questions before they can even be spoken. Tragic because there *is* Someone home in the universe; God is not dead; and everyone who seeks, shall find.

CHAPTER 14

Your Child's Discovery Channels

Every trade has its tricks. A farrier knows how to make a horse stand still while he hammers on a new horseshoe. Fly fishermen know how to snap the rod and make the line float out over the water. Knowing these tricks makes work a sport, and sport more enjoyable.

Learning can also be a sport. The difference between the duffers and the champions is that the champions know the tricks of the sport and care enough to put them into practice.

I would now like to share with you some very simple tricks and resources that can make a huge difference in how much you and your children enjoy learning.

Your Special Discovery Channels

Jack Sprat could learn by chat
His wife could learn by sight
Their son, named Neil, could learn by feel
They were a funny sight!

Everyone is born with a special discovery channel—not a cable network but a favorite way to discover new facts about the world. Some, like Jack Sprat in the ditty above, learn best by listening. Others, like his wife, learn best by seeing. Still others are sensuous types who need to have real objects to handle. If you are taught through the channel that suits you, fantastic! If you're not, it's frustration time.

Educrats, in their slow grappling with reality, have recently rediscovered discovery channels and christened them "modalities." Don't expect any sudden changes in the schools from this discovery, though. The best you can hope for is that *after* your child has been labeled "dyslexic" or "hyperactive" or "learning disabled," some up-to-date remedial teacher will discover that Johnny really just has a discovery channel that his classroom did not accommodate.

Now let's discover *your* best discovery channel.

Why Not "Learning Styles"?

Your overall learning style includes both

- the channel through which you learn best (eye, ear, hand)
- the ways you are most motivated to learn (your "thinking style")

We will be finding out how both of these work in this chapter and the chapter following.

The traditional classroom, which is set up to teach mostly to the auditory mode, is serving only about 34% of its students!
—*Mariaemma Willis &*
Victoria Hodson, Discover Your
Child's Learning Style *(Rocklin,*
CA: Prima Publishing, 1999)

The Way They Learn

Parents. Suggested donation, $11. *Focus on the Family Publishing, CO. (719) 531-3400, www.family.org.*

Of all the learning styles books I've read, **The Way They Learn** is by far my (Renee's) favorite. If you're at loggerheads with a child you just can't seem to teach, *The Way They Learn* may be just the help you need. Credit goes to author Cynthia Ulrich Tobias for making the subject matter interesting, easily understood, and applicable to all individuals—no matter where the learning takes place.

Her book is based on five sets of independent research on the way people learn. Here are the five models:

1. Four ways people perceive and order information: Abstract-Random, Abstract-Sequential, Concrete-Random, and Concrete-Sequential. Abstract versus concrete refers to the way we take in information, while sequential-random describes the way we organize it. Questions and illustrations are provided to help you get a feel for your style. Detailed chapters illustrate what each style "looks like" in an adult or a child.
2. Ideal study environments
3. Modes of remembering (auditory, visual, and kinesthetic)
4. Analytic vs. global approach to new information
5. Seven types of intelligence (spatial, musical, etc.)

She condenses it all in this very readable, parent-friendly 168-page hardback.

The overarching theme is that people's thinking/learning styles are

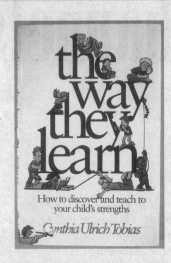

distinct and follow specific patterns. By recognizing these patterns in ourselves and our children, we can reduce needless arguments over how they should approach learning a subject and instead help them use their strengths to learn what they need to know.

Ferreting out a child's strengths using any of these models will un-doubtedly give him more knowledge of himself and enable him to tackle the learning process from a perspective that suits his style. In that sense the book is both useful and correct. But we note two cautions, one of which Mrs. Tobias rightly raises herself. Don't pigeonhole someone into a particular learning style; we usually have some of the characteristics of several. We would also add: Don't rely on these secular theories as the end-all in learning styles—use them only as general guides.

This book is most useful as an easygoing introduction to the idea that we all do things differently. It's a good reminder for us that some conflicts and difficulties are simply a matter of not knowing how to accommodate those differences. As educators, that's something we should all be aware of. But as a Christian educator, I have to ask how Scripture comes to bear on these very issues. While there is nothing in the Bible about four personality types, there is plenty written on learning and teaching. How come a book from a Christian publisher has nothing to say to this question? Are we going to be content to let someone sift through the findings of the secular psychologists for us? Or will someone be brave enough to tackle the subject with concordance in hand? Any volunteers? *Review by Renee Mathis and Charles and Betty Burger*

Seeing Is Believing—The Visual Learner

Are you easily distracted by new sights? Do you remember where you put things? Are you good at catching typos and doing puzzles? Are you very aware of visual details in drawings? Do you remember names better when you see them on a name tag? If you answered "yes" to these questions, you are a *visual* learner.

Visual learners need to *see* what they are supposed to do. You should write out a model, or demonstrate visually the skill to be learned. Some materials that are good for visual learners are:

- Flash cards
- Matching games
- Puzzles
- Instruction books

- Charts
- Pictures, posters, wall strips, desk tapes
- Videos and DVDs
- Simulation software

The visual sense is, if anything, *over*developed in many children of the TV generation. That is why it's so easy to find instruction geared to the visual learner. The visual learner often gets an artificial "head start" in academic success, thanks to the match between his favorite learning style and the school's favored teaching style. Later on, though, visual learners can get into trouble. Being able to follow printed directions is not the same as being able to follow oral directions, for example—and neither necessarily translates into knowing how to assemble the bikes you bought the kids for Christmas!

Even though such great stress is put on visual learning in our culture, visual learners should be encouraged to develop their auditory and hands-on abilities.

Learning by Hearing or Talking: The Auditory Learner

Do you like to talk a lot? Do you talk to yourself? As a child, were you a "babbler?" Do you remember names easily? Can you carry a tune? Do you like to "keep the beat" along with the music? Do you read out loud or subvocalize during reading? Can you follow oral directions more easily than written directions? When taking tests, do you frequently know the answer but have trouble expressing it on paper? Then you are an *auditory* learner.

Some auditory learners learn best by hearing. They need to be *told* what to do. These auditory learners will listen to you reading for hours, but you may not think they are paying attention because they don't look at you. They like to memorize by ear and can easily develop a good sense of rhythm. Naturally, auditory learners have a head start when it comes to learning music. Good materials for this type of auditory learners are:

- Cassette tapes or CDs
- Educational songs and rhymes (like the ABC song)
- Rhythm instruments

Let's talk for a second about how musically minded instruction can help the "I gotta hear it to understand it" kind of auditory learners. Before the movie character Mary Poppins informed her rapt young charges, "A Song Will Help the Job Along," parents and teachers were using music to teach

- The alphabet
- Phonics rules
- Arithmetic facts
- Character lessons ("Dare to Be a Daniel!")
- Bible verses
- Manners
- Handwriting ("Down and Over/Down some more/That's the way we make a Four!")
- Cultural history (Mother Goose)
- General history ("We fired our guns and the British kept a-coming . . .")
- Science ("The hipbone's connected to the . . . legbone")
- Oh, yes, music itself
- And a few thousand other things!

Print & Picture Learners

Willis and Hodson, in their book *Discover Your Child's Learning Style*, reviewed in the next chapter, divide visual learners into "print learners" and "picture learners." According to their book, "While Picture Learners are busy trying to convert language into pictures, Print Learners are converting pictures into words."

As a Print Learner myself, I find relatively few times I need to convert pictures into words, while Picture Learners have to constantly translate the other way. *Discover Your Child's Learning style* contains many useful hints for this type of learner.

You will find musical resources sprinkled throughout the volumes of this series. Some of the best are in the Phonics, Geography, Bible, Foreign Languages, and of course, Music chapters of the other volumes. Try balancing these with a variety of interesting visual and hands-on resources to both encourage your auditory learner's natural talents and help him develop more visual and tactile learning strengths.

Finally, some auditory learners need to hear *themselves* repeat the instructions or information before they really grasp it. The Charlotte Mason method, which emphasizes students narrating what they have learned, is tailor-made for this type of learner. If your child can't seem to follow written instructions, have him try reading them aloud to himself. If that makes a big difference, he's the "talking" type of auditory learner.

Fine Tuning: An Auditory-Visual Training Program

Book 1: Primary/Intermediate,
Book II: Intermediate/Advanced,
$17 each.
Academic Therapy Publications, CA.
(800) 422-7249, www.atp.com.

"Ok, now listen up!"

"Did you hear me?"

Can listening be taught, exercised, and practiced? If material isn't making it from the child's ears to the child's brain, perhaps some simple drills to improve auditory skills might help.

The concept behind **Fine Tuning: An Auditory-Visual Training Program** by Ray Barsch is very simple: The child is given a grid, listens to instructions, enters the necessary information on the grid, and is rewarded with a completed picture or saying.

Two types of grids are given in this book. A Progression Grid consists of evenly spaced rows of numbers. Instructions are "Draw a line from 7 to 32" and so on, resulting in a simple line drawing. A Signs and Sayings Grid is composed of blank squares, with letters labeling horizontal rows and numbers labeling vertical ones. "Place an H in square D-5 . . . place a T in square R-11," etc., until you've completed a well-known saying.

The primary-level grids, 40 in all, are simpler and contain fewer numbers and easier sayings. (Keep off the grass. Apartment for rent.) The 45 intermediate grids feature more numbers/letters and sayings along the lines of "To know how to wait is the secret of success."

You get masters of all grids for you to copy and re-use as needed. For those who'd like the extra drill and practice, this book might be the answer you're looking, er . . . make that listening, for!
Review by Renee Mathis

BOOK ONE
Primary–Intermediate Level

FINE TUNING

An Auditory–Visual Training Program

RAY BARSCH

Learning by Moving and Grabbing: The Kinesthetic/Tactile Learner

Now for the physical types! Here are your so-called "hyperactives." As a child, did you have difficulty sitting still? Were you always grabbing for things? Did you always run your finger across the boards when walking past a fence? Do you move around a lot, and use animated gestures and facial expressions when talking? Can you walk along the curb without losing your balance? Do you prefer hugs from your spouse rather than verbal praise? Do you like to take things apart? Are you always fooling with paper or something on your desk when you're on the phone? If so, then you're a *kinesthetic* learner.

Hands-on learning is a must for kinesthetic learners. They need to mold or sculpt or whittle or bend, fold, and mutilate in order to express themselves. Kinesthetic learners learn to read best by learning to write. They like math manipulatives and sandpaper letters. Kinesthetic learners do *not* like sitting at a desk for hours staring at the blackboard—it's like blindfolding a visual learner to do this to a kinesthetic learner.

For kinesthetic learners, try:

- Long nature walks
- Model kits
- Yard work and gardening
- Textured puzzles
- Typing instead of writing (it's faster and less frustrating)

Be sure to have kinesthetic learners write BIG when they are first learning. Large muscle action zips through to the brain more easily than small, fine movements. Manipulative materials and a good phonics program cure reversals in kinesthetic learners, who are the group most frequently labeled "dyslexic." Couple this with small doses of rich visual and auditory materials to increase your kinesthetic learner's attention span for these different types of learning.

You *can* be all three: visual, auditory, and kinesthetic. God designed people to learn through *all* their senses. But since most of us lean more to one learning style, you can increase your learning abilities by deliberately practicing with your weakest discovery channels . . . and increase your learning enjoyment by adapting more input to fit your dominant discovery channel.

Varieties of K/T Learners

Discover Your Child's Learning Style breaks kinesthetic/tactile learners into:

- Hands-On Learners
- Whole-Body Learners
- Sketching Learners
- Writing Learners

If your child fits the k/t profile, I suggest that you try teaching using all of the above. Your k/t child may learn well through her hands, through whole-body motions (e.g., drawing letters in the air with whole-art movements), *and* through sketching, for example! This is just one more reason why all children should be taught how to draw well at a young age.

CHAPTER 15

Your Child's Thinking Style

Learning Style theory can be taken to extremes. The first mistake is to narrow yourself down to fit into a single discovery channel. Few people only learn visually, auditorally, or kinesthetically.

The second mistake is to think each person falls into a single category. Categories are useful for defining major areas of interest, strength, and weakness, but they are not good for defining your total personality. Most of us fit into many categories at the same time. Take, for example, People Who like Ice Cream for Dessert and People Who Like Chocolate Candy. Or Sports Fans and Philosophers (there's more crossover between these than you think!). Or Energetic, Outgoing types and Sympathetic, Listening types (you can be each of these at different times).

There is also a danger of accepting everything about a person as that person's "style." Taken to extremes, immature or bad behavior could become enshrined as a valid temperament difference. Was it just Hitler's perfectly valid "style" to be fanatical and Himmler's "style" to be cruel? Some people are fanatical *and* cruel. Shall we call this the "National Socialist Temperament Style"? I don't think so!

Yet another problem is the introduction of occult Eastern religious techniques under the umbrella of "helping children with their learning styles." One book, for example, under the heading "Visualizing Success in Learning," says the following:

Picture a teacher that knows everything. This is your very own "inner teacher." Anytime you have a question about something, you can ask this teacher and get the answer. If you're taking a test and the answer doesn't come to you, ask your inner teacher for the right answer. If you're reading a book and see an unfamiliar word, ask your inner teacher to help you with it. If you're having a hard time understanding a new idea in school, have a conversation with your inner teacher about what is unclear, and your inner teacher will help you understand the idea.

Most Pegs Don't Fit the Holes

Classrooms, for the most part, are arranged for children who are well-practiced or naturally gifted in the Producing Skills. . . .

I have found that children with the Producing Disposition comprise between 8% and 16% of a regular classroom—or roughly, three to six students out of thirty-five.

—*Discover Your Child's Learning Style*

The Middle Ages & Temperament Voodoo

Middle Age folks were the first to invent "temperaments." They thought people were either melancholy, sanguine, choleric, or phlegmatic, depending on which bodily "humor" controlled them. Bodily fluids were thought to consist of four "humors." The one that predominated determined your personality.

Sanguine people were supposed to be cheerful because they were what we'd call "red-blooded" types. "Sang" comes from the Latin for "blood." Choleric people were easy to anger because they were bilious—full of choler. Melancholic people were sullen because they were full of black bile. 'What, me worry?' phlegmatic types were full of—you guessed it—phlegm.

Unlike more modern temperament theories, this actually had some small basis in fact. Obviously if you're healthy, you'll tend to be happier than if your liver, gall bladder, or spleen are irritating you. However, these "temperaments" are based on outdated anatomical thought. They totally ignore the spiritual aspect of our emotions and the effect that life experience can have on people. Many a Happy Harry has turned sour under life's blows, while many a Miserable Marvin has found joy and peace through a new relationship with God.

Finally, medieval temperament classifications are useless for our study of how children learn best since there is no way to design a method specifically for Gloomy Gus or Angry Angela—as if you'd want to! We don't want our children to settle for being chronically gloomy, angry, or apathetic. We want them to know how to *overcome* feelings of despair, anger, and unconcern.

If the author of that book really believes this "inner teacher" is just the child talking to himself, he is making unrealistic promises. If the child doesn't know a word, he doesn't know it, and no amount of chatting inside his head will substitute for looking the word up in the dictionary. However, if the author actually expects the "inner teacher" to provide information the child does not know, what we're looking at is boys and girls being encouraged to call upon supernatural beings other than God (our forebears called these "demons") and to submit to them as infallible guides.

Long-dead psychologist Carl Jung, a favorite of many involved in learning type theory nowadays, actually had frequent experiences of this nature, although he never recognized that the "beings" he was chatting with could have been more than simple projections of his subconscious mind.

I find it ominous that Jungian theory is being repackaged for Christians nowadays via the Jung-derived Myers-Briggs Type Inventory. The bottom line of all these Jungian "discover your temperament" books and packages is their insistence that character flaws like self-centeredness and the refusal to bow to any absolutes are perfectly valid temperament styles. Some of these books go even further and insist that even our basic beliefs are simply reflections of our temperaments. This amounts to saying, in an exceedingly doctrinaire fashion cleverly disguised by the rhetoric of tolerance, that Jung was right and Jesus Christ was wrong.

The buyer, in other words, must learn to beware. Just because a theory claims to be cutting-edge doesn't mean it is scientifically valid or religiously neutral.

Temperament, in any case, is not an inflexible king to whom we are doomed to submit. As renowned nineteenth-century educator Charlotte Mason said in volume 1 of her Home Education series (now republished by Tyndale House and available from Charlotte Mason Research & Supply),

> *The problem before the educator is to give the child control over his own nature, to enable him to hold himself in hand as much in regard to the traits we call good, as to those we call evil. Many a man makes shipwreck on the rock of what he grew up to think his characteristic virtue—his open-handedness, for instance.*

For terrific insight into how we parents can help our children not only recognize but also rule their natural temperaments, I highly recommend Charlotte Mason's books.

Does Knowing Your Thinking Style Help?

Having said all that, it is worthwhile to understand one's basic tendencies, whether to cultivate them or fight them. Parents, in particular, can benefit enormously from the knowledge that their "difficult" child is just a different personality who doesn't necessarily respond to the same things in the same ways as the parents. You can then play to the audience—give the kiddies assignments they will really like—while fostering growth in the less-liked areas. One good example would be buying Junior a fischertechnik construction kit (Junior loves working with his hands) and teaching him to type (Junior hates to write, but you want him able to put creative thoughts on paper). A less savvy mother or father would be fighting it out every day with Junior over undone writing assignments, whereas you have successfully navigated to your real goal.

Children do owe their parents obedience and honor, and not every childish rejection of a task calls for negotiation. It's also important to recognize that such things as character flaws, weaknesses, and downright sins do

The "Four Temperaments"?

Professor David Keirsey has re-fashioned the "psychological types" of Carl Jung and Isabel Myers into "sociological types." Net result: two books about discovering your personality type—*Please Understand Me* and *Portraits of Temperament,* both published by Prometheus Nemesis Book Company.

Please Understand Me starts with a personality test. After scoring your answers, you end up as one of four types, each with four variants, for sixteen total possible combinations:

- *The Dionysians*—promoters, artisans, entertainers, artists
- *The Epimetheans*—administrators, trustees, sellers, conservators
- *The Prometheans*—field marshalls, scientists, architects, inventors
- *The Apollonians*—pedagogues, authors, journalists, questers

These are based on four pairs of preferences: extrovert/introvert, sensation/intuition, thinking/feeling, perceiving/judging. The rest of the book first explains Dr. Keirsey's views on how temperament and character determine your behavior in marriage, child-training, learning, and business, illustrated with various literary excerpts featuring different temperament types.

Portraits of Temperament takes a more popular approach to the same subject. Here you get both the Person Classifier and the Temperament Sorter, but instead of personality types being named things like Promethean NJs, the four types presented earlier are now described as:

- *Artisans*—operators and players
- *Guardians*—monitors and conservators
- *Rationals*—organizers and engineers
- *Idealists*—mentors and advocates

Both books strongly stress the belief that even our beliefs are simply the reflection of our basic temperaments, and that we owe it to others to accept them exactly the way they are. This actually is an argument for the Dionysians/Apollonians being right in their basic outlook on life and the Epimethean/Prometheans being wrong. (Is that why the distributing company calls itself Prometheus *Nemesis?*)

Another book, by Dr. Keith Golay, entitled *Learning Patterns and Temperament Styles* presents four basic temperaments: the Dionysian (free spirit), Epimethean (dutiful citizen), Promethean (natural scholar), and Apollonian (crusader for self-actualization). I seriously question the use of these categories, mainly because the Bible says everyone should make the search for wisdom his top priority (the Promethean). The Bible also has some severe things to say about self-love and the consuming desire to be a self-actualized big shot (the Apollonian) and the rejection of absolute laws in the quest for personal autonomy (the Dionysian).

In fact, the four "temperaments" turn out not to be four equally valid personality types, but to be unbalanced to one degree or another. The Dionysian, for example, is like a baby that has never grown up. He lives only in the present and has no patience. The Bible would say this person needs to learn endurance and perseverance, and also needs to start putting others ahead of his own impulses. Golay, however, says that "to assign this type a paper-and-pencil task is deadly," ignoring the fact that millions of this type of boy could and did sit in rows in rural schools working with papers and pencils in the days before learning theory. This is not to say that some people are not validly more physical or action-oriented than others—just that we can and should grow to be more than our "natural" selves.

exist. In real life, I'm so-so and you're so-so and we both have things we need to work on. Still, wise moms and dads take care to understand each child's fundamental gifts and preferences.

So, what is your "thinking style"? It's not your preferred discovery channel(s), which we discussed in the last chapter. Discovery channels are the way you prefer to receive information. Your thinking style is the type of thinker you are: abstract or concrete, action-oriented or thoughtful, people-oriented or turned on by ideas, progress, or experiments. Each thinking style is motivated by a different "learning button." Find your child's top learning buttons and you'll know which educational methods will literally "turn him on."

Temperament or Thinking Style?

Your thinking style is *not* your "temperament."

Personality Is Good

In our eventual callings we may need enough courage to do what goes against the grain of our natural selves. But our education is not supposed to violate the personalities God gave us! Jesus, in the three and a half years He spent with His disciples, did not turn out twelve Peters or twelve Johns. Each of those men came out of his training period more of what he went in. Peter was more courageous, John more spiritual-minded, and Paul the Apostle, who received his teaching directly from the risen Lord, was more of an excellent arguer and scholar when Jesus had trained him.

If we can learn to think of students as people, each with his or her unique contribution to give the world—which may include being the one who does not fit into society, but instead helps change society—then we will realize we have an obligation to treat each one differently. One moral rule fits all—e.g., "Thou shalt not smite thy classmate"—but one academic rule never will fit all. We must try to quench those little twinges of wishing Johnny were more like Suzy, who sits so nicely and quietly. Students are all different . . . but would you really want a classroom of robots?

Vive la différence!

—*Schoolproof*

This is important to stress. First, temperament theory is useless for helping children learn. Second, Jungian temperament theory has as its subtext that faithlessness and being willing to change your beliefs at a moment's notice is as much a valid "temperament" as faithfulness and belief in unchanging absolutes. To take this to its logical conclusion, atheism, New Age, the Nazi Party, hedonism, and Christianity are all just really the outworkings of equally valid temperament styles. Which is baloney.

A more fruitful approach has recently been developed, based on the ways people prefer to attack problems and the types of problems they prefer to attack. In the chart to the right, you'll see how four different authors and organizations identify these learning approaches. You'll also see my attempt to correlate these with characters from the popular "Star Trek" show of the 1960s. I threw that in to add some fun! (By the way, if you find it hard to think of Dr. McCoy, *aka* "Bones," as the sensitive, caring type because of how he verbally abuses Mr. Spock, just substitute Deanna Troi from the "Star Trek: Next Generation" show.)

Here's how it breaks down:

- **Spock is the Puzzle Solver.** He loves analyzing and coming up with theories. (I'm going here with Willis and Hodson, who combine these characteristics into one person. This makes more sense to me then separating them into "analytical" and "imaginative.") Names and terminology don't mean as much to this person as *how* and *why* things work. He loves to ponder.
- **Kirk is the Action Man.** He loves to face challenges head-on and wants to do something "right now." He thinks "outside the box" and loves to discover new things—to "boldly go where no man has gone before."
- **Bones is the People Person.** On the show, his character is if anything too emotional, to form a foil to the impassive Mr. Spock. Concern for others is his hallmark, as is an ability to easily remember names and details about people and their actions. Again, if you have trouble with his abrasiveness (which only comes to the fore when he thinks Spock or Kirk are unconcerned about the needs of others), think of Deanna Troi instead.
- **Scotty is the Progress Person.** He is organized and can handle any job on time and under budget. However, he prefers *not* to have huge hairy challenges thrown at him. His idea of joy is cruising along sweetly with the ship running at greater than 100 percent efficiency.
- **Sulu is the Performer.** Several episodes brought out Sulu's underlying "swashbuckling" style, as have the books in which he is the main character. A razzle-dazzle pilot by training, and a swordfighting enthusiast, Sulu likes to impress others with his skills and flair.

You may legitimately question whether "Performing" is a thinking style, an out-of-balance personality, or anything to do with thinking styles at all. An extreme desire to draw attention to oneself would be labeled "sinful pride" by the Mennonite materials I have reviewed, for example. And three out of four learning-styles sources I referenced do not even list Performing as an option. The fact remains that some children just naturally love to entertain others, and you can choose to work either with this or against it.

Learning Approaches by Author/Organization

"Star Trek" Character	Alta Vista College *Learning Styles* packet by Cheryl Senecal	Marlene LeFever *Learning Styles*	Diana Waring *Beyond Survival*	Willis & Hodson *Discover Your Child's Learning Style*	What I Decided to Call That Thinking Style
Spock	Analytical	Analytical	Thinker	Thinking/Creating	Puzzle Solver
Kirk	Intuitive	Dynamic	Intuitor	Inventor	Action Man
Bones	Imaginative	Imaginative	Feeler	Relating/Inspiring	People Person
Scotty	Practical	Common Sense	Sensor	Producer	Progress Person
Sulu	n/a	n/a	n/a	Performer	Performer

	Success Is	What They Say	What They Like
Spock	Figuring it out	"I see it now"	Finding the answer; puzzles; theories; new ideas; logic
Kirk	Completing a challenge	"This just might work!"	Action; experiments
Bones	Happy & healthy crew	"I know how you feel"	Harmony; working with others
Scotty	Perfectly functioning ship	"I built that"	Results & efficiency
Sulu	Doing it with style	"Look at me!"	Applause & attention; spontaneity

	Favored Homeschool Methods
Spock	Classical Education/Great Books, Laptop Homeschooling, Principle Approach (if allowed to figure out new applications of principles), Robinson Method
Kirk	Contests, Unit Studies, Unschooling
Bones	Charlotte Mason Method, Montessori Method
Scotty	Basics, Contests, Maloney Method, Unit Studies (projects & experiments), Unschooling
Sulu	Classical Education, Contests, Unschooling (with heavy emphasis on real-world activities that employ his talents)

Of greatest importance to us is the fact that

Today's schools do not push most children's learning buttons.

Just the opposite occurs. Spock types are not encouraged to be absorbed in thought—they're supposed to pay attention to the teacher every minute. As a Spock type myself, I could relate to this line in *Discover Your Child's Learning Style*: "She might doodle or look out the window with a glazed stare while the teacher is talking." I have several old report cards that accuse me of exactly that! "Action Man" types may do great on the football team but get easily frustrated by a schedule controlled by the ringing of bells. And don't even ask about what happens to Performers. These kids end up *living* in the principal's office. The charge? "Disrupting class" with their impromptu performances.

Today's schools were initially designed for the Progress Person. Grinding away at small, systematic steps towards a final goal is what this personality is good at. However, even the Progress Person might be double-crossed by educational fads that outrage his built-in sense of logic and order. Meanwhile, the People Person is happy as a clam as long as she has a few good friends. This does not mean she is *learning* anything, though.

Did you ever see or hear of a teacher doing this?

- Force a Puzzle Solver into a "cooperative learning" situation with a bunch of kids who refuse to do the work

- Make the Action Man do workbook pages for hours
- Tell the Performer to sit down and shut up
- Give the Progress Person an assignment where "it doesn't matter if the answer is right as long as you are thinking creatively"
- Punish the People Person for socializing during class time

I don't usually like to blame "the system" for what individuals do, but in this case, I really don't blame the teachers. If you had 30 strange kids staring at you, and you had to not only keep them from killing each other but try to teach them something, you'd do exactly the same thing (except, I hope, telling your students that right answers don't matter!).

Designing a classroom to accommodate all these thinking styles is just about impossible, and separating them into groups of like personalities would make school very strange. Imagine a classroom full of nothing but class clowns, and another full of people whose deepest desire is to socialize. Spock types would hide out in the library and never meet another soul, while Action Guys and Gals would be fighting over the lab equipment. Not a pretty sight.

The only solution that works, especially for those whose children don't fit the "I love to do worksheets" mold, is homeschooling.

Now, here are some tips.

For the Puzzle Solver

Give him lots of time alone. This personality will willingly learn, and even assign himself problems to solve, but does so best without distractions. Load up on strategy games (chess, checkers, Risk, Scrabble) and computer games of the "figure it out" variety. Go the the library frequently and bring a large plastic tote for all the books you'll be lugging home. Show him how much you expect him to complete during the school year, and don't be surprised if he gets all the math done in a month. Expect to spend extra time on drilling terminology, dates, and other "irrelevant facts" that the Puzzle Solver figures can just be looked up anytime in a reference book. *Some* names and dates are important!

Extra help with social skills may also be needed, particularly if the child has poor vision, which makes it harder to see people's facial expressions.

I have a theory that the "nerd" personality, which seems to go along with thick glasses, has something to do with the fact that children who start out with fuzzy vision don't learn to "read" people's facial expressions, and thus grow up relating to people mainly by the words others say, and at best the tone with which they say them. Some instruction in reading facial expressions and body language might help, since college is a little late to be figuring all this out.

Some regular physical activity is a must, since the Puzzle Solver will happily sit all day with a book or a computer unless you get him in the habit of exercise. Preferably the exercise should have a definite goal, such as improving lap time or getting her next Karate belt.

For the Action Man

. . . who of course may also be an Action Grrrl! He or she likes ideas just as much as the Puzzle Solver. The difference is that the Action Man likes to solve *concrete* puzzles, while the Puzzle Solver lives for *abstract* puzzles.

Supply with: things to take apart and put together. Science lab kits. Construction kits. Lots of projects. Lots of physical activity. Remember, the word "hands-on" was invented for this kid!

For the People Person

Friends are all-important to the People Person, so make sure you sign him up for some clubs and activities where he can meet other kids. Since you, the parent, are a person too, encourage this child's natural desire to please you. Pick materials that focus on loving and serving God (another Very Important Person) and that teach about people around the world and people in history. Fiction of all kinds is good, especially historical fiction and biographies of people you'd like your child to emulate. See if you can team up this child with another of your children who is slightly older or younger, so they can study the same material together.

For the Progress Person

This kid needs to know where he is going. Show him the plan. Buy the workbooks. Hand out the assignments. Avoid nebulous, squishy, and time-wasting work, as this student will see right through it all and resent being stuck doing it. (Be sure to read Chapter 18 if you're not certain of your own abilities to spot this stuff!)

Don't let anyone put you down for being a "Workbook Mom" if this is in fact the way your child learns best.

For the Performer

You're going to have to cultivate some patience here. Your entire school training will have you reaching for the duct tape to strap this kid into his seat and cover up his motor mouth.

Fight those instincts. Try actually listening to what he is saying and watching what she wants to show you. Once you have filled up his or her "applause" bucket, you are more likely to get an audience for what *you* are trying to say or show.

If you can show this student how to do an assignment with flair and pizzazz, you have him. Don't just ask for a book report: Have him pretend he is a radio announcer and "read" his book review "on the air." Don't just read a Bible chapter: Act it out. A few props add verisimilitude. An old bathrobe can become an Israelite garment, topped off with a birdseye diaper wrapped around the head or hanging down for a veil. You can either use your imagination here or just buy the KONOS curriculum (not KONOS-In-A-Box, but one or more of the original three volumes). These are just chock-full of great ideas tailored for the Performer personality.

Gregg Harris's *The Christian Home School* offers up some more neat ideas for a less-showy Performer personality. If you think your child would like to learn to do flip-chart presentations, for example, Gregg is your man. And you know he knows how to do it, because his oldest son Joshua is one of the most entertaining and inspiring speakers I have ever heard.

Remember These Hot Buttons

- The Puzzler's hot button is *ideas*.
- The Action Man's hot button is *trying it out right now*—preferably something that involves making, fixing or experimenting.
- The People Person wants to *meet, help, and inspire others.*
- The Progress Person *has to see progress* to stay motivated.
- The Performer yearns to be *noticed*. Try to give him attention (and lots of it!) for work done well—and let him pursue his own fierce interests as much as possible.

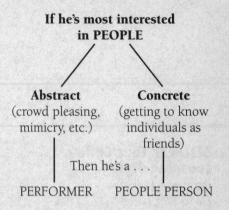

Here's a visual way to uncover your child's thinking style

If he's most interested in PEOPLE

Abstract (crowd pleasing, mimicry, etc.)   Concrete (getting to know individuals as friends)

Then he's a . . .

PERFORMER   PEOPLE PERSON

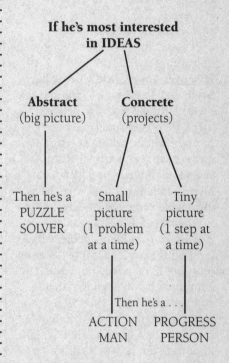

If he's most interested in IDEAS

Abstract (big picture)   Concrete (projects)

Then he's a PUZZLE SOLVER   Small picture (1 problem at a time)   Tiny picture (1 step at a time)

Then he's a . . .

ACTION MAN   PROGRESS PERSON

33

It's common to be strongest in one thinking style and still score high in one or two more. This just gives you more buttons to push!

We understand, of course, that children are not machines. I came up with the "buttons" metaphor to make this discussion less confusing and more memorable, not to encourage untoward parental manipulation. You love your children and want to help them. Getting to know them better—their real needs and interests—is an important step towards homeschool success. I strongly urge you to get a copy of *Discover Your Child's Learning Style* and take that step.

Discover Your Child's Learning Style

Parents. $16.95.
Home Life, Inc., PO Box 1190, Fenton, MO 63026-1190
800-446-6322
www.home-school.com/catalog

If you're the slightest bit interested in learning styles, you need **Discover Your Child's Learning Style** by Mariaemma Willis and Victoria Kindle Hodson. Between them, these credentialed teachers (both of whom hold master's degrees) have been working over 50 years to develop their educational model, including many years helping a wide variety of students.

Their book is well-organized, easy to read, and personable, which right off the bat makes it better than most books on education written by educators. It's directed to parents, and though it stops short of recommending homeschooling, it does recognize that "parents are the most important teachers in a child's life."

Part I of *Discover Your Child's Learning Style* includes:
- An introduction to their philosophy that children are naturally eager learners and can succeed at learning
- Their "C.A.R.E.S." model of how parents should "coach" their children to academic success.

The C.A.R.E.S. model has these five suggestions:
- Celebrate your child's uniqueness rather than criticizing
- Accept your role as teacher rather than avoid it

- Respond to your child's feelings by following his lead as much as possible rather than reacting with blame or threats
- Expand your idea of where education can happen rather than excluding the home
- Stop supporting labels based on a "bell curve" where some children *must* fail to make the curve look right

Includes "learning style" assessments for all ages

"Parents who understand the principles in this book will be better parents!"
—RICHARD AND LINDA EYRE, authors of *Teaching Your Children Values*

Discover Your Child's Learning Style

Children Learn in Unique Ways— Here's the Key to Every Child's Learning Success

Mariaemma Willis, M.S., and Victoria Kindle Hodson, M.A.

You need this book

Part II, the heart of the book, introduces these five ways to unlock your child's learning personality:
- Dispositions: Performing, Producing, Inventing, Relating/Inspiring, and Thinking/Creating
- Talents
- Interests
- Modalities, which they subdivide as follows: Auditory (listening learners, verbal learners),

Visual (picture learners, print learners), and kinesthetic/tactile (hands-on learners, whole-body learners, sketching learners, writing learners)
- Environment: whether your child learns best when it's warm or cool, bright or subdued, noisy or not, etc.

There's a Learning Profile self-test for each of these right there in the book.

Part III explains how to apply your new knowledge, including how to talk to your child's classroom teacher about accommodating his learning style. This part also includes a stunning chapter entitled "What About Learning Disabilities?" which totally debunks the testing-and-labeling model and the National Educational Goal, which defines coming to school "ready to learn" in terms that make it clear *only* children with the Producing Disposition will be recognized as "ready to learn"! They contrast this with their own Learning Style Model of education, show how the latter accommodates *all* children and pretty much does away with the ADD and "dyslexic" labels, and address special topics such as light sensitivity and food allergies. If your child has ever been labeled, this chapter alone is reason enough to buy this book.

I can't imagine how a single book could present this entire field of study more helpfully—and I can't imagine a book with greater potential to immediately improve your home-school results than this one. Very highly recommended.

PART 4

Education 101

Melissa Mason of Austin, TX, a homeschooler from fourth grade through twelfth grade, graduated with high honors from the University of Texas . . . at the age of 19! She was elected to the honor society Phi Beta Kappa in her senior year of college, at an age when most kids are still seniors in high school.

CHAPTER 16

Getting Them Ready to Learn

What is the secret to homeschool success? What have we got that the schools haven't got?

Your first advantage is simply who you are: a parent and a child, with your special bond and years of relationship. Your second advantage is the vast amount of help available for homeschoolers and the way we cooperate to help each other succeed. Your third advantage is homeschoolers' freedom from bureaucratic hindrances and the relatively modest effort required to teach a handful of your own children rather than a classroom full of strangers. Your fourth advantage is that you now understand how to tailor teaching materials and methods to your individual child's discovery channels and thinking style—a task the schools have not yet begun to face, and in fact may never be able to manage, given their institutional nature.

But you're not home free. You still have to actually *teach* this child! This means you need to understand

- How to motivate him
- How to design an effective learning environment
- How to detect and ditch time-wasting twaddle
- The many ways children can absorb information from the world
- The many ways you can help your children process what they are learning
- The many ways you can determine what they have and have not learned

That's what this section is about. It's your educational tool kit, your "Education 101" course in homeschooling. Pay attention: You *will* see this material again!

> Kids are born with a natural desire to please their parents. The more your children trust and respect you, the easier your job will be.

The basic function of a liberal education is to expose people to fields they normally wouldn't investigate. Whether you believe the purpose of education is to shape one's character in a democracy or to prepare Johnny for his job, neither is accomplished when kids get to study only what they want.

—TIME, *August 27, 2001*

Classical Conditioning vs. Operant Conditioning

In **classical conditioning**, the behavior is elicited by some specific stimulus [e.g., dog food] and we learn to transfer the response to some previously neutral stimulus [e.g., the sound of a bell]. In **operant conditioning**, the behavior is emitted by the subject voluntarily, rather than triggered by outside events. A student raising his hand in class to get the teacher's attention is an example of operant conditioning. The behavior is designed to operate on the environment in a way that will bring some kind of satisfaction to the individual. . . .

In operant conditioning, correct responses to approximations to correct responses are rewarded. Incorrect responses are ignored or even punished. . . .

—*Michael Maloney,* Teach Your Children Well (*Cambridge Center for Behavioral Studies, 1998*)
Emphasis mine

Motivation Comes First

The 1992 Republican Party National Platform stated (among many other things):

We are confident that the United States can, by the end of this decade, reach the six national education goals that President Bush and the Nation's Governors have established: **that all children should arrive at school ready to learn;** *that high school graduation rates should be at least 90 percent; that all children should learn challenging subject matter and become responsible citizens; that American children should be first in the world in math and science; that there must be a literate and skilled workforce; and that schools must be disciplined and free of drugs and violence. [Emphasis mine]*

Whatever you may think of these goals (including the obvious fact that they have not been met), that first goal makes a lot of sense. Not as part of a government plan, because government has no business extending its tentacles into our babies' playpens in order to make them "ready to learn," whatever that may mean to a government bureaucrat. But as a list of objectives for parents, it's not bad.

The first goal is the key to all the rest. Once your child is "ready to learn," that is, motivated and willing to make some effort, all you really need to do is provide good learning materials and answer his or her questions. Once your child learns to read, he can become a partner in his own education . . . if he wants to. Even in the face of active opposition (which of course you have no intention of providing), a truly motivated child will find the materials himself and research the answers to his own questions. With your help and support, such a child can go far indeed.

So, what form should your support take? How do you "motivate" a child if motivation comes from within? *Does* motivation come from within? Can an unmotivated child be consciously inspired by his parents, or do you just have to wait for a bolt from the blue?

To answer these questions, let's summarize the two motivational theories prevalent in our schools and then check out three more motivational techniques inspired by an author well-known to veteran homeschoolers.

Punished by Rewards?

Behaviorism is a model of human nature based largely on laboratory observations of animals in controlled conditions. Its basic assumption is that man is an animal, a programmable mix of chemicals, and that a science of behavior can discern exactly how to program this organic machine.

Educational behaviorists strive to create a controlled classroom environment with carefully selected "inputs," to associate desired "outputs" with a signal and/or (initially) a reward, and to discourage or punish undesired outputs.

Don't make the mistake of thinking that this motivational method is only about rewards and punishments, carrots and sticks. **Classical conditioning is about *training kids to respond "appropriately" to a "trigger" signal*,** so that even when the reward is no longer offered, the behavior remains.

This is the method that the Russian scientist Ivan Pavlov used to train dogs to salivate when they heard the sound of a bell. The bell was rung when the dogs were about to be fed. Eventually, the dogs so associated the sound of the bell with food that they would salivate whenever the bell was rung, even when food ceased to be provided at that time. It is also the method used to train elephants in India to stay in place at night. When the elephant is a young calf, he is chained to a stake. He learns that he cannot break free from the chain. Years later, when the elephant is perfectly capable of yanking up the stake, he will still stay in place when he is chained for the night. Putting on the chain has become the "signal" to stay in place, and it is so firmly associated with the concept that the grown elephant won't even test it.

If that's too exotic, think of a less drastic example from our own Old West. If you've ever seen a cowboy movie, notice how a cowboy loops the reins over the horse's head and leaves the horse standing there, expecting it to be there when he gets back. The horse has been trained to "stay" when the reins are looped over, even though nothing is holding it there.

In my opinion, **classical behaviorists have captured the ancient idea of "habit" and given it a new twist.** Their "conditioned responses" are simply the *habit* of behaving in a certain way in response to a given circumstance.

This powerful motivational tool can be used for good or evil. An example of evil classical conditioning is in George Orwell's famous dystopian novel *1984*. In Orwell's book, a future society is totally enslaved by a totalitarian government that even watches individual citizens in their homes through their TV sets. That's why Orwell invented the phrase, "Big Brother is watching you!" The citizens put up with this because they have been trained to. For example, at the sound of "a hideous, grinding screech" from the "telescreen" and the sight of "Emmanuel Goldstein, the Enemy of the People" flashing on the screen, every citizen in the room automatically goes into "the Two Minutes Hate," an uncontrollable emotional state of rage designed to dissipate their feelings of discontent at the "bare, unsatisfying" lives they are forced to lead.

In the world of *1984,* operant conditioning also is used for evil as children are taught to "crimestop." This complicated mental contortion is "the faculty of stopping short, as though by instinct, at the threshold of any dangerous thought," a mental process "as complete as that of a contortionist over his body." Crimestopping is "taught even to young children," since it is "the first and simplest stage in the discipline" of total obedience to the Party.

In other words, in Orwell's dystopia, which was meant to warn people about the dangers of communist society, people are trained using both types of conditioning to behave *against* their nature and even their common sense. The book's hero, Winston Smith, eventually sees through the facade and tries to break free of the system, but is himself broken in the end by severe physical and psychological torture geared to his own personal weaknesses.

What we're talking about is **brainwashing**, an extreme form of conditioning. Brainwashing is only effective when (1) the victim is so young and inexperienced he is unaware of any other intellectual position than the one the brainwasher trains him in, or (2) the victim first has his spirit broken, typically by sleep deprivation, sensory deprivation, starvation, and disorientation. There is also a third category: (3) those who find it useful to believe what the brainwasher is telling them. E.g., prison guards in Stalin's Russia or Hitler's Germany undoubtedly found it helpful to believe their prisoners were animals deserving of their dire fate.

So behavioral conditioning is all bad, right? Not necessarily. For a positive example of conditioning, consider the case of a child who immediately after supper goes out into the kitchen to wash the dishes. Everyone rising from the table has become the signal to clear the dishes and get to work. Another example: When you sit at your desk (or your sewing table

BEHAVIORIST MOTIVATION WORKS . . . SORT OF

In certain circumstances, behaviorism works. In others, it doesn't, which is why we still have prisons. If it were possible to train humans to behave exactly as desired, then a controlled prison environment should form the ideal laboratory for demonstrating this.

Behaviorists' theories as to *why* their method works (when it does) are wrong, I believe. People have often been wrong in the past about why things work the way they do. We no longer believe Thor is flinging his mighty hammer at the sky when we hear thunder; we don't think rotting meat spontaneously generates maggots; and we don't think the cows in England died of mad cow disease because some witch hexed them. In each of these cases, people of the past observed the *effect* (thunder, maggots, and dead cows) and came up with a totally inaccurate *cause* because they were operating under false assumptions.

As a theory of human nature and *why* we learn, behaviorism is repellent. As Ruth Beechick, author of *A Biblical Psychology of Learning* (Mott Media, 2002; previous edition, Accent Publishing, 1992), whose own motivational theories we'll be looking at later on in this chapter, eloquently puts it, for behaviorists, "Learning is measured by outer responses only. There is no person inside to be concerned with." But humans *do* have a spirit as well as a body, and that spirit will inevitably wish to rebel if it sees you are playing a trick on it. Even the desired outer responses vanish once the inner person catches on to what's going on if he doesn't agree with the teacher's goals for him.

Reinforcement & Punishment

Once the behavior has been produced, reinforcement increases the probability that it will be produced again. . . . Reinforcement strengthens behavior even when the learner doesn't know that he is being reinforced. . . .

There are two kinds of reinforcers—positive and negative. Following a response with an outcome which is desirable to the learner is an example of positive reinforcement. Praise, being done, getting a good mark, feeling satisfied with your performance are positively reinforcement. Negative reinforcement ends a difficult or unpleasant situation. Finishing a hard term paper that has kept you up all night, shutting off an alarm clock that has just wakened you from a sound sleep are examples of negative reinforcement. Negative reinforcement is very different than punishment.

Punishment consists of something unpleasant happening in order to change or terminate an unacceptable behavior. Punishment can be either the introduction of some aversive condition or the withdrawal of some reinforcer. . . .

Generally, punishers are to be avoided for a number of reasons. . . . To maintain their effectiveness, punishers generally have to be increased over time to get the same effect. . . Punishment also has dangerous side effects in that it often breeds fear and suspicion and undermines trust. People tend to avoid individuals and situations which they find punishing.

—*Michael Maloney*
Teach Your Children Well

or your workshop bench), do you find yourself going into "work mode"? No bell has been rung, but you associate the sight, sound, and even smell of that environment with the need to get to work.

We are talking about the power of *habit*, and it is powerful indeed. Research has shown that once you have done the same thing at the same time 11 days in a row, it becomes a habit. So if you can make it past the first few weeks of an exercise program, for example, you become used to exercise at that time and actually feel upset if you *don't* get to exercise.

As a motivational system, associating pleasant things with a desired output and a visual, auditory, or sensory "trigger" with getting into "learning mode" works well for:

- Extremely young children
- Mentally challenged children (insofar as they are still childlike in their outlook; some such children can be quite the little skeptics)
- People who wish to motivate themselves

This last bullet point is the key to the difference between brainwashing and motivation. **As soon as possible, you should reveal the "trick" to your children.** Explain to them the power of habit and how associating a "trigger" with a mode can help them get into the frame of mind to tackle difficult challenges. You and they can then *cooperate* in developing habits, inventing rewards for tasks completed and helping them find personal "triggers" that help them concentrate.

The Quest for Power and Success

Classical behaviorism falls down the most in its stunted ideas of what constitutes a reward. For mature human beings, tangible rewards are the least valued. Learning can be rewarding for its own sake, and a child may not be as motivated by the sticker you just gave him as by the sense of accomplishment he received for finishing the task successfully. Honor, glory, fame, and fortune all require "future" thinking—something a science designed with the help of rats and pigeons is ill-equipped to model.

For a motivational philosophy that emphasizes these types of rewards, we must now turn to the "E" movement: **elitism.**

We're looking at prep-school humanism, as exemplified in films such as *Dead Poets Society, Finding Forrester,* and even *Chariots of Fire.* This is its most attractive face: holding the world of success, fame, and glory before kids and saying "*Carpe diem,* lads! Go for it! Make something of yourselves!"

Success! Achievement! The ability to look down on others who have not studied Latin! **Beware of this.** These motivations *seem* more worthy than the simple desire to earn a gold star but are actually more subversive, which of the films mentioned, only *Chariots of Fire* recognizes. When Satan took Christ to the top of the mountain to tempt Him, He didn't offer him gold stars. He offered him the world.

For elite youngsters, the ultimate reward is to be accepted by the elite as a fellow human in a world full of lesser-evolved animals. According to their Nietzschean thinking, everyone else is one of the herd, but you are an *übermensch,* literally a "superman." The masses are stupid; you and your friends are smart. You were either born to lead, as a trust-fund baby, or showed such obvious superiority that you were let in via scholarship. Acceptance by the elite as "one of them" is the ultimate prize. Social punishment for not accepting the group's goals and values, or for falling short of their expectations, can be severe, as seen in the Brendan

Fraser movie *School Ties,* in which one of the schoolboy characters attempts suicide when he fails to get accepted at Yale University.

The desire for success alone is not the problem. The question is, "What kind of success—and what happens if you fail?" Elite students may hope for grand social goals, but the quest for success can fail even at a much humbler level. That's why so many Japanese youths fling themselves off high buildings when their career and university hopes go awry—their entire social upbringing has stressed university entrance as the sole purpose of their life's existence. The expelled student in Erfurt, Germany, who picked up a gun and slaughtered his teachers seemed to be operating from the same impulse.

There's real danger, in other words, in telling kids "You can be anything you want to be," and "Pursue your dream, no matter what." Not only is this a basically selfish message, it's not always realistic. I'd love to fly like Superman, but I can't be Superman, and if I decide to obsessively pursue the dream of becoming Superman, I'll end up in a nuthouse or going postal on those who I blame for thwarting my unrealistic dreams.

So, what sort of long-term, future-oriented motivations *can* we use?

First, the motivation should be *internally validated,* not at the mercy of some group's judgment. We want our kids to have the character to do the right thing, even if everyone is against them. For Christians, this is a matter of knowing God's will and following it. Pleasing God in the present requires doing one's schoolwork, which will enable one to serve God in the future.

Second, the motivation should be *for the benefit of others.* Again, for Christians, right after love of God comes love of neighbor. These are supposed to be the two great motivations for our lives. Personal pride, fame, glory, success, and wealth are irrelevant; what matters is being of use to God first and the world second. This distinguishes our goals from those of elitists, who basically see their role as first pleasing their elite group and second controlling the unwashed masses, who are NOKD—"Not Our Kind, Dear."

Ruth Beechick and Three More Motivations

We've looked at short-term rewards and punishments, and also at long-term rewards and punishments. But something still is missing. Why do some people *love* to learn, even if they are punished for doing so? Why did young J.S. Bach sneak into his brother's room to copy his music sheets, even when his brother smacked him for doing it? Why did so many black Southern slaves secretly teach their kids to read after laws were passed severely punishing this? Why is there a known class of schoolkids called "geeks" and "nerds" who insist on doing well in their courses even though their classmates mock, harass, and even beat them up? Why do some kids wreck their eyesight reading under the bedcovers after they've been told again and again to turn out the light and go to sleep?

Elitism and behaviorism can't explain this longing for learning. These kids are being *punished* for learning, and it's doubtful most of them have lofty future ambitions in mind while they're doing it, so why do they persist?

When the elitists and behaviorists fail you, it's time to turn to Ruth Beechick. In her most excellent book *A Biblical Psychology of Learning,* Dr. Beechick lists these three additional motivations:

- understanding, not just knowing
- the thrill of creation
- time and freedom for total absorption

REWARDS THAT WORK

In the last few chapters, you learned how to find your student's "hot buttons." These are areas in which your student should already be motivated, and rewards that will motivate him. To put this in the framework of rewards:

- The Puzzle Solver is motivated by the promise of free time
- The Action Man is motivated by the promise of resources for his projects and/or free time to pursue her own active projects
- The People Person is motivated by the approval of the teacher and the promise of time to spend with friends or on social outings
- The Progress Person is motivated first by seeing her own progress and secondarily by a "pat on the back" acknowledging her advancement—maybe even a gold star!
- The Performer is motivated by applause

In other words, just because *you* would think something is a great reward, don't assume your child feels the same way. Rewards and punishments can misfire when you assume your student is like you. For yet another *Star Trek* example, in the famous episode "The Trouble With Tribbles," Captain Kirk (who as an Action Man never could stand being cooped up anywhere) tried to punish Scotty the engineer by making him stay in his quarters during shore leave. Scotty thanked him: "Now I can catch up on my technical journals!"

Understanding, Not Just Knowing. Some kids are born with a rage for this, but all kids are born with *some* yearning to understand. It's the motivating factor that causes babies to learn to speak—so they can understand and be understood.

To increase your children's motivation, help them see how the world works. In Charlotte Mason lingo, you present them with "living ideas."

Don't just hand them a math book; rent a video about the space program and let the see the results of applied math in a successful rocket launch. My own teachers impressed on me that a math error could send a rocket crashing to Earth that was meant to go to the Moon—and I've never forgotten it!

The same applies to science, economics, history, literature, and every other subject that requires some wisdom to understand. Let your children know there are issues . . . and various sides to the issues. Let them read articles and books and view videos by leaders in the field, past and present. Old-style liberal educators called this becoming part of the "**Great Conversation**" and treated it as an end in itself. The point of the exercise, however, is not just to know what everyone is saying but to decide which (if any) side is right. With such understanding comes passion . . . and a whole lot of learning.

The Thrill of Creation. Pigeons and rats do not create, so we can see why behaviorists tend to miss out on this motivating technique. It's also probably no coincidence that the artistic legacy arising out of modern humanism is called *de*-construction. That being said, kids are born loving to make things. Sandcastles. Block towers. Crayon pictures. Gingerbread men.

The most unmotivated child will often respond to the chance to build or make a hands-on project. The best project is one you are doing, as an adult, that they can help you with. The worst project is a contrived school exercise that will be dumpstered upon completion. Generally, projects that you can really use for something (or really wear or really eat) are more motivating than projects-for-the-sake-of-projects. Some kids really like projects they can show off. Can you guess these kids' thinking style?

Time and Freedom for Total Absorption. Other thinkers, such as Maria Montessori, who we will meet later, have noticed that children naturally get absorbed in tasks when they are provided the freedom to do so and an environment free of worthless distractions.

We'll be talking more about the uses of environment as a learning tool in the next two chapters.

CHAPTER 17

Preparation of the Environment

Have you ever thought of your home as a learning tool? How about your yard? Your car? Your neighborhood? The whole world? The virtual world?

This chapter is about four ways you can structure your child's learning environments. Entire theories of education have been built around each of these four ways. As usual, the proponents of each theory tout it as the one best way. The truth is that certain skills are best taught in one environment, while other skills are best taught in another. Knowing your options will make you a much stronger home educator—and open your children's horizons!

Basically, at home you can teach your child in a

- Microworld—a very limited environment in which children have free use of a small set of tools
- Miniworld—a scaled-down version of a real space, minus the distractions that would lead a child away from the desired studies
- Regular world—we live in this one
- Virtual world—way too many of our kids want to live in this one!

Microworlds, the Land of Constructivism

Constructivism is one of those slippery educational terms. Its advocates tend to swing back and forth between constructivism as

- Building things
- Building things in an environment devoid of everything except tools and materials for the desired constructions
- Reinventing the wheel (since to really know anything you have to invent it yourself)

The last definition is obviously ridiculous as a complete educational method. Life is too short for kids to discover calculus or the Theory of

What Is Constructivism?

Under the name **constructivism**, this theoretical movement argues that learning happens best when it is self-directed. It complains that much traditional teaching is based on a model of a pipeline through which knowledge passes from teacher to student. The name constructivism derives from an alternative model, according to which the learner has to "construct" knowledge afresh every time. Piaget, the most influential advocate of constructivist education, popularized the slogan: "To understand is to invent." The role of the teacher is to create the conditions for invention rather than to provide ready-made knowledge.

—*Seymour Papert*, The Connected Family (*Longstreet Press, 1996*)

"Nyah, Nyah, Teaching Is Boring" Quoth the Progressives

In his latest book, *The Schools We Need, and Why We Don't Have Them,* E.D. Hirsch very adroitly puts his finger on the major reason for North American school failure. He attributes it to the current philosophy of learning that has permeated classrooms across North America for the past 50 years. It is generally known as the "**Progressive Model of Education**" and is part of the American Romanticist philosophy espoused by writers and philosophers like Thoreau and Emerson. When misapplied to education, it has led to the disastrous international test results and the growing illiteracy and incompetence today's schools are producing. According to this philosophy, anything that is "unnatural," such as confining children to desks in rows, is inherently bad; anything demanding stressful effort or tedious practice is to be avoided, as it is not immediately rewarding for the child and decimates his natural curiosity.

The application of this naturalistic, discovery-oriented approach became dominant in the early decades of the 20th century. It gained prominence because it effectively polarized the thinking of Americans about educational practices by the language used to describe the major philosophies of the day. Opponents were labeled "conservative" as opposed to "progressive." Their methods were characterized as traditional, teacher-directed, lockstep, boring, repetitive, and failing to teach the "whole" child. Progressive educators, on the other hand, were seen as modern, hands-on, integrated, interesting, individualized, and developing the entire child.

—*Michael Maloney*
Teach Your Children Well

Special Relativity on their own. As if they could! No amount of willingness to "invent" new theories allowed anyone before Newton and Leibnitz to come up with calculus, and the odds of every kid turning into another Einstein approach zero. So strict constructivism, if I may invent such a term, flat doesn't work for advanced math or science.

Constructivism is sometimes referred to as "**discovery learning**," but technically it is the process of inventing knowledge for yourself, based on resources handily provided by your teacher, or should I say "facilitator"?

Constructivism works best in a "microworld," a term invented by Dr. Seymour Papert of M.I.T. The idea is that you provide a small set of integrated tools. With these the student can build freely. "At-risk" kids who have been given access to such a microworld often show great jumps in their overall school abilities.

Here are some examples of microworlds:

- The computer language LOGO, also invented by Seymour Papert, which allows kids to build Etch-a-Sketch type designs by programming an onscreen cursor called a "turtle"
- "Discovery" type software that allows children to create with the program tools—e.g., *Widget Workshop* or *SimCity*
- LEGO bricks, especially when interfaced with a computer through a robotics module
- Gears—playing with gears is how Dr. Papert intuited many math relationships as a young boy
- Math manipulatives that enable you to model arithmetic concepts
- Chess and other strategy games

After giving this a lot of thought, I believe that the excitement over microworlds and constructivism is overblown. The kids are responding to the chance to utilize logic and creativity. If you're an inner-city kid, your chaotic neighborhood environment encourages you to react to the very dangerous threats that pop up around you rather than to reason and to plan. Your neighborhood environment also actively discourages creativity, since anything nice that shows up in public will get trashed or stolen. Given the opportunity in a safe environment to use your built-in reasoning capabilities and creativity is a very powerful stimulant to such a child. However, kids whose home environments already encourage creativity and logical thinking have proportionately less need to spend time in a microworld.

Miniworlds, the Land of Montessori

Among the many other accomplishment of Italian physician and educator Maria Montessori (yes, the lady all those preschools are named after) was the concept of "preparation of the environment." In simplest terms, this means putting the resources you want the child to study into his environment and removing any distractions from that environment.

The typical Montessori classroom thus resembles a somewhat altered home environment. Neatly organized groups of materials for stacking, sorting, counting, etc. abound, while random elements such as coffee tables, a skateboard someone left near the front door, and yesterday's mail are not to be found.

The philosophy behind miniworlds is sound. Provide easy, organized access to the materials you want your child to use; get rid of mess and twaddle. That's easier said than done in a homeschool environment. However, if you have an area (or several areas) of your house that you can devote to homeschooling, the chapter in this book on how to get organized has some great suggestions that will help you make miniworlds out of chaos.

Other miniworlds include sports and fitness miniworlds: Martial arts academies, skating rinks, and swimming pools are examples. And there are the planned learning environments such as museums, zoos, and science centers. Homeschoolers spend a lot of time in these miniworlds. See the chapter on field trips!

Real World, the Land of Unschooling

You know this world! It's down the block, in the center of town, out in the country, and on the map. We call it the "Real World," and kids can learn a lot in it.

In the real world, your children can:

- Work on the crew of a community theatre
- Act in the play!
- Volunteer at a local charity
- Start their own business!
- Wander around town and sketch the buildings
- Visit a nursing home and listen to the residents' life experiences
- Hang around the horticultural center and pester the owners until they reveal everything they know about taking care of plants
- Tour the USA by bicycle
- Hike the Appalachian Trail
- Save up, buy a sailboat, and learn to sail it
- Build their own airplane (I know one homeschool family that did this!)

You'll notice these aren't contrived classroom projects, which is why an education largely made up of such projects is called "unschooling." Grown-ups actually do these things of their own free will. That word "grown-ups" is the key. The Real World is the world of adults, not the artificial world of the classroom or the kiddie hangout.

The big question when dealing with Real World experiences is how much guidance you, the parent, will provide. The younger and more inexperienced the child, the more likely you will have to come up with the bright ideas and supervise the results. Don't forget to document all this real-world learning; see the chapter in this book on How to Keep Great Records for ideas on how to do this.

Virtual World, the Home of Hypertext

The encyclopedia that talks like a man. The bulletin board for the whole world. A raunchy peep show that routinely hawks its wares in uninvited emails. The world's biggest library. The ultimate party line. The Internet has been called all that and more.

When thinkers used to talk about using computers in education, just a few years ago they were thinking of stand-alone software products whose rules children would have to obey. Today, getting an "online education" can be the equivalent of the kid who used to read the encyclopedia for fun . . . or of the rebel who used to cut class and hang out in the bad side of town.

From years of experience, I would say that online education is best for older kids who can be trusted to stay on task and not get distracted with random chatting and random Web surfing.

Or am I contradicting myself? Teenagers *love* random chatting and random Web surfing!

The Web is great when you need to find something out. Its links can also draw you in to an entire research project when you only intended to be online for five minutes, or distract you completely from your original topic. But if a kid has the time and the character for that kind of unguided browsing, he or she can definitely learn a lot.

Microworlds. Miniworlds. Real world. Virtual worlds. They're all your children's worlds now!

But there's an enemy hidden in each of these worlds. Yes, we're talking about **twaddle**, that strange visitor from another planet which, disguised as meek-mannered "fun" and "clever" activities, lurks in lesson plans, messes with your math manipulatives, clogs up your community projects, and weaves its subtle way through the web of online learning. Many is the homeschool mom who has lost her way under the subtle spell of twaddle.

Fear not, gentle reader. That horrible fate does not await *you*. To become prepared to meet and defeat twaddle, just continue on to the next chapter!

CHAPTER 18

Twaddle, Begone!

This is the chapter for Slasher Moms—those of us who recognize much curriculum is saturated with activities that fatten the teacher's manual but add no educational mass. In some cases, *super*saturated. You, too, can become a Twaddle-Slashing Mom or Dad. In fact, you'd better if you want to survive your homeschooling adventure. All that ugly twaddly fat will weigh you down and burn you out. So let's *slash* it!

Twaddle Happens

Curriculum authors are very creative people. Unfortunately, *their* creativity often does not take into account *your* need to get through the activities and projects in a reasonable amount of time.

Novice homeschoolers don't realize

(a) most activities are designed for enrichment and can be skipped without missing an educational beat
(b) how to recognize and slash all this unnecessary twaddle

That's why you need Pride's Top Ten Twaddle List. An activity is skippable twaddle if it is:

- Too big
- Too long
- Too silly
- Too unprepared
- Too unrealistic
- Too intrusive
- Too incomplete
- Too unimportant or trivial
- Too expensive
- Too time-consuming or too much effort

Let's take these one by one. I promise you'll never look at a teacher's manual the same way again!

Too Big

Would you ask your five-year-old to paint a hundred-foot fence? Would you expect your eight-year-old to run for Congress?

I'm betting your answer is no. Yet curriculum authors often casually drop overblown and overresponsible assignments on kids. The worst offender is the guilt trip whereby kids are supposed to "save the planet" by becoming baby lobbyists and preteen political activists. Leaving aside for now the question as to whether the planet is really on its deathbed, surely a little common sense reveals that lobbying and activism is a job for mature, informed adults. Shoving this task onto kids is exploitative at best. So let me make it official:

Your kid does not have to save the planet.

"The planet" is too big. "Our city" is too big. "Our neighborhood" is too big. "Your bedroom" is just the right size. I fully support teaching kids to detrash their bedrooms.

In a similar vein, asking kids to create a mural, a tapestry, or a life-size statue is asking too much. So is asking them to complete a foot-by-foot graph of your backyard, a street map of your neighborhood, and so on. These activities qualify as twaddle for other reasons as well, but I wanted you to get the main idea here: too much is . . . too much.

Too Long

Some activities are stretched out over too long a period to mean much to the age group to which they are assigned. Making a graph of family members' heights over a year is *not* an efficient way to teach graphing skills.

Never measure anything that changes slowly over time for a school project.

Go ahead and measure the kids just because *you* want to. Don't make it into schoolwork.

Planting a garden in order to emphasize certain character qualities and Bible verses is another example. Gardens are great, but by the time a kid has been pulling weeds for a few months you will have moved on to another unit. The example (what weeds are like) follows too far behind the instruction (parable of the sower and the seed) to make an impact unless you teach that lesson all over again each few weeks.

Never grow anything or get a pet for a school project.

Do it for its own sake or not at all. These long, slow lessons are really about gardens, animals, work, and love, not school assignments.

Too Silly

"Make up an imaginary animal/plant/alien. Then draw it/write a story about it/make a puppet of it." What *exactly* does this teach? My point exactly.

Again, if your student *wants* to do this, that's fine. But don't *assign* silly stuff like this.

More silly assignments: "Pretend you're a tree/a flower/a giraffe/anything else nonhuman. Then wave your little leaves in the breeze/sway your little petals/galumph around and eat stuff off the top of the refrigerator." Unless your child plans a future career as a mime or drama coach, pretend you never saw these assignments.

Too Unprepared

Curriculum authors *love* to include drawing assignments in the early grades. These vary from the specific ("Draw Puss in Boots") to the annoyingly nebulous ("Draw a picture that shows how you feel about summer"). Two things here:

- The kids are never taught to draw first.
- Most kids *hate* these assignments because they were never taught to draw first.

One more point courtesy of the Slasher Mom:

- How much math, language arts, science, and history are they learning by making bad drawings? Or even good ones?

I believe every child can and should be taught to draw and paint. As an *art* course. For resources on how to do this, see the Art chapters in the other two volumes of this series.

Your moral:

Slash every assignment for which kids have not yet been taught the skills to triumphantly complete the assignment.

Too Unrealistic

Asking kids to create simulations or models that do not in fact simulate or model the item being studied is just plain stupid. My personal favorite example: "Create a 3-D model of the human body out of toilet paper rolls." What are we trying to say here, people? That people are fat cylinders with scraps of T.P. attached?

Also popular among heavy caffeine users from the curriculum designer crowd: assignments that require kids to write or put on plays or skits about historical figures. Since we don't know exactly what they said or their precise motivations, and kids are not about to put in the kind of serious research that writers of historical fiction and biographies sweat through, this teaches kids to *make up the facts*. A career in network news awaits!

Worst of all: the "interview" of a biblical character or other famous historical personage. "And just what did you think, Mr. Joshua, when the walls of Jericho came tumbling down?" "Why are your teeth wooden, President Washington?" Does anyone really think that any important person of the past would have put up for one second with this nonsense? The "interview" assignment chops great men and women down to the size of the stupid pet tricks on Letterman. (Which, amazingly, I know about even without owning a TV set.) Drop the phony nonsense and read another good book on the character you are studying instead.

Too Intrusive

"Write a paragraph about how much you love God." "Write about the worst fight you ever had with your parents." I cringe whenever I encounter this kind of assignment. All the more so since they usually occur in materials designed to be used in *classrooms*.

> Forcing kids to parrot piety they may not yet have achieved is a great way to teach hypocrisy.

> Making them reveal personal feelings or embarrassments as an *assignment* is just plain evil.

Rule of thumb: If you curriculum designers want our kids to write about this stuff, *you* do the assignment too and let us all read what *you* wrote. Better yet, write out your answers and send a signed copy to your boss or some other authority figure in your life. This may provide a clue as to why kids' privacy should never be forced like this.

Too Incomplete

Don't you just love vocabulary lists with no pronunciation clues or definitions? How about huge lists of books to read that don't throw you a clue as to which are the *most important* books? Spelling word lists apparently picked at random (the words share no pattern or common topic)? Assignments that tell you, "Look up all the Bible verses on 'family'"?

> Don't beat yourself to death trying to do the curriculum designer's work for him.

Nobody is paying you for this. Call, fax, phone, or email the company that put out these incomplete materials and *demand* updated, useful, *complete* information. In the meantime, skip all the incomplete assignments and replace them with complete materials from another publisher. Or just have the kids read more. Vocabulary building without pain!

Too Unimportant or Trivial

Always ask yourself,

> "Why am I teaching this? How much of my life and my student's life is it worth?"

An example: "Animals have fur." I figure that's worth about three seconds of my life. Yet I have seen a curriculum that orders parents to collect magazines with pictures of animals, then cut out those pictures and make a collage of animal furs. This swell creative idea has now expanded your time investment to somewhere between hours and days. Your child will also learn the valuable skill of chopping up magazines. All without ever *touching* a furry animal!

Another popular example: "Research and write about the history of your town." Since the average American family moves once every three years, this is less than a worthwhile assignment. It can, however, soak up unlimited amounts of your precious time.

For the technically minded among you, I offer this equation. Where T = minutes to complete a project, M = minutes it would take to just *tell* your child the facts or *show* him the skills, F = the "fun" value of the project on a scale of 1 to 10, and S = how much spare time you have on a scale of 1 to 10:

$$\text{If T divided by M is greater than } \frac{FS}{10}, \text{ forget it.}$$

Too Expensive

Does the project or activity require expensive materials you don't already have on hand? Then either substitute less-expensive, more-available materials, or slash it. Comfort yourself with the thought that rich kids will be wasting time with this stuff while *your* student is zooming ahead in his workbook.

Too Much Effort

Some valuable educational activities may be more trouble than they are worth.

I am sure that visiting Cape Kennedy is wonderfully educational . . . for those who live or vacation in Florida. Making a seashell collection is great . . . if you live near a beach. Learning to rope and ride makes sense . . . if you live in Montana. Visiting the theater on a regular basis is fine . . . if you're a rich New Yorker.

When we lived in St. Louis, we were Zoo Members and regularly visited the museums, planetarium, and botanical garden. Here in Fenton, Missouri, a trip to Denny's is usually more than I can manage. Are my kids deprived? I think not. We have substituted activities that are near us (Tai Kwon Do and swim team) for the faraway stuff.

You can't do everything for your kids . . . but you can do enough. If an activity is a major strain on your family in travel time, planning, or preparation, drop it. *You* are the teacher, not the curriculum designer. Slasher Moms everywhere are probably skipping that exact same activity!

So there you have it. Ten ways to identify twaddle—and now you know them all. Take out that chainsaw and hack out the undergrowth—your kids will love you for it!

THINK I'M MAKING THIS UP? CHECK OUT "POSTER MANIA," THE LATEST TWADDLE EDU-FAD

Assignment: Think of 8 different phrases that would describe a main character in the book. Find these words in magazines. Cut them out and paste them on poster board.

Project: Spend hours searching through magazines and newspapers with sharp scissors in hand. Get frustrated when the 'words' can't be found. Run to the store to buy more resources. Sneak to the library and cut words from the magazines there!

The result: A poster that looks like a ransom note is presented to the class and displayed in the hallway.

Poster Mania is alive and well in all grades and subject areas. This arts and crafts teaching approach has taken the place of rigorous writing assignments. Why? To boost student grades and self-esteem. But what are the real results? To answer this question just look at a state like Florida in which 81% of eighth grade students are rated "non-proficient" in writing tests.

—Education Advocate
Jan/Feb 2000

CHAPTER 19

What Goes In

We've looked at how to motivate your student, how to choose an environment suitable to the topic to be studied, and how to slash your way through time-wasting distractions.

In these next three chapters, you will complete the second semester of Home Education 101 by learning:

- Ten ways to provide information and experiences to your children
- Five ways you and your children can process new learning, so it becomes a permanent part of them
- Twelve ways you can draw upon your close relationship with your student to pinpoint just what he or she knows (more traditional testing methods are in the Evaluating and Testing chapter)

This is the chapter for checking out the various ways you can present information to your children. We'll start with the most traditional and teacher-guided methods, and end with the least traditional and most child-controlled methods. The point of this exercise is to help you learn to think about teaching "outside the box" of the traditional classroom—the only place most of us have ever been programmed to associate with serious learning.

Talk to Me

[To be sung to the tune of "War"]

> "Classrooms! Huh! What are they GOOD for? Absolutely NOTHing!"

Well, that's not exactly true. The classroom environment is perfect for the **lecture** mode of instruction.

A lecture is where a teacher, presumably older and wiser, tells his students, who are usually younger and less experienced, the way things are.

Sometimes you'll want to be a "guide on the side." Other times it works better to be the "sage on the stage." It's not an either/or choice!

HERE'S AN IDEA: Video lectures are a great way to supplement your teaching, especially once you teach your children how to take effective notes.

It's great for sharing old war stories, presenting logical sequences of thought, and explaining terminology with visual aids.

At home, the lecture is probably the most incongruous form of instruction. Mom at the blackboard? Dad flipping easel pages or flashing Powerpoint slides on a screen? Give me a break! These methods are fine for large-group instruction but look silly in your living room.

Instead of the lecture, try the **story** and/or the **demonstration**. **Reading aloud** to your children (which many bad teachers confuse with lecturing) also is a great way to convey information. Please note you don't have to stop reading aloud just because the children are now in their teens! Even adults will stop each other and say, "I just read the greatest article. Here it is! Let me read the good parts to you."

How to Read a Book Aloud to Your Children

This is probably the least expensive therapy you will ever encounter. And unlike the various brands of psychotherapy, it actually works!

I say "therapy" because with the exception of the irrepressible Performer People among us, most of us learned to *fear* reading aloud in school. There the point of the exercise was for the teacher to catch our errors, with the humiliation greatly increased because our classmates heard our every stutter and our every misspoken word. If you are like most of us, the budding performer in us was squelched by this experience. How liberating to rediscover this long-suppressed part of your personality!

The truth is, we all have a little Performer in us. With the uncritical and enthusiastic audience of your own children, you'll eventually learn to let yourself go.

When reading a storybook aloud, get into the characters. Use different voices and pacing. Sound mysterious when you're reading a spooky part. Add sound effects when a rocket takes off. (You can find books at your library that tell you how to do all kinds of great effects with your mouth alone!)

When reading a textbook aloud, remember that *you* are the teacher, not the textbook. Feel free to stop and comment on or even argue with the text. Add your own personal stories. Throw in examples from current events or your historical reading that illustrate the point. The more you interact with the book, the more interesting it is for the students.

How to Dramatize a Lesson

One step up the ladder from reading material aloud is enlisting your children's help in acting it out.

You can:

- Take parts and verbally put on a play (great for studying Shakespeare and other classic dramatic literature).
- Re-enact scenes from a book or play (this is a popular way of enlivening Bible lessons!).
- Go up another notch by adding simple costumes and props.
- Use handmade puppets to put on your drama.
- Create scenery and backgrounds for your puppet theater.

The key here is to distinguish between doing it and *over*doing it. The "drama" method is great for subjects directly related to it: literature and plays. It can be used to *occasionally* jazz up your history studies, provided you don't end up spending more time on the costumes and scenery than

HERE'S AN IDEA: Try recording some of your read-aloud sessions. Kids love listening to tapes!

on the history. Or you can turn it around and consider your scenery construction as lessons in a very practical art form. The amount of this you do should probably depend most on how much of a Performer personality your child is . . . and how much of a Performer you are!

How to Tell a Story

Your personal history, and the history of those you know, is endlessly fascinating to young children. Your kids will hang on every word of what you learned when you faced the bully, or got your first job, or made the biggest blunder of your life. (Yes, even your mistakes turn out to be educational!) Every kid wants to know where he or she came from, and stories about Mom and Dad, Grandma and Grandpa, uncles and aunts, and ancient ancestors all provide a sense of "rootedness."

This is real history; don't kid yourself about that. I had no trouble remembering who was fighting whom in World War II when my Hungarian mother told me of her family's narrow escape, one jump ahead of the Russian occupation force, only to end up starving for three years in Nazi Germany where as despised outsiders they couldn't even gather fallen wood from the forest for fuel without special permission of the burgomeister. The lessons learned during your tough times and good times also provide great teaching material for character education.

A talented enough teacher can present *any* history as a story. This explains the enduring appeal of such works as *A Child's History of the World,* which is basically a series of stories about historical eras told by Calvert School's first headmaster, Virgil Hillyer, a book that has remained in print for a hundred years.

How to Sing a Song

Much information can be transmitted through music. From the "Alphabet Song" to "The Star-Spangled Banner," we are rich in songs we all know that teach many things. The "Wee Sing" tape series from Price/Stern/Sloan has collected hundreds of these songs.

Today, educational song cassettes and CDs that teach subjects from math and science to personal hygiene and world history are also available from many publishers. You'll find reviews of many of these in my *Birth to Grade 6* homeschool book.

How to Lead a Chant or Chorus

Repeating aloud as a group is a good way to increase rote memorization, and it works with a group as small as two people. You tell your child or children, "Say it with me." If this is too hard, you say, "Repeat it after me." GEN-esis, EX-odus, LeVITicus, NUMbers, DeuterONOmy . . . Repeat as often as necessary, and your child will know the names of the first five books of the Bible. Do it often enough, and he will *never* forget them.

This technique is best used for lists and for verses or sayings you want to sink down into your child's bones.

How to Give a Demonstration

Gather the materials. Gather the kids. Do the demonstration, explaining step-by-step. Let them help as gofers, fetching materials or turning off the lights. Have them help you clean it up.

> HERE'S AN IDEA: I've suggested elsewhere that the best way to improve your home teaching is to spend time yourself studying the subjects you plan to teach. Do so with an eye for interesting stories you can tell the kids, and you'll become an *excellent* teacher!

The second time, you walk them through it. They do each step after you model it first.

Then let them try it another time with you watching. Do this until you can see they understand.

Let them continue to perform the task. Spot check from time to time.

This is more or less what research has found to be the best way to teach a new *skill*, as opposed to a new *concept*. These steps—modeling the skill, leading the student through performing the skill himself, guided practice with the skill, and unguided practice with the skill—are essential features of the Maloney Method, which has an entire chapter devoted to it later in this book.

How to Teach a Scripted Lesson

Another feature of the Maloney method is called **scripting**. A technique arising out of behavioral science (which, remember, misses the boat in its view of human nature but is not *all* bad), "scripting" means that everything the teacher is to do or say is already written out. So is what the student is expected to reply. If the student does *not* give the correct answer, a "correction procedure" in your script tells you what to do and say to correct their misunderstanding.

Scripted lessons are great for novice teachers who need help teaching specific skills, assuming the curriculum designer knew what he was doing. You'll never be at a loss for what to do next!

How to Teach with Visual Aids

Here are three ways to teach with visual aids:

- You draw it for them on the whiteboard (much more fun with wipe-off colored markers than with plain old boring chalk!).
- You bring it into the house and show it to them.
- You bring them into the world and show it to them there.

Let's say, for example, you live in a remote, moose-rich area of Alaska, and you are studying the moose. You could draw a picture of a moose on the whiteboard, showing all its basic anatomy and organs. You could catch a moose and drag it into the house for study (not recommended). Or you could lie in wait in a likely location and try to observe a moose in its native habitat.

Visual material can best be captured with quick sketches. This is another good reason for teaching every child at least the rudiments of drawing—so he can learn to take "notes" on what he sees, as well as on what he hears.

How to Teach with Guided Exploration

The phrase **hands-on learning** is one of those buzzwords that sounds so great, but is a bit slippery when you try to define it. Technically, anything you can touch is "hands-on." Reading Braille is "hands-on," although it's exactly equivalent to information a sighted person takes in through his or her eyes.

In practice, most advocates of hands-on learning are really talking about our old friend **discovery learning**, another slippery term whose most useful definition is "learning through research or through building things." It could just as well be called "Aha! learning," since the point is for the student to have an "Aha!" experience.

Providing your children with books you want them to read is a form of *guided* exploration. Taking them to the library and letting them pick out their own books is a form of *unguided* exploration.

More useful than either of these phrases are the terms **guided exploration** and **unguided exploration**. Instead of focusing on the sense of touch or the end result of discovery, these terms tell us what type of learning is taking place and how much teacher help is or is not required.

Let's start with guided exploration. The student is going to learn about a subject by "exploring" it. This can be through such means as:

- Books on the subject
- Magazines on the subject (a commonly overlooked but great way for a kid to rapidly gain the same knowledge as an expert adult)
- Encyclopedia articles and other reference material on the subject
- Websites on the subject
- Businesses or ministries related to the subject (e.g., to explore the subject of veterinarian science, a student could start by visiting, or even volunteering to work in, an animal shelter or a vet's office)
- Entertainment related to the subject (e.g., to continue our vet science example, the video *All Creatures Great and Small*)
- People who know about the subject, whether online, in person, by phone, or by mail
- Events devoted to the subject (e.g., pet shows, state fairs, rodeos, 4-H fairs)

You get the idea!

In guided exploration, the teacher provides *goals* and *feedback*. In other words, you actually give the student an *assignment*. The assignment may be strictly defined—"Look up 'ants' in the *World Book Encyclopedia*" or loosely defined—"See how many styles of art you can find in this wing of the gallery." You and your student then agree on a feedback method (written report, verbal report, photo portfolio, etc.).

As the teacher, you may increase the amount of guidance you provide to include the *method* of investigation ("Start at this website and follow all the links related to Ancient Egypt") and even *hints* ("Try looking in the atlas").

Remember, you are teaching two things: (1) the subject itself and (2) how to find things out. The second topic is more important in the long run, as it is one of the "tools" of learning. Your directions and hints should be geared to helping students discover new ways of finding things out so they can move on to the next step.

How to Teach with Unguided Exploration

And that next step is **unguided exploration**!

Believe it or not, students functioning at this stage still need a teacher. Yes, they know how to find things out. But they might not yet have the judgment as to the best strategies to use or the ability to figure out what is important, unimportant, or downright wrong about the information they have obtained through their explorations. So we will see how to teach children to process new information in educationally useful ways in the next chapter.

CHAPTER 20

Thinking It Through

As we saw in the section on "How Kids Really Learn," it's not enough to just feed kids information or even for kids to find information on their own. In order for them to remember it and ultimately understand it, that information needs to be organized inside their heads into

- Frameworks—the overall organizing scheme for a topic
- Categories inside frameworks
- Patterns inside categories

And finally, they need to make new connections between what they have just learned and what they already know.

Here are some ways you can help your student process what he's learned, so it turns into wisdom and understanding.

Writing It Down

The first, but not necessarily best, way a student can process new information is by *writing it down*. By summarizing the information (repeating it in his own words), adding any of his own thoughts and comments, and then reading what he wrote, the student is able to come to grips with what he does and does not understand about the new information.

Notebooks and journals are the usual tools for this processing method. In a notebook, the primary emphasis is on summarizing course information, as well as repeating choice bits verbatim. In a journal, the main emphasis is on the student's thoughts about the new information.

Parents may be drawn to this method because it allows the student to do most of the "processing" on his own, with the parent just jumping in to explain tough concepts. It also provides a handy way to show authorities that learning is taking place.

However, here are some cautions to keep in mind:

YOU HAVE TO PROCESS IT BEFORE YOU KNOW IT

Education involves starting with a novice and helping the novice become an expert who has strong, readily accessible background knowledge. . . .

Experts not only have well-developed knowledge, they also have strong connections between different parts of that knowledge. . . .

For example, if you mention one thing about the Civil War to American history experts, they are able to connect that information to the intellectual, the economic, and the political knowledge they have about the Civil War. Not only can they connect, but the connections are firm, and are readily accessible because they have been practiced. These knowledge structures are called schema and experts have well-developed and well-connected schema.

—Professor Emeritus Barak Rosenshine, as interviewed by George Clowes, School Reform News, *May 2002*

HERE'S AN IDEA: **Why not combine the best features of notebooks and journals into a single method? And why not add to that sketches, marked-up photocopies of source documents, scraps of fabric, pressed flowers, timelines, or any other reasonably flat objects related to your study? You can even use a photo album—place photos and other "loose" items in the photo pages, and three-hole-punch your student's writings to slip into the binder's rings.**

- If your student hates to write, this is *not* the primary method you should ask him to use.
- The student's privacy should be respected; if he wants to keep a deeply private diary or journal, let that be separate from the writings he does for inspection.

Principle Approach curricula rely heavily on notebooking. These may provide forms with questions for your student to answer about each person, place, event, and so on studied. The Charlotte Mason method also encourages notebooking, this time with an eye to noticing and preserving beauty. Lab science courses also require lab notebooks, which describe each experiment and its expected results, list the actual data for the experiment, and end with the conclusions arising out of the actual data. Finally, many traditional curricula require students to maintain notebooks in which they write new terminology and definitions.

Spitting It Out

Narration is another great way for kids to process information. They tell you what they just learned! This also has the second benefit of giving you immediate feedback on their level of understanding.

For more details on the narration technique, see the chapter on Charlotte Mason education.

Talking It Through

Discussion is a processing technique that actually works in the home, whereas it tends to fail at the classroom level from kindergarten on up. Only in graduate-level symposia do students begin to emerge from their catatonic state to share their thoughts when the teacher asks a question.

The real key to fruitful discussion is to let the *students* ask as many of the questions as possible.

The more your children become your friends, the more energetic your discussions become. (I'm referring here to shared interests and enthusiasms, not to confusion about who is in charge of the home!) When you treat their opinions with interest and respect, and show you care about what *they* care about, it's easy to keep the "feast of reason and the flow of soul" going.

Many curricula include "discussion questions." These are usually fine as discussion *starters,* provided they are somewhat open-ended. As ever, feel free to argue with your child, argue with the text, and let your child argue with you as you quest after truth together.

Socratic Dialogue

The best-known technique for arguing with your child is the **Socratic Method**. Named after Socrates, the Greek philosopher who taught Aristotle (and who ended up drinking hemlock as an alternative to banishment from Athens), the Socratic Method consists of

- Interrogating the student
- Questioning his opinions
- Making him provide proof for his assertions

In this method, the teacher typically reserves his knowledge of the right answer until the student has struggled his way towards the light. The teacher's role is to guide the student by helping him see for himself why certain paths are wrong and illogical and others are right and make sense.

If you want to use this method, you'd better

- Have a student or students who trust and respect you
- Thoroughly understand your subject
- Have a good understanding of human nature
- Know when your student is losing patience!

The last point is especially important. As the daughter of a philosophy professor who used this method extensively in daily conversation, I can attest that it can become annoying at times!

The Socratic Method is a "gadfly" method. The teacher "stings" the student verbally every time he strays into illogic and false assumptions. It will enthrall the Puzzle Person, bore the Action Man, frustrate the Progress Person, and cut the Performer down to size. A People Person might love it or hate it, depending on the emotional feel of the "group" (again, this group may be just you and your child). If there's lots of laughter and bonding, the People Person can enjoy it.

The Socratic Method is mostly used in classical education. But that does not mean you have to go for the whole Latin-Iliad-Odyssey-rhetoric thing to use it. Whenever you answer a question with a question, or challenge a student's thinking or assumptions, you're using the Socratic Method.

The moral here: **Don't be too quick to always give out the answer.** If your students are ready for it, let them at least occasionally sweat their way to an answer, with you guiding them.

Good questions to ask are:

- "How would *you* go about figuring that out?"
- "How do you know that?"
- "What evidence does the writer provide for his thesis?"
- "What are you assuming when you say that?"
- "If [this] is true, does [that] necessarily have to be true?"

The point of the Socratic Method is to train students to *think*. They move beyond "processing" data to *analyzing* it. Originally, Socrates used this method to encourage his students to come to grips with the great questions of life. And you can, too.

Using It

Finally, a really great way to process new information and skills is to **use** them. Watching other people do something is all very well, as is having the theoretical knowledge in your head. Putting your knowledge and skills to work both increases motivation to remember this suddenly useful material and creates actual brain paths through the repetition involved.

Sadly, many opportunities to practice new skills and techniques are no more glamorous than a workbook page. This is the weakest form of using a new skill: a contrived exercise to be graded.

One step up is an assignment that requires creativity *and* the use of your new skills. For example, once you have learned some elementary digital engineering, you can try making your own circuit board. Once you have learned some piano basics, you can try writing your own simple pieces. Once you have learned to write by hand or type on a computer, you can write letters to friends or start noodling on a play.

LEARN ABOUT IT OR LEARN IT?

If I wished a boy to know something about the arts and sciences, for instance, I would not pursue the common course, which is merely to send him into the neighborhood of some professor . . . to survey the world through a telescope or a microscope, and never with his natural eye; to study chemistry, and not learn how his bread is made, or mechanics, and not learn how it is earned; to discover new satellites to Neptune, and not detect the motes in his eyes . . .

Which would have advanced the most at the end of a month—the boy who had made his own jackknife from the ore which he had dug and smelted, reading as much as would be necessary for this—or the boy who had attended the lectures on metallurgy at the Institute in the meanwhile, and had received a Rodgers' penknife from his father? Which would be most likely to cut his fingers?

To my astonishment I was informed on leaving college that I had studied navigation! Why, if I had taken one turn down the harbor I should have known more about it.
—*Henry David Thoreau, "Economy,"* Walden

This brings us to **hands-on projects**. Although they are usually thought of as an "input" method, actually, most hands-on projects are less about "teaching" than about "processing." Students are *applying* what they have learned in order to construct the model boat, build the birdhouse, sew the dress, or cook the medieval feast. The act of creation then helps cement the facts and skills in the learner's mind.

As you saw in the sidebar on the previous page, Henry David Thoreau once asked rhetorically who would understand metallurgy better: a boy who had read a book on metallurgy, or another who had dug his own ore, smelted it, and made his own penknife. Obviously the second young man would know metallurgy in his bones and would probably have found his studies more interesting as well. But would he have all the tools to tackle a different project, such as goldsmithing? So, as ever, be wise in balancing the pleasure and memorableness of a project with the depth and width of information your child will gain and the value of the time it will take.

One thing you can say for the kid with the penknife, though—at least he has something to show his friends and relatives. In the next chapter, we'll examine other ways of finding out how much your child has learned, and perhaps also demonstrating it to others.

CHAPTER 21

What Comes Out

How can you tell how much your child has learned? The modern answer is, "Give him or her a standardized test!" Yes, homeschoolers have been taking such tests for years and doing better on them than their schooled counterparts.

But once-a-year standardized testing doesn't give you the feedback you need from day to day.

Keep reading for some strategies that do!

Timed Drill

In this era of child-centered education, good old timed drill has gotten a bad name. Yet this is still the most effective way to determine how well your children have mastered certain types of material.

For more detailed information on how to use timed drill most effectively, see the section on Precision Teaching in the chapter on the Maloney Method.

The Quick Verbal Quiz

If you know the subject well enough, you can quickly find out where the student is in his level of understanding simply by asking a few questions. Make sure your questions aren't too predictable, though, or a smart slacker will just study "the kind of stuff Mom always asks me about."

Educational Software

Most "educational software" is actually *testing* software. It asks questions rather than teaching new material. There's nothing wrong with this, if you're using it to take the place of boring flashcards. The extra practice will reinforce what was learned. As a bonus, the program often automatically grades the child's work and provides motivation in the form of high scores or some other onscreen reward.

Making the Grade by Lesha Myers ($19.95, Cameron Academy, P.O. Box 21383, Concord, CA, [925] 798-2097, www.cameron-publishing.com) is the best book ever on how to grade and evaluate home-schooled children. It covers every grading and evaluating method, explains how God Himself grades by examining His evaluation of Judah, shows how to grade individual subjects, and includes all the forms and examples you need.

Repeat It for Me

How can you tell your child has memorized his Bible verse/the poem you assigned/the planets in order/the Gettysburg Address?

You sit there with the verse/poem/etc. in front of you and check him while he recites it to you.

You knew this already, of course!

The Little Red Schoolhouses of the past relied more heavily on this method than they should. Groups of children would arise to "recite" all sorts of material, not just the sort we naturally expect our children to memorize. The definitions of parts of speech, science concepts, historical events, and much more were memorized by rote. As "progressive" critics justly complained, being able to spit out a bunch of words doesn't mean the student *understood* any of it.

Simply put, material that is unchanging (the words of a Bible verse or poem, for example) is appropriate for rote memorization. For material that requires understanding, the learner needs to be able to say it "in his own words." That brings us to the next output method.

Tell Me About It

Remember "narration" from the previous chapter? The child summarizes for you verbally what he has learned.

Narration is not only a great way to get kids to process new information; it's also a great way for you to find out what they know. See the Charlotte Mason chapter for more details.

Write Me a Report

Beloved of school officials everywhere, the written report hopefully shows the student's understanding of the subject.

Extremely important: For reports to mean anything real educationally, and also for the sake of doing the right thing, you *must* teach your student not to plagiarize. Quotes from source material *must* be noted as such. Even paraphrased material should be attributed to its source.

Today's kids . . . and even some adults . . . are blissfully ignorant of the ethics of copying other people's work. That's why so many "reports" are just rewritten or copied encyclopedia material, and why writers such as myself keep finding material in other people's books, not attributed to us in any way, that we really wonder how they could have found out without having read our articles and books . . . since we invented the terms they are using, we were the first to promote the methods they are discussing, we actually reviewed the hundreds of curricula they airily pontificate about, the contact information they provide contains errors identical to those found in outdated versions of our books, etc.

See Susan Richman's article "How to Teach Your Children Not to Plagiarize" on the opposite page for more information on this vital topic.

Copy It for Me

Often mistakenly thought of as a "teaching" method, **dictation** is actually an "output" method used to test memory, handwriting, spelling, and grammar. Popular in the past, it hardly ever appears in today's public schools.

Here's how it works.

MOTIVATIONAL TIP

A huge motivating factor in my early school studies was hoping to earn the chance to finally use a fountain pen.

In the early grades, my teachers made us do all our schoolwork and dictation in pencil. Fountain pens were for *big* kids.And how we desired them! Even today, in the land of the Bic Clic, a pen with real ink cartridges just *feels* better, and the writing *looks* better.

Having to earn the right to use a particular tool (in this case, a fountain pen) can be a big thing to a little kid.

How to Teach Your Kids Not to Plagiariz

by Susan Richman

Has plagiarism ever come up in conversation at home with your kids?

Maybe it should.

I think my own kids' first intro to the idea of plagiarism was way back when our oldest son, Jesse (now 24 years old), was about seven. We had a huge stack of old *Highlight Magazines* that a retired teacher friend of ours had given to us, and we especially liked looking through the pages with kids' original writings and drawings. And there it was—blatant plagiarism by a child. One of the submitted poems was *not* really written by an 8-year-old, but instead was a poem I'd read in a professional anthology of poetry for children. I found the original poem, showed it to my kids, and we talked about how terrible this was that the child had lied and said the poem was his when it wasn't. **Plagiarism was just like stealing.**

Later we had other glimpses into plagiarism, sometimes through books we were reading aloud. We found out about the time Helen Keller was accused of plagiarizing a story while in high school—and the hurt and confusion this caused her. . . .

My kids also knew about the story I'd later share in our book *Writing from Home,* in the intro to a chapter about creative alternatives to report and research writing:

> *I remember many years ago a young 9-year-old neighbor came up to visit at our house, with Volume K of a borrowed school encyclopedia under his arm. He told me that he had to write a "report" for school about the Kremlin. On talking more with the boy, I gradually became aware of something shocking—he actually believed that the teacher wanted him to copy verbatim the encyclopedia entry on the Kremlin. He thought that's what writing a report meant—copying the dry words somebody else (an anonymous someone at that) had already written. He had no notion of the wrongs of plagiarism— that stealing someone else's words and passing them off as your own was very wrong. And he had even less notion that the goal probably was that he actually learn something about his topic. The Kremlin meant nothing to him at that point, and I'm sure it didn't mean much more once he'd finished his "report.".* . . .

Plagiarism isn't just seen among young kids who maybe really just don't understand fully what they are doing. It happens even with Advanced Placement level homeschool students. I've uncovered plagiarism at least four times in my own AP US History online course, and have had to discuss this issue at length with these students, and bring the issue up for discussion at times with the whole class. I now have plagiarism warnings right in my syllabus. I let kids know that if caught a second time in this, they will be dropped immediately from the course. All offenders were strongly religious kids, from good families—the types of kids who would never steal *things*. They just didn't think of *words* as *things*. . . .

In my class, plagiarism has almost always been in a biography assignment, where kids are pulling info off the Internet. Computers just make it so very easy to copy-and-paste and be done with an assignment when you're pressed for time. **Now whenever I see something odd in a biography essay**—things out of chronological sequence, ideas or even whole sentences repeated in different paragraphs, or simply a very choppy presentation, **I do a quick *Google* search** on a few sentences from the piece. The plagiarized website quickly pops up on the screen. . . .

How to help your kids avoid plagiarism? First, tell them some of these stories. Read this whole article around the lunch table and discuss it. . . .

Next, see that assignments are structured to almost make it impossible for a student to plagiarize. At the suggestion of some wonderfully creative students in my AP online course, I've encouraged the kids to write their Biography Essays in innovative ways. . . . Students have been remarkable in the range of formats they've developed now for this assignment. They've done mock interviews, funeral orations, series of imagined letters from the famous person to a grandchild, or from an invented friend to the famous person. They've written mock news articles from different periods of the person's life—often making sure they write from different perspectives in each "article" so we get a sense of how opposing groups reacted to the person. They've created journal entries spanning a lifetime. . . .

Students who take this sort of creative approach can't possibly plagiarize—they have to *use* the info they've gathered in really novel ways, showing us both personality as well as facts, and they have to make true decisions about what is really important to include. Students caught doing cut-and-paste from the Internet are always those trying to get by with a straightforward, bare-bones, factual, and usually *short* essay. They then must rewrite it completely, this time using one of the creative approaches. The difference is remarkable. Next year, I'm requiring inventiveness from everyone, right from the start.

—Susan Richman, "Teaching Kids Not to Plagiarize," Practical Homeschooling *May/June 2002. With Sue's permission, and of course crediting her as the author, the* Practical Homeschooling *piece was based on an article that appeared in issue #78 of* Pennsylvania Homeschoolers, *Susan and Howard Richman's quarterly newsletter.*

First, you pick the excerpt you plan to dictate. A literary excerpt works well. So does a Bible verse.

Then you read it to the child, sentence by sentence. For younger children, first you read the sentence, then you read it phrase by phrase. Each phrase can be repeated once more upon request.

The final output is then graded for accuracy, spelling, and grammatical correctness. Did the student remember to start each sentence with a capital letter and end with a punctuation mark? Are quote marks used properly? Are all the words there, and spelled correctly? In addition, some teachers grade the handwriting.

Show Me Your Project

Whether it's a finished job or a work in progress, check on your student's project often enough to let him know you care. Then, when it's finished, take a photo of it for the portfolio or videotape it.

Lab science experiments should definitely be documented this way, to prove to college officials that your student didn't just read the book. Since lab science is an entrance requirement at many better schools, it pays to document this work.

Do It for Me

Let your child demonstrate to you what he knows while you watch. Let him bake a cake, change a tire (with you right there, of course!), do ten push-ups, brush his teeth correctly, conjugate a French verb, or make a baking-soda volcano. Don't forget to be impressed!

Show Me Your Notebook

Want to know if your child is actually studying his textbook? Want to know if he's just watching those educational videos or trying to learn and remember the information?

His notebook will tell the tale.

Granted that one person's notes can be another person's gibberish, you might want to ask him to summarize and repeat what he's learning while looking at the notebook. If it all makes sense to him, and he can in turn make it make sense to you, learning is occurring. But to make *extra* sure, you can always ask him to . . .

Show Me Your Portfolio

At every level from kindergarten through graduate school, a well-done portfolio convinces even skeptics that your child has learned something.

The most important points to remember when assembling a portfolio:

- **It must look professional.** This means holding it all together in a professional "container" such as a three-ring binder or an art portfolio, or having it all bound with a nice cover at a local copy center. We have successfully used photo albums to hold our children's college portfolios, which resulted in scholarship offers from every institution to which they applied!
- **It must be organized.** Complex portfolios include an index or table of contents. Like material should be grouped together.
- **Each piece should be identified.** We simply taped a description of each item to the acetate overlay for each page.

- **Three-dimensional or large items should be photographed.** These can then be included in your relatively flat portfolio.
- **Pick the best pieces.** Papers should be neat and well written. Art examples should be finished and attractive. Photos should be clear, not grainy or blurry. The idea is to put your best foot forward while simplifying the amount of material to look at.

Draw or Model It for Me

Building a model or making a drawing is a great way to demonstrate knowledge of some topics: the relative positions of the planets or human anatomy, for two examples. If your child can draw the planets in order or model the skeletal system from clay, he has definitely learned those lessons!

Teach Me

The apex of understanding is when you can teach what you've learned to someone else. If your daughter can teach the topic to you or to a younger sibling, she really knows it. The very process of teaching further cements the information in the brain, while thinking about *how* to teach it helps the brain form some of those helpful connections we've been talking about!

Teach Us

This is the pinnacle of the pinnacle; your child making a presentation to a group that shows what he has learned. Non-performer types may not love this assignment, but except in cases of exceptional shyness, every child can benefit from knowing how to present information to a group.

The presentation can be as simple as a verbal report or as complicated as a major science fair project or a proposal to the city zoning commission.

This feedback method requires much more preparation than any of the others, so is best saved for important occasions, such as family reunions and Homeschool Day at the state capital.

Review . . . Review . . . Review

Got all that? Then close your eyes and repeat the 14 feedback methods I just described. I thought so. This is why **review** is so important in education, and why I saved mentioning it for last. Constant review is the key to ensuring your student will remember what he was taught, even years in the future.

You can review using any of the methods in this chapter. The more intense the method, the less often you will need to use it. I can still remember the major projects I did in grade school, though I did each one only once. On the other hand, you will probably need to repeat the alphabet backward about 40 times before your kids really "know" it. (I'm not kidding; knowing the alphabet backward as well as forward is a great help when looking up alphabetical information.)

Generally, curriculum that includes **cumulative reviews** (review of everything taught up to that point in the book) is superior to curriculum that only has reviews once at the end of each chapter, which in turn is superior to curriculum that has no review at all. You can, however, improve a review-free curriculum by creating your own simple review questions or quizzes.

Congratulations! You've made it all the way through Education 101. Now you're ready to do what experienced educators do: analyze, review, and pick the best parts of the available educational methods for use with your own students.

The next two sections will introduce you to a dozen of the most popular homeschool methods. I want to emphasize that **you do not have to pick just one method!** In fact, the last "method," the Eclectic Method, is actually the practice of using *other* methods as a menu of choices. **You also can use different methods with different children.** This requires a bit more teaching effort but can be very worthwhile when you have children with wildly different thinking styles.

Think of these next two sections as "Education 102." This is graduate school for homeschoolers. Even veteran educators don't know everything that's in these chapters . . . but you will, just as soon as you've finished reading them!

PART 5

Popular Homeschool Methods

Homeschooling isn't just academics.
Real-life projects can play an important part.
Here's an example! Hannah Coley, a 14-year-old
homeschooler from Goldsboro, NC, was cast in the role
of Helen Keller in the play The Miracle Worker in a
local theater production. While researching her part,
Hannah learned sign language, which she still uses
often. The Coleys then planned a trip to Washington,
D.C. in the spring, to visit Helen Keller's
tomb at the National Cathedral, among other places.
Hannah told us she feels that local theater and
historical plays would be a great way for other homeschoolers to become far more involved in history.

CHAPTER 22

Back to Basics

The basics. The "3 R's." Reading, 'riting, and 'rithmetic. Most parents fervently agree that whatever "education" means, it surely must include these.

Until compulsory attendance laws were passed—a fairly recent development in our history—children were normally taught to read and count at home *before* attending school, and many well-educated people never went to school at all.

Even when children went to school, until partway through this century "school" was not at all like what we experience today. A typical school experience would last six years, with three semesters of 6–12 weeks each, scheduled so kids could take time off to help with planting and harvest on their family's farm. In that short amount of "school" time, they were expected to learn how to read material we would now consider "college level" fluently, handwrite beautifully, and solve complex word problems involving what we now deem "college level" consumer math. They were also familiar with the early history of America, its founding documents, and the principles set down in those documents—making them better-educated citizens than most of our current elected representatives and judges!

Our great-great-grandparents were expected to learn all this in one-room schoolhouses whose accessories included pot-bellied stoves and outhouses. They were taught by a single teacher with no teacher's assistants except for the older children, no classroom TV, no audio-video equipment, no computers, no math manipulatives, no bulletin-board cutouts, and (very importantly) *no* teacher's unions and almost *no* Federal or state bureaucracy interfering with every step of her teaching.

Those who had their sights set on college, which at that time was a special experience achieved only by a relatively few, typically added more advanced math and science, Latin and perhaps Greek, and a European language or two to their studies, plus a reading course in the "Great Books." Following such a course, it was not unusual for students to be ready for college at age 14 or 16.

Back to Basics Curriculum

- A Beka Book (textbooks & workbooks, correspondence school option)
- A Beka Video School
- Accelerated Christian Education, formerly School of Tomorrow (worktexts, associated correspondence school option)
- Alpha Omega Publications (worktexts, software option, and online academy option)
- Bob Jones University Press (textbooks & workbooks)
- Christian Liberty Academy (workbooks & textbooks, correspondence options)
- Christian Light Education (worktexts, correspondence school option)
- Landmark's Freedom Baptist Curriculum (worktexts)
- Rod & Staff (textbooks & workbooks)

Please note that most of these publishers also offer a variety of support and enrichment materials, plus curriculum for higher grade levels.

Sam Blumenfeld's excellent **How to Tutor** ($24.95, Paradigm Company, 208-322-4440, www.howtotutor.com) presents the theory and instructions behind his Alpha-Phonics program (reviewed in *Mary Pride's Complete Guide to Homeschooling from Birth to Grade 6*). Plus how to successfully teach 'ritin' and 'rithmetic in one-on-one situations. Stripped-down, no-frills, easy to read and easy to do. Step-by-step instructions, with explanations of why Mr. Blumenfeld has such success with his approach. This last feature, the reasoned explanations of why you should follow classic methods of instruction, sets *How to Tutor* apart. Not a bad price for learning how to teach your child the three R's from preschool through grade 6.

Why the Cry of "Back to Basics"?

The public schools have been experimenting for decades with methods designed to bypass what progressive elements considered the "mindless drill" and "rote learning" associated with the way these basics had been successfully taught for centuries. Parents and many teachers watched in dismay as Look-Say, the New Math, Whole Language, and other fads left generations of kids in need of remedial reading courses in college and unprepared to make correct change at McDonald's.

The "Back to Basics" movement was a response to these falling academic standards. A handful of curriculum companies, some secular and some Christian, came out with workbooks and textbooks that employed traditional teach-'em-and-drill-'em techniques. Some even reprinted classic texts from the early days of public schooling, such as the famous McGuffey Readers. The burgeoning Christian school movement snapped these up, as did many in the emerging homeschool movement.

Since the skills at issue were those taught in the early grades, for the purposes of this book we will consider "back to basics" to refer to materials for grades K–6. However, publishers of "back to basics" materials often carry the same no-nonsense approach on through junior high and high school.

Basics curricula have this in common:

- Authoritative instruction that tells students the facts and how to do the work (as opposed to encouraging them to guess or invent their own methods)
- Step-by-step approach to teaching new skills
- Lots of practice problems
- Lots of rote drill to ensure mastery

Where basics curricula differ from each other is not in their approach (though there are minor differences). They differ in the amount and kind of spiritual emphasis they include and in the medium they use to present the basics.

You know what kind of spiritual emphasis you are looking for. So, for the rest of this chapter let's look at the different ways—textbook, worktext, audio, video, and software—you can purchase a peck of basics today!

Traditional Textbook

"Traditional Textbook" is what most people think of when they first contemplate homeschooling—children setting at desks, reading textbooks and writing answers down. Just like school. But at home.

Textbook learning follows this familiar school sequence:

- Give an assignment.
- The child reads the lesson and you answer any questions.
- The child does the "exercises" at the end of the section or chapter.
- You grade the exercises and explain what the child missed.
- The child takes quizzes and tests, and does some reports or projects, which you also grade.

Textbook learning lends itself well to the "X pages a day method." Simply stated, you take the textbook, divide its pages by the number of days in which you desire to complete it (200 days for a 40-week school year, for example), and assign the child that many pages per day.

Advantages of textbook learning: Ease of assignments (X pages per day); only one study book (there may be additional exercise books, answer keys, teacher manuals, etc., though); lends itself somewhat to self-study; minimal teacher preparation; no shopping for additional resources or books; easy to provide a "grade" for each course; covers all material in the public-school sequence, so you're all set for standardized tests. Exception: Christian biology texts do *not* prepare you well for the heavily evolutionary CLEP, SAT II, or AP biology tests, and Christian literature courses leave out many politically correct/sexually oriented readings now included on the CLEP/SAT II/AP literature tests.

Christian publishers such as A Beka Book, Bob Jones University Press, and Rod and Staff are the most popular vendors of textbooks to the home-school market.

Many secular vendors offer a variety of individual texts of value in preparing for elementary and high-school level studies, but none of them offer an entire packaged curriculum targeted to homeschoolers. You'll find reviews of many of these individual texts in my other books.

WHO IT'S BEST FOR: Puzzle Solvers, Progress People, and visual learners benefit most. The "wiggle worm" kinesthetic/tactile child may need some seatwork time to learn self-control, but an overdose of textbooks will kill his or her motivation, so keep it light. Auditory learners love to be read to, but most textbooks don't exactly cry out to be read aloud, and they don't provide the "people" connection that People Persons crave.

Traditional Worktext

A "worktext" is not exactly a textbook, and it's not exactly a workbook. It's a consumable booklet that includes both the instruction normally found in a textbook and the exercises and quizzes normally found in a workbook. Many worktexts are "reproducible," meaning the publisher grants you the right to photocopy the pages for your own use. At home this is a mixed blessing, since few of us have home photocopy machines, and the price of photocopying an entire book can easily outweigh the cost of an additional copy. However, if you only need to photocopy a few pages (e.g., chapter exercises and tests), it can save you some money.

Worktext advantages include low initial cost and simplicity of storage— everything is in the one book. Since answer keys are either in the worktext itself or available for sale separately, grading the child's answers is no problem. Except that there are *so many* answers to grade!

The worktext route is designed for more self-study and less parental involvement than the textbook route. You likely won't need a separate teacher's manual, except for the answer key. You will, however, have to do *lots* of grading. What you gain in lesson preparation time you lose in grading, filling out the umpteen record sheets that record the grade, and calculating final grades for every quiz, test, and the course itself.

WHO IT'S BEST FOR: Puzzle Solvers, Progress People, and visual learners benefit most. "Wiggle worm" Action People find worktexts less onerous than textbooks since worktexts are usually thinner and it's easier to feel like you're getting somewhere. Plus, the "write on me" nature of worktexts is more appealing than having to do your work on separate paper. Auditory learners don't especially benefit. People Persons might enjoy a worktext that is written personably and illustrated charmingly (e.g., the *Simply Grammar* worktext, reviewed in my *Birth to Grade 6* volume).

To find educational videos for homeschoolers online, go to **www.home-school.com/mall**, click on "Curriculum Hall," and select the Educational Videos category. There you'll find links to sites that sell a wide selection of educational videos.

Video Teachers

Go to class . . . without going to class. Yes, you can bring the teacher home. Just purchase his or her video series!

To date, phonics instruction on video has not been popular or successful. Phonics video instruction has worked best for showing parents how to do the teaching themselves. Math and science, however, both lend themselves well to the video format. A video teacher can demonstrate fractions with manipulatives, show you how to use a number line, demonstrate science experiments, and take you to the zoo.

You'll find math and science video series reviewed in the other volumes of this series. These are not all "white-bread" products: For example, the "Standard Deviants" video review series for high school in spite of its MTV-like look actually utilizes a "basics" step-by-step approach.

WHO IT'S BEST FOR: If done right, a teaching video can hit everyone's buttons except the Action Man. The beauty of math is enough to enthrall the Puzzle Solver, while seeing it tidily organized step-by-step on screen appeals to the Progress Person. Be aware that both these types need to work out some problems on paper themselves to feel fully happy with the instruction; a videotape alone is not enough. If the video teacher is personable, the People Person will enjoy his company, while the Performer is naturally interested in the presentation's style. Videos and DVDs are auditory *and* visual; and if you give the kinesthetic/tactile student the means of taking notes and stop the tape or pause the DVD to "act out" new facts, you've got all the discovery channel bases covered.

Audio Drill Materials

Since now you're missing the picture, audio materials are good for topics you don't need to see demonstrated, and better for information you want the student to memorize and repeat. For the "basics," start with classics like the Alphabet Song, skip-count math drills, and so forth. Bible verses, the names of books of the Bible, and the catechism are great for audio drill. In fact, you can find audiocassettes and CDs for drilling facts in just about any school subject area. See my *Birth to Grade 6* volume for lots of examples.

To find educational audiocassettes for homeschoolers online, go to the Curriculum Hall as described above and click on "Audio."

WHO IT'S BEST FOR: Auditory learners. The type of auditory learner who needs to hear information can pick facts up easily this way, while the type who needs to hear himself say the information needs to "sing along" or "echo back" as well. Kinesthetic/tactile students can indulge their need for movement while learning. Visual learners should practice with at least some auditory materials to strengthen important listening skills. As for thinking styles: Puzzle Solvers will not find a tape intriguing unless there's a mystery to be solved. Action People can't experiment much with a tape. Progress Persons may enjoy a logical organization of facts, while Performers enjoy mimicking the voices (simultaneously learning those facts!). A People Person may enjoy listening to a tape just because she likes the friendly voices.

Tutoring Software

Tutoring software may be text only. It may be mostly text plus some pictures and animations. Or it can basically be a teaching video plus advanced interactive drill and practice.

Everything I said about video teachers applies to even the text-only type of tutoring software. Many parents don't realize that kids react to the computer itself as a separate personality. Software that is text-only is like communicating with a teacher through email. Software that features video clips of a teacher is like videoconferencing with a teacher. This means that, contrary to what you might think, even People Persons can be found glued to a computer monitor from time to time.

Kids perceive even the dullest software to be more fun than all but the most exciting educational video. That's because you can hit a button and make things happen. In a kid's world, where almost all of his life is under adult control, the illusion of being in control of your computer is very compelling. (I say it's an illusion because the software programmers have limited your options to what they want you to do.)

While I still think phonics instruction belongs in Mama's lap, you can now purchase pretty good phonics tutoring software. Math tutoring, science tutoring, grammar lessons, history lessons, and much more are available on low-cost CD-ROMs.

WHO IT'S BEST FOR: Visual learners, Progress Persons. If the tutoring software makes the "patterns" of the subject clear, Puzzle Solvers will be interested.

Drill & Practice Software

This is basics at its most basic. Practice and drill those facts! If you don't feel like serving on permanent flashcard detail, grab a handful of drill and practice software. Instead of your kids groaning and moaning while you spend hours flipping cards, they will happily drill themselves on their phonics, math facts, science terminology, history dates, and lots more while you find something more fulfilling to do.

WHO IT'S BEST FOR: Visual learners (for visual drill), auditory learners (for spoken drills as in foreign-language software). Make sure the software type is geared to your child's thinking style. If the reward for completing a drill is to get another piece of the ongoing Hangman puzzle, for example, this will appeal most to a Puzzle Solver. If progress can be clearly seen (as in the "words per minute" and "words without errors" statistics in learn-to-type software), the Progress Person will be motivated.

Beyond the Basics

Yes, just about everyone agrees our children should learn the basics, and just about every homeschooled child will end up using some "basics" style curriculum, whether it be textbooks, worktexts, videos or DVDs, audiocassettes or CDs, tutoring software, or drill-and-practice software.

These questions now remain:

- How far beyond the basics will he or she go?

- How many of the basics will the child be expected to discover through his or her own exploring, research, and experimentation?

The remaining methods in this section answer these questions in very different ways.

CHAPTER 23

The Charlotte Mason Method

If textbook methods and Principle Approach seem designed for the Progress Person . . . if classical education and Robinson Method appeal to the Puzzle Solver . . . if unit studies and unschooling appeal to the Action Man and Performer . . . then what kind of education is tailor-made for the People Person? Is there a homeschool method for the child who has a great heart and is most motivated by love and beauty?

Meet Charlotte Mason

Charlotte Mason was a Christian educator who lived and worked in Britain during the latter part of the nineteenth century. An idealist, she developed a Christian philosophy of education. When we speak of anyone being an idealist and/or philosopher we are usually implying that the person is preoccupied with high thinking but leaves the practical application to others. Unlike Dorothy Sayers, Charlotte did not do this. She was no armchair philosopher. She was one of those rare spirits who, having probed the depths of thought, could not rest content until she saw how it all worked out.

Today Charlotte's work is undergoing a revival in homeschool circles.

What's It All About, Charlotte?

For Charlotte Mason, education was not a list of skills or facts to be mastered. Education was **an atmosphere, a discipline, a life.** She saw education as a life process that is not confined to the classroom. Homeschoolers who follow her method do not attempt to duplicate the public school classroom regimen in their homes. They emphasize educating their children for life, not for achievement tests.

In the Charlotte Mason method, **whole books** and **first-hand sources** are used whenever possible, rather than textbooks.

Miss Mason advocated what she called **"living books."** Children, she thought, should read the best books, not graded readers or textbook comprehension paragraphs. Educators think they are doing children a favor by taking scissors to cut out pages of the best books. Charlotte called this putting literature in "snippet form." She felt children deserve to have more than just a nodding acquaintance with the best authors.

This chapter was written by Karen Andreola and Mary Pride, and is partly based on the following articles: *Parents' Review* 1923, "A Brief Account of the Life and Work of Charlotte Mason," by E.K. and *Parents' Review* 1910, "An Educational Union," by Mrs. Kirwain.

Karen Andreola

Karen Andreola is widely regarded as the world's foremost authority on Charlotte Mason education in the homeschool. She is the former publisher of *Parents' Review*, a newsletter dedicated to reviving the educational principles of Charlotte Mason. With her husband, Dean, she is the founder of Charlotte Mason Research & Supply Co., PO Box 758, Union, ME 04862, www.charlotte-mason.com.

What Drew Me to Charlotte Mason Education

by Karen Andreola

Living Books

One of the first things that impressed me about Charlotte was her method of using whole books and first-hand sources. . . . Textbooks compiled by a committee tend to be crammed with facts and information, at the expense of human emotion. This dryness is deadening to the imagination of the child. Miss Mason advocated what she called "living books." Whole books are living in a sense that they are written by a single author who shares his favorite subject with us and we pick up his enthusiasm. Textbooks written by one author might make this claim, too.

Narration

With living books a child gains knowledge through his own work, digging out facts and information. He then expresses what he has learned by clothing it in literary (conversational) language—in short, narrating it back to you.

Miss Mason believed that narration is the best way to acquire knowledge from books. Narration also provides opportunities for a child to form an opinion or make a judgment, no matter how crude. Because narration takes the place of questionnaires and multiple-choice tests, it enables the child to bring all the faculties of his mind into play. The child learns to call on the vocabulary and descriptive power of good writers as he tells his own version of the passage or chapter.

No Homework

Another attraction to Miss Mason's philosophy is that her schools never gave homework (under the age of 13). When a child follows her method there is no need for homework in the elementary years because the child immediately deals with the literature at hand and proves his mastery by narrating at the time of the reading.

Studies have proved homework to be less effective than this form of immediate feedback.

Instead of homework, my children enjoy an atmosphere of a cozy evening with a good book and parental attention.

No Grades—Short Lessons— Motivation of Lasting Value

Miss Mason was an idealist. Unlike some idealistic persons she worked out her scheme and saw it put into practice. She wanted children to be motivated by admiration, faith, and love instead of artificial stimulants such as prizes (stickers, candy, or money), competition, and grades.

Miss Mason managed to retain a child's curiosity and develop a love of knowledge in a child that he would carry on all through his life. The children took examinations where they narrated orally or on paper from "those lovely" books that they read that semester. Each child learned first to acquire the habit of attention by listening to and narrating short stories, and by accomplishing short lessons in the drills and skills. Short lessons discourage dawdling; they encourage the child to concentrate and make his best effort. Because the Charlotte Mason method employs whole books, narration, and short lessons, a child taught this way will try his best even though he will not be graded.

Free Afternoons

Bookish lessons in the Charlotte Mason scheme of things end at 1:00 P.M., or earlier if the children are quite young. High-school students will probably need some afternoon study time, but overall the afternoon is free for leisure. This is another aspect of her philosophy that so easily finds its way into the modern homeschool.

Leisure for children usually means running, climbing, yelling, and so forth—all out of doors. It has been observed that boys, particularly, cannot flourish without this opportunity. Handicrafts, practicing an instru-ment, chores, cooking, visiting lonely neighbors, observing and recording the wonders of nature may also be accomplished during this time.

Sadly, public-school children (young or old) must endure such long lessons and long hours that they are frequently tranquilized with drugs in order to pass through the system. They ride the bus home just in time to see the sun set and do homework.

Few Lectures

I was also drawn to Miss Mason's philosophy because it doesn't require me to give lectures. Charlotte pointed out that I need not be a certified teacher trained in the skill of giving lectures in order for my children to learn. This was a relief to me.

Through Charlotte's method, children gain the ability of educating themselves. Students do not depend upon notes they have taken from a teacher's lecture where most of the information has been predigested by the teacher. With Charlotte's superior method of narration from books, the carefully chosen words of an author are commented on by the child in essay form, either oral or written, starting at age 6 or 7. Too much explaining by the teacher can be a bore because, in actuality, the only true education is that of self-education.

Ideas and Culture

Inspiring children to love knowledge depends on how well ideas are presented to them. The mind feeds upon ideas. To quote Miss Mason, "Ideas must reach us directly from the mind of the thinker, and it is chiefly by the means of the books they have written that we get in touch with the best minds." This includes all forms of human expression. This is why Charlotte said the Bible and "varied human reading as well as the appreciation of the humanities (culture) is not a luxury, a tidbit, to be given to children now and then, but their very bread of life."

Charlotte's curriculum enabled children of all classes to experience books and culture in abundance when in Victorian days the arts and humanities seemed to belong only to the "well-to-do" classes.

Today, with so many pictures and art print books available, children can observe museum pieces and learn to recognize the works of dozens of artists over time just by changing what goes under the thumb tack once every two weeks or so. Our children can easily become familiar with the music of great composers by listening to cassettes and CDs, when years ago they would have needed to visit a concert hall. . . .

Education Is a Discipline

What Charlotte meant by "discipline," in Victorian-day terms, is that proper education inculcates good habits. The mother who takes pains to endow her children with good habits secures for herself smooth and orderly days. On the other hand, she who lets habits take care of themselves has a weary life of endless friction.

The mother needs to acquire her own habit of training her children so that, by and by, it is not troublesome to her, but a pleasure. She devotes herself to the formation of one habit in her children at a time, doing no more than watch over those already formed. Remember, to instill habits:

- Be consistent. It's dangerous to let things go "just this once."
- Forming a habit is using perseverance to work against a contrary habit.
- Formation is easier than reformation. Nip each weed in the bud!

Sane Education

If the above ideas sound as sane and sensible to you as they have to me, perhaps it is because Charlotte Mason hasn't been the only one sharing these "open secrets." Other voices in homeschooling are now sharing conclusions similar to those that Charlotte Mason advocated so many years ago. Many of us have come to similar conclusions about what goes into a well-brought-up person— "great minds think alike." Happily, many children are benefiting from a Charlotte Mason-style education in homeschools across the nation.

From the article "What Drew Me to Charlotte Mason Education," originally published in Practical Homeschooling *July/August 1996*

Miss Mason said that **asking children to narrate back what they have learned** is the best way to acquire knowledge from books. Because narration takes the place of questionnaires and multiple choice tests, it enables the child to bring all the faculties of mind into play. The child learns to call on the vocabulary and descriptive power of good writers as he tells his own version of the story.

Miss Mason's schools never gave homework? Correct. If you follow her method there is **no need for homework** in the elementary years.

Charlotte Mason believed in **introducing the child to the humanities while he is still young,** while he is forming his personality. In her view education is for the spiritual and intellectual benefit of the child, not just to provide the skills needed for making a living. Short goody-goody stories are shunned for whole books that follow the life of an admirable character. Morals are painted for the child, not pointed at the child.

Miss Mason wanted children to be **motivated by admiration, faith, and love** instead of what she felt to be "artificial stimulants," such as prizes, competition and grades. There were no grades in her elementary schools. No As, Bs, Cs, or Fs. No happy-face stickers or gold stars.

Lessons in the Charlotte Mason scheme of things end at 1:00 P.M., and **the afternoon is free for leisure.**

Homeschoolers following Charlotte's philosophy and method try to give their children **abundant portions of the humanities** at regular periods. They don't allow themselves to get stuck in a routine that emphasizes skills alone. *"Oh, we only had time for math drill, spelling, and grammar, and a few pages from our history textbook today. Tomorrow we will hopefully have time for poetry, and maybe a little music appreciation."* Charlotte Mason-style educators believe that when fear of a poor showing on the achievement test allows skills to take precedence, humanities take a back seat. The result: lessons become wearisome, children become fed up, mom gets burned out.

In the Charlotte Mason method, **lessons are kept short,** enabling children to develop the habit of attention and preventing the contrary habit of dawdling over lessons. *"Oh, you're not finished with your one math page yet? Well, then there is no time for a short romp in the backyard. Perhaps you can finish your math page in less than 15 minutes tomorrow."*

Curriculum Suitable for Use with the Charlotte Mason Method

At **AmblesideOnline.homestead. com** you can find "a free curriculum that uses the highest quality books and costs no more than the cost of texts. The curriculum uses as many free online books as possible, and there is no cost to use this information or join the support group." What I saw was a suggested booklist for each grade, plus weekly schedules of readings. They also had a good group of links to articles on Charlotte Mason education.

At this point, we have not yet seen any commercial elementary curriculum developed according to the Charlotte Mason Method. However, thousands of families are using this method by following the suggestions in the books at the end of this chapter.

At the high-school level, Far Above Rubies and Heart of Wisdom are two Charlotte Mason-style curricula.

How Narration Works

When I tell new homeschoolers about Victorian-era British educator Charlotte Mason's technique of having children narrate what they have read or studied instead of filling out endless workbook exercises, everyone asks the same question: "How do you do that?"

Here are some ways you can prompt your children to narrate what they have learned.

Charlotte's favorite—**"Tell me all you know about. . . ."**

- the habits of a shark.
- the landing of the Pilgrims.
- Heidi's visit to Peter's grandmother.

"Explain how . . ."

- a rose is pollinated.
- sedimentary rock is formed.
- Jesus healed the blind man.
- the U.S. Constitution came to be written.
- cheese is made.
- Robinson Crusoe settled on the lonely island.

"Describe our . . ."

- trip to the Oregon coast.
- nature walk.
- visit to the nursing home.
- planetarium experience.

"Tell about anything new you have just learned in this chapter."

"Tell the story (passage, episode) back in your own words."

"What four things have you learned about —— in this chapter?"

"Ask or write six questions covering the material of this chapter."

"Draw a picture, map, or likeness of —— ."

"What impressions have you on the life of (Abraham Lincoln, Queen Elizabeth I, Abigail Adams, William Tyndale, Frederick Banting [the inventor of insulin], Ebenezer Scrooge, Achilles, King Arthur, Black Beauty) in this chapter?"

—*Karen Andreola*

Charlotte didn't concern herself with **grammar lessons** until the children were well into the habit of narration. She thought it was more important that the child learn to express himself correctly. He should have daily opportunities to have an opinion, make a judgment, no matter how crude, develop a train of thought, and use his imagination. She felt that grammar lessons for first, second, and third grade children should not replace this free use of expression.

How It All Began

Charlotte Maria Shaw Mason was born on January 1, 1842. Her home was in Liverpool, where her father was a merchant. Just like her father and mother, she was an only child. When orphaned at the age of 16, her greatest desire was to help children. She decided to devote her whole life to them. After a short time training, and some experience in schools of various kinds and in a vocational college, she began to see a need for reform in the theory and practice of education. She told part of the story in the introduction of *Philosophy of Education*. In 1885, after 25 years' experience, she proposed these theories and methods in a series of lectures about training and educating children at home. In 1886 her book *Home Education* was published. Mothers wanting something better for their children eagerly accepted the advice in this book. Friends gathered around Charlotte, and they decided to start a society to advance these principles "for the children's sake." Parents wrote letters requesting further lectures, and in 1887 Charlotte Mason was invited to speak before the British Association, held that year at Owens College, Manchester.

Lots of Letters

In 1887 Charlotte held a meeting in the living room of Mrs. Francis Steinthal to discuss starting the Parents' National Educational Union (PNEU), for Miss Mason always made her first appeal to parents. A further meeting and much correspondence with the educational leaders of the day led to meeting in London, at which the Union was made official, with a council and an executive committee. Miss Mason continued to lecture, and in 1890, with the help of her friends, launched the *Parents' Review,* a monthly magazine for home training and culture. The magazine was supported entirely by donations. She also set up a free lending library of books chosen to help parents and teachers.

A Training Center in the Country

Then came the question of how to further advance Charlotte's work. Miss Mason had for some years spent her vacation time in the Lake District, and she came to realize that this would be an excellent dwelling place for the center of her work—a spot full of beauty and literary associations, "an unwalled university," as she once called it. She founded the House of Education here in 1891. In the same year she sent out the first complete curriculum program to help parents or governesses teach children at home. In 1892 she opened a college to train teachers. A mother's course gave mothers needed confidence to use her method in their homes. For a time Charlotte carried on her work from Ambleside, and she did much of the lecturing herself, but soon she needed an office in London from which the propaganda work of the Union could be carried out. The Union held an annual conference in various parts of England. Members of the Union began providing an ongoing series of free lectures to the public and formed support groups throughout the United Kingdom.

12 Quick Tips to Charlotte Mason Success
by Karen Andreola

1. Take courage and take the "real book plunge." The act of replacing a history, science, or literature textbook with the many fabulous real books available in homeschool catalogs may be an experience similar to that of jumping into cool water on a hot day. Once you are in, however, you are glad you had the courage because the water is wonderful.

2. Let your young children chatter. Charlotte Mason said that this was an amazing gift that every normal child is born with and that it should be taken advantage of in their education. Children of any age can start to narrate using an Aesop fable, for example. Over time a child's habit of narrating what he knows will carry over beautifully to his writing ability.

3. Pitch the worksheets. Develop the habit of narrating. Use it in place of so many worksheets.

4. Those who read twaddle may just as well twiddle their thumbs. Most children are bored by easy vocabulary found in "graded readers." Try reading aloud from a page or two of any well-written children's book. I recently finished reading aloud from the story *Ginger Pye* by Newbery medalist Eleanor Estes. In it we read that the dog named "Ginger was a *purposeful* dog. When he found something he "thoughtfully and *earnestly* breathed in the *essence* of Jerry until it *permeated* his *entire* being . . ." Are the words I put in italics third-grade vocabulary? fourth grade? fifth grade? sixth grade? I don't know. What I do know is that my eight-year-old son delighted in hearing it read aloud. He always looked forward to hearing the next chapter at bedtime. Listening to vocabulary in context like this is the best way to become familiar with new or strange words.

5. Make a nature notebook. It's a pity when children can name all the Star Wars characters but do not know the names of the birds, trees, flowers, and insects in their own neighborhood. My children's Nature Notebooks, filled with crayon drawings of the nature they have observed, are more precious than a pile of workbook pages could ever be.

6. Display at least six pictures of one artist's works over a period of a semester. This is all it takes for a student to become acquainted with some of the world's greatest works of art. Display six or more of Leonardo DaVinci, six of Jean Francois Millet, six of Michelangelo, or whomever you choose. Let the children look and look and look and then describe what they see.

7. Do the same for music. Just pop in a cassette of greatest hits of Mozart, Beethoven, Scott Joplin, or Gershwin. One composer at a time is suggested. Play that composer's music over and over again while you wash dishes, sweep the floor, ride in the car, draw, or give the little ones a bath. Music is the universal language, and classical music is another part of a cultural heritage we can pass on to our children.

8. Hooray for the strong-willed child! My prayer is that all my children will be strong-willed children, that they develop the will-power to do what is right, to choose to follow God's will and to do it with all their might. My job as a parent is to guide and inspire. I place in the curriculum stories that invite "hero admiration." The Bible, biography, and historical fiction can supply heroes with virtuous characters that children may choose to emulate.

9. Good habits need constant attention until they are formed. Faithfulness at a task involves consistency. To be consistent takes great effort until a habit is formed. Once a good habit is formed another can be added to the list of acquired attainments. And good habits can take the place of bad ones this way, too.

10. Keep lessons short in the early years of school so that a student can focus all his attention without being tempted to dawdle. Over time a habit of attention is formed that enables the students to do harder work without fretting.

11. Some 20 "habits of the good life" can be instilled in the lives of our children during their school years. A mother only needs to develop one habit in her children at a time, keeping watch over those already formed. Her homeschool days will go by more smoothly with some routine and good manners. Saying "thank you" and "please," sharing, taking turns, sitting up straight at the table, waiting patiently, and remembering daily prayer can become habit. Speaking the truth in love, using determination, and counting our blessings (to avoid self-pity and depression) are virtuous actions that do not need strenuous moral effort once they have become habit.

12. You don't have to be perfect. I'll admit to you that I was not brought up by way of Charlotte Mason's guiding principles of education. I was an "all right kid" so I got through the system of public school okay with slightly above-average grades. But I graduated without reading more than one or two real books. I acquired little knowledge of literature, poetry, great art, classical music, history or science.

When my own children were small I was desperately in need of the wisdom and confidence to homeschool my children. So I asked God's help and searched for His answer to my prayers. This was the answer. I would learn along with my children. I cannot say I've never had a down, insecure, or confused moment during my homeschool adventure. However, I can say that I am so glad I decided to homeschool 14 years ago. We've been learning a lot together. And I am grateful Charlotte Mason's guidance was made available to me.

A Curriculum

The Parents' Union School (a correspondence school) arranged first for home schoolrooms and later extended membership to private schools. Soon thousands of British children from six to eighteen around the world were receiving a generous education under the Union's auspices. The Parents' Union School sent out a timetable and fresh syllabus of work each term, and examination papers at the end of the term in which children wrote narrations about what they learned. The hours were short; the youngest class only took two and a half hours per day. The children took delight in the work, which was varied and interesting. The chosen books were of great literary value and worth keeping for a lifetime. There was no danger of "cramming." Students learned good habits (paying attention, doing their best without grades). Because their curiosity was protected, a love of learning carried them easily through their lessons. Through discipline, students gained wisdom and developed strength of character. Through the method of narration they learned to recall, reason, analyze, and finally evaluate what they read. The courses never used long lists of questions, true or false, multiple choice, fill in the blank, match the columns, and other sorts of "devices of the idle." Children were asked to tell, describe, and explain what they remembered from a book or an experience. The fee for a family of one or more children under ten was (in 1910) only one guinea a year, and two guineas for a child over ten (less than three to six dollars!). Much time was taken for activities like outdoor nature study, art and music appreciation, crafts, or an annual Shakespeare play for the older students.

In 1902 the Board of Education issued regulations enabling the head of any state school to use (with the approval of the local education authority) any method of teaching that seemed to benefit the children under his or her charge. Finally, Charlotte Mason's lifelong vision of "A Generous Education for All" had come true. In 1913, the state school started in Yorkshire (setting of the story *The Secret Garden*) became the first to use Charlotte's method. From that time onward examination papers came to Ambleside from children in every rank of life. Even poor children with illiterate parents in mining villages were learning to love knowledge and enjoy their "lovely books."

Retirement?

The Training College at The House of Education (nicknamed the House of the Holy Spirit) started with four students but very quickly increased to twenty-five. Here Miss Mason trained her students, speaking to them about her educational method, guiding her work in a small school in which the Parent's Union School's programs were carried out, and providing a quiet place for her students where for two years they might study nature and receive joy from simple life and high thinking. Everything needed for a generous education was shown in the college curriculum. As her prospectus said, "the aim of education presented to the students is to produce a human being at his best, physically, mentally, morally, and spiritually, quickened by religion and with some knowledge of nature, art, literature, and handicraft."

Miss Mason lived at The House of Education until her death. She not only remained in daily contact with the students and with the children in the practicing school, but also stayed in touch with the many thousands of children working in home schoolrooms all over the world. She passed away in 1923, still in active work at the age of 81. She left her students

Covering the Basics the Charlotte Mason Way

by Karen Andreola

From what Charlotte Mason wrote in her book *Home Education,* first published in England in the 1880's, I can give you a peek at how Charlotte taught children the basics—those fundamental areas of learning. Perhaps these few paragraphs will welcome you to explore her words further.

General Knowledge—Most of a child's knowledge will come from books. A very young student cannot read much for himself, so it must be read aloud to him. It used to be thought that the chief function of a teacher was to explain; with Charlotte Mason's emphasis it would be to read. She said a teacher's chief function is to distinguish information from knowledge.

If a child can put what he is learning in his own words, he has proved he is knowledgeable. The child who has only information can only fill in the blanks in the stereotyped phrases of his test-book.

To narrate is to know. Narration, retelling reading in one's own words, can be called "the art of knowing." But a child often finds it awkward to narrate from a dry, factual textbook. This is one reason real books on a variety of subjects are better to be used in acquiring knowledge.

An author of a real book is a person who decided to write on what strongly interested him. He shares his favorite subject, and any personal experience of it, with us. The writing is often touched with human emotion. And as we read, we pick up his enthusiasm for his subject.

Reading—Where there are no lovely little sentences there can be no reading.

"Lessons in word-making help the young student take intelligent interest in *words;* but his progress in the art of reading depends chiefly on the 'reading by sight' lessons. [Some of you may be gasping at this, but I successfully taught my children to read this way and they all *loved* learning to read. You start by teaching the sounds of the letters, and then . . .] The teacher must be content to proceed very slowly, reviewing as she goes. Say—

Twinkle, twinkle, little star,
How I wonder what you are,

is the first lesson . . . . Read the passage for the child, very slowly and sweetly. Point to each word as you read. Then point to *twinkle, wonder, star, what,* and expect the child to pronounce (sound-out) each word in the verse taken randomly; then, when he shows that he knows each word by itself, and not before, let him *read* the two lines with clear enunciation and expression. If these lines are written in a good size on paper, the words may be cut out to allow the child to piece them together. The cards can be kept for review.

"In this way the child accumulates a little capital; he knows eight or ten words so well that he will recognize them anywhere, and the lesson has occupied probably ten minutes. Lines can be taken from short tales, fables or poems. 'But what a snail's progress!' you are inclined to say. Not so slow, after all: a child will thus learn, without appreciable labour, from two to three thousand words in the course of a year . . . The master of this number of words will carry him with comfort through most of the books that fall in his way."

Some teachers keep their young students "in phonics" for a long, long time before anything interesting is given to them to *read.* "I should never put him into words of one syllable at all. The bigger the word, the more striking the look of it, and therefore, the easier it is to read, provided always that the idea it conveys is interesting to a child."

It is sad to see an intelligent child toiling over a reading lesson infinitely below his capacity—*ath, eth, ith, oth, uth*—or, at the very best, "The cat sat on the mat." "He ate cool noodles at noon with a spoon" is silly. How about: "He ate red lasagna at noon with spoon." This is reading, not just "sounding-out."

Reading lessons should not be twaddle.

Writing—Penmanship is a skill acquired by daily short lessons. After a child is somewhat fluent in it he can go on to gradually fill up his "copy book" with verse and prose that he has chosen. The old-fashioned black-and-white composition books are perfect for this activity. When a child narrates, a parent can take dictation. The child can then copy the dictation (or parts of it if it's a long one) into his copy book. He can tell about his trip to a museum, or tell back an Aesop fable, or tell about anything he is learning. These little narrations can be written in his copy book. Pictures and maps can be drawn and photographs added.

After a child is familiar with narrating orally, he can then begin written narration. This more independent skill should be started no younger than age ten. Instead of "telling aloud" he can "tell" on paper while the teacher makes herself available to any younger students. The teacher may assign a "narration question" such as, "Give a description of Columbus' first voyage to the new world," or "Tell how a honey bee makes honey," or "What four things did you learn from this chapter?" The student need not be overly concerned with spelling in his rough draft but should write freely. The following day attention can be given to the finer points of his writing. Through the regular use of oral narration a student's power to "tell" naturally carries over to his writing.

His written narration is his composition or essay.

Mathematics—Charlotte's book *Home Education* teaches us to begin teaching numbers through the evidence of the senses. Sets or groups of objects such as apples, beans, Lego bricks, buttons, or shells can be arranged in such a way to show addition, subtraction, multiplication, division or fractions.

But true mathematics is when a child begins to *think* in numbers and not in objects. At this point, the illustration should not occupy a more prominent place than the concept being illustrated.

For mathematics, "nothing can be more delightful than the careful analysis of numbers and the beautiful graduation of the work, only one difficulty at a time being presented the mind." The most delightful little word problems are those that have been invented by writers in sympathy with children.

Science—A young child strengthens his powers of observation in his young years by acting as a naturalist. Many children will be able to tell you the names of all the Star Wars characters, but do they know the names of the living things in their own backyards? To lie on his stomach beside a busy ant hill, to lie on his back to follow the drifting clouds, to dig in the soil for earthworms, to stare at a bumble bee, to take note of what time of day the petals of flowers open and close and to recognize their fragrance, to collect fallen leaves, acorns and seeds—these things and more can all be part of a child's "school."

When he is a little older, he can create his own nature notebook, filling it with drawings of his observations and a written record of his findings. These personal notebooks are priceless to their owners because they represent time spent in the glorious outdoors. Glorious it is because nature is one way in which God reveals himself to us. Poems and verses of hymns exclaiming the beauty and wonder of nature can be copied into these nature notebooks.

In a day and age when there is much concern for a child's attention span, the powers of attention and observation gained in the young years through nature study are valuable powers to be used later in any other of the higher sciences (filling out lab reports, etc.).

House Mouse

Wild Strawberry (Fragara Vesca)

April 26 I was glad we hadn't cut the grass yet because I found so many delicate flowering weeds and wild flowers. The girls came running to me calling, "Can we eat these?" They discovered an expansive patch of wild strawberries surrounding the oak tree.

April 29 There was a down pour of rain. I was about to close the sliding glass door when a scurrying creature caught my eye. A gray mouse hid in the dry spot behind the drain pipe. With a loud whisper I waved the girls over. We stood staring. "It's the mouse from Peter Rat," giggled one sister. "No," argued the younger sister. "There's no large pea in its mouth."

Karen Andreola

Pages From My Nature Diary-1989-Tennessee

March 30 Sophia and Yolanda spotted Wild Violets beside the driveway in the shadowy woods.

April 19 My son Nigel was born. The Red Bud trees were in full bloom.

April 22 The girls waded in the creek as the baby and I laid on a quilt. I made the girls wear their bonnets to keep the ticks out of their hair, and their old sneakers to keep the leaches off their toes. Sophia excitedly caught little crayfish with a pet store fish net. Yolanda piled up smooth stones from the creek bottom. Above our heads, high in the blue sky, a hawk circled. I wondered if it had its eye on my baby.

Wild Violet (Viola adunce)

Crayfish

History—Charlotte Mason strongly believed in focusing on the *story* part of history while children are developing their wonderful powers of imagination. Myths and legends have a place, too. This appeal to the imagination in history gives emphasis to its literary side.

According to Charlotte, no history should be read to young children unless it is in literary language. She dwelled on the pleasure derived from a study of former ages—the culture and refinement it affords, the enjoyment and mental profit that is gained through narrating it. She wrote that it is a fatal mistake to think young children must learn "outlines" or overviews of the whole of history of Rome or England [or America]. Isn't this what many history books do by including mostly names, and dates, and events with very little story aspect in between? Instead, Charlotte asserted,

"Let [the child] on the contrary, linger pleasantly over the history of a single man, a short period, until he thinks the thoughts of the man, is at home in the ways of that period. Though he is reading and thinking of the lifetime of a single man, he is really getting intimately acquainted with the history of a whole nation of a whole age. . . . Let him know the great people and the common people, the ways of the court and of the crowd. Let him know what other nations were doing while we at home were doing thus and thus."

Books that are biographical in nature provide examples for imitation as well as for warning. The deeds of heroes give us the opportunity to admire and form higher ideals.

If you venture to implement Charlotte's ideas in mid-stream, expect a period of transition. Take patience. You will start to recognize little accomplishments, and then bigger ones. Believe in God, believe in your children (and their natural-born curiosity), believe in Charlotte's principles for a gentle art of learning, and you will find joy.

Passages in this article have been taken and used with permission from the new book, A Charlotte Mason Companion—Personal Reflections on the Gentle Art of Learning *by Karen Andreola. All passages in quotes have been taken from Charlotte Mason's Original Homeschooling Series.*

with work so full of life from her principles that it has continued to be passed down from person to person since her death.

Times Changed

The training given in the House of Education was so famous that, at one time, it was impossible for them to supply the demand for governesses and teachers. However, over the years, especially after the Second World War, governesses and nannies and home-taught children were fast becoming a thing of the past. Parents sent their children to more competitive schools, and then the government sanctioned a national curriculum. Today, there are little more than a handful of PNEU schools left. Of these, some have strayed from the original intent and style of the program.

However, homeschoolers today have rediscovered Charlotte in a big way! Today's Charlotte Mason movement in home education traces its roots to the publication of Susan Schaeffer Macaulay's *For the Children's Sake*. Mrs. Macaulay had discovered Charlotte's works while living with her family at the L'Abri mission in England. Her book stirred in many the desire to try this warmhearted and wise-headed form of education, and led ultimately to others making the effort to republish Charlotte's original works.

Charlotte Mason Materials

The slipcased six-volume **Original Charlotte Mason series** is the only series of how-to-teach books I know about that comes endorsed by Her Majesty Queen Elizabeth of England!

Charlotte Mason understood the need to respect the child while not worshipping him. She stressed the importance of the "fallow" first six years of life, when according to her, children ought to spend much time out-of-doors playing and observing nature. Among her other contributions: geography taught the way adults like to learn it, through the medium of interesting travel stories; history centered around interesting people and their environments rather than as a list of dates to memorize; the importance of beauty in the child's life and the value of living with great art (in the form of inexpensive art prints); and how to train children in the habit of perfect obedience. This is only the tip of the iceberg, as Miss Mason had many fascinating things to say, all based on her personal experience of decades of teaching.

Having heard of Charlotte Mason, I went years ago in search of her books, only to find that they were not available anywhere, even in the entire St. Louis library system! Dean and Karen Andreola have solved this problem for us. While visiting England, they tracked down the books in the library of Charlotte Mason College and got an American publisher to put out this very nice facsimile edition of six Charlotte Mason books. The series includes *Home Education, Parents and Children, School Education, Ourselves, Formation of Character*, and *A Philosophy of Education*. All are easy reading—remember, British *parents* were inspired by these books!

After you've read *For the Children's Sake*, **A Charlotte Mason Companion** should be the next book on your Charlotte Mason reading list. In its 384 pages, Karen Andreola, the world's foremost expert on Charlotte Mason homeschooling (and a *Practical Homeschooling* columnist for several years!), has distilled, amplified, explained, and illustrated Charlotte's methods for today. Even if you've read—and reread—all six volumes of the Original Charlotte Mason series, you're sure to find much to treasure in this book's 49 chapters.

The Original Charlotte Mason series
Parents. $58.95.
Charlotte Mason Research & Supply, www.charlotte-mason.com.

Charlotte Mason Companion
Parents. $18.99.
Charlotte Mason Research & Supply, www.charlotte-mason.com.

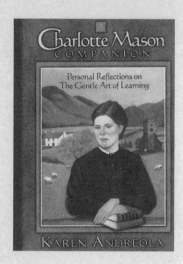

After years of editing her own Charlotte Mason method magazine, the *Parents' Review*, Karen knows the questions parents face when they try to re-arrange their thinking and lives to fit this new way of living and learning. Where Charlotte's own writings scatter nuggets here and there, Karen has collected these insights together, rephrased them in more understandable language, and added numerous examples from her own experience and that of other Charlotte Mason families. Whether you want to understand more about how to train a child's will, how and why to use narration instead of written reports, what to do when a child doesn't want to narrate or does poor narrations, how to teach composition and grammar, why and how to study Greek mythology, the right and wrong way to handle picture study, or any of the other special features of Charlotte Mason education, *A Charlotte Mason Companion* will gently and thoroughly lead you like a good friend.

Unlike some other authors, Karen is not just *organizing* Charlotte's thoughts for us, but *explaining* and *applying* them, with many real-life illustrations.

I personally must admit that *A Charlotte Mason Companion* has clarified many things for me that I found obscure in Charlotte's books. But above all, you will enjoy the book's gentle, loving spirit. It's truly, as it is subtitled, "Personal Reflections on the Gentle Art of Learning." Highly recommended.

Charlotte Mason Study Guide

Parents. $10.95.
Penny Gardner, UT.
members.aol.com/CMSGpenny.

In her **Charlotte Mason Study Guide: A Simplified Approach to a "Living" Education**, Penny Gardner has organized Miss Mason's ideas topically. The first of the 20 chapters (or "study topics") of this 166-page book is, appropriately, a study of Charlotte Mason herself. Following topics include Discipline, Geography, Nature Study, Narration, and more on philosophies, goals, and methods of education. Each study topic has brief quotes from the six-volume series, refer-enced for those who want to read further.

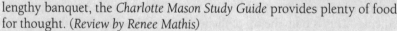

Penny Gardner weaves in just enough addition-al comments to be helpful and practical without detracting from the central focus of the book. Either as a tasty tidbit or the first course of a lengthy banquet, the *Charlotte Mason Study Guide* provides plenty of food for thought. (*Review by Renee Mathis*)

For the Children's Sake

Parents. $12.99.
Crossway Books, IL. (800) 635-7993,
www.goodnews.gospelcom.net.

For the Children's Sake: Foundations of Education for Home and School is not a "how to" book as much as a beautiful "why to" and "in what manner."

I have never read a book that was more full of joy. Addressing the relationship of Christianity and education, Susan Macaulay shares with us the in-sights of Charlotte Mason, a teacher extraordinaire from the last century. The sweeping freedom that a child raised God's way can know, and the depth of beauty he or she can enjoy, shines through on every page. The author includes many of her per-sonal experiences as a homeschooled child and the experiences of her own family as they searched for appropriate education for their children.

A historical note: This is the book that got Dean and Karen Andreola in-terested in Charlotte Mason's works, which led to Charlotte's books being reprinted, which led to "Charlotte Mason education" becoming one of the main homeschool methods! This is one powerful book.

CHAPTER 24

Classical Education & Great Books

In this chapter you'll learn about classical education from some of its main proponents:

- **Fritz Hinrichs** is the founder of Escondido Tutorial Service and a pioneer of classical education via the Internet in the homeschool community. He is a graduate of St. John's College in Annapolis, MD, which is based on the classical model, and of Westminster Seminary, in Escondido, California.
- **Andrew Kern** is the founder of the CiRCE Institute, a research and consulting service for classical educators, and the coauthor of *Classical Education: The Movement Sweeping America*. He is a homeschooling father of five children.
- **Douglas Wilson** is a founder of Logos School in Moscow, Idaho, one of the first modern American day schools founded on classical learning principles. To promote these principles he has written *Recovering the Lost Tools of Learning* (Crossway Books, 1991), as well as texts on introductory logic and Latin grammar. A prolific author with many other books in print, Douglas edits the monthly magazine *Credenda/Agenda* and is the father of three teenage children.

Fritz Hinrichs on Why Classical Education Is Undergoing a Revival

Most anyone familiar with history has come to the humbling realization that even our sharpest minds do not match the mental capabilities possessed by the shining lights of history. Many have found that the writings of our own nation's founding fathers show an eloquence and depth of thought that put us to shame. In the past, homeschoolers have desired to simply return to a wholesome "back to the basics" type of education—something like that had by Laura Ingalls Wilder. Today, many homeschoolers want to know how to raise an orator such as Patrick Henry or a man of the political insight and principle of George Washington. Increasingly, homeschoolers have been turning to classical Christian education for answers to these questions. Classical Christian education attempts to glean

Curriculum Based on the Principles of Classical Education

- Classical Free Academy (online)
- Escondido Tutorial Service (online)
- Kolbe Academy (correspondence)
- Scholars Online Academy (online)

Curriculum with Some Classical Elements

- Calvert School (correspondence; combines classical principles and texts with modern educational theory and texts)
- Covenant Home Curriculum (correspondence; combines classical principles and texts with some modern texts)
- Seton Home Study School (correspondence; upper grades are somewhat classical in content)
- Our Lady of Victory (correspondence; upper grades are optionally classical in content)

"Great Books" Curriculum

- Great Books Academy (correspondence)

Christian Classical Education

by Douglas Wilson

Pagan Classicism

When people talk about classical education, they often are thinking of the classical world of ancient Greece and Rome, with special emphasis placed upon the "golden eras" of Athens under Pericles or Rome under Augustus.

While the art and literature produced in classical antiquity has great value and we ought to study it, Christians face one problem in using classical antiquity as the central point of reference in understanding classicism. The problem is, of course, the *paganism*. Many Christian parents rightly have a problem with an education that prominently features the gods and goddesses of the ancient world, pagan myths and heroes, etc. As a Christian classicist, I am not calling for a return to the paganism of the ancient world, or any attempt to revive a "kinder, gentler" paganism, as was partially seen in the Renaissance.

Mixed Classicism

The second type of classical education is a compromise, so it is sometimes harder to see the problems it brings. Here we see the basic ideas, categories, and concepts of classical antiquity combined in assorted ways with Christian theology and terminology.

Obviously, given the nature of biblical truth, it is the integrity of Christian theology which suffers in the mix. An example of this would be Thomas Aquinas' attempt to combine the philosophy of Aristotle with the theology of Christianity, resulting in a theology called Thomism. In the field of education, a recent example of this would be the educational theory of Mortimer Adler, which is unabashedly Aristotelian. In his book *Reforming Education*, Dr. Adler makes the statement that the liberal arts are neither *pagan* or *Christian*, but rather *human*. This elevates the liberal arts into a religion of their own, midway between Christianity and paganism, and superior to both. Any consistent Christian educator must obviously reject Dr. Adler's statement, along with the worldview behind it.

Christian Classicism

The third type of classical education—*biblical* classical education—is what we are looking for. It attempts to provide a timeless introduction to knowledge, based not on the insights of great thinkers but on the Bible. Once the student's presuppositions have been formed and instructed by Bible study, he is then set free to consider the breadth and depth of human achievement—for example, what some call the "Great Books." The difference is that the student is trained to evaluate human insights by the yardstick of the Bible's teaching, not vice versa.

The classically trained Christian student doesn't have to hide from history. Without worshipping the past, he knows he can—and must—learn from it. In fact, without these studies in history, literature, rhetoric, and theology he will become a slave of the passing popular opinions of our day, incapable of leading others back to the timeless ways of God.

Modern Protestant educators, unhappily, have often tended to ignore the past. Many evangelicals mistakenly assume, for example, that to appreciate Latin you must be a Roman Catholic traditionalist. This indicates just how much of our Western heritage we have lost—and must recover. The Latin language is not the exclusive language of Catholics; it is the language of the West. John Calvin and Martin Luther wrote many works in Latin!

Because we have failed to educate our children properly, we have lost touch with our own Founding Fathers—the everyday Christians and church leaders of the past. While our culture has made much technological progress, in the liberal arts our culture is almost completely at sea. We have forgotten our heritage.

Our model for understanding culture—art, literature, history, etc.—will be the apostle Paul, who was the first biblical classicist. Thoroughly trained in classical languages, literature, and philosophy, he consistently refused to trim God's message to fit the classical pagan mold. Yet Paul was never a "fundamentalist know-nothing." We must remember that Paul demonstrated in his writings a thorough knowledge and use of classical culture. He knew classical poets (Acts 17:28), classical playwrights (Acts 26:14), the language (Acts 21:37), classical philosophy (1 Timothy 6:10), and so on. But as a consistent Christian, his intention in all of this was no secret—to bring every thought captive to the risen Christ.

What better time could we find for bringing our children to love and serve Christ than the time we spend teaching them? But because a large part of this work has been done before, it would be foolish to undertake the work "from scratch." Others have gone before us and already thought through how to accomplish these tasks. Is it not better to learn from almost 2,000 years of Christian civilizations—and learn to avoid copying the mistakes of the pagan civilizations—than to try to reinvent the wheel?

What's the Difference?

	"Modern"	Classical
Phonics	Emphasizes "creative" interaction with words—look/say & whole language.	Emphasizes a thorough mastery of the units of sound.
Reading	If literate, the student progresses to basal readers.	When literate, the student begins reading great books.
Maths	Emphasizes trying to get the student to understand the *concept*. Discourages rote learning of tables, rules, etc.	Emphasizes mastery of tables, rules, etc. as well as repetitive drills to make certain math processes *habitual*.
Bible	Bible? Are you crazy? Bible?	Emphasizes systematic Bible reading as soon as the students are literate.
Spelling	Concentrates on avoiding rules. The focus is to foster creativity and maintain the student's self-esteem.	Concentrates on being prescriptive, rule-guided, autocratic, unforgiving, unyielding, rigid, puritanical, dictatorial, and harsh.
History	Debunks or ignores the achievements of western civilization. Uses history as a tool to support the ideological agenda currently in vogue.	Emphasizes the fact that history is under the providential hand of God and that it therefore has a purpose. Holds that our heritage should be understood, and, unless at variance with Scripture, *appreciated*.
Rhetoric & Speech	As with many subjects, stresses "creativity" and self-expression, resulting in a stream of consciousness approach as opposed to the more rigorous discipline of wordsmithing.	The point is to teach the student to recognize the structure of available means of persuasion, and avail himself of them.
Political Science	One of the largest liberal political organizations in the US is the NEA. The students are the NEA auxiliary. Their grasp of politics is limited therefore to whatever the current "issues of the month" may be.	The emphasis is on the history of constitutionalism and the application to current events.
Thinking Skills & Logic	Concentrates on getting the student to express an opinion, along with whatever reasons he may have for holding it. The key is self-expression.	Emphasizes the difference between truth and validity. Teaches the student to identify fallacies of form and distraction.
Languages	Modern foreign languages are not required for the non-native speaker. They are present, however, because a zeal for "multiculturalism" and "diversity" insists that non-English speakers shouldn't have to learn a foreign language either.	Foreign languages are taught to those who are not native speakers as a form of intellectual discipline, which has certain practical side-benefits.
Latin	Once fairly common in the government schools, Latin is now virtually extinct and is viewed as a monstrous irrelevance.	Latin is seen as a foundation for precise thinking, English vocabulary study, appreciation of classical and English literature, study of the Romance languages, and, of course, *et cetera*.
Literature	The purpose is to bring books down to the level of the contemporary student—books that will not overwhelm a limited vocabulary, limited fluency, cultural isolation, and reluctance to read anything unfamiliar.	The object here is to bring the student up to the level of great and classical literature and to teach appreciation of challenging books from all ages.

Top Ten Tips for Classical Education

by Marlin Detweiler, founder of Veritas Press

10 Don't believe everything is "classical" that says it is. A book or resource may be "classic," i.e., trusted by many people for a notable length of time, without being "classical"—part of the enduring tradition of centuries past.

9 Hard work is good.

8 Children are far more capable of hard work—and understanding—than we give them credit for today.

7 If you want your children to love learning, make sure they see your excitement when you learn something new. Emulate Archimedes in all but your choice of clothing.

6 A complete classical education won't happen in three hours a day.

5 Latin isn't really a dead language. And it didn't kill the ancient Romans, either.

4 Reading *Recovering the Lost Tools of Learning* is a must.

3 Books . . . good. Internet . . . good and bad. TV . . . bad.

2 When we talk about classical literature for your eighth grader, don't confuse the Boxcar Children and Nancy Drew with *The Epic of Gilgamesh* and Plato's *Republic*. Even Coke can be "Classic" without being classical.

1 Learning to distinguish between good and evil is only the first step. Learning to love the good is better. Learning to do the good is the whole point.

Digging Deeper

For more information on the use of the trivium in a classical curriculum, Fritz invites you to peruse his Web page—**www.gbt.org**. You might also be interested in obtaining a copy of Dorothy Sayers' "Lost Tools of Learning" essay. This may be found as an appendix or section in many of the books reviewed in this chapter, or in her book *Are Women Human?* which can be ordered through your local bookstore or online through major distributors.

Stages of the Trivium

A child begins a classical education by proceeding through the three stages of the trivium—*grammar*, *dialectic*, and *rhetoric*. Each of these stages is perfectly suited to a child's learning development. The *grammar* stage is appropriate for young children as it focuses on the memorization of facts. Young children are very quick at picking up facts, even though they are not yet capable of logically analyzing their significance. As children grow older, they gradually become aware of the logical relationship between facts and the potential for logical contradiction to arise. At this time, children can move into the *dialectical* period. During the dialectical period, children are taught logic in order to hone their developing natural abilities and equip them to analyze the information they have accumulated. After becoming proficient in logic a child moves into the *rhetoric* period and learns to present what he has learned in a manner that is not only logical, but also aesthetically pleasing and persuasive.

—*Fritz Hinrichs*

from the experience and wisdom found in the past in order to understand why our own contemporary attempts at education seem to fall so short.

Douglas Wilson on What Is Classical Education?

Classical learning is called "classical" because future leaders have been trained in its methods for centuries. In fact, some parts of the classical curriculum have been around for millennia.

Classical learning follows a particular pattern called the **trivium**—which consists of grammar, dialectic, and rhetoric. The students learn the **grammar** of each subject (that subject's "particulars"). They then learn **dialectic**, or the relationships of these particulars to one another, and then go on to learn **rhetoric**. That is, they learn how to express what they have gained in an effective and coherent fashion. The purpose of following this pattern is not to teach the student everything there is to know, but rather to establish in the student a habit of mind which instinctively knows how to learn new material when the formal schooling process is only a faint memory. The student is not so much taught *what* to think, he is shown *how* to think.

As Dorothy Sayers, author of the "Lord Wimsey" mysteries and a friend of C.S. Lewis and J.R.R. Tolkien, points out in her famous essay, "The Lost Tools of Learning," the three stages of the trivium match **the developmental stages of growing children** quite nicely. The very great value of this method is that it provides a rigorous education suited to basic human nature and tested over centuries, rather than one developed from the theories of educational faddists.

Another significant part of the value of classical instruction is that it teaches students the rigors of **logical analysis.** Our society abounds in bunkum; we desperately need to train people to recognize it so that someone might take it away. In short, we need more epistemological garbage men. This requires training in logic and the apologetics of Christian worldview thinking. Classical education supplies this in a way not seen elsewhere.

Third, the student learns that **our culture and civilization is an outgrowth of the classical, medieval, and reformation world**. Modern students must learn that our culture was not purchased for them by their parents at the mall. As C.S. Lewis pointed out, by reading old books the student is protected against some of the sillier mistakes of modernity.

Fritz Hinrichs on How Classical Education Is Different

Classical education differs from most educational philosophies in that it attempts to step back from the parade of educational theories that seem to keep us in a state of continual bewilderment and asks,

- "What was education like in the past?"
- "What books were used?"
- "What goals were thought important?"

Dorothy Sayers, in her well-known essay "The Lost Tools of Learning," attempted to answer these questions and in so doing gave us some very sage advice for education in our own day. She began by investigating the medieval model of education and found that it was composed of two parts: the first was called the Trivium and the second, the Quadrivium.

The Trivium contained three areas: Grammar, Dialectic, and Rhetoric. Each of these three areas were specifically suited to one of the stages in a child's mental development.

The Grammar Period. During his early years, a child studies the Grammar portion of the Trivium. The Grammar period (ages 9–11) includes learning a language—preferably an ancient language, such as Latin or Greek— that will require the child to spend a great deal of time learning and memorizing its grammatical structure.

During their younger years, children possess a great natural ability to memorize large amounts of material, even though they may not understand its significance. This is the time to fill them full of facts, such as the multiplication table, geography, dates, events, plant and animal classifications: anything that lends itself to easy repetition and assimilation by the mind.

The Dialectic Period. During the second period, the Dialectic period (ages 12–14), the child begins to understand that which he has learned and begins to use his reason to ask questions based on the information that he has gathered in the grammar stage.

The Rhetoric Period. The third period Sayers mentions is that of Rhetoric (ages 14–16). During this period the child moves from merely grasping the logical sequence of arguments to learning how to present them in an persuasive, aesthetically pleasing form.

Fritz Hinrichs on Learning to Learn

In modern education, we have put the proverbial cart before the horse by expecting students to master a great number of subjects before they have mastered the tools of learning. Even though the study of language and logic may seem dull in themselves, they are the tools that one needs to develop to be able to approach the task of mastering any particular subject whether it be Scottish political history or carburetor maintenance. Sayers ends her essay with this line: "The sole true end of education is simply this; to teach men how to learn for themselves; and whatever instruction fails to do this is effort spent in vain."

"Learning to learn for oneself" certainly well summarizes the pedagogical goal of classical education. However, once you can learn on your own, where do you go from there?

Fritz Hinrichs on Great Books of the Western World

Another educational truism is helpful: "Education is merely selling someone on books." To this end we must ask, "Which books are worthy teachers?" The answer to this question usually lies in what we are attempting to learn. If we merely ask in general "Which are the truly great books?" we find there is actually a fairly broad agreement on the answer to this question. Throughout history, certain books have generally come to be viewed as central to the development of Western culture and have had an unusually large impact due to the profundity and eloquence with which they have expressed their ideas. These books form the core of the Western intellectual tradition. The ideas contained in them have formed the saga that we know as Western History.

Anyone who has grown up in the West—by which I mean Greece, Rome, Israel, and the cultures descended from them, which include America, the British Commonwealth nations, and Western Europe—and desires to understand the cultural milieu in which they have been raised, should read these books.

Andrew Kern on the Modern Classical Movement

The war for the soul of America, contested in the realm of educational theory, was fought fiercely around the time of World War I. The progressives,

For more information on classical education:

- The Association of Classical and Christian Schools. One hundred schools and some homeschool groups are associated with ACCS. www.accsedu.org.
- The Canon Press catalog (1-800-488-2034, www.canonpress.org) carries most of the resources below, plus classical education resources such as elementary Latin and formal logic courses.
- *The Abolition of Man*, C.S. Lewis (New York: Macmillan, 1947). A classically trained mind examines modern education. The book is readily available in Christian bookstores.
- *Classical Education and the Home School*, Douglas Jones & Douglas Wilson. This short booklet outlines the basic features of a classical education and shows what parents should do if they want to provide this kind of education for their children at home. Now available free in Adobe Acrobat format on the Canon Press website given above.
- *On Christian Doctrine* (Book IV), Augustine. This can best be found in volume 18 of the "Great Books" series. A good library should have it.
- *On Secular Education*, R.L. Dabney. A critique of the government school system, which was in its infancy when Dabney wrote. From Canon Press.
- *Recovering the Lost Tools of Learning* by Douglas Wilson. This book contains as an appendix Dorothy Sayers' seminal essay, "The Lost Tools of Learning." From Canon Press.
- *Repairing the Ruins*, a collection of 14 tapes from the first conference of the Association of Classical and Christian Schools. $50. From Canon Press. Also collected as a book; see review at the end of this chapter.
- The Veritas Press catalog, (800) 922-5082, www.veritaspress.com.

What About Mythology?

by Rob & Cyndy Shearer

- Should Christians teach their children about Zeus?
- Should they know who Wodin, Loki, and Thor are?
- Would our children benefit by knowing anything about Heqet, the Egyptian goddess of birth? (Hint: She was usually depicted with the head of a frog.)

We are strong proponents of teaching more than just American history to our children. In fact, we advocate beginning with the Old Testament (as history) and teaching our children about western civilization in sequence, moving through ancient Egypt, ancient Greece, ancient Rome, the Middle Ages, the Renaissance, the Reformation, Explorers, etc. so that our children understand both the context and logical development of our culture.

There are a number of sound reasons for doing this. But attempting it does confront one with a different set of problems. If you begin with the cultures of Egypt, Greece, and Rome, you will immediately have to make some decisions about how you will (or won't) cover the topics of evolution and mythology with your students.

The "mythology" issue is one we have thought a lot about. Christian parents have legitimate concerns about teaching mythology. We don't want to teach falsehoods to our children, or lead them to confuse falsehoods with the truth; and we don't want to encourage any fascination with or inappropriate attention to the occult.

Having said that, we think that the study of mythology (Greek, Roman, Egyptian, and Norse) is still appropriate and profitable for our children when set in the proper Christian context for three reasons:

- It inoculates them against false religion.
- It gives them a deeper understanding of Greek and Roman culture (and Egyptian and European).
- And it builds a foundation for them to understand the great literature of western civilization.

What the Bible Says About the History of Religion

The key phrase in the paragraph above is "the proper Christian context." Whenever we approach the topic of mythology, we introduce it by reviewing with our children what God has to say about the history of religion.

Modern man spins a tale about primitive man beginning by worshipping anything and everything: trees, rocks, thunder, streams, grasshoppers, etc. Then (the wisdom/foolishness of the moderns speculates), man "progressed" to worshipping only a few specific deities. Then, as he began to walk completely upright, he moved from many gods to monotheism, the worship of only one god. The last step in this sequence you won't find spelled

---

What the Puritans Thought About Greek & Roman Myths

Tubal-cain, whom (as the learned conceive, and the agreement of the name and function makes probable) the heathens worshipped by the name of Vulcan, the god of smiths; and his sister Naamah, by the name of Venus. He first taught men how to make arms, and other instruments of iron. Naamah; so called from her beauty, which her name signifies.—Matthew Poole, Commentary on the Holy Bible, *commenting on Genesis 4:11*

Jabal was their Pan and Jubal their Apollo. Tubal Cain was a famous smith, who greatly improved the art of working in brass and iron, for the service both of war and husbandry. He was their Vulcan.—Matthew Henry's Commentary, *commenting on Genesis 4:11*

The Puritans believed the Greek myths were "tall tales," based on ancestor worship and a few notable exploits of living men, which were later magnified into tales of godlike prowess, with a few nature myths thrown in for good measure.

Whereas other cultures based their myths upon literal "doctrines of demons"—stories relayed to them by unclean supernatural messengers (as per the Aztecs and Babylonians)—the Greeks, and after them the Romans, seemed to have been content with "gods" who were just larger-than-life-sized human heroes.

By the time of Jesus many Greeks had come to look upon their myths the same way we look at our own American larger-than-life-sized heroes, Paul Bunyan and Pecos Bill. The myths were good stories that might include some character lessons, but they should not be taken seriously. That's how the Puritans considered them, and how we should consider them today.—*Mary Pride*

out explicitly, but it is the logical completion of the "evolution of religion": the step from monotheism to atheism, the worship of no god.

This progression, from many to few to one to none, is not found in Scripture anywhere. Beware of authors who present this as the way man's religions developed!

What the Bible says about the "development" of religion is quite different:

For the invisible things of him from the creation of the world are clearly seen, being understood by the things that are made, even his eternal power and Godhead; so that they are without excuse: Because that, when they knew God, they glorified him not as God, neither were thankful; but became vain in their imaginations, and their foolish heart was darkened. Professing themselves

Myths to Avoid

"LIVE" MYTHS believed today by substantial numbers of people. These should be studied under the category of "false religions," as a bare outline of those beliefs, *without* getting heavily into the actual stories and rituals behind the beliefs. Thus, we would not recommend making a detailed study of Hindu or Shinto myths. Native American myths might now fall in this category, as the public schools are making a mighty effort to get children to take them seriously, even requiring them in some cases to re-enact tribal religious rituals.

"SCANDALOUS" MYTHS. Some people's myths are graphically violent, anti-family, and sex-laden. Greek and Roman myths do *not* fall into this category, because the *details* of the sex and violence are unimportant to the stories. In fact, it's still easy to find editions of those myths that leave them out altogether. What counts is that Oedipus inadvertently married his mother, not how they conducted themselves as husband and wife. In contrast, sexual details are an integral part of Hindu mythology and of many African, South American, and South Seas tribal myths.

"FORBIDDEN" MYTHS. God specifically forbade the Jews to inquire too deeply into the religious practices of the Canaanites (Deuteronomy 18:9). The myths of Baal, Ashtoreth, Molech, and other Canaanite gods should therefore *not* be studied. It also seems to me that little is gained by studying Egyptian myths. Although it is quite true that knowing the titles of the Egyptian pantheon is helpful in understanding the plagues of Egypt, the stories themselves are depressing. They focus on death and actually *condone* incest and other gross sins.

In Greek and Roman myths, ill behavior and *hubris* (pride) lead to disaster. When Tantalus serves his guests with the flesh of their own children, he is condemned to eternal hunger and thirst. If Pandora had only kept her curiosity under control, the human race would have been spared countless ills. Because Zeus was unfaithful to his wife Hera with Hercules' mother, Hera brought many evils upon Hercules and his family. And so on. Thus, although the Greek gods and the humans in whom they interest themselves may not always act morally, moral results do follow their actions. This contrasts sharply with the myths of most other cultures, which often legitimize the grossest behavior.—*Mary Pride*

to be wise, they became fools and changed the glory of the uncorruptible God into an image made like to corruptible man, and to birds, and fourfooted beasts, and creeping things (Romans 1:20-23).

The picture here is of the "devolution" of religion. The Bible says that men fall into false religion and the worship of idols when they reject the truth about God, refuse to honor him, exchange the truth for a lie and suppress the truth in unrighteousness. There's nothing here about "progressing" towards God by way of mythology.

Our recommendation then is **not to teach mythology until you have taught Genesis.** And begin your study of mythology by reviewing with your children what God says about man's religion in the book of Romans. Once set in proper context, there are valuable lessons to be learned while reading the Greek myths. Without setting it in context, you risk confusion and error. So by all means, include mythology in your history lesson plans about Egypt, Greece, and Rome, but set it in context.

Moses, Paul, and Mythology

One last note about including mythology in your course of study: Moses clearly knew Egyptian religious stories and Paul clearly knew about Greek and Roman religion. This can be seen in the way each of them deals with the false religions of the culture they are dealing with. Paul even quotes from Greek poetry (a poem that discusses the pantheon of Greek mythological gods). To understand the conflict between Moses and Pharaoh, it is tremendously helpful if you understand the relationship between the plagues and the Egyptian pantheon. It turns out that each of the plagues is God's challenge to a specific Egyptian deity. If you don't know who the Egyptian deities are, you can't really understand what God is saying.

This does not mean that we need to dwell on detailed descriptions of immoral practices associated with the false religions. We use common sense . . . and rely for the most part on texts published before 1965. But a study of the themes and major characters of Egyptian, Greek, Roman, and Norse mythologies will have much to teach us and our children.

Three Reasons for Studying Mythology

To return to our three reasons for including mythology as a part of history:

(1) The best protection we can give our children from false religion is an early inoculation/exposure to it under controlled circumstances. Set in context as described above, we have an opportunity to discuss with our children the contrast between true and false religion. We can highlight the foolishness of the false gods. They will always remember the comparisons and will be much less likely to be taken in by "new age" repackaging when they are older.

(2) To understand the Greeks, Romans, Egyptians, or North Europeans, you need to understand what they believed about their gods. By including a study of the myths when you read biographies or study these cultures you can ask key questions about how the false religion affected the culture. You can ask, "If the Greeks believed the gods behaved this way, how do you think they would behave themselves?" With Greek religion you can discuss the reasons for Socrates' execution (one of the charges against him was that he taught the youth of Athens that there could be only one god and that the myths had many contradictions and couldn't be true). You can talk about why Paul went to Mars Hill and preached about the unknown god. You can talk about the background to the controversy in 1 Corinthians over eating meat that had been sacrificed to idols. These issues are much easier to understand if you have some knowledge of Greek religion.

With Roman culture as well, there are close links between morals, behavior, and religion. The Romans adopted the Greek gods, and then went further and began to deify the emperors. Christians who refused to sacrifice to the emperor found their lives in danger. Note well, it was not illegal to worship Jesus; it was illegal to worship only Jesus! The worship of the emperor fit Roman "statism" very neatly and meshed with the respect all Romans were taught toward "the fathers" (Latin *patria*, whence we get our English word *patriotism*). We cannot fully appreciate the issues facing early Christians unless we are familiar with Roman religion.

(3) The myths are an integral part of our literary heritage. One cannot fully appreciate any great writer (Shakespeare, to name one) unless one is familiar with the stories from the myths. Knowing them does not mean we must accept them as true. But we should know them in order to intelligently converse with and present the Gospel to our culture. The great works of literature in the western tradition all use symbols and images drawn from the myths of the Greeks, Romans, and Scandinavians. We cannot appreciate the nuances or the ideas themselves unless we recognize the references.

An acquaintance with the myths of the Greeks, Romans, and Norsemen has seldom proven a snare to adult Christians or their children. Quite the opposite seems to be true. For scholars like C.S. Lewis and J.R.R. Tolkien the myths and legends (what Lewis called "northernness") aroused in them an appreciation for beauty and drama and a longing for "joy" that Lewis said was instrumental in his final conversion to Christianity.

Our conclusion then? Do not teach mythology as a separate subject or in a way that encourages or entices. But do teach mythology as a key part of the history and culture of the Egyptians, Greeks, Romans, and Europeans. And do teach it in the context of what God himself teaches about man and his turning aside to false religions. In this way you will make your children better able to serve God, to communicate to the pagan culture around us, and to stand as godly men and women in their own generation.

"Great Books" or Classical Education?

A classical education is more than reading great books, and a Great Books education is not exactly like other classical education programs. The "Great Books" movement promotes, not just a certain group of classics, but a Socratic method of teaching in which the professor leads the student to think out the answers for himself. For more information, see the Great Books Academy review in *Mary Pride's Complete Guide to Homeschooling Grades 7–12.* For a suggested list of Great Books, see the appendix in that volume.

Classical Homeschooling

Once upon a time, thousands of years ago, classical education happened at home. In fact, Cicero declared that state involvement in education was contrary to the Roman character. When the Renaissance brought about the renewal of ancient learning, children were frequently taught classically at home. Since then, many of the most important minds of western culture, such as Pascal, John Stuart Mill, and Abraham Lincoln, have been home-schooled.   —*Andrew Kern*

led by John Dewey and his school, believed that education was a forum for experience and training. The classicists believed that the goal was wisdom and virtue. The progressives won all the major battles, and, frankly, most Christians of the time, being practical Americans trained in favoring "a good job" over "fruit for eternity," were comfortable with the results.

A movement back to classical education began almost immediately. Its most important leader has been Mortimer Adler, who has written a number of brilliant books on education and founded a movement called The Paideia Program. In addition he edited and promoted the 52-volume Great Books of the Western World.

Dorothy Sayers fired a volley from England with her seminal article "The Lost Tools of Learning," in which she described the trivium as the key to an educational revival. Douglas Wilson's *Recovering the Lost Tools of Learning* propelled the ideas of Dorothy Sayers to the vanguard of popular reform theory.

As the classical ideas of Adler, Sayers, Wilson, et al., were filtering down from the theorists, homeschooling formed into a powerful movement. The two ideas joined hands in the pages of *The Teaching Home* magazine, which published the "Lost Tools" article by Dorothy Sayers some 15 years ago. It sparked a tremendous interest among homeschoolers, but many felt frustrated because detailed curricula and methodology were not yet developed.

Nonetheless, in characteristic homeschooling fashion, **a number of families stepped forward to pioneer the old path.** The Bluedorns created Trivium Pursuit. In the early 90's Canon Press began making its materials available. Laura Behrquist published an excellent manual (*Designing Your Own Classical Curriculum*, Ignatius Press) specially written for the Catholic homeschooler but eminently useful for any interested in classical education. Douglas Wilson, Doug Jones, and Wes Callihan wrote a handbook on the classical Christian homeschool (*Classical Education and the Home School*, from Canon Press). And homeschooling has always been well-represented at the Association of Classical and Christian Schools (ACCS) conferences.

Then classical homeschooling hit the Internet. Linda Robinson and others began Scholars Online Academy. Fritz Hinrichs, a graduate of St. John's College (another of Adler's great achievements) joined them with his Escondido Tutorial Service. Recently, David and Jennifer Hoos have published a weekly Internet newsletter for classical schoolers, called *CCS Digest*. Most of the readers are homeschoolers.

Meanwhile, Foundations Academy pioneered the **classical school/homeschool co-op.** It makes seminars available to homeschooling high schoolers on such subjects as logic, Latin, classical history and literature, and composition. Finally, Veritas Press developed a full-fledged classical curriculum catalogue, a giant step further, presenting in its pages not only the books needed but an implicit scope and sequence as well.

Andrew Kern on Classical Education for All

Many homeschoolers are classical without knowing it because of their educational goals. In fact, most of the people who buy into the classical vision don't do so because it is new and exciting but because it ties together and explains so many of the things they have long desired: virtue and wisdom, skill using words and numbers, and a heart to value and sustain their heritage (Christian, Western, American, and family).

The classical curriculum gives a form to those desires. It does not exclude apprenticeship or training. It simply recognizes that everybody needs wisdom and virtue, skill at using words and numbers, and respect for their heritage while not everyone needs to be able to use a computer or fix a tractor. Classical education puts everything in its place and thus enables everything to fulfill its purpose.

Books on Classical Education

Like any educational movement, the philosophies of classical education continue to be refined and articulated by those from within. **Classical Education: The Movement Sweeping America** is the revised edition of *Classical Education: Towards the Revival of American Schooling.*

Like the previous edition, this book answers the question, "Just what *is* classical ed?" Co-authors Andrew Kern and Gene Edward Veith bring years of experience to this 144-page work, which serves as a much-needed summary and concise explanation of where we currently stand in relation to classical ed.

Beginning with a brief explanation of the problems with modern and postmodern education, the book proceeds not only to define classical education but to show how it looks in different forms.

For example: Christian Classical schools (Logos School in Moscow, Idaho), Democratic Classical schools (Mortimer Adler's Paideia Group), Moral Classical Schools (Renaissance Humanism), and finally classical education in the inner city (Marva Collins and Westside Prep) are all explained. Two new chapters in this edition also look at Catholic classicism and classical education in homeschooling.

Taking things one step further, this book addresses the rise and fall of liberal arts colleges as the authors explore the current state of higher education. Rounding out this brief volume is a list of current resources to further your own study into this subject. "We do well to avoid the fatal and arrogant conceit of jettisoning our heritage" say the authors, but they combine this with a reminder: "Heritage is not solely a gift of wisdom and virtue. It also contains cautions and forewarnings. Classical education reminds us of the bigger picture." And this book frames that picture quite nicely. *Review by Renee Mathis*

If you think classics are stodgy, dusty tomes . . . think again. By the time you finish reading **Classics in the Classroom**, you will be motivated to reach for these treasures and share them with your children.

Michael Clay Thompson, the author, obviously enjoys what he's doing and imparts this excitement to you. He explains how to identify a classic,

It's Our History

We live in the continuum of Western history. In order to evaluate this stream that we are part of, we must step back from it and discern the ideas that have shaped it. To attempt to ignore the ideas that have shaped our cultural history is to guarantee ourselves not only cultural irrelevance but also entrenchment in the Christian ghetto.—*Fritz Hinrichs*

Classical Education: The Movement Sweeping America
Parents. $10.
Capital Research Center, DC. (202) 483-6900, www.capitalresearch.org.

Classics in the Classroom
Parents. $10.
Royal Fireworks Press, NY.
(845) 726-3333, www.rfpress.com.

Repairing the Ruins

Parents. $14.
Canon Press, ID. (800) 488-2034,
www.canonpress.org.

Teaching the Trivium

Parents. $27.
Trivium Pursuit, IA. (309) 537-3641,
www.triviumpursuit.com.

the "whys" of reading them, and practical ideas for encouraging your student to enjoy them as well.

The first three chapters are the meat. The last is an amazingly long list of 1,300 classics that can be used as a reference point for your own lists.

Even though this was written for classrooms, the ideas can be adapted easily. There are some really wonderful ideas here, although I found myself disagreeing with some of his assertions. For example, he recommends the reading of "rascally" (i.e. censored) books and the suspension of disbelief when reading, so as to allow oneself to be enfolded into the story. Be aware the list of classics runs the gamut from *Malcolm X, The Oresteia,* and the *Koran* to *The Deerslayer, The Divine Comedy,* and the Bible. All the books are coded and tell you if the book is a Newbery winner, on the Great Books list, or has, in one way or other, received recognition. *Marla Perry*

Repairing the Ruins: The Classical and Christian Challenge to Education begins with an introduction by Marlin Detweiler of Veritas Press. Then come three sections, with articles contributed by a variety of authors, including Douglas Wilson, who edited the book.

The first section, "The Scriptural Worldview," attempts to bring out the importance of worldview as a foundation for education and make the case for classical education as distinctively Christian education, as opposed to public schooling or "Christianized" public schooling in the form of private schools. Doug Wilson's point in the first article is that truly Christian education presents Christianity as the antithesis to other worldviews, not as merely one of a multitude of equally valid options to study.

The first part of section two, "The Classical Mind," still is geared to educational philosophy more than how-tos. These chapters include "Egalitarianism: the Great Enemy," "The Trivium Applied in the Elementary," "The Classical Model: Trivium 101," and "The Seven Laws of Teaching." This section also includes a chapter apiece on the "why and how" of teaching logic, Latin, history, literature, rhetoric, and apologetics the classical way.

Section three, "Making It Work in This Century," is practical advice for those interested in starting a classical school. Chapters tackle the topics of bylaws, policies, and guidelines; planning and overseeing curriculum; the "Servant School"; the responsibility of a school to "take the place of the parent"; and practical steps in starting a school. There's also an optimistic epilogue on "The Rise and Fall of Government Education," and a suggested reading list (though not, unfortunately, an index.)

Although obviously not written primarily for homeschoolers (it began life as a series of talks at an Association of Christian and Classical Schools convention), *Repairing the Ruins* has many interesting and practical ideas homeschoolers can use.

Note that an earlier book meant for homeschoolers by Douglas Wilson, Wes Callihan, and Douglas Jones, **Classical Education and the Home School**, is available free on the Canon Press website. See the sidebar on page 191 for more books and curriculum available via Canon Press.

Teaching the Trivium: Christian Homeschooling in a Classical Style is by Harvey and Laurie Bluedorn, the world's reigning experts on this subject. As long ago as 1989, the Bluedorns were writing on classical education for homeschoolers—long before any other book on the topic emerged—as well as promoting it through their speaking at hundreds of conventions. They certainly know how to teach you how to do classical homeschooling from a Christian perspective. Their 640-page book holds you by the hand and takes you right through all the how-tos.

The first ten chapters of *Teaching the Trivium* make the case for homeschooling, for the trivium model and method, for teaching the trivium subjects, for what the authors consider a biblical approach to history and literature, and for approaching all this with some flexibility. The next five chapters amplify and extend two articles they wrote for my magazine, *Practical Homeschooling*. These provide "Ten Things to Do" with children before age 10, from ages 10 to 12, from ages 13 to 15, from ages 16 to 18, and from ages 19 and onward. These ages and stages are respectively dubbed the Early Knowledge level, the Later Knowledge level, the Understanding level, the Wisdom level, and the Finishing level. Each of these chapters provides a suggested course of study, a suggested daily schedule, and a wealth of practical tips for teaching each school subject.

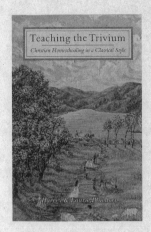

A massive Appendix One contains 16 articles on various educational topics. These include, of course, Dorothy Sayers' famous "Lost Tools of Learning" essay plus various essays by the Bluedorns of which the most noteworthy are "The Trivium in Scripture," "A Comparison of Ancient Alphabets," "The Christian Use of Logic," "Family Bible Study by the Trivium," and "Outcome-Based Education Versus Trivium-Based Education." This appendix also contains some ancient essays, such as "On Christian Doctrine" by Augustine, a Bluedorn article apiece on "Beginning a Homeschool Speech and Debate Club" and "Pointers for Public Speaking," and the Bluedorns' "Contests in Your Curriculum" article. The latter includes the 2001 version of their Trivium Pursuit contest list: basically, contact info and a couple of phrases to let you know what the contest is about and what ages it is for.

Finally, as with all books of this type, you get the Bluedorns' hefty "Resource List" appendix. This is a mostly unannotated list of resources divided into all sorts of categories. Some resources have contact info; others simply have the name of the publisher. Sadly there is no index to the book, which would have been a *great* help. (Next edition, perhaps?)

The Bluedorns depart from Dorothy Sayers' dicta in several cases. By reading their arguments as to why doing it *their* way makes more sense than the prep-school way, you will become aware that even classical education can be "done" several differing ways, and start forming your own opinions on educational philosophy. And the incredibly practical nature of the many tips scattered throughout the book will give you a big "leg up" on your own educational efforts.

I should mention that the Bluedorns' kids have demonstrated educational excellence along the way, winning or scoring high in various academic and creative contests, from large science fairs to a NASA contest to the "Written and Illustrated By" contest. So this is not another "how to" book by wannabes who can't show any academic results.

If you're a Bible-believing Christian who is drawn to classical homeschooling, I urge you to buy . . . and study . . . this book.

It has been said that the real test of the modern homeschooling movement will come as the children of those pioneering families in the 1970's and 1980's have children of their own. Will those children continue to build on that foundation as they educate their own little ones?

Fortunately for all of us, in the case of classical educators Jessie Wise and Susan Wise Bauer, the answer is a resounding, "Yes!" A former public school teacher, Jessie Wise began crafting an educational plan for her own three children in the '70's. Laying aside the fluffy, mind-numbing contemporary educational philosophy in which she'd been steeped, she reached back for a set of tools proven over time to build solid, thinking adults. These tools, known as the trivium, have been popularized in the homeschool world by

The Well-Trained Mind
Parents. $35 plus shipping.
W.W. Norton & Company, Inc.,
(800) 223-2584. Available in bookstores.

A new book from Susan Wise Bauer, *The Well Educated Mind,* has just been released by W. W. Norton, & Co. Subtitled "A Guide to the Classical Education You Never Had," it presents a 30-minute-a-day, four-days-a-week reading plan for adults who would like to come to grips with the classics of fiction, autobiography, history, drama, and poetry. It's not just lists; you get the background information you need as well.

Dorothy Sayers' seminal essay on the subject and by Douglas Wilson's 1991 book entitled *Recovering the Lost Tools of Learning*. Jessie Wise, nearly two decades earlier, did just what Wilson's book title suggests. The result was that her daughter Susan Wise Bauer now teaches literature at the College of William and Mary and yes, homeschools her own four children.

In **The Well-Trained Mind**, these two women have created a definitive guide to classical home education that is second only to the Bluedorns' book, *Teaching the Trivium* (which came out first, and which is reviewed above). The Bauers' 764-page hardcover book is a careful, detailed description of how to use the tools of the trivium (grammar, logic, and rhetoric) to prepare your child to think, read, and reason. The book not only tells you why (though it does that eloquently) but tells you how . . . specifically. The authors explain each developmental stage and offer a philosophical base for teaching each subject area within that stage, complete with detailed curriculum suggestions. This section of the book alone weighs in at over 500 pages. The remainder of the book is devoted to the nuts and bolts of home education, including scheduling, socialization, homeschooling with babies and toddlers, how to start home educating "midstream," and a terrific section on the college application process.

The Well-Trained Mind is a tremendous resource and is a valuable read not only for those of you interested in using the classical model for your homeschool, but for most everyone who cares about learning well. The only weakness in this text is the very fleeting mention of faith. In discussions of teaching ethics or theology, the authors steer you back to your own religious traditions, and move off the subject quickly. Without anchoring education to transcendent truth, a classical model of education will create a great big frontal lobe detached from a heart.

Even with that one weakness, this book is of incredible value and comes highly recommended. *Michelle Van Loon*

Bonus Article: Classical Colleges for Homeschoolers

by Andrew Kern

This morning, at Gutenberg College in Eugene, Oregon, students are gathering for discussions over a great text. The tutor, serving as mentor and coach, will guide them through an intense dialogue on what Plato, Milton, or Melville have to say to the young adult of the twenty-first century. Each student will form and defend his opinion and then confront the challenges his position engenders.

Gutenberg students lead the way among the growing number of college students following the classical model.

Homeschoolers with a bent toward classical education have been especially eager to find schools to round out their work, schools that interact with great ideas, teach with an emphasis on discussion and interaction, and respect the scholars while preparing them for moral responsibility and leadership. Yet homeschooling parents often run into a dilemma when selecting their children's college. Parents and students yearn for a school where learning occurs, the law of God is not mocked, and students are prepared to make godly decisions in an ungodly world. But where to look?

The most famous "classical" college is **St. John's College** in Annapolis. Chartered in 1784 by the State of Maryland, and with a campus in Santa Fe, New Mexico, St. John's is famous for pioneering the Great Books/Great Discussion approach promoted by Robert Hutchins and Mortimer Adler. The curriculum consists of seminars in which the great books are discussed; language, math, and music tutorials; and science laboratories. Once per week students listen to a lecture by a tutor or guest. Afterward, students and faculty question the lecturer. In the junior and senior years a preceptorial is added. Now the student engages in tutor-directed study of a topic or text.

St. Johns is a secular institution known for raising questions without answering them. The Christian who needs an intellectual challenge may thrive here, but the moral tone is liberal with an undertone of despair. Christianity is treated with respect, but the Bible is not regarded as authoritative.

Admissions are based primarily on an application essay and interview, strong academic background in the secondary years, and letters of recommendation. SAT or ACT scores are not required but may be useful. Tuition is expensive.

Thomas Aquinas College is a Catholic Liberal Arts college founded in 1971 in Santa Paula, California. Believing that only the truth sets men free and that truth concerns both natural and supernatural matters, TAC seeks to ground its students in the arts of thinking, while developing a wide-ranging, integrated vision of life and learning. The curriculum parallels the St. John's program, using tutorials, seminars, and laboratories to explore the great ideas in groups of 14–20 students. Socratic discussions and great books replace lectures and textbooks.

Thomas Aquinas is particularly homeschool friendly. 76 percent of their 301 students come from home or private schools. Admissions are based on essays, transcripts (including a list of courses and books read for homeschoolers), letters of reference, and SAT or ACT scores.

The University of Dallas is a Catholic liberal arts college founded in 1956. While St. John's and Thomas Aquinas offer few or no electives, Dallas's Constantin College offers a core curriculum and majors. The core includes Philosophy, English, Mathematics and Fine Arts, Science, Languages, American and Western Civilization, Politics, Economics, and Theology. After finishing the core curriculum in the first two years, the student proceeds to his major in the humanities or sciences.

The curriculum seeks to develop the intellectual and moral virtues needed to understand oneself and one's relationship to God, nature, and other humans in order to live responsibly in the changing world.

Admissions for homeschoolers are based on an application essay, a letter of recommendation, a high school transcript, SAT I or ACT scores, a personal interview, and the Home Education Information Form provided by the school.

Two recently founded colleges appealing to the classical student are Patrick Henry College in Purcellville, Virginia, and New St. Andrew's College in Moscow, Idaho.

New St. Andrews College (NSA) in Moscow, Idaho, is a ministry of Christ Church, where Douglas Wilson is pastor, and an extension of the classical Christian renewal occurring through the Association of Classical and Christian Schools. After opening with four full-time students in 1994, NSA expanded to 134 students in 2003. NSA rejects the notion of academic neutrality, believing that, "In the business of the classroom . . . confessional, applied Christianity is tragically absent" from many modern Christian colleges. NSA emphasizes the study of classical antiquity, Western civilization, and Christ's lordship over every human endeavor.

Teacher-student interaction and scholarship are the keynotes of the NSA approach. The courses are divided into colloquia, or yearlong courses, in language (Latin and Greek) and culture (Lordship, Rhetoric, Theology, Music, Literature, Classical culture and history, and electives). Students meet for seminars 1–3 times per week and for occasional recitations with tutors. Disputations take place weekly. Oral exams occur at the end of each term. Seniors seeking a B.A. degree must present and defend a thesis in public.

NSA welcomes homeschoolers. Admissions are based on high-school transcripts or homeschool course work descriptions, SAT or ACT scores, a statement of faith, an essay written by the student on why he wishes to attend NSA, a copy of an academic essay, and a questionnaire filled out by the student's pastor.

Patrick Henry College in Purcellville, VA, is the first college founded primarily for homeschoolers. Michael Farris, founder and president of HSLDA, is also the founder and president of Patrick Henry College. Promoting Christian character with a smile, PHC teaches the classical liberal arts from within the Christian worldview to nurture American leaders endowed with virtue, leadership skills, and understanding of the traditions of freedom.

The core of the PHC curriculum is the classical liberal arts program. The government major is built on this foundation and involves "the most intensive apprenticeship program in the nation," while also covering every facet of government and public policy. The other classical liberal arts majors are creative writing and education. Future majors will include business, media arts, information technology, and journalism.

Admissions to PHC are based on academic preparation, test scores, letters of reference, and evidence of Christian maturity. Tuition is inexpensive.

Finally, the new and small **Gutenberg College** grew out of the McKenzie Study Center, a mission to the students at the University of Oregon in Eugene. Gutenberg believes that education should go beyond preparing students to earn a living to preparing students to live a good life. Tutors seek to develop the students' reasoning skills, to teach a broad knowledge base, and to help students learn to live wisely.

In 2001, Gutenberg's 22 students followed a Great Books/tutorial curriculum in a warm family environment. Eighty-three percent of the students came from homeschooling backgrounds. Since most of the Gutenberg staff also homeschool their children, the students have found an understanding environment. The program, though similar to that of TAC and St. John's, is approached from a Protestant perspective.

Gutenberg College regards learning as an apprenticeship. Students are not told what to think; rather, they are presented with perennial issues, shown various solutions, and trained in how to evaluate them.

Admissions to Gutenberg are based on written essays, high school performance, SAT tests, and a meeting with a school representative. Along with the Great Books discussions, scholars study mathematics, writing, science, Greek, and German. And tuition is inexpensive.

CHAPTER 25

Contests

Contests as a homeschool method? What possessed you to make this an entire chapter?"

Here's what happened. Over the years, I have been chronicling the achievements of homeschooled children in my magazine, *Practical Homeschooling*. I began to notice that some families frequently had "Show & Tell" pieces to submit about their children. It seemed that those families were using contests as a major part of their curriculum.

"Interesting," I thought. "I know my own children get really serious about a subject as a contest approaches." We're talking kids who *pressure* me into signing them up for the Spelling Bee, Art Fair, and every local math contest that comes down the pike. I knew from experience that most of these contests involve learning facts and skills above and beyond the regular curriculum. Plus, we have discovered that many of them have curriculum available to help you study for the contest—whether it's math problem sets from previous years, or spelling lists, or geography lesson plans and online quizzes . . .

So, yes,

Contests are a *motivational* method.

And if you so desire,

Contests can form an entire curriculum.

Homeschoolers have done well in many of them—taking first place at the National Geography Bee and first, second, and third place at one year's National Spelling Bee, for instance. The Richman kids alone must have won or placed in several dozen contests, judging from the reports in the Pennsylvania Homeschoolers newsletter, and I must admit I've had to designate a "ribbon drawer" for the smaller awards of my own kids!

See Appendix 4

for a huge list of contests your homeschooled children can enter.

Ugh! Contests!

I know some of you might be thinking, "Contests?! Ugh! Competition between children is something we wanted to get away from by homeschooling! Forget it, contests aren't for us." I'm sort of that way too—I don't feel comfortable with the kind of nastiness over rankings that can develop *at school* when kids compete. Worthwhile contests *at home* can be a whole different experience—something that you as parents can fully monitor, discuss, and assess. You can choose just what to encourage your child to participate in, and there is no peer group to taunt losers.

—*Sue Richman*

Contests are an educational experience especially suited for home-schooled students. What can contests do for your child academically? Consider:

Laurie Bluedorn on Contests as Motivators

Laurie and Harvey Bluedorn are the founders of Trivium Pursuit, a provider of classical education products for homeschoolers. Laurie's insights on this page were taken from a column she wrote for *Practical Homeschooling*. To request their catalog, contact Trivium Pursuit, PMB 168, 139 Colorado Street, Muscatine, IA 52761, (309) 537-3641. You can sign up for their email loop and see their catalog and many helpful articles and links online at **www.triviumpursuit.com**.

Envision a typical homeschool assignment. Mom asks Henry to write a composition on "What Valentine's Day Means to Me." Henry is not particularly interested in Valentine's Day and knows his finished composition will go no further than Mom's eyes and then into the three-ring binder on the schoolroom bookshelf. As a consequence, his motivation level is mediocre and his effort halfhearted.

But suppose Mom tells Henry she wants him to draw a scene from intergalactic space and write a scientific narrative of that scene. Henry, who is the local expert on space exploration, lights up at this idea. When she tells him they will enter his drawing and narrative in the Intergalactic Art Competition (part of the Space Science Student Involvement Program), and he might win an all-expenses paid trip to the National Space Science Symposium in Washington, D.C. . . . well, the fire is lit; and look out world, Henry has a lot to say on that subject. It was a combination of good topic, competition, and reward that did the trick.

How Contests Develop Research Skills

To be sure, writing a scientific narrative on space exploration will take more than your 1952 *Encyclopædia Britannica*, so off to the library you go. Here is the perfect opportunity to teach the lad how to research. You will want to use a good college or university library along with your own local library. Arrange for personal interviews. And don't forget to tap into the Internet.

A contest can bring together all the skills you've taught your children into one exciting finale. To write this paper on space exploration, numerous subjects will be covered: grammar, spelling, punctuation, science, penmanship or typing skills, logic (construction of arguments), and rhetoric (expressing your point in an eloquent manner). So this one essay contest is not just "another composition" to write, but an entire unit study in itself, with the final product bringing—as Jessica Hulcy says—"closure."

How Contests Develop Character Qualities

Many of these contests take a long time to complete. Some, such as a Science and Engineering Fair science project, will take an entire school year. It develops perseverance and diligence. Contests can seem overwhelming and unmanageable if you only look at the whole picture, but by planning and organization the process can be broken down into bite-size pieces. The student strives toward his goal, doing his best, and in the end can obtain the "satisfaction and pride of a job well done" (as Ranger Bill would say).

Some contests require teamwork. The national "Written & Illustrated By . . ." awards contest provided an opportunity for my oldest daughter, Johannah, to teach her younger sister Helena watercolor techniques.

Because of their flexible schedules, homeschooled students are at an advantage in contest participation. The first contest we ever entered was a local science fair. I learned about this competition only two weeks before it was held, so we devoted those two weeks full-time to the contest. What an exciting experience! That was back in 1989, but all the kids remember the fun of those days. Two weeks of pure science, not to be distracted by Latin declensions.

Sue Richman on Types of Contests

Here are a few things to keep in mind:

There are many types of contests. Some will be more suitable for your family and your children than others. I have a broad definition of a contest. Sending a piece of writing or artwork into a children's magazine for possible publication is like a contest in many ways, as is preparing for and passing an Advanced Placement (AP) exam in the late high school years.

Some contests have many winners. An art contest my daughters entered offers about 1,000 awards to the 4,000 US entries. Last year both girls were thrilled to get silver and bronze medals and simple art supplies as prizes. Other contests have only a very few winners, which may be discouraging to some children.

Winners must sometime meet certain criteria, as in the AP program or the Presidential Sports Award program. Everyone who meets the established scale of excellence receives credit; you're not competing against others, you are competing against a clear standard.

Money rewards or trips, like to Washington, D.C., for final award ceremonies, are a part of some contests. Others offer plaques, certificates, or other formal recognition.

The "Written & Illustrated by . . ." contest publishes several wonderful books created by children each year. Each winning student also receives scholarship money and full royalties on his or her book. For the history buff, the *Concord Review* is a professional journal that publishes high school students' history research papers. Often college scholarships are offered, as in the National Merit Scholarship program for high school juniors who take the PSAT exam. Again, the thing to keep in perspective is that the better the prize, the fewer the winners. Prepare your kids accordingly!

Contests are local and national. Locally, our daily paper ran an editorial cartoon competition for high school students. Nationally, NewsCurrents sponsors an annual editorial cartoon contest for kids. It's up to you to decide which type of contest you want to encourage your kids to enter.

Sue Richman on Eight Benefits of Entering Contests

It's a Wednesday morning. A group of elementary-age kids are gathered around a table cluttered with test papers, math games, and manipulatives, all listening to another child explaining how she solved a tricky problem from this month's Math Olympiad set. She's diagramming her solution on the large chalkboard, and others are waving their hands to share how their ways of going about the problem were somewhat different.

Think this must be a school classroom? Wrong! It's our monthly homeschool Math Olympiad meeting. What's the Math Olympiad? It's a wonderful international competition for elementary-age students that annually involves about 80,000 public and private school children in challenging math problem solving. We started the very first homeschool team 11 years ago, and now groups of homeschoolers all across the country are starting to take part.

The Math Olympiad is just one national program that our four homeschooled kids have taken part in over the years. Many team or group

Sue Richman is a former *Practical Homeschooling* columnist and the co-founder of Pennsylvania Homeschoolers. Among many other things, they offer a terrific set of AP online courses. Check out their website at **www.pahomeschoolers.com**.

Yet More Types of Contests

Don't forget local **sports contests.** Our children have participated in swim meets and martial arts tournaments so far, with soccer looming in the future. Such events provide goals that help kids measure their progress realistically against others and provide incentive for some extra workouts.

4-H and **state fairs** are another arena in which homeschooled children often compete—and succeed!

Outcome-Based Contests?

When it comes to the Olympic Games, everyone seems to understand that competition produces the winners and the record-breakers. It's unlikely that the athletes could reach such heights of achievement and endurance if they were not competing against other athletes who are closely matched in skills and putting forth their very best.

Some people, however, are at war against the whole concept of competition. They think it is undemocratic, unfair, and elitist. It's a sign of the times that, in Cecile County, Maryland, basketball is now played by some very unusual rules. If one basketball team is ten points ahead of the other, additional baskets don't count until the underdog team catches up. No record is kept of who scores how many baskets, so no player can ever be recognized as the star of the team.

This system should be called Outcome-Based Basketball because it's just like the Outcome-Based Education (OBE) that has spread through our public schools like a contagious disease. OBE is sometimes called Performance-Based Education.

OBE does not allow any student to progress faster or farther than the slowest child in the class. This system conceals the fact that some children aren't learning much of anything. What is the teacher to do with the faster learners after they complete the assigned material? They are required to do peer tutoring (trying to tutor the slower pupils) or "horizontal enrichment." The former is a frustration for all students, and the latter is just busywork.

"Self-esteem" is OBE's mantra. Since the lack of self-esteem is postulated to be the cause of all social ills (crime, illegal drugs, teenage pregnancies, AIDS, and low SAT scores), OBE's primary goal is to inculcate self-esteem. There is no evidence that lack of self-esteem causes

contest programs welcome homeschoolers. Here are some of the benefits we've found in taking part in these types of activities:

1. **Learning to cooperate with others.** Cooperate while competing? Yes, that's actually the focus of many of the programs we've been in. A competition may be the culminating event, but the hours of working together with other kids and learning together is probably what carries much of the real value. The Math Olympiad wouldn't be nearly as much fun and so energizing for the kids if they were all doing these challenging math problems at home just on their own. At our meetings we encourage the kids to help one another, play math games together, share ideas with the group, and even present special projects they've done at home. It's positive socializing—and fun.

2. **Ease of organizing a group activity.** National team contests are already well-organized, making it possible for even this very busy mom of four to take part. For instance, the Math Olympiad program sends local teams all the needed materials for each monthly contest. I don't have to do a lot of last-minute planning or head-scratching about what to do on Wednesday when I'm faced with a dozen bouncing kids. And if we want to add extras, there are lots of ideas in the Olympiad newsletter.

3. **Provides focus for getting a group together.** Sometimes support groups want to provide kids' activities, but it can be hard to decide just what to offer. An agreed-upon group contest, such as the Geography Bee, can sometimes give that focus and lets everyone know clearly what they are involved in. This can be especially important at the high-school level.

4. **We get excellent, often free, guidelines** for developing an area of our curriculum that maybe we had been pushing to the background for too long. I think of the great materials from the National Geographic Geography Bee; they really got me realizing that we needed to focus more on this area. Or there's the MathCounts coaching books with all their sample problem sets and ideas for using calculators and advanced problem-solving techniques with junior-high-age kids. Many times these contest materials have spurred interests that last for years.

5. **We get an unusual chance to let our kids measure themselves** against kids who are traditionally schooled. Sometimes this is energizing—as when our Jesse at 16 came in third place for eleventh graders in the national current events competition Global Challenge, and the same year our Jacob at 13 came in fifth place for eighth graders. This was out of thousands of kids in the country, and probably our team comprised the only homeschoolers. Sometimes competitions are humbling and let us realize that there indeed are really bright and hardworking kids out there in the public and private schools. Good for keeping a bit of perspective! Our kids get an equal chance to reach high goals with other students and see how they measure up.

6. **Entering contests gives someone else the job** of setting parameters for a project, not just Mom. I can go over the contest guidelines for the American Statistical Association's annual project and poster contest with Jacob and his team partner and help them devise a plan to meet the requirements. I become a coach and guide, not someone who is just dishing out assignments, or someone who is just weakly making

watery suggestions. Proofreading is not Jacob's favorite thing, but we proofread his statistics paper with a fine-tooth comb (it was on the demographics of homeschooling in PA!). That was our language arts work for a week. And it was authentic and needed, with no doubt about the purpose of it all.

7. **It doesn't hurt to have team contest accomplishments** listed on a homeschooler's high-school records. Last year when Jesse applied to a special high-school summer program on the workings of the free enterprise system, he had many recognizable things to list when asked about any special awards or honors he'd earned in his high-school years. Many people might think that homeschoolers wouldn't have anything to put down—after all, aren't these types of activities only available through schools?

8. **Participating in contests can be good public relations work** on the value of homeschooling. People in my hometown come up to me all the time to say, "Oh, I see how well all you homeschoolers are doing—saw the article just last week in the paper about that math competition your group won!" Sometimes people outside of homeschooling really need to hear about these sorts of accomplishments before they can believe this "nutty" idea of ours is working. Impresses legislators too. And our PA Department of Education always notices how many homeschoolers make it each year to the state level Geography Bee. This year 6 out of the 100 state-level kids were homeschoolers!

   Just remember—when taking part in a national contest, your homeschool group must follow all the program rules. A few years back the Geography Bee threatened to disqualify all homeschoolers when one family had a child take the written test for the state level without actually having a local oral Bee with the required number of students. Let's show these national organizations that we can be trusted by being scrupulous about following all guidelines.

Laurie Bluedorn on Picking the Right Contest

A word of warning about contests. Avoid politically correct contests. If the registration form *requires* you to list your race, then it is possible that winners will be chosen on the basis of race, not simply merit. Some contests require you to travel long distances or cost large sums of money. MathCounts, a very popular math competition, recently started charging $40 per school. Avoid contests that just want to sell or promote a product (some of the poetry contests will do this) or build a mailing list. Some of the Internet "contests" are sweepstakes and not really contests at all.

Which contest should you pick for your child? If your child is extra good at math, then any of the numerous math competitions will stretch his skills, and there are plenty of art contests for the artistically inclined.

To integrate contests into your curriculum I suggest this plan. For the first year, pick one of the fun contests that coincide with that child's interests: robotics, chess, crafts, spelling, art, geography, model rocketry, etc. Check out the deadline for the contest and make out a rough schedule for progress. For example, by October have the project topic decided, have outlines finished by November, rough drafts by December, etc. Break the process down into manageable bite-size pieces.

The next year, have the student enter one of the project contests (National History Day, science fairs, or invention projects). By the third year you will be considered a contest pro and can even make contests a major part of your

those problems, nor is there any evidence that having self-esteem causes students to score better in academic subjects.
—*The Phyllis Schlafly Report*

Why Cooperation Is Not Always Better than Competition

Cooperative Learning, in which students receive a group grade, is another means of concealing who does the assignment accurately and who goofs off. The brighter students soon learn that their effort is not rewarded, and the slower students learn that there's no reason to try because someone will give them the answers.
—*The Phyllis Schlafly Report*

curriculum. The student can enter a writing contest, a speech contest, and a project contest each year, making for a well-rounded curriculum. You can also use contests to help your student work on areas he is weak in.

Contests let the student bring together the skills he learns at home and apply them in his everyday schooling. This is the ultimate in practical homeschooling.

CHAPTER 26

Laptop Homeschooling

Are you one of the few . . . the proud . . . the wired? Do your kids yawn at workbooks but thrill to computer games? Do you have oodles of kids . . . but not oodles of time to grade dozens of workbooks? Is your schedule overloaded, or are there subjects you'd like the kids to learn that you don't feel confident enough to teach?

Then welcome to Laptop Homeschooling.

Disclaimer

As I've said before, and will probably say again, **you don't need a computer to give your children a great education.** If you have the time, hands-on learning and print curriculum can do a great job. In fact, if you're looking to calm down and return to the simple virtues, I recommend sitting side by side on the couch with your student with no louder sound effect than pencil on paper.

However, you can obtain *some* of the same family closeness by moving from Desktop Education to Laptop Education. More on this later!

Advantages of Using a Computer in Your Homeschool

Later in this chapter we'll be dealing with some of the *dis*advantages of homeschool computing (and how to get around them), so let's first consider why we want to bother with educational computing at all. Ponder these major advantages of educational software:

- Saves you the time—and the stress—of making your child do old-fashioned flashcard-style drill
- Can *show* and *tell*—especially helpful in subjects such as music and art instruction, but also great for providing more colorful illustrations than it would be practical to print in a textbook
- Interacts with your child, so there's immediate feedback. Even the fastest mom can't grade every problem instantly!
- Animations and other 3-D teaching devices can demonstrate how things work.

> You cannot stop an idea whose time has come.
> —*Victor Hugo*

See the "Online Academies" section in the Quick Resource Guide at the back of this book to find some popular choices, including some that offer complete grade-level curriculum.

- Highly motivating: Kids love to use computers, and most software has a high "fun factor."
- Great for teaching research skills
- Encourages kids to write more, especially boys, who often hate handwriting but are much more positive toward keyboarding
- Kids "get into" it and are often willing to spend more time on homework at a computer than with a workbook.

So far, we're just talking CD-ROMS, DVDs, and disks. When it comes to online education, here are some additional benefits:

- A real, live teacher who knows the subject can interact with your child.
- It's possible to make friends with online classmates and develop "school spirit."
- The Web is a vast treasure trove of information; well-constructed online courses (and much new educational software) make use of this by directing the student to preselected and checked-out links.

Now, all of this information and interactivity can have a dark side. And here it comes . . .

Laptops vs. Desktops

Wondering why I called this chapter "Laptop Homeschool" instead of "Desktop Homeschool"? The fact is, you probably already know quite a bit about desktop education. You've used some educational software and read some articles about online academies. But we're not just talking about a little bit of computer biz you can add to your homeschool day. We're taking computerized education to the max, to show you the current state of the art.

But first, here's the problem with desktop computers.

1. They sit in one place.
2. If they're Internet-capable, they're usually plugged right into the phone cord, so a user can log in anytime.

Why is this a problem? Because . . .

- Sitting at a desk for any length of time is only comfortable to certain types of learners, and most desks don't have a lot of useful room for school-related materials.
- If Mom (or Dad, if he's the main homeschooling parent) needs to move about to get work done, the kiddie user has nobody supervising his work while Mom or Dad is out of the room.
- If the computer is plugged into the phone line, Junior can be going online to who knows where while you're not watching.
- If Junior happens to prefer computer games to educational software (like every other kid on the planet) and the desktop computer in question has even *one* real game on it (like the *Solitaire* and *Minesweepers* Bill Gates thoughtfully built into Windows), major slacking may occur while Mom and Dad aren't around.

Most of the above can be avoided by putting the children's educational software on a laptop, to which you (the parent) retain the phone wire. If you or a child need to go online, *then* you plug into the phone outlet. Meanwhile, it's easy for different children to use the same laptop in different locations and for Mom to keep the computer user together with his or her siblings instead of off alone at a desk by himself.

If you own a desktop computer, don't stress too much over this. But if you still have the choice—laptop or desktop?—we'd say, **"Go with the laptop,"** even though the desktop computer will be less expensive.

Let me put it this way: After years of reviewing every educational software product known to man, we had no luck getting our children to actually *use* most of the software we wanted them to until we discovered the joys of laptops. It has made all the difference in the world to our homeschool management. And, if worst comes to worst and computer use is unproductive for a time until your child gains more strength of character, you can always pack your laptop in its case and stick it in storage, or loan it to a friend—and your child will know this is no idle threat. This is much harder to manage with a bulky, heavy, desktop computer and monitor.

Now, I know *your* kids would never go online to download unauthorized games, or visit nasty websites, or play during homeschool hours. But for the sake of all the less-blessed out there who still see many advantages to computers in the homeschool, and who may have been struggling with some of the *dis*advantages, we'd like to share some tips we've learned over the years.

The Elementary Child: Software Only

Homework tutoring sites and online courses for young children are beginning to sprout up. Should your preteen child go online to use these sites and make friends?

At this point, we would say no. Totally apart from the problem of online stalkers and inappropriate language in chat rooms, this is not when you want your child disappearing into a virtual world. Constant parental supervision is wearying but necessary because online porn sites are just an accidental mouse-click away. And why bother? A combination of educational software and traditional tools can easily supply all the educational needs of a child in this age group.

One good software collection (e.g., the Elementary Edge programs from Encore Software available for sale in stores or online) can provide plenty of educational power at an affordable price. This might be a good place to start if you're counting the pennies.

TIP: We have found CD-ROM wallets very helpful. If you have enough software to warrant it, you can organize the software by age level, child, or subject. List the contents on it with a gel pen (regular pens and markers don't work, and stickers and labels don't stick to these wallets!). Teach each child how to put away a disc after use. This will prevent the common problem of scratched and lost software, especially if you purchased a laptop case (also recommended) where wallets can be stored between uses.

The Middle Years: Software and Learning the Rules of the Internet

Young teens can learn the rules of online safety, but there's more going on here than just following rules. If your child has a tendency to slack, remember that the Internet is the original black hole of time. Offsetting this, some excellent online academies offer courses for this age group, and with

NEED HELP KEEPING TRACK OF YOUR KIDS ONLINE?

Once you decide to let your kids go online, it might be wise to invest in an online usage monitoring program, such as **Specter 2.2** (available via CD or download for both Windows and Macintosh from **www.software4parents.com**). This program continually captures shots of the user's screen and saves them in a hidden folder. Later, you can play through it like a movie with fast-forward, reverse, and frame-by-frame, to see exactly what your student is doing on his computer. As their website blurb says, "You get recordings of all chat conversations, instant messages, e-mails typed and read, all web sites visited, all programs/applications run, all keystrokes typed—EVERYTHING they do on the computer and on the Internet." Although this analogy might strike some as Big Brother-ish, it's like having a surveillance camera pointed at the computer in question.

A more expensive program available from the same website, **Specter Pro**, even includes a feature that causes the computer it's installed on to automatically send you an email when any of a list of key words crop up on the computer screen. You can pick the key words to ensure that you'll be notified of any untoward chats, emails, or web pages. This one is unfortunately only available for Windows at the time of writing.

With the very real risk of online sexual predators, and the easy availability of even the most degenerate porn to a user of any age, it's not overdoing it to let your kids know in advance that Mom and Dad will find out if any hanky-panky is going on. This is true even if you are using "filtering" or "blocking" software; none of those programs is perfect, and you have a right to know if your kids are spending an obsessive amount of time with people or in places online where you don't want them (e.g., gaming sites).

more complex schoolwork, homework help sites might start making some sense for the first time.

TIP: I wouldn't turn over the keys to the online kingdom indiscriminately, however. Hang on to that phone wire so you have some control over how much time your student is spending online. Even if this means you're spending a lot of time under a desk plugging in the wire, it's worth it. And *do not,* under any circumstances, let a single Nintendo-style computer game in the house! If you wish to allow your children to play this type of game, have them play it on a console, not on the computer. Boys of this age are especially prone to becoming game addicts in the blink of an eye, and you do not want the computer becoming another portal to this time-wasting (and in many cases, morally offensive) universe.

The High School Years: Online and Loving It

Unless you're using a computerized curriculum such as Switched-On Schoolhouse, educational software fills less of your educational basket at this age. Kids need to be doing a lot of real-world projects and writing assignments to prepare them for college. SAT-prep software is great, though, and far less expensive than attending SAT-prep classes in person.

This is the age where online academies are most helpful—and needed. We would never have had the time to put our children through Advanced Placement courses ourselves, or teach them Latin. If you want to provide your children with a homeschool education to rival that found in elite prep schools, and you have a lot of children or relatively little time, some online classes are the way to go. Plus, they help meet the intense social needs of this age group, in which finding friends who share your interests is more important than simply having people of your age to hang around with.

TIP: Life is much more bearable if at the same time you enroll your student in his online courses you obtain a separate phone line for his modem, or sign up for DSL. Unless you enjoy having your friends get busy signals day and night when they try to call you.

To put you fully in the picture about what's available today in online academies, we asked our two Class of 2001 high-school-graduate consultants, Joseph and Sarah Pride, to share their experiences with four such academies. Before going to college, they took online courses for eight years. Joseph in particular served as a beta tester for one of these academies! Both Joseph and Sarah, like a good number of their online classmates, are National Merit Finalists and have been accepted with full-tuition scholarships at top colleges. Incidentally, they both chose to use laptops rather than desktop computers with their online courses, which is what originally inspired the title of this chapter!

Real-Time, Text-Only with Institute for Study of the Liberal Arts and Sciences

ISLAS (www.islas.org) was one of the very first online academies. It offers a full high-school curriculum, and some middle-school courses as well, through its Scholars' Online Academy (SOLA). Its sister school, Regina Coeli Academy, has a specifically Catholic emphasis, while SOLA is more generically Christian. Both Sarah and Joe took Latin and some other courses from ISLAS.

Sarah says, "I always loved ISLAS because I made really good friends with all my classmates. Although it was text-only, I had the feeling of being in a 'real' class. We'd all chat together before—and sometimes during—the weekly classes. We could send private messages through a separate window

The Cyber Option Is Here to Stay

A snapshot of a cyber school student might include:

- Special-needs students for whom inclusion has not been successful
- Students who do not thrive in a structured, traditional model
- Pregnant teens and teen mothers who need to balance school, motherhood and employment
- Elementary school students whose parents desire more traditional instruction
- Gifted students who are better served by advanced courses
- Expelled students who are at-risk of dropping out
- Students who are concerned with safety issues in schools
- Students who want a career-specific curriculum to supplement the core requirements

Despite this wide variation, successful cyber school students are self-motivated learners who have full parental support and oversight.

Flexibility makes a cyber school attractive to students and their parents:

- Flexibility to transcend socioeconomic and geographic constraints
- Flexibility in selecting from several world-class curricula
- Flexibility in scheduling since school is available 24/7 year round
- Flexibility for students to work at their own pace
- The most important asset of cyber schools . . . may be the opportunity for students to utilize 21st-century technology, enabling them to access cutting-edge opportunities.

Although the future guidelines for cyber schools may evolve in the legislature and through the courts, one certainty exists: cyber schools are an idea whose time has come; there is no turning back.

—Education Advocate, *July/August 2001*

while attending class in the main window, although of course the teacher didn't encourage this! When the teacher figured out one or more of the students were having a long lag in answering, she'd 'ping' us to see if we were still online. This way she could catch us while we were 'passing notes.' When the teacher asked a question, everyone would type an exclamation point when they had the answer. The first person to type the exclamation point would get first shot at answering the question; if they were wrong, the next person in line would do it. The downside was that not every student was a fast typist, so we didn't always get through as much in a class as we wished. It got less formal in Latin 3, where everyone took turns typing in portions of the translations for others to critique.

"All the ISLAS teachers created their own courses, so they really knew what they were talking and emailing about. I would say they all are good teachers, and the instruction is of high quality.

"Another good thing about ISLAS was their graduation ceremony, held in real time and real space. I got to attend the 2000 ceremony here in St. Louis and actually meet the people I'd been chatting with online for years. It was great!

"My favorite online class was my first: 'Molding Your Prose,' taught by Dr. Bruce McMenomy, and taken when I was 12 years old. At the beginning of the year, we each chose one well-known story and then rewrote it in many different forms: news story, humorous story, short-short story of less than 100 words, and so on. It was like a big writing club online. Some of the other students are still my friends."

Joseph echoes Sarah's comments about the friends he made and the quality of ISLAS instruction and adds, "There is no computer so ancient it can't run ISLAS. Everything is set up through email and online chat, so if your computer can connect to the Internet and accept keystrokes, you can take an online course here."

The difference between e-learning and e-ducation (see the grey box on the opposite page) is the teacher. Online academies have teachers; multiple-choice quiz sites don't.

If a teacher, whether Mom or an online instructor, is grading your writing, answering your questions, and provoking you to think, that's e-ducation!

And if you have online classmates with whom you can discuss course material, whether live in real-time online classes or at your own pace via class forums, so much the better.

Real Time with Whiteboard and Internet Audio: Escondido Tutorial Service

Fritz Hinrichs' Escondido Tutorial Service (www.gbt.org) started years ago with classes for local students, added distance learning via speakerphone, and then discovered the Internet. Best known for Fritz's "Great Books Tutorial," which covers the Great Books of the Western World over a period of six years, ETS now offers a variety of other courses as well. Joe took two years of Great Books Tutorial; Sarah took one.

Sarah says, "Escondido Tutorial Service's 'Great Books' online courses were the most interactive courses I had. Although, annoyingly, my Macintosh software did not allow me to literally talk to the other students (I had to input text), I did get to hear what they and Mr. Hinrichs were saying. Attending just one class in real time seemed normal at the time, as I had only attended ISLAS courses before, which also used real-time chat.

"Real-time audio discussions—as opposed to lectures—are a good instructional medium. We'd read the book and then discuss it, which I felt led to much better understanding than just reading it alone would have."

Joseph says, "ETS is still pretty chummy, but you're only likely to find any chat happening during class time, unlike ISLAS, which runs its own Internet Relay Chat (IRC) server. You'd better *love* ancient books if you're going to be in any of Mr. Hinrichs' classes. Don't forget, he graduated from St. John's!"

24-Hour Message Board plus Email: PA Homeschoolers

A lifesaver when we found them, Pennsylvania Homeschoolers (www.pahomeschoolers.com) was the first online academy we know of that offered Advanced Placement courses to homeschoolers. Today, they offer a wider selection than ever. Our children have taken many courses from a variety of teachers through PA Homeschoolers.

Sarah says, "PA Homeschoolers Advanced Placement courses, of which I have taken five over four years, are always of top quality. These courses are 'asynchronous,' meaning you don't attend at a specific time of the day. Rather, you get posted or emailed assignments due by a specific date. Expect *lot* of written assignments because they are the best way to prepare for AP exams. Each course also requires lots of time-consuming discussion, either through their website or email.

"The AP Economics course taught by Howard Richman did an especially good job of preparing us by going over and over and *over* the exact topics that we needed to be prepared to write about. Each course had a detailed syllabus also, which let parents and students know what was due when."

Joseph says, "There always seems to be a spirited discussion going on at PA Homeschoolers courses. One major component of these courses is commenting on your fellow-students' essays and comments. These courses are especially good for the non-science and math AP subjects, the ones that require a lot of discussion between teacher and students."

All the Bells & Whistles: APEX

APEX Learning (www.apexlearning.com), founded by Bill Gates' buddy and Microsoft cofounder Paul Allen, also offers Advanced Placement courses. It features:

A Cautionary Note:
The Perils of Mistaking E-learning for E-ducation

by Paul Glen

At a conference I recently attended, a speaker billed as a "futurist" confidently predicted that within ten years universities will be irrelevant and that corporations will control the entire educational system. In his view most education would be delivered through the Web in small five- to ten-minute increments that can be easily digested at a desk in a cubicle.

He wasn't the first person I've heard make that claim, but what bothered me was that most of the audience seemed to bob their heads in agreement. "Oh yes," they said, "Education will all move to the Web, and universities will go away." This crowd of well-educated professionals seemed very enthusiastic about the prospect of replacing teachers with web browsers and social contact with isolation.

It seemed to me that this futurist, a former university professor with a Ph.D., was confusing *education* and *training.* He failed to see the differences between them and the importance both have in developing an intelligent and aware citizenry as well as a competitive work force.

Training is an activity in which students learn immediately applicable skills to apply to the workplace. Whether they're learning how to install a new computer, configure a new software package, program in a new language, use a new methodology, communicate with colleagues more effectively, or enhance team performance, training students are learning information and techniques to enhance their professional performance. Training is designed to transmit factual information about how to perform specific work tasks.

But education is different. The purpose of education is not to transfer technology, techniques, or skills. **Education is about learning to think, about developing the ability to apply reason and judgment to any situation.** Education is exercise for the mind, designed to help students grow into whole, competent citizens of society, something much more than just competitive workers.

E-learning may be a good approach to training for some job-related skills, but only time will tell how pervasive it becomes. Personally, I think it will be very useful for task-level training. When you want to know how to change the toner in a specific model copier, or how to customize Microsoft Word, the Web is a great place to go. Learner-directed, immediately available task training is well suited to the Web environment.

But it's become all too common to dismiss the importance of education to the health of a professional career. It's much more important to be able to think clearly and creatively than it is to know how to change fonts in a word processor. Online training is great for simple tasks, but if you want add high-value for your clients or colleagues, clear thinking and synthesis are much more important. I've yet to hear of any online training that will educate your mind for a high-powered career and I have a hard time believing that it ever will.

My advice is to use each technique for which it is best. Use the Web for information, but don't confuse e-learning with e-education. In the long run, ignoring education will limit your career and circumscribe your life, no matter how much training you get.

Paul Glen, an adjunct professor at University of Southern California and Loyola Marymount University, is the author of the book Healing Client Relationships *and an upcoming book I am anxious to read entitled* Leading Geeks. *He is Principal of C2 Consulting (www.c2-consulting.com), a company that helps clients build effective IT (information technology) organizations.*

- Online course syllabus, including assignment descriptions and how long they should take
- Continually updated online report cards, with grades and percents posted for assignments as soon as they are graded
- Online video lectures, sometimes also available on a CD-ROM they send you
- Automatic grading of many assignments, with the remainder to be faxed in for hand grading
- All the course material is right there on the site; no separate textbooks, workbooks, etc., are needed.

As a parent, I *love* the APEX interface. It makes it super easy to see exactly what the kids have done and what they need to do. From a management standpoint, my only gripe is the weird scheduling of units according

UN-L ISHS ONLINE

Now available online: courses from University of Nebraska-Lincoln's fully-accredited Independent Study High School. Basically, they have put the syllabus material online, where it is much more colorful and attractive. The self-check tests are online, with instant grading and the ability to retake the tests at any time. Written assignments can be submitted and stored online, and evaluations can also be taken online. Plus there are links to sites that contain relevant information for extra study and instruction. It's all very neat, clean, and easy to use.

The new "Way Cool" management system installed in 2003 lets you check on grades and work online, and even take tests online with instant grading.

Just about every required high-school course you can imagine—and a number of nifty electives—are now available through "Way Cool."

to their topics and not according to the calendar. A unit can be anywhere from three to eight days long, and weekends and holidays are included just like other days. Weekly unit assignments would make much more sense from a scheduling standpoint.

Sarah doesn't share my love affair with APEX. She says, "I found APEX far too automated. When you got the assignment, if a question was confusing or had mistakes in its input, then you had to try to email the teacher and maybe—or maybe not—get a response back in time to make sense of your assignment. All the other online courses I've attended had assignments written by the actual online teachers. Typically, those other courses emailed assignments or gave them out during chats, so if you had any questions or confusion you could sort it out right then.

"Exception: Mr. Robinson, my APEX AP Physics teacher, was very good about getting back quickly with answers. I think this was partly because he had been one of the people who developed the course. My AP Calculus teacher, on the other hand, was horrible about getting back to me. Several times, assignments weren't graded for two weeks, which made it hard to learn anything from my mistakes and really killed my motivation to get the assignments in. Her email answers to my questions weren't very helpful, and she didn't comment on my assignments at all.

"APEX is not the place to make online friends. The online student lounge was usually deserted, and the required discussions seem to end up fulfilling only the minimal requirement of posting a comment and commenting on one other post. There is no real-time chat and no school spirit. Most of the kids taking courses are public schoolers. The two classes I took both consisted mostly of a group of kids from one public school, plus a few strays from public schools around the country, plus my brother Joseph and me, the lone homeschoolers."

Joseph agrees with all the above. His comment: "It's like taking a course via educational software, except that you do have teacher input and grading added throughout the course. The systematic, automated approach is great for science and math. You just grind through it day or night, whenever you have the time. Run the lectures from the CD-ROM, if you can, is my advice, as otherwise you will end up wasting lots of time reestablishing broken connections in the middle of the lecture. As a side note, the physics course has web animations rather than video lectures, and those always ran right. I'd recommend a Pentium or an iMac to make your APEX experience as smooth as it can be."

Since our kids took those APEX courses, APEX has shifted its main focus to providing online AP courses for entire *states*. Public-school students in those states can take APEX courses for free. Homeschool students can still sign up for APEX courses but have to pay full price.

SARAH'S FINAL TIP: "Don't get overexcited about all the neat courses out there and overenroll your student. I talk to homeschooled kids online all the time whose parents have signed them up for too many online courses, so they're spending all their time struggling with academics."

Good point, Sarah! Whether it's educational software or online courses, start off small. Where you go from there is up to you!

CHAPTER 27

The Maloney Method

A feisty self-starter from Ontario, Canada, for more than a quarter of a century, Michael Maloney has been a different kind of educator. Like thousands of other beginning teachers, Maloney started his teacher career in 1964 in the usual way, teaching history and geography to high-school students. He coached, helped with the school newspaper, and worked on school committees.

But Maloney's students were different. They were the hard cases, the repeaters, those with severe academic problems who had been side-streamed into nonacademic courses.

One thing these children all had in common: an inability to read fluently.

Knowing little about teaching basic literacy, Maloney became so frustrated when the school principal failed seven of his hardest-working students that he quit public education.

After five years of graduate psychology studies and a stint teaching community college, Maloney was eventually enticed back into public school classrooms, this time as a behavioral consultant. Again he worked with students at risk of failure. While teaching these students, their teachers, and their principals, Maloney and his colleague Eric Haughton developed an instructional system that consistently created startling academic results.

Despite the obvious and dramatic changes in the students' skills in their more than 60 schools, the district administrators elected to dispense with the programs and released the staff involved in the project . . . just as was happening elsewhere with other successful programs based on Follow-Through research.

The Quinte Learning Centers

Maloney decided to strike out on his own and create his own learning center for children and adults. The center rapidly grew into a full-time private school where children who were failing in their public school classrooms consistently gained two or more grade levels each year. Illiterate adults completed a year of schooling for each month they attended and were usually college-ready within a year. More than 90 percent of the center's students succeeded in their next academic placement.

As the word spread and others visited the school, the demand for more centers resulted in the eventual formation of 20 others across Canada and

Michael Maloney, shown here holding the 2001 National Literacy Award he received from the Canada Post, is the founder of the Quinte Learning Centers. He is also the author of the best-selling educational software *Math Tutor*, the book *Teach Your Children Well*, and its associated curriculum series. Although he did not invent any of the techniques covered in this chapter, he was the first to combine them into a method directed at homeschoolers—and my magazine, *Practical Homeschooling*, was the first homeschool publication to report on his method.

What Does the Maloney Method Offer?

Born as a result of the Western world's largest and most comprehensive study of learning methods, and proven for decades in his own Canadian learning centers, the Maloney Method offers two years of academic advancement in one year of studies—even if your child has been labeled learning-disabled or educationally handicapped. Plus an entirely new approach to instruction, testing, practice, and more.

the USA. The chairman of the local school board pulled his son from one of the public schools he helped to administer and enrolled him full-time in Maloney's classroom for three years. His son rewarded him by graduating from college despite his "learning disability."

Other centers have sprung up using similar methods. Because those who have adopted the model are researchers, the results of students' programs are published in professional journals.

Consistently students are tested at the beginning and end of each school year and consistently they produce gains of two or more years for each year that they are enrolled. Whether the school is in Connecticut, Utah, Washington, California, or Ontario, the results have been consistent for the past two decades.

Each center develops its own unique character determined by its owner and clientele. Each may place a slightly different emphasis on some component of the model, but each gets consistently positive results. (Maloney's book *Teach Your Children Well*, reviewed later in this chapter, describes the work of many of these centers.)

Software Developer

As computers entered schools, Maloney realized that once again his students could be disadvantaged when they returned to their original classrooms by being the only one unable to operate a classroom computer. But his staff were unable to find any software that actually taught anything. (Remember, this was years ago!) Seeking to remedy the deficiency, during the next two years Maloney and his colleague, Michael Summers, a 19-year-old computer whiz, created *Math Tutor,* a set of eight arithmetic programs that taught all of the elementary concepts of math from addition to algebra. Scholastic Inc. of New York immediately bought the licensing rights and marketed *Math Tutor* around the world. The software won its share of awards and sales and became Scholastic's leading line of math products for the next 15 years. It will soon be available in a Windows version.

Teach Your Children Well: Book & Curriculum

Even though Maloney published research and made presentations at national and international education and psychology conferences, the Maloney method wasn't making any headway in North American public schools. After 20 years of successfully teaching children and adults the basics of reading, writing, spelling, and math at rates at least double the norm, Maloney decided to chronicle his work and that of his mentors and colleagues in a book called *Teach Your Children Well*.

As a rookie author, Maloney set out to do book signing appearances in over 200 bookstores, accompanied by his editor, Lynne Brearley. Much to their surprise, it was not the public school teachers who flocked to his signings, but homeschooling parents looking for better instructional methods. The interest of homeschoolers and the buzz in their many communication networks pushed book sales and resulted in Chapters, Canada's largest book chain, selecting Maloney as one of their rising new authors three months after *Teach Your Children Well* was published. It is now a bestseller in its third printing.

Reading about the successes of children who were not supposed to learn well, let alone excel, homeschoolers persistently asked for the materials used in Maloney's centers. Their requests were sufficiently frequent and pressing that Michael, Lynne, and her sister Judie, both retired teachers, decided to write a reading series for elementary school children that would be similar to the ones used in the learning centers. The *Teach Your Children to Read Well* series (reviewed later in this chapter) made its first appearances at annual statewide conferences of the Christian Homeschool Association of Pennsylvania in May 2001 as part of the Creative Kids booth, and at the Christian Home Educators of Ohio conference in Columbus in June.

All this activity was crowned in September 2001 when Michael Maloney was awarded the "Literacy Educator of the Year" award by the Canada Post (no, it's not a newspaper, it's their national mail service!).

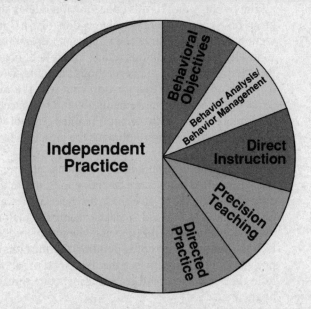

The Maloney Method

Maloney's method was derived from the educational research literature over a 40-year period, which of course included Project Follow-Through, as described in the sidebar.

The Maloney Model has five components:

- Learning Outcomes/Behavior Objectives
- Student Management/Behavior Analysis
- Direct Instruction
- Precision Teaching
- Practice

These five components include the only two (out of 16 tested) from the Follow-Through project that demonstrated consistent academic gains for children at risk of school failure, plus three more Maloney added during his teaching career. As Maloney's book *Teach Your Children Well* explains,

Of the two methods which were successful, the Direct Instruction model from the University of Oregon accounted for the largest share. . . . The second model, Behavior Analysis from the University of Kansas, accounted for much of the remainder. . . . They also ranked first and second in affective measures, that is to say, how the children felt about their involvement and their learning.

Each component is described briefly below.

What Is Project Follow-Through?

It is 1968, and the results of the first stage of Project Follow-Through have just been released. You say you have never heard of Project Follow-Through? Neither have most school-teachers and administrators. This is odd, because **Project Follow-Through eventually became the largest** (250,000 children), **most comprehensive** (16 methods), **longest-running** (20+ years), **most expensive** ($2.2 billion) **comparative study of educational methods ever done in the Western world.**

The Follow-Through study was an attempt to systematically determine what methods worked . . . and what methods didn't . . . when teaching basic skills to "at risk" children considered likely to fail in school. It compared 16 different methods for teaching reading, spelling, language, and arithmetic to more than a quarter million primary school children nationwide over more than a 20-year period. Only two of the 16 methods proved to have any effect: Direct Instruction and Behavior Analysis.

Based on this study, attempts were made in several places to implement these new teaching strategies. For a number of political reasons and in spite of their academic success, all the public school programs based on Follow-Through research were eventually abandoned.

The Maloney Method is based on the techniques shown by Project Follow-Through to be the most successful for teaching basic skills to at-risk youth.

Teach Your Children Well: The Book

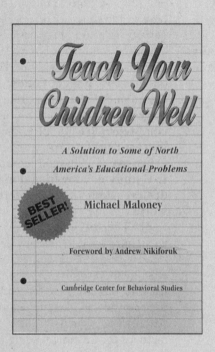

Teach Your Children Well: The Book

Parents. $16.95.
Teach Your Children Well, Ontario, Canada.
(877) 368-1513,
www.teachyourchildrenwell.ca.

This is the book by the man himself, Michael Maloney. And it's well worth reading. In fact, reading **Teach Your Children Well** is what inspired me to ask Mr. Maloney to let me interview him for a *Practical Homeschooling* cover feature.

Chapter 1 is a brief recap of Maloney's own educational odyssey, leading him to found the Quinte Learning Centers and his software and books. Chapters 3 and 4 recount how both Canada (Maloney's home country) and the USA are sliding into an appalling gulf of illiteracy and innumeracy, and just what this is costing us all in both money and the tragedy of wasted lives. The next two chapters chronicle the major educational research into how to successfully teach basic skills to "at risk" children and briefly introduce the "QLC" model, which for ease of remembering and discussion I have rechristened the "Maloney Model," after its foremost synthesist. Chapters 6 through 10 then explain the model in depth, with one chapter each on Behavioral Objectives/Learning Outcomes, Behavioral Analysis/Behavior Management, Direct Instruction,

Precision Teaching, and Directed & Independent Practice. The next part shows how the model has worked in real life in a wide range of academic locations. Finally, Part Six answers the question we're all asking by this time, "If this educational model is so great, how come the public schools don't use it?" In this section, Maloney outlines the political and personal reasons why teachers, administrators, and school board members can and do prefer methods that don't work over proven methods that do work and why the various "educational reform" movements all tend to concentrate on school *structure* rather than "the nitty gritty of what will happen in the classroom once the structure has been altered."

To keep you from suffering in suspense, it turns out that his method takes more teacher effort, and school officials usually fail to give those teachers any rewards for their success. Instead, a teacher using the Maloney Method will usually end up being given *more* problem kids to teach, with no corresponding rise in status or pay. Also, such teachers face the likelihood of sabotage from their less-successful colleagues who are threatened by their success.

Maloney decries the current lack of *measurable* academic standards (when is the last time you ever heard of public school students being given a timed test of how many words aloud they could read without errors?), the erosion of standards via social promotion and (in Canada) "life experience" credits for simply existing, lack of sanctions for ineffective teachers, the pain of change, the pain of success (extra problem kids to teach), staff tension between teachers using proven methods and those using ineffective methods (who may sabotage or backbite their rivals), and so on. His cultural critique doesn't delve as deeply as, say, John Taylor Gatto's, whose *Underground History of American Education* laid out a persuasive case for why our political and cultural elite actually *wants* most kids to graduate with poor academic skills. Still, his capsule descriptions of the various "reform" movements is quite an education in itself.

Teach Your Children Well ends with the usual list of suggestions for changing the system, but of course a parent who needs help *now* doesn't have years to wait for change that might come late or never. Hence the need for educational tools a parent can use at home. You'll find some in the review later in this chapter.

Learning Outcomes/Behavioral Objectives

If you've used homeschool curriculum for any length of time, you've probably run across a set of lessons with "objectives" or "outcomes" listed at the beginning of the lesson, or even a "scope and sequence" of the entire curriculum. Objectives provide a road map for learning. Gathered together into an orderly sequence, they become a "scope and sequence." The "scope" of what will be taught—e.g., the content—is outlined, and the sequence in which skills will be learned is given, usually in a chart format.

Ideally, outcomes are written so that they can be easily observed and measured. An example of a Maloney objective: "The student reads aloud from his/her story at 200 words per minute with no more than 2 errors." It is relatively easy to listen to a child read for a minute, to count the errors and the words read correctly to see if they have achieved the objective.

Student Management/Behavior Analysis

No one can teach effectively in chaos. So here are Maloney's classroom rules:

- Work quickly and quietly.
- Bring all of your materials.
- Keep your hands and your feet to yourself.
- Say only good things.
- Raise your hand to address the group.

All these can apply just as well at home as at school, except that "raising the hand to address the group" bit.

In this portion of the Maloney model (which is similar to that proposed by National Academy for Child Development founder Robert Doman and other "positive-reinforcement" advocates), teachers pay attention to those who follow the rules and systematically ignore those who break them. The closest compliant student is singled out for attention, rather than directing attention to the rule breaker. This is not a sneaky way of tricking kids into compliance; rather, students are actively taught the rules, to the point that they can state any or all of them verbatim if asked. The goal is to catch the student doing something *right* rather than punishing them for doing something *wrong*.

In the safety of the home, the parent can and should deal with genuine moral infractions rather than just ignoring them, *as well as* praising good behavior. However, as Doman points out in his materials, often parents fall into the trap of continuous negativity. It is important to remind ourselves constantly to notice and praise good behavior rather than taking it for granted.

Scripting/Direct Instruction

Most of the results of the massive Follow-Through study were accounted for by one of the 16 methods, the Direct Instruction method.

The idea behind Direct Instruction is to enable any teacher to teach basic skills in such a way that every single child in the class will learn them.

Direct Instruction employs **scripting**. Everything the teacher is to say, and that the student should reply, is written out in an actual script. Among homeschool materials, you may have seen this in the Cornerstone Curriculum Press materials, among others.

"Correction procedures" that tell the the teacher what to say when faced with specific wrong responses are also included in the script. All errors are corrected immediately.

Teach Your Children Well: The Curriculum

Teach Your Children Well series

Grades K–4. Instructor's Manuals, $29.95 each. Student Reader, $16.95 each. Student Workbooks, $8.95 each. Complete set of 3 books (any level), $54.95.

Teach Your Children Well, Ontario, Canada. (877) 368-1513, *www.teachyourchildrenwell.ca.*

Daily lessons. A way to easily measure student progress. Reading selections with measuring tools built in. Nice large print. Cookbook style "scripted" instructions. These are just some of the distinctive features of the easy-to-use **Teach Your Children to Read Well series**.

Currently, five levels are available.

- Level 1A, for grades K–2, has 30 lessons
- Level 1B, also for grades K–2, also has 30 lessons
- Level 2, for grades 3–4, has 60 lessons. These start by reviewing all the basic decoding skills taught in levels 1A and 1B and continue on to more complex decoding strategies to develop fluency.
- Level 3, for grades 5–6, also has 60 lessons. It launches immediately into sentence composition and vocabulary improvement.
- Level 4 for grades 7–8 is another 60-lesson course with more advanced vocabulary and English skills.

Each level includes an Instructor's Manual, a Student Workbook, and a Student Reader.

Instructor's Manual. Scripted lessons tell you exactly what to say; if the student responds incorrectly, "correction procedures" tell you exactly what to do.

Each Manual begins with a detailed explanation of the method. Count on a day or two of study to feel comfortable with all the phonics sounds and teaching techniques if you have never encountered them before.

Student Workbook includes handwriting practice (standard manuscript style: You may wish to substitute another series of your choice for this portion or adapt the instructions to pre-cursive) and a variety of reading activities, beginning with letter recognition in level 1A and progressing to open-ended (*not* multiple-choice!) comprehension questions in Level 2. Crosswords, unscrambles, mazes, and other typical kid-pleasing drill materials are also included. Depending on the level, in the back of the book you'll also find an Alphabet Letters Fluency Chart, Sound Fluency Chart, Word Fluency Chart, and/or a Story Reading Fluency Chart, in which you record daily student measurements. Finally, you measure day-to-day progress with a Points Chart, which ties together your student's overall score. This is based on 1 to 10 points each for working hard, paying attention, following instructions, workbook exercises, and fluency checks. See how the "behavior analysis" is built right in?

Student Reader for each level is where you'll find practice stories for the student to read aloud, beginning in level 1A with individual sentences. The Word Fluency Chart in the workbook tracks your child's score on the Word Fluency Checks found in the readers. These are lists of individual words, in no particular order, to be read aloud and timed. The words are numbered by fives both horizontally and vertically, so you can easily see exactly how many words were correctly read in a given time period. Similarly, each line of the story has a number next to it that tells you how many words the child has read so far. A great time-saver!

Learning starts with the back cover of each and every book, where you'll find a short reading excerpt. If your child reads this with less than four errors (miscalled words, added words, or omitted words), you can proceed to the next level in the series and try the test on the back of *that* book. Hopefully these quick placement tests will be placed on the website, so you don't have to physically have a book in your hands to determine your child's correct level.

The most successfully marketed Direct Instruction program of all time, the DISTAR program from Science Reading Associates (SRA), failed to dominate in the schools partly because of parent disgust with the odd content in the reading assignments. That's only fair: No amount of good techniques can make up for objectionable content. With that in mind, I carefully looked over the reading selections in the Teach Your Children to Read Well volumes. I found they contain a mix of fascinating facts (e.g., the origin of the sandwich), thrillers ("Lost in the Dark," "Shipwrecked," etc., many of which are continued over several reading sessions as cliffhangers), and fantasy ("Timothy the Timid Troll" and "Backwards Land"). The fantasy selections were clearly intended for kids to take as cute but impossible stories, and at home of course a parent can choose to skip any content he or she finds objectionable.

Direct Instruction employs a three-part sequence called "Model – Lead – Test." First, the teacher models the task. Then, the students perform the same task along with the teacher. Finally, when the teacher is sure the student can do the task correctly, he or she is allowed to practice it alone.

To organize learning as much as possible, Direct Instruction teaches children rules whenever possible, rather than asking them to memorize baskets of facts. For example, in his *Teach Your Children to Read Well* phonics series, Maloney and his coauthors teach students that there are two possible plural endings for nouns: *s* and *es*. They then present a set of nouns and teach the following rule. "If a noun ends with *ch, sh, s,x,* or *z,* use *es* to make it plural. If it does not, use *s*." Next, they present them with examples (e.g., *brush*) and with non-examples (e.g., *tree*) and ask them to say the plural ending *s* or *es* based on the rule. There are 20 such spelling rules, all of which are taught in the series.

There's much more to Direct Instruction than this. If you want to know more, the quickest way is to read Maloney's book!

Measurement/Precision Teaching

In the Maloney Method, after the instruction is completed, the teacher measures performance to ensure that the learning occurred. If the student didn't learn, the teacher didn't teach.

Usually the method used to measure performance is to take a timed sample of the student's new learning and compare it to a known standard. The same measurement taken each day provides information about the rate at which the student is learning.

Humans speak at approximately 200 words per minute. Once they learn to talk, children speak at about the same rate as adults. If the child were a fluent reader, the child should be able to read words at or about the same rate that he or she speaks. So when Maloney measures oral reading, he expects the child to read at a conversational rate. The standard is achieved when the child can read grade level material at 200 words per minute with

Aside from this, I found one story about creatures on another planet who are concerned that people on earth kill each other (a theme you may well find unsuitable for young children), and an amazing number of stories about fishing and frogs, one from the point of view of a frog that is being hunted for use as bait. It could be a little unsettling for kids to switch gears from treating frogs as animals who it's OK to catch, to a frog thinking about how he does *not* want to be caught. There's also a story about a sea monster that wants to eat children (they give it cake instead), and one about boxing (which for me is no problem since all our kids take martial arts).

On the obviously positive side, several continued stories revolve around the theme of how helpful it is to learn to read well, and there's a story about how silly it is for athletes to be superstitious (wearing "lucky" socks that are never washed—yuck!).

Another feature some disliked about DISTAR was the unusual orthography. Letters were shaped differently, depending on the sounds they made. If you've used *Teach Your Child to Read in 100 Easy Lessons* you've seen a similar approach. The only such tactic used in the Teach Your Children to Read Well series is a bar across the top of some long vowels in words such as *the*. In keeping with Maloney's philosophy of teaching rules that cover a multitude of words, rather than relying on visual crutches, it is *not* applied to words that follow the "silent-e-at-the-end" rule, such as *game* and *home*. All long-vowel bars are phased out by level 2.

Bottom line: this series has all the features of the Maloney Method in one handy package. If you liked *Teach Your Child to Read in 100 Easy Lessons,* you should love this program. It has all the benefits of the former, with no awkward "conversion" period from nonstandard to standard orthography, and much better teaching tools. If your child is a late bloomer or has special needs, you especially should check this new series out, as it is based on the best research about teaching these very groups. And if you are a literacy volunteer, special educator, or early grades teacher, you definitely should buy both Maloney's book and a set of this series.

no more than two errors. Any behavior that can be seen and repeated can be counted and charted to show current performance, rate of learning, and distance from the standard.

In Maloney's method, objectives are set and changed based on data from thousands of children doing the same or similar tasks. Thanks to this research, it is known what level of performance constitutes "fluency" in a given skill. Children and teachers then both know exactly what they are aiming for, the amount of improvement, and how far they have to go.

To be fluent in reading, a child or adult should be able to:

• See/say sounds in isolation	60–80 sounds/minute
• See/say single words in lists	80–100 words/minute
• Think/say alphabet in order	300–400 letters/minute
• See/say sound-out words	20–30 words/minute
• See/say words in sentences	200+ words/minute

To be fluent in math, you and your children should be able to:

• Hear/write numbers (random)	80–100 numbers/minute
• Think/write numbers in sequence	120–160 numbers/minute
• See/say numbers (random)	80–100 numbers/minute
• See/write math facts (answers to single-digit problems)	80–100 facts/minute

These are just a few of the many "pinpoint" objectives in the Maloney Method. As you can see, it takes only a minute to determine exactly how fluent your child is in any of these skills.

Directed Practice

Directed practice is where the teacher holds your hand while you attempt the task you have just been shown. This allows the teacher to determine whether or not you are ready to practice that skill independently. Regardless of the teaching method you are currently using, smart homeschoolers always take the time to do this! We spot and correct errors so that our students do not practice mistakes.

Independent Practice

Maloney says, "Directed and independent practice comprise 60 to 70 percent of teaching and learning. Independent practice is by far the largest and most time-consuming aspect of learning."

Students are allowed to practice independently when their errors have dropped to an acceptable level so that the skill is being perfected. In math, for example, they are making occasional "stupid" mistakes (such as mistaking an addition problem that follows three subtraction problems for another subtraction problem) rather than organic mistakes, such as giving wrong answers although they understand the problem. At this stage, the child is able to catch his own errors or resolve a problem correctly himself once it is marked wrong and returned to him.

Putting It All Together

The Maloney Method was based on research and experience with "at risk" children. It is highly successful at teaching basic skills to this group.

The benefits I see it bringing to homeschoolers are:

- Great help for those with special-needs children
- Scientific help in measuring your child's progress from day to day, regardless of his or her ability
- Generating more thought on curriculum design
- Generating helpful discussion on the benefits of teacher-centered rather than child-centered educational methods.

Maloney waxes passionate on the decline he feels child-centered methods such as Discovery Learning have brought to the public schools. This could lead to a helpful balance, since up to this point the rhetorical advantage has all gone to the child-centered camp.

Education is more than facts and skills, as Maloney himself agrees. You can't use pinpoint objectives and precision measurement to determine how wise a student is becoming, or to interest students in a career. Worldview subjects, such as history, literature, and Bible, should be explored as well as studied. However, we will be much more effective at teaching the *facts* of subjects ranging from history, music, and literature to Bible study if we adopt at least some of Maloney's techniques.

Most of my children learned to read at age 4 or 5. But one daughter, even at age 8, could only read small words very slowly. We started using Maloney's curriculum with her, and in just a month she was reading grade-level texts fluently!

Not every kid needs this approach. But for those who are slow in a "skills" subject, it can work wonders.

CHAPTER 28

The Montessori Method

Have you ever bought your children a set of stacking toys, or a "shapes" puzzle, or a set of textured objects to feel and play with? Did you ever get your baby a set of objects that he or she needed to place precisely into fitted holes? Did your kiddies ever use child-sized tools to learn clean-up jobs, or sandpaper letters to learn the alphabet?

If so, you've already encountered the Montessori Method in action.

If you were to take a visit today to an upscale "developmental toys" store, you would be surrounded on all sides by Montessori inventions. The very idea of a self-checking toy—one that directs the user to practice a skill and only allows "correct" answers by its very design—was a Montessori invention, as was the idea of sparking children's observational senses with the help of "sensory objects"—items with distinct textures, sounds, and smells. These are just a few ways in which Maria Montessori, although she receives little credit for it, has changed our children's world.

So, who is this Maria Montessori?

Maria Montessori: medical doctor, philosopher, and educational innovator

Meet Maria Montessori

Maria Montessori (1870–1952), Italian founder of the educational philosophy that has led among other things to a network of "Montessori Schools" worldwide, was a medical doctor who carefully observed children and made notes about what they liked and disliked. Asked to take over the education of all the "deficient" children from the public schools of Rome and the "idiot" children in Rome from the asylums in which they were housed (these were the terms for mentally challenged children at the time!), she taught them so well that they passed the same tests "normal" children were given. Rather than basking in the acclaim this feat brought her, Dr. Montessori, who sounds like a lady we'd all enjoy meeting today, said, "While everyone was admiring the progress of my idiots, I was searching for the reasons which could keep the happy healthy children of the common schools on so low a plane that they could be equalled in tests of intelligence by my unfortunate pupils!"

Given the chance to form schools for Italian slum children within their own tenements, she put her now more refined theories into practice and stunned the world by turning these children into adept scholars, capable

A Highly Original Method

Certain aspects of the [Montessori] system are in themselves striking and significant: it adapts to the education of normal children methods and apparatus originally used for deficients [mentally challenged children]; it is based on a radical conception of liberty for the pupil; it entails a highly formal training of separate sensory, motor, and mental capacities; and it leads to rapid, easy, and substantial mastery of the elements of writing, reading, and arithmetic.

—Harvard professor Haney W. Holmes, from his introduction to the book The Montessori Method

THE BOOK YOU SHOULD READ

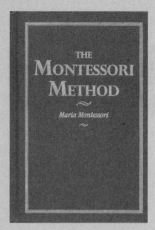

THE
MONTESSORI
METHOD
~
Maria Montessori
~

Many books have been written about the Montessori method. The one you should start with is appropriately titled **The Montessori Method**. Its author: Dr. Maria Montessori. She tells how she researched her approach, how she put it into practice and refined it, and exactly how it works, all in the most practical and poetic terms.

"Practical" and "poetic" don't normally go together. Rarely is both the practical "make it work" and the poetic "sense of wonder" combined in one individual along with the patience to continually refine and test and the cleverness to continually invent new ideas. This is undoubtedly part of Montessori's enduring appeal, and also a reason why her method works so well. The lady seems to have been blessed with a copious helping of *every* learning personality style, and therefore her method embraces them all.

Published in 1912, this translation into English of Dr. Montessori's original writings has recently been reissued in a handsome hardcover edition with gilt accents by Roger A. McCaffrey Publishing (CT), (970) 490-2735, www.booksforcatholics. com. The price for this keepsake edition is $24.80. Highly recommended.

(for instance) of writing lovely letters without a single error, and in lovely handwriting, at the age of four. These children, from a class thought of at the time as naturally uncontrolled and rough in behavior, astonished visitors who saw 40 or 50 children aged 3 to 6 working quietly in a room on a variety of separate projects. These children took care of their class pets, cared for their own garden, and were capable of group intervals of absolute silence upon teacher request.

How did Dr. Montessori accomplish these seeming miracles? **She gave the children pieces of equipment carefully designed to help them learn adult skills:** wooden frames with canvas attached and string for practicing lacing, frames for buttoning, frames for using the button-hook devices of that day. These materials were designed to **correct any errors**; by their very design, the child could tell whether he was doing the task correctly or not. **She gave them materials they could feel with their hands:** textured blocks, letter stencils, number stencils. **She gave them grown-up tools scaled down to child's size:** pots and pans, brooms and mops. **She gave them responsibility** for doing as adult a job as possible. Children in Montessori's own school served themselves lunch and cleaned up afterward, although they were only three to five years old.

Having prepared the environment as carefully as she could to be free of distractions, Montessori and her teachers sat back and watched. They might show a child how to use a piece of apparatus; then they would back off and let the children learn as much as they could totally unaided.

The data was there—hands-on experiences by the roomful. The framework was there—carefully graduated exercises led the children almost imperceptibly to reading, writing, and figuring. The children learned.

Awed by Montessori's success, teachers all over the world descended on her. In time she ended up writing several books and teaching others to carry on her work. The Montessori method is now taught by several different societies and in hundreds of schools and preschools, as well as homeschools.

What Is the Montessori Method?

Here are a few of the method's main features:

- **Start with the senses.** Montessori made much of the importance of training children to carefully observe, not only with the senses of sight and hearing, but with various aspects of the sense of touch (tactile sense—roughness versus smoothness, general "feel"; baric sense—discerning weights of objects; thermal sense—discerning relative temperatures; stereognostic sense—discerning an object's shape by touch alone). She felt this aided a child tremendously in developing his scientific powers of observation.
- **Preparation of the environment.** I have already touched on this in a previous chapter. For Montessori, this meant removing all twaddle, nonsense, distractions, and unhygienic materials, and arranging the environment to optimally accommodate learning. Child-sized furniture designed to be light enough for the children to move was one of her classroom innovations.
- **Observation of the child.** The child was not the only one supposed to develop powers of observation. For Montessori, observation was the teacher's main job. The teacher noted carefully each child's progress and personality, and only intervened when necessary to suppress bad behavior or prevent harm.

How to Teach Each Age

At ages 3 to 6 it's important to give your child lots of practical activities to do, with the steps broken down for the sake of mastery. You can find many good sources of Montessori activities on the Web for this period. I might make substitutions, like using Cuisenaire Jumbo Rods instead of Montessori materials, but I make sure I understand how to use the new materials to teach the desired skill in a similar fashion.

For ages 6 to 12, I have found a few products that are like Montessori's original ideas. I modify such programs by creating a wall chart that shows the big ideas and adding homemade vocabulary cards, color coding, symbols, and hands-on activities as needed. I also rely less on auditory mnemonics than these programs ask me to.

From ages 6 to 12 I teach my children the "content areas" (subjects such as history, science, and geography) through key lessons. Each area of study is on a list that spans three years, so we have no pressure to complete it all in one year. The skills in each area move from concrete objects, to the more abstract labels and cards, to the more abstract still: writing and research. I share these subject/skill lists with my elementary children so they can chart and monitor their progress. It is a way to give them the big picture of what they're learning, and a key to mastery.

From ages 9 to 12, learning is more research driven. But I still provide research ideas so the children can imagine the possibilities. In the case of studying the moon, I might suggest researching manned space flights to the moon and giving a rocket-launching demonstration. In each stage of my student's work, I am there with suggestions and resources if he gets stuck.

and tries to build words . . . when she tries to read road signs and enjoys following your finger under a line of print while you read.

The First Plane of Development: Birth to Age 6. The first **plane of development** in Montessori-speak (other writers usually call these **stages of development**) is the period from ages 0 to 6, where the infant develops into the child. In the first half of this plane, from ages 0 to 3, the child transforms from a baby to a young child. His random movements become coordinated and controlled: grasping, touching, turning, balancing, walking. In the second half of the plane, from ages 3 to 6, he will classify and categorize his sense impressions.

Each specific skill area develops quickly during its sensitive period, almost to the exclusion of other skills during that time. As Jane Healy, author of *Endangered Minds,* says, "The child actually changes the physiology of the brain through interaction with the environment at specific stages of development." If your child misses the opportunity to develop a skill during its sensitive periods, he can learn it later on, but it will be much harder.

More detailed information on these sensitive periods is presented in Montessori's books and can be found searching the Web under that topic.

The Second Plane of Development: Ages 6 to 12. During the second plane of development the child's physical state is stable. While he is still growing, there are no major hormonal changes. It is an intellectual period, so the child's appetite for knowledge is big. Children of this age want to grasp the big picture of facts and ideas in relation to each other.

The Third Plane of Development: Ages 12 to 18. During the first half, ages 12 to 15, these young teens are unstable intellectually because of the great physical changes they are experiencing. They need extra sleep, and are interested mostly in practical work related to supplying food, shelter, transportation, etc. Intellectual work during this plane is best when it follows the student's interests without pressure. I try to limit the amount of coursework and encourage more work and social time.

In the second half of this plane, from age 15 to age 18 and up, I say, "Their brains come back into their bodies." Older teens are ready for more rigorous intellectual work along with ministry and apprenticeships in the work world. I introduce standard high-school curriculum at this point, due to its efficiency in preparing the student for college.

The Fourth Plane of Development: Age 18 and Up. In the fourth and final plane, the child has fully transformed to an adult. The years from age 18 to 24 are a time of specialization and preparation for careers. Parents often feel their job is completed by age 18, but great parental energy is still needed to support our young adults as they make many lifelong decisions. Good mentors who help the student find his way into the right field of specialized learning are also important.

Dr. Montessori thought universities should have students find work experiences in the community so they could achieve their financial independence while still in college, even if it means taking a few more years to complete their studies. An interesting thought for our debt-ridden day!

How Kathy Does It

My homeschooling needs a fence to keep us in good places. The first side of my fence is my **prepared room** and **overall skills list for each child.** The list lets me know where my children should be heading and

- **Respect for the child and his individuality.** The lockstep education Montessori called "old fashioned" in her 1912 book is still with us today. Montessori was absolutely opposed to this. She believed each child's distinct personality should be encouraged.
- **The goal of independence.** Montessori didn't believe in doing anything for children (or, for that matter, adults) that they could do for themselves. As opposed to the "kindergarten" invented by Froebel, where the children are all grouped around the teacher, through whom all knowledge is mediated, the goal of Montessori preschool was a child who would learn on his own as much as possible and be as responsible as possible.
- **No external rewards or punishments.** While Montessori occasionally would show approval by letting the "most silent" child go first, for example, she frowned on stars, smiley faces, medals, and other special honors for academic work or behavior. Her goal was to train the child's spirit to love learning and righteousness so that they would be motivated inwardly.
- **Practical life training.** From buttoning their own shoes and personal cleanliness to cleaning the room themselves, from care of animals to gardening, Montessori taught children the practical life lessons valuable in their daily lives.
- **Ingenious self-correcting didactic material.** Montessori adapted or invented many teaching tools still used today: shape puzzles, sandpaper letters, buttoning frames, stacking toys, etc. All these materials were designed to naturally draw children to learning the proper lessons. When tracing sandpaper letters, for example, the child could instantly tell by the shift from rough sandpaper to smooth cardboard that his or her finger had left the correct path.
- **The three-period lesson.** In **period 1** the teacher associates the child's sensory perception with the name of the item. E.g., "This is a red card. This is a blue card." In **period 2** the teacher tests the child's recognition of the item. E.g., "Give me the red card." In **period 3** the child's memory of the name is tested. E.g., (holding up a red card), "What is this?"

Building on Dr. Montessori's work, today's Montessori educators have gone far beyond the initial preschool material. At a recent convention of the American Montessori Society, middle school and high school education was a very hot topic. One such school, the Barrie school (www.barrie.org) has had 20 percent of their students become National Merit Scholars (as opposed to about .25 percent—that's ¼ of 1 percent—of public school students who ever achieve this honor).

For the rest of this chapter, I turn you over to *Practical Homeschooling's* reigning "Montessori at home" expert, Katherine von Duyke. Kathy is currently involved in trying to pioneer connections between the Montessori school community and the homeschool community. We're hoping for some exciting new developments over the next few years.

Ideally, we'd like to see Montessori teacher training available for homeschoolers, more Montessori materials readily available through homeschool catalogs, and Montessori schools that open their doors to homeschool students, who could attend part-time. This could be especially helpful for both communities at the middle- and high-school level.

For more on this, keep reading *Practical Homeschooling!*

EVERY PARENT A MONTESSORI TEACHER

When one reads [Montessori's] eloquent "Inaugural Address" it is impossible not to wish that a "School within the Home" might stand as a center of hopeful child life in the midst of every close-built city block. Better, of course, if there were no hive-like city tenements at all, and if every family could give to its own children on its own premises enough of "happy play in grassy places." Better if every mother and father were in certain ways an expert in child psychology and hygiene.
—*Haney W. Holmes*

MONTESSORI IN THE HOME

As to the use of the Montessori system in the home, one or two remarks must suffice. In the first place, parents should not expect that the mere presence of the materials in the nursery will be enough to work an educational miracle. A Montessori directress does no common "teaching," but she is called upon for very skillful and very tiring effort. She must watch, assist, inspire, suggest, guide, explain, correct, inhibit. . . . It will do not harm—except perhaps to the material itself—to have the Montessori material at hand in the home, but it must be used under proper guidance if it to be educationally effective. And besides, it must not be forgotten that the material is by no means the most important feature of the Montessori programme. The best use of the Montessori system in the home will come through the reading of this book. [See review of the book on the previous page.]
—*Haney W. Holmes*

Katherine von Duyke is *Practical Homeschooling's* expert on using the Montessori method at home. She has homeschooled her 12 children for 17 years and teaches algebra and earth science for Towle, a homeschool high school. Kathy is also the author of the *Month by Month* spelling guide, a companion guide to *The Writing Road to Reading,* and *The Home Education Copybook,* a resource for developing and using unit studies.

Except where noted, the rest of this chapter is based on articles Kathy wrote for my *Practical Homeschooling* magazine.

Home as a Prepared Environment

The family is meant to be a place of grace. We were created to interact heart to heart, and mind to mind, knowing each other, caring about each other, being involved, and encouraging one another. Authority is used to bring up and nurture and support the weak among us, our children. Weakness may be in many forms—this one is undisciplined, that one is fearful; one struggles with math, that one isn't ready to read. But how to create a home environment that allows such beauty to unfold among the members within? And how does one do this in the swing between rigidly disciplined lessons with accountability, and child-led studies that perhaps leave a parent breathless trying to give such freedom to a houseful of children?

Enter the **prepared environment** of the Montessori Method. It is both child-directed and yet parent-directed. I find that all of my favorite homeschool resources work well and perhaps even better within a prepared environment and in the context of the Montessori teaching methods.

In this method, developed early last century by Italian doctor Maria Montessori, lessons are presented in three **periods**. Information is *presented, practiced,* and finally *checked for mastery,* all with attention to the dignity and *intrinsic desire to learn* within a child.

Hands-On First

Dr. Montessori researched and found that all children past the age of babyhood learn through their hands first. In fact, she concluded that children needed sensorial training (senses). She developed many beautiful, clever materials that are satisfying to the touch and that allow for exploration and development of the senses. This attention to the senses is then incorporated into higher learning. For example, a child builds multiplication tables through the use of an attractive wooden set of counters and a board. Through the use of satisfying touch and hands-on patterning, a very young child can build a mental pattern for mathematics.

Preparing a Neat Environment

On one of the first days of school I demonstrate how to take a rug, unfold it, and lay it out. I will choose an activity from the shelf and bring it to my rug. Materials are laid out left to right and bottom to top in order of difficulty on the shelves. Children are encouraged to work a shelf in this fashion so that they build each small skill upon the preceding one. When I am finished, I will put the activity back in its original form and place it back on the shelf.

Neatness, order, thoughtfulness towards others, and grace are incorporated into each activity. If only they would do this with the toilet paper roll, right? Using the rugs helps children define their space. This keeps them from worrying about encroachment and from encroaching on others. In fact, this is one of the first ways we teach them to love their neighbor as themselves.

Obviously, setting up such carefully prepared materials in a home environment takes time, and a curious one-year-old can unshelve it mighty quickly. Justin (eight months) was allowed to play in the bean bowl with the cups, but each time his father popped his head in the room, he would become startled and toss the cup of beans over his shoulder and all over the floor. While this was cute, he didn't have the skill to clean it up, and it wouldn't be a safe play area apart from my careful attending. So Tim

hinged two long, low purchased bookcases that had backs. He set casters under them and a lock on the outside. With this setup, I can carefully lay out several weeks' worth of materials and lock it up at the end of our school day. This leaves the room free for later play without overuse or abuse of the materials.

With a prepared environment, meaningful and engaging activities, some beautiful violin pieces or Irish harp in the background, and a clear set of expectations for school-age children, we have experienced some incredibly peaceful and productive school days.

Practical Life Training

As homeschoolers, we love a strong focus on practical life training. The Montessori method developed a whole curriculum around this goal. Practical life training has brought a much greater sense of order and peace in our school day. The repeated practice of useful tasks is very engaging to young children, absorbing their concentration, training them in independence, and modeling how to perform family tasks, making them both a delight and a help.

I had initially assumed I could do this training at chore times, but many of those tasks needed to be broken down and practiced in much smaller pieces. In one activity I created for my two-year-old, Heidi, I cut a hole in a large plastic bin top and seated a plastic bowl down into it. I filled the bowl with kidney beans, adding a scoop and six plastic cups around the perimeter of the bin. After demonstrating to her how to scoop from the middle of the bowl into the middle of the cup, and later carefully pour back into the bowl and clean up her spills, I let her have a go. I was moved by the level of intense focus she applied to her task and the length of time she spent working to perfect her ability to scoop and fill and pour. In time she will easily pour her own cups of milk without a spill.

Sensitive Periods and Planes of Development

I have spent the past four days wearing the same pair of pajamas, holed up in my basement, staring at a computer screen 12 inches from my face. Occasionally, on emerging, my children ask if I'm the real mother or just the virtual reality. Tim, my muscled other half, has somehow kept an eye on the house and kids in between his myriad of business tasks.

Any veteran homeschooler knows this is a picture of lesson planning time. So how do I plan in the Montessori way? "The education of our day is rich in methods, aims, and social ends, but one must still say that it takes no account of life itself," said Maria Montessori.

We see this in children who are learning to read. Presented with the right teaching at the right time, a child will learn to read. Forced to read before he is ready, and then crushed under loads of remedial work, a child becomes an adult with poor reading skills. Why? Because the myelin sheath development needed for optimum brain connections must first be in place. **Children naturally gravitate to those activities that follow their brain development.** They have an urge to exercise those new brain connections, much as a child who is teething has an urge to chew. Forced laborious reading with unformed or partially-formed brain connections results in a mental habit that destroys reading enjoyment for life.

How do we know when it's the right time for our child to learn to read? When he begins to notice and show interest in print . . . when she begins to ask questions about reading . . . when he grabs onto learning the sounds

Choosing Materials

When choosing materials fo... 3 to 12 I often start by asking ... self, "Is it fun?" If it doesn't app... me, it probably won't to them e... Then I ask, "Do they want to wa... me demonstrate it or do it them-selves?" If possible, I change the a... tivity so they can do it themselves, making up a way to self-check, and adding question cards that include the main ideas I want them to learn. I want them to be able to fiddle with the material and gain their own sense of how it works, and I want them to know key ideas through the questions I ask them. I then think of a way to use the knowledge. Can they get out in the real world and use it/do it/collect it/sort it? I might keep an ongoing samples table. I present the big ideas in a chart, and have the children commit those ideas to memory. Finally, as the children become able to read and write, this is followed by simple research models and report writing.

what to set up in my schoolroom so they might have opportunity to pursue it. Keeping myself accountable this way helps me stay alert to what areas need more work and what areas have become old for each child.

The second side of the fence is **the syllabus I write for each subject my child will work on for the year.** I have an overall plan for the year written out, but I fill in the syllabi monthly. This allows me to stay close to my child's interests and abilities. I feel Peter, our fifth grader, will get lots more learning out of all the terrific books we have filled our school room with over the years, and he loves to read. So I emphasize reading, but he may research a topic. I want to build his research and writing skills, but I like to key these to what I see he is excited about. For Timmy, our third grader, the books he can read are fairly simple, but he can gain a lot through projects that encourage his attention to the subject. His research must be very simple: a short list of questions I make for him, which he answers and then rewrites into a paragraph format. Often, I will create a shelf of job choices and leave out a stack of library books, further increasing their chance to choose what interests them. Sometimes I simply write "your choice" under a heading and they fill in what is completed.

My simple syllabus for each course is the same. It shows a block:

	Day 1	Day 2	Day 3	Etc.
Read				
Activities				
Research				
Computer				

Of course, the blocks are bigger than this example!

"Read" is followed by a book title or free choice. We always start here because the human brain was not designed to absorb facts but to respond to story. I keep this in mind when I scour for books. "Activities" usually consists of jobs I've created, creative projects, or nature hunts. This is the adventurous part of schooling that woos them into the subject. "Research" may consist of a worksheet or a list of questions to look up. I keep the list short for children under fourth grade because young children are emotional creatures and don't think inductively. "Computer" may be a software choice, a website to explore, or nothing in the blank.

The rest of our school is fenced on two sides by two routines.

Morning line time. The children check their checklist, which simply lists the subjects they are to cover that day, and write out their plan of work for their day in their log book. This may seem redundant with young children, but I'm building a lifelong habit in them of checking their day and deciding what to do with it. They have the choice of which subject to do first, and except for those subjects that I teach in small groups, may clump courses any way they like as long as the list is finished by the weekend. For core courses, the checklist will state "history," but the children check the history syllabus I have on file under their name and pick which activities for the week they would like to do that day. This respects my children's thinking because if they are really enjoying a subject, they need not put it down just as it becomes interesting. On the other hand, it makes sure that other subjects don't trail too far behind.

Afternoon checkpoint. I gather the children on the line again before breaking for chores and lunch. They bring their journals and write a short entry about what they have learned that day. I feel this both creates a sense of ownership about the work they are doing and a chance to "think about

Some Montessori Catalogs to Request

- **Appleseed Educational LLC,** CA. (408) 260-7333, www.appleseededucational.com. Wide variety of classic and clever Montessori hands-on materials. Cute stuff!
- **Edu Aids USA,** CA. (866) 611-0036, www.eduaids.com. Leading supplier of hands-on materials to Montessori schools. Handles large orders only (no individual orders). Homeschoolers can order as co-ops.
- **Educational Sounds and Images, Inc.,** OH. (937) 431-0900, www.esii.cc. A hands-on phonics course to die for. Very expensive in its entirety but very beautiful!
- **Hello Wood Products,** TN. (800) 598-2432, hellowood.com. "Your best choice for Montessori materials and classroom furniture." Seconds are available at reduced price!
- **Lord Company** www.lordequip.com. Beautiful furniture, sawing job.
- **Montessori Services** (877) 975-3003, www.montessoriservices.com. A terrific catalog. I highly recommend their beginning practical life kits. You'd have a hard time finding the right materials and purchasing them for less. The pictures are wonderful and give great information for setting up activities.
- **North American Progressive MTTC,** B.C., Canada. (877) 531-6665 www.montessoritraining.net. Pricey but very durable and beautiful training manuals.
- **Sevenoaks Montessori Equipment** us2uk2k@aol.com. A source for a less expensive grammar farm and some very clever math mats.
- **Waseca Learning Environment,** GA. (706) 546-8633, www.wasecalearning.com. A great source for cursive writing and biomes activities.

their learning," a mind habit important for retaining and connecting their subjects in their minds. This is also the time to engage them in conversation about what they have learned and to teach respectful listening skills.

This should be a relaxed time, a time to share a few thoughts and jokes together. It is an extremely important time because I have cues to their understanding, can often extend a thought for them, and remind myself of ways I can enhance what has now become a part of their field of interest. My creative juices get going as I am inspired by what is inspiring them!

Our ground rules do not change, and that's the key here. Once these habits are built in, we can count on them for sure signposts of mastery and growth.

We need an opening to our day and a closure. I need checkpoints to oversee their work and hear their thoughts on what they are learning. I need a plan for them, but also a connection with their thinking so I can best work that plan or be willing to change that plan.

More than that, I need to hear them as people and be flexible enough to respond to them.

Enjoying and knowing my children is why after 17 years of homeschooling, I'm still going.

Maria Montessori on the Liberty of the Child

The liberty of the child should have as its limit the collective interest; as its form, what we universally consider good breeding. We must, therefore, check in the child whatever offends or annoys others, or whatever tends toward rough or ill-bred acts. But all the rest—every manifestation having a useful scope—whatever it be, and under whatever form it expresses itself, must not only be permitted, but most be observed by the teacher. . . .

In our system, she must become a passive, much more than an active, influence, and her passivity shall be composed of anxious scientific curiosity, and of absolute respect for the phenomenon which she wishes to observe. . . .

It is of course understood that here we do not speak of useless or dangerous acts, for these must be suppressed, destroyed. . . . It is necessary to hinder, and little by little suppress, all those things which we must not do, so that the child may come to discern clearly between good and evil. . . . The task of the educator lies in seeing that the child does not confound good with immobility and evil with activity, as often happens in the case of the old-time discipline.

No one can be free unless he is independent: therefore the first, active manifestations of the child's individual liberty must be so guided that through this activity he may arrive at independence.

—*Maria Montessori,* The Montessori Method

CHAPTER 29

The Principle Approach

"What is the Principle Approach?" you ask. It is designed to make children "active producers rather than passive consumers of the educational process." It is also designed to steep them in the worldview of America's Founding Fathers (and Mothers), with an eye to raising a generation who will once again demand—and lead—a constitutional government, rather than our present "government" of whatever the media and the judges say is the law, is the law.

How is this done? Through:

- **Reading copiously in American source documents** (upper grades), **biographies of famous patriots** (lower grades), **and classic pro-liberty fiction** (all grades)
- **Looking up word definitions** in Noah Webster's 1828 dictionary, *The American Dictionary of the English Language*)
- **Learning the "principles" that make up the Principle Approach**, including principles for how each and every school subject should be taught and learned
- **Learning to use the "4 R's,"** otherwise known as the Notebook Method

Curriculum Based on the Principle Approach

- Judah Bible Curriculum
- The Noah Plan

The Notebook Method

The Principle Approach is based on "4 R's": *research, reasoning, relating,* and *recording*. **Research** means getting back to the real facts of "America's Christian history" and looking up word meanings in the 1828 Noah Webster dictionary. **Reasoning** means figuring out the basic biblical principles involved in what you just researched. **Relating** means using various ways to "echo back" the biblical principles in your studies and life. **Recording** means *writing* or *drawing* in a notebook: making a memorable record of what you have learned, in your own words or illustrations.

As you can imagine, this approach involves a *lot* of writing. "Wiggle worm" types actively resist all writing assignments. So if you just adore what this approach teaches, and your child is a Performer or Action Man personality, consider learning the material yourself and then adapting it to your child with activities that are more "hands on" and less "pencil on."

The Seven Principles

The Principle Approach is also based on seven principles:

1. **God's Principle of Individuality** Everyone is unique and special. This does not seem earth-shaking—in fact, it sounds kind of like the first principle of public education, "you are so special and deserve self-esteem." The difference here is that they are for individuality *as opposed to* socialist collectivism.
2. **The Christian Principle of Self-Government** In The Noah Plan's own words, "In order to have true liberty, man must be governed internally by the Spirit of God rather than by external forces."
3. **America's Heritage of Christian Character** "The model of American Christian character is the Pilgrim character, which demonstrates these qualities: *faith and steadfastness, brotherly love, Christian care, diligence and industry,* and *liberty of conscience.*"
4. **"Conscience is the Most Sacred of All Property" (James Madison)** This principle teaches the value of both property and conscience.
5. **The Christian Form of Our Government** Teaches that separation of powers, checks and balances, and reservation of most power to the individual (as opposed to any level of government) are derived from the Bible.
6. **How the Seed of Local Self-Government Is Planted** This principle teaches the necessity of salvation, "education in God's Law and Love," and the "Chain of Christianity," which traces the influence of the Bible from Israel to Europe to America.
7. **The Christian Principle of American Political Union** Standing together with others of like mind to form a "more perfect union"—starting with individuality and self-government—you end up with a self-governed society of people who can work together well.

How It Works: Start with Words & Ideas

According to the Principle Approach, each school subject is approached in the same way.

First, the student looks up the name of the subject—e.g., History—in Noah Webster's 1828 dictionary and copies down its definition.

Second, he looks up and records biblical passages related to the word and its definition. Sometimes these come right out of the *1828 Dictionary.* Sometimes the curriculum provides them. And sometimes the student is encouraged to look them up for himself in *Strong's Exhaustive Concordance,* a h-u-g-e book that lists every word in the Bible, its original

Principle Approach Principle	Biblical Principle	Opposing Principle
God's Principle of Individuality	Christian Individuality	Collectivism
The Christian Principle of Self-Government	Christian Self-Government	Anarchy (External Force)
America's Heritage of Christian Character	Christian Character	Degradation
Conscience is the Most Sacred of All Property	Biblical Stewardship	Communism
Our Christian Form of Government	God's Sovereignty	Autocracy
How the Seed of Local Self-Government Is Planted	Sowing & Reaping	Centralization
The Christian Principle of American Political Union	Covenant	Social Engineering

Greek or Hebrew root and root meaning, and all the passages in which it occurs.

Third, he is given the basic vocabulary for the subject—its most important terms or "key words"—and asked to look them up in Noah Webster's 1828 dictionary. Key words associated with the subject civics (also called American Government in many schools) may be *freedom, slavery, ruler, citizen, state, king, noble, law,* and *justice,* for example. Again, he copies down definitions and biblical passages related to these key words. This is intended to help him understand the "properties" of the subject.

All this is merely preliminary to the *real* point of the student's studies: determining how the "Seven Principles" govern each discipline. Then, the actual study of the discipline begins, ideally run along the lines of the principles, and with continual efforts to discern the cause/effect relationship between any application of or disobedience to biblical laws on the part of current or historical figures or theories. **The student also learns the "Christian history" of the subject:** its discoverers and chroniclers (even if they weren't Christians), how the subject has been used throughout history, and its place in the "Chain of Christianity." The methods used are research and outlining the major people and events.

Every subject, even math, has a history. *Someone* had to invent the Pythagorean Theorem, and I bet you know what his name was! The net effect is to learn the history of ideas and to see how the ups and downs in human history relate to those ideas and their foundations. The student learns that, in the famous words of Richard Weaver, "Ideas have consequences."

Follow with Facts

When it comes to how to teach ideas and theories, Principle Approach advocates pretty much agree. But what about the *facts* of a subjects—e.g., addition and subtraction facts, states and capitals, etc.? Here, the consensus is that whatever was good enough for the Founding Fathers is good enough for us, with some slight modifications reflecting the fact that this *is* the twenty-first century.

Early American children learned phonics from a "horn book"—a thin piece of transparent animal horn with a one-page alphabet primer based on Bible characters. Example for the letter "A": "In Adam's fall we sinned all." Principle Approach students use more modern phonics materials, back-to-basics type math drill, diagramming, and traditional (but not Early American) penmanship.

So what you have here is an extremely defined, step-by-step, highly organized approach to learning, with a strongly American Christian worldview built in. Not surprisingly, history and government are emphasized as early as possible, from a this-is-how-the-world-*ought*-to-work perspective.

The chart above was created for *Practical Homeschooling* magazine by Principle Approach advocate and speaker Lori Harris of Landmark Distributors (CA), (559) 597-2156, landmarkal@hotmail.com.

Who Invented the Principle Approach?

It started with Verna M. Hall's study of US history. In 1947 she founded a Constitutional study group. The group's studies revealed clearly that America had taken a 180-degree turn from its original Constitutional principles. But this study alone did not make it clear *why* this had happened or what could be done about it.

Provoked to deeper study, Miss Hall began unearthing original source documents that shed light on just where America came from.

During the 1960s, the Foundation for American Christian Education (FACE) began putting out large reference books containing the fruits of Miss Hall's research. The bottom line of her findings, which mostly consist of copious quotes from source documents written during the early years of the colonies and the republic: The United States of America was instituted as a Christian nation based on Christian character.

Rosalie J. Slater, a teacher who joined Miss Hall's study group, decided to dig deeper and try to find the common threads that tied America's Christian history together. It was Miss Slater who coined the phrase "The Principle Approach" and who rediscovered the methods used to educate America's Founding Fathers and the informed citizens who supported them. The "4R's" and the "Seven Principles" were first articulated in her book, *Teaching and Learning America's Christian History: The Principle Approach.* Since then, FACE has produced an entire K–12 curriculum, the Noah Plan, based on this method.

FACE, however, was not the only group that helped to implement and popularize the Principle Approach. As their own catalog said, "Today a number of ministries continue the work throughout the nation."

FACE is currently seeking to trademark the phrase "The Principle Approach." If they succeed, it will be harder for other materials based on this method to be recognized as such. Knowing the distinguishing characteristics of this method, as outlined in this chapter, will help you spot future materials in this vein.

What Is the "Chain of Christianity"?

The **Chain of Christianity** is Verna Hall and Rosalie Slater's term for the spread of biblical civilization. In their view, it began in Palestine, was spread throughout the Roman Empire, and flowered in Britain, where a serious attempt at biblical law and government was launched. It then spread to America, which began as an entire political and legal system largely based on biblical principles. Presumably, the torch could be passed from America to another nation, but at present Principle Approach scholars prefer to concentrate on trying to revive biblical government, law, and lifestyles here.

FACE is currently attempting to trademark the phrase "Chain of Christianity," which could result in limiting its use to within their own curriculum and materials.

Supplement with People Skills

A study of the Seven Principles, combined with an intense study of American history and its founding documents, will leave most of us with a burning desire to change the world around us. A lot. That burning desire, and the knowledge (if not the people skills) to back it up, are exactly what the Principle Approach offers.

But if you really want to change the world, it's not enough to be right, or smart, or informed. People have to want to follow you.

It's true that most other methods, with the notable exceptions of Charlotte Mason, the Montessori Method, and character-trait-based unit

Books You Need to Understand the Principle Approach

Christian History of the American Revolution, $42. Christian History of the Constitution, Volumes I and II, $40 each. Teaching & Learning America's Christian History, $35. American Dictionary of the English Language, $65. Rudiments of America's Christian History & Government, $15.
Foundation for American Christian Education (FACE) (VA), (800) 352-FACE, www.face.net.

FACE is reviving the "Principle Approach" to government, an approach based on biblical law, on which they say the USA was founded. Their material traces America's roots through source documents. Political freedom begins with self-government, FACE says, and self-government begins in the home.

A complete curriculum based on the Principle Approach —the Noah Plan—is now available from FACE. However, you can also purchase individual books separately. Many of you who never plan to use the Principle Approach for your basic curriculum will nonetheless be interested in FACE's offerings on the subject of government and American history.

Before we proceed any further, let me make it clear that these are not workbooks for young children. The theory is that you are going to work through this information yourself and then present it according to a set of complicated teaching suggestions that require you continually to flip back and forth between books.

The Christian History of the Constitution, Volume 1, formerly entitled "Christian Self-Government" (this is now the subtitle) documents that America is a Christian nation (that is, it was dedicated to Christ once upon a time) with a Christian Constitution (that is, one based on Christian principles). The "Chain of Christianity" is traced westward to America as the gospel spread from Israel to the Roman Empire and thence to the uncouth white tribespeople who, once Christianized, spread it over the world. A large book, consisting almost entirely of quotes from source documents. Volume 2, previously titled "Christian Self-Government with Union" (again, this is now the subtitle) is more history from source documents, emphasizing the colonists' voluntary union that led to self-government.

Teaching and Learning America's Christian History is the original how-to manual of the Principle Approach. Each principle is spelled out, precept on precept, line on line.

Rudiments of America's Christian History and Government is a workbook for students filled with source quotes from distinguished American Christian leaders of the past and questions designed to develop both Christian thinking and an awareness of our Christian heritage. For teens and adults.

The Christian History of the American Revolution, previously titled "Consider and Ponder" (this is now the subtitle) covers the Constitutional Debate period of 1765–1775, during which Americans wrestled with the question of what an ideal government should look like.

studies, don't teach students how to be winsome. And only Classical Education includes training in the art of persuasiveness in its basic mission. But these other methods are not necessarily geared to producing graduates who are reformers, like the Principle Approach does. From what I have seen, it devotes little attention to helping students become persuasive and winsome. This is an area you should plan on "shoring up" with additional instruction and resources.

Final Thoughts

One last thing to remember about the Principle Approach: **It is highly prescriptive.** You'll find lots of "shoulds" peppering the pages of Principle Approach materials and a disinclination to let children skip any of the many steps or assignments, which the authors believe build character.

The Principle Approach excels in teaching kids to be systematic, methodical, logical thinkers and hard workers at desk work. It excels in preparing them to know a host of facts and skills. Visual learners, Puzzle Solvers, and especially Progress People may be drawn to this highly reading-and-writing, reasoning-and-logic based method.

CHAPTER 30

The Robinson Method

The "Robinson Method" is so called because it has been popularized among homeschoolers by Dr. Arthur Robinson, who has also produced a curriculum based on this method.

This method is designed to make children independent learners ASAP. It can be used with the curriculum designed for it—see the Robinson Curriculum mentioned in the sidebars of this chapter—or with any set of materials well suited to self-study and individual reading.

What makes the Robinson Method unique is that **it seeks to eliminate the teacher's role as soon as possible.** This makes it perfect for parents who have motivated, well-disciplined children who are good visual learners and abstract thinkers, when the parents have little free time to actively teach their children.

At last report, about 32,000 children were being homeschooled with the Robinson Curriculum. Presumably some thousands more are being homeschooled according to this method using other materials.

Since we have been fortunate enough to have Dr. Robinson as a regular *Practical Homeschooling* columnist in the past, we have his own "take" on his method. Thus the rest of this chapter is Dr. Robinson's own description of his method.

Dr. Robinson Explains His Method

There is a growing possibility that, if the homeschooling movement continues to expand, it may become the most important single force in American public life.

In order for this to occur, however, some current weaknesses in the homeschool movement need to be corrected. These include:

- **No full-time homeschooling parent.** Homeschooling is very difficult for parents whose circumstances prevent at least one dedicated parent from giving a very large percentage of his or her time to the homeschool. While it is fine to argue that a family should always include one full-time parent in the home with time to teach the children, many families find themselves in circumstances that do not permit this.

Dr. Arthur Robinson is a scientist who works on various aspects of fundamental biochemistry, nutrition, and preventive medicine. He is President and Research Professor of the Oregon Institute of Science and Medicine. His wife Laurelee, who was also a scientist, homeschooled their children until her death in November 1988, when the children were 12, 10, 9, 7, 7, and 17 months. During the past 13 years, Dr. Robinson and the children have continued their homeschooling by developing a program entirely based upon self-teaching.

The **Robinson Curriculum** is currently the only one available using this approach. It's available for $195 from Oregon Institute of Science and Medicine (OR), (541) 592-4142, www.oism.org.

The Work of a Solitary Mind

A book is the permanent record of the work of a solitary human mind, to be read, marked, learned, and inwardly digested by another solitary human mind. A committee can no more make a book than it can play the violin, but almost every "book" used in schools—and in teacher-training academies—is written collectively and for collective purposes.

A magnificent education, as countless examples attest, can come from nothing more than reading and writing. In the one we behold the work of the solitary mind, in the other we do it, but we do it in such a way that we can behold again, and understand, and judge, the work of a solitary mind—our own. . . . But the gimmickry of the schools . . . is an integral and large portion of a general program designed to prevent solitude. And while the children themselves are pestered with values clarification modules and relating sessions and group activities lest they fall into solitude, they are also protected from dangerous exposure to the fruits of solitary thinking in others.

—*Richard Mitchell*
The Graves of Academe
(1984, Little, Brown & Company)

The Robinson Curriculum is a set of 22 CD-ROMs in a storage case, containing 120,000 scanned-in pages of text from over 250 mostly classic and out-of-print books: about 70 percent literature, 10 percent autobiographies, 10 percent textbooks, and 10 percent "other." Some exercises and answer keys are also included.

- **Undereducated parents.** Many parents themselves lack the education that they so earnestly want for their children. As a consequence, homeschooled children have a difficult time rising above the level of academic achievement of their parents. This is true of many homes in which both parents are college trained and may even have advanced degrees. A large fraction of college graduates, for example, are not trained to do simple calculus—a level of academic achievement easily possible for most properly educated 16-year-old children. Even parents holding doctoral degrees in mathematics and science are often poorly educated in literature, history, and the foundations of our civilization.

- **Not reaching the child's full academic potential.** The average level of academic achievement in homeschools at present looks good only when compared with the disastrously poor results currently the norm in public schools. While it is true that SAT scores are a little higher for homeschools than for public schools, the average public school child comes from a generally poorer home environment and a school environment that is not conducive to learning.

We Need Higher Hopes

Some parents react to these difficulties with various forms of resignation. They hope that more families will find a way to rearrange their lives for homeschooling. In their homeschools, they emphasize subjects such as spelling and grammar and spend less time with difficult subjects such as mathematics and science. They hope that by the age of 18 their children will be strong enough to resist the evils that they encounter at the universities, or else they deny the children a higher education and direct them into occupations where that education is not required.

They are comforted by the fact that they have achieved slightly higher educational performance than the public schools while, at the same time, sparing their children the depravities of the secular world for at least part of their formative years. These are dedicated people who are doing their best for their children. I believe, however, that they should be thinking beyond the current homeschool situation.

In order to take our country back, we must do more in our homeschool movement than we are doing now. Our children must be not a little better educated when compared with those in the public schools—they must be so much better educated that they are entirely beyond such comparisons.

Our children must be able to think—and to think so much more effectively than their opponents that they are able, in one generation, to become a superior force in science and engineering and in industry and government.

Our children must be such shining examples for the homeschool movement that the majority of American families demand the same quality for their children.

Our children must be such superior performers in America's colleges and universities that they not only resist the corruption in those institutions—that they destroy, by their example, the corruption itself.

Interesting rhetoric, you may say, but how can this be done?

I respond, it MUST be done, and now I will describe an experiment that indicates the beginnings of a way in which it may possibly be done.

How It All Began

Like most successful experiments, this one reveals only part of the truth and suggests further experiments that may be worthwhile. Also, like a great many experiments that point in a different direction, this one was done by accident. If it ultimately proves to have been worthwhile, then the credit belongs to the Lord—not to the participants.

As our children reached school age, my wife, Laurelee, undertook their instruction. A highly educated scientist herself, she understood what they needed to learn, but she had no experience in teaching children. Moreover, she worked virtually full-time with me in our research work; she was still bearing new children and caring for infants; and she was carrying out a significant amount of farm work in addition to the usual household chores.

As an aid to her growing homeschool (all of our children have been entirely homeschooled), Laurelee purchased educational materials and curricula from a wide variety of sources. These she melded into a curriculum along with a large amount of Christian materials that she purchased. (She purchased so many Sunday school materials that the people at the local Christian bookstore thought that we were operating a church.)

Not knowing whether or not these materials would be available to us in the future, she created an entire 12-grade curriculum for each of the six children and obtained all of the necessary materials for that curriculum. These she organized meticulously in the order that they would be used. That curriculum occupies the equivalent of about five large filing cabinets and is in perfect order.

This effort, in degrees that vary according to the resources, education, abilities, and motivations of the parents, is one that is being undertaken today in tens of thousands of homeschools across America. It is being made increasingly effective by the growth of many excellent businesses that supply materials and curricula to homeschools.

Laurelee's effort was truly outstanding. It allowed for every academic eventuality and it utilized the very best materials available. It even included life insurance on me, so that she would be able to continue the homeschool in the event of my death. Her plan had only one flaw—a flaw that neither she nor I ever considered. The plan assumed that she would be alive to teach.

Six Children Who Teach Themselves

When Laurelee died suddenly years ago, after an illness that lasted less than 24 hours, her class contained Zachary, Noah, Arynne, Joshua, Bethany, and Matthew—ages 12, 10, 9, 7, 7, and 17 months—a class now without a teacher.

As I assumed her work, including cooking, laundry, and other household tasks, and continued the farm and professional work without her by my side, there was no possibility that I could even read the curriculum that she had so carefully created—much less have the time to teach it to the children. Friends tried to help, but the problem seemed to be intractable.

What happened then, with the Lord's help, was remarkable. Gradually, over the next two years and building upon the environment that their mother and I had already created for them and some rules of study that I provided, the children solved the problem themselves. Not only did they solve it themselves, they created a homeschool that, in many ways, points toward answers to some of the difficulties enumerated above.

Gradually, with occasional coaching and help from me, they created a homeschool that actually needs no teacher and is extraordinary in its effectiveness.

A Visit With the Robinsons

My husband and I were also intrigued by the article by Dr. Robinson in *Practical Homeschooling* #5 ("My Children Teach Themselves"), especially when Steve realized that he had been reading a book written by Dr. Robinson about civil defense.

We were going to be traveling through Oregon, so we called the Robinsons and asked if we could stop for a short visit. Dr. Robinson was very gracious and gave directions to his home.

When we arrived, the Robinson children were helping their father construct a building. The children were courteous with one another and all were working very hard. Steve and I visited with Dr. Robinson for 45 minutes in the building where their family has school. He told us about the literature project they are working on, which will provide a systematic curriculum for reading for all grades. Many of the books in the program will be older books with no copyright, and they will be included on a CD-ROM. [This is the Henty Books on CD-ROM. See sidebar on page 244.]

As we were leaving, Dr. Robinson gave us copies of two newsletters he edits and publishes. One, called *Access to Energy*, used to be published by a famous physicist named Petr Beckmann. He asked Dr. Robinson to continue it after his death. It provides commentary on the anti-science being propagated in our society and provides real science with which to combat it. It is pro-science and pro-free market and well-written as well as easily understandable. It costs $35 for 12 issues to individuals and can be ordered from PO Box 1279, Cave Junction, OR 97523.

Dr. Robinson's methods may sound too streamlined to those always looking for newer and better curriculum or teaching styles, but it obviously works in his family!

—*Carmon Friedrich*

More to Robinson Than Meets the Eye

My favorite homeschooling philosophy is Dr. Arthur Robinson's (Robinson Curriculum). Let me warn you, this requires a lot of trust, but it doesn't need to be as formal or rigid. Dr. Robinson proposes two hours of math a day (which may be too much for a young child, but he's a mathematical person so he puts more emphasis in that area) and composing a one-page paper (the child's choice of topic) that will be corrected by you and returned for a possible rewrite. The remainder of the time is spent reading anything in your personal library (the books are there because they're good, right?).

Dr. Robinson proposes the right combination for education: reading, 'riting, and 'rithmetic. The three R's. There doesn't seem to be much exploration or hands-on activity in his style, right? Ah, but that's where you're wrong, because he lives on a farm that needs to be taken care of exclusively by him and the kids (he's a widower). This also means that the kids need to cook and clean. Do you see what I see?

> He covers the basics, and all the life skills are part of their real world.

—Kristina Sabalis Krulikas
Homeschooling by Heart
(1999, Solomon's Secrets)

In judging its effectiveness, I have some experience for comparison.

I, myself, was fortunate to attend one of the finest public schools in Texas—Lamar in Houston—during the late 1950s when public schools in America still retained reasonable standards. I performed well and was admitted to every college to which I applied—including Harvard, M.I.T., Rice, and Caltech. After graduating from Caltech, I obtained a Ph.D. in chemistry from the University of California at San Diego and was immediately appointed to a faculty position at that University. There I taught introductory chemistry to 300 students each year and supervised a group of graduate students.

I can honestly say that the six Robinson children in our homeschool are, on average, at least two years ahead of my own abilities at their ages and have a far higher potential for the future than did I. Moreover, by the age of about 15, they are surpassing at least 98 percent of the college freshmen that I taught at the University of California at San Diego.

The oldest, Zachary, who is 16, is already completing a math and science curriculum that uses the actual freshman and sophomore texts from the best science universities in America. Last October he took the Scholastic Aptitude Tests for the first time (the PSAT). His scores of 750 in math and 730 in verbal for a sum of 1480 (and a NMSQT score of 221) were above the 99.9 percentile among the 1,600,000 students worldwide who took the test. The other children are, for their ages, performing at least as well.

During the past four years, I have spent less than 15 minutes per day (on average) engaged in working as the children's teacher. They are teaching themselves.

Moreover, each one of them has spontaneously, without suggestion or demand from me, taken over an essential aspect of our farm and personal lives. They do all the work with the cattle and sheep; they do all the laundry, cooking, and housework; and they are working beside me as Laurelee used to do in the scientific research and civil defense work that is our ministry and our professional life. One by one, my tasks just disappeared as the children assumed them.

In general, they prefer to work independently. They tend not to share tasks and have not divided them as one might expect. For example, 11-year-old Joshua is the cook—and already a better cook than I. Zachary does all the work with the cattle (about 30) and the chickens; Arynne cares for the sheep (about 100); Noah is in charge of all farm and laboratory repairs; and Bethany does the washing and teaches Matthew. Some tasks are shared, such as house cleaning, sheep shearing, and watching over Matthew.

This sort of extracurricular work is especially valuable as reinforcement for the homeschool. While self-confidence can be built somewhat in sports or other "activities," the confidence that comes to a child from the knowledge that he is independently carrying on an activity that is essential to the survival of the family is valuable indeed.

It is important, however, not to take advantage of this situation. The development of a young mind takes place in a few short years. A parent must always make certain that the children have more than enough time for their academic studies and for essential recreation. When children show an aptitude for productive work helpful to the parent, there can be a tendency for the parent to let them do too much. This can deprive the children of mental development necessary to their own futures.

I generally consider each child's time to be more valuable than my own. If I provide them the time for optimum development and direct them to the necessary tools, then each of them should be able to surpass my own abilities and accomplishments. If they do, then my goals for their academic work will have been fulfilled. Remarkably, they have spontaneously responded with efforts that provide me also with more time for productive work.

Our home is not as neat and clean as some, our spelling (including mine) is not all that could be desired, and our traditions have become somewhat unusual (they leave the Christmas tree and nativity scene up for six months each year—from December through June), but these children know how to work and they know how to think.

Their homeschool is a success. This school is entirely self-taught by each student working alone. It depends upon a set of rules that can be adopted within any home in America. As their parent, my sole essential contribution has been to set the rules under which they live and study.

How the Robinsons Do It

For those who consider adopting these procedures, I offer the opinion that they will work in any home and with any children, regardless of ability. Obviously children differ in innate ability. I believe, however, that these rules will achieve remarkable results with any child when compared with other alternatives.

These are not, however, "suggestions." They are rigorous requirements. I know what has happened here. I do not know what would happen in different experiments under different conditions. If, therefore, these suggestions are all followed in the same way, I expect the same result.

No TV. There is no television in our home. We do have a VCR. As a family we watch a videotape approximately once every six months. Television wastes time, promotes passive, vicarious brain development rather than active thought, and is a source of pernicious social contamination.

Most American children are addicted to TV. Their brains spend four hours or more each day learning bad, passive habits from the TV and another few hours (if they are fortunate to have good activities, too) unlearning the bad habits. Then, if there are any hours left, they can make positive progress.

Moreover, when TV is used as a tranquilizer, it can mask other problems that should be solved early in life. Children need to work out the ways in which they interact with other people. Even though their behavior while doing so may be more distracting than their behavior when pacified by a television set, the TV may be retarding this aspect of development, which is then undesirably transferred to the classroom instead.

No Sweets. The children do not eat sugar or honey or foods made with these materials and have never done so at any time in their lives. Sugar alters the metabolism in such a way as to increase the probability of diabetes, hypoglycemia, hyperglycemia, and immune deficiencies that can lead to cancer and other fatal illnesses at a later age. Most importantly to a homeschool, sugar diminishes mental function and increases irritability and mental instability. Most children are able to learn regardless of these effects, but why burden them with this disadvantage?

These points about sugar have been expanded upon in several texts that may be available in your library. I recommend these books: *Sweet and Dangerous* by John Yudkin, Peter D. Wyden, Inc., 750 Third Ave, New York, NY 10017 (1972); *Sugar Blues* by William Dufty, Chilton Book Company, Radnor, PA (1975); and *Food, Teens & Behavior* by Barbara Reed, Natural Press, PO Box 2107, Manitowoc, WI (1983). These books contain a substantial number of appropriate references to the scientific literature.

Though Laurelee and I (both sugar addicts) established this rule, it is now out of my control. Two years ago, when some visitors whom we greatly wished to please came for dinner, they brought sweet rolls and donuts. I suggested to the children that they should eat just one so as not to offend. They all refused.

Practical Advantages of Self-Study

Besides the great advantage of developing good study habits and thinking ability, self-teaching also has immediate practical advantages. Many children should be able, through Advanced Placement examinations, to skip over one or more years of college. The great saving in time and expense from this is self-evident. These and other comparable accomplishments await most children who learn to self-teach and then apply this skill to their home education.

Even children of lesser ability can, by means of self-teaching and good study habits, achieve far more than they otherwise would have accomplished by the more ordinary techniques.

—*Arthur Robinson*

The Robinson kids did almost all of the work of putting together the Robinson Curriculum. The younger ones scanned in books; the older ones did most of the computer work. Likewise, they scanned and assembled the **G.A. Henty CD-ROMs** (pictured above: a 6-disc set including 99 complete books by the Victorian-era historical fiction writer known as "The Boy's Own Author," 53 short stories, and 215 additional short stories by other authors of the same era, $99) from a large set of rare books that took over two years to collect. They even constructed the building the Robinson Curriculum is sold from. They take the orders, do the shipping, everything! Basically, it's their business.

Five Hours, Six Days, Ten Months. Formal school work occupies about five hours each day—six days per week—twelve months per year. Sometimes one of them skips his studies for the day as a result of some special activity, and we take an occasional automobile trip. With these diversions, their actual annual school time occupies about ten full months of six-day weeks.

School First. These five hours each day are the most productive hours—the morning and early afternoon. As soon as they wake—and with time out only for breakfast and milking the cows—they study. Each has a large desk in the school room. My desk is also in that room. I try to do my own desk work during the same time, since my presence keeps the school room quiet and avoids arguments about noise.

Phonics. The five older children were taught to read with the phonetic system—learning the individual sounds of our language. Laurelee taught them all. Matthew (five years old) is currently learning to read by phonics. The children are teaching him.

Lots of Good Books. The teacher-presented materials that Laurelee obtained are not used, but the history, science, and literature books that we accumulated, which include a good selection of classics, are essential to the curriculum.

Saxon Math. Each day, before beginning any other work, each child (except Matthew) works an entire lesson in the Saxon series of mathematics books. This usually involves working about 30 problems. If the 30 problems seem to be taking much less than two hours each day, we sometimes increase the assignment to two lessons or about 60 problems per day. If the lessons seem to be taking much more than two hours, then we reduce to one-half lesson or about 15 problems per day. This is an excellent series of texts. The children work their way through the entire series at a rate that finishes calculus, the last text in the series, when they are 15 years of age.

They grade their own problems and rework any missed problems. They must tell me if they miss a problem and show the correctly worked solution to me. The younger children tend to make one or two errors each day. As they get older, the error rate drops. The older children make about one error each week. On very rare occasions, perhaps once each month, an older child will actually need help with a problem he or she feels unable to solve.

This emphasis on math with the help of the excellent Saxon series teaches them to think, builds confidence and ability to the point of almost error-free performance, and establishes a basis of knowledge that is essential to later progress in science and engineering.

It is also absolutely essential preparation for the non-quantitative subjects that do not require mathematics. The ability to distinguish the quantitative from the non-quantitative—the truth from error—fact from fiction—is an absolutely essential requirement for effective thinking. Otherwise one will tend to confuse independent, truthful thought with opinions based upon falsehoods and propaganda.

Our society is filled to the brim with public school graduates who imagine that they are independent thinkers when they actually are programmed to believe anything they perceive as fashionable. This cultlike behavior is not limited to graduates in "soft subjects." Many people supposedly educated in the sciences and engineering also practice this ritual of non-thought.

I believe that much of this difficulty stems from poor early education in mathematics and logical thought. It is essential to understand that physical truths are absolute and can be rigorously determined. This must be learned by actually determining absolutes. Mathematical problem solving is an excellent mechanism for doing this.

Grim examples of failures in this area are everywhere. Earlier today, for example, a local bureaucrat telephoned in an effort to get my help in fashioning a community compromise on environmental issues between the solid citizens of this valley and some pseudoenvironmentalist political agitators who have been disrupting the community recently.

During the discussion I mentioned that the agitators had filed a document with the federal government that contained a graph condemning the local lumber industry for destroying local game fish. Actually there was no correlation between fish population and timber harvest. The agitators had created a correlation by leaving out about half of the data for the last 40 years—the half which proves that their premise is false.

"Oh well," the bureaucrat replied, "we all do that sort of thing."

An Essay a Day. After completing the mathematics work, each child writes a one-page essay about any subject that interests him and gives it to me. Some of the children enjoy writing these essays more than others. The remainder of the five hours is spent in reading history and science texts.

I read these pages and mark misspelled words and grammatical errors that the child must then correct. Sometimes I fall many weeks behind with these corrections, but the children just keep writing.

There is an unusual bonus in these short essays. Sometimes the student will write things that he or she would not (and sometimes should not) say to the parent otherwise. These essays have educational value, and they also open a new line of communication with the children.

College-Level Science. Zachary (16 years old) has a more rigorous curriculum, since he finished calculus about a year ago. He is working his way through freshman and sophomore college physics and chemistry texts in the same way that he previously worked his way through Saxon math. After those years of self-taught math, he has simply gone on to self-taught science—and in the toughest college level texts that I was able to obtain. His mind has become used to the fact that there is nothing in the well-known sciences that he cannot understand and learn and no problem that, with a proper book, he cannot work correctly. His error rate is negligible.

No Computers. No child is allowed to use a computer until after he or she has completed mathematics all the way through calculus. (At one point Saxon calls for a little use of the hand-held calculator. I permit this, but only on a very few occasions.)

Constant Recreational Reading. Since they have no television, the children are prone to spend a substantial part of their non-school hours reading. They read whatever interests them from our library—which Laurelee purged of all books that she thought it best for them to avoid. By recreational reading, the children pick up most of their vocabulary and grammar and most of their knowledge about the world. Regarding current events, they do not listen to the radio, but it has become increasingly difficult to maintain control of my copy of the *Wall Street Journal*.

No Formal Bible Teaching. The Bible is not a required part of our formal curriculum. We have a family Bible reading before bed each evening, and we discuss elements of Christianity as they happen to arise in our everyday lives.

Like Isaac Newton, no one in our family ever questions the truth of the Lord's Word as provided to us in the Old and New Testaments of the King James Bible. We only seek to understand these truths by repeated reading. That reading is rarely accompanied by interpretive comment. Each of us must understand these things for himself and build his own relationship with God.

What We Leave Out. This curriculum is important for what it contains and also for what it does not contain. It contains about two hours of math

Good Study Habits

Since certain skills need to be acquired at an early age—particularly mathematics and reading, writing, and thinking in one's native language—it is sensible to arrange the homeschool so that learning these essential skills will automatically lead to the development of good study habits. This is one reason that self-teaching homeschools have a special value.

Consider, for example, the teaching of math and science. Many homeschools use Saxon Math. Although produced with teachers and classrooms in mind, this series of math books is so well-written that it can be mastered by most students entirely on their own without any teacher intervention whatever. This self-mastery usually does not happen automatically, but it can be learned by almost any student with correct study rules and a good study environment.

While the subject matter can be mastered with or without a teacher, the student who masters it without a teacher learns something more. He learns to teach himself. Then, when he continues into physics, chemistry, and biology—which are studied in their own special language, the language of mathematics—he is able to teach these subjects to himself regardless of whether or not a teacher with the necessary specialized knowledge is present. Also, he is able to make use of much higher-quality texts—texts written for adults.

—*Arthur Robinson*

Mom & Dad as Living Books

To avoid misunderstanding, let me add that Dr. Robinson is not suggesting that parents should never answer their children's questions. Providing your children with information that is not "in the book" again reduces the educational equation to two participants: you (the source of this knowledge) and the child. You become the "living book" the child is studying!

What he is saying is that our children need to learn to ferret out new information and skills on their own. Obviously, this is easier if we give them excellent resources that provide the information in easy-to-understand, step-by-step fashion. So for those who choose to follow this method; choosing great resources is vital in the early years to avoid discouragement. An older child who is trained in this method can squeeze juice out of even the driest resource, but let's not start our little ones with anything but the best!

How Did the Robinson Kids Turn Out?

Since this chapter was written, four of Dr. Robinson's children have taken SATs with an average score above 1400 and entered college. Zachary and Noah are finished with college; both earned Bachelors degrees in Chemistry after only two years at the university. Zachary is in graduate school at Iowa State University, studying for a Ph.D. in Chemistry and a Doctor in Veterinary Medicine simultaneously. Noah is studying for his Ph.D. in Chemistry at Caltech. Arynne, Bethany, and Joshua are in college. Matthew is still in homeschool.

or science problem-solving followed by about two hours of directed reading and a short essay each day—all self-taught by the student.

What it does not contain is also very important. Each additional subject that is added to the curriculum creates a demand upon the brain's 24 hours of time. If an unnecessary subject is added, it wastes not only the curricular school time but also a fraction of the extracurricular time. It is therefore important to be very careful not to add unnecessary subjects.

Our public schools and also many of our homeschools have so many subjects in their curricula that the children's brains do not have time to give adequate attention to the fundamentally important subjects.

Although the children take piano lessons and engage in a rich variety of extracurricular activities oriented around our farm and laboratory, their formal curriculum consists of "reading, writing, and arithmetic" and *nothing more.* It also essentially has no teacher—a fact that I have come to realize can be an *advantage.*

Just Say Nothing

When your eight-year-old child is all alone at his large desk in a quiet room with his *Saxon 65* book and has been there three hours already—with most of that time spent in childhood daydreams—and says, "Mommy, I don't know how to work this problem," give him a wonderful gift. Simply reply, "Then you will need to keep studying until you can work the problem."

For a while, his progress may be slow. Speed will come with practice. Eventually, he will stop asking questions about how to do his assignments and will sail along through his lessons without help.

These study habits can then spill over into the other subjects—with astonishing results.

Learning to Think

In the formative years, it is absolutely essential that children learn how to think and how to learn independently. They have a lifetime to accumulate facts and will do so more effectively if they acquire a correct foundation—not of facts, but of ability to read, think, and evaluate for themselves.

The ability to think is the most important. A very large percentage of our public school graduates lack the ability to think. Most of them can, however, articulate acceptably. When we give the brain a small number of the most important tools to learn and use, we give it an opportunity to learn to think.

The Experiment Works

In this experiment, I have watched a group of children educate themselves in a far superior manner than I could have done for them if I had spent every waking hour teaching them in the usual manner. I am convinced that, had I done so, their progress would have been far less.

Although I have occasionally helped them with specific questions, that help has been so infrequent that they would have advanced almost as far if I had not helped. Moreover, the level of academic accomplishment that they have achieved is truly extraordinary.

Children learn by example and by doing. They do not learn effectively by being lectured to or by vicarious involvement as in television viewing. Our educational method works, and it involves almost no parental time once the school room and curriculum have been provided and the rules have been established.

CHAPTER 31

Unit Studies

What is a unit study? If you are only beginning to think about homeschooling, you may have no idea. If you have friends who do unit studies, you may have a vague notion of lots of time spent sewing costumes, cooking ethnic meals, and acting out history and science lessons. Depending on your personality, this either sounds like a horrendous waste of time or scads of fun.

Despite the impression many people seem to have, unit studies are not undirected fun and games. They are a highly effective way to:

- Integrate school subjects—that is, you'll be using and learning skills and facts from many "subjects" all at once instead of in lessons separated into "math," "science," "history," and so on.
- Include many family members in the same learning experience
- Liven your homeschool up
- Make a seemingly stuffy topic more memorable and enjoyable
- Prepare your child for real-world learning

How Units Work

A "unit" starts with a topic or theme. Theoretically, this could be anything. However, in homeschool curriculum circles, unit themes tend to be:

- **Character traits** (the ATII curriculum and KONOS curriculum)
- **Literature/authors** (the Calvert School units on Beatrix Potter and Laura Ingalls Wilder and the Five in a Row series, for example)
- **Science topics** (Kym Wright's units and the Media Angels Creation Science Units, for example)
- **Countries** (Teaching with God's Heart for the World)
- **Historical figures and events** (Beautiful Feet, TRISMS, KONOS History of the World)
- **Fun topics** (Amanda Bennet's units on Baseball and Olympics, for example)

> A unit study is a formal guided exploration that organizes many subjects (traditionally taught as separate courses) around a central theme.

> To find unit-study curriculum, check out the Quick Resource Guide at the back of this book.

> [A unit study] is a complete immersion into the topic so that the student will see things as a "whole" instead of bits and pieces learned throughout their education.
> —*Amanda Bennett, noted unit study author*

Once you've picked your theme, you then come up with a number of activities designed to shed information on your topic.

The Purely Hypothetical Star Trek Unit Study

Let's see how this works in practice by going through a totally fictional unit I just made up: the Star Trek unit study.

In case you're wondering why I keep mentioning Star Trek, it's because research has shown that over 50 percent of the American public consider themselves Star Trek fans, and just about all of the other 50 percent have watched the show at least a few times. Plus, this is a topic you will *not* see in any curriculum package soon, so we can concentrate on how a unit works without worrying if you should do any of these activities.

Let's hypothesize that you are obsessed with Star Trek. You want to learn all about the show and everything related to it.

This is the very definition of a unit study. In the real world, whenever you say,

"I want to learn everything I can about this,"

you are embarking on a unit study.

So, what would a serious Star Trek fan do?

- Watch every episode
- Learn all about the actors
- Purchase reference works, such as *Scotty's Guide to the Starship Enterprise*, and memorize the blueprints
- Engage in online or in-person discussion with other fans about the episodes, the ship design, the actors, the writers . . .
- Make a costume
- Play games based on the show
- Attend conventions
- Collect action figures and other "stuff" related to the show
- Learn Klingon

If you doubt any of this, see the video *Trekkies*. Real fans go a *lot* farther than this!

The Match Game

It's also important to match the depth of your unit study to the interest of your students.

A "shallow" unit study is one that merely introduces a theme. Continuing our Star Trek example, you'd read *one* Star Trek book or watch a couple of episodes of the show. Then you'd do a few simple related activities that take no more than a hour or two combined. For example, you could model the solar system by pacing off relative distances in a parking lot, placing balls of various sizes at each planetary location. You could also go online to the NASA website and browse around. Just about any kid can suffer through this much, even if he has no interest in Star Trek.

A "medium" unit study might include all this, plus add more books on the theme topic, such as *Scotty's Guide* or some biographies of the actors, more related studies (in this case we've picked outer space, so it's books about astronomy and the space program), and more time-consuming activities (e.g., making a space station model and a space program timeline).

A **"deep" unit study** would take everything in the list above and add to it. Perhaps you'd join an online Star Trek newsgroup or go to a convention. You might study the book *Moby Dick* and the history of seamanship—two recurring themes on the "Next Generation" show. Spurred by an interest in Mr. Worf, you might investigate codes of honor throughout history or do a report on the uses of Shakespeare in Star Trek. The science-minded may dig into astronomy, while artistic types learn portraiture and landscape painting in order to memorialize their favorite actors and scenes.

A truly intense interest in this one particular show could lead to studying set design, lighting, and special effects . . . acting and directing . . . detective fiction (those holodeck adventures!) . . . sociology (the interaction of different cultures is a constant series theme) . . . leadership and management . . . military history and protocol . . . aviation history and technology . . . newsletter design and production (fanzines) . . . website design and production (online fan sites) . . . math (to be like Mr. Spock) . . . science (to be like Mr. Spock) . . . medicine (to be like the Star Trek doctors) . . . robotics . . . the list is endless.

Your child could literally become a rocket scientist as a direct result of pursuing interests arising from Star Trek. In fact, during the period when I attended engineering school, a large percentage of my classmates were at least partially influenced in their chosen career path by good ol' Scotty. According to the biography of actor James Doohan, who played Scotty, he found this to be true among engineering students everywhere he toured.

As you can see, **the central unit-study topic leads to *related* topics.** Picking appropriate related topics is one secret of good unit studies. You use the initial interest to get things rolling and then often *transfer* that interest to something more real-world or more academically useful. You can't become an Enterprise crewman, but you *can* become an astronaut, an engineer, a writer, or an actor. You can't serve on a ship with Horatio Hornblower, or explore Africa with David Livingstone, but you *can* join today's Navy or become a tour guide or archaeologist. You can also study the Napoleonic wars (when the fictional character Horatio served) and the colonization and subsequent liberation of Africa (the era partly ushered in by Livingstone). An interest in stamp collecting can lead to studying the history and geography of the countries whose stamps you collect. A rock collection naturally leads to the study of geology, famous geologists, gemology, jewelry design, orienteering (rocks are in the great outdoors!), fossils, creation vs. evolution, and much more.

Don't worry if you haven't figured out yet how to go about picking *which* topics for your unit theme or how to choose helpful related subjects and projects. Right now, you're just getting familiar with what unit studies *are*. We have an entire section on how to choose and create unit studies coming up after this one!

Teaching Many Kids at Once

A highly touted advantage of unit studies is that the whole family can study the same unit at the same time, thus cutting down on Mom's workload.

This is partly true (students of all ages *can* study the same unit at the same time) and partly not (unit studies do not necessarily cut down on your workload). What you save in time that would be spent grading workbooks for different age levels will likely be soaked up in time spent shopping for and organizing materials needed for the clever unit projects, and in time spent doing those clever projects!

These are the main tricks to teaching children of different ages using the same unit study:

- Let an older child read the books to the younger ones who can't read that well yet.
- Give the older children more intense research and writing assignments.

For example, if the whole family is studying Dickens' *A Christmas Carol,* the oldest child can read this aloud while the younger ones gather around. Then the twelfth-grader can research and write about the plight of workers in Dickens' England, the tenth-grader can write a page of Dickensian dialogue, the fourth-grader can write an invitation to Tiny Tim's house, and the first-grader can practice printing simple vocabulary words from the story. Everyone can join in on the group projects: singing carols, cooking and eating a Christmas feast, making and wearing a nightcap like Scrooge's, and acting out the scenes where the Ghost of Christmas Past confronts our heroic villain (or is it our villainous hero?). The whole family can also join in on the discussion of why Scrooge started out so mean, how God feels about employers who fail to provide for their employees, why some people have no friends while others have plenty, and other fascinating topics that arise naturally from the story.

Now, for a more in-depth look at unit studies, I turn you over to *Practical Homeschooling*'s original unit study expert, Jessica Hulcy. Jessica is the coauthor (with Carole Thaxton of KONOS Connections) of the popular KONOS unit-study curriculum. She is a genuine homeschool pioneer and curriculum innovator, and is currently the leader of our Unit Studies forum at www.home-school.com.

Jessica Hulcy on the Difference Between Public School Units & Homeschool Unit Studies

Public education and homeschool have different goals for unit studies. While one may seek to camouflage the actual course of study, the other seeks to preserve children's sense of wonder.

In public schools, unit studies are usually called "study units."

More than the name is different, though. Although both "study units" (or just "units," as they are often called) and "unit studies" bring many subjects together under one main unit topic, the goals of most public school "units" is either to fill up the time with trivialities such as constructing a shoe box village to make holders for valentine cards (here the "subjects" employed are art and holidays) or to indoctrinate children in a politically correct worldview.

Such public school units often blur the lines of separation between the different academic subjects, so parents have difficulty determining what subjects are actually being studied and what material is actually being covered. Conscientious parents may become frustrated when their ability to oversee their child's education is nullified because the all-in-one teaching of units obscures the fact that Johnny is really not learning science or history, but instead is studying politically correct ways to preserve the rain forest.

Units Are Naturals at Home

At home it is a different story. Here, integrating subjects allows subjects to be taught naturally in an unfragmented approach. Units preserve the

Jessica Hulcy is perhaps the world's foremost expert on the use of unit studies in the homeschool. Jessica is coauthor of the popular KONOS family of unit-study curriculum and products available through KONOS Inc. (TX), (972) 924-2712, www.konos.com. Except where noted, her remarks quoted in this chapter and those in the Unit Studies section were taken from her columns in *Practical Homeschooling* magazine.

unity, the interrelatedness, and the wonder of God's creation. Unit studies work well for homeschooling because the art teacher is the history teacher and the English teacher all rolled into one—Mom! The only faculty meeting necessary to correlate the subjects is in Mom's mind. An art project, say a papoose carrier, can fit right into a history demonstration and an English report on the Apache Indians. When students dramatize the Constitutional Convention, they are covering the subjects of history, drama, speech, debate, and even art through the making of their costumes. Yes, the lines are blurred between the subjects, yet when subjects are meshed together, each is enhanced by the others.

Cynthia Pilling, the KONOS representative in Florida, recently trained a group of parents in "How to Teach with Unit Studies." Instead of telling them how to integrate subjects and make learning hands-on and fun, she decided to teach them by giving an actual lesson. Her unit topic was "birds." Naturally, she would have included sketching birds as well as reading about John James Audubon, but her real goal was to have the parents participate in a hands-on activity. Laying out an assortment of tools that represented the birds' beaks as well as an assortment of birds' food, the parents were instructed to choose the best beak for the various foods. Nuts were cracked by pliers, a coffee filter was used to catch flying insects (mini marshmallows), while tongs were used to dig through peanut butter (mud) to pluck out a prized gummy worm.

For exercise, Cynthia had the parents stand up and flap their *wings* to see if their muscles tired easily. Then she told them how fast the hummingbird flapped its wings. They were amazed! As they talked about nests of birds, Cynthia passed out a milk carton cap to each parent. Placing one navy bean in each cap, she told them that the cap was the size of a hummingbird nest and the bean was the size of a hummingbird egg.

Although there had been much talking and bantering by the "students" during the other activities, as soon as the size of the hummingbird egg was revealed, all became quiet. The sense of wonder had overtaken them.

Units Are More than Projects

I encourage homeschooling parents who desire to raise thinkers to employ the methods of discovery *and* dialogue. Real thinkers cannot help but be educated. As my friend Erin Blain says, "Be obsessed with education, not graduation." Allow graduation to take its proper place as the icing on the cake of education.

Product-oriented education is obsessed with the answer rather than the thought behind the answer. Dialogue, on the other hand, draws answers out of students while demanding that students think in the process.

Anyone who has seen the movie *Shadowlands*, recounting the life of C.S. Lewis, has seen the art of dialogue at its best. At Oxford and Cambridge, young men came to class ready to dialogue with their mentor about what they had read. C.S. Lewis posed question after question to the students, each time insisting that the views they held be proved and supported.

While a workbook asks for a single word to be regurgitated, dialogue asks for an original thought to be articulated and supported.

Because homeschool class sizes are small, homeschooling parents have the unique opportunity to use dialogue to stretch their child's reasoning and thinking ability by asking open-ended questions, such as "What would

The KONOS Method

Unit studies the Jessica Hulcy way include dialogue (the Socratic method) and discovery (guided exploration that includes both research and hands-on projects).

Beware of unit activities that end with phrases such as, "tell your children ..." or "read to your children ..." as the consistent bottom line. Of course, as parents we are continually speaking and reading to our children, but if your curriculum ends there, you are merely teaching on the surface. Only when you engage in dialogue with your children do you dig into the heart of learning, encouraging your children to think and understand.
—*Jessica Hulcy*

happen if . . . ?"; "Which solution do you think is best?"; "Can you support your belief?"

Projects make your units memorable; research projects teach your children how to learn; dialogue makes your children wise. And wisdom, not a mere discovery and regurgitation of facts, is the real goal of all education, including unit studies.

CHAPTER 32

Unschooling

"Unschooling": What is it? Some people refer to the act of removing one's children from the schools, or refusing to enroll them, as "unschooling." This is actually not the right usage, as it confuses unschooling with homeschooling.

Rightly understood, "unschooling" describes both a very popular homeschooling *philosophy* and a popular homeschool *method*.

Unschooling Techniques

Unschooling is actually a constellation of methods. One of these methods is practically unique to unschooling, while the others are used much more in unschooling than in any other method. These are

- Preparation of the environment
- Constructivism
- Guided exploration (including mentoring)
- Unguided exploration
- Involvement of the parent

Preparation of the Environment

We already looked at this in the Preparation of the Environment chapter in Part 4 and in the Montessori Method chapter. In fact, if you read the back issues of the (sadly no longer published) *Growing Without Schooling* magazine, you'll find that many of the contributors said they drew some of their inspiration from Montessori.

As you'll recall, in its most basic form preparation of the environment means *removing* items which contradict the orderly development of the mind and *including* those items that promote logical learning. It turns out that the home is full of such items, so classrooms that follow Montessori principles end up trying to emulate a well-ordered TV-free home environment! Socks come in matching pairs, cooking pots nest inside each other, cleaning implements have their proper storage places, and so forth. As a child gets older, he

John Holt and "Invited Learning"

John Holt can justly be called one of the fathers of the modern homeschooling movement, particularly its "unschooling" wing. While Holt, sadly now deceased, never married or had any children, he was a keen observer of children and a pioneer thinker in the field of alternative education. When his efforts to reform the schools failed, like all other such efforts, he turned his attention to homeschooling. The result was the first homeschool magazine, *Growing Without Schooling,* and a series of books outlining his theories and findings.

John Holt is the prophet of real-world learning. For years Mr. Holt quietly but insistently taught that children can learn *all by themselves,* without any well-intentioned adult interference. He sees the idea of programmed learning as positively evil. As he so tellingly put it in *How Children Learn,*

> The difference between fond and delighted parents playing "This Little Piggy Went to Market" with their laughing

baby's toes and two anxious home-based would-be clinicians giving "tactile stimulation" to those same toes, so that the child will one day be smarter than other children and thus get into the best colleges, may not on the face of it seem to be very much. But in fact it is the difference between night and day. Of two ways of looking at children now growing in fashion—seeing them as monsters of evil who must be beaten into submission, or as little two-legged walking computers whom we can program into geniuses, it is hard to know which is worse.

John Holt did not reject all of Montessori's thought, but he fiercely defended the right of children to tackle the *real* environment. Where Montessori would carefully create a lacing frame for children to practice on, Holt would let them mess with Daddy's shoes. Where Montessori would carefully exclude from her prepared environment all randomness and chance, Holt would be happier in the mess of normal living.

John Holt's motto was "Trust Children." Based on his own observations of children learning and not learning, garnered in real-life situations, Holt believed children really want to learn and that they will learn what they need to know if left entirely to themselves. In actual practice Holt advocated involving children in our adult activities rather than begging them constantly, "What do *you* want to do today?" His theory almost eliminates "teaching" as a profession, other than a master/apprentice type of relationship where the apprentice is eager to learn a particular difficult skill. What a person can learn on his own, Holt says, he should learn on his own—our teachers are not there to tyrannize us, but to offer the help we need.

discovers that mail is sorted into logical piles (bills, junk mail, letters), books in the home library go on appropriate shelves, the encyclopedia volumes are in A–Z order . . .

It's no coincidence that the homes of successful homeschoolers are both rich in items to read and use, and that there is an order, understood by the entire family, underlying what may seem to be a riot of books, tapes, art supplies, carpentry tools, etc.

Constructivism

At this point you might want to go back and reread Chapter 17. This outlines the various "input" methods available to homeschoolers, including, among other things, constructivism.

An educational method popularized by Dr. Seymour Papert, inventor of the LOGO programming language and author of several influential books, constructivism holds that children learn best when they discover facts for themselves.

Jean Piaget, the Swiss educator, and a name that unschoolers have been invoking for decades, came up with the slogan, "To understand is to invent." Papert puts it this way in his book *The Connected Family*: "The role of the teacher is to create the conditions for invention rather than to provide ready-made knowledge."

This sounds like our old friend John Dewey, who brought the Prussian educational system back to the United States, and his belief that all knowledge is based on personal experience—i.e., book-learning stinks. But actually, constructivism is far more complex than that. Where Dewey espoused "learning by doing," constructivists espouse "learning by building."

As long as we're talking real-world projects based on an intense interest, learning by building is a good thing. I know of homeschool families that have built airplanes, cars, houses, rafts, playhouses, corrals, and museum exhibits. But of course, no one family can do *all* of this! It's also clear that the sum of human knowledge can not be achieved through hands-on real-world projects. It's also clear that lawyers, unions, and available space all conspire to make large-scale, permanent, meaningful projects of any kind impossible in today's classrooms.

As I pointed out in Chapter 17, constructivists have risen to the challenge by inventing **microworlds**. These are specialized learning environments, usually in the form of computer software and/or construction kits such as Lego bricks. By playing with these materials, children are led to discover facts about school subjects on their own.

In the most famous example, the LOGO programming language teaches children not only the rudiments of programming, but also logic and strategy, as the children attempt to "tell" the LOGO turtle to draw various shapes on the computer screen.

Microworlds of this nature are **excellent** at teaching logic and strategy, which probably explains why teachers of underprivileged children whose students use LOGO and other constructivist microworlds report such huge improvements in their students' school skills. These students tend to live in the present moment without much concern or hope for the future consequences of present actions. A little training in logic and strategy can go a long way toward encouraging such children to take charge of their own lives. In contrast, homeschooled children have many other ways to learn logic and strategy, starting with Dad's old chess set.

Microworlds are **good** for getting deeply into some aspects of math and science, since these subjects are themselves simplifications of what we see in the real world around us. They are also suitable for computer art and music, which by their nature work with limited media and a limited number of musical notes and rhythms.

Microworlds are **lousy** for any non-mechanical, descriptive, or research-oriented discipline. As my husband, Bill, says, "You can't build history!"

Microworlds are an extreme example of preparation of the environment. They tap into our deep human urge to build and make sense of the universe, which is why some students become obsessed with them. The more chaotic and unstructured the child's environment, the more benefit he gains from a logic-based microworld.

In the unschooling world, children tend to create their own microworlds. One of the first homeschooling books, *Better Than School,* chronicled among many other things how the author's children spent weeks creating miniature worlds with small toys, using them to tell deeply involved stories. I have observed my own children doing the same thing with their Beanie Babies and, before that, with dolls they made from old-fashioned wooden clothespins. They have also assembled furniture with a hammer and nails, sewed simple clothing, and created their own recipes. They have *not* made a puncheon floor, milled their own lumber, made their own cider, or done any of the other thousand things our ancestors did because they had to.

However, as a part of the unschooling educational mix, constructivism does provide an additional motivational and learning pathway.

Guided Exploration

Think of guided exploration as "tours" or "field trips." A trusted older person, who knows his way around, takes the student to places he has never been before. Once at the "tour stop" or field trip site, the student is free to explore, with a guiding eye upon him.

Unschoolers believe in adults sharing their real lives with their children, so in the beginning, the baby goes everywhere the parents can reasonably take her, rather than being left in daycare. As she gets older, the parents start planning special outings designed to expose her to options she might later like to pursue—e.g., symphony concerts, art museums, an architect's office, the United Nations . . .

Mentors

Mentors are a big part of guided exploration. Again, successful unschoolers try to add as much richness to their children's lives as possible, realizing that sticking only to what interests the parents may shortchange a child whose deepest interests may eventually lie elsewhere.

For more information on guided exploration and the next topic, *un*-guided exploration, see chapter 19.

Unguided Exploration

Recognizing that children throughout history have taken on adult activities and responsibilities at what we today would consider a young age, unschoolers start training their children quite early to be independent. And yes, I said "train." Even though some unschoolers are philosophically opposed to the whole idea of child training, constant encouragement for the child to make his own decisions, and to recognize the consequences of his decisions, is certainly training in independence. Some of this training is in the area of life skills—e.g., a preteen child can learn to handle the stove properly and cook safely rather than being told to stay away from the

What Unschooling Doesn't Mean

- Unschooling does not mean raising your children without discipline.
- Unschooling does not mean allowing your children to do nothing all day except watch television and play video games.
- Unschooling does not mean you are too lazy to teach your children the "proper way."
- Unschooling does not mean anti-Christian. True, there are unschoolers who are Jewish, Muslim, Buddhists, agnostics, etc. However, we are Christians and we are unschoolers . . .

—*Teri J. Brown and Elisa M. Wahl,* Christian Unschooling *(Champion Press, 2001)*

Real Books vs. Textbooks

Textbooks are one type of book you're not likely to find a lot of in most unschoolers' homes. . . . Unschoolers prefer what we usually call "real" books—books written by and for people who are interested in their subjects, without excessive concern about the level of vocabulary or sentence complexity, whether the book meets state guidelines, or how many supplementary workbooks, study guides, and coordinated manipulatives are available.

—*Mary Griffith,* The Unschooling Handbook *(Prima Publishing, 1998)*

What Unschooling Does Mean

The common theme is allowing your children the freedom to choose, in many cases, what they will learn. . . .

We are diligent in finding mentors for them, in searching out creative ways to satisfy their curiosity, in being there for them every day to facilitate their learning. . . .

Teaching our children is, I believe, a mandate from God. But for me, one of the most important parts of unschooling or raising children is teaching your children to teach themselves what they need to know. . . .

Why should I choose packets or curriculum to teach my children when Christ did not have one for His disciples?
—*Christian Unschooling*

stove. Some of this training consists of encouraging the child to pursue ideas and projects that take him away from the home environment. Sometimes the child ventures into environments that have been made familiar through guided exploration, for example trying out for a role in a local theatre production. Teen children might take extended trips on their own or with friends, apprentice to an out-of-state mentor, or simply bike around the town or city to see what's there. I did plenty of this when I was 14 and 15! Eventually, this unguided exploration should result in the child discovering serious interests that result in serious projects that serendipitously develop academic skills.

The outstanding example of how this theory works in practice was given by the first homeschool speaker I ever heard. It was a small meeting, just a few of us, over 20 years ago, and I have forgotten her name, but I remember the story. Her eight-year-old son hated school so much that his behavior became more and more out of control. The final straw came when he dropped on his teacher from an overhanging tree limb, where he had been lurking, and bit her! The school was quick to agree (in a time when schools *never* agreed to this) that this particular child should be educated at home.

Needless to say, we're not talking about a child with huge academic motivation. The parents wisely did not bring out any textbooks, but gave him time to unwind and try out new interests.

One day, the boy told his dad that he wanted to build a raft to float on their pond. The dad asked him, "How many board feet of lumber will you need?" This led to a discussion of how area is length times width. Eventually the son had to learn to multiply, divide, add, and subtract, all in the context of building his raft. The use of tools was learned, and books about

Unschooling or Homeschooling?

Unschooling has become associated with the particular style of homeschooling in which no set curriculum is used. Homeschooling carries an implication of schooling-at-home, while unschooling connotes that what you are doing is the opposite of school. . . .

The reason that unschooling is hard to explain and hard for some people to understand is that it is not a technique that can be broken down like a typical curriculum, lesson plan, or even unit study. Rather, unschooling is an attitude, a way of life. Where most homeschooling puts the emphasis on what needs to be learned, unschooling puts the emphasis on who is doing the learning.

In a typical school environment, the student is taught that learning is something that takes place in a certain location, at certain times, requiring a desk, textbooks, tests, etc. Children are taught that they cannot learn on their own but must be taught. . . . Children taught this way tend to wait for more input rather then seeking it on their own. . . .

In unschooling, learning can happen anywhere and at anytime. . . . There is no sense of relief that school is out because learning is always happening. Students also

know that they are responsible for their learning. They do not need an "expert" to teach them. If they have an interest, they can go out and pursue the knowledge they need. Children are encouraged to be self-learners who know how to search after information and knowledge. Letting the children pick subjects that interest them helps to achieve true learning. . . .

Here is what can best sum up this learning method if you had to shorten it to a paragraph:

The main educational objective is to keep alive the spark of curiosity and the natural love of learning with which all children are born. Children need to accept learning as a natural consequence of living, and an ongoing incremental process that continues throughout life. Learning is an integrated process in which all subjects are interrelated. (Einstein wrote on this specifically.) Children should be allowed the time to pursue a subject as fully as they want, rather than imposing artificial time constraints on them. These aspects of learning are limited by the traditional implementation of a curriculum and this is why we homeschool this way.

— *Billy Greer, "Unschooling or Homeschooling?" www.unschooling.org. Home of FUN Books and the Family Unschoolers Network News.*

John Holt's Books and Back Issues of Growing Without Schooling

How Children Learn, $11.40. How Children Fail, $11.40. Growing Without Schooling book, $26.95. Grab bag of 30 GWS back issues, $30. Complete set of all available remaining back issues (67 of them, or about half of those ever published), $100.50.
Fun Books (MD), (888) 386-7020, www.funschooling.org and www.fun-books.com.

How Children Fail and **How Children Learn** are John Holt's firsthand observations of children doing both, along with some very penetrating analysis of why children learn, or fail to learn.

Growing Without Schooling, John's magazine, continued publication after his death for quite a while, but recently ceased publication. However, back issues are still available from Fun Books. The first 12 issues have been collected into a

book; the remainder are available as a full set of remaining available issues or as a "grab bag" of 30 issues.

I own every single GWS issue ever published and can tell you this is extremely enjoyable reading if you don't mind the small print and lack of layout fanciness. The cumulative sum of all those hundreds or even thousands of parents' observations and conclusions will add much to your own homeschool background, whichever method you choose to use.

raft and boat design were dug out. Now the boy had to learn to read, which he did. By the time he had built his raft, he had learned all the math and reading the school was trying unsuccessfully to teach him, plus some.

Because of the many true stories like this, **unschoolers tend to believe that *any* interest, faithfully followed, will lead to a child learning all the basics**, plus of course the additional math, science, diplomatic skills, or whatever is involved in the particular area of interest.

Involvement of the Parents

The part of unschooling that successful unschoolers often take for granted, and that those who confuse "just goofing around" with unschooling always miss, is the *heavy* attention and involvement of the unschooling parents.

Montessori's influence is clearly evident in the way many unschoolers almost obsessively observe their children. Year after year of *Growing Without Schooling* is filled with the most meticulous possible observations of children learning in home and real-world situations. It's no coincidence that **journaling**, for both parents and children, is a favorite unschooling activity.

Unschooling parents don't just lie on the couch while the kids do whatever they feel like. They engage in active projects and outings of all kinds, taking the children along from babyhood onward. They anxiously select the best possible educational resources and build more and more bookshelves to house them. Often they strictly control TV watching or don't even own a TV. The same applies to console games, although computer and online games are a bit tougher proposition!

Unschooling parents tend to be well educated, highly verbal, and voracious readers. They may not realize how much their own background and innate resources contribute to their success. However, I feel it's important that this point is brought out.

> In many ways, "preparation of the parents" is even more important to unschooling success than preparation of the environment.

Many Names for Unschooling

Whether we call it *Christian unschooling, relaxed homeschooling,* or *flexible homeschooling* (I've even heard it called *God-ordained, parent-directed, child-implemented relaxed homeschooling*) it still remains an educational philosophy and option worth exploring by the homeschooling family.
—*Mary Ann Turner. All M.A.T. quotes in this chapter are taken from her columns in* Practical Homeschooling.

SHOW ENTHUSIASM

The most important gift you can give your eager learner is enthusiasm. If he doesn't see you get excited in the quest for education, his excitement will soon die. Give him space to explore the world around him, but be handy in case he wants to include you in his explorations. Be open to the learning opportunities in your everyday life. Should he suggest a walk in the woods, take time to walk with him. Listen to his questions, because when he asks, he is opening the door for you to be an active part in the learning process.
—*Mary Ann Turner*

Living Is Learning Curriculum Guides

Grades K–12. Guide for K–1, 2 & 3, 4 & 5, $13.50 each. Guide for 6–8, $19.99. Guide for 9–12, $22.50. *Fun Books (MD), (888) 386-7020, www.funschooling.org and www.fun-books.com.*

"How do we know if our children are learning what school covers? How do we report unschooling/homeschooling to schools?"

Nancy Plent, the founder of the Unschoolers Network of NJ, compiled the curricular goals for each year of school and translated them into real-life situations unschoolers can relate to. Packed with suggestions for meeting and exceeding these guidelines, the **Living Is Learning Curriculum Guides** double as record-keepers to help you organize your children's learning into an "after-the-fact" curriculum that

schools can recognize. Compiled from national and state curricular guidelines, these books help you see what is going on in most schools for each grade level. A confidence builder for anyone wondering if they have what it takes to "cover" a year of learning without going to school. *Used by permission from the original write-up in John Holt's Bookstore catalog*

MOM & DAD AS LEARNERS

The first thing you have to do to be a successful unschooling family, is to educate yourself. Research and read about different methods to present basic educational objectives, so when the opportunities arise, you will be prepared. For instance, when your 6-year-old becomes enamored with the idea of reading like Mommy does, you need to have a plan of action ready to guide him to becoming a reader.

—*Mary Ann Turner*

CHILDREN ARE NATURALLY MOTIVATED TO LEARN

What is unschooling? Among the many different definitions that have been tossed about, the one that best describes unschooling is "allowing your child's natural curiosity about the world and natural desire to learn become the motivating factors in education." As parents, our job is to guide and help our children as they pursue their interests at their own pace according to their unique abilities. Children are natural learners, and they want to learn about the world they live in. So if their lives are rich in learning possibilities, great books, and parents that care, children will absorb all the information around them like a sponge.

—*Mary Ann Turner*

If John Taylor Gatto was stuck on a desert island with a group of kids, those kids probably would rate as geniuses on whatever test you chose to give them by the time they made it off the island. But if a typical "absent in spirit" American dad who slumps in front of the TV set all day was given a houseful of every educational resource known to man, his kids would probably end up couch potatoes.

It's up to you: Just how dedicated and attentive are you? How much time do you have to spend *with* your kids (not just in the same room working on some project of your own)?

If you have the energy, the time, the creativity, and the fire to try unschooling, then read on!

The Unschooling Philosophy

While unschoolers like to argue among themselves as to the fine points of their philosophy, all subscribe to some extent to these main tenets:

1. Trust children.
2. Learning happens best in the real world.
3. Prepare a rich home learning environment.
4. Draw freely on mentors.

Trust Children. Unschoolers may differ as to the degree of trust they offer their children and at what age the children should be allowed to make what decisions, but in general unschooling is a philosophy that encourages children to take charge of their own education. The motto is,

"Back off! Let the kid do as much as possible on his own."

While this might sound like the Robinson philosophy, actually it's the opposite. In the Robinson Method, students follow a course of study designed by the parents or by Dr. Robinson and do the work on their own. In unschooling, the child defines the course of study as much as possible and may enlist the help of a legion of people, if desired—friends, relatives, mentors, and outside experts. Actually, unschooling is more in tune with the Montessori Method—whose techniques many unschoolers freely adapt.

Real-World Learning. You might, for example, teach writing the traditional way by assigning essays, poems, etc., which are then graded and filed away in a little folder. Alternatively, a child might learn to write the unschooling way by writing actual letters to Grandma, writing shopping lists, writing stories to be submitted to a children's magazine, and so on. A child can learn to read the traditional way by following a strictly tracked "primer" series; on the other hand, he might begin the unschooling way by reading books he picks out himself from the library.

The Unschooling Handbook

Parents. $15.95.
Prima Publishing (CA), (800) 632-8676, www.primapublishing.com.

The Unschooling Handbook: How to Use the Whole World as Your Child's Classroom by Mary Griffith was one of the first home-schooling books Prima Publishing put out before they apparently decided to corner the homeschool book market by publishing a title on every conceivable homeschool topic. Appearing in 1998, it starts out a bit defensively, painting "traditional" homeschoolers as considering unschoolers to be engaging in "benign neglect at best" and often sometimes "publicly criticiz[ing] unschoolers as giving homeschooling a bad name." No footnote was provided for this statement, so I'm wondering just where these public criticisms were vented, since I surely haven't seem them.

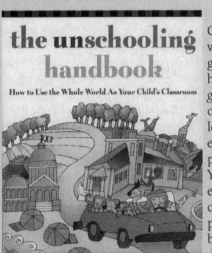

Once we get past this little chip on the shoulder, the author provides a crisp overview of her book:

> *The first four chapters give an overview of unschooling. Chapter 1 tells how we define unschooling and how we view learning and our children, and looks at the research support for an unschooling approach to education. Chapter 2 covers the materials we learn from: everything from traditional curricular materials, toys, and games, to friends and acquaintances, to completely unconventional learning resources. In Chapter 3, we'll look at learning and technology—in the form of television, videos, and computers in learning with our kids, and some of the debate over their value. In Chapter 4, we'll talk about evaluating the documenting the whole process . . . The next five chapters give examples of unschooling approaches to learning in basic subject areas . . . The final four chapters look at some of the larger issues involved with unschooling. Chapter 10 addresses typical changes in the unschooling process as our children grow older. . . . Chapter 11 introduces the practical considerations of legalities, siblings, and managing time and money. Chapter 12 looks at some of the ways to find help and support for an unschooling approach to education. Finally, Chapter 13 considers some of the societal implications of the*

unschooling approach: How does it affect family life? What are its long-term consequences? Can conventional educators learn anything from unschoolers?

Like most unschoolers, Mary Griffith is an excellent; readable writer with a lot of passion and a flair for organizing. (I'm not being contradictory here; the best unschooling parents are *great* organizers, since the highest art of organizing is to make it appear artless.) This is an impressive shot at covering everything *secular* that the prospective unschooler needs to know. You'll find annotated resources at the end of every chapter, quotes from a couple dozen unschooling families' experience scattered throughout, sidebars with yet more quotes, and an index at the end of the book.

Although brief bios of the contributors can be found in the back of the book, they are referred to by first name or first name and last initial only, presumably to shield them from the attentions of social workers and truant officers who aren't clued in to the value of unschooling.

I was unable to locate even one reference in the index to any well-known Christian homeschool leader, curriculum, book, magazine, or organization. This is odd, because all must admit that Christian homeschoolers were by far the largest segment of the homeschool movement in 1998. Nor was unschooling ignored in the Christian community: An entire chapter on it has been in every edition of my *Big Book of Home Learning* since 1987 to the present book you are holding in your hands. From 1996 to 1998, when we began to move away from the "one column per homeschooling method format," we ran a regular column on the topic by Mary Ann Turner in my magazine *Practical Homeschooling*. During this same period (1987 to 1998), the most comprehensive and best-selling guides available to curriculum resources for homeschoolers, including hundreds of products of interest to unschoolers, were my *Big Books of Home Learning* and Cathy Duffy's *Christian Home Educator's Curriculum Manuals*, neither of which are mentioned in this book either.

Whether by omission or intent, for all practical purposes the Christian unschooling and homeschooling movements do not exist in the pages of this book. I hope this omission will be rectified if there is a future edition. In the meantime, turn the page to find a book that fills this gap.

> You have to decide what are acceptable ways for your child to spend his time each day. If you surround your child with learning opportunities, he will almost invariably use those opportunities to learn... but if you surround your child with "twaddle" he will twaddle away his education. So as an unschooling parent, you are still responsible to make sure that your child's environment is rich in opportunity, example, and encouragement.
> —*Mary Ann Turner*

Even more than this, **children's *motivations* are hoped by unschoolers to arise from real world needs.** Thus, a young unschooled child may want to learn to read because he always sees his parents reading and he naturally wants to imitate them (most unschooling parents are voracious readers). In this case, the parent is operating as a **model**, which all unschoolers agree is a good thing, not just as a **teacher** telling the child what to do. An older child who has resisted reading in the classroom might decide on his own, once unschooling begins, that he wants to learn to read because reading is a necessary means of gathering information for a desired project.

A Rich Home Learning Environment. We already dealt with this earlier in the chapter. I venture to say this is part of unschooling philosophy (as in, "To be an unschooler, one *must* provide oodles of enticing resources"), as well as unschooling technique (as in, "It's easy to get kids to learn on their own when lots of great resources are lying around"). You can prove this to yourself by ridding your home of most of your educational resources, inviting over an unschooler, and observing his or her reactions.

Draw Freely on Mentors. Here we come to the heart of the biggest debate among unschoolers: how much to teach?

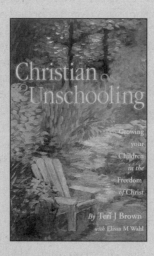

Christian Unschooling

Parents. $13.95.
Champion Press, Ltd (WI), (414) 540-9873,
www.championpress.com

Christian Unschooling: Growing Your Child in the Freedom of Christ is the first book on this topic. Its authors, Teri J. Brown and Elissa M. Wahl, are concerned that until now, unschooling has been quite suspect in many Christian circles. (Although actually my magazine, *Practical Homeschooling,* ran a regular column by Mary Ann Turner on Christian unschooling as long ago as 1996.) The authors attempt to both remedy this perceived anti-unschooling bias and give readers a taste of what unschooling is like. At this, they succeed. However, as a complete guide to the subject, more work is needed.

The book is divided into two sections. The first section, written by the two authors, attempts to define unschooling and show that it is not only compatible with Christianity but the best available homeschooling method, although several other methods are shown to make a good first step to unschooling (e.g., unit studies

and Charlotte Mason). Several "how to" chapters follow: one each on what can be only called "unscheduling," on ideas for unschooling the four main subjects, and on teaching vs. facilitating.

The second section consists first of four "collaborative" chapters of essays on the chapter topic by other Christian (or not, since the authors decided not to have contributors sign a statement of faith) unschoolers. These chapters include "Why We Unschool," "A Day in Our Life," "Lessons and Learning," and "Guided by the Lord." Contributors are not identified in any way except by name, but some names will be familiar to veteran homeschoolers (e.g., Barb Shelton and Patricia Moon).

The final three chapters are an extremely brief look at support groups, Web resources, and other resources. In these chapters the authors show their allegiance to the *Home Education Magazine* wing of homeschooling.

Some questions still remain to be raised and answered: The authors' own treatment of how to "unschool" math, for example, was brief and unsatisfactory. I can't see a kid getting into M.I.T. with only this much background. Yes, the authors admit to their own math phobia, but since unschooling is supposed to be a *child*-led method, in theory the parents' own deficiencies in a subject should make no difference. Also unexamined is the obvious fact that successful unschooling families all seem to have well-educated, highly verbal parents with many interests of their own. Can this be a method for all when so many parents do *not* fall into this category?

That said, this 150-page book is an OK, even brave, first attempt to open up the topic of Christian unschooling. However, a future edition would benefit from interaction with some tough-minded advocates of parent-led teaching, such as Michael Maloney, and more proponents of Christian education from both inside and outside the Christian unschooling wing.

It is generally concluded that non-parental experts are free to teach the child any way they want, short of an actual course with textbooks. A moving example of this was shared by *Practical Homeschooling*'s unschooling columnist Mary Ann Turner in our November/December 1997 issue:

> We were so blessed by a very special lady that lived in our community. She was a wonderfully talented artist. She was battling cancer and unable to continue her very busy schedule, so she offered to teach our children art. Yet she taught them so much more than art! She took them into the fields to sketch what they saw. She brought the wonders of nature inside for them to watercolor. She talked about creation and God's design, and she taught them to respect life and God's plan. She told them of the things she had experienced in her lifetime. She took them places with her wonderful stories. Places that they had never been before. She even taught them to rescue box turtles from the middle of the road.
>
> She was very special and unique, and I feel God brought her into our lives for many reasons. [The children] learned things about art that I never could have taught them. But more importantly, they learned lessons about life, and unfortunately death, that only Miss Sharon could have told them in her own words. We lost Miss Sharon a few months ago, and it was a very sad experience for our children, but the lessons she taught the children will last a lifetime.

When it comes to acting as mentors themselves, many unschooling parents suffer angst. Some feel guilt at the idea of *telling* a child to do anything, or even at preparing a set of real-world exercises for him *a la* the "Wax on . . . wax off" instructions from the wise old karate mentor in the movie *The Karate Kid*. I suspect this arises from popular modern child training methods that encourage children to think of their parents as peers and thus to ignore their parents as possible mentors who are older and wiser and to be respected. I also suspect that parents who are proficient in the martial arts, which encourage students to respect teachers, do not have this problem.

Unschoolers believe they should trust children . . . but how much? Must the child *always* lead the way? If so, at what age? Can or should parents compel *any* form of teaching that the child might not immediately enjoy, such as piano lessons?

Finding the Balance

James Muncy, in his essay "Unschooling Unchristian?" included in the book *Christian Unschooling*, perhaps analyzes it best. He breaks unschooling into an "environmental component"—the rich educational environment we have been discussing—and a "social component." In his case, the latter refers to being "active participants with our children in the educational experience . . . what we do *with* our children and not what we do *to* our children." Although Muncy doesn't specifically mention outside mentors, most unschooling families would eagerly include them in this social component. Finally, Muncy also refers to a "compulsory component." As he says,

> We are not pure unschoolers because we do force our children to learn certain things. But this is the smallest part of our educational experience. We only do this in areas where the child might not see the educational value before the learning experience. Perhaps I am of little faith, but I can't see our children memorizing their multiplication tables "just for fun."

MAKING THE TRANSITION

I know when I made the switch from a more structured atmosphere to an unstructured one, it was very helpful to take a couple of weeks off to get used to the feel of freedom again. My children were not accustomed to having so many educational choices and it took them a while to want to "study" anything. Once freed from the constraints of a structured atmosphere, they were ready to veg out and relax all day. I casually offered fun trips and projects. Soon both were ready for more "solid" activities. . . .

Many people use **literature** as a stepping stone toward unschooling. The library is the perfect place to start doing this. Allow your children to get their own library cards, then let them browse for books. . . .

I've noticed **unit studies** are another common bridge between structured learning and nonstructured learning. . . . Once your children do several unit studies they will begin to learn how to approach learning in diverse ways and to look at topics with an eye for the unusual.

Many [**Charlotte Mason**] techniques are so child-friendly that they lend themselves wonderfully to the unschooling method. . . . For those who are wanting to relax their homeschools into an unschool, but who are reluctant to make such a leap, some of the Charlotte Mason methods might be just right for you.
—*Christian Unschooling*

The most exciting part of unschooling is watching your children learn to think for themselves, watching the excitement in their eyes when they are working on some elaborate project they've invented, and watching them enter the adult world one step at a time, with confidence.

—*Mary Ann Turner*

What About College?

Now you say, what about math? Biology? History? If a child reads well, and his lifetime has been filled with listening, learning, and exploring, then he naturally explores these topics, too. If college attendance has always been a priority in his education, then by his teen years he is aware that upper-level math will probably be a necessity for acceptance into a 4-year-college program. At that point, it becomes his responsibility to use all those already acquired learning skills to attain his goal . . . learning what he needs before he begins his college years. As a parent, your job is to help him research what the college he hopes to attend requires for acceptance, and help him decide how he can fulfill those requirements. This varies from college to college, so research is necessary. Please don't make any assumptions; call to find out.

If he has mastered the reading, writing, and communication skills, the rest will take a very short time. Four years of upper-level math can be covered in a year, if need be. A biology text can be read in a week or two. History, more likely than not, was learned long ago with great books from the library. So the entire high school process could possibly be completed in a year. On the other hand, your child can spend all that extra time studying wonderful topics of interest and expanding his knowledge well beyond college level. That choice is up to your family

—*Mary Ann Turner. Her daughter Jamie was accepted into college at age 12, and got a 4.0 her first semester, before deciding to return to homeschool.*

I wonder if the difference between the "pure" unschoolers and those who, like Muncy, recognize the need for *some* compulsory training, is actually a difference between the math-and-science parents and the humanities parents—between the Geeks and the I Hate Math crowds. I say this because I have yet to encounter an unschooling parent with a heavy math and science background who was content to let his or her kids just "noodle around" with math or any other subject he or she considers vital to the children's future. Such parents might employ clever strategies to teach the math facts without seeming to teach them. They might play card games that require lots of fast addition and subtraction. They might encourage the use of software that disguises math drill as a game. They might make mental math into a mealtime game. But although they may be content with history studied via videos and random reading, or composition lessons that consist of shopping lists/online chats and forums/letters to the editor, they will *not* let the child learn math facts and concepts only if and when he or she so desires.

The Top Ten

Unschoolers live or die by how well the learner is motivated. True motivation comes from *inside*, but it comes as a response to something *outside*: an interest, a person, a piece of the community that a child wants to be a part of. With that in mind, I humbly present this list of the top ten characteristics of successful unschooling families. They:

1. Go lots of interesting places and take the kids
2. Own lots of books and leave them where the children can handle them
3. Read a lot in front of their children
4. Talk to their children on an adult level from a very young age
5. Teach their children the rules of analysis, logic, and debate, through critical watching of videos, discussion of educational issues and political topics, drawing the child's attention to obvious hype in an ad, etc.
6. Are observant of their children's abilities and moods and like to journal them
7. Involve the children in necessary chores
8. Involve the children in meaningful family projects, not as a "schoolish" attempt to drag in education, but because the work is important, it has to be done, and the children are able to help
9. Have interesting adult friends to whom they introduce their children, encouraging them to become comfortable in the company of adults and to look upon adults as potential resources and mentors from an early age
10. Connect to other unschooling families online, through magazines, or in person

Unschooling is an adventure, for the adventurous. If all you do is sit at home and watch TV, you'd better skip this method. But if your life is filled with friends and activities, if you live where children are free to explore (here city or country both beat suburbs), or you simply feel it's time to break the mold and go boldly where you've never gone before, unschooling may be for you!

CHAPTER 33

The Eclectic Method

So, which homeschool method do you pick? How about *all* of them? Typically dubbed the "Eclectic Method" of homeschooling, this is the "Chinese menu" approach. For a given child, at a given age or stage, you might use parts of two or three methods, while for another child you pick a different approach entirely.

Since we now know children have wildly varying learning styles and thinking styles, this makes sense. While *overall* you might pick a given method as your favorite, some kids and some subjects just won't fit in that box.

You are now seeing one of the huge advantages of homeschooling: **your ability to experiment until you find what works for each part of each child's education.** As Maria Montessori put it,

> The teacher must not limit her action to *observation,* but must proceed to *experiment.* The lesson corresponds to an *experiment.* The teacher must always *test* whether or not her lesson has attained the end she had in view.

If the method you've chosen doesn't seem to be working for your child, feel free to try another more suited to the situation. You can mix and match: a bit of Charlotte Mason narration *here,* some unschooling-style journaling *there,* some Precision Teaching drill *here,* some hands-on projects *there.* It's OK for an unschooler to occasionally use a textbook and for a "back to basics" mom to do a unit study.

The "5 D's" of WholeHearted Education

Perhaps the most successful "eclectic" organizational scheme I have seen is "WholeHearted Education," the brainchild of Clay and Sally Clarkson. The Clarksons break homeschooling down into five "areas of focused studies." As they put it in their article that appeared in the September/October 1998 issue of *Practical Homeschooling* (my comments are in brackets):

Value of the Eclectic Method

In its actual procedure school work must always be thus eclectic. An all-or-nothing policy for a single system inevitably courts defeat; for the public is not interested in systems and systems, and refuses in the end to believe that any one system contains every good thing. Nor can we doubt that this attitude is essentially sound. If we continue, despite the pragmatists, to believe in absolute principles, we may yet remain skeptical about the logic of their reduction to practice—at least in any fixed programme of education. We are not yet justified, at any rate, in adopting one programme to the exclusion of every other simply because it is based on the most intelligible or the most inspiring philosophy. We must try out several combinations, watch and record the results, compare them, and proceed cautiously to new experiments.

—*Harvard professor Haney W. Holmes from his introduction to the book* The Montessori Method

Educating the WholeHearted Child

Parents. Book, $20.95. Tape sets, $20 each.
Whole Heart Ministries, CO.
(888) 311-2146, www.wholeheart.org.

As I said, the most successful eclectic approach I have seen is that of Clay and Sally Clarkson in their book, **Educating the WholeHearted Child.** They divide school subjects into the "5 D's"—Discipleship Studies (Bible and Christian living), Disciplined Studies (the "basics"), Discussion Studies (the humanities), Discovery Studies (nature, science, the arts, and personal interests), and Discretionary Studies (real-life skills, field trips, etc.). They then explain how to complete these studies using the best techniques of the various methods.

Their oversized, 220-plus-page book includes much more than this: character training, whether you should homeschool, the practicalities of organization, realities of dealing with the spiritual blues, and sources of support. Much helpful advice and inspiration is included, as well as a hefty appendix of planning forms you can use in your homeschool.

For more details and insights, now there's *The WholeHearted Child* tape set and *The WholeHearted Mother* tape set. Each set is four audiocassettes in a protective slim case. Recommended. *Reviewed by Mary Pride and Charles & Betty Burger*

1. **Discipleship Studies.** We start with the study of God's Word to gain wisdom. Our goal is to shape our children's hearts to love God and to study and know his Word. [Take your pick from these appropriate methods: Back to Basics (for Bible facts and memory), Charlotte Mason, Maloney Method (for instant recall of Bible facts), Principle Approach, Unschooling, Unit Studies]

2. **Disciplined Studies.** Then we study the "basics," such as math and language arts, that require a more disciplined approach. Our goal is to develop our children's foundational learning skills and competencies. [Back to Basics, Contests, Laptop Homeschooling, Maloney Method, Principle Approach]

3. **Discussion Studies.** Then we spend the bulk of our studies in the humanities, reading and reading aloud literature and history, and studying the fine arts. Our goal is to feed our children's minds on the best in living books and the fine arts. [Charlotte Mason, Classical Education & Great Books, Montessori Method, Principle Approach, Robinson Method, Unit Studies, Unschooling]

4. **Discovery Studies.** Next, we direct our children into the "study of learning" in areas such as nature, science, the creative arts, and all other interests. Our goal is to stimulate in our children a love for learning by creating opportunities for curiosity, creativity, and discovery. [Charlotte Mason, Montessori Method, Unschooling, Unit Studies]

5. **Discretionary Studies.** Finally, we turn to the "study of living," focusing on natural gifts and interests, community involvement, and life skills. Our goal is to direct our children in developing a range of skills and abilities according to their drives and gifts. [Montessori Method, Unschooling, Unit Studies]

As you can see, each of the Clarksons' "5 D's" can be approached in a variety of ways, including mixing and matching the methods most appropriate to each area of study.

You can also torture a method to use it for an area it is *not* best suited for, such as trying to teach a slow learner to read the "unschooling" way when the research shows that slow learners need the additional structure and correction provided by methods such as Back to Basics and the Maloney Method. But why bother? Isn't one of the reasons we homeschool to get away from labels? You owe no loyalty to a *method* or *system.* Like Maria Montessori said, it's all about what *works*, not what *ought* to work! In that sense, we all should be eclectic homeschoolers.

Next: Unit Studies

Well, we're at the end of the Homeschool Methods section, but there's still more that needs to be said about one of the very most popular homeschool methods: unit studies. This is no mistake: Unit studies are so complex that we decided to give them an entire section of their own. Just keep reading to find out the difference between a unit and a sloppy mess, the basic steps you'll need to create your own successful units, and how to develop units based on authors, history and geography, and science.

PART 6

Taking the Mystery Out of Unit Studies

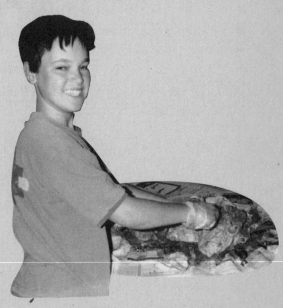

Wonder what "hands-on learning" is all about? Here is an example! Arlene Hartley of Millington, TN, sent in this picture of her son, Kyle, investigating the heart and lungs of a pig (obtained from a slaughter house). As you can tell by the use of gloves, the Hartleys were hesitant to "feel" these parts. In the end, Kyle learned a lot about these body parts, a lesson long to be remembered.

Nathan Harter, a 12-year-old homeschooler from Madison, NY, has apparently been learning more than academics at home. His 4-H project, a Windsor Chair that he made in his father's shop, won a blue ribbon at the Madison County 4-H fair. It was then taken to the New York State Fair and put on display with items from around the state. The picture shows Nathan with his chair and poster at the state fair. Nathan spent about 20 hours working on his chair, starting right from the log! Add an essay to this picture, and some study of wood types, and you've got one really memorable unit study!

CHAPTER 34

Ingredients of a Successful Unit Study

As we saw in last section's Unit Studies chapter, unit studies have a number of advantages. They are *multilevel* (meaning you can use the same curriculum for children of various ages, all at one time). They *integrate school subjects,* helping kids see the "big picture" and simultaneously teaching them how to apply skills from many areas. They make learning *memorable* and *enjoyable*. They help kids develop *research skills*.

But even with all this going for them, unit studies are still the single most confusing homeschool method for many people.

In this chapter, we will begin to brush away the cobwebs by answering these questions:

- Does merely investigating an interest count as a "unit study," or is there more to it than this?
- Is there a difference between poorly designed units and excellent units? If so, what should you look for?
- Can you teach *everything* with unit studies?

Then, in the remaining chapters of this section, we'll look at the steps of designing a quality unit study and show you how to use these tools to create your own literature, history, geography, and science units.

Unit Splatter and Hyperwandering

This is where the confusion about unit studies arises. Some prepackaged unit studies have activities with little or no direct connection to the theme. Such units seem to be constructed like this:

- We're going to study trees.
- Trees are used to make cardboard.
- Cardboard is used in boxes.
- So we will do a bunch of crafts using cardboard boxes and we'll study the history of boxmaking.

Can anyone tell me what this has to do with our original theme of "trees"?

Projects Are Not Enough

There are many new unit study curricula out on the homeschool market, yet a closer look reveals that all unit studies are not created equal.

Successful unit studies not only have a central theme and offer many related activities and projects based on that theme, they also encourage discovery learning.

Discovery learning is not merely the absence of instructions; it is the absence of instruction plus the presence of carefully constructed open-ended questions that lead children to the next thought, then the next thought, and finally to the big concept that connects their single activity to the larger issue being studied.

—*Jessica Hulcy*

- I call this **unit splatter**. Someone drops the theme on the floor and you wind up studying the splatters that land two yards away.
- Another good word for it, especially as it applies to online units, is **hyperwandering**. I thought I invented this term, but a quick check at yahoo.com showed that actually a U.K. marketing expert published an article using it a year ago, and for all I know he had in turn seen the term somewhere else. Whoever first came up with it, "hyperwandering" is a great way to describe the process that takes a person from website to website, pursuing links as the whimsy takes him. It's also a great way to describe

Should I Use Unit Studies for Everything?
by Pam Maxey

Unit studies have become more popular of late for a variety of reasons.

- For many parents, unit studies offer a chance to teach their children of different grade levels at the same time. This is a huge benefit to a parent educator.
- You can also incorporate a variety of subject areas into a unit. For example, a unit study can easily incorporate literature and history activities.
- Most of the time, children and parents alike consider unit studies fun activities to do together.

In my opinion, there is nothing wrong with fun learning in a homeschooler's day. There are many opportunities for creative activities that still teach valuable information. With unit studies, parents get a break from structured, workbook activities. This explains why the students enjoy them as well!

In addition to the material and the presentation of that material, there are other benefits for the parent. Unit studies offer more freedom and less structure than traditional curricula. I talk to many parents who are ready for a break from a rigid schedule. For many of these parents, unit studies can provide a welcome relief that adds variety to their day.

These studies are typically offered at an affordable cost, but this is where parents can get into trouble. Some parents with whom I have spoken have decided to make an "either/or" decision and pick a unit study because it is the less expensive, more exciting alternative. This decision could cost you down the road if your child lacks the reading or mathematics skills he needs to excel in life.

Unit Studies Plus Sequential Studies

Unit studies and curricula are like bread and butter—they each have a place at the table. I like my bread buttered! Bread, like curricula, can be a bit dry going down.

Unit studies, like butter, are meant to supplement and enrich curriculum, not replace it.

There are some wonderful unit studies available to homeschoolers, but they do not totally take the place of a sequential curriculum in all subject areas. The KONOS curriculum, for example, states clearly that their unit studies are not a substitute for phonetic reading and math curriculum, so you need to buy separate curriculum in these areas as well.

Danger! Danger!

The danger in using unit studies with no reading and mathematics curriculum is that you have no set of sequential skills that you are teaching your child. As the name suggests, "sequential skills" are taught to build upon one another. Without this sequential system of learning, there is no logical means by which to reach the end. As you might imagine, this could lead to major problems down the road.

Unit studies may have reading and mathematics activities but still not cover all the skills needed in a specific grade level. Neither do they teach a parent how to teach a child to read or solve mathematics equations.

In my household, when that warm bread comes out of the oven, we reach for the butter. We wouldn't think of having one without the other. What are you doing at your house? Are you buttering your bread, or are you trying to eat the butter without the bread?

There is a time and a place for everything. The best option is warm bread with butter. Similarly, the best teaching option is to use curricula for the subject areas in which sequential instruction is necessary plus unit studies for those areas in which research and hands-on activities work best.

Pamela Maxey home educates her two sons and is the author of Classic Start Curriculums and Themed Unit Studies. You can visit her website at www.classicapple.com. This column initially appeared in Practical Homeschooling magazine.

a random so-called "unit study" that goes from trees, to cardboard, to boxes, to crafts with shoeboxes, to shoes, to dancing, to wherever, and on and on. . .

I have found a way of visualizing what unit studies should look like that will help you spot the difference between an actual "unit" (a well-organized approach to a topic) and a random walkabout through a number of unrelated subject areas.

Picture an archery target. In the center is the bull's-eye. This is your unit theme. The first ring around the bull's-eye encompasses *essential* studies and activities. These are on the topic of the theme and designed to help you learn and remember what you need to know about the theme. In the second ring are *useful* studies and activities. These are closely related topics that will give your understanding of the theme added depth. In the next ring, we find *contrived* studies and activities. These are those that (like the relationship between cardboard and trees) bear *some* relation to the unit theme but aren't essential or even necessarily helpful in understanding it.

How to Spot & Avoid Mindless Unit Studies

Some units can verge on the ridiculous. Such units seem to be arduously contrived instead of flowing together naturally. Here are three red flags to beware of in units.

Beware of Units That Miss the Big Picture

If a unit revolves around American history, *The Witch of Blackbird Pond* is a natural book to read. If the unit launches off into pond life, for the sake of adding science to the unit, then the entire point of the book has been lost as well as the point of the unit. *The Witch of Blackbird Pond* is about Puritan history, tolerance and intolerance, obedience and disobedience, love and hate, not about pond life.

For a unit to be well constructed, each activity should contribute to the big picture rather than strain at minutia or incidentals. All activities should build on the same general theme, rounding out the unit.

Units should be as carefully woven as fabric is woven. It makes no sense to be weaving with yarn and then to insert a piece of barbed wire.

Beware of Units That Integrate Every Subject in Every Unit

Sometimes integrating every subject in every unit simply does not fit. A unit on air pressure should not "force" art into the unit just to check art off the list of subjects covered. While an art activity such as "paint or draw air" is a definite waste of time, another art activity "paint with a straw" is not a waste of time. As the child sucks paint into the straw, places his finger over the end of the straw, and then releases his finger and slings paint on the paper, he is using the principle of air pres-

sure he has just learned. This art activity reinforces the main theme of the unit.

Let's face it. Some units are heavy on science or history while other units are heavy on art or music. Many moms are frustrated when they cannot have 30 minutes of each subject balanced perfectly in each unit. This attitude causes the natural flow of a unit to be lost.

Beware of Units That Have No Higher Purpose

Christians should teach children not only units of WHAT but also units of WHY. All knowledge should further our understanding of God as well as equip us to operate in the world. Units on simple machines, inventions, and the Industrial Revolution should emphasize the common character traits of the inventors, such as resourcefulness and persistence. Children should focus on the character traits of those they study. While studying grains and bread, parents should point children to "the bread of life," which is in the Word of God, and to the bread of communion, which represents the body of Christ. As we study units on stars and planets, the goal for our children should be to crack open a door of wonderment revealing an incredible God of orderliness, creativity, and design.

Pointing to a higher purpose need not be contrived. Beyond all facts, figures, and activities is the Creator of the universe whom we want our children to know personally. The more Christian parents study His Word, the more we will see it evidenced in everything from gardening to Beethoven, and the more we will pass this wonder on to our children.

—*Jessica Hulcy, from her article in the first issue of* Practical Homeschooling

Finally, in the outer darkness . . . I mean the outer ring . . . we have *irrelevant* studies and activities. To continue our example, shoeboxes may be made of cardboard, but a study of how cardboard boxes are made in a factory will not teach us anything relevant to a study of trees.

Here is a picture that shows the same thing:

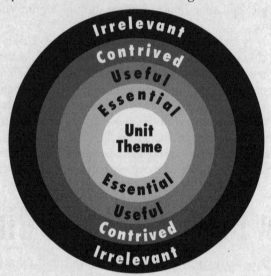

Here is the same thing visually as it pertains to hyperlinks:

Unit Theme

First Link

Essential Studies & Activities

Second Link

Useful Studies & Activities

Third Link

Contrived Studies & Activities

Fourth Link

Irrelevant Studies & Activities

As you can see, the further afield you get from the basic unit theme, the more contrived and irrelevant the studies and activities become.

The one exception to the above visuals is a *deep* unit with *sub-units*. In that case, the sub-unit theme is an actual unit study of its own. This means you have a string of archery targets, each with its own "bull's eye."

For example, the KONOS Character Curriculum has units based on character traits. These are divided into sub-units. Each of these sub-units is what would in itself constitute a light to medium unit study and has its own theme. For "Attentiveness," one of the sub-units is a study of the eye.

Now, let's look at the central, usable portion of our archery target (the grey circle labeled "Essential") in another way—as a pie to be divided up:

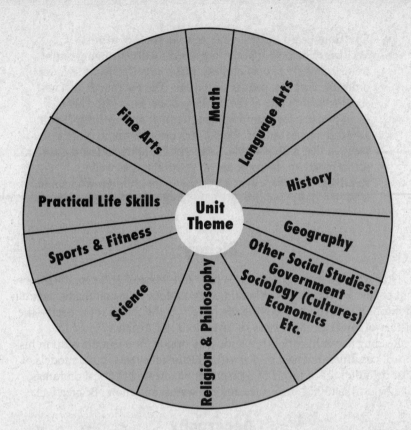

We can quibble about the subjects I've picked for the slices, and the sizes of the slices. In fact, the subjects and slice sizes will change depending on your central theme, as you'll see in the next chapters. Regardless, the "pie" metaphor works well as a way to see how a unit study is put together.

A Whole Unit Pie or a Few Scattered Crumbs?

The word "unit" means "whole." Thus, the ideal unit includes *all* the subjects, and the ideal unit "pie" includes *all* (or very close to all) these slices pictured above.

Or, if you prefer to think in terms of what goes into your pie, the ideal unit study should have a complete set of tasty and nutritious subject "ingredients."

You can't tack a few activities onto a topic and magically turn it into a unit, any more than you can have a whole pie with half its slices missing (or half its ingredients missing). For your "pie" to be complete, you need to add a solid bite of academic content in a wide number of subject areas.

Let's see how this works as we examine our friendly pie visual above.

> If one of these subjects is less important to you, think of it as the whipped topping—an optional extra—rather than as a slice of the pie.

Language Arts

Starting at the top right, you see Language Arts. As Pam Maxey said in her sidebar on page 268, unit studies are not a good way to teach phonics or grammar. However, language arts naturally fit into unit studies in many ways.

- **Vocabulary.** Each unit theme has its own unique vocabulary associated with it. These words can be looked up and then written onto flashcards or in notebooks, used in sentences, or simply learned.

- **Spelling.** Learn to spell your new vocabulary words!
- **Writing.** The potential writing assignments springing out of unit studies are almost endless: plays, reports, business letters ordering supplies, poems, and more. The parent can dictate sentences from one of the books you are studying: This is good practice for grammar, handwriting, and spelling. If you are studying an author, the student can attempt to write a piece in that author's style. Oral reports, narration, and even songs based on the topic are all possibilities as well.
- **Reading.** Was there ever a unit study for children who could read that didn't involve lots of reading? I don't think so!

History

Now we answer the questions "Who?" and "When?" Who are the important people for your topic? What time period does your unit theme *naturally* fit into? Or will you be studying the history of the theme topic itself—the history of music or the history of inventions, for instance?

Reading about history is not your only option. You can dress up in historical costumes, re-enact or dramatize historical events, build models of historic buildings or forms of transportation, create historical dioramas, take field trips to historical sites and museums, and more. Be creative!

Geography

The question is now "Where?" What locations are associated with your unit theme?

Physical geography studies the "lay of the land"—rivers, tundra, mountains, climate. **Political geography** studies the man-made features: countries, states, cities, transportation routes, imports and exports, and so on.

A good reference atlas and a good globe will help you look up places you are studying. If the places in question were in ancient times, you might also need a cultural or historical atlas for background information.

Online you can locate websites devoted to just about any modern or historic location. Be careful to note *who* is providing the information. Is this a site designed to entice tourists, or an academic site based on deep research? Is it the work of a dedicated amateur, or a professional who might be less inclined to give you the "inside" story? Who checks the facts on the site? These are good questions to ask about any educational site, not just geography sites!

Now that you have your background information, you can flesh it out with projects. Making your own maps or filling in blank maps is one good way to solidify geographic information. Sampling the food of another region, making regional doll costumes, creating folk jewelry, singing folk songs, and dancing folk dances are some other ways to "get into" geography.

Other Social Studies

The government and economics of a time period or a region go naturally with a history or geography unit. They may also enter into an author or literature unit, or even a holiday study. Consider the works of Charles Dickens, many of which were written to protest the economic conditions of his day, or the political significance of the Fourth of July.

If you want to get more deeply into other cultures, don't forget our next area of study . . .

Religion & Philosophy

Here we have Bible study and memorization, comparative religions, and philosophy. For a history unit: What thinking was popular at the time? Deism? Medieval Christianity? Sophism? Roman paganism? What world-views were at war for the hearts and minds of the people? What major thinkers were alive at the time? For a geography unit: What are the religions of the region? What do they teach? Have any of them immigrated to your country, and if so, do they still have the same form as in their land of origin?

Science

In the elementary grades, science as taught in the schools is just a mishmash of projects and terminology, little of which is remembered. You can easily match this level of academics by adding experiments related to your theme from books such as the Backyard Scientist series or Janice van Cleave's various series. Related reading from non-textbook sources, especially the great Usborne "fact" books in various science topics, will actually put your student ahead of schooled counterparts. Plus there's field trips, nature walks, and just lying in the backyard with your nose to the ground watching the ants and grasshoppers. More on this topic in the Science Units chapter.

Sports & Fitness

I happen to believe that exercise is another of those areas that should be systematic, not haphazard. Tossing one little physical skill in here or there will not add much to your unit study.

The Nutrition aspect of fitness also really is a subset of Science, and belongs in that particular pie slice.

Finally, actual participation in a sport is obviously well beyond all unit studies except one devoted to that sport. Exception: A unit study can kick off interest in a sport.

So what does this leave that we can weave into our unit studies?

- Sports and games of other times and cultures
- The physical training of soldiers in that time and place
- The importance of fitness and sports to the persons, times, or places that are the central theme
- Fitness techniques of that time or culture
- The relative health levels of people at that time and place (e.g., the amazing lung capacity of Andean Indians or the intellectual dullness ancient Romans experienced once they began using lead pipes to carry their water)
- The factors responsible for those health levels (e.g., a study of the Horatio Hornblower novels will naturally lead to investigating the Black Death and scurvy, two diseases that are major plot elements in the novels)
- Medical treatments current in the time and culture, and how they correspond to medical treatments in our time

Practical Life Skills

Typing. Computer literacy. Washing the car. Cooking dinner. First aid and CPR. Volunteering. Gardening. Fixing small machines. Building a radio from a kit. Making a kite. Covering a sofa. Sewing a dress.

Real Units Are Great!

Unit studies are great when done right. In fact, I believe *every* homeschool should include at least *some* unit studies, even if you choose another method for your core curriculum.

The warnings against "twaddly" and "mindless" unit studies in this chapter are meant to help you avoid bogus units so you can experience the joys of *real* units—unit studies that allow a child to get deeply into a beloved or much-needed theme, pulling it all together in the same way that adults do when we find a topic that fascinates us.

If you think about this list, you'll realize that many unit-study projects employ or teach practical life skills. If you sew your own Medieval Princess costume, you are engaged in historical research (for an accurate costume), art (for an attractive design), *and* sewing (a practical life skill). Making a bird feeder not only teaches about birds but also about woodworking. Cooking your KONOS-inspired feast for the close of your unit requires not only researching the recipes and the mode of presentation but also actual cooking skills.

If you make a list of all the practical skills you know and want to teach your children, plus those you want to learn together with your children, you can work backward from this list, using it to come up with projects that both employ the skills *and* add depth to your unit theme.

Fine Arts

Drawing. Painting. Cartooning. Photography. Music. Dance. Film. These can relate to your theme as you study

- The art of the time and place
- Art *about* the time, place, or topic

Listening to music about trains and watching movies that show trains of different periods would be appropriate for a unit on trains. A unit on French royalty could well include a visit to a ballet performance, since ballet was invented in order to provide entertainment to the French court. You can do units on painters and musicians, or include painters, musicians, and their works in units on the history or geography of their times. A Christmas unit *needs* Christmas songs, and a study of Iwo Jima *needs* that famous photograph of the American men lifting the flag.

Studying art is also a great introduction to learning at least some of the techniques of the artist. Public schools have been teaching folk artist techniques for decades (in places where the art program hasn't been cancelled to provide more money for the football team)!

CAUTION: Some art and music techniques were designed to ornament religious ceremonies. Public schools often use a study of such techniques as a back door to inculcating interest in non-Christian religions. I would clearly separate the technique from its religious use. You don't have to make an actual totem or worry doll to learn the techniques involved. See for instance how famous Jewish artist Marc Chagall has adapted Christian stained-glass techniques for a variety of nontraditional pieces.

Math

Finally, at the top of our pie, we have Math. As you saw in the box on the second page of this chapter, unit studies are generally *not* a good way to handle math study. For that, you need systematic instruction.

However, as you'll see in the following chapters, some math topics do arise naturally out of certain types of unit themes and projects. Many homeschooled kids got their first introduction to fractions while measuring out fractions of tablespoons and cups for baking projects, for example.

What to Look for in a Ready-Made Unit Study

And there you have all your ingredients. Now, let's see how you can use this shopping list to evaluate ready-made units—units written for sale (or placed online for free) by a curriculum developer.

A good ready-made unit study will provide the following:

- **No splatter.** Activities and discussion questions are directly related to the theme.
- **Activities that include a variety of school subjects that naturally fit a study of the theme.** Typically, you'll read and do some research, do some writing, act out or dramatize persons or things studied, make models of things studied, do demonstrations or experiments that illustrate scientific principles studied, memorize some facts or famous sayings, build a working something-or-other, and play some educational games. Math problems may also be included, but beware, as this tends to be the fake and useless part of most unit studies. The most popular units curricula all suggest you study math separately and systematically.
- **An excellent annotated reading list**—so you can tell which of the books you want to bother obtaining and studying
- **Lists of materials needed** lesson by lesson
- **Activities for both older and younger learners**

Top 10 Questions for Ready-Made Units

Now that you're familiar with the ingredients of a quality unit study, let's make a list of questions that you can ask when considering any unit designed by someone other than yourself.

1. **What size is it?** Is this a light, medium, or deep unit? Generally, you can answer this question by seeing how long the unit designer says the unit should take to complete.
2. **Is the unit theme** either (a) a topic you need to cover at the moment in your homeschool or (b) a topic that really excites your learners *and* draws them into areas you want to cover?
3. **What is the academic value** of the theme and related topics? Do you just skim shallowly over the surface of a number of topics, or are you actually learning an equivalent amount to what would be taught in more traditional courses?
4. **Are the topics actually related** to the theme?
5. **If it's a deep unit** (one that lasts for a month or more), **does it require a usable amount of readily available references** (books and other media you'll use repeatedly)? Most ready-made units refer again and again to a central core of necessary media (generally, books and/or software). You should count the cost of purchasing these reference materials into the unit cost, since it's unlikely that your library will let you keep them for as long as the unit lasts, assuming the library has a copy in the first place.
6. **Are the projects** efficient or twaddly?
7. **Are the supplies you need for the projects readily available?** If they aren't household supplies, is ordering information provided (where to get them)? Are they expensive?
8. **Are there discussion questions, quizzes, or tests?** If so, **are answers or answer keys provided?**
9. **Are teaching aids** such as charts, maps, graphs, and time-lines (blank or otherwise) included or available?
10. **Does the unit have closure?**

One Last Question

And here's one more question I personally consider very important. This one is for veteran homeschoolers only:

Is it full of projects and ideas that are suspiciously similar to the projects and ideas in other publishers' unit studies?

A lot of people these days have the idea that, because ideas can't be copyrighted, it's OK to borrow other people's project ideas and curriculum outlines. Actually, it's not, unless you do it for your own personal use. Feel free to create your own family curriculum based on bits and pieces of whatever you wish. But don't put it online, even for free, or photocopy and hand it out, let alone try to sell it, if it includes projects and ideas from someone else's work. You could get into a lot of trouble!

If you as a veteran homeschooler spot what seems to be a lot of borrowing in a ready-made unit study, the courteous thing is to alert the person whose work appears to be borrowed. Contacting the person who did the borrowing is *not* a good idea—at worst, you are warning a plagiarist to take action to defend their plagiarism, and at best, you might end up looking silly or annoying. If the plagiarist is one of those people who believe they have a God-given right to "help homeschoolers" by appropriating other people's work, you also might find yourself embroiled in a long, fruitless, and painful discussion ending in them threatening you if you dare to warn the victim—which you should have done in the first place. In any case, *you* are not the offended party—the injustice was done to the person whose work was stolen. Don't gossip or speculate about it online—let the people in question deal with it.

A good product description will answer most of these questions and clue you in to what the curriculum author is trying to accomplish. Reviews will then let you know how successfully the curriculum accomplishes its declared goals.

Putting It Together: The 10 How-Tos of Unit Studies

In this chapter, we've covered the first four important points you need to know about unit studies:

- **You can't use units to cover every subject.** For phonics, language-arts basics such as grammar, high-school science, and other deep, sequential subjects you need sequential (not topical) curriculum.
- **Start by picking your size**: shallow (or, if you prefer, light), medium, or deep. A deep unit might have sub-units; each of these should have a strong central theme just like a regular smaller unit.
- **Pick your theme.** If possible, make it one of high interest to the learner. If not, pick one you need to cover anyway.
- **Group related topics around a central theme** using my model of a pie divided into slices. Avoid all unit splatter and hyperwandering.

In the next chapter, you'll learn about how to:

- **Pick your starting point.** Professional curriculum developers such as Amanda Bennett heavily research each unit theme before starting to design their units. You don't have time for this. Just pick a starting book, video, TV show, project, field trip, or event to create interest. The following chapters will show you just how to do this.
- **Fill in your unit** with reference sources and deeper research.
- **Make it memorable** with projects, trips, and activities.
- **Create understanding** by talking and writing about the theme; modeling it; dramatizing it; in short, any and all of the techniques in the last two chapters of the "Education 101" section.
- **Create retention** by organizing the material you've studied (timelines, flashcards, graphs, maps, journals, portfolios, etc.) and drilling it with games, projects, presentations, or even just plain drill.
- **Add closure** to your unit by ending with a big project, research paper, demonstration, or even a quiz.

It may seem like a lot of effort at first, but it's worth it. You don't always have to create a complete unit to benefit from an understanding of how unit studies work. Virtually any school subject can be made more interesting and memorable by slipping a few unit-study ingredients into the mix. In fact, I'd venture to say that the difference between great teachers and mediocre teachers is that the great teachers know how to "jazz up" their lessons in just this way—not just to be clever, but because their main goal is to have their students *remember* their lessons.

So get ready to learn more of those tips 'n tricks that will make your homeschool not just good, but great!

CHAPTER 35

Mary's Secret Unit-Study Recipe

There is a secret recipe for quickly creating successful unit studies. It's not the only way to do it, but it works, and you don't have to be a genius at research or a huge educational expert to use it. My secret recipe has six steps:

1. Inexpensive, fun, and readily available idea sparkers you can use to kick off just about any unit
2. The easiest ways to quickly find . . .
3. . . . the in-depth material for filling in your "pie slices"
4. My secret weapon for great unit-study projects
5. Secret tips for improving retention of what was learned
6. Jessica Hulcy's unit topper: the magic of closure

Ways to Kick Off Your Unit

You need an **idea sparker**—something that your children will find interesting and that will also open the door to further study. An idea sparker can be:

- **A "living book."** This term invented by Charlotte Mason describes a book written by an individual who is both knowledgeable and passionate about the subject, as opposed to a "dead book," neutered of interest and usually written by a committee. Most but not all textbooks are "dead books."
- **A movie or video.** Again, you can have "living videos" (created with passion, interest, and insight and based on solid

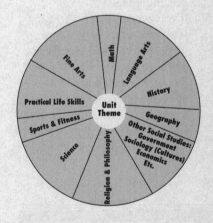

Remember our old friend Mr. Unit Study Pie? The doughnut hole in the middle represents the central unit theme. Pick the right materials to introduce the theme, and you'll gets your kids hungry to tackle the rest of the pie!

Where to Start?

I recommend the following sequence for those new to unit studies.

1. Pick a "light" ready-made unit and go through it. This will familiarize you with the basic "feel" of a unit study.

2. Purchase all three volumes of the KONOS Character Curriculum and the invaluable Index to the KONOS Curriculum. Now you have a huge, easy-to-use library of clever educational projects (with illustrated directions and supply lists) and related reading for every conceivable school topic.

3. Use an Usborne or other "fact" book (the kind with double-page spreads) as the kick-off point for your first home-made unit study. (More about "fact" and "list" books and their uses in the upcoming chapter on creating your own history units.)

4. For further unit ideas, try to kick off with a project or fact book that follows your learner's existing interests.

5. If you eventually find creating your own units to be too much work, but you still love *doing* units, go back to Step 1. Only this time, pick your choice of light, medium, or deep ready-made units, evaluating them in advance with the help of the lists found in the previous chapter.

research), "dead videos" (factual but deadly boring), or "lying videos" (the facts are wrong, so the quality of the presentation is irrelevant). Most historical dramas at least get the clothes and architecture right. Most movies set in foreign lands at least show the actual landscape and some of the actual inhabitants. Movie scriptwriter David Guterson, in the book he wrote about homeschooling his son for one year (*Family Matters,* available in bookstores and online), suggests a number of interest-sparking movies you can rent from your local Blockbuster.

- The incredibly creative Jessica Hulcy thinks every unit should start with **a hands-on project.** These are easy for her to think up, or for you to glean from her KONOS curriculum. But for sheer ease of use, you can't beat starting with . . .

- **A fact book.**

Step 1: Start with a Fact Book

With short, lavishly illustrated two-page chapters, each introducing another topic directly related to the book's theme in the most eye-catching way possible, fact books are my secret weapon for creating the effort-free unit study.

It couldn't be simpler. You simply read the book with your child, and then investigate the chapter topics that interest you more fully with the help of living books, reference books, videos, websites, and activities that go into each topic more deeply.

Since fact books are almost always designed to cover an entire topic thoroughly but not very deeply, they make an ideal starting point for a unit study. Plus, you can multiply the effect by getting several fact books on the same topic.

Take, for example, an unpretentious little book from the Usborne Starting Point History series titled **Who were the Vikings?** It's only 32 pages long, including the index, yet it introduces all these topics (in the form of questions):

- *Who were the Vikings?* On this double-page spread is a map showing where Vikings came from and where they went, a description of when and where the Vikings came from, what the word *Viking* means, how we know about the Vikings, and more, plus illustration including a statue of Leif Ericsson (with a brief description of him), some Irish treasures looted by Vikings, the city of Novgorod, Viking merchants trading with Arabs, a Viking warrior, and much more

- *What did Vikings look like?* (Clothing, hairstyles, jewelry, face painting)

- *What was a Viking family like?* (An illustration of a settlement showing various types of work going on, descriptions of their schooling, what crops they grew, what animals they kept, and how they hunted and fished)

- *What were Viking houses like?* (An inside view, showing people going about their daily activities, plus breakout illustrations of a Greenland turf house and a chief's bed)

- *Did the Vikings believe in God?* (Some Viking mythology)

- *What happened if they were ill?* (Health care, burial, afterlife beliefs)

What Is a Two-Page Spread?

Instead of a "chapter" format, the two-page spread presents information in two-page chunks. Open up one of these publishers' books and you may see something that looks like this . . .

This Peter Bedrick book looks like a pop-up book, but it isn't; the art is so detailed it just pops off the page!

Note the sleek, futuristic look of this Millbrook spread.

Some Usborne Books from EDC Publishing use this "around the edge of the page" format.

Signs of the Times series spread: Oxford University Press

A typical spread from *Disaster!* by Dorling Kindersley. The book is oversized, hardbound, and a great read!

Just a small sample of the most recently published Usborne books. Too bad this isn't on a four-color page—they are beautiful!

All these, and more, are from Millbrook Press

Circle of Learning Workbooks

The Candlewick Press History News series. Cool!

Dorling-Kindersley has tons of titles. These are just a small sample.

Oxford Press is loosening up. Note the "Smelly History" series. Most titles still reflect a classical background.

Some of the best series from Peter Bedrick books

Generally, the longer your unit is supposed to last, the more involved your projects can be. For beginners, a good rule of thumb is to **spend no more time on projects than you do on reading** (this includes the reading your student has to do in order to research his or her project). This will keep the projects from overwhelming your focus on historical facts.

I've only begun to describe half the book, and I'm already exhausted! There's more:

- *What was Viking food like?*
- *What did the Vikings do for fun?*
- *Could the Vikings read and write?*
- *How did the Vikings get around?*
- *Did the Vikings go shopping?*
- *Did the Vikings have kings?*
- *Did they have an army?*
- *Were all Vikings ruthless raiders?*
- *How far did Viking settlers go?*

Where Can I Find Fact Books (Two-Page Spread Books)?

Usborne books, from EDC Publishing, have been for many years a staple in the homeschool market. With their colorful, fun format, affordable prices, and wide variety of educational subject matter, the hundreds of Usborne books have won their way into the hearts—and onto the shelves—of homeschool families everywhere.

Sensing that they had a winner here, several years ago the folks at EDC Publishing expanded their traditional sales to bookstores, libraries, and schools to include home "party plan" sales. Homeschool moms, in particular, enjoyed the opportunity to earn free books or commissions by showing and selling a subset of the Usborne line to friends and neighbors. (See the "My Life as an Usborne Consultant" sidebar.) EDC also covered its bases by making sure that the most prolific homeschool reviewer, namely, me, got a copy of every new Usborne book to review. (Yes, I have every single Usborne book ever published. Eat your heart out!)

Meanwhile, some other publishers began using—and in some cases, improving on—the Usborne format. **Random House** issued their **Eyewitness Books** series (now mostly out of print), which used a combination of crisp photographs and old-timey illustrations to accompany their educational text. **Peter Bedrick Books**, visually a cross between Usborne books and Eyewitness books, created dozens of series, many on the identical subjects of the Usborne books. **Kingfisher** brought out a line of educational books and reference books, many using the two-page-spread format, covering a wide variety of academic topics. **Dorling-Kindersley** (known to the trade as **DK**) also produced an impressive lineup of books in the two-page-spread format, as well as a number of CD-ROMs. **Millbrook** picked over the European market and licensed (and translated) a number of series. **Candlewick** and **Crabtree**, among others, brought out Usborne-style series. Even the venerable **Oxford University Press**, best known for its huge, stodgy dictionaries and textbooks, has recently jumped into this market, with the release of titles in an Eyewitness format

such as their "Signs of the Times" series (*Story of Communications, Story of Writing and Printing, Story of Numbers and Counting,* etc.).

The Usborne line shrugged off these challenges, at least as far as homeschoolers were concerned. The other publishers were selling *some* books: EDC was selling a *ton* of books.

The **Eyewitness** lineup (which reverted to Dorling-Kindersley in the meantime) is attractive, but personality-free, as well as tending towards political correctness and a ratio of too many captions to too little text.

Kingfisher's lineup is better, but like Random House, they have not pursued homeschoolers. In fact, I couldn't even get them to send me the additional review samples that I had requested for this article!

Peter Bedrick Books also hasn't pursued homeschool catalogs or direct sales. Many of their books aren't designed to appeal to conservative homeschool sensibilities.

Millbrook's books are more family-friendly, but like Bedrick, so far they have not advertised or promoted their products to homeschoolers.

DK signed up some homeschool reps, and then canceled this plan, and like the others has made no special effort to market their books or bring them to the attention of homeschool writers and reviewers. DK books, while highly attractive and educational, go for the "authoritative" tone rather than Usborne's more personal look and feel.

Oxford University Press has just entered the fray, so in their case it's too soon to tell, but the authoritative, impersonal tone used in their books has not historically had tremendous appeal to homeschoolers.

Crabtree has succeeded in getting Sonlight Curriculum to carry a number of their "Peoples, Lands, & Cultures" series titles (these are *great* for introducing a geography unit), so perhaps we'll hear more from them. They continue to send me review samples of their various series, so I know they're interested in selling to you!

These latter spreads introduced Viking runes, sagas, games, a Viking fairy tale, boat-building, archaeology (how we know about all of this!), a Viking town, import and export, money, crafts, Viking government, warriors and their weapons, Viking settlements and seamanship, and more besides.

The point is not that you should rush out and plunk down $4.95 for a copy of this book (although it *is* an excellent book). Rather, **just one fact book can introduce *dozens* of high-interest topics related to your theme** with enough basic information to point you to the next step in your studies. For example, the Vikings book we were looking at has good enough illustrations of Viking buildings that you might decide to invest in a copy of of EDC Publishing's *Make This Model Viking Settlement*, a book you can actually cut out and piece together to make a 3-D Viking village. If Viking mythology interests you, you can go to the library and take out books on the subject. Or read some old back issues of a *Thor* comic book from Marvel Publishing, to get a different take on Mjolnir and the Rainbow Bridge! This could spark all kinds of lively discussions about true religion vs. false. If Leif Ericsson interests you, Beautiful Feet Books carries the classic illustrated children's book *Leif the Lucky* by Ingri and Edgar D'Aulaire. If Viking ships interest you, go to <u>yahoo.com</u> and type the words *Viking longboats museum* in the Search box. You'll find photos and text about longboats from both amateur museum-goers and the official museum sites.

With a good fact book, you can go through it spread by spread and dig a little deeper into each topic using outside resources. **The fact book itself forms the structure, the "backbone" if you will, of your unit.** It will then be up to you to come up with a project or activity to close the unit.

Here's another example of how you can spark a unit with a fact book: the **Alphabet Book** series by **Jerry Pallota** (Charlesbridge Publishing, MA. (800) 225-3214, www.charlesbridge.com). Again, the books are inexpensive: just $6.95 for the paperbound version or $14.95–$15.95 for a hardbound edition. Each book devotes one page apiece to an illustration

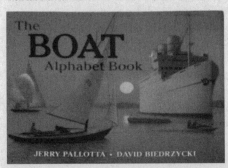

and text about a word beginning with an alphabet letter, in order from A–Z. For example, in *The Airplane Alphabet Book*, *A* is for the AT-6 plane, while *F* is for the Ford Tri-Motor. In *The Boat Alphabet Book*, *A* is for Aircraft Carrier, *B* is for Barketine, *C* is for Canoe, and so on. The two-page spread devoted to Aircraft Carrier shows

Jessica Hulcy's Top Ten + One Unit Study Tips

1. **More with Less Stress.** Teach all you can to everyone at one time.
2. **Fit, Not Fat.** Include as many academic subjects in each unit *that fit,* **BUT** do not force every subject into every unit.
3. **Read On!** Read deep and wide, from classic literature to reference books.
4. **First Things First.** Cover your basics in the morning.
5. **Write What You Know.** Teach language arts by writing from firsthand experience.
6. **Awe Them.** Teach multi-level by starting with a single hands-on activity that produces a sense of wonder.
7. **Efficiency Counts.** Choose only worthwhile, multipurpose activities that kill more than one purpose with a stone.
8. **Handle with Care.** Use textbooks as a resource/information overview *only.*
9. **Dejunk.** Use only the workbook pages necessary for remedial use; throw the rest away.
10. **Teach Them to Learn and to Love to Learn.** Be obsessed with *process,* not *product,* in the younger years.
11. **Closure.** Wrap up each unit with a bang, such as show-and-tell at the dinner table, a medieval feast, a kid-created natural history museum, or a field trip.

Nancy Lotinsky

Need some help sorting out those hundreds of Usborne books? **Teaching with Usborne Books** by Nancy Lotinsky, now in its third edition (available for $5.95 through her website, **www.nancy.lotinsky. com**) is a handy tool that solves this problem.

Each chapter of this 134-page book is devoted to an academic subject area or age group: baby books, preschool books, science, computer science, history, geography, art, music, sports and physical education, "brain-stretchers," and foreign languages. In each chapter, books and series are described in non-alphabetical order, including which awards they have won. Some of the short descriptions include how-to-use tips. Each chapter then ends with a graph showing which book or series in the chapter is appropriate for which age levels. A chapter on "Who Uses or Recommends Usborne Books" provides short descriptions of some publishers and educational methods that use these books. Finally, the handy index lets you quickly locate any individual book.

Updates to this book are available free to buyers of the book on Nancy's website.

you a full-color illustration of a carrier, while the detailed text tells you how many aircraft and people populate a carrier, how many haircuts the barbers give every day, how many loaves the cooks bake, how many cans of soda the crew drinks, how many hamburgers may be served at a time, and much more.

Just start with one of these books, look up the entries that interest you in an encyclopedia or take out library books for added details, draw pictures or make models of some of the entries, or whatever else comes to you. Voila! Instant unit study!

The series currently includes:

- *The Airplane Alphabet Book*
- *The Bird Alphabet Book*
- *The Boat Alphabet Book*
- *The Butterfly Alphabet Book*
- *The Desert Alphabet Book*
- *The Dinosaur Alphabet Book*
- *The Extinct Alphabet Book*
- *The Flower Alphabet Book*
- *The Freshwater Alphabet Book*
- *The Frog Alphabet Book*
- *The Furry Animal Alphabet Book*
- *The Icky Bug Alphabet Book* (an *Icky Bug Counting Book* is also available!)
- *The Ocean Alphabet Book*
- *The Spice Alphabet Book*
- *The Underwater Alphabet Book*
- *The Victory Garden Vegetable Alphabet Book*
- *The Yucky Reptile Alphabet Book*

Some fact books include activities and projects right in the book. Others may require you to use a bit more imagination to make the learning "hands on." In either case, knowing what is available in the world of fact books can make putting together your own units a snap!

The Best of the Best Fact Books

Each of these publishers I mentioned has its strong side. Let's take a look!

Usborne definitely wins the Charm Award. Their books are cuter and friendlier than anyone else's. No matter *what* school or after-school topic you're looking for, Usborne has a book (or, more likely, five books) on that subject. However, the "raggedy" cartoon art found in so many Usborne books is not a match for the near-photographic illustration and actual photographs in books from their competitors. Also, most Usborne books don't *teach,* they *present.*

Usborne Kid Kits each include an Usborne book, plus some materials to use with it, all in a reclosable plastic pouch. In other words, you get your fact book *plus* some built-in activities *and* the supplies for those activities. These kits are way more educational than most of what Klutz puts out, and include way more materials than kits from other publishers. Kits are available for all sorts of topics, with more coming out all the time.

Dorling-Kindersley wins the Eye Candy Award. Talk about *beautiful* books! Many are oversized and hardcover, but still quite affordable. Some of their more impressive titles include the Art Pack (with pop-ups and play-withs on most pages), the Stephen Biesty and other cut-away series (like David Macaulay in explaining how things work, only more realistic and more colorful), the Eyewitness Science series (I'm a sucker for those silver covers), their hundreds of sticker books, and more. Like Usborne, DK has something on every conceivable educational topic.

The **Millbrook Press**, who you've probably never heard of before, wins the **High-Tech Award** and the **Discovery Award**. With not quite as huge a selection as either DK or Usborne, some of their titles (the ones licensed from Aladdin Books in England) are not only visually futuristic, but they incorporate ways of helping children actually *learn* the neat facts presented on the pages. For instance, on each spread readers are asked to find the answers to certain questions, and in the back of the book there is a review set of questions. Another innovative feature: sideways spreads. Hold the book sideways to see a very long picture (e.g., human body) with captions pointing out all the interesting features.

The **History News** series from **Candlewick Press** beats all other such attempts, including Usborne's Newspaper Histories. The concept may be the same—retell history in sensationalized tabloid form, to make it more fun and relevant—but where Usborne's offering is loaded with inside jokes that turn history on its head, Candlewick's series is just as interesting but far less confusing. And it's hardbound. And it's prettier.

A Few More Fact Book Series

There are coloring books . . . and there are **Bellerophon coloring books.** Coloring is permutated, transmogrified, and otherwise rendered ineffable in this unique (I can use the word safely) series of over 100 educational coloring books.

Regular coloring books are sold in supermarkets. Bellerophon coloring books are sold in museum shops. The reason is that (1) Bellerophon books concentrate on classical cultural topics such as fine art and ancient civilizations and (2) the art itself is not designed for little kids. These are really coloring books for preteens and right on up to adults.

The art in Bellerophon books is mostly line-drawing reproductions of original art from the time period covered in the coloring book. Thus, in *A Coloring Book of Ancient China*, when you see a page-sized picture of a bird to color in, small print at the bottom of the page informs you that the bird actually is a line drawing of a bronze vessel from the Late Chou dynasty. Similarly, the two-page spread of Chinese men on horses is from *The Tribute Horse*, an early Sung painting in the Metropolitan Museum of Art.

Scattered throughout each Bellerophon book is text explaining historical details of the art and the scenes the art portrays. In a book like *A Coloring Book of Great Composers: Bach to Berlioz*, the text outweighs the pictures. Here again the coloring pictures themselves are based on famous portraits or caricatures of the composers.

A sampling of Bellerophon titles: *A Coloring Book of Rome, A Coloring Book of Great Explorers, Magnificent Helmets in Gold & Silver to Cut Out and Wear, Gorgons, California Missions, Cowgirls, Paper Soldiers of the Middle Ages, A Coloring Book of the Old Testament, Castles to Cut Out and Put Together, Peter and the Wolf,* and *A Coloring Book of Our Presidents.* As I said, this is merely a sampling. You do notice, however, that Bellerophon also sells ornate cut-out books, and that these too have some historico-cultural significance.

These books should be colored with markers or coloring pencils. You'll need watercolor markers, not the heavy-duty permanent kind—these bleed through the paper.

Art of the past often included lots of nudes, sometimes as the subject of the art, other times in the guise of mermaids and other fanciful decorations. Those who object to such decorations (frequently found in these books) can disguise them by overcoloring with the darker shades of felt-tipped markers.

Because Bellerophon art is copied from such diverse sources, flipping through one of these books can be rather unsettling. On one page you might find an ornate, grotesque woodcut, while on the next could be a simple classical line drawing.

Bellerophon Coloring Books

Grades 5–adult. $2.95–$4.95 each. Quantity discounts on orders of 25 or more books.
Bellerophon Books (CA), orders: (800) 253-9943, inquiries: (805) 965-7034, www.bellerophonbooks.com.

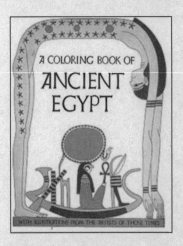

For me, accustomed as I am to supermarket coloring books, it took a while to get used to Bellerophon's user interface. Once I did, though, I was really impressed by how much you can learn from one of these books. Remember, these are not just coloring books, but introductions to large hunks of (mostly) Western civilization. You know, as in, "Hey, hey, ho, ho, Western Cultcha's gotta go." (I have news for them. It already has.) And don't forget Bellerophon's trendier titles on non-European cultures, too, even if you're not allergic to WASPs.

Millbrook "I Didn't Know That!" series

Ages 6–8. Each book, $19.90.
The Millbrook Press, orders (800) 462-4703, inquiries (203) 740-2220, www.millbrookpress.com.

The very cool-looking hardcover books in **Millbrook's I Didn't Know That series** are cover-to-cover color. The pages of these beautifully designed books have no "white space"; the background of each page is either a full-color, almost-photo-quality illustration, a colored text box, or a combination. White text on black or colored background gives an up-to-date look. Beyond the usual fun and fascinating facts, you get true/false questions meant to inspire interest (example: True or false? The sloth eats its meals upside down") with the answer provided below the question, quickie experiments, "search and find" activities such as "find the five monkeys in this picture," and bonus "amazing facts" in the margin of many pages.

Available so far are *Dinosaurs Laid Eggs and Other Amazing Facts About Prehistoric Reptiles, Some Birds Hang Upside Down and Other Amazing Facts About Birds, Some Bugs Glow in the Dark and Other Amazing Facts About Insects, Some Snakes Spit Poison and Other Amazing Facts About Snakes, Some Trains Run on Water and Other Amazing Facts About Rail Transport, Spiders Have Fangs and Other Amazing Facts About Arachnids, The Sun is a Star and Other Amazing Facts About Space, You Can Jump Higher on the Moon and Other Amazing Facts About Space Exploration, Some Planes Hover and Other Amazing Facts About Flying Machines, Some Plants Grow in Mid-Air and Other Amazing Facts About the Rainforest, People Chase Twisters and Other Amazing Facts About Violent Weather,* and *Sharks Keep Losing Their Teeth and Other Amazing Facts About Sharks.* We've only seen four so far: *Sharks, Weather, Rainforest,* and *Flying Machines*—but aside from a very slight bit of mainstream ecology and the obligatory nod to evolutionary dating, the facts seemed accurate.

Usborne Book series

All ages. Most Usborne paperback books, $2.95 and up. Hardbound versions, $10.95 and up. *EDC Publishing, Division of Educational Development Corporation (OK), (800) 475-4522, www.edcpub.com.*

Usborne Books are tremendously popular among homeschoolers because (1) there are hundreds of them, so you can find one that teaches just about anything you want your children to learn, (2) they are amazingly inexpensive, and (3) they are designed differently than American textbooks. Although these books cover the basic subject areas (science, math, reading, history, geography, and so on), you will not find one speck of scholarly mumbo-jumbo, nor subheadings, chapter summaries, "Things to Think About," or questions to answer at the end of each chapter.

Instead of putting the student through the laborious process of memorizing bland text, Usborne Books are designed graphically to draw him in, make him *want* to learn the material and help him remember it forever. Typically a page will have one or more large, colorful illustrations with a minimum of text explaining what is happening and more text under each visual "subplot," labeling and explaining it. Example: Usborne's *How Your Body Works* uses the

metaphor of the body as a machine. The section on the circulatory system shows white blood cells dressed as policemen zapping germs in the "blood river," which itself is being pumped through all the (labeled) organs. I also already told and showed you how the Usborne book *Who were the Vikings?* works, earlier in this chapter. These are just two books out of hundreds.

Do children remember this material? I've quizzed our six- and seven-year-old about anatomy and have been surprised at how much they retained from *How Your Body Works*. Of course, it helps that they *voluntarily* read these books over and over and over . . .

The more Usborne Books you buy, the more you will buy. Lasers! How films are produced! Chemistry! Natural science! History! Whatever subject you found boring in school, there's an exquisitely-cartooned full-color Usborne book that makes the same dull old subject fascinating.

Although EDC will sell to you directly, in the homeschool market lots of Usborne books are sold through "party plan" distributorships. Homeschool moms pay a small fee to sign up as distributors, and then show the Usborne lineup to friends and neighbors. Becoming an Usborne distributor is not a way to get rich quick, but if you like the books enough, it's a way to stay home and still put some money in the cookie jar.

My Life as an Usborne Consultant
by Judy Smith

I have been a consultant for six years. It has been the perfect home business for me. I enjoy working flexible hours out of my own home. My children enjoy reviewing each new title, which Usborne publishes twice a year.

My best consultants are homeschooling parents because they are thoroughly familiar with the products. They use our books in their curriculum. In addition, homeschooling families are usually one-income families who are choosing to live with "less" so that they can homeschool. As consultants, they earn extra spending money as well as build up a quality home library on a shoestring. They like setting their own goals and working as much or as little as they choose.

When I purchased my start-up kit in January 1993, I immediately began doing home shows. If you've ever attended a Tupperware or Pampered Chef or Discovery Toys home party, you're familiar with how this works. The hostess invites her friends to come over to her house. As the consultant, I gave a simple presentation about the history of Usborne and showed everyone my favorite books. The customer response was great! Everyone who loves reading appreciates the quality of Usborne Books. As I got more involved with EDC and the products, I realized what a wonderful ground level business opportunity this was.

My whole family is involved in the business. My husband, Joseph, helps with the big events and takes care of the financial records. Our three children contribute by reviewing new titles and helping with repetitive office activities, such as putting on labels or stamps. The oldest two are quite proficient at setting up and taking down the book display. However, Joanne (11) and Jeanette (8) say their favorite aspect of the business is getting to read these wonderful books. Jeremiah (4) enjoys having mom at home.

Here are some facts about the Usborne Books at Home (UBAH for short) program you might not know:

- The UBAH catalog selection includes books and products not available through their regular catalog.
- Each month, customers who purchase $30 or more are allowed the option of purchasing the Customer Specials for that month at a discount.
- If you are willing to host an Usborne party, you can earn free or half-price books. The amount depends on how many are sold at the party.
- A start-up kit now costs $199 plus $15 shipping. The kit includes many books for you to show customers (and to enjoy with your children), plus sales helps such as catalogs, training sales videos, hostess guides, postcard invitations, and a whole lot more.

After six years with Usborne, I now have trained 8 people to supervise new consultants, and have over 300 consultants in my downline. Over the course of a year, our family makes about $40,000 before taxes and expenses. Some other families make less; others make more. It depends a lot on how much time you put into it. Some folks just do it long enough to earn themselves a huge free library of Usborne books!

If you like people and love books, you probably would enjoy being an Usborne hostess or consultant.

In her book *How to Create Your Own Unit Study* (latest revision published 1994 by Common Sense Press and available through Christian Book Distributors, (800) 247-4784, www.christianbooks.com), Valerie Bendt points out that some encyclopedias include outlines with their more important, lengthy articles. Such an outline can form the framework of a unit study. As a bonus, some even come with discussions questions! *World Book* is particularly helpful in this regard.

by Valerie Bendt

WHERE TO FIND OUTLINE MAPS

The following outline maps are available from Geography Matters, KY. (800) 426-4650, www.geomatters.com:

- **Uncle Josh's Outline Maps Book**, $19.95. 104 reproducible maps of "continents, ancient historical regions, all 50 states, and more."
- **Uncle Josh's Maps on CD-ROM** for Win and Mac, $26.95. All the maps in the book plus 21 more, all in Adobe Acrobat pdf file format
- Laminated **"Mark-It" Maps** of all continents, USA/World, Ancient Civilizations, and Israel/East Mediterranean, $6.95–$9.95 each. Also available as sets in paper or laminated.

Step 2: How to Find What You Need to Look Up

If you're new to unit studies, ready-made units can almost look like they were created by braniacs from another planet. "How did they know where to find all these great books, videos, and background information?" you wonder.

I'm going to give you one secret tip and another not-so-secret tip that will help *you* hunt down your own resources.

First, the not-so-secret tip: **look up your theme in the encyclopedia.**

Second, the secret tip: **write down or type in all the names** of the important people, places, events, weapons, clothing, food, jewelry, dances, sports, scientific discoveries, and other topics associated with your theme that you find in your fact book and in the encyclopedia article.

In just one step you've created both your unit's vocabulary list and your list of possible "pie slice" topics to research.

Step 3: Where to Hunt

Now that you have your list of topics that you intend to cluster around your central theme, where do you find the background information that you need to bring them to life?

- **At the library.** Valerie Bendt's *How to Create Your Own Unit Study* has a particularly helpful section on how to use the reference section of the children's department of the public library. This reference section, where books may *not* be checked out, includes many books which point to *other* books: books about books, if you get my drift. You then check out the appropriate books, both fiction and nonfiction, relating to your central theme and the "pie slice" topics.
- **On the Internet.** Valerie's book, and its companion volume *The Unit Study Idea Book,* were last revised in 1994, and therefore don't include Web destinations. You can find scads about any topic online by typing the appropriate phrases into a search engine, such as *yahoo, altavista,* or *google.* If you don't already know how to do this, see page 50, which explains how to do your own online research.
- **In your encyclopedia and home reference books.** You may actually prefer to have your children do this part: It's excellent training for them! Look up the related topics you uncovered in your encyclopedia, *starting with the index.* You'll miss some articles of interest if you just look up the topic directly! For locations, use your atlas and globe. You might also want to have them fill in the locations they study on a blank "outline" map, such as those available from Geography Matters. Depending on your interests, you might have a home dictionary or encyclopedia of medical terms, herbs, science, legal terms, etc. You also doubtless own cookbooks with various ethnic recipes.
- **In what I call "list" books.** These are books that, by subject, provide tons of the information children need to learn, in list form rather than as attractive, illustrated two-page spreads. Lists of grammar terms and their definitions. Lists of Bible verses pertaining to a school subject. Lists of state tourism offices. Lists of state abbreviations. List of books on science topics. Lists of earth science terms, with definitions. And on and on . . . List books fill in what fact books introduce.

List Books

The best way to tell you about list books is to show you some. Below are the most popular list books for homeschoolers currently on the market.

Would you like to turn your encyclopedia into a dynamite Christian unit studies curriculum? Here's how to do it. Either look up all Scripture references for every subject in a concordance, study them, and create a framework for approaching each subject. Or buy **The Encyclopedia of Bible Truth for School Subjects**. Originally published as a four-volume set of paperback books, and now available in several languages as a single combined hardcover volume, it organizes all the passages of Scripture related to over 30 subjects of school study. For each subject you get a concept summary and scriptural overview. By looking through the concept summary you can identify the places in your encyclopedia or regular text where passages of Scripture will be illuminating.

Ranging from Art to Zoology, Dr. Haycock gives the complete verse or passage (or a synopsis of a lengthy passage) along with historical information concerning the Bible's accuracy in areas under study. You'll be amazed at the amount of revelation the Bible offers on subjects like biology, mathematics, and athletics, subjects that most people think it doesn't address at all!

Under Social Studies, it covers history, geography, economics, government, leadership and administration, social relationships, the family, the church, and social problems. The Language Arts/English section gets into reading, writing, literature, speech, listening, and foreign languages. The Science/Mathematics section looks at astronomy, earth science, physics and chemistry, zoology, botany, human biology, and mathematics. Finally, the Fine Arts and Health section covers creativity, arts and crafts, music, health, sex education, physical education, athletics, and death education—all from a point of view you'll never hear in public school.

The Encyclopedia of Bible Truth for School Subjects also includes a vast list of resources for further study, including books for students and teachers, tapes, curriculum guides, textbooks, resource units, supplementary materials, audiovisual materials, periodicals, and an index for each section.

It's hard to see how anyone could go wrong with a book like this; it's easy to see how someone might go wrong without it. This is the classic on integrating the Bible into school studies, whether at home or in the classroom.

A 250-page almanac of essential information perfect for homeschoolers, **Facts Plus** is packed not only with textual information but also eight full-page maps, over 50 charts, and 133 diagrams, illustrations, graphs, and time lines. A self-published effort that has been enthusiastically received by home educators, it includes scads of facts on such topics as holidays around the world, human body systems, notable people throughout history, state tourism offices, how to use the library, alphabets from other lands, handwriting examples, common abbreviations, and many more. Newbery award-winning books. Caldecott award winners. Grammar rules. How to outline and take notes. Letter writing. I could go on and on! An invaluable resource for any home schooler.

The **Facts Plus Activity Book** is 182 reproducible pages of activities based on *Facts Plus*. This means you can copy pages freely for use within your own "classroom," which for homeschoolers means for use with your own children. The book starts out with a series of activities designed to teach your child how to research all kinds of facts. "The Facts Game" is a

Encyclopedia of Bible Truth for School Subjects
Parents. $65.
ACSI (CO), (800) 367-0798, www.acsi.org. Available through homeschool catalogs.

Facts Plus
Grades 3–12. Facts Plus, $15.95. Activity Book, $19.95. Add $2.50 shipping.
Instructional Resources Company (AK). (907) 345-6689, www.susancanthony.com.

make-it-yourself board game with question cards you cut out and laminate and a board you cut out and back with cardboard. "Calendar Capers" allow you to make your own perpetual calendar. This section also includes a series of events for you to look up and mark on the calendar. "On This Day in History" is another game with pages and pages of question cards, one for each day of the year. Using Facts Plus, you look up the events for each day. "Our Place in Time" includes make-it-yourself timelines, starting with an evolutionary timeline of geological history. Plus activities for astronomy, U.S. maps and facts, country comparisons, and miscellaneous challenges such as learning your way around a computer keyboard and the periodic table.

Facts Plus and its accompanying activity book won't cover everything your child ought to know. They are short in science, the activity book has no math-only activities, and Biblical content is nil. Still, for less than $40 overall, you get an awesome amount of information and a way to put it into practice on those rainy days.

Home Schooler's Complete Reference Guide

Parents. $25.
Kay Milow (NE), (402) 895-3280, www.members.aol.com/kaymilow.

This spiral-bound, 208-page, oversized **Home Schooler's Complete Reference Guide** is an encyclopedia of learning for K–6. Homeschooling mother Kay Milow draws on her experience teaching at both school and home to provide all the lists, rules, definitions, project ideas, and teaching tips you are likely to need for reading, English (including an extensive section on sentence diagramming), spelling, math, social studies, science, health, Spanish, and art. Everything is organized by subject in a sequential manner, so it is ultra-easy to use. Need to find a glossary of geometric terms? Information on noun suffixes? How to outline? Conservation projects? State abbreviations? Roman numerals? Basic math exercises using money? Irregular English verbs? Literature reading lists for each grade level? All this and tons more, plus sample exercises and projects and suggested library books to read for each topic, are in this one handy volume.

You won't have any holes in your home curriculum if you diligently use this book. In fact, you may not need any home curriculum if you diligently use this book! As Jill Johnson of Waverly, Nebraska, a satisfied user of this book, says, "Kay's book, a set of encyclopedias, and the occasional use of the public library are all you need."

The Reading Teacher's Book of Lists, 4th Edition

Parents of kids grades 4–8. $29.50. Also available: Science Teacher's

Book of Lists, Social Studies Teacher's Book of Lists, $29.95 each. *Published by Prentice-Hall and used as a search example on their website,* phdirect.com, *but impossible to find there. Available through bookstores, catalogs, and online.*

The Reading Teacher's Book of Lists is the sort of book that a public school teacher would own. Is there a place for it on your shelf?

Flipping through nearly 400 pages will give you a bird's-eye view of every list imaginable: synonyms and antonyms, portmanteaus and compound words, phonograms, signal words, foreign words, and homophones (a really fun list). This only skims the surface. Are you looking for the Braille alphabet? It's here. Morse Code? Radio voice alphabet? Punctuation or capitalization guidelines? They're here too. There are even reading lists, including "All-Time Favorites", Caldecott and Newbery Award winners, and read alouds. Be careful, though. Some books would likely make the "Don't Waste Your Time" list!

One of my favorite lists has three columns of words on the page. You are advised to choose one word from each column to make a wonderfully inarticulate phrase—in other words, "doublespeak." Exceptional orientation evaluation. Sequential accelerated capacity. Ooh, this is fun!

Some of the lists are pure trivia, others are merely useless. Some are good for diversions on a rainy day and a few have some real educational value. One list even gives parents ten tips on helping your child read better. (Hint: parental involvement is one of the ten.) Does it deserve shelf space? You decide. *Marla Perry*

Step 4: My Secret Weapon for Great Unit-Study Projects

So you've picked your central theme, come up with topics for your "pie slices," and hunted down enough background information to make this unit academically valuable *and* interesting.

Now, what about projects?

It is possible to do an entirely reading-and-writing based unit, without a speck of discovery learning except more reading (while doing research). But such a unit is like the old Jewish legend of the *golem*—a hunk of clay shambling around that *looked* like a person but had no soul.

Hands-on projects are what your kids will remember fondly for years. Sure, they're more work for you and a lot more mess to clean up—but so is baking a cake from scratch as opposed to buying one from the supermarket. And guess which tastes better?

The big problem with unit-study projects is that it takes a certain type of mind, backed with lots of knowledge and teaching experience, to think them up.

Once you've been homeschooling for years, you will develop this kind of mind. In the meantime, welcome to my secret weapon—the **KONOS Character Curriculum**!

In the three hefty volumes of this complete unit-study curriculum for grades K–8, you'll find *hundreds* of truly creative and memorable projects for every school subject—projects with actual academic value as well as kid appeal.

Whether or not you elect to use this as your family's curriculum, you can certainly benefit from the massive amounts of creativity and research that went into these volumes.

How?

By using the handy **KONOS Index: A Cross Reference to Every Subject in the Three Original KONOS Character Curriculum Volumes.** Every topic is indexed two ways. First, in the general index. Second, in a subject index. So, for example, you can find "Coal" in the general index, or in the Science Index under the Geology topic. There's a Bible index, English/Literature index, History/Social Studies index, Science index, Arts & Crafts index, Music index, Physical Skills/Games index, Practical Living Skills index, Speech/Drama index, and Movies & Videos index. Simply looking through any of these indexes is bound to give you lots of ideas for unit themes—and all you have to do next is to look up the referenced pages in the specified KONOS volume in order to find oodles of resources and activities.

Newcomers are often overwhelmed by the huge amount of possible activities that KONOS provides for each topic. You won't be, because *you* picked the initial theme and the topics you want to cover that are related to it. Keeping your own unit-study goals firmly in mind, you can quickly zip

KONOS Character Curriculum with Index

Volumes I–III, $95 each. Index, $20. Compass, $25.
*KONOS, Inc. (TX), (972) 924-2712,
www.konos.com.*

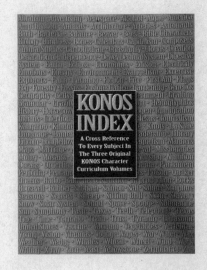

down the list of suggested KONOS activities and pick just those that fit your theme and topics best.

Step 5: Increasing Retention with Memory Tools, Drill, & Games

You've had your fun. Your student has read his books, done his research, and created his projects.

How much of all this will he remember?

Some facts just are so interesting they soak in and stay there. Others need a little more help. That is why unit-study mavens typically enlist the help of:

- Outline maps
- Timelines
- Notebooks
- Games
- And sometimes drill

I already mentioned **outline maps** earlier in this chapter and told you where to get them. These are blank maps that the student fills in himself or herself with the aid of a complete map or atlas. Filling in the information tends to cement it in the brain, plus the completed outlines look very nice in a portfolio of student work.

Timelines are another unit-study favorite. A timeline is a way of visually showing history in chronological order. Events and people are shown along a line divided up by centuries or decades.

Several ready-made unit curricula come with their own timelines and/or timeline figures to cut out and place on the timeline.

For those of you with limited wall space, there are some alternatives. Calvert School has students make **a timeline on a roll of adding-machine paper.** This obviously is a "text only" timeline, short on illustrations and heavy on what comes before what. Valerie Bendt, in her book *How to Create Your Own Unit Studies,* suggests making a **timeline portfolio.** Her book includes complete instructions on how to construct one of these from a 14″ x 17″ binder with plastic sleeves, poster board, and index cards. The poster board is cut into three strips to form the timeline and placed in the binder. The index cards are cut in half and filled out with drawings and the information you want the children to remember, and fit into slits on the poster board. Finally, there's my own down-and-dirty method of timeline cards. Here there's no actual "line" showing dates. You just write a name on one side of an index card and put the facts you want your children to associate with that event, place, or person name on the other side, along with the dates. You can then play games with the cards, or practice putting them in order on the table or floor. This is a self-checking exercise, as your child only has to turn the cards over to check if he or she got it right. Each time your child puts the cards in order he or she in effect creates a timeline.

Notebooking is another popular way to increase retention. This can be done in many ways. One way is for the children simply to journal what they have done each day. They can make a little book about the unit theme by hand or on the computer, illustrated with maps, charts, graphs, illustrations, timelines, photos of completed projects, and so on. They can videotape an oral presentation or a project. They could even create a website devoted to the unit theme.

Games are another popular way to increase retention of academic matter related to your unit. Kids generally perceive games as a fun treat, which will rarely be the case with workbooks! (Unless you're Jason Foxtrot.) However, most (but not all) educational games take quite a bit of time for relatively little skills practice. Educational software games generally fare better at this than board and card games, but you miss out on the personal interaction which is one of the big reasons for pursuing unit studies. Electronic games, such as the Talking GeoSafari Globe or Odyssey Atlasphere III talking globe, can provide both instant feedback and personal interaction with other players.

I review educational games for all sorts of school subjects in my *Birth to Grade 6* and *Grades 7–12* volumes. To tide you over until those books come out, you might try visiting your local teacher's store. (You should do this anyway, just to see all the great stuff they have!) Their game offerings will likely have more educational value than those you find in family superstores.

Finally, there's good old-fashioned **drill and practice.** Even this can be made less painful by choosing homeschool-friendly drill materials. Competitive children will enjoy being timed while they do a set of math problems or a page of grammar drills. You can have the children do a "spelling bee" with more difficult words for the older children and easier ones for the younger, or shout out mental math problems. Using a few books of logic puzzles from Critical Thinking Press or even doing the daily crossword online can provide practice with pizzazz.

The final step in creating a successful unit is closure. I haven't seen a better description of this much-neglected final step for the perfect unit study than the following article that Jessica Hulcy wrote for one of the first issues of *Practical Homeschooling*. From this point to the end of the chapter, while the reviews in the sidebars continue to be mine, the words in the main text column are Jessica's. And away we go!

Step Six: How Do I Wrap It Up? Jessica Hulcy on Closure

When my oldest son, Jason, was six years old and had just begun homeschooling, he thought school lessons should end at a definite time each day. Jason had been learning to read, so I asked him to read a word on a sign "after school hours." He balked and asked, "I'm not supposed to read after school, am I?"

For Jason, "reading" equaled "school," and school had come to an end. He saw no point in extending school after 3:00 P.M.

Naturally, in a typical homeschooling, biblical-perspective, Christian-world-view manner I informed him that according to Deuteronomy 6:7, school never ended. Parents were commanded in Scripture to teach our children when we sat with them, when we walked with them, when we lay down with them, and when we rose up with them. I was sure that covered "after school hours" too. Besides, I knew Jason desired to be a lifetime learner—didn't he?—and that meant learning every minute of every day.

School Lessons Need Closure

At that point my husband, Wade, intervened on behalf of Jason and suggested a new word to me: "closure." Shouldn't school have closure to it? Did school have to go on and on and on? After all, even adults want closure to a daily job.

Closure is a good thing. It gives people a sense of completion, an ending or pausing point to work, an event, or a unit. Yes, Jason had to read "after

How to Create Your Own Unit Study
Parents. $16.
Common Sense Press, FL. (352) 475-5757 to locate a retailer near you. They don't sell direct to the public. Valerie's books are available at discount through Christian Book Distrubutors, (800) 247-4784, www.christianbook.com.

Seriously intrigued by units and want even more information on how to build a unit study? Valerie Bendt's **How to Create Your Own Unit Study** (104 pages, oversized paperback) simply has it all. Valerie explains how to schedule, what to study when, how to involve high schoolers, how to keep your records, how to use the library, how to use games and teaching aids, how to use textbooks as a "frame" for your own unit studies, how to get involved in writing and literature, and much more. Her specific curriculum advice is excellent—the particular programs she recommends do cover phonics and math quickly and thoroughly. The sample unit studies included give a good idea of how to design your own. An extremely helpful "Introduction to References" section provides you with dozens of short reviews of reference books you can find at the library. These books were chosen because they greatly ease your unit-study planning. A brief resource list at the back tells where to get every resource mentioned in the book but does not give prices or detailed reviews.

Every page of this book has some practical tidbit of advice on how to simplify your homeschooling life. You do not need to be a super-organized person, or even a dedicated unit-study fan, to put Valerie's recommendations to immediate use. If you want to create your own unit studies, or just find scads of creative ideas for tackling the major school subjects, this is the book to get. Highly recommended.

The Unit Study Idea Book
Parents. $14.
Common Sense Press, FL. (352) 475-5757 to locate a retailer near you. They don't sell direct to the public. Valerie's books are available at discount through Christian Book Distrubutors, (800) 247-4784, www.christianbook.com.

Valerie Bendt's **Unit Study Idea Book** (103 pages, oversized paperback) deserves an "A" for organization and thoroughness but only a "C" for practical helpfulness.

The book is mostly made up of sample units, with some general directions for how to create similar units of your own. However, it reads more like a set of published unit studies than a unit-study construction kit.

Under the heading "Literature" there's a library unit, children's authors unit, and three literature-based units, one each for *Heidi, The Swiss Family Robinson,* and *The Plant Sitter.* Under "Science" you'll find one unit each for aviation, astronomy, ants, birds, human body, and electricity. Under "History and Geography" you'll find general directions for a foreign countries unit, followed by one sample unit each for Korea, ancient Egypt, and ancient Greece. Under "Fine Arts" you'll find animation, the orchestra and great composers, the impressionists, and painters of the American Revolution.

school hours." Yes, parents were commanded to train our children constantly. Yes, learning was an ongoing process. But I was not to remain in my "broadcast teaching mode," creating a 30-minute lesson complete with maps, reference books, and additional assignments out of every question or every situation after 3:00 P.M. "Turn off the teaching machine!" was the command.

Closure to each school day is the break, the change of pace and focus each person needs to relax and rejuvenate for the next day.

Without Closure, Students and Teachers Are Frustrated

When I taught science in public school eons ago, I realized the value and importance of hands-on learning. I was delighted when my school was chosen to teach a pilot physical science program that used the total experimentation method instead of only the textbook method.

I couldn't understand why teachers who had initially been delighted with the class were totally frustrated with the class by the Christmas holiday. Then it dawned on me. The new program had children doing experiment after experiment after experiment with no wrap-up, no end, no conclusion. There was no mental closure to an experiment or unit. No scientific principle was ever extrapolated from the hands-on experiments. Doing experiments was the sole purpose and focus of the classes. Never did the students come together and compare data to discover any scientific principles. Classes never dialogued about experiment results. Teachers never drilled on what had been learned because nothing had truly been learned or mastered. It had only been experienced.

First Experience, Then Closure

I have known homeschoolers who have had field trip after field trip or experience after experience without any wrap-up or closure. For them, as with the pilot science classes, the focus was solely on the experience.

Don't get me wrong; for years I have been trying to get homeschoolers to increase experiential learning, especially for younger children. But when some homeschoolers brag about taking 12 field trips per week, I wonder if their children are able to take in the experience, much less have any closure on the first experience before jumping to the second and third experience. Even if all the experiences are related to the same topic, digesting them takes time—time the children must have. Successfully digesting the experience also requires closure, so the children can internalize what they have experienced.

The 5 D's of Experience-Based Learning

As Carole Thaxton and I wrote our KONOS curriculum, which is largely experience-based, we grappled with different teaching methods and the order in which they should be used. Carole came up with the 5 D's of KONOS.

Actually, these 5 D's are what we consider properly sequenced teaching methods that apply to all experience-based learning, not just KONOS. The first D is **DOING** the experiment or hands-on activity. From DOING, **DISCOVERIES** are made, principles are extrapolated. Next we **DRAMATIZE**. Though dramatizing applies mostly to history, KONOS has been known to ask children to dramatize parts of the body or a car distributor and a spark plug.

The last two D's, **DIALOGUE** and **DRILL**, provide the wrap-up. Dialogue between students and between students and teacher helps to identify major points of what was discovered and aids in internalizing those points. Drill is any repetition that crystallizes everything learned, so subjects will be retained and mastered.

Ways to Add Closure to Your Experience-Based Studies

Games. Most parents think the only way to drill is by test or with flash cards. Drill for our purposes should be defined as any process that causes knowledge to be crystallized in a child's brain. Though tests and flash cards can be used, there are a variety of more exciting ways to crystallize and close a unit. Games are great vehicles to test knowledge. We have closed units with competitions such as Family Feud, Jeopardy, Olympics of the Minds, and Trivial Pursuit. We let the children make up the questions, form the categories, etc. We find that they make up far more difficult questions than the questions parents add to the question pot. Competitive games prompt unsolicited studying as teams study to beat each other on game night.

Show and Tell. The simplest way to test knowledge is to let children explain what they have learned. If they have learned the parts of the ear and created a large model "ear" to crawl through, then they need to show Dad the parts of the ear when he comes home. If Dad wants to crawl through the ear while the children tell him about each part, so much the better! Explaining to another person reinforces the explainer's knowledge as well as informing the explainee of the information. Good ol' Dad is not the only person children can share their new knowledge with, either. Older children may first read information and then impart it to younger siblings, or vice versa. Statistics show the child doing the explaining learns and retains more than the child hearing the explanation.

Creative Expression Projects. While studying the character trait of cooperation, we studied systems of the body. To culminate this unit children cooperatively wrote a book entitled *Traveling Through the Human Body*. Parts of each body system and how it functioned had to be completely understood to write such an epic. Likewise, under the character trait of honesty, we studied newspapers, their parts, how they were written and published, what made news newsworthy, etc. What better way to test our children's complete understanding of newspapers than to have them produce their own newspaper?

Cut, Sort, and Match. This is an excellent way to test specific knowledge such as capitals of states, countries on continents, duties of each branch of the government, characteristics of different phyla in biology, etc. For example: Write down the states and capitals on paper or cards, cut them apart, and place them in a plastic baggie. (You may want to photocopy several sets first before cutting if you have more than one child.) Give each child a baggie and time him as he matches the states to the capitals. You can do the same for the duties of the branches of the government. We wrote down all the duties of the Senate, the House of Representatives, the Executive Branch, and the Judicial Branch. Then we cut them apart and placed them in a baggie. Our children then sorted the duties under each branch. This exercise also could be timed or not timed—your choice.

Wrap Up with a Play or Project. After studying a Kings and Queens unit our children were well acquainted with the feudal system and who had to obey whom during medieval times. But instead of a test covering the unit, we had a medieval feast that put into practice all our children had

Under "General Knowledge" are a unit apiece on sign language, the Civil War, dolls and stuffed toys, and construction. The last three units were actually designed by Valerie's children, and serve as examples of kid-created unit studies (a somewhat similar concept to Gregg Harris's "delight-directed studies").

As unit studies, the sample units themselves could be improved. The reader is frequently instructed to take a side trip into some enormous field of study—for example, getting out a book on trees—in the midst of a study of something entirely different. Just because the Swiss Family Robinson encountered certain specific tropical trees does not mean this is the time to study *all* trees!

For the price, *The Unit Study Idea Book* is not a bad buy. Just discipline yourself to read it in the spirit of, "How interesting! So that's how she does it!"Then take out your copy of Valerie's excellent *How to Create Your Own Unit Study* (reviewed earlier in this chapter), turn to the "References" section, go to the library, and plan a unit study that fits your family and schedule!

learned about the period. Cooking chicken on a spit, stitching tapestries to decorate the walls, speaking Old English dialect, dressing the part of a knight or lady-in-waiting, juggling for entertainment, and even placing the lower classes "beneath the salt" at the table were activities that reinforced details as well as the big picture. What a review!

As you can see, adding closure to your studies is not just a necessary chore. It can be fun! Whether it's fun or not . . . whether it takes the form of games and drama or just an old-fashioned tests . . . we all need closure. Closure helps us crystallize and internalize the new information we have learned. It also brings our unit to a climax and gives us a breathing space before we turn our attention to a new unit. Once the door has been closed on one unit, we can confidentially turn our attention to a new unit without feeling like we have left unfinished business or loose ends hanging.

CHAPTER 36

Create Your Own Character Unit

Good character is important. But that's not what this chapter is about. We're talking about *characters,* not character *traits* such as honesty and faithfulness. Character trait units are a whole different story!

A "character" unit is one that focuses on a real or fictional person. The "person" can be a real or fictional human being, a talking animal (think Peter Rabbit), or in fact any fictional being that people tell stories about (think The Little Engine That Could).

Characters make great unit themes because we're all interested in our favorite characters. Why struggle to find a way to fascinate your child when all you have to do is to find out who his favorite characters are?

Learning about the character can be the main point of your study when the character is a Very Important Person. Or the character can just be a "door" into the history and culture of his place and time (or his topic, which in the case of the Little Engine would naturally be trains, for example). Both approaches are valid, and both can yield a successful unit.

In the category of Very Important People, you'll find the kinds of people you read about in history books:

- Authors
- Statesmen and warriors
- Inventors, scientists, and engineers
- Explorers
- Artists and musicians
- Philosophers and theologians

Start with an Author Unit

Homeschoolers all love to read. So a good place to start for your very first homemade unit study is an "author" unit. Don't let the name fool you—you'll be studying much more than the life of one author. The books written by this person, as well as his or her life and times, become the portals for learning in all those subject areas of our "pie" drawing.

Let's refresh our memory of the various topics covered in the pie chart:

Pamela Maxey, whom you will see quoted often in the text and sidebars of the next few chapters, is the author of the Classic Start Curriculums and Themed Unit Studies. She is the homeschooling mom of three sons. You can visit her website at **www.classicapple.com**. Her quotes are taken from articles she wrote for *Practical Homeschooling* magazine.

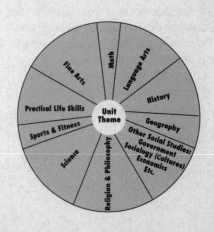

HOW TO PICK AN AUTHOR

Picking an author for a unit study is one way to create interest in different types of literature and expand your children's interest in reading. Creating your own author unit is a wonderful experience that will increase their love of reading. . . .

If you choose to create your own author unit, the first step is to pick your author. You can choose from many wonderful writers such as Robert McCloskey, E.B. White, and George MacDonald. Another place to start: Caldecott or Newbery Award winners. Look for an author from your hometown or state. You can pick an author who is one of your child's favorites or one whose work will create interest in new types of literature.

—*Pamela Maxey*

ADDING BOOKS AND WEBSITES

After you pick your author, gather books by that author. Try and use your local library as much as possible. Also look for a biography about that author. If you are unable to find a biography, check an encyclopedia or reference book at your library. I have used *The Young Reader's Companion* by Gorton Carruth. It gives short descriptions of a large variety of children's literature and authors. Many current authors have websites with information about their books and some include coloring sheets or activities that correspond to their books.

—*Pamela Maxey*

A Charles Dickens Unit Study

Dickens is a great author for a unit study for many reasons. For one thing, he wrote a *lot* of books. This gives you a wide range to choose from, with the added bonus that if your child gets "into" Dickens, there's a lot more to read! Dickens also had a significant effect both on his age and on the English language itself. His characters are both memorable and somewhat cartoony, making them excellent mnemonics for certain character traits: The slimy Uriah Heep and the ever-optimistic Mr. Micawber come immediately to mind. The lengthy sentences and extensive vocabulary employed by Dickens will improve your student's ability to analyze and to express himself, while the plots are strong enough to make kids *want* to keep reading this difficult (by today's standards) prose.

As we go around our pie, here are some ideas.

- **Language Arts.** Read a few/some/many/all of Dickens' books (depending on time available). Improve your vocabulary with words from the writing of Dickens. Start slipping phrases and characters from Dickens into your everyday conversation. Write a short story in the style of Dickens. Discuss the stories in the books.
- **History.** Read a biography of Dickens. Study the culture of England during the time of Dickens. Make a costume so you can dress up like a Dickens character and/or act out scenes from a Dickens book. Make crafts mentioned in the book you read. Play games mentioned in the book you read. Cook and eat a type of food mentioned in the book you read. (Christmas goose and plum pudding are good!)
- **Economics.** Dickens had much to say about some of the economic institutions of his time: the workhouse and the treatment of the poor, for example. Were his depictions of lower-class life accurate? How do economic conditions today differ from conditions then? You might even be inspired to do a sub-unit on the treatment of the poor from Dickens' time until now.
- **Philosophy and Religion.** What are the religious motivations of the various characters? What doctrines were familiar to the readers of Dickens' day? What were Dickens' own religious and philosophical beliefs?
- **Fine Arts.** Maybe get distracted by the art in the Dickens book you read and read a biography of his most famous illustrator as well as studying his techniques.

I could go on, but you get the point. You're immersing yourself in the world and work of Charles Dickens. Along the way you are practicing the following skills: reading, writing, analyzing, discussing, sewing, constructing, cooking, vocabulary improvement, and history. If you feel the need, you could add

- **Science**, by studying inventors who lived at the time of Dickens or whose inventions solved some of the problems people experienced in Dickens' books
- **Geography** of the British Isles
- **Sociology**, via the class structure of Dickens' England
- and so forth.

Such topics as nuclear chemistry or genetic engineering would have to be grafted onto the topic of Dickens, as they do not flow naturally from the subject matter. This is one reason why it's important to either use a packaged curriculum that covers all school topics over time, or have a game plan of your own that ensures you won't miss any important topics.

Of course, if what you really want to study is science, you're better off with the books of Jules Verne or David Macaulay!

With this in mind, here is a sampling of authors and some of the areas of study into which their many books naturally lead.

Authors for Younger Children

- **Stan and Jan Berenstain.** The Berenstain Bears series needs no introduction. The first few were simply fun (usually at the expense of dear old Dad, who was made to look like a fool). In recent years, the series has tackled negative behavior and childhood worries in a very charming way. The solutions are not always biblical but are worth discussing. Great cartoon art for kids to trace and copy, too!
- **Beatrix Potter.** Author of *The Tale of Peter Rabbit* and many other delightful illustrated books for children. Small animals, English countryside, socialism (sadly so). A ready-made Beatrix Potter unit is available from Calvert School.
- **Beverly Cleary.** Author of the Ramona and Beezus books and many more. Realistic yet charming depictions of the secular childhood of about 30 years ago. The characters (especially the parents) do not always act well, even when the author seems to think they do. Great grist for intelligent discussions.
- **Robert McCloskey.** Author and illustrator of many charming children's books, such as *Make Way for Ducklings, Blueberries for Sal, One Morning in Maine,* and (for slightly older children) the *Homer Price* books. A ready-made McCloskey unit is available from Calvert School.

Authors for Preteens and Up

- **Walter Brooks.** Author of the fabulous "Freddy the Pig" series about the quintessential American talking farm animal and his friends. My personal favorite as a child. Liberty vs. tyranny, community and neighborliness, farm life, newspaper publishing, banking, poetry (the many hats of Freddy!). Too many positive character traits to list.
- **Walter Farley.** Author of the Black Stallion series. Horses, animal training, racing, loyalty, courage.
- **Jean Fritz.** Series of history books from an ironic, secular point of view. Early American history mostly. Character traits noted but sometimes sly fun is poked at good traits. Idea sparkers for historical figures.
- **C.S. Lewis.** Author of the Chronicles of Narnia and (for older students) a large number of science fiction and Christian apologetic works. Allegory, Bible, mythology, beauties of nature, character traits of courage, honesty, and leadership. A

WAYS TO EXPAND YOUR UNIT

Use the books you choose to expand reading to other creative areas. If your books are historical fiction, you can explore the customs, clothing, food, art, and religion of the time period represented in the book. Draw pictures of the clothing worn in that time period. Act out a scene from the book. Explore a character in the book and write a journal entry pretending to be that character. Ever wish you could change the ending of a story? Include creative writing by writing a new ending for a book you have read.

[For younger children:] Make new illustrations for the book. Use clay to sculpt the creatures or characters in the book. Create a book cover with a new cover illustration, a biography of the author for the back cover, and a biography about the illustrator, your child. You can use illustrations in the book to create math story problems for your child. During your author unit, you could have story problems using Dr. Seuss's Snitches, Horton the elephant, or any of his wonderful characters.

[For older children:] Compare and contrast books by the same author. Use the books to pick out spelling words for a weekly test. Have your child pick his favorite character, write a biography of that character, and compare it to his own life.

After reading a book, brainstorm for ideas that you can do as a family that were represented in the book. For example you could go on a picnic, go to the zoo, or take a hike in the woods.

—*Pamela Maxey*

In the world of literature, besides Author units you can have Book units (here the main unit theme is the book itself) and Genre units (science fiction, Russian plays, or humorous poetry, to name three examples).

Some of these authors will show up on the AP, SAT II, and CLEP literature tests. Others will not. If your only concern is to cover the types of authors who show up on those tests, get a test-prep book and find out who the usual suspects are this year.

Some of the new so-called "classics" are semi-pornographic, vile in language, and despairing or hateful in content, and in such cases, I strongly advise the judicious use of Cliffs Notes rather than even reading such books, let alone devoting the additional emphasis of a unit to them.

ready-made Narnia unit is available from Cadron Creek Christian Curriculum

- **L.M. Montgomery.** Author of the Anne of Green Gables series. Turn-of-the-century life (early 1900s), imagination, self-sacrifice, orphans. A ready-made unit is available from Cadron Creek Christian Curriculum.
- **C.S. Forester.** Author of the Horatio Hornblower series. Napoleonic Wars, seamanship, courage, honesty, loyalty, leadership.
- **Robert Heinlein.** Science fiction books for young readers, such as *Starship Troopers.* Astronomy, military, space, honor.
- **G.A. Henty.** Prolific writer of adventurous historical fiction, covering many periods. Many positive character traits.
- **David Macaulay.** Author of many "how things work" type books and videos, including one by that very title. Engineering, math, design.
- **Scott O'Dell.** Historical biographies of many individuals. History of many periods, geography of many countries, courage, loyalty.
- **William Shakespeare.** The most important English author, with dozens of plays and hundreds of poems. Every important literary theme and many important historical periods. Every character trait, both good and bad. Smart preteens *can* understand Shakespeare. He's my son Greg's favorite author!
- **Robert Louis Stevenson.** A judgment call here. Hefty vocabulary, but adventure books written for boys.
- **Gertrude Chandler Warner.** Author of the Boxcar Children series, where children are trusted on their own and live up to it. The later books in the series written by others aren't as good. Family loyalty and dependability.
- **Laura Ingalls Wilder.** Everyone's favorite author unit study. Several ready-made studies available. Pioneer history, customs, practical life skills. Good and bad character traits explored in strong, spare, easy-to-read prose.

Authors for High School

- **Jane Austen.** Ironic observer of upper-class English life in the late 1700s and early 1800s. Marriage customs, emotion vs. sense, the class system, historical customs of the period.
- **Ray Bradbury.** Classic sci-fi and horror, great writing.
- **The Bronte sisters.** Gothic atmosphere galore!
- **Homer.** Classics of ancient Greece. Mythology, history, character traits.
- **Walt Morey.** Best known as the author of *Gentle Ben,* Morey wrote many more books with the themes of outdoors life and a boy becoming a responsible man. Alaska, horses, bears, fishing, and positive manly traits
- **Ellis Peters.** The Brother Cadfael series. Wonderfully warm and evocative tales of medieval Christian life written in the murder mystery genre. Courage, honesty, and loyalty are uplifted, although Cadfael (a returned Crusader) has a rather loose view of chastity (on the part of the others and of his own past behavior). Lots of history, deep character development.

- **William Shakespeare** again!
- **J.R.R. Tolkien.** Fantasy with strong Christian themes.
- **Mark Twain.** Not a happy writer, despite his reputation. Settings of mid-1800s America. Slavery, friendship, adventure.
- **Jules Verne.** Author of many early "science fiction" books that were actually much more science than fiction. Some of his fictional inventions have become reality. Science of all kinds, revenge vs. forgiveness, honor.

Books About Books

Want to find your own characters to study? The following "books about books" will help you do just that! One of them will even help you find books and historical figures related to a desired time period.

Books Children Love: A Guide to the Best Children's Literature goes far beyond a reading-list approach. Most reading lists deal exclusively with fiction, but *Books Children Love* lists hundreds of books from more than two dozen subject areas, with comments on each one. Author Elizabeth Wilson has selected "excellently written, interest-holding books on as wide a range of topics as possible—books that also embody ideas and ideals in harmony with traditional values and a Christian worldview." Susan Schaeffer Macaulay wrote the foreword to this lovely thick book.

Books Children Love
Parents. $14.99.
Crossway Books, IL, (800) 635-7993, goodnews.gospelcom.net.

Have I got a book for you! Zondervan's **Honey for a Child's Heart**, subtitled *The Imaginative Use of Books in Family Life*, is the most fantastic, inspiring book about books that I have ever read. Gladys Hunt, the author, expertly deals with the questions of what makes a good book a good book and explains how to make family reading a rich part of your life, as well as providing 224 pages of suggested reading for different age levels. The book is illustrated with pictures from recommended books and is an absolute delight to read. Gladys Hunt says everything I wanted to say about literature, and says it better. Highly recommended.

Honey for a Child's Heart
Parents. $12.99.
Zondervan Publishing House, MI, www.zondervan.com. Available in Christian bookstores.

Let the Authors Speak is "A Guide to Worthy Books Based on Historical Setting" by Carolyn Hatcher. The book begins with an extended essay promoting the Charlotte Mason system of education. But the heart of *Let the Authors Speak* is two book lists. The first "Guide sorted by century/location," lists books by title, author, type (a two-letter code— "RH" for example stands for "realistic historical"), century-location (e.g.,

Let the Authors Speak
Parents. $18.95.
Old Pinnacle Publishing, TN, (615) 746-3342. Available through some online homeschool catalogs.

"17 NA NE" means "17th century A.D., North America, New England"), and a very brief comment (e.g., "Indian princess, married settler"). This very condensed listing, which is sorted by historical era and location, helps you instantly pick out relevant literature to accompany any geographical or historical studies you may be involved in. The second list contains the same information, only sorted by author. Little codes by each book title lets you know if that book was reviewed in *Books Children Love* or *Honey for a Child's Heart* (two books that write up classic children's books and that I reviewed above), whether it is on the recommended reading list for Marva Collins' Westside Prep School, and whether it has won the Newbery Medal or the Pulitzer Prize.

This book and an encyclopedia are all you need to plan some really good unit studies. Well worth the price.

CHAPTER 37

Create Your Own History & Geography Units

Let's take a look at the possible types of history units. A history unit can have as its central theme:

- A character (e.g., Napoleon)
- A group (the early American colonists)
- An era (Victorian England or World War II)
- An event (the Battle of Gettysburg)
- A topic, that is, the "history of" something (e.g. the history of medicine or the history of American fashion)
- A place (the history of Zimbabwe)

Possible geography unit themes include:

- A person who traveled a *lot*, such as Marco Polo, Alexander the Great, or the Apostle Paul
- A city, state, or country
- A physical or political region (e.g., the tundra or the European Economic Community)
- A landscape feature (the Nile River or Mt. Everest)
- A group indigenous to that region
- The history of something that happened in that region (e.g., the history of Christian missions in Brazil or the history of trade along the Silk Road)
- Here's a nifty idea from Pam Maxey: "If your kids are interested in sports, you could even have a unit where you look at favorite teams, where they are located, and something unique about each city where the college or team plays."

Marco Polo for Kids

HIS MARVELOUS JOURNEY TO CHINA

21 ACTIVITIES

JANIS HERBERT

Learning about a famous explorer or a famous leader of another country can be a great way to kick off a geography unit. For a history unit, you can "draft" a famous historical figure of that era for your unit kick-off. With the help of a good fact or activity book about that person, such as **Marco Polo for Kids** from Chicago Review Press (800-888-4741, *ipgbook.com*), at least half of your preparation work is done for you already.

As you can see, history and geography studies tend to be related. When you study history, you usually end up at least noticing the geography of that historical era. When you study geography, you usually end up at least noticing the people who live in that place and their history.

What this means to you is that you can use the same approach, and many of the same "pie slices," when creating history and geography units. The central theme may differ, but most of the surrounding topics and activities can be the same.

Pie Slice Topics for a History or Geography Unit

Language Arts. We already dealt with this in the "Ingredients" chapter, in which you met the (hopefully by now familiar) pie on the left. Vocabulary, spelling the words from the vocabulary, oral narration and reports, writing assignments, and reading lots of books—these are all obvious ingredients of the language arts "slice."

Research skills also typically fall under the "language arts" category, as do foreign languages. Any "deep" unit lends itself to the practice of research skills, as long as you let the kids do most of the work!

Since most colleges require at least two years of a foreign or classical language as an entrance requirement, keep your eyes peeled for which language might interest your child. Depending on the place and time studied, it could be appropriate to introduce at least a smattering of the vocabulary and grammar of a particular foreign or classical language. This might in turn lead to an interest in studying that language formally.

History. If this is a history unit, you're all set! You already have an event or era to study. If this is a geography unit based on a particular place or landscape feature, you should of course include the history of that place or feature in your study. Make a timeline!

Geography. Again, if this is a geography unit, you're already focused on a geography theme. If it's a history unit, simply drag out the historical atlas and an outline map and start mapping the important locations and routes introduced via your history study. Crabtree's excellent "Lands, Peoples, and Cultures" series (which you'll find reviewed under "Geography Unit Study Starters" later in this chapter) is an excellent starting point for any of the many modern nations included in the series.

Other Social Studies. Here's where you start making your unit "real." Give your children a taste of the customs, food, clothing, money, stamps, jewelry, housing, and form of government of the time and place.

This area of study is one of the best sources for hands-on projects. Cooking the kind of meal the people of that time and place ate is one popular project. So is sewing or constructing a costume of the place and time, and perhaps even using it in a folk dance or dramatic production. You could make a banner, heraldic crest, or flag related to your theme. You could build or cut out a model dwelling of the time and place.

When you think about it, a Renaissance Faire or Civil War reenactment is a practical demonstration of many of the kinds of hands-on projects you can do in a history or geography unit! So is any historical movie. The costume design, scene setting, artifacts and weapons used by the actors, dwelling and mode of transportation shown in the movie all show just how far your unit study could go if you only had a few spare millions of dollars!

Religion and Philosophy. What did the people of that time and place believe, and how does it compare and contrast to what you believe? (Hint: Cultural behavior is a good clue to what the people *really* believed and how much impact the supposedly major religion had in the lives of the people.) What developments took place in the history of philosophy in that time or

SHOW THE CONNECTIONS

Be sure to relate how this person or event helped shape history and where the events took place. Many times children do not see the connection between past events and the present day. Many do not relate Bible accounts with historical accounts read in other books. They also become confused about where things happened.

If possible, use a globe to locate where you live and where your event took place.

Timelines are also helpful in establishing when events occurred.

Exploring history through people and events will make the past come alive for your child!

—*Pamela Maxey*

region? Don't believe what modern texts tell you on this topic area. They are written in order not to offend anyone (except Bible believers!), including the *descendants* of anyone who may have practiced a truly awful religion of the past. So behavior that today would rightly be condemned as evil and tyrannical is now soft-pedaled or even excused. You will never understand the fear and bondage the Aztec and Mayan people lived in by reading "bookstore" books about them, for example. These tend to focus on the massive architecture, crafts skills, and organizing abilities of these nations, while the horrific realities of a culture centered around the idea that the gods can only be appeased by human blood are largely ignored.

If you'd like a *real* look at animistic religions and tribal paganism, head to your nearest Bible-believing church library and borrow some missionary books. These tribes live in daily fear of the spirits. They do not love their gods. Their greatest hope is that the gods will ignore them!

It's particularly interesting to study the difference between "martyrdom" and "duty" in Christian and non-Christian cultures. Christian martyrs are people who were tortured or killed for their faith. Muslim "martyrs" in today's world appear to be young people who attempt to kill as many people as possible, their own deaths being the means of attacking others. Kamikaze pilots from Shinto Japan fulfilled the role they were trained in from youth, that dying for the Emperor was the greatest thing they could do. Suicide is honorable in traditional Japanese religion, but the Christian church has categorized it under the sin of despair. Meanwhile, General Patton, who his worst enemies wouldn't call a fundamentalist Christian, but who did read the Bible, informed *his* troops that it wasn't their job to die for their country, but (as soldiers) to make the enemy die for his. You can't find a plainer speech *against* the idea of soldierly martyrdom than opens the movie *Patton.*(Those with young kids, watch out for the rough language. Though Patton was in the Army, he swore like a sailor.)

How is this relevant to you? Well, unless you're Jewish, your ancestors were deluded spirit-worshippers who wore odd hats and engaged in blood sacrifice. That may seem harsh, but you check far enough back in history and then tell me if you still think I'm wrong. If you're Scandinavian, check out the movie *The Vikings* for a glimpse of some of the milder aspects of pagan European society. If you're descended from the Celtic peoples of France, Ireland, and Wales, your folks burned people alive in huge wicker baskets. If you're from India, it's only a century ago that women in your culture were burned alive when their husbands died. My own ancestors include some from the misguided followers of that prince of sweetie-pies, Attila the Hun.

I could go on and on, but why bother? *You* do the unit study and look in the right places (check out *Operation World*, reviewed later in this chapter), and you'll find out for yourself that all religions are *not* alike.

Science. As Pam Maxey suggests, "A science theme can be combined with a history theme when you study an inventor or scientist. First you need to decide whom you will study about in your unit. Pick your person and find as much information about the person as possible. Begin with an encyclopedia but also look for a variety of science books or biographies. For instance, if you are studying Ben Franklin, find a variety of textbooks and biographies, but also have your child read *Ben and Me,* the humorous story of Ben Franklin's mouse, Amos. Include information about the person and where they lived. It is also important to have background information about the person's times to place that person in history. Most importantly, discover how this person and his contribution to science have changed the world. You can easily incorporate writing practice if you choose to have your child write a report about your scientist or inventor. You may also include some simple experiments, science texts, videos, and craft projects."

LOCAL HERO?

I live in Lee's Summit, Missouri, where every fall our fair city recognizes its favorite son with a festival bearing his name—The Cole Younger Days. We also have a park and road named after him. For all of his notoriety, most locals probably have no idea who Cole Younger really was. This year, my boys and I created our own history unit to discover more about our local "hero." You too may have someone famous from your area. Why not find out more about them with your own history unit study? If you're like me, it may help you dispel popular myths with less than heroic facts!

In our case, my sons' eyes were opened when they learned that our local "hero" was really an outlaw. Unfortunately, Hollywood and local myths don't make for good historians. We learned the *true* Cole Younger story. His legend started as a guerrilla fighter in the Civil War and he later became an outlaw. He helped form and rode with the James gang with whom he robbed banks, trains, and exposition centers. We discovered that after having been shot 11 times during his escapades, he wound up in prison with a bullet lodged in his right eye.

In a few weeks we are heading to Minnesota for a fishing trip. Thanks to our unit study, we're planning to stop and visit Northfield, Minnesota. It was there, once upon a time, the locals didn't appreciate our "heroes" from Missouri attempting to rob their bank!

—*Pamela Maxey*

MANY AGES, ONE UNIT

You can also plan for different age and maturity levels within your unit. If you study the Civil War, a younger child may read different books and understand the war on a more surface level. An older child will read different books and will be able to understand the many issues involved with the war. Both children could easily participate in listening to a variety of music from the time, cooking food that the soldiers ate, and making costumes from both sides of the war. A younger child may make a drum for the drummer boy and an older child could make a representation of a famous battle scene. Both are studying the war with combined and separate activities and goals.

—*Pamela Maxey*

I'd like to add that every place and time uses some form of architecture, communication, transportation, hygiene, medicine, animal husbandry, agriculture, and weaponry, to name a few fields in which scientists and engineers have played significant roles throughout history. What people knew, or *thought* they knew, about biology, chemistry, earth science, physics, and so on affected what they built, how they cared for themselves and their animals, what level of weaponry was available, and so forth. The Bronze Age and the Iron Age, for example, were named after the metals used in the swords of the times—which in turn were as advanced as the metallurgy of the time.

You don't have to pull a Thoreau and build your own smelter (this is a backyard activity in which I bet your local fire department would be highly interested). However, working backward from the buildings, clothes, medicine, etc. of the time and place to the actual science behind them can be quite interesting. David Macaulay has made a career showing us "How Things Work." His books and videos, and others by additional authors, can peel back the layers and add some scientific spice to your unit.

Sports and Fitness. Every culture around the world has its own games. When these are played professionally by adults, we call them "sports."

Every historical era also has some unique sports. Plus, every sport started sometime and somewhere. I bet you didn't know that tennis first became an open-air game in England in 1351 and that the Black Prince (1330–1376, Prince Edward, eldest son of Edward III) loved to play it. It was *smart* to lose to the Black Prince. One courtier had the misfortune to strike the Prince with an errant tennis ball, and had to give up several of his castles, which he was glad to do, as facing the royal wrath without appeasing it tended to be fatal in those days.

A study of tennis throughout history (remember that the "history of" a topic counts for a history unit?) leads straight to Shakespeare's *Henry V*, in which the French Dauphin inspires the young English king with enmity by sending him the present of a box of tennis balls, thus implying that Henry, who like his ancestor the Black Prince enjoyed tennis, was a lightweight as a ruler. So here comes some literature for your Language Arts pie slice!

Until recent times, the average man had little interest in or need for special "fitness" activities. However, soldiers have always been trained with exercises, and every time and region except Amish Country has always had soldiers. So here's another way to drag some physical education into your history or geography unit!

Practical Life Skills. In every era in history and in just about every other place in the world right now, adults did (and do) far more hands-on, real-world *work* than we do today. The "Little House" books of Laura Ingalls Wilder, for example, owe much of their appeal to the way they show the reader how to do *real* things, such as churn butter or make a puncheon floor.

You may never need to "read" the waves and locate a land mass beyond the horizon like the ancient Polynesians, or plow with musk oxen like many kids are doing this minute on the Indian continent, but it broadens your world just knowing that people *can* do these things.

Then there are all those wonderful practical life skills we actually use today. How to operate various forms of machinery (dish washer, dryer, lawn mower). How to sit at a desk and process paper (keyboarding, photocopying, faxing, using a multi-line phone system). The first batch doesn't need to be dragged into a unit study. The second batch may well be used in the course of your child's research.

Sewing, quilting, gardening, animal husbandry, playing Mr. Fixit, and all the other "farm house" skills are not really necessary to city or suburban life. It's the lack of such skills that has turned America from the land of "good old American know-how" to the land of "something's broke, let's call the repairman." Happily, these skills are practiced in just about every place and time that's not part of the modern Western world, and your history or geography unit may very well be the excuse you need to teach your child how to actual *make* and *fix* things.

The "Kids Around the World" series reviewed later in this chapter shows how kids cook, celebrate, and create in different countries. It's an excellent starting point for some of those hands-on activities you're hungering to add to your unit.

Fine Arts. Usually you won't expect to do more than art appreciation studies, and perhaps some simple native crafts, in a history or geography unit. Becoming skilled in an art medium takes serious study of its own.

As I pointed out in an earlier chapter, you can bring in art and music from the time and place or art and music *about* the time and place. That should be a big enough clue to get your creative juices flowing!

Math. I personally favor leaving special math activities out of history and geography units unless you're studying a mathematician or scientist or it naturally arises in the context of one of your "how to" activities. Exception: A unit study on the history of math is a *great* idea. You'll find books on the subject at your library or bookstore.

History Unit Study Starters

In an earlier chapter, I suggested using "fact" books as history unit starters. In my upcoming homeschool volumes for birth to grade 6 and for grades 7 to 12, you'll find dozens of additional great history resources. To tide you over until they come out, here are two excellent unit study starters.

This is the best jumping-off point every for Western civilization history units for Christians and those seeking spiritual truth. In the **How Should We Then Live?** video series, Dr. Francis Schaeffer, one of the great philosophers and theologians of our time, has provided a key that can help any high school student, adult, or wide-awake sixth-grader make sense of history, philosophy, theology, and the arts. This three-video series, directed by his son Franky Schaeffer and filmed around the world, follows the history of human thought. It shows not only that ideas have consequences, but what the consequences are. Why the Renaissance? Whither the Reformation? Whence our modern angst? *Pourquoi* Picasso? The answers are all in these twelve 30-minute episodes.

Starting with the Roman Age, Dr. Schaeffer takes us through the Middle Ages, Renaissance, Reformation, Age of Revolution, Scientific Age, Age of Non-Reason, Age of Fragmentation, and today's shining glory, the Age of Personal Peace and Affluence. Yea, all hail the Economy. At each stage, he contrasts historic Christian faith with the errors of the times and shows what flowed from each belief.

How Should We Then Live?
Grade 9–adult. $99.95.
Gospel Communications International, MI, (800) 253-0413, www.gospelcom.net.

The book stands on its own. Get this first if you're not sure about the video series.

Jackdaw Portfolios

Ages 12 and up. Each portfolio, $41. *Jackdaw Publications, Division of Golden Owl Publishing, NY, (800) 789-0022, www.jackdaw.com.*

The Westward Ho portfolios available, as shown on the Jackdaw website.

Tape 3 includes two bonus interviews with Dr. and Mrs. Schaeffer, "Living with Suffering and Sickness" and "God's Leading in L'Abri and Our Lives." The former is particularly poignant, since Dr. Schaeffer, who looks hale and hearty on the tape, knew he was dying of cancer at the time.

This series is the ideal foundation for any number of unit studies. If nothing else, it is bound to spark powerful interest in the Great Books and the major historical figures and artworks shown in the video. An ideal "core" course for high school or college level. One warning: a few of the artworks involve non-erotic nudity. Specifically, Michelangelo's "David," Botticelli's "Venus," somebody's "Madonna" which turned out to be the king's mistress (her breast is exposed to nurse the baby), and a few others I forget. Really, it's easy to overlook these parts, although personally I wish they had been filmed more circumspectly.

For less than $100 you can buy this film series, show it to your family, lend it to your friends, and show it to your whole support group. (It's cleared for small-group viewing in "face-to-face instructional settings." In other words, don't rent the local theater to show it.) For considerably less than that ($17.99, to be exact), you can buy the book of the same name from Crossway Publishers (1-800-323-3890). For maximum impact, watch the video first, then read the book.

Want some extra information on a historical period or event? Try "Jackdaws"! A **Jackdaw portfolio** includes primary source documents from the period you are studying. Examine reproductions of actual letters, diaries, telegrams, cartoons, tracts, newspaper articles, court decisions, maps, and so on.

Each portfolio includes eight to fifteen facsimiles of original documents, plus four to eight illustrated Broadsheets (written by historians to explain and supplement the documents), detailed notes on background and source material, transcriptions or translations of hard-to-read/archaic/ foreign documents, all in a sturdy portfolio jacket.

Example: *California Gold Rush* includes Gold Rush Bill of Fare, "The Miner's Ten Commandments" poster, a page from President Polk's 1849 diary, map of the gold regions, sheet music for "Oh! Susanna," and a panoramic daguerreotype of San Francisco harbor during the Gold Rush, plus five other source documents.

Multiple Jackdaw portfolios are available in each of the following US history areas:

- New York State History
- American Indians
- Colonial America
- Economics
- Government & Civics
- Immigration
- Slavery & Civil War
- Westward Expansion
- Conflicts & Social Issues

World History portfolios are available in these topic areas:

- Greek & Roman Series
- Ancient Civilizations
- Explorers
- Global Studies & Cultural
- Conflicts & Social Issues

- Literature
- Science

Most Jackdaws are sold to schools, not homeschoolers, so expect some of that outlook in the teacher materials. The source documents and materials, however, speak for themselves.

Geography Unit Study Starters

The **Crabtree Lands, People, and Cultures series** is an easy-reading, clear-sighted look at other cultures. With just enough written details, and lots of vibrant large photos and illustrations, these are a great introduction to each of the countries covered.

Most countries have three volumes: *Lands, People,* and *Cultures.* The *Lands* book talks about the landscape, the country's history, and how people live there today. The *People* book introduces the various ethnic and religious groups that share the land and talks about what it's like growing up and living there. The *Cultures* book covers such topics as religions, holidays, clothes, and art.

The series includes *Land, People,* and *Cultures* volumes for Argentina, Canada, China, Egypt, France, Germany, Greece, India, Japan, Mexico, Nigeria, South Africa, Spain, Russia, Israel, and Vietnam. It also includes a single volume for Tibet, two volumes apiece for Peru and El Salvador (*Land* and *People and Culture),* and a volume entitled *Canada Celebrates Multiculturalism.* One side note of interest (to me, anyway): The teenage girl on the cover of *Israel: The People* looks almost exactly like me at that age!

New books come out continually, and older ones in this series are revised from time to time.

If you are studying any of these countries, I can highly recommend these books. The entire set would make a wonderful support-group library purchase—or perhaps you could talk your local public library into getting the more expensive set with reinforced library bindings.

Operation World began in 1963 as a sheaf of facts, country by country, for use during a week of prayer for the world. Since then, author Patrick Johnstone fell prey to the same syndrome as yours truly—he kept adding *more* and *more* facts and updating the information while his book got bigger and bigger!

Crabtree Lands, People, and Cultures series

Grades 4–9. Each book, $7.95 paperback, $20.60 reinforced library binding. Complete set pricing available. *Crabtree Publishing Company, NY, (800) 387-7650, www.crabtree-pub.com.*

Operation World & Window on the World

Operation World, grades 7–adult, $17.99. Window, as early as you can read it to them, $19.99. *Bethany House, MN, (800) 328-6109, www.bethanyhouse.com.*

In its new and much more attractive form, *Operation World* provides almost 800 pages of densely packed information on every country in the world from a Christian and missionary point of view, plus lots and lots of statistics (sometimes arranged in handy charts), historical background information, ethnic information, and prayer and praise requests. This is information you can't find in your *World Book of Facts* or encyclopedia: stuff like, "What is the ratio of missionaries to the number of people in that country?" "How many languages are spoken in the country, and into how many of them is the Bible translated?" "How are Christians treated in that country?" and "What is the history of Christian missionary activity in that country?" Along with this are geographical, social, population, and other facts. The reader is given specific prayer requests arising from the recent history of each country, plus names and addresses of mission groups operating in that country and a section on "special ministries" such as medical missions and student ministries.

All this is arranged by country and date. New this edition: Helpful black-and-white maps of each country make it even easier to use this as your geography unit starter.

In previous editions, the suggested prayer calendar format assigned you a country or ministry to pray for each day of the year. This was hard to manage, mainly because it takes more than one day to digest all the information about a country or mission! In response to this concern, the new edition gives you several days for larger countries—16 whole days for India, for example—while smaller countries such as Yemen and individual ministries such as "Medical Mission Work" still get only a day apiece.

For behind-the-scenes information on every country from a Christian perspective, *Operation World* is unsurpassed.

A sister volume for younger children, **Window on the World**, is now available. Laid out in colorful two-page spread "fact book" style, replete with lovely color photos, sidebars, and maps, it's the kind of book kids will enjoy reading to themselves and that you will enjoy reading to them. Countries and people groups are arranged in alphabetical order, each with its own "tag" to help you remember them. For the Jolas group found in Gambia, Senegal, and Guinea-Bissau, for example, the "tag" is "Who pray to the spirits in poems." Some of the people groups who need prayer are quite recognizable, such as Children of the Streets and Missionary Kids. Others most North Americans have never heard of—unless they read this book!

Each spread has a sidebar of prayer and praise requests, a "fact file" with statistics about the people or country, a "Do You Know?" fun fact to remember, and of course all that lovely text and photos. In addition, the book has short chapters on animism, Buddhism, Christianity, Hinduism, Islam, and Judaism; a World List of vocabulary words; a world map; ideas about how to get involved in missions; and a resource directory of Christian agencies who can help you learn more about these countries and people groups.

If you have younger children, you can start them on *Window on the World* and break off into units on any group or country that catches your interest. If you have older children, or wish to pray systematically for the world, I suggest you get both books.

These are the best resources ever for giving your children a heart for missions. And they are just loaded with solid behind-the-scenes facts and academic value. Add some mapping activities and geography vocabulary, and you have a head start on the National Geography Bee as well!

Some General Activity Books for Geography Units

Thanks to the multicultural fad, the world is full of books like the ones you are about to see. They tend to have the same strengths and flaws.

Strengths: Lots of good recipes and crafts activities, plus varying amounts of background information about a number of countries. Flaws: I have noticed an increasingly heavy push to include *religious* crafts in these books, (e.g., crafts that were or are practiced as part of non-Christian religious observance) while they continue (as a rule) to leave out Christian holidays and crafts and ignore or misrepresent Christian doctrine.

The underlying theme of such books is that children around the world are all alike (true) and that all cultures and religions are equally good, quaint, and valid in all areas (demonstrably false).

Here's an example. If you liked the Salem Witch Trials (which were kicked off by the accusations of some girls who were practicing witchcraft, and ended by Cotton Mather, a Christian minister—bet you didn't see *that* in your school textbooks!), you'll love this one. Among animistic believers, the belief is widespread that misfortunes can be caused by an enemy's curse, and only cured by killing the enemy.

Killing one of two twins (to get rid of the supposed bad luck), self-mutilation, female castration, worship of various living human beings, revenge and deceit seen as positive virtues, smoking or ingesting hallucinogens, animal sacrifice, and much more you'd be appalled to see in your neighborhood are all parts of religions practiced today around the world by millions of people. Read *Operation World* or *Window on the World* for an antidote to the Disneyfied versions of cultures and religions presented in these books.

However, if you keep your head and are aware of these potential problems going in, you can still glean quite a few hands-on ideas from series such as the following.

Have you ever wondered what kind of festivals and feasts are observed by other children around our world? What makes each celebration uniquely different or similar to holidays you may celebrate?

Kids Around the World: Celebrate! The Best Feasts and Festivals from Many Lands (120 pages) introduces 16 celebrations in four separate categories that will expand your cultural knowledge of foreign customs and traditions. Categories include four celebrations that welcome the New Year, four that commemorate fasting periods, four that give appreciation and thanks and four that are meant to renew the spirit. From Mardi Gras in New Orleans to the Chinese New Year in China, from Hanukkah in Israel to Iriji in Nigeria, everyone will be sure to learn something new. A description of basic beliefs associated with each holiday, as well as history, customs, crafts, and recipes are included in each section. Be aware the origins of some holidays may not line up with your own religious beliefs.

For those seeking to better understand and explore multicultural differences, this book offers a good starting point.

Now, care for some afternoon tea from Great Britain? How about dishing up a bowl of Cuban Black Bean or Polish Strawberry Soup? Slice up some Jamaican Coconut Bread or dig your fork into some Sweet Rice with Coconut Custard from Thailand. If that doesn't pique your curiosity about food from other lands, you'll find 16 more recipes in **Kids Around the World: Cook! The Best Foods and Recipes from Many Lands**.

A section on kitchen safety is followed by five other topics including beverages, breads, soups and starters, main courses, and finally desserts. Historical and cultural backgrounds accompany each dish, as well as ingredient lists and real-life illustrations of the finished product. For an interesting blend of youth-centered Home Economics and national Social Studies, this fascinating book packs a load of fun and worthwhile information.

What kind of crafts and activities do other children all around our world make? What tradition or story is behind each craft?

Kids Around The World: series
Grades 3–6. Each book, $12.95
John Wiley and Sons, Inc., IN, (800) 225-5945, www.wiley.com. Available in bookstores.

Kids Around the World: Create! The Best Crafts and Activities from Many Lands (107 pages) offers a collection of 24 exciting and original projects that will introduce your family to unique cultural and ethnic customs. Most all crafts can be made by using common items found in your own home such as craft sticks, plastic cups, yarn, material scraps, and aluminum foil. Discover the fun in creating your own South African Zulu basket or piecing together an Amish quilt. Practice Sudanese face painting or shake your Caribbean maracas. Some may find the pagan origins of some projects offensive or in opposition to their own religious beliefs.

Step-by-step instructions follow a brief history of each item, as well as simple illustrations and a glossary of terms. If you seek a fun way to teach multicultural appreciation, this book is a must. *Sharon Fooshe*

CHAPTER 38

Create Your Own Science Unit

Science is usually taught in schools as a separate subject that has nothing to do with history, geography, religion, or language arts. Even the individual science topics are usually studied in isolation from each other.

In the upper grades, this makes sense to a certain extent, as we will see. Science that is mathematically based needs to be presented in a certain order. Even so, students should be shown how biology, chemistry, physics, and the other sciences connect to each other and to the real world.

Science units provide a way to drag science out of the lab and into real life. They also allow you to:

- Get kids excited about science (textbooks rarely do this!)
- Keep their sense of wonder alive (even non-scientists need this!)
- Produce thinkers who can invent their own experiments, not just drones who know how to follow science "recipes"
- Help your science-oriented children grow into socially responsible real people, not nerds oblivious to the effects of their work on the world

Why Not Just Add Experiments & Activities?

If unit studies are supposed to be hands-on (which they are), then couldn't you create a science "unit" by tacking some fun experiments and activities on to a regular science text?

This question misses the boat in two ways:

- Most modern science texts already include some experiments.
- A "unit" is supposed to integrate many subjects to provide a bigger picture and fuller understanding. It's much more than just text-plus-activities.

Experiments and activities are essential to a science unit. But first we need to understand the difference between an experiment and an activity.

Hobbies Make Great First Units

Is it possible to teach science to three-year-olds (or to five-year-olds either)?

I suggest you watch for those aspects of the physical world that seem to fascinate her—and then provide materials to encourage hobbies along those lines.

—Dr. Arthur Robinson, of the Oregon Institute for Science & Medicine, posted on his Science forum at www.home-school.com

High-School Science Units

High-school students seeking to attend college need to be careful to cover at least two basic sciences *in depth* before graduation. When I say "in depth" I mean "with enough depth so you could pass the SAT II test for that subject with flying colors."

That being the case, I feel that **in the upper grades, science either should be studied separately** from unit studies as regular sequential courses, **or** (if your student is really intent on this) **as several *very* deep unit studies** with the particular science as the central theme.

This can work. Grant Colfax, the oldest son of David and Micki Colfax, got into Harvard partly on the strength of his research into goat breeding. Although the Colfaxes consider themselves "unschoolers," I think it's fair to say that the work Grant put into his studies about goats and genetics strongly resembles a deep unit study on these topics. You can read all about it for yourself in the Colfax's book, *Homeschooling for Excellence.* Originally self-published in 1992, it's now available in a snazzy new edition from Warner Books in bookstores and online at major book sites.

What Is an Experiment? What Is an Activity?

Let me explain the difference. An **experiment** first presents a hypothesis: "Under these conditions, this should take place." A real-world test is then devised. Ideally, this real-world test should be able to **falsify** the hypothesis—that is, prove it is wrong if in fact it *is* wrong. An apparatus is set up, data is gathered and written down in *ink* (not pencil) in a science notebook, and then the data is put into a mathematically sensible form such as a table, chart, or graph. Finally, a conclusion is reached.

An experiment checks something out in the real world. An **activity** *models* the real world. Turning out the lights and shining a flashlight on a globe as you rotate it *models* the way sunlight shines on only part of the Earth at a time. It is not an "experiment." You are not holding the actual Earth in your hand and shining an actual sun on it. What you are witnessing *only* tells you something about the sun, the Earth, and sunlight *if* the model's assumptions about the Earth's rotation on its axis and its orbit about the sun are correct. When you build models of molecules with Styrofoam balls and toothpicks, you are demonstrating something about the way molecules are formed out of atoms . . . but real molecules aren't connected with sticks and real atoms and electrons are only statistically in certain positions.

Because the education majors who put together science texts don't understand this difference, the experiments found in textbooks are often rather limp and pallid, with results predictably obvious in advance, and requiring no actual scientific techniques. Often the supposed "experiments" actually *model* scientific facts, rather than testing them as a real experiment would.

It is vital that we teach our kids to discern the assumptions behind what they're being taught. For this, unit studies can work well if you follow the suggestions in this chapter.

The Science Notebook

For real scientists, the keeping of a *true* (not faked up after the fact) lab notebook is of utmost importance. Nothing can be erased or deleted. Every bit of data should also be supported as much as possible. Devotion to this ideal of scientific truth is what made the vast progress of the last few centuries possible. Without the lab notebook, no real scientific investigation is taking place.

This was drilled into me in my public-school science classes, but oddly, since then I have scarcely seen science notebooks mentioned it anywhere. Maybe that's why we're now hearing so much about "junk" science: researchers faking or misrepresenting lab data in order to reach a financially profitable or politically correct conclusion.

Kicking Off Your Science Unit

By now, you know that I think fact books are a great way to kick off a unit. There are even more science fact books than history and geography fact books. The Usborne book series alone has hundreds of science fact books.

Even better than a science fact book is a science kit. You're probably imagining one of those old Radio Shack "50 Electronic Projects" kits, or one of those "101 Chemistry Experiments" kits that a certain kind of parent likes to buy for birthday presents. That's not the kind of kit I had in mind. Such kits tend to teach little about the science topic, and in fact are usually no more than recipes for the kid to follow. "Put this wire here and that transistor there" is just about as fun, challenging, and educational as "Add the contents of X packet to the water in the test tube." Yawn.

Lately I've seen a new breed of science kit. Typically, these come with (wait for it!) a fact book, plus all the hard-to-find components and ingredients necessary for the activities and experiments in the fact book. With one of these in hand, you're already halfway done with your unit study preparation.

I've included a few sources for such kits at the end of this chapter.

Picking Your Topic

I suggest that you start with a topic that interests both you and your child. Ideally, it's a subject you'd like to know more about but never had the time to pursue. This means you'll be learning along with your child, not tempted to lecture.

Here are just a few high-interest topics:

- The Solar System
- Weather (especially violent weather!)
- Earthquakes (and maybe other natural disasters as well)
- Magnetism
- Creation vs. Evolution

Teach Science with Units? Yes!
by Jessica Hulcy

Textbook/workbook loyalists often view hands-on curriculum as fun-focused and less academic. Quite the contrary. If the object is to get the information into the child's brain, then learning by doing will win hands down every time. For example, the study of the ear is a typical learning objective in science/health. The child would read about the different parts of the ear, draw and label the parts of the ear, and read about how the ear works in humans. He might study hearing sensitivity in a variety of species and then read about causes of hearing loss. His vocabulary words will include *lobe, inner canal, tympanic membrane, hammer, anvil, stirrup, cochlea,* and *auditory nerve.* He will fill in two pages of answers in the proper blanks in his workbook and is ready to move on to the sense of smell. Sounds pretty exciting, doesn't it?

On the other hand, you could have your children make a crawl-through model ear by draping bedspreads or blankets over the dining room table down to the floor. They would then make a giant earlobe out of cardboard and place it at the end of the table. The kids would actually become the sound wave themselves as they crawled through the earlobe, under the table, which is the inner canal, then out the other end where they have positioned a plastic-wrap-covered oatmeal box for the eardrum and tympanic membrane. They

have had to use their brains to problem solve how to come up with their own hammer, anvil, stirrup, cochlea, and auditory nerve. When dad comes home from work, all of the kids including the toddlers pull him into the dining room and make him crawl through the ear too. He has to tell them, "Whoa, one at a time!" as they all try to explain how the ear works at once. Dad, who was very skeptical about this hands-on science, is thinking to himself, "These are the smartest kids I've ever seen, my wife is the world's greatest teacher, and I love homeschooling!" For family night, mom suggests a video entitled *The Miracle Worker,* Helen Keller's biography. Doris, who does the signing for the deaf at church, will give the family a lesson in signing and then the children will spend the rest of the day learning and talking to each other in sign language. Mom is convinced that her children will never forget this study of the ear.

Incredibly, the only difference in her teaching from her usual was not in *content,* what was taught, but in *methods,* how it was taught.

Almost any area of science can be taught hands-on without owning a fully equipped laboratory. If you are not creative enough to invent your own activities, there are several curricula on the market with the ideas already listed. You just supply the household items and a bored kid or two!

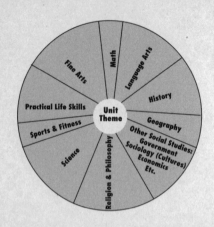

NO MORE "PRETEND" SCIENCE

Avoid gee-whiz, trust-and-parrot "science" books that really teach the child nothing and are written for general interest.

The worst mistake you can make —a mistake contained in most "science" programs for kids—is to mislead the child into thinking he is actually learning or doing science that is not within his capabilities. ["Physics" without calculus, "chemistry" without an algebra background, etc.]

Pretend science is the norm now. The result—even when they are older, American kids score last in the developed world in science skills. They are fooled about science at an early age—and never do the hard work of developing the basic skills.

My son Noah is now a graduate student at Caltech. His skills developed so well that, when he applied to graduate school Ph.D. programs in chemistry, M.I.T. told him that he was their top-ranked applicant of that year.

I just fed his interests with books that were over his head—and he reached up for them (and after great efforts managed to partially master them).

In short, respond to the child's interests by making available first-rate *real* science books [*or magazines!*— *Mary*], regardless of their complexity, in the subject he self-selects.

The parent, of course, will usually not understand these books either (except in part), but this is irrelevant. The child is the one that will be reading them.

—*Dr. Arthur Robinson*

Pie Slice Topics for Your Science Unit

This time, I'm not going to take the slices in the order they show up around the "pie," but in the order that makes sense for this type of unit.

History. Who were the famous scientists and inventors who discovered the properties you will be studying? Even more importantly, what cockeyed theories were the "received wisdom" of scientists of the past? You may have to dig some for this, since science textbooks are weak in this area and fact books tend to skip it. To help with your research, check out *Christian Men of Science* (Ambassador-Emerald International, (800) 209-8570, www.emerald-house.com, $14.99) and *Men of Science, Men of God* (Master Books, (800) 999-3777, www.masterbooks.net, $7.99). Between them, you'll find biographies of just about everyone who pioneered the branches of modern science.

Current Events. Is your topic in the news now? Has it been in the news recently? Knowing how to use online search engines and having a good shortlist of online news sites comes in really handy here. Often the debate over a scientific issue will give you lots more understanding than a passionless textbook description.

Politics. This also falls on our pie under "Other Social Studies," but don't be fooled into thinking that it's an unimportant topic. What political and financial considerations govern how much money is spent on research in this area, what results are considered "acceptable," and what social changes are proposed as a result of (or in spite of) the scientific data?

Religion and Philosophy. You can do this two ways. First, you can look up Bible verses on the topic. If you're doing "weather," for example, look up *wind, whirlwind, storm, clouds, rain, frost, snow,* and other "weather" words. With a software Bible program, you can automatically print out the verses and three-hole-punch the sheets for your binder. These can then serve both as memory verses and information about what the Bible says about the topic.

The second way requires much more biblical knowledge. You bring the Bible's teaching to bear on the ethical issues associated with your topic. For human cloning, for instance, the Bible makes it clear that *life* and *spirit* come from God. No lab can "make" a person. They can manipulate genetic material, but the breath of life comes from God. Therefore no lab or corporation can *own* a person. Other verses make it clear that the strong are supposed to defend the weak and the parent is supposed to care for the child, so whether you consider a clone the "child" of the person cloned or not, either way it's wrong to harvest his or her cells for the benefit of the person cloned or anyone else.

Math. In the lower grades, science units are great for teaching the *importance* of math, and also for practicing those seldom-used estimating, averaging, measuring, graphing, and charting skills. In fact, you could make a good case for yanking those skills *out* of the math texts, where they merely interfere with the systematic presentation of the arithmetic skills younger children need to learn, and putting them *in* the science texts instead. If you are a textbook publisher, feel free to steal this idea.

Lab Techniques. We touched on this above. Observing carefully, measuring accurately, notebooking, and safely using scientific apparatus and chemicals all need to be taught sometime. A couple of the resources found later in this chapter will help you with this.

Language Arts. Scientists are notoriously poor writers, whether you're talking about handwriting or creative writing. The more your kid fixates on science, the harder you'll likely have to work at pointing out that the purpose of scientific research is to *communicate*. A camcorder or tape recorder might help the truly pen-phobic to get started: Oral dictation and visual presentation are part of language arts these days. Other suitable language-arts topics to meld into your science unit are Greek and Latin roots (the basis of scientific terminology) and of course the scientific vocabulary itself—including how to spell those words correctly.

Physical Education. Rather than trying to work phys ed into a science unit, try it the other way around. You can do a science unit centered on phys ed. Blood pressure, resting heart rate, the muscular system, the action of a wide variety of sports-supplement chemicals on the human body—all this and much more is of great interest to athletes, a group who in general are *not* fascinated by science and other perceived "geeky" subjects. Many fascinating, up-to-date topics in sports nutrition and the physiology of sport are dealt with in entertaining style in every issue of *Muscle Media* magazine (the most family-friendly of the bodybuilding/men's health mags). Which brings up one very important tip when studying science: **Magazines on the science topic written for adults often appeal to kids who have an interest in that topic.** Once a student can read at an adult level, even if he only understands some of the magazine, he will pick up far more than with a normal kiddie book. I am of course referring to popular magazines, or magazines for amateur enthusiasts, not to deadly dry and overwritten scholarly journals.

Fine Arts. This one is a bit of a stretch. You can study the chemistry of paint and the physics of sound, but that doesn't exactly get you into the spirit of art. You can look at art and listen to music about your science topic, especially if it's something like "weather" or "the human body." But if nothing jumps into your brain, feel free to skip this subtopic.

Practical Life Skills. Since so much of modern science is technical and lab-based, this is another area you might find hard to fill. I suggest you think in terms of "folk" wisdom—folk and alternative medicine, farmer's almanac tips on predicting the weather and the best time to plant, gardening skills, plant and animal identification, pest insect identification and eradication—all that "Little House on the Prairie" type of knowledge that people used to get by listening to their parents and personally observing the world.

Some Science Kits to Kick Off a Unit Study

What is a Do-It Tube? Well, that's the first thing you'll set out to discover with the **Test Tube Adventures: Science for New Scientists** kit from Wild Goose's **Fun-Sized Science** series. While the Do-It Tube is used in this kit (and some others in this series) as a test tube, you'll also find out its real story. It's very interesting. From there you move on to experiments with color, melting peanuts, and floating things.

The parent instructions encourage your child to think scientifically: developing a hypothesis, experimenting, recording and analyzing the results. The included instruction cards for

Fun-Sized Science Kits
Ages 4 and up. Each kit, $12.99
The Wild Goose Company, NC, (888) 621-1040, www.wildgoosescience.com.

Other kits available in this "Fun-Sized Science Kits" series:

- Flying Things
- Rainbow Recipes (activities with color and light)
- Oozers and Bouncers (various safe chemical compounds)
- Sparks and Zaps!
- Extreme Solar
- Wild Wacky Weather
- Dark Shadows
- Pit Stop Science (rubber-band dragsters and balloon racers)
- Diggin' Dirty Science (activities with plants and seeds)
- Outrageous Ooze
- Air-Amazing Mysteries
- Water Jelly Crystals
- Growing Gators (polymers that soak up water)

Jumbo-Sized Science Kits

Ages 8 and up. Each kit, $21.99
The Wild Goose Company, NC, (888) 621-1040, www.wildgoosescience.com.

Wild Goose has several other science-at-home series, including a "3-in-1" series that covers similar territory to the Fun-Sized Science series reviewed above but with fewer materials and experiments, at $6.49 each.

Wiz Kits

Ages 5 and up. Each kit, $19.95.
Home Life, Inc., MO, (800) 346-6322, www.home-school.com.

your children will encourage them to think. Using the cards, your children can also explain why they think something happened the way it did and record it by writing or drawing on the back of the card.

Sometimes they will have the wrong answers, but that's OK, they're learning! Don't worry if you don't have all the answers, the parent's guide will help you out.

This kit includes almost all you need for the ten activities. You need to add some common household items. This is a fun way to introduce your young child to lab science! *Jo Dee Soles*

Don your lab coat and get ready for some fun with the **Jumbo-Sized Science kits** from Wild Goose!

Included in the **Soda Bottle Science** kit I reviewed are instructions for 20 activities that make use of 1- and 2-liter soda bottles. The kit includes the 1-liter bottles as well as many of the other materials you'll need. Other things you will already have or be able to get easily.

You and your child will enjoy doing these gravity, air pressure, and water-pressure experiments. Try to knock a brass nut into the bottle, make Cartesian divers (and keep one or more as a "pet"), try to blow a small piece of paper into the bottle, blow up a balloon in a bottle, and watch water stay in a bottle full of holes. You will double over with laughter during several of the activities. Your children will be laughing at themselves and then laughing at you trying to do the same thing. Who said learning couldn't be silly, too?

Also available in the Jumbo-Sized Science Kits series:

- After Dinner Science
- Just Add Water
- Water Rocket

If you have children who don't like science, they will learn to love it. If they already love science, they will enjoy it all the more. You may even have to step aside as everyone makes up their own experiments! I did. *Jo Dee Soles*

The best way to turn kids on to science is to let them do science. And the best science kits I've seen are the award-winning **Wiz series** for ages 5 and up.

With these kits, even young children can learn science that's normally not taught until middle or high school!

Each kit comes with a full-size, full-color book illustrated in kid-pleasing 3-D style. The book systematically teaches basic science concepts and includes illustrated step-by-step experiments.

Not just another collection of random activities, the Wiz kits are designed to systematically teach more serious science than many of us learned in school.

The series includes:

- **Electrowiz Magnetism.** What is magnetism? Safety rules. Fishing game. Attraction. Repulsion. Magnetic poles. Compass. Electromagnet. More!
- **Electrowiz Electricity.** Make circuits. Add a motor. Explore buzzers & LEDs. Switch & Morse code. Conductivity. More!
- **Wave Wiz Light.** Light sources. Prism. Rainbow wheel. Reflection. Refraction. Making lenses. Kaleidoscope. Pinhole camera. More!
- **Chemistry Wiz.** My personal favorite. You start right at the beginning and investigate properties of solids, liquids, and gases. A great first introduction.

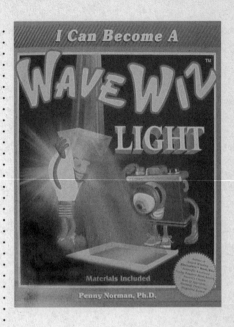

Each Wiz kit comes loaded with goodies: all needed materials except common household supplies such as salt. For example, Wave Wiz Light (pictured open above: Notice the heavily illustrated instructions and the supplies inside the plastic box on the bottom of the right cover) comes with gelatin molds, magnifying lenses, feather, wires with alligator clips, switch/light bulb, prism, motor, filters, mirrors, kaleidoscope tube, and more. The Chemistry Wiz includes pipettes, balloons, wax crystals, paper clips, string, cord, marbles, wax candle, clay, test tubes, iron filings, baking soda, filters, and cups. The others are just as generously supplied with serious, usable components and ingredients.

This entire series is a great hands-on introduction to these science topics that will probably teach *you* things you didn't learn or remember the first time around.

A Few Other Handy Science Unit Starters

Do you need hands-on activities for science that will capture your children's attention instead of having them roll their eyes at you? In the **Science Mini-Unit series**, Evan-Moor Publishers tries to accomplish just that. The series titles include:

- *Magnetism*
- *Electricity*
- *Light*
- *Sound*

Evan-Moor Science Mini-Unit
Grades 3-6. $5.95 each or set of 12 for $71.40.
Evan-Moor Educational Publishers, CA, (831) 649-5901,
www.evan-moor.com.

- *Matter and Energy*
- *Earth, Sun, and Moon*
- *Making Scientific Comparisons*
- *Solving Science Mysteries*
- *Hands-On Geology*
- *Playground Physics*
- *Backyard Biology*
- *Outer Space*

Each book is only 16 pages long, but each includes a double-sided poster. One side of the poster presents information on the topic and the other side is a learning game. The book includes teacher demonstrations, hands-on student activities, and student journals. There is also a jacketed, spectacled "professor" rat to lead you on your journey. For instance, in *Magnetism*, you will predict which of a group of items will stick to a magnet. Then, you will test your predictions, using the items and a magnet. In other exercises, you will determine how a magnet works, you will make a magnet, you will "fish" for iron, and you will make a paper clip float. (No, I will not disclose the secret—buy the book and discover it for yourself!)

These books cover a wide variety of topics in a mini-unit format. They work great on their own or to reinforce a difficult subject. *Barbara Buchanan*

Science Through Children's Literature

Grades K–3. $24.50
Teacher Ideas Press, CT. (800) 237-6124, www.lu.com/tips.

Just a glance at the title **Science Through Children's Literature: An Integrated Approach Second Edition** impressed me. I could hardly wait to open the book to find out what this was all about.

Part I of the book compares "traditional" to "contemporary" science teaching and how to integrate various school subjects into a unit, including how to choose books and plan activities. This first part includes a sample unit, which uses *Mike Mulligan and His Steam Shovel* as the starting point. Parts II through IV provide 31 different chapters for the various branches of science.

Each chapter suggests a book for a starting point and provides a summary of the book, the science- and content-related concepts, content-related words (vocabulary), suggested activities, and related books and references. That's 31 different unit studies, each based on a different child's book.

As an example, chapter 20 gives a study on lighthouses and oceans based on the book *Keep the Lights Burning, Abbie* by Peter and Connie Roop. The concepts include physical oceanography, lighthouses, tides, storms, and navigation. Some of the suggested activities have to do with geography (finding where the lighthouse is located and why it may be there), showing the effect of ocean tides via a model, showing how to magnify light, etc. Twenty suggested activities are listed for this study.

Even if you don't use the books listed (you may have one of your own), you will be able to get many ideas for activities. If you are someone who has always wanted to do a unit study, but had a difficult time figuring out how to put it all together, this book will help you get started. Before long you'll be able to create your own from scratch. *Jo Dee Soles*

Science Around the Year

Grades 3–6. $12.95.
John Wiley & Sons, NY, (800) 225-594, www.wiley.com. Available in bookstores.

Author Janice VanCleave needs no introduction—with over two million books in print, her 40 books have introduced children to hands-on learning fun in science for years.

Science Around the Year treats you to 52 topics (one for each week of the year) and four pages of important dates (one for each season). The 122-page oversized softcover book presents each topic on two pages in a user-friendly format filled with black-and-white line drawings.

Each topic includes the following:

- *Did You Know?* starts with a fun fact, such as "Autumn leaves have a 'sweet tooth'!" and then proceeds to explain it in clear, concise English.
- *Fun Time* describes an activity that you can do to understand the fun fact. The activities are easy to put together and do. VanCleave provides step-by-step processes and the expected results, so you can verify what you found.
- *The Book List* recommends three or more books to explore the topic in more depth.
- *More Fun* is a science or craft activity related to the topic.

The activities are well designed, making use of materials that you generally already have, and the procedures are written in step-by-step fashion. It isn't all experiments; sometimes it's easier to understand a science concept through an activity instead. Did you know that you can learn why chameleons change color with only two sheets of colored plastic and a black magic marker?

There's a combination of the familiar—stringing popcorn, cutting snowflakes, decorating jack-o'-lanterns—and activities you may not have encountered before, such as making pinecone hygrometers, and imitating chicken clucks using a sponge, a paper cup, some water, and a string.

Try your own activity with *Science Around the Year*: Next time your children are looking for something to do, introduce them to one of the topics in the book and see how much fun they'll have. They won't even realize it's educational. *Teresa Schultz-Jones*

Science Is Golden discusses "how to implement an inquiry-based, problem-solving approach to science education." What this means is that you ask your children a question or give them a problem to solve and have them brainstorm. You write down their answers and direct the discussion with more questions that are designed to lead them to an experiment. Many examples of brainstorming and experiments are given to help you visualize how this is done.

With this book, your children should learn how to ask good questions, do research, plan and design an experiment using controls, collect and analyze data, and be able to present this information. This book holds your hand the whole way.

A sample laboratory notebook is in the back so you can see how one should be filled out. There is also a list of questions if you're not sure where to begin or if your children aren't used to asking questions (although I don't think this will be a problem).

This book may be a bit overwhelming for some, since you will be doing most of the initial work, but your time investment will pay off when you see your budding scientists learning to work on their own and to think scientifically. *Michele Schindler*

Science Is Golden
Parents of ages 5–10. $19.95.
Michigan State U Press, MI. (517) 355-9543 x100,
www.msupress.msu.edu.

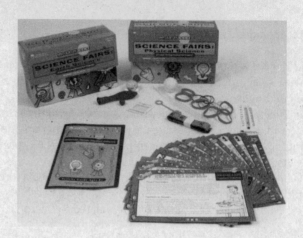

Spotlight on Science: Science Fair Kits

Grades 3–6. Earth Science, Physical Science: $14.95 each.
Learning Resources, IL. (800) 333-8281, www.learningresources.com.

Stuck for an idea for a science project? The **Spotlight on Science: Science Fair Kits** will remedy that by providing background, inspiration and a few objects in a 9 x 5½ x 3″ box.

Each box comes with eight project-starters, each related to a different question such as: "Can uncommon minerals be found in common places?" (Earth Science) or "What's the solution to making the best bubble mixture?" (Physical Science). Three laminated 8½ x 5″ cards guide you through each project start by giving you the following:

- Project Description—connects a question to an idea that can be studied for answers
- Questions to Consider
- Procedure—a very general outline, such as making and testing three different bubble solutions on a plastic bag surface
- Tips
- Background Information—definitions and how-to's
- Vocabulary
- Display Ideas
- Charting and Table Ideas
- Variations and Further Investigations
- Sources of Information

These are not canned experiments—the project starter questions suggest ideas that you can pursue. The Bubble Mixture questions ask what is "best" when making bubbles: size? durability? flexibility? aesthetics? Depending upon what you think is best, you'll need to come up with different ways to test each batch of mixture that you make.

An eight-page activity guide explains the scientific process, pointers to successful science projects, the importance of documenting your results, and an overview to the project starters. Between the cards and the guide, you already have the basics to inspire your project, but each kit also contains things to allow an eager person to start right away. The Physical Science kit contains a thermometer, balloon, diffraction grating, rubber bands, a tape measure, bubble wand, Ping-Pong ball, and more—nothing fancy, but it saves you the trouble of trying to gather some of the more obvious implements.

Science fairs force you to look beyond the textbook by developing and testing your own ideas. These kits take the mystery out of figuring out what goes into a science fair project, letting you focus on the science.
Teresa Schultz-Jones

PART 7

Planning & Record Keeping

If you keep really great homeschool records, will a Congressman want to shake your hand? Well, if your child enters the right competition, a Congressional handshake may indeed be on the agenda. Take, for instance, Joyce Watson of Kleinfeltersville, PA. At 16, Joyce won the grade 10–12 category of the National Student Zinc Essay Contest sponsored by the American Zinc Association and the U.S. Bureau of Mines. As part of her award, Joyce spent the day in Washington, D.C., where she met with her senator and congressman. "I am very pleased to have a student from my district selected as the winner," said Congressman Gekas, pictured here with Joyce. Joyce, along with her three younger sisters, is taught at home by her mother, Laura-Jean Watson.

Taking good notes and writing up projects is a skill children can learn . . . and use to win prizes! Both Meredith Novak, age 15, and Pauli Novak, 12, homeschoolers from Embarrass, MN, won purple ribbons, the highest award possible, at the Minnesota State Fair. Meredith, on the right in this picture, won with her 4-H project about forestry's use of prescribed burns. Pauli, on the left, won her ribbon with a food and nutrition project titled Potica. Both girls went on to win the Grand Champion Awards in their respective project areas at the St. Louis County Fair.

CHAPTER 39

How to Get Organized

Books and magazine articles make it sound so easy . . . "To organize your life, start by labeling a set of boxes A–Z. Get file folders and label them as follows: Accounting, Aster seeds, Acts (book of), Articles . . ." With enough file folders, you can conquer the world!

Well, maybe *you* can conquer the world. As for me, I'll be in the middle of filing and inevitably start reminiscing. "Oh, I remember this article!" "Someday I'm going to try this craft." "Look at this college paper; I really did have a mind once." And I'll stop to read it.

I've avidly read books on organization since my first baby uncovered this hidden inadequacy in my life years ago. Over the years, six principles have emerged that have remained true friends in my struggle to conquer clutter and pursue beauty in my home. These are:

- Organize around themes
- Less is more
- Plan in blocks
- Prioritize space by time, money, and use
- Put it in plastic
- Weed consistently

Organize Around Themes

A theme directs your thinking, prayers, and creativity and helps turn them into reality. A theme should feel satisfying and whole. It weeds out the fuzzy decisions from the productive ones.

As I stood back and looked at the work produced in my kitchen, its own theme emerged: simple and natural. My children are allowed to use the kitchen for all kinds of messy food experimentation. Therefore, the kitchen is kept simple, with plenty of counter space and replacements for most of the important equipment. Places for things are clearly marked so the children can clean up without my help.

Our decorations usually consist of a bunch of drying herbs, a tray of recently planted seeds, an onion someone is sprouting, and rows of assorted grains and legumes in antique canning jars. I can easily see that stoneware,

This chapter originally appeared as a series of articles in *Practical Homeschooling* magazine. It is by organizing expert and all-around homeschooling ideas person **Katherine von Duyke**.

Kathy has home taught her 12 children for 17 years, and teaches algebra and earth science for Towle, a homeschool high school. She is the author of the *Home Education CopyBook*, reviewed in this chapter, as well as the *Month by Month* spelling guide, a companion guide to *The Writing Road to Reading*. For years she also published the excellent *KONOS Helps* newsletter. Her latest project: helping homeschoolers gain access to Montessori training and materials.

Clutter Free!

Grade 7–adult. $12.95.
Don Aslett's Cleaning Center, ID.
(800) 451-2402,
www.cleanreport.com.

Dejunking is an essential first step of getting organized. **Clutter Free!** is the first book on de-junking mostly written by the junkers themselves. Find out how real people just like you deal with the agony of packrat relatives, dust-catching "treasures," and all the other detritus of a mass "consumer" culture that never actually "consumes" anything that can be stored in the attic instead. Like all Don Aslett's books, it's warm, human, fun to read, and motivating. *Mary Pride*

wood, and dried herbs will complement the look, while fussy decorations would be a source of tension. Decorative canisters that can't be knocked around or knick-knack shelves would work against my goals.

Some themes slowly develop as we stand back and look at the whole of the work we do, as in our kitchen, and some themes are decided at the outset. I'm currently working on building a western theme into my boys' room. I started by picking red, white, and blue, with touches of green, for my palette. My boys and I keep finding little ways to make the theme come alive: denim patchwork quilts, coiled rope lamps the boys can make, a collection of old horseshoes on the wall, stuffed fabric cacti, and tab curtains with bandanna tie backs.

A theme can also help to simplify. I use one for clothing decisions. I'm usually blessed with bags of outgrown children's clothes. Initially, I saved and catalogued everything. This job was tiring, and the results were disappointing. I'd find that this year's neon colors were a poor mix with last year's pastels. My children were dressed, but the result was an fashion nightmare. I took a lesson from the Amish and chose a palette of colors and styles for my children. Anything outside of that palette, with no match, goes to a local thrift store where patrons have a better chance of finding matches from a larger selection.

We picked jeans, turtlenecks, and sweatshirts in the primary colors for our everyday pattern. Winter dress outfits are in black, red, white, and gold. Summer outfits follow a sailor look. Some of my children look better in fall colors, while others look better in pastels, so we chose the colors that looked best on everybody (off-white, royal blues, and orange-reds). Though my choices are not unique, I'm thrilled with the time I save on Sunday mornings. Plus, since we seem to add a new baby to our family every two years, whatever clothes survive can be mixed and matched with new purchases or hand-me-downs.

Less Is More

I've always loved the way Japanese homes are decorated. They often use blank space to offset one exquisitely curved floral arrangement. I use this example to remember that "less is more." As I plan my theme I ask myself, "Which are the simplest choices?" I then rule out the rest. For example, if the children's drawers are stuffed with outfits, they won't be able to keep them neat. So I remove some of the clothes. They only need a week's worth of outfits in their drawers. A few extras can be kept in storage.

Picking themes limits the amount of crafts we will do, instruments we will play, businesses we will attempt, or units we will study. I'd like to do pottery, but don't have the time or space for it now. In the meantime, I'm not collecting pottery materials; they would clutter and detract from the themes I am faithful to now. The fewer themes I follow in the present, the more potential there is for developing new themes in the future. Less is more.

As our homeschooling has progressed, our family learning style has developed a few themes. We love fun, unit-style activities that weave in practical skills along with history, science, literature, writing, and a basic survey of art and music. I love sharing these studies with my children, but I recognize that I would burn out fast if I tried to teach everything this way. We balance our schooling by teaching math, foreign languages, grammar and spelling, and a sequential art program (I confess, PHS has influenced me!). In addition, I want my children to have some time available to pursue their own interests. I make my purchase decisions while keeping in mind the aim of our homeschool. I won't be buying a complicated science textbook or an intricate, activity-based math program. They don't fit our scheme. I want to invoke the "less is more" principle so that I'm not saturating my children with more material than they can possibly absorb.

Plan in Blocks of Time

A study once noted that men are usually convinced that whatever they are doing is what they should be doing, while woman are almost always sure they should be doing something else. So we need to prioritize time as well as space.

A rigid clock-watching schedule doesn't work for me. I need time to initiate tasks, but I also desire the flexibility to respond to the people in my life. Schedules should follow a progression of priority, energy, and natural setting. My priorities begin with the Lord, then my husband, then my children, then my physical home, then business, etc. When I have time left over, I can dedicate it to items lower on my priority list.

I've learned that my family is most faithful to anything scheduled before lunch—probably because that's when we have the most energy. Therefore, we clean the house, have school, practice instruments, and write in our school journals early in the day.

I usually don't have a lot of energy in the afternoon, but I can accomplish mending and sewing and be available to answer questions as my children work on individual assignments.

Many tasks have natural settings and times. For example, we take an exercise break midday because that seems to be what we all physically and mentally need. While I am cooking, I can do laundry because my washer is in the kitchen. Your environment will shape when you can accomplish some tasks. You can't fight your surroundings, so you have to figure out how to efficiently work within them.

Big Blocks or Little Plods?

Many women have enjoyed the benefits of grouping their cooking tasks into one block of time. They save on preparation work and cleanup. One clever woman simply rethought a task normally done in little bits and chunked it into one large block.

As you plan your schedule, try to visualize yourself maximizing performance while completing tasks in organized blocks of time. Should I clean one room every day or clean the entire house in an eight-hour period once a week? Can I remodel the kitchen over a period of days or should I set aside an entire concentrated week?

On a yearly basis, I may need to schedule a whole week for one task. For example, I like to map out the entire school year in the summer. I also enjoy taking a few major sewing and craft breaks throughout the year.

On a weekly basis, I need chunks of time to spend on organizing, cleaning, schoolwork, desk work, homemaking, and errands. All of these jobs need more than an hour to complete. While I could do a little bit every day, the time it takes me to gather my thoughts, locate the materials, and clean up afterwards is too costly. I save time by minimizing these steps and working at the task longer. The activities I perform within these blocks of time change throughout the year and involve some trade-offs. If I'm on a writing hiatus, I can use the extra time to paint. If I am gardening heavily in April, I won't sew much that month. My goals and duties may change, but I still know when the best time is to work on each block.

On a daily basis, I need bits of time to keep the small jobs from adding up. I write better if I work at an article over many days. Mending is less

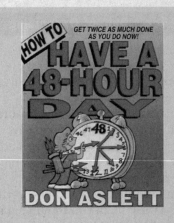

How to Have a 48-Hour Day
Grade 7–adult. $12.99.
Don Aslett's Cleaning Center, ID.
(800) 451-2402,
www.cleanreport.com.

The real trick to packing 48 hours into your day is, of course, to be born as Don Aslett. Parents, this is what your "hyperactive" kids can accomplish if they just put that energy into something productive instead of swinging from the chandelier. Don exhibits that kind of restless energy, and it's helped him write dozens of books, found and run a multi-million dollar cleaning company, personally build his second home in Hawaii, appear on TV almost everywhere . . . do I need to go on?

However, for those of us without that extra "zip" in our genes, there is now hope, thanks to this book. **How to Have a 48-Hour Day** is dedicated to all us slackers out there who get "workaholic" and "productive" confused. Don first explains why it's nice to get lots more done than you're accomplishing right now; then he tells you how to eliminate the time-wasters *and* add more useful things to your life. He cajoles, preaches, even nags you to make your life count for something besides rest stops and play periods. If this volume you're reading ever makes it into print, like it's supposed to, it's because I've started taking Don's advice. *Mary Pride*

After being taught for years that a good wife never throws anything out (it might be useful some day, you know!), I finally found out that time is worth more than junk, the less junk you have the less you have to organize, and that you should organize your things if you hope to ever use them, and that if you don't expect to ever use them you should pitch them. Revelation! Hence, my one contribution to Home Organization Theory:

Pride's Rule:
If it's not worth finding a special place for, throw it out. You'll never find it again anyway.

—Schoolproof

monstrous if it doesn't pile too high (though some prefer to mend all in a day). The house needs to be picked up often or it looks like "eclectic clutter."

With my time blocked out, I now have the ability to tie up those nagging loose ends. I use business cards to list my tasks (you could also use sticky notes). I then file these in a card holder under the appropriate day/time heading (Monday—10:00, Tuesday—3:00, etc.). All of my business ideas get filed under Wednesday since that's when I establish my office hours. Each Wednesday, I scan down my list, decide which tasks take priority, and work my way through them. Any "leftovers" stay under the Wednesday heading until that block of time comes up again. The card holder saves me from having to rewrite lists, and I don't have to look at a whole mess of different jobs to do, just those that apply to the current block of time.

Space, the Final Frontier

Once your time is blocked, you can decide how to store materials. You may only cook once a month, so a lot of your big pots and pans can be put in storage. If you sew only once a month, your supplies can be kept in the closet. However, if you sew every day, you'll want your supplies accessible. Your house may not readily lend itself to a sewing corner, but if you are an avid sewer, get creative. If experimentation is a big part of your homeschool, an extra bathroom could function as your lab.

My point: Balance what you want to accomplish with the traits of your home. Leaving out lots of lab equipment isn't feasible, so we have a lab box that can be readily taken down and used in the kitchen.

Ask yourself three questions when deciding where to store an item:

- Will it be stored in the open or hidden?
- How frequently will the item get used?
- How much manhandling or hard use will the item receive?

Bookshelves, walls, and tables are easily accessible and open to public view. Frequently used items are often stored there because they make for interesting conversation and are not easily lost. Items that receive hard use, like dishes and utensils, should have the most stable storage. Items used only on a weekly basis can be stored in harder-to-reach areas, such as high cupboards, and seasonal items can go into deep storage.

We had a problem that demanded high priority in all three areas. Our house had no front closet, and coats are usually stored in the entrance hall (first point of public view). Coats are used frequently and the children are not always gentle in pulling them down. My husband spent time and money building an attractive, sturdy shelf and hook system so that each child would know exactly where to put his things.

We didn't need to expend the same amount of time and money to organize the children's drawers. Each top drawer has a homemade set of containers to hold socks, belts, "treasures," etc. This helps to keep drawers neat and teaches categorization.

In a large family where everyone is responsible to help with the laundry, it is important that everyone knows where things go. I can remember spending many frustrating moments weeding through our children's drawers trying to find the baby's socks! Organization makes problems more clear and makes them easier to isolate and identify. We can also come up with creative solutions. We keep a bin on the back of the dryer labeled: "Personal: Lonely Crew Seeks Same for Mate" for all the single socks that turn up.

I also seek the minimum level of organization that yields the maximum time benefit. For instance, my spices are divided between savory and sweet. I know many people who alphabetize their spices, but since I don't alphabetize well, I'd have to sing the alphabet song every time I wanted the salt! I would use more time than I would save.

Now, I'll share some of the ways I store our materials.

How to Store for Success

When was the last time you went to the library and noticed all the books on the floor? When did you hit the grocery store and have to rummage through piles of boxes? I know storage containers are expensive, but by prioritizing your storage you know where to rely on homemade containers and where to invest your money.

I remember babysitting for a friend who had a very nice play area, with all the toys categorized and shelved in homemade containers. Unfortunately, the shelf and the containers were poorly made. When her little boy scrambled up to get an item, the whole system came tumbling down. We were looking at several hours of sorting!

My friend's carefully selected categories helped her child play in a purposeful way, unlike a child who is distracted from deep play by the mess (usually created when the toy box gets dumped to find that one special toy). However, her system wasn't up to the hard use under which it was required to perform. As a result, she bought sturdier shelving and clear containers with lids that snapped on securely. She hadn't felt she could afford the containers until she saw the valuable time it was costing her to not have them.

My favorite organizers are:

- Velcro
- Clear slip-in report covers
- Large plastic containers with lids

Here's how I use each:

Velcro. This sticky-backed tape comes in three decorator colors: white, beige, and black. I keep some strips on the wall space designated for posters. The wall gets the fuzzy side, and the poster, which I laminate, gets the looped side. This makes it easy to rotate posters or maps according to our needs without leaving lots of holes in the walls. Unfortunately, you can't take the Velcro off without removing the paint, so I use the color that best blends in. I also use Velcro on the back of a clipboard to attach notes to my work station. A piece of Velcro keeps the VCR remote stuck to the monitor and pencils stuck to pads near the phone. Velcro is also wonderful on felt. I stick it on little timeline people to fit them on a large piece of felt. The figures come off but don't constantly fall. In humid climates, where basement walls spit off tape like a baby spits spinach, posters stuck on with Velcro will stay.

Slip-in Report Covers. I originally began using these pocketed report covers to make up my children's school portfolios, and they work great. The younger children enjoy browsing through their older siblings' work, and we have no fear of damage. The artwork can also be beautifully displayed. One reader told me that she had used this idea and built an art portfolio dating back to the time when her child was scribbling. She keeps it on the coffee table with other display art books. What a way to motivate a child!

Organizing Rules for Kids

Renee Peters, time-management and organizing expert with AT-A-GLANCE [a series of planning products now produced by the Mead Consumer & Office Products Division] and member of NAPO (National Association of Professional Organizers), has developed the following tips and suggestions just for kids to help them get organized now and acquire the skills to keep organized in the future.

- **Write it down, never frown!** Use a daily planner or calendar to write down the important stuff! You know, like birthday parties, practices, due dates for homework—anything you don't want to forget.
- **Color it in!** Use colored markers or pens to stand for different kinds of stuff in your planner. For example, use blue for regularly scheduled appointments like practices; use red for important stuff like tests . . .; use purple for fun stuff . . . ; use green for family activities like vacations and trips.
- **Check it out!** Make a list of stuff you do on a regular basis and tape it up where you'll see it every day, like the refrigerator or closet door. List things that need to be done regularly, like clean your room, homework, or taking out the garbage. Then when it gets done, check it off the list!
- **Tomorrow is only a day away!** Put everything you need for tomorrow . . . in a place where you will remember . . . them. You can even pick out the clothes you would like to wear the next day. Remember, the more you do tonight, the less you have to do tomorrow morning.
- **Take a bite out of it!** If you have a big project to do, break it into smaller bits and tackle it one bit at a time. For example, cleaning your room might be a BIG project, but *(continued next page)*

breaking it down into making your bed, putting away clothes, and cleaning off your desk makes it easier to handle.

- **Keep it together!** Keep all related gear in one spot. Put musical instruments and sheet music, football helmet and spikes, baseball hat and gloves, or whatever you may have, in one place, or even a container, like a crate in the corner. That way, you'll always know where your stuff is!

—From a press release from Mead

Since we keep a large supply of these plastic sheets handy, we've found other ways to use them. I organize my sewing patterns with them. The illustration on the pattern envelope goes in front of each plastic pocket. Each size I design goes into its own cover. When I want to make PJ's or sweats for several children, I can readily find the sizes I need. I keep women's dress patterns in one binder so I can easily flip through to the pattern I want. In another binder, I have collected iron-on appliqués with coordinating fabric in each pocket.

In the kitchen I use the covers to hold our favorite recipes. I told you about my themes; well, this works in cooking, too. Monday is Mexican night, Thursday is stir-fry night, Friday is always Dad's homemade pizza. Under my Monday tab I'll find several of our favorite Mexican dishes, plus whatever else I've planned to make that day of the week.

In my teaching binder, I keep my master chore sheets in one cover and our monthly timeline people in another. I've also been known to tape a report cover opposite the toilet and fill it with poetry or Scripture we are attempting to memorize.

I generally buy report covers in bulk through Viking Office Supplies. They also carry Velcro and ship free to your door, usually by the next day.

Don't Put It Down, Put It Away

Once you've organized your materials, you need to teach yourself and your children to put things away. When a new area is established, I have difficulty getting in the habit of putting items in the right bins. My children may toss items anywhere. I will go through and rearrange misplaced items until my children catch on. After a while, they know where things go and begin to put them there themselves.

When they neglect to follow through, I will remind them to "put the details away." If needed, I will ask a child to pull a whole section of drawers and put away each detail that they've allowed to pile up. I point out how much easier it is to maintain the system if they put things away directly after they use them.

I keep a little bin or basket for odds and ends that I pick up throughout the day, and designate one child to go find the homes for the items. This has helped keep us from losing scores of minuscule game pieces.

Believe it or not, the children really like to have things organized. They like to know where to get what they want, when they want it.

Staying organized is much easier if everything is in its proper place. I have found plastic to be a natural solution for many of my organizing woes.

Put It in Plastic (Bins, That Is)

How I love my plastic bins! Naturally, we use them to store toys. Most large families come to the conclusion that toys are best stored in a central location and not in bedrooms. This also works if you are a small family but your children are little. Most young children don't have the ability to keep their rooms neat if there is much in them. The central location also promotes shared use of toys and allows you to build on (here I go again) themes. The toys go in labeled bins, which go on a labeled shelf. By specifying for my children, I make it easy for them to help me clean up. Our shelves are metal, the kind used in workshops, so they can take some climbing. We have a huge open bin of Duplo blocks on the bottom, then smaller bins with lids for things like the castle set, plastic zoo animals, and math manipulatives. Exploration of manipulatives is an option at any time of day.

From the Big . . .

Caution! Some of these bins are large enough for a child to fit inside. Any large plastic container can form an electrostatic seal with carpeting and can suffocate your child. When we first purchased the large bins, I would wake up at night with nightmares of my children suffocating in them. During the day I would get busy, and it seemed too hard to ask Daddy, tired from work, to watch the kids. One day, while my children were playing, I came around the corner to find one child under a bin, with another child humming and sitting on top of it. I think I shook for a full hour while I dumped every bin we owned and stacked all 20 of them by the front door! My husband drilled holes in the sides and bottoms of all the bins and I started sleeping better at night.

Even with the holes, these large bins are very effective. My favorite use: **unit-study bins.** Over the years, we've collected a lot of homeschooling stuff, mostly in themes (of course!). A reader told me about a terrific storage solution and business idea. A woman in her area has organized 45 bins, which she rents out on a monthly basis for a fee. Taking that idea home, I was able to ease the crunch on our bookshelves, our game closet, and our videos and tapes, and put them in unit bins. We never have time to use those items while on a different theme because we are usually too

MARY SAYS: The best way to get your homeschool organized is to teach your kids to keep themselves organized. As with so many things, the tools adults use to organize their lives often work better for kids—and are far more motivating—than cutesy-poo "kiddie" organizers. Chore charts may be necessary for *family* organization, but as soon as kids can write, give them a professional-looking planner. Your teen might enjoy a PDA (personal digital assistant) handheld planner for a birthday present! Mead makes some inexpensive models designed to slip into pockets on their binders made just for kids.

How to Avoid Interruptions
by Joyce Swann

Interruptions often steal many hours of our homeschool day. Robbing us of precious hours that should be spent teaching our children, these time thieves can keep us from accomplishing our goals and leave us feeling inadequate and guilty. Yet, by planning ahead, we can make provision for both internal and external interruptions.

Most external interruptions fall into one of several categories:

- phone calls from friends
- appointments with doctors, dentists, hairdressers, etc.
- appointments with plumbers, appliance repairmen, and other service personnel

External interruptions are easier to control since you usually can anticipate them ahead of time and plan to make them less intrusive.

Phone Rules

When we began homeschooling, the first thing I did was let my friends know what we were doing and tell them our school hours. Most were considerate enough not to call while we were in school, but when one did, I talked to her for few seconds and then told her that we were in school. I then asked if I could return the call and set up a specific time to do so. This usually worked quite well. Some, of course, were displeased with the arrangement, but I soon discovered that they were not so much opposed to having their call returned as they were to the idea of homeschooling.

Now that my children are older, I try never to answer the phone during school hours. If someone calls, I have one of the children take the name and number, and I return the call as soon as we finish school.

Appointments

I also quickly discovered that a successful homeschool depends on strictly adhering to school hours and planning the rest of our lives around school—not vice versa. Appointments with doctors, dentists, hairdressers, etc., were set up so that they would not cut into school hours. I made it a rule to tell everyone that I could not take any appointment before 3:00 P.M. Of course, the receptionists tried to talk me into taking the appointments most convenient for them, but I always responded, "That is not possible. I cannot come in before 3:00." After all, *I* was paying *them,* and I felt that I had every right to insist on appointments that worked best for me.

I handled appointment for plumbers, appliance repairmen, and other service personnel a little differently. If I knew that all I had to do was open the door and point the way to the appropriate repair job, I allowed them to come during school hours. Since these kinds of appointments are not usually disruptive to school, I felt it best to accommodate the repairmen.

Ready to Teach

Internal interruptions require a little more effort since they are more difficult to control. Generally, internal interruptions stem from one of the following:

- Lack of preparedness on the part of the home teacher
- Lost or missing school materials
- Breaks—bathroom breaks, recess, etc.
- General discipline problems

Coming to school prepared to teach prevents many major disruptions to your school day. This means you must know what you are going to be teaching before the school day begins.

If you do not use a curriculum that includes a daily lesson plan, make up a written plan in advance so that you will know how many pages each student will be covering in each subject. In my lectures I recommend that this daily lesson plan be made up several months before the school year begins.

You should also make certain that you have read the material your students will be covering that day and that you are prepared to answer questions and help them with math when problems arise. Having your students sit idly while you prepare to give them assignments, look for answers, or try to figure out how to solve a math problem, robs them of valuable study time and plays havoc with your school day.

School Materials in a Box

Lost or missing school materials can also be the source of major disruptions.

In our house, we assure that everyone has his materials on hand at all times by giving each child his own cardboard box in which he keeps his text books, syllabus, a pad of paper, pencils, erasers, a ruler, a compass, a protractor, a pocket-sized spelling dictionary, and any other materials, such as flash cards and art reproductions, that may be included with his course. When it is time for school, the children bring their "school boxes" to the table, and we are ready to begin. When school is over, they return their materials to their boxes and store them in their closets. Thus, we NEVER waste time looking for materials.

Breaks & Recess

Breaks are planned interruptions that should either be eliminated or kept to a minimum.

In our home, we are in school for three straight hours with no breaks. While it is sometimes necessary for someone to use the bathroom, it is rare for any of my students to leave the school room until school has ended for the day. By having children use the bathroom and get a drink before they come to school, these kinds of interruptions can be largely eliminated.

Another major disruption for many homeschoolers is recess. Because most of us are products of the public school system, we tend to believe that recess is necessary. However, in my 19 years of homeschooling I have never given a recess and do not believe that it serves any useful purpose. Homeschooling mothers who do give their children a recess tell me that these breaks frequently extend to 20 or 25 minutes since children often do not return to their seats on time. In addition, it takes a while for them to "settle down" and resume their studies. With thought processes interrupted, children often have a difficult time picking up where they left off. The homeschool teacher often finds that what was supposed to be a brief break to refresh her students has turned into a serious interruption, which results in a longer school day for everyone.

The most obvious interruptions to the homeschool day are likely to stem from general discipline problems. Children sometimes try to manipulate the classroom by bringing up subjects unrelated to their school work.

Since we want our children to know that we value their ideas and think their questions are important, we may feel it is necessary to put aside lessons and discuss those subjects immediately. This approach will, however, probably result in everyone being distracted from his studies for an extended period.

I handle this problem by telling my students that I am "very interested" in what they have to say but that we will have to discuss it after school. Later that day I remind them that we were going to talk after school, and I then spend as much time on the subject as they like.

Classroom Rules

I discovered quite early that the key to a well-disciplined class lies in establishing a few simple rules to ensure a quiet, orderly atmosphere in which little scholars can thrive. Here are my rules which have governed our homeschool for 19 years:

- No talking about anything that does not pertain to the lessons being studied.
- No staring out the window.
- No food or drinks in the classroom.
- No talking to other students.
- No wasting time.

While no one can create a homeschool that is entirely free of interruptions, each of us can eliminate many of the predictable interruptions by planning ahead. Controlling the external interruptions and setting up guidelines to minimize the internal ones is the best way to provide your students with a quiet, stress-free atmosphere, which encourages learning and promotes good scholarship.

Joyce Swann and her amazing family are featured in chapter 50.

engrossed in our present topic. So, now we have bins for the 1700s, the War for Independence, the 1800s, the Middle Ages, and Creation.

One bin may combine several units until I find I need to split them up. To accommodate the flow of items from bin to bin, I've labeled each with an index card and black marker, which I put at the front of the bin on the inside. To change the contents I only need to mark or change the card instead of trying to peel and stick on new labels. These unit bins can be made from cheap containers and stored in out-of-the-way places.

Out-of-season clothing seems to store best under beds. This allows me to claim all under-bed areas for my own use, keeping the territory free of junk and dirty clothes. Containers may be of any sort, but they must fit snugly under the bed and have some sort of cover. Otherwise, the children may be overwhelmed by the temptation to stuff the containers with their own items. This system works beautifully: New or outgrown clothes are stored under the bed of the child who will next wear them. The bins can be pulled and riffled through whenever someone grows and changes size.

The quickest way to work through a seasonal change of clothing is to have each child bring their bins to the living room. Then, starting with the oldest, each shows the contents of their drawers in turn and leaves with outfits that fit and match. The oldest is first to "shop" for clothes, so he can have the broadest range of choices (you know how clothes can be mis-sized). Meanwhile, I set aside unmatched clothing and take notes on what each child needs from the store. One of my children loves to function as fashion coordinator, so this job gets easier all the time.

. . . To the Small

Smaller, clear bins organize craft items near their point of use, but high enough not to tempt the little children. My children don't get these down without permission, and we are careful about putting them back. This has saved us from loads of disasters.

These craft bins consist of paints (some toxic), glues, glitter, and assorted craft items. In my sewing area, I keep bins for elastics, thread, buttons, bias, and lace. I have a separate storage bin for tools that I don't use as often.

Rubbermaid makes cute little clear drawer bins which offer easy-access storage for daily homeschool supplies. We have one with colored pencils, another with office supplies (tape, stapler, glue sticks), another with math manipulatives, another with pattern blocks, another with cards and envelopes, and another with rubber-stamp stuff. We have a set for frequently used games, labeled "Bible games," "Math games," "Chess and checkers," and "Geography games." The game boards are stored on top. The preschoolers have a set of drawers on the floor that include cars, pegboards, snap cubes, inch blocks, and small puzzles. We can quickly locate the drawer we need for the task at hand. I'd much rather spend my energies helping my child understand a difficult math concept than hunting for pencils.

Being organized is like a bank account: I can draw from it in bad times and add to in good times. And with money in the bank, I no longer feel like I'm drowning.

Teach Yourself How to Organize

The following products are designed to help you organize your life so your homeschooling will be successful. Additional reviews of record-keeping systems can be found in the next chapter.

Blueprints Organizer: A Planning Guide for Home-Schooling Parents

Parents. $9.95.

Hewitt Homeschooling Resources, WA. (800) 890-4097, www.hewitthomeschooling.com

Help for the Harried Homeschooler

Parents. $13.99.

Random House, MD. (800) 733-3000. They prefer you to order from bookstores. www.randomhouse.com

The Home Education CopyBook and Planning Guide!

Parents. $25.

KONOS etc, UT. (425) 613-1321, www.konosetc.com.

Blueprints Organizer: A Planning Guide for Home-Schooling Parents is a set of 116 reproducible sheets "to help you manage your life—not only school." Its three sections cover Organization, Prioritizing, and Scheduling, which should seem to cover the territory. Worksheets include family goals and expectations, children's goal sheets, quarterly subject goals, sample schedules, daily planning sheets, yearly calendar of months, month-at-a-glance calendars, weekly planners, progress summaries for each month, yearly summary by subject with comment blocks on the back, grocery list with teaching suggestions for shopping trips, memo sheets, and certificates. All master sheets are undated, so you don't have to buy a fresh pack every year. It comes loose in a plastic bag "for easy copying."

Is your daily routine more like a juggling clown in a three-ring circus? If the answer to this question is yes, then **Help for the Harried Homeschooler** by Christine Field will benefit you. Part I deals with homeschool basics including balance, chaos control, and discipline. Part II delves into the homeschool classroom such as structure vs. freedom, making curriculum choices, character and life skills training, teaching multiple ages and stages, and setting and meeting standards. Part III focuses on family homeschool issues like sibling fights, dealing with toddlers, how homeschooling can affect marriage, and school ties vs. family ties. The final section looks at the personal issues of homeschooling through a crisis, disapproval of others, discouragement, and burnout. Anyone who is feeling doubtful about their homeschooling decision should grab this book and read it. *Sharon Fooshe*

Information, inspiration, and lots of practical advice! This latest version of **The Home Education CopyBook** is no longer just a book of reproducible forms—though it *does* include forms, forms, and more forms!

Using these forms, you can customize your planner to meet your needs regardless of the homeschool method you use. Forms for organizing and running your household help you to maximize your time. Then with all the extra time on your hands, you can use the wonderful homeschool planning forms. You get yearly forms, daily lesson plan grids, unit study plans and evaluation sheets, journal sheets, maps, book lists, resource lists—you name it and it's in here.

Veteran homeschool author Katherine von Duyke explains in detail how to do the needed decision-making that goes into planning. Within each chapter are filled-in forms taken from her own teaching notebook. A magnifying glass ought to be included in each book because you can squint out some great ideas from these samples!

"Planning 101" is for the new-to-homeschooling mom. Kathy cuts out all the glitz and clutter of the early school years and focuses on the most needed skills: reading, math, and housework! This chapter provides a detailed look at what a home with four young children can actually accomplish for school, plus helps moms focus on foundational habits needed for future years. She includes such nitty-gritty issues as when to do laundry, what to have for lunch, and when to take a potty break! You even get her own program for preschool math and phonics, which if followed, the author says, will prepare your child to tackle high-school sciences well before high school.

"Setting Objectives" covers spreading units over the course of a year to make the most of each season, teaching units over a four-year cycle, and includes a month-by-month discussion of typical homeschooling and home management activities. Next, grade-level objectives are broken down so that you decide the best method to teach each subject, your standard of excellence, your documentation method, and what will end up in your child's portfolio. Kathy shows you how to document loosely-taught subjects so they look official. These objectives are then translated into assignment sheets with several options for different styles of documentation. Her best advice? Plan out where you can double up on tasks, and don't assign out any work you can't "freelance."

"Unit Planning" takes the rest of the subjects you wish to teach as a unit and helps you unravel the unit for subject-by-subject documentation, without giving up any of the spontaneity of a unit study. Described in detail are how to plan a unit, the elements of a successful unit, and how to document your unit—not to please the state, but to get more mileage out of your teaching. Typically, you get several cute forms with lots of different ideas for using them.

"High School (and College)" gets very personal. There's a bit of a philosophical discussion about the purpose for the high-school years and a discussion of inner vs. outer motivation. High-school courses are evaluated according to what is required, the level of student interest, the level of pursuit, and the means and methods chosen per course. To illustrate this she discusses her own high schoolers and how she has coached them into being responsible for their own education. She tells her own story of struggling with her then 13-year-old son who no longer wanted to do school "Mom's way" but ended up graduating two years early! She concludes with some strategies for completing college work at home. The high-school log form allows for very fluid record keeping so that students can keep official records for everything from textbooks to lifestyle learning.

The *Home Education CopyBook* is a wonderful addition to any homeschool family's library of homeschool helpers. This book is especially suited to homeschooling veterans who are ready to take more control over their children's work and want to build a lifestyle around deep learning. Lots of information packed in this book! Recommended. *Mary Pride and Maryann Turner*

Popular among homeschoolers for over 12 years (at the time I wrote this), **The Homeschool Organizer** by famous homeschool pioneers Gregg and Sono Harris is an extremely complete organizer designed to help Christian families set up a methodical schedule of family ministry and homeschooling.

This organizer has a system of major and minor planning keys that allows you to jot only key references on the month-at-a-glance or weekly planner sections. Details are recorded only once, on the Planning/Record sheets.

Now, what do you get? A three-ring binder with 250 pages separated by 13 divider tabs. After Gregg's inspiring introduction on the adventure of family ministry, each section includes blue Master Copies (store and save these), and enough white copies for your first year's use.

Let's look at these one by one.

Organization is most of what the old *CopyBook* used to contain, but even this has been updated. Kathy tells you how she has changed over the years. She discusses when to do tasks (e.g., daily schedules, chores), where to put stuff, and where to stuff papers (filing). Included are directions for setting up a teaching notebook and a purse-sized notebook. A little more philosophy comes through as the chapter ends with a discussion of life themes. In the appendix is a listing of her favorite tried-and-true products. Kathy states that her goal in organization is not a perfect home, but a prepared home fit to meet the needs of her family.

The book and planner sheets are bound together with a removable, slide binding making it easy to take the forms out to copy for your use. Then you can just put everything back together. If only all of life could be that simple!

The Homeschool Organizer by Gregg and Sono Harris
Parents. $34.95.
Noble Publishing Associates, WA.
(800) 225-5259,
www.noblepublishing.com.

Notice that Gregg and Sono's organizer does provide schedule and chore sheets for the children, making it a true household (not just parent) organizer. Also, because it is reproducible, large families will have enough sheets for everyone.

- **Household Management.** Master sheets only. You get a Weekly Menu Planner with a clip-off shopping list, a Recreation Planner (this sheet is my idea of being overorganized!), Lending Library Book Marks sheet, and Borrowing/Lending Record.

- **Personal Records.** This includes master sheets only for personal study recording, an Idea Keeper, Reading List, and Reading Review sheet. The latter would be quite helpful to any budding author or speaker since it gives you room to record strong passages to remember, quotable quotes, and bibliographic references, plus your thoughts about the book. You photocopy as many of each of these as you find helpful.

- **The Weekly Planner.** Fifty-two sheets. One side covers Phone Calls to Make and Letters to Write, Things to Do (broken down by personal, homeschool, business, hospitality, and civil influence), Appointments (by day: includes a space for a Bible text), a very complete Household Maintenance chart that gives you an open-ended list of possible maintenance activities for each location plus codes that tell you at a glance whether the job is assigned or done, Projects to Complete, Items to Obtain, and Projects to Plan.

- **The Monthly Planner.** Each month covers two sides of the sheet: Sunday through Tuesday plus a column listing the Planning Keys on one side, and the rest of each week on the other. There's also a section for Notes and Events to Plan. At the end of this section are five Notes to Remember pages, cross-keyed back to the Monthly Planner pages.

- **The Daily Checklist** holds a very complete Baby-sitting Instruction Sheet, as well as a list that holds kids accountable for their hygiene, devotions, and personal and family chores. You're going to want to make a lot of copies of this sheet!

- **Family Business.** Six Master Pages. One page records names, addresses, and phone numbers of advisors and professionals. There is also an Estate Net Worth Worksheet (find out the sorry truth!), a Household Budget Planner, Auto Maintenance Record, and a Record of Generosity. The Home Business Venture Planning/Report Sheet works better as a take-off point than a sheet to fill out.

- **Church.** For personal/family Bible study and sermon recording.

- **Hospitality.** Master Pages only. The Guest Room Planning Record is the most useful of these six planning sheets.

- **Civil Influence.** Five Master Pages. The most useful ones here are the Prayer List for Those in Authority and the sheet for you to fill out with political and media contacts.

- **The Household Profile Sheet.** A place to write down important facts like your passport numbers; vehicle make, ID, and license numbers; children's birthdates, blood types, Social Security, and driver's license numbers; where to find your insurance policies, what each policy number is and who your agent is; bank information; and emergency contacts.

- **Homeschooling Plans and Records.** Forty pages of Weekly Lesson Plan sheets. Each has room for basic comments, six subjects (you could squeeze in seven kids under each subject), and lesson planning codes down the side so you can condense your info into the smallest possible space. This section also includes eight Quarterly Attendance and Grades by Subject sheets.

- **Homeschool Helps.** Another section with Master Pages only. Some of these sheets are helpful, some are more work than they are worth. Quite helpful is the Weekly Assignments sheet—copy up bunches of these and use them to help your children form independent study habits.
- **The Directory.** Two Master Pages. Your basic name/address/phone number sheets.

This organizer comes in a three-ring binder, complete with a full year's worth of materials. You can use it practically forever because every buyer has permission to reproduce the entire organizer for personal use only for the rest of his life. At year's end, just pop the entire year's organizer in an envelope and there are your school records for the year in easy-to-find order. Use your Copy Masters to reproduce the new year's sheets, click them into your binder, and you're ready to roll again.

This organizing system takes some time to master—learning the codes for the planning keys and what goes where. You probably won't use *all* the sections: Select the ones you need now and leave the rest for later.

Once you cut the organizer down to size this way, you wind up with a useful planning tool that covers many areas others don't.

I really, really like this book! **Homeschooling by Heart** is just the juice disorganized types need to become successful homeschoolers. After all, the book's original title was going to be *So You Want to Quit Homeschooling?*

Yes, this book has charts, tables, and scheduling forms galore. What makes it stand out from the herd is that (1) this is *not* a book for those who naturally love to fill out forms and (2) the warm human touch author Kristina Sabalis Krulikas brings to the book. You're not exhorted to picture-perfect conformity. Rather, she takes you through first reexamining your reasons for homeschooling and recognizing homeschooling is a lifestyle and motherhood is a job. She then encourages you to simplify, build community bonds without going crazy with activities, and *not* compare your family to others.

After this overview of your homeschooling "road map," Krulikas takes you step-by-step through goal setting, child training and discipline, a detailed step-by-step guide to organizing your entire house room by room, scheduling, menu planning, budgeting, and kids' allowances. The rest of the book is taken up with helping you plan a curriculum that focuses on wisdom first, the love of learning second, and having fun third, including an entire chapter on why you should homeschool through high school. I think I found one sentence I disagreed with in the entire book!

If you're looking for from-the-trenches advice and organizing helps that will make you feel better instead of guilty, get this book.

Do you need a book filled with copies of every form or chart imaginable? If so, **Organization with Ease** will register high on your "must buy" scale!

I was quite impressed with the variety of forms included in this book. They are all there for you to copy until your heart's content.

Homeschooling by Heart
Parents. $19.95.
Solomon's Secrets, 27 Azalea Drive, Weaverville, NC 28787.
www.solomons-secrets.com.

Organization with Ease
Parents. $25 postpaid.
Carla Hofstee, www.organizem.com.

For us organizer wannabe's, the sky is the limit. There are forms for chores and responsibilities, grocery lists, meal planners, babysitter's instructions—and the list goes on and on! A checklist for your daily housecleaning is even included. You can copy what you need to make your household run more efficiently and save the originals to copy again later.

Interspersed among the array of goal sheets and diet sheets is wonderful organizing advice on almost any topic. The author, a mother of 12, shares a wealth of information on making your household run more smoothly. She even includes a sheet to help you evaluate how you spend your time!

Although this book isn't specifically for homeschoolers, it is chock full of valuable information and encouragement. Recommended. *Maryann Turner*

The Organized Homeschooler

Parents. $11.99.
Crossway Books, IL. (800) 635-7993, www.crosswaybooks.org.

I need new shoes after reading **The Organized Homeschooler,** as the author, Vickie Caruana, stepped all over my toes! This small book is just full of wonderful suggestions. Even veteran homeschoolers can benefit from the guidance and encouragement found in this concise book, based on the suggestions in Vickie's most-requested homeschool workshop. The optimism and desire the author takes from God's instruction is very motivational. I found myself eager to start reorganizing our homeschool library. The author's wisdom is evident as she encourages all her readers to organize not only their physical space and schedules, but also their thinking. With forms in the back of the book, multiple suggestions, and additional reading lists, this is a must-have if you are organizationally challenged.

The 144-page paperback book is very usable. Vickie shows you how to organize so you can overcome common household and homeschool roadblocks, emphasizing that the point of doing this is to provide time for more important things. Starting with the very basics, she talks about all the "good" excuses we all use for why we are not organized. Then she leads you through the painful process of getting rid of clutter, all those papers that pile up, and deciding what is actually junk. As you read this you can see what you are going to tackle next.

Throughout the book, Vickie uses small steps to reach the ultimate goal. So even if you are organizationally challenged this will help you. This is a wonderful addition to any library. *Tammy Campbell*

Step-by-Step Family Organizer

Parents. $34.95.
Homeschool with a Purpose , NY, (585) 682-4348, www.homeschoolwithapurpose.com.

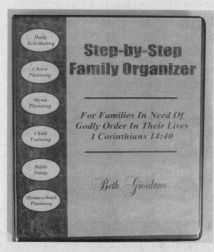

If you need help in getting your family organized the **Step-by-Step Family Organizer** by Beth Giordano would be a great investment for you and your family. This three-ring binder has 290 pages packed full of step-by-step information on "establishing godly order in your home."

Each of the eight sections begins with a description of exactly what it will help you accomplish. Throughout each section, the author walks you through how to organize your family, your home, your school, and the thing we all never have enough—time. Great emphasis is placed on time spent with God. Many of the suggestions are reinforced with Bible passages from the KJV, using them to show that God as the great organizer gives us guidelines on how to be better organized.

I found the clip art pictures for the goal charts to be very inspiring for the younger children or just the young at heart. Even if they cannot read, they can understand the pictures that encourage them to pick up their rooms, make the bed, brush their teeth, etc.

The Organizer helps you organize your chores, schedule, activities, appointments, menus, shopping, recipes, child training, and Bible study time, and also includes a homeschool planner with basic forms for scheduling your homeschool day. The author tells you in the beginning that in an effort to save you money on the expense of the book, you will need to photocopy the needed forms and suggests that you keep one of each form for an original.

This organizer is very well thought out, and very easy to use. One suggestion: The pages will last longer if you reinforce them with a plastic strip along the outer edge of the paper (the part that you will three-hole-punch). *Tammy Campbell*

Chore Systems

A neat new development (in more ways than one) is the chore record-keeping system. Realistically, homeschooling is half studying and half trying to keep the house clean. Thus no mere system for preserving academic records can do justice to your pressing need to have the kitchen floor mopped.

The best way to do your chores, of course, is to train the children to do them. However, this means you need some way of deciding which child does what and checking up on them. If you believe in rewarding your children for chores well done, you will also need some way of totting up their pay.

Here are some systems that do nothing but teach children how to do their chores and organize who does what when. If you have more than one or two children, such a system might be a worthwhile investment.

Author Patricia Sprinkle has tackled the topic of household chores and children in this chatty 198-page softcover book. "I'm convinced that we as parents do ourselves a disservice if we carry the full load of regular household chores and fail to share them with our children," she writes. Overflowing with quotes from parents and a plethora of other experts, **Children Who Do Too Little** examines why our children need to work, as well as many parents' reasons for not making them work. The last two-thirds of the book are where you'll find the how-tos: how to have a family meeting, how to teach skills, not chores, how to teach by natural consequences, and more. The appendix section of the book profiles some of the parents who shared in the book (a nice touch) and also has a group discussion guide.

The tone of this book may remind you of that found in many mass-market women's magazines: tons of bite-sized quotes and thoughts advance Sprinkle's basic thesis that our children need to help shoulder the load in our families. You may find the wide variety of approaches and ideas helpful if you have children who don't have a sense of how to work, and you're not sure how to get them to start. But for many of you, this book may feel like too much information about a fairly straightforward topic. In order to func-

Children Who Do Too Little
Parents. $9.99.
Zondervan Publishing House, MI.
www.zondervan.com.
Available in Christian bookstores.

tion as a family, particularly if you have several children, each one in the family needs age-appropriate responsibilities and a patient and realistic parent to train them to do the job well. *Michelle Van Loon*

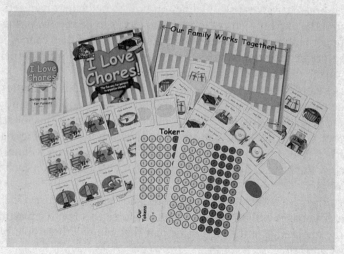

I Love Chores

Grades preK–12. $18.95.
Coffee House Publishers, OR.
888-896-4568.
Available online through homeschool catalogers.

Every homeschool family wants to teach their children to learn the value of contributing to the household through chores. Unfortunately, many of us find ourselves nagging our children to complete just basic chores. **I Love Chores** may end that nagging forever. To begin, just take out the included chore chart and place it on an easily accessible place. The chore chart proclaims, "Our Family Works Together" and contains enough little pockets for four children to write their names. One side of the chart has four pockets with "To Do" listed at the bottom while the other side has four pockets with "Done" listed. Fifty full-color chore cards in addition to 12 custom chore cards are also included in this handy set. The chore to be done is clearly depicted along with the written words. For example, "Fold Clothes" has a picture of clothes in a laundry basket. Even my non-reading four-year-old had no trouble deciphering what the picture cards meant. Once you have all the cards ready you're ready to assign chores. Just put the chore cards in each child's "To Do" pocket. Once the chore is completed your child can move it to the "Done" side. An optional set of cardboard tokens is also included that will allow you to establish a point system for each chore. To simplify this process, each chore card has a colored background corresponding to the token. For example, making beds is assigned one point while raking leaves is assigned two points. You decide what can be done with accumulated points. Spending time with mom or additional allowance, your family makes the choice. I Love Chores allows your child to complete assigned chores while learning how valuable his contribution is to your family. *Irene Buntyn*

CHAPTER 40

How to Keep Great Homeschool Records

I'm going to tell you the truth—I don't especially enjoy reviewing record-keeping products for homeschoolers. Too often they consist of huge binders loaded with forms you could just as easily design for yourself. Then there's the difficulty of trying to figure out whether *this* system would meet a lot of people's needs, or if *that* system might be better. If Family A uses textbooks, and Family B relies on unit studies, how can anyone possibly compare the record-keeping systems they use?

Aha! A way out of this dilemma! Let's look at the different *types* of record-keeping systems instead of at single products. Let's determine which kind of system fits which kind of home schooling. Then you will be able to decide which type of product you prefer, or whether you'd really rather invent your own.

Who Am I?

Are you a Portfolio Person or a Diarist? A Daily Planner Dad or a Mondo Mom? Take this simple test to find out.

- **Do you create individual lists** for each member of the family, listing what they should do and what they should take, before you go on vacation? Does it make you feel more secure to have everything written down in advance? Then you are a Planner Person. Maybe even a Mondo Mom.
- **Do you have a completely filled-out baby book** for every one of your children? Do you truly enjoy taking the time to chronicle your children's achievements? Then you are a Diarist. Do the journal thing.
- **Do you love to collect** knick-knacks? Do you enjoy taking pictures? Videos? Audio taping the kids' cute sayings? Then you are a Portfolio Person.
- **Is your life a series of random disasters** that kill all your plans and leave you too exhausted at the end of the day to write down what each child actually did? You're a Mini-System Mom! Get some workbooks in the major subject areas, break them down into pages per day, write it on the workbooks, and you'll be able to ensure that *something* is getting done every day.

Keep the Results and Nothing But the Results

Those of us who teach our own children, or run our own schools, are in a strong position to make our record keeping and grading useful rather than destructive. For starters, we can determine to throw away the steps and keep the results. This is what we do in the real world. No businessman saves the first drafts of his memos. No homeworker treasures up her botched dress seams. Instead, the businessman tosses the first drafts as soon as he has the final copy in his hands, and the homeworker rips out the botched seam and replaces it with one sewn properly. As adults, we quite rightly want to be judged on our final products, not on our missteps along the way.

—*Schoolproof*

If you can't decide, then remember that less is usually more (the more sheets, the more guilt). Try keeping your own records your own way for a while, and you'll find yourself falling into one of these categories. Big on To-Do lists? Get a daily planner. Like to write at length about your children's charms? You're a Diarist. Love checklists and filled-out forms? Get a mondo system. Always changing your plans on the fly? Try a card-based system. Too much work, too little time? Add a chore system. Children discouraged by their chores or work? Add an incentive system. No matter what, keep a portfolio of their best work—this is an encouragement in itself—and remember to take some time to smell the roses.

The Daily or Weekly Planner

These are the familiar planning books used by executives. Each double-page spread has the weekdays across the top and hours across the left side. Each box on the page represents a specific day and hour.

You can use a daily planner two ways:

(1) As a lesson planner. You write the assignments in for each hour of each day.

(2) If you prefer to use the "journaling" method, you write in what you actually did after it is done.

The lesson planning method obviously works best if you use textbooks, while a journaling method is usually better for unit-study and project-oriented homeschools. The more unpredictable your daily schedule, the more likely you are a candidate for journaling.

One tip to help you fit many children and courses onto a daily planner: **Assign each textbook a code.** You might want to write a list of all the texts you are using on one of the other forms in the planner, along with their codes. Then you can write, say, "ABM7 12, 13" instead of "A Beka Math Grade 7, pages 12–13."

If your children tend to work a lot on different assignments, you might want to consider getting a separate planner for each child. Then even if the children aren't all in the same location while they are doing their work, each child can follow his own assignments. This also is a good idea if you have many children, as it can be hard to write six assignments in one teeny-weeny planner box!

Daily planner systems usually also include monthly and yearly planning sheets. These are handy for writing in field trips, projects, and errands.

One drawback of the daily planner is that you can't both plan and record what you did without a lot of erasing or arrows pointing from one block to the next. If you don't do exactly what you thought you would exactly when you thought you would do it, the lesson plans fail to serve as a record of your actual homeschool hours. Conversely, just writing down what you did in a journal form means you miss out on the comfort of seeing your plans written out in advance.

CLASS Lesson Planner
Parents. $7.95.
Christian Liberty Press, IL.
(847) 259-4444, www.homeschools.org.

"No school profits from disorder," say the folks at Christian Liberty Academy. They've come up with a professional-looking, quality planner to ensure this doesn't happen to you.

Designed for families who are members of the CLASS (Christian Liberty Academy Satellite School), the **CLASS Lesson Planner** will nevertheless benefit anyone using a traditional, structured curriculum. Sufficient record-keeping sheets are included in this spiral-bound book for one child anywhere from kindergarten up through high school. Requirements are suggested for families with college-bound students as well, in order to help you map out their course of study.

Unlike most lesson planners, the CLASS planner groups subjects in weekly blocks. You're provided enough room to record the week's assignments, quizzes, and items still needing review. Report card forms, transcript form, and a quarterly evaluation form are all included. Even if you don't use all of the forms, the price makes this especially affordable for families with more than one student. *Renee Mathis*

Although it's actually a book about how to home educate, **Educating the WholeHearted Child** keeps winning the "Best Organizer" award in our annual *Practical Homeschooling* Reader Awards. Perhaps it's the huge appendix of planning forms? See the complete review on page 264.

Educating the WholeHearted Child
Parents. $20.95.
Whole Heart Ministries, CO.
(888) 311-2146, www.wholeheart.org.

The Home School Organizer by Ericka and Craig Brown has to be the most complete and concise three-ring binder that I have seen. It is easily expandable to include all your curricula, lesson plans, and forms. Extra dividers are even included, in case you want to organize some categories the author may not have thought of. In my case, I'd use these for an elective or to organize field trips. And it comes in your choice of black, blue, burgundy, or green covers!

After an initial three pages of suggestions and examples, the first section is 180 lesson plan pages. Each page is well arranged, with room for all general subjects from Bible to an elective area. Also included at the bottom of each page is an area for reminders and homework. Ample room is given for each subject, and each page can be used for up to five children. Refills are available when the original planning pages are filled up.

The remaining dividers are labeled Math, History/Geography, English/Grammar, Spelling/Reading, Science/Health, then a blank one, followed by attendance/grades, schedule, curriculum, general info, and another blank divider. Blank calendars are provided for you to fill in your personal system.

Many helpful tables and other extras are included on the dividers themselves. On the Math divider you'll find the multiplication table, weights and measures, and conversions. The History/Geography divider has states and capitals. The Science/Health divider shows the skeletal system, major bones, and blood circulation. On the Grading divider is an easy grade-calculation table, and so on.

One last bit of added usefulness: The organizer has two pocket folders in the back for any extra worksheets or papers for field trips, etc.

This organizer is great for on-the-go people, whether you are a brand-new homeschooler or a veteran who wants to keep your school more

The Home School Organizer by Ericka and Craig Brown
Parents. $35. Refills, $30 each.
Home School Organizers, FL.
(866) 243-8476,
www.homeschoolorganizer.com.

together and easily accessible. This easily manageable addition to your curriculum doesn't have a lot of nonsense; it just gets to the heart of most everything you need to be organized. You really get your money's worth with this one. To find out more, take the tour of its features on their website. While you're at it, you can also download their free *Basic Home School Record Keeping Workshop* notes and *High School Record Keeping Workshop* notes, both available right on the main page. And one last FYI: They also offer a weekly planner, all sorts of forms packets, denim planner totes, and both custom and stock diplomas through their site. *Tammy Campbell*

The Home Schooler's Journal
The Homeschooler's High School Journal

Parents and teens. Each journal, $9.95.
FERG N US Services, NY.
(315) 287-9131,
www.fergnusservices.com.

These are the very popular planners with the distinctive wire-bound "jelly-proof" covers. A several-time winner in the Practical Homeschooling Reader Awards, **The Home Schooler's Journal** includes:

- Daily Subject Log for 200 days
- Field Trip Logs
- Check-Off List for Yearly Requirements
- Calendars
- Objective/Resource Pages
- Individual Library Lists for up to five students

The Subject Log is set up in a five-day planner format with a wide "notes" column. With careful thought, you can use one of these planners for up to five children. Not fancy; it's just straightforward record keeping.

The Homeschooler's High School Journal is meant for one student's use for one school year. The student records his or her daily assignments, attendance, and grades, plus library books read and other educational products studied. Community service projects, objectives, resources, and field trips can also be logged. A transcript planning section includes a Yearly High School Requirement Log, in which you log individual complete courses, grades, and credits earned. The journal also includes a four-year calendar.

The Homeschool Planbook

Elementary Edition, $9.99. Double-Decker Elementary Edition, $15. Family Edition, $15. Unit Studies Edition, $15. High School Edition, $9.50. Shipping extra.
The Homeschool Planbook, MO.
(636) 338-9218,
www.homeschoolplanbook.com

Sarah Crain, a 13-year-old in her fifth year of homeschooling, decided in 1993 the best way to get a planner to suit the needs of her family was to design it herself. That is how she came out with the **Elementary Edition** of **The Homeschool Planbook**.

This is a very nice effort that is designed to keep records for one student. As an individual assignment book it could work very well.

The author has included enough pages to keep track of school hours. She has a page each for yearly goals, curriculum used, weekly planning pages, field trips taken, projects completed, verses memorized, books read (you can fit 68 books here), and a four-year calendar. Also included is a section for keeping track of your goals, subjects, curriculum, and resources. The 52 weekly planning pages are very simple: seven days of the week down one side and nine subjects listed across the top. You can also tally your hours at the bottom of each weekly page. If you are in a state that, like Missouri, wants you to keep track of hours spent on academic goals, you'll find the 12 monthly "hours of instruction" pages in the back helpful. These are set up according to Missouri standards of "core" and "non-core" hours, and also include space for separating hours spent away from home (e.g., on field trips, at the library) from hours spent at home. The pages are spiral-bound and the cover is now "jelly proof," so your copy should survive longer under ordinary use.

The **Double-Decker Edition** is for two elementary students. It has two sets of "hours of instruction" pages. All the rest is the same as the *Elementary Edition.*

The **Family Edition** has the same information as the Elementary Edition, with enough planning pages for four students doing separate assignments.

The **Unit Study Edition** can handle four students doing unit studies together, and language arts and math separately. Great idea!

The **High School Edition** is quite different. Sarah designed this one when she became aware that high school requires different record keeping from earlier grades. What you get: a four-year calendar, a four-year course planner with accompanying requirements checklist (important for college-bound and those who plan to earn a high school diploma), space for writing out course descriptions (room for 16 courses now—another improvement from the previous edition), an official-looking grades/credits sheet, another official-looking transcript sheet (suitable for photocopying and sending to college admissions officials), a "Books Read" form with room for 68 books, a "Project Report" form with room for six major projects, an "Extracurricular Activities" form, and 52 weekly planning spreads, with subjects left blank.

You will need a *High School Edition* for each year of high school, just as you need one *Elementary Edition* per child—or one *Family Edition* or *Unit Study Edition* for every four children—for each earlier school grade. *Renee Mathis and Mary Pride*

Managers of Their Homes by Steve and Teri Maxwell is a book dedicated to talking about the importance of *scheduling* in a busy homeschool mom's life. Scheduling is presented as a tool that the Lord can use to help homeschool moms accomplish what He has called them to do. There also is a chapter by Steve directed at dads to let them know how they can support their wives' scheduling efforts.

Managers of Their Homes
Parents. $25.
Managers of Their Homes, KS.
(913) 772-0392, www.titus2.com.

You'll find lots of how-to hints specifically directed to homeschool families. A scheduling kit is included in the book, along with step-by-step instructions on how to use it. It has all the forms for a mom to create a schedule for herself and for each of her children, and chore worksheets for the children. Once you register your book, you have the right to copy the forms for multiple children for personal family use only. It comes with enough forms for eight people, so if you have seven or less kids, you're all set!

In fact, if you tell them at the time you order that you have more than seven children, they'll add the extra forms into your packet at no extra charge. How nice!

There is a planning sheet for each person. Each person's forms are color-coded. You take the colored pieces of paper and put them on an 11 x 17" master schedule, so you can see what your whole family is up to (or should be up to) at a glance!

Wonder how other families do it? Then you'll enjoy reading the several dozen sample schedules in the back of the book, which explain how other families schedule their homeschools.

One thing I can tell you—this is a very popular record-keeping system. Thousands of copies have been sold, and it consistently places in our annual *Practical Homeschooling* Reader Awards!

Dear Diary

Once you get started journaling, you find that seldom do your projects divide themselves up neatly by hours. You might then prefer to keep more of a "daily diary" type of journal, in which you write down the events of the day all at once.

To give more structure to this approach, some record-keeping systems include sheets you can regularly fill out with weekly, monthly, and yearly objectives. The style and topics of these sheets seem only to be limited by the imagination of their publishers. I have seen spiritual objectives sheets, character-traits objectives sheets, marital relationship objectives sheets . . . you get the idea.

More useful to my mind than blank "objectives" sheets are checklists, out of which you can pick your objectives. At present you will have to invent your own checklists, as I haven't seen any published systems with such checklists. Ideally churches would have such checklists for their own members' spiritual and academic growth. The more specific the objective, the better—e.g., "Memorize Ten Commandments," is better than, "Do more Bible memory."

Daily-diary systems also often include sheets for you to record your impressions about your children's progress. If you like to do this sort of thing, you'll find it lots of fun, and you'll have it to read later when your children are grown.

Relaxed Record Keeping

Parents. $6.95 plus shipping.
Elijah Company, TN.
(888)2ELIJAH,
www.elijahcompany.com.

Relaxed Record Keeping will be appreciated by you relaxed homeschoolers out there. (If you're like me and like to see neat little squares filled in, this is probably not the book for you.) The intended audience for this 26-page large-format booklet is those who adopt a very unstructured approach, yet are required to make an account of their year to the local authorities. If this applies to you, then heed her instructions on how to make your assessments sound "official." *Renee Mathis*

Card Systems

A switch on these approaches is to keep your plans and/or records on cards. The cards can then be filed by child, subject, project, date, or whatever.

I have seen two card-based systems that impressed me. One uses index cards and coded lesson assignments. The child gives you assignment cards as the assignments are finished. You then file them as a record of his work. The other uses special square cards and an executive-type binder with staggered panels, so the top line of each card is always displayed. This makes it much easier to see where all your cards are.

Card-based systems are more flexible than daily planner systems. If your plans change, just change the date on the card. You never have to scratch over a written page. Your child can complete assignments at his own pace without messing up your records. You lose the ability to see your week at a glance, but this only matters if you want to know exactly who is doing what each hour. If you prefer to start at the beginning of a study or project and continue on to the end without worrying about how long it takes, consider a card-based system.

Unlike other planning systems, the **ScanCard System** uses cards. You write the project name of top of a card, jot down whatever you want to remember to do, and stick it in one of the pockets of your organizer. Every day you quickly scan all your cards to see what ought to be done next.

Like most really useful inventions, the ScanCard system happened almost by accident. Founder Marvin Williams was fed up with project lists and overstructured time management systems. So he developed a system of filing project cards into staggered pockets, with the project name peeking out on top. Everywhere he went, his fellow businessmen wanted one. Getting the hint, Mr. Williams formed a product line featuring these organizers.

The ScanCard system's best feature is that it is not tied to particular dates and times. Instead of writing in the date and time you intend to do a project, you just write the project down on a card. Then, when interruptions inevitably mess up your schedule, you don't have to cross out boxes on your calendar, draw little lines back and forth between pages, and so on. No guilt, no pain, no projects forgotten because they weren't done on the right day and you forgot to write them in again on a later page. If you need to do something by a certain date, just say so on the card. The card format also makes it super-easy to add or subtract projects.

It would take too much space to list all the different styles, colors, and bindings in which ScanCard comes. So here are the most popular:

- **The Organizer** is made to fit the needs and budgets of most people—executives and professionals, homemakers, teachers, students, and the clergy. It is 9x12" and only about 3/4 inch thick. Inside its two covers you find on the left 24 ScanCard pockets and a small year-at-a-glance calendar that sits in a plastic pocket of its own just beneath those pockets. On the right is a yellow legal pad, a one-sheet phone/address index on thick stock with room for 100 names that becomes visible when you flip forward the legal pad, and a "TrapFile" vinyl pocket behind it all where you can hold important papers. In between is a narrow little pocket where you can keep your pen or pencil. It comes with 100 ScanCard project cards.
- **The Chairman** is the deluxe model. It comes with three ScanCard panels that handle up to 120 projects, and is expandable (with purchase of additional panels) to a total of 200 projects. It also has an appointment calendar, phone index, built-in multi-function calculator, business and credit card compartments, and concealed pocket files for important papers, plus everything included in the Organizer model. It comes with 500 ScanCard project cards.
- **The Manager's Companion** combines a ScanCard planning system with a daily planner. Sized 9½" x 12¼" x 1¾", it comes in vinyl or full-grain leather and includes a zippered, double-file pocket, a removable 24-project ScanCard panel (more can be added), ruled notepad, double pen/pencil holder, and more.

The beauty of this system is that you can keep your personal, business, home, and ministry projects all in the same place, and the ScanCard system can be adapted easily to homeschool lesson planning. One organizer per child is ideal. It has plenty of space for homeschool record keeping with room left over for Junior to do his own kid's business and chore planning. Then just save the completed project cards, and you have a complete "paper trail" of your home-schooling activities for legal purposes.

ScanCard System

Organizer: vinyl, $39.95; leather, $89.95; Italian leather, $119.95. Chairman: vinyl, $109.95; leather, $159.95. Manager's Companion zip-around ScanCard folio: vinyl $59.95; leather, $99.95. Other models available. Shipping extra. *Scancard Systems, LLC, OH.* *(800) 848-2618,* *www.executivegallery.com.*

ScanCard Organizer Model

ScanCard Chairman Model

We recommend the Chairman model for business owners and the Organizer model for children and most other uses. The Zip-Around model would be ideal for someone who has to carry his organizer out and around with him.

Mondo Systems

Mondo systems are very popular with the people who design home-school record-keeping systems—although I'm not sure how many people actually use all those fancy features! Basically, a mondo system is designed to organize your entire life. One sheet will tell you which library books you have out. Another will list the Bible verses you are memorizing. A third will hold your personal address list. A fourth will tell your spouse, in the event of your unfortunate demise, where the insurance policy is hidden. And so on. In the middle of all this will also be found sheets for keeping your homeschool records. Lists of textbooks. Lists of objectives. Daily planning sheets. Monthly planning sheets. Yearly planning sheets. Auto repair checklists. Etc.

Mondo systems appeal because they promise to bring your helter-skelter life under control. Unfortunately, even the best mondo system won't work unless *you* take the time to fill in all the records! Only you know if you have the discipline to do this or even really *want* to do it.

Most of us will find that we can live very nicely without some of the sheets in a mondo system. For example, we take out about 50 library books each time we visit the library, and there's no way I'm going to write those titles down every week or two. I already have a separate address book, so I don't need the address-list features. I prefer to write my appointments on a huge wall calendar, where I can't miss them, and I *never* write down objectives (too busy trying to achieve 'em!). Someone else might live and die by the library book list, but not me. Determine how many of those "extra" sheets you are really going to use before you pay the hefty price for one of these systems.

I confess. I've had flings with planners before. I've succumbed to the siren song of the supple leather covers. I've fallen for the tantalizing tapestry binders, the pristine pages waiting for the penciled notes that would bring joy and order to my life. Alas, these dalliances were all too brief, and before long I was back to finding Post-it notes stuck to the bottoms of my shoes. So much for organization.

Could **The Noble Planner** help someone like me? Or you? Yes, yes, and yes! Gregg Harris has come up with a planning system that far outshines the other big guys on the block. The difference is that he fully bases his method on the truths of Scripture. You'll learn how loving God with all your heart, soul, mind, and strength can translate into specific purposes, goals, plans, and actions. You'll discover the ultimate in team management techniques as Gregg teaches from Genesis, Chapter 1. You'll understand how planning on Sunday afternoon, "in the afterglow of worship" can lead to a week that's focused and centered. This goes way beyond keeping track of dentist appointments.

Your starter kit contains the binder, seven-hole-punched like most day planners, and a supply of basic forms to set up your system. The 38 pages of instructions lead you through the process of setting up your system. You're given sample copies of all the basic forms. Some of these will be more or less useful to you depending on your situation. You get two months worth of two-page-per-day and two-page-per-week calendar pages. After using them, you'll need to choose your preferred style and then order

The Noble Planner

Starter package in 7-ring binder with 2-pages-per-day, $89.95. 2-pages-per-week starter package, $67.95. Starter package conversion kit (without binder) 2-pages-per-day, $59.95. 2-pages-per-week, $49.95. 2-pages-per-day daily planner pages, $24.95. Week-in-view weekly planner pages, $14.95. Shipping extra.
Noble Publishing Associates, OR. (800) 225-5259, *www.noblepublishing.com*

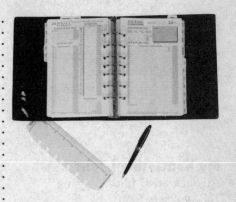

a year's supply to fill out your binder. The gorgeous binder even has room to store your wallet and cash. Bet you won't be tempted to forget it now! If you already have a planner cover, you can ordering just the forms themselves. Some of what's available:

- Sermon notes
- Inductive Bible study
- Business expenses
- Detailed project and goal planning
- Relationship maintenance
- Communication log
- Household records
- Honey-do list
- A note-keeping system that actually makes sense.

Although not specifically a homeschool planner, using this to organize the "non-school" part of life would put your homeschool miles ahead. As for me and my Noble Planner, well, I can already sense a long-term relationship in store for both of us. *Renee Mathis*

Portfolio Systems

One problem with "planner" systems is that they combine your personal requirements (keeping track of or deciding what your children should do) with other people's requirements (proving to family members and government officials that your homeschool program is legal, educationally sound, and fat-free). Generally, your rule of thumb should be

(1) **Do the planning or record keeping *you* feel is necessary** to help you keep track of your educational program. Don't overdo it; your job is home teaching, not Administrator of Public Records.
(2) **Add anything impressive that pops up.** Did your fifth-grader get 700s on the SAT? Did she win the science fair grand prize? Is he Paper Carrier of the Month? Did she write a three-page report on how chocolate bars are made? Standardized test scores, contests, any lengthy written work, any major science or crafts projects, any outside jobs or volunteering— this is the stuff you should keep. Not just because it will impress the neighbors, but because your child will enjoy sharing this with his or her own children some day.

Take one hanging file folder (or catalog-sized envelope, or artist's portfolio, or photo scrapbook, or box, or all the above). Place your child's dated work in this container. File away. It's done!

The portfolio system is one good way to document your child's work. Many states have dignified the portfolio system with the same status as a planner or journaling system. If you can show the authorities what your child did, plus perhaps some good test scores, they'll be satisfied.

The trick here is to not let the portfolio swallow your house. The problem is that your child's most creative work just won't fit in a few square feet. A few dinosaur dioramas and fischertechnik robotic creations will overflow any decent-sized portfolio.

The solution: Take pictures or videos of sizable projects. Date them (announce the date on a video) and file in your portfolio. Then dispose of the masterwork itself in humane fashion when it has outlived its usefulness.

Simplified Homeschool Record Keeping

Parents. $3.95 plus $2 shipping.
JoyceHerzog.com, CA.
(800) 745-8212, www.joyceherzog.com.

My Homeschool Year

All ages. $8.95 plus shipping.
The Sycamore Tree, CA.
(800) 779-6750,
www.sycamoretree.com.

By homeschool author Joyce Herzog, **Simplified Homeschool Record Keeping** tells how to keep a notebook/portfolio for all ages. General divider headings, plus a sample list of topics for each grade from K–6. This scope and sequence makes a great guideline for unit studies as well. Junior high and up have a page for suggested topics to include in a Lifetime Notebook. 16 pages.

Memories Systems

Okay, so one of the drawbacks of homeschooling has been that your children don't get a yearbook with pictures of their school, teachers, friends, clubs, etc. in it. Some large support groups now band together to have yearbook pictures taken. If you don't live in an area with a large support group, or if your group isn't into yearbook mode yet, **My Homeschool Year** is the solution to this problem.

The oversized book is printed on sturdy card stock and comb-bound so it will lie flat when open. The cover has a charming color drawing of a home with several children and a cat peeking out of the windows, with the Bible verse Joshua 24:15 printed beneath it. The rest of the black-and-white pages have lots of space for you or your child to paste photos and other memorabilia. Each page has a title and some pen-and-ink drawings near the edge.

Topics include My Family, My Chores, Holidays, Things I Like to Do, Special Friends, Subjects I Studied, Books I Used for School, Sports, Field Trips, Favorite Bible Verses, Some of My Best Work, Photographs and Autographs.

The title page has blank lines for your child to fill in his or her name and the year, as well as a spot for a picture. Thus, the book is more suited to use by a single child rather than a family; families with more than one child will probably want a copy for each child.

My Homeschool Year seems to be intended to be used more like a scrapbook than a portfolio, since at least half of the pages have non-academic topics. There are few totally blank pages, but titles could be altered or covered over if you find them limiting. *Melissa Worcester*

Software Planners

The first thing you notice when looking at homeschool software-based planners is how many there are now. The second thing you notice is how alike their names are. I guess there are only so many ways to combine the words "organize," "plan," "record," "journal," and "homeschool."

PC owners are in luck, with ten programs to chose from. Macintosh users have a few, as well.

Since all of these are online, and most offer demos or online tours, I suggest you pick those that sound most promising and then check them out online.

e-Home Journal 1.0

Parents. $28.95. Win 95/98/2000/ME. Windows 2000 users, check website support page for special ordering and installation instructions.
Innate Source, CO.
(877) 646-6900,
www.e-homejournal.com.

The **e-Home Journal 1.0** is a homeschool planner, record keeper, time and test keeper, previewer, reporter, and archiver that can easily handle up to eight students' records (its Microsoft Access-based database slows down with each student you add over this number). You can enter all of your information and then let this software keep track of everything. It will generate reports for you. You can archive all of your records at the end of the year and still use this planner for the next year. That makes this software very reasonable in price.

Basically, the e-Home Journal replaces all of your planning and record-keeping paper work. Navigation is easily done on pull down arrows for students, subjects, week, etc. Separate Planning and Recordkeeping modules let you make plans and then record what actually happened (since plans often change!). The colors are a gray with pink and white contrasting colors, which is not uncomfortable on your eyes. There are many helps included within the software to make it easy on the user.

It is obvious this software was designed by a homeschooler. You can even keep records of how long your child spends on each subject—useful in states that require this information. Repetitive entries only have to be entered once. Even so, I found that at times the initial setup of each student is somewhat monotonous.

On initial installation a file has to be loaded separately, which is not really hard, just a hassle. This software runs without the CD. It is a one-time installation. You do need to back up all data.

The e-Home Journal comes with a very helpful user's guide that should answer most of your questions. In the back of the guide is an e-mail address if you experience technical problems. *Tammy Campbell*

If you own a PC, this next homeschool recordkeeper might make you feel like you're in hog heaven. **Edu-Track Home School** tries hard to include all the best features of other systems while being super easy to use. It even has a version that works on a handheld Palm organizer, if you're so inclined.

You start by following the ten-step Setup Wizard. School data, student data, and lessons and activities are all very easy to enter. A "repeating activities" feature lets you set up hundreds of lessons (e.g., Math at 10 A.M. for a whole semester) in seconds. Unit studies are provided for: In fact, you can even use one unit study as a template for the next!

What goes *in* is one thing. What comes *out* is another. In the case of Edu-Track Home School, you can print over 80 built-in reports, including progress reports, activity summaries, lessons & assignments, student data tracking, fill-in forms of all kinds, report cards and diplomas, and dozens of awards & certificates. Topping it all off is the ability to print very impressive transcripts that include everything a "real" school transcript does.

Search for "lost" records, sort on any category, track hours and attendance, and lots more. Edu-Track Home School will calculate hours, grades, percentages, credits, and Grade Point Averages for you. You can instantly view each student's progress for user-defined subjects, courses, grade-level, and core vs. non-core studies—a real help in states that require this information.

If you're the type who really likes to keep *detailed* records, you'll love the Teacher's Journal and File Cabinet features. Each include a built-in word processor that allows you to bold, underline, tab, import pictures, change fonts, make bulletized lists, and lots more. The Journal is for creating and organizing entries by day, while the File Cabinet lets you create and organize entries by categories *you* define. One suggested use of the File Cabinet: Organize your educational Web links.

When your whole homeschool life is collected in one planner, you'll want to back it up frequently. Edu-Track Home Schooler even makes this easier, with a "1-Click" backup and restore feature. You can back up to a hard drive, floppy disk, Zip disk, CD-R, CD-RW, DVD-RW, or a network shared disk—and it takes about ten seconds.

Edu-Track Home School

Parents. Homeschool version, $59. Add $20 for Palm version. One year unlimited upgrades, $15 (downloaded version only). Bound Help manual, $25. Free e-Help. Demo CD-ROM, $5. Pentium and up, Windows 95 and up. Handheld version requires Palm compatible. *ConTECH Solutions, Inc., MO. www.edu-track.net.*

So, if you have a PC and like to keep *very* complete records, this software planner is one you should check out.

Home School Easy Records 2.0

Parents. $39.95 plus $3 shipping. Windows 95 and up.
DataPlus Solutions, CO. (888) 328-7587, www.dataplus.biz/HER.

Homeschooling dad Vince Dugar had a need for a good multi-purpose record-keeping program. Since he couldn't find one on the market to suit his needs, he created one from scratch. (Well, not completely from scratch; **Homeschool Easy Records** is based on the Microsoft Access database platform.)

This program is not extremely flashy. No glitzy animated startup screens. But it does have a lot of depth and capability, and allows for flexibility in customization (e.g., setting up summer school and weekend schooling days). This program keeps almost all of your records in one place, and with its automatic data backup and restore capabilities, the data will be secure.

There is a fair amount of setup involved, but the program walks you through it, step-by-step.

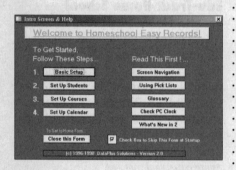

1. **Basic Setup.** You input the starting and ending dates of the current school year, the number of hours per day set aside for school, and the grading scale.
2. **Setup Students.** You enter the names of your children, the students, into the form and assign them a unique ID number.
3. **Setup Courses.** You enter information about each course subject the students are taking, such as the course name, number of credits, and any textbooks and materials and special notes about the course.
4. **Setup Calendar.** You enter special school days and holidays into the school calendar—based on the "quarter" system.

If this seems daunting, plenty of setup help and assistance is available, from the 50-page printed manual that comes with your CD-ROM or diskette to the pop-up windows and "Help Tips" boxes throughout the program.

Once the initial setup has been done, keeping records up-to-date is fairly easy. The commonly used features are accessible from the "Home Form." The options are:

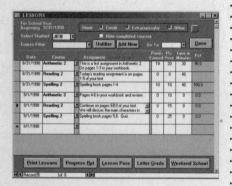

- **Lessons.** Here you enter information for each lesson, including the date, the particular assignment, and the number of points possible.
- **Reports.** This is a very handy feature, and part of the heart of Easy Records. There are five different Report options: Progress Report, Report Card, Course/Curriculum Report, School Calendar Report, and Transcript. All nicely formatted. Organized parents especially will like being able to print out individualized weekly lesson plans for each student.
- **Calendar/Attendance.** Here you can modify the school calendar by adding any special days, and note which days the student misses.
- **Quit.** Close down the program and save the files.

Home School Easy Records will certainly make the administrative side of your homeschool more organized, especially for those in states with comprehensive record-keeping regulations for homeschoolers. To top it all off, there is a 90-day money-back guarantee. *Christopher Thorne*

If you're needing a *little* assistance in the organizing arena, and don't want to keep buying printed organizers, here's a CD that could help. The **Home School Manual 2000 CD-ROM** is the twin of Ted Wade's book in software form. Among its 62 chapters on everything from the basics of homeschooling and inspiring motivation to teaching subjects and finding what Dads can do, plus (if you're online) links to hundreds of publishers, home school organizations, sites recommended for learning activities, etc., you'll find 17 printable forms. In other words, this is not an organizer you fill in electronically, but a source of forms you can print and then fill in with pen or pencil.

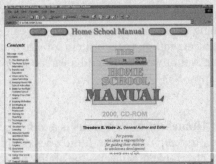

Your autoplay feature should automatically bring up this e-book's intro window, allowing quick access to the manual, the forms, extra information and instruction, and Gazelle's website. (The link takes you to www. hoofprint.com, which is incorrect. The correct one is www.gazellepublications. com.) No installation is necessary for most of the information.

Viewing the forms requires either a word processor or a browser. The best choice is to use your word processor, which gives you the advantage of typing into the form, changing the font style, or even adding graphics rather than just writing on a generic printed form. The forms incorporated on this CD include: Master schedule, Household responsibilities, Weekly home management plans, Daily responsibilities, Individual evaluation, Curriculum sources, Curriculum calendar, Subject or unit worksheet, Weekly plans and progress, Weekly studies log, Grade and attendance record, Attendance log & evaluation summary, Books read (young children), Books read, Field trip plans, Standardized or achievement test, and Solving a problem.

With computer access, you can print all the forms your heart desires over and over again. For those who like to fill their notebooks with lots of forms, be sure to check this one out. *Judy Scott*

The **Home School ORGANIZE** organizer first came out in 1998 and has only been updated slightly since. If you like to have everything planned out ahead of time, or you've been driven to chore charts so your kids will do their share, here is a product that can ease the paperwork involved. It provides five different forms, as well as chores charts for your kids and a wonderful resource-tracker. As a bare-bones product, it won't have everything you want, but the author is eager for suggestions for future releases.

Home School ORGANIZE generates lesson plans, chore charts, unit study theme charts, weekly planners, and menu planners. Text screens prompt you for information before you print a form. I found it hard to answer some of the prompts without seeing the way the form was organized first, so I was glad there were some samples to print. It would have been easier if there were illustrations in the documentation, or better yet, previews on the screen. The program does let you enter information into the lesson plan forms, allowing some degree of customization. A good spreadsheet program would give you more flexibility, but if you don't have one, this might give you something to start with.

The resource tracker, on the other hand, is very well designed. With a little initial work in entering the hundreds (thousands?) of books, magazines, videos, and computer programs you've acquired since you started

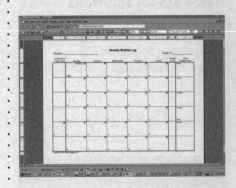

homeschooling, you'll never again have to wonder who you loaned something to or where you stored it. You can print reports sorted by location, subject, author, type, or item, or you can get a list of items on loan. Now, if the author would just add a way to keep track of *borrowed* items, I'd be happy. *Kim O'Hara*

Home School Solutions

Parents. $35. Windows 95/98. 486 and up.
Home School Solutions, IL.
www.homeschool.solutions.com.

Homeschool Solutions is another popular PC-based homeschool record-keeping system. It includes many of the most-requested features of an electronic organizer—the ability to "repeat" data from form to form, grade averaging, GPA calculation and transcripts, onscreen help—and some extras, such as optional password protection (to keep the kiddies from accidentally wiping out all your data) and a Continuing Education screen for keeping track of educational events and courses you attend.

A School Information screen lets you add very comprehensive data about your homeschool—much more than just name and contact information. You can also log information about each "instructor" (helpful if you use tutors and outside classes).

The Students screen is where you store the typical information that appears on transcripts (name, address, birthdate, Social Security number, and grade level).

Click open separate windows to log attendance, courses, books read, video tapes viewed, CDs/audiotapes listened to, software used, educational games played, field trips, grades, expenses, long term goals, and short term goals. Want to keep track of borrowed and loaned items? There's a screen for that, too.

That's nice, but what you really need is to store lesson assignments and hours spent "on task." A year's worth of assignments can be entered for each child. You can choose the starting and ending date for each course—handy!

If you like to grocery shop with a checklist of everything you are likely to buy, just checking off what you're getting this time, you should like the School Supply List screen. Like my grocery list, it comes set up with a list of suggested supplies. Simply move any of these you wish to a new list and then add any items not on the original list. Print it out and take it when you go to the teacher's store!

The program also allows you to enter all sorts of detailed information about your Friends and Contacts. This may not be as important if you already have some sort of computerized address book.

Each student can have a list of courses that they are taking during a school term. For each course, you can also set the starting and ending dates in the lesson planner.

You can take a tour of the program online, and also download a free 30-day trial version.

HomeSchool Planner 2.1

Parents. $20 for registering emailed version. Add $3 if you want diskette mailed to you. Mac OS 6.0.7 and up.
France & Associates, CO. (303) 841-5003, www.franceandassociates.net.

If you're a Macintosh owner who doesn't have or want OSX, your choice comes down to this: the **HomeSchool Planner**. (If you're an OSX user, check out the next review, of a product with a very similar name but a totally different interface.)

HomeSchool Planner has a very simple "hypercard" look to it. Data is very easy to enter. You can you assign lessons and activities on any day of the week and any hour of the day. You can also enter starting and ending times, and the software will automatically calculate the duration of the activity. Entering grades is easy, and the program automatically calculates GPAs. You can print out quarterly, semester, or yearly reports.

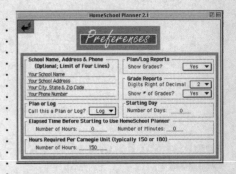

If you live in a state that requires you to keep track of how many hours are spent teaching individual subjects, the program will provide these reports for you as well.

In the newest edition, you can assign "weights" to assignments. So, for example, a midterm could be 20 percent of the grade, while daily quizzes are 1 percent apiece.

Like other popular programs, it has a "repeating entry" feature that allows you to copy one day's plan to as many other days as you wish, and one student's plan to another. You can then just update any parts of the plan that differ from student to student.

Like field trips? You can keep quite extensive notes on each one with this program.

Library lover? Keep track of the books your children have read, including title, author, date finished, and number of pages.

High-school students can keep track of Carnegie units earned. Just tell the program how many hours the student must complete per subject to earn a Carnegie unit.

In short, while this does not have every single "bell and whistle" of the most advanced PC programs, it will do the job. It won't organize your whole life, but it will organize your homeschool.

Before you run to your computer to buy this planner, plant yourself in a chair and see what **Homeschool Planner and Portfolio 2.0** can do for you. Refreshingly user-friendly, this planner is made for those who prefer not to do their record keeping with paper and pencil. Even so, you have the option of printing off every worksheet if the need arises.

After the quick install, you are welcomed by a title page that's pleasing to the eye. Just a touch of colorful graphics with a school theme has been added to keep your tasks from becoming monotonous. The first thing on the agenda is to add your students. A student profile provides room for a full name, current age and grade, birthdate, health record, and anything else you care to stick in.

Each student has his own set of worksheets on which you record. These include: Daily Lesson Plan, Monthly Lesson Plan, Books Read, Curriculum, Resources Used, Educational Videos, Extracurricular Activities, Classes, Field Trips, Report Card, Sports, and Class Credits. In addition to these, you may create your own worksheets. If there are some you don't want or need, a Show/Hide feature lets you display the ones of your choice. No information is shared, so if you take your three kids on a field trip, you'll need to enter the same info three times—once for each child.

If that's not enough to keep you organized, Esposoft also added a directory, calendar, to-do list, and journal. The directory is akin to a computerized phone book with additional entry fields for email, website addresses, and personal notes. Your monthly schedule is easy to see with the calendar feature. Keep track of meetings, music lessons, sports activities, and more. Entering them is even easier. Just click your cursor on the date you wish to enter an activity and begin typing. The to-do list is a two-column worksheet. The left column has a checkbox and the right column is where you put the to-do item. Lastly, the journal is a blank slate where you may keep anything you wish. No dates or checkboxes—just a plain notepad.

All in all, I would highly recommend this planner. It's simple and easy to use and makes record keeping enjoyable. The only drawback that bothered

Homeschool Planner and Portfolio 2.0

Parents. $19.95 plus $4 shipping. Windows 95 and up (except NT). Version 2.2 runs on Mac OSX and Windows.
Esposoft. www.esposoft.com.

me was the inability to install this software to a desired directory. It is automatically put on your C drive. I have been informed, though, that will be an option in the next version. *Judy Scott*

Version 2.2 includes new features that allow grade and time calculation.

Other new features being released shortly include: transcripts, attendance calculation, and improved journal capabilities. Purchasers receive regular updates for free as they become available.

HomeSchool Record v2.0 for Windows

Parents. $39.95. Win 98.
Digital Information Guild, MD. 866-413-0524 . HomeSchoolTech.com.

School Tool Lesson Planner

Parents. $20 (download) or $30 (postpaid CD-ROM). 486 or better, Win 95/98/NT.
Red 17 Development, GA.
(404) 918-1464,
www.red-17.com/stlp.htm.

Records, records, and more records! With **HomeSchool Record v2.0**, you have in your hands just about the only software you'll need to keep track of every resource or activity you could possibly think of for your homeschool students. This is one major database! And three main working windows are all it takes.

Starting off, you select what you want to do—use the Recorder, Reporter, or the Daily Planner. The Recorder is the obvious first choice if the database is empty. This window allows you to enter anything—no joke. Nine customizable categories cover pertinent info: student name, activity type, work product, grade level, goals, subject, and resource media type, copyright date, and author. Some of these fields already have entries, but the great thing is—they are editable. For example, if you watched a video, you might want to select that for your activity. But when you find that term not listed, no problem. Just select "add new" and put it in. Records can be saved as an activity, a work product, or educational resource. There are also fields to enter activity length, evaluation (grade), activity date, Carnegie Units, and description. And if you forget how to do something, check out the "How Do I?" menu option.

Once you've created several records, you are able to have some fun with the next feature, the Reporter. Want to see one student's work for the month? You got it. How about all resources related to one particular activity? It's right there. Maybe you need a list of all field trips that were science-oriented. Piece of cake!

Now let's take it one step further with the Daily Planner. With this, you can organize everyone's activities, enabling you to keep track of who's doing what when. You may view all the entries, only those for specific names you select, or just the ones with a certain subject(s). An individual daily list may also be printed out for each student as a reminder of the day's requirements—nice touch.

Although HomeSchool Record has no bells or whistles for those fun-loving personalities, I don't think they'll be missed. The time and effort that's saved coupled with the convenience of stress-free reporting overshadows any colorful graphics or fancy interface you might find in other applications. It's easy to get up-and-running with this one. *Judy Scott*

Organizing lessons in your homeschool can be difficult, especially when you don't have the knack for organization. **School Tool Lesson Planner** tries to help in these situations by allowing you to assign lessons and book reading lists to each of your children via the computer.

You start by entering in your school name and your children's information. You then move on to the Core Information. Here is where you show all subjects, in as much detail as you want, list your resources for each (books, software, etc.), and create your lessons by resource. The lessons include fields for the name, activity, level, objective, evaluation, notes, and supplies.

The template manager is next, where you create a week's worth of lessons for your child from your previously created lessons. The lesson templates can then be assigned for any week you wish. Reading lists can be created and assigned here as well.

Reports include attendance (even in official format if submission is necessary), a student schedule, and a supply list, and you can even print your templates.

Keying in the information is time-consuming, and many will find it easier to continue to use your current, manual methods. The first day of the week used is Monday, and it cannot be changed. I did like the list of resources. It helps you remember little-used resources, because when you create a template, there you see it listed. Another good feature is exporting and importing templates to share between friends.

In reviewing the program, I found many glitches. Some were very frustrating. Most major problems were taken care of when I downloaded the update from the website—others still need correction. The company has done a good job discussing these problems and trying to come up with solutions. *Jo Dee Soles*

Do you wish you had a form for nearly every possible homeschool-related topic you could think of? If so, take a good look at the rundown on this collection. **The Ultimate Homeschool Planner** now includes **The Ultimate Homeschool Plan Book Forms & Worksheets CD**. All the forms located within the Planner binder have been placed on a CD, so now you have the capability of changing and modifying them to your heart's desire. Try using a different font or even adding graphics from your computer. All you need is Microsoft Word 97 or better. No installation is necessary, which makes getting started a breeze. And if you don't have very many fonts, there are 40 on the CD for you to install on your computer by following the simple directions. These allow you to view the worksheets as originally designed.

Of the 53 forms, you'll find some not-so-common along with the typical: student knowledge inventory, student school questionnaire, goal planning, goal overview by subject template, special events, weekly planning sheet by subject, week at a glance, daily planning detail, books to consider for next year's schooling, wish list, future study, supply list, expense summary, daily learning log, attendance for the month, high school record, assessment template, unit study outline, homework card, field trip summary, nature journal, food log, and many more.

Some of the more uncommon ones include:

- **The Mom's Keeping It All Together Sheet.** This form has spaces to put appointments for the day and separate sections for menu planning, school notes, just for me, a to-do list, and what needs to be done in the home.
- **Week in Review.** Record the week's accomplishments for one student by filling in what was done, new skills learned, where improvement was seen, areas needing more work, and ideas for the following week.
- **Creating an Action Plan.** Get help in organizing your household by listing your top organizational nightmares and dreams and then implementing the four-step process described in the binder.

Within the pages of the binder, you'll find form-usage instructions at the beginning of each of the five sections: getting started, curriculum planning, logging your learning, templates & units, and home management.

At first glance you may be tempted to put this system back down. No frills, few graphics, lots of words. But don't let that sway you. Because whether or not forms are your thing, chances are you'll find something very useful in this treasure trove of organizational remedies. *Judy Scott*

The Ultimate Homeschool Planner with The Ultimate Homeschool Plan Book Forms & Worksheets CD
Parents. $29.95. Windows 95 and up, Microsoft Word 97 and up. *Champion Press, Ltd., WI. (414) 540-9873. www.championpress.com*

Making Your Own Planner

If you really want the ultimate in customized planners, don't overlook the option of making your own. It's not as hard as you might think. With a word processor or typewriter, felt-tip pen, and some clip art, you can do a very nice job as well. Make the desired number of copies and you're in business. Once you've decided on the forms that best suit your family, you can decide whether you want to go the loose-leaf notebook approach or spiral bound.

Your first decision: "To bind or not to bind?" Three-ring binders are great for adding your own materials (support group newsletters and mailing lists, for example) and customizing the number of pages. You are usually given permission to reproduce the forms within your family as well. Unfortunately they can also be bulky, and pages tend to rip out. Spiral-bound volumes, on the other hand, often aren't as durable (get out the "jelly-proof" contact paper) but they are more portable. If you go the spiral-bound route, you'll also need to re-invest every year in a new planner.

Just a suggestion: If you're buying a notebook, splurge and make it one you really like! This is going to be your friend and constant companion day in and day out, so save the office rejects for the kids to play with.

While we may not be creating miniature classrooms in our dining rooms, there is no reason not to have the best tools available at our disposable. Nothing is more frustrating than having to search in umpteen different drawers and cabinets to find your teaching materials (or your HSLDA membership number, or the name of the person who's going to test your kids, or the address of that catalog you've been meaning to send away for . . .). The costs you pay for being organized in the present can pay off many times over in the future!

Renee Mathis

Mary's Mini System

The very simplest way to plan is to not use planners at all. For all courses involving workbooks, I do the following:

1. **Write the child's name** on the front of the book or on the title page.
2. **Calculate how many pages** per school day he must do to finish the book in the allotted time. If it's to be completed in one school year, divide the pages by 160 school days.
3. **Write how many pages per day** are to be completed on the cover or title page.

You wind up with something that looks like this: "Franklin, 3 pages/day." Then all you have to do is figure out which day of the school year it is. "We're on the first day of the second week, so this is Day 6. He is supposed to do 3 pages a day, so he should have finished page 18 by the end of the school day."

Once you have written the daily page allotment on each workbook, all you have to do is keep track of which school week it is. Then when the child finishes the workbook, write the completion date on the cover and file the book on a shelf in the basement along with all the other completed school workbooks. If anyone ever wants to check out your homeschool, the sheer boredom of evaluating dozens of ratty workbooks will elicit the response you're looking for: "Never mind, I can see you've been doing a lot of schoolwork here." For better results, also make sure to give each child a bulletin board where he can pin up his ribbons from the math competition, science fair, art show, and whatever other homeschool events he enters. For best results, combine with yearly standardized testing, so you can also demonstrate the children's actual achievement levels, if asked. Easy!

Hourly Logs

Some states require you to log the hours each child spends on schoolwork. Missouri, the worst in this regard, requires you to log core academic subjects differently from non-core subjects, and hours spent at home separately from hours spent on field trips. If you're stuck with a situation like this, the best thing to do is ask your local support-group or state leader what forms (or ideally, software) they recommend homeschoolers use in your state, or to use one of the software systems reviewed above that supports tracking subjects by hours.

PART 8

Testing & Standards

Monique Harris, a 17-year-old homeschooler from Vilonia, TX, received a perfect 1600 on the SAT, and 34 out of 36 on the ACT. She's a National Merit Finalist, with a scholarship of $9,000 per year for four years. She also received the Governor's Distinguished Scholarship, which pays for complete tuition, room and board, and all mandatory expenses for four years of college. While still deciding, Monique is considering medical college.

Monique has homeschooled for her entire life, except for two years of high school. She found that "regular" school didn't offer any additional academic challenges, so she home-schooled this last year again, getting her lessons over quickly and saving time for other worthwhile activities. Monique has volunteered with Family Council, filing papers, taking notes, and performing legal research. She has been playing piano for years and has attended the Pensacola Music Academy camp for the last three summers. Monique now gives piano lessons. It's no wonder the world's beating a path to her door!

CHAPTER 41

National & State Standards

Testing your child to see how well he has learned what he needs to know. What could be controversial about that?

As it turns out, a major national and state-by-state battle is raging over how children should be tested and evaluated. This is a battle with more than two opposing sides. On one side are those who believe that all testing is innately unfair and unreliable, possibly racist, and that it distorts the teaching process. On another side are those who believe we should have a national curriculum and that the best way to achieve this is to force all children to take the same tests, thus forcing teachers in turn to spend the bulk of their time teaching the content and attitudes that will be tested. On the third corner of the triangle are parents and educators who find value in the traditional standardized test, provided parents choose if and when such tests are taken, but who are very wary of the drive toward state standards and criteria-referenced tests.

Why does any of this matter? Because he who controls the tests controls the curriculum . . . and homeschool freedom depends on your right to control your child's curriculum.

Achievement Tests vs. State Assessment Tests

Most parents remember when they were herded into the cafeteria or library for their annual group testing. These tests were used to analyze each student's strengths and weaknesses in specific academic areas as well as their overall performance. Test results also compared individuals with other students locally and nationally. Tests such as these, including the Iowa Test of Basic Skills, the California Achievement Test, and the Stanford Achievement Test, have long been utilized as validated measures of student achievement.

Today, when students miss classroom instruction to take time-intensive state assessment tests, parents automatically think that their children will be taking the same achievement test that they took 30 years ago. However, these new state assessment tests, which have become the center of a national controversy, represent a radical departure from the kind of tests that are familiar to parents.

What's in a Norm?

Children take one of two types of standardized test, one "norm-referenced," the other "criteria-referenced." Although those names have an arcane ring, most parents are familiar with how the exams differ. **Norm-referenced tests give percentile scores**, as when a student is said to be at the 40th percentile; that means the child did better than 40 percent of a sample of students who took the test in an earlier, base year, and worse than 60 percent.

Criteria-referenced tests, on the other hand, tell if a student has learned the assigned curriculum: a child who meets the state's standard is termed "proficient," one at a higher standard is "advanced," one at a lower standard is "basic," and one even lower is "below basic."

The difference between the two exams has now become important, because a group of liberal Democratic senators are insisting that the new federal education law be interpreted as requiring the use of criteria-referenced tests.

—New York Times, *May 22, 2002*

The portion of this chapter beginning on the previous page with the section header "Achievement Tests v. State Assessment Tests" and continuing up to the header "The Standards Testing Movement" is from the *Education Advocate* of May/June 2000 and used by permission. This publication of Commonwealth Education Associates is put out by every day folks in the trenches who have done the work of researching this and other issues on behalf of families like yours and mine. They deserve a round of applause, don't you think?

How Are Achievement and Assessment Tests Different?

The **Iowa, California and Stanford achievement tests** measure the attainment of knowledge and skill using questions that cover essential academic material for each specific grade level. Historically, the multiple-choice tests are objectively scored by machines that read the answers entered in bubbles with #2 pencils. These tests are nationally normed so that students are compared across the country. Scores are reported in simple local and national percentile rankings, so that each student is ranked using a good cross-section of U.S. students the same age. Specific skills in reading, math, social studies and science are scored individually, including spelling, capitalization, punctuation, maps and diagrams, math concepts, estimation, etc.

State assessment tests determine student performance relative to predetermined criteria with scoring that is scaled. While some parts of the test are objectively scored, open-ended math and reading questions are subjectively scored. Subjective scoring can reflect various interpretations by the individual scorers. Scores are based on the degree to which students meet the *current* criteria, which makes it difficult to compare scores from year to year. Scores often do not compare students across a school district or the nation.

The Pennsylvania System of School *Assessment* (PSSA) is the state *assessment* test taken by almost all Pennsylvania students in grades 5, 8, and 11. Requiring up to ten or more hours to take, the *assessment* tests includes objective and open-ended questions. Student results are reported 5 or 6 months later as a single score in reading and a single score in math with matching state percentiles. These results are so general that they cannot be used to identify individual student strengths and weaknesses. The State, however, will use these scores to categorize student proficiency as *below-basic, basic, proficient,* or *advanced.* The composite results of an individual school are compared with *only* 19 other Pennsylvania schools with similar social and economic characteristics.

Pennsylvania is not alone in the development of state assessment tests. According to *Education Week* (5/3/00), over 50 percent of states now use assessment test scores to make decisions on student promotion and/or graduation as well as school and teacher incentive rewards. As this high-stakes testing trend spreads, so do the concerns of students, teachers, administrators and parents. In fact, the April 2000, *American School Board Journal* warns of the "onslaught of future lawsuits from teachers who are fired and students who are denied diplomas because of high-stakes assessment tests."

What's Happening Across the Country?

- **Massachusetts:** A *student* boycott of the state assessment test captured the national headlines this spring. Students are protesting the use of one single snapshot test as the gatekeeper for promotion and graduation.
- **Wisconsin:** Parents worked together to have the Wisconsin state assessment repealed as a graduation requirement.
- **Minnesota:** An outcry against an invasive essay question caused school administrators to defy the state mandates and pull the test. The writing prompt asked students, "If you could change one thing about yourself, what would it be?" Many believed that such questions step over the academic line into the realm of psychology and have no place in a state mandated test.

- **Texas:** In 1999, parents sued over the Texas Assessment of Academic Skills, claiming it violates the constitutional and civil rights of black and Hispanic students.
- **New York City and Austin, Texas:** Allegations of widespread cheating has brought attention to administrators who don't allow poorer performing students to take the tests, change student answers, and even provide questions to the students before the test.

What Do Education Professionals Think?

At the annual meeting of the American Education Research Association in New Orleans, scholars expressed their concerns that rather than improving student learning, these high-stakes tests are narrowing the curriculum as teachers spend inordinate time drilling and teaching-to-the-test.

Pressure on teachers and administrators to constantly improve test results has led to extreme measures. According to *Education USA* (1/99), "over 16,000 schools have either curtailed or eliminated recess stating that more time is needed to focus on the requirements."

Unpatriotic Civics "Standards"

Behind frequent protestations by public officials about local control of the schools, a federal curriculum has been quietly imposed by law. All the pieces are now in place for this major goal of the Clinton Administration. And it's all hiding behind that good conservative word "standards." . . .

In a remarkable inclusion of special-interest legislation, the third law named and funded a private organization, the Center for Civic Education (CCE), to develop the national standards for teaching civics and government. This cozy relationship was reconfirmed in the 2002 education law called "Leave No Child Behind" and means that CCE is empowered, with the force of federal law and a stream of taxpayers' money, to decide what is taught in our nation's schools about civics and government.

CCE produced a 180-page volume called *National Standards for Civics and Government,* plus textbooks, teacher's guides and other materials for elementary, middle, and high school levels. This great quantity of words is short on facts but long on inculcating attitudes.

CCE's textbook called *We the People: The Citizen and the Constitution* admits a peculiar aversion to facts: "The primary purpose of this text is not to fill your head with a lot of facts about American history and geography. Knowledge of the facts is important but only insofar as it deepens your understanding of the American Constitutional system and its development."

"Deepens your understanding," that is, of a pre-scribed worldview without cluttering your mind with hard facts about American history and what is actually in the U.S. Constitution. For example, the fact that the U.S. Constitution contains a Second Amendment doesn't exist in the book called *Standards.* Many pages of *Standards* are devoted to the Bill of Rights but, funny thing, the Second Amendment is completely censored out.

The 180 pages of *Standards,* of course, contain much that is informative, but the information is peripheral to the selling of a political agenda designed to change the student. The book admits that *Standards* is trying to teach "certain dispositions or traits of character."

One major theme is a put-down of allegiance to national sovereignty. . . .

Six of the eight references to national sovereignty use the same curious wording: "The world is divided into nation-states that claim sovereignty over a defined territory and jurisdiction over everyone within it." Do we only "claim" national sovereignty, or is it a historical fact that we won our national sovereignty in a War of Independence and we jolly well need it to protect ourselves against foreign aggressors? . . .

The last page of *Standards* gives its final advice to the students: Citizens have "the ability to reaffirm or change fundamental constitutional values." Is that what a federal curriculum is all about—changing our constitutional values?

—Phyllis Schlafly Report, *March 2002*

An underlying problem with state assessments is that they are often based on vague and poorly written state standards. According to the Fordham Foundation's *State of State Standards 2000,* "42 states (including Pennsylvania) still hold mediocre or inferior expectations for their K–12 students, at least in most subjects. . . . The news gets bleaker when we look at the next steps: assessments and consequences."

Despite concerns, few educators are opposed to high standards and accountability. However, many believe the use of a single score on a single test on a single day should not be the sole determiner of a child's future. Donald Gatz, writing for *Phi Delta Kappa* (5/00), dislikes using high-stakes tests because they "are poorly constructed, not validated, too hard, politically driven, and shrouded in secrecy."

Controversial state assessment tests are the major trend in today's education. Researchers and state governments "are not willing to give up on the kind of leverage that high-stakes testing programs provide for school reform," according to Debra Viadero of *Education Week* (5/8/00). *This "leverage" refers to the reality that state standards often force schools to revise proven curricula while state assessment tests act as a compliance checklist for those changes. This "leverage" thereby takes away local control of curriculum and accountability.*

What can local school boards do? First, recognize existing problems related to state standards and assessment tests. Second, recognize that other more reliable time-tested student evaluation tools must also be used. *Third, do not abandon the use of national achievement tests, which, according to the Fordham Foundation, "provide exceptionally reliable and valid information about student achievement."* [Emphasis theirs]

The Standards/Testing Movement

States have been forced by federal legislation to participate in the standards movement—developing lists of skills and content required at each grade level. The weapon of enforcement is testing. New tests are being developed that reflect the content of the standards. These tests are supposed to judge student mastery of what is actually being taught rather than the general competence measured by standardized tests of the past. If students are or are not learning (as shown by test scores), schools and teachers are rewarded or penalized. There are two underlying assumptions: that every child is capable of learning the identical information at the same time as every other child, and that all the standards selected by each state are academically sound and worthwhile. If children were programmable robots, the first might be possible. If politics and public pressure played no role in the standards, the second might be possible. The experiences of the left-leaning Coalition for Educational Justice and the right-leaning Kansas State School Board demonstrate the fallout from these two false assumptions.

Leftist Group Decries Standards

On May 8, 2001, the left-leaning Coalition for Educational Justice (CEJ) orchestrated a demonstration against the Los Angeles School Board's use of the Stanford 9 test, labeling it a racist test. They also protested the use of high-stakes testing to dole out monetary rewards and punishments. The basis of CEJ's arguments is that biased tests and unequal school funding are the cause of low test scores among schools serving low-income students of color. Thus, they stand strongly opposed to the increasing use of test scores for determining what schools and teachers get extra money and which lose funding or get taken over by the state.

The remainder of the chapter text (the part not in gray sidebars) is by homeschool pioneer, author, and speaker Cathy Duffy.

Cathy began educating her three sons at home in 1982, graduating the youngest from high school in 1997. She is best known for her books, *The Christian Home Educators' Curriculum Manuals* (two volumes), which she began publishing in 1984. Cathy is also the author of *Government Nannies: The Cradle-to-Grave Agenda of Goals 2000* and *Outcome-Based Education* as well as numerous articles on home education and broader education issues.

Cathy's article can also be found on the main page of Homeschool World at *www.home-school.com.* For the research-minded among you, the online article includes links to the articles it cites.

"Right Wing" School Board Members Cause Brouhaha by Change in Standards

In Kansas, school board members were labeled right-wing radicals in 1999 when they voted to not include questions on macro-evolution in state tests. [Footnote: Macro-evolution means one species changing into another species; micro-evolution means adaptations or changes within species.] Teachers were not forbidden to teach macro-evolution, but it wouldn't be included in a standards-based test. Evolutionists viewed the decision as a challenge to the very fundamentals of science education. As reported in the Kansas City Star of April 11, 1999, Adrian Melott, a University of Kansas physics professor told the board, "I see this as an attack on science in general, not just biology."

CEJ and the Kansas School Board members appear to have little in common on the surface. But their respective battles over testing and standards are merely the tip of the iceberg, illustrating just a few of the problems stemming from school reform efforts centered around development of national standards and high-stakes testing. Problems for private and home-schools promise to be even worse.

Control of Private School Curricula

While the standards and testing movement is certain to create enemies across the political spectrum from far left to far right, it poses the most serious threat to private schools who wish to pursue their own "standards" based on philosophical outlooks and values that differ from that which buttress the standards/testing movement. For example, classical education is the latest movement in private schooling. Many new classical schools have opened in recent years. Their courses of study usually differ dramatically from those of government schools. High-school students study works of Aristotle, Plato, Cicero, Keynes, Marx, and other influential thinkers rather than reading through typical textbooks. They study Latin, logic, and debate. They don't take classes in Conflict Resolution, Sex Education, or Cultural Awareness. They are not well prepared to pass tests that assume

Dumbing Down Standards

When it comes to the standards to which assessments are tied, have we so quickly forgotten the uproar about the federally funded National History Standards of 1995 which omitted or downgraded some of America's greatest achievers and used obscure and third-rate figures to teach diversity revisionism? Those standards were so anti-American they were denounced by the U.S. Senate in a vote of 99 to 1.

Have we so quickly forgotten the national math standards, which were denounced by 200 prestigious mathematicians, including four Nobel Laureates, because they failed to teach basic skills? Their criticisms were published in a full-page ad in the *Washington Post* (11-18-99), but that had no effect on the U.S. Department of Education's determination to induce schools to adopt fuzzy math curricula.

A stated goal of the school reformers is to "narrow the achievement gap." But the gap can be closed by bringing top and bottom together, not necessarily by raising the bottom to a higher level of achievement.

Then there is the announced goal called accountability, a word that cries out to be followed by a preposition and an object. Accountability has no meaning unless one is accountable to someone or something. Federal bureaucrats, plus those who still subscribe to the unpopular Goals 2000/School-to-Work paradigm, want to make the schools accountable to the U.S. Departments of Education and Labor. But what parents want is accountability to parents and local school boards, not to a federal or state agency.

—Phyllis Schlafly Report, *March 2001*

Math "Standards" Give Standards a Bad Name
by Phyllis Schlafly

The U.S. Department of Education last October officially endorsed ten new math courses for grades K–12, calling them "exemplary" or "promising" and urging local school districts to "seriously consider" adopting one of them. The recommended programs were approved by an "expert" panel commissioned by the Department of Education.

But many parents believe that the "experts" are subtracting rather than adding to the skills of schoolchildren. **Parents are starting to realize that "fuzzy" math courses** (variously called "whole math," "new math" or "new new math") **are producing kids who can't do arithmetic**, much less algebra.

Scholars are criticizing the new courses, too. They say that most of the panel's "field reviewers" who made the initial recommendations were teachers, not math experts, and that the panel making the final decisions did not include "active research mathematicians."

Within six weeks of the Department of Education's announcement, **more than 200 mathematicians and scholars banded together to denounce the government-anointed curricula** because they fail to teach basic skills. The group wrote a joint letter to Education Secretary Richard Riley criticizing the "exemplary" programs and asking the Department to reconsider its choices.

The group then published the letter as a full-page ad in the November 18th *Washington Post*. Despite the prestige of the letter's signers, including four Nobel Laureates and two winners of the Fields Medal (the highest mathematics honor), Riley refused to back away from the Department's endorsements.

Riley defended his Department's recommendations because they conform to the so-called "standards" adopted in 1989 by the National Council of Teachers of Mathematics (NCTM). **But the nationally created math "standards" are just as off the mark as the nationally created history standards** that caused such an uproar when they were released in 1995. The history standards were denounced in the U.S. Senate by a vote of 99 to 1, but that didn't faze the educators determined to indoctrinate students with "politically correct" history. After a few cosmetic changes, revisionist history masquerading under the label "standards" has infected nearly all new social studies textbooks.

The schools appear just as determined to force fuzzy math on children despite its obvious failures and the opposition of scholars and parents. In Illinois, parents have clashed with schools over one of these "exemplary" courses called "Everyday Math," or "Chicago Math" because it was produced by the University of Chicago Mathematics Project, complaining that the curriculum neglects basic computation.

Last August, parents in Plano, Texas filed a lawsuit against their school district over another of these Department-approved courses, "Connected Math," accusing the district of failing to give their children basic math instruction. In December, parents in Montgomery County, Maryland kicked up vigorous opposition to Connected Math even though the district was being enticed into using it by the prospect of a $6 million federal grant.

Another of these Department-approved courses, "Mathland," directs the children to meet in small groups and invent their own ways to add, subtract, multiply and divide. It's too bad they don't know that adults wiser than those now in school have already discovered how to add, subtract, multiply and divide.

Critics charge that these fuzzy math programs, which are touted as complying with "standards," do not teach traditional or standard arithmetic at all and actually give the word "standards" a bad name. They are based on such theories as that "process skills" are more important than computational skills and that **correct solutions are not important so long as the student feels good about what he is doing.**

The arguments for fuzzy math are that it is supposed to spare children the rigors of teacher-imposed rules and teach them that all they need is a calculator. Fuzzy math omits drill in basic math facts, fails to systematically build from one math concept to another, and encourages children to work in groups to "discover" math and construct their own math language.

According to mathematician Joel Hass of the University of California at Davis, one of the signers of the letter to Riley, "Saying that we don't need to teach children how to compute now that we have calculators is like saying we don't need to teach them how to draw now that we have cameras or we don't need to teach them how to play music now that we have CD players." Mathematician William G. Quirk, whose career includes teaching 26 different math and computer science courses at three universities, says, **"Nowhere in the NCTM's 258 pages of standards do they suggest that kids should remember any specific math facts."**

Critics complain that failing to teach children the division of fractions precludes their moving on to algebra. David Klein of California State University, another signer of the letter to Riley, said, "In shutting the door to algebra, Connected Math also closes doors to careers in engineering and science."

In 1989 23 percent of freshmen entering California colleges needed remedial help in math. This figure has now risen to 55 percent. If parents want their children to learn arithmetic, they will have to teach them at home.

—Phyllis Schlafly Report, *April 2000*

all students are being taught the same things, but they seem to be better educated than the average government school graduate.

The danger of undermining such private schools with government testing and standards mandates has gone largely unremarked because most families enroll their children in government schools and have little or no interaction with any private schools. However, private schools—a category which includes homeschools and religiously-affiliated schools up through very prestigious prep schools—are valuable not only to those whose children attend such schools, but to the public at large, even though they are largely unaware of this. Why? For one thing, because private schools pose a continual challenge to government-financed schooling. They offer a "product" that is perceived to be significantly different enough from the "free" public schools that many parents make the necessary sacrifices so that their children might attend. Whether those differences are academic, social, religious, ethical, emotional, or physical, many parents pay twice through taxes and tuition for their children to get "a better education."

Such parents seem to believe they are getting value for their money or they wouldn't continue to pay, but the rest of the country also benefits from the competition posed by this alternate "system" of private schools. Yes, it reflects poorly upon a government school when a private school in the same geographic area, serving a similar socio-economic group, produces better-educated graduates, a safer environment, or other temptations for parents to defect to the private school. And this might force some government schools to do a better job than they might without any competition. But the real value of private schools lies in their ability to teach what they believe to be right or best without dictates from the government. They are free to develop a more challenging or alternative curriculum and then let the marketplace decide whether or not they are successful. If they do a good job, they will have students.

It should surprise no one that innovation and creativity is much more common in private schools than government schools. In fact, the most-private schools—homeschools—are the most innovative of all. Why else would so many online education providers first target homeschool students? They understand the openness and flexibility of parents who constantly look for the best methods of providing education for their own children. Homeschoolers can pick and choose from among the wide world of options: traditional texts, programmed learning, student-initiated projects, video courses, computer programs, tutors, group classes, and online learning.

Because of this, homeschools operate as a laboratory for the development of new and unusual content and delivery methods in ways that traditional private schools cannot. And the evidence is clear that homeschooling is producing both academic and personal excellence. As more and more homeschoolers have gone on to college, they have done so well that college recruiters across the country actively court homeschoolers to attend their institutions.

Redefining Education as Vocational Training

The standards/testing movement has the potential to cripple private schooling by constraining it within its own narrow boundaries. Those boundaries are the result of Goals 2000 and School-to-Work (STW) legislation passed in 1994, coupled with other, older efforts from the Departments of Labor and Education to redefine education as "training for the workforce." Documents such as *Learning a Living,* published by the Department of Labor in 1992, have explained the economic necessity of preparing stu-

See Chapter 4 if you'd like to refresh your memory of how the School-to-Work program has redefined "education" to mean only "training for a specific job into which you will be tracked starting in grade 8."

dents to compete in the global economy of the twenty-first century as the justification for educational restructuring. Goals 2000 and STW allowed the federal government to dictate restructuring requirements to the states.

Floretta Dukes McKenzie helps us understand the thinking behind the "school as training" agenda. McKenzie voices support for this view of education in a book *Equity: A Call to Action* published in 1993 by the NEA spinoff organization, Association for Supervision and Curriculum Development. Notice McKenzie's emphasis on economic competition, "marketable skills," and workers as the primary focus of education "equity." She tells us,

> *Educators and policymakers must join forces with other government agencies to bridge the gap between the haves and have-nots. This gap threatens the safety of our cities today, as well as the economic survival of our society into the next century. . . . From a purely economic point of view, failure to pursue educational equity for minority youth is a form of slow suicide. The internationalization of the economy will require an increasing economic competitiveness. . . . We must transcend the common practices of focusing on basic skills and marketable skills for minority students without providing the thinking and learning skills that will help them adapt to the 21st-century career environment. The continued development and use of leading-edge technology will require a high-quality work force. On a more selfish note, the next generation of workers will require three workers to support each person on Social Security. . . . today's older workers must maximize the learning skills and, therefore, the earning skills of tomorrow's minority workers, on whom they will rely for their retirement incomes.*

While McKenzie is on the right track with her recognition of the need for improved "thinking and learning skills," she and others seem to view the purpose only as success in the workforce. Neil Postman labels this educational outlook as "Economic Utility" in his book *The End of Education* (Vintage Books, 1996): "If you pay attention in school, and do your homework, and score well on tests, and behave yourself, you will be rewarded with a well-paying job when you are done. Its driving idea is that the purpose of schooling is to prepare children for competent entry into the economic life of a community."

Contrast this view of "education solely as job preparation" with the idea of "liberal" (in the classical sense) education as described in the Summer 2000 newsletter of Great Books Academy, a new online classical school: "Liberal education is ordered toward making the student a free and happy individual. This freedom and happiness arises within the student as he is freed from ignorance and becomes better equipped to recognize the truth and beauty of the world around him. And it is truth which in turn leads him to freedom and happiness."

A liberal education, as traditionally understood, was designed to produce a wise young adult with a wide breadth of tools for learning and evaluating any new situation or task—the very result politicians and educators have been clamoring for. These "tools of learning" are accompanied in a liberal education by a solid grounding in the great thinkers and events of the past. A student so educated is capable of holding a wide variety of jobs—whatever his innate talents and desires draw him to—not just one that is chosen for him by state planners. However, the most important part of such an education, once the basic tools of learning are mastered, is the student's growth in understanding—a quality that can only be measured through ongoing interaction with wise teachers and mentors.

The effect of the theory of economic utility in education is to transform it into a commodity that can be easily measured, tracked, and quantified and that requires no special wisdom or insight to administer. That transformation happens as reformers come up with specific, measurable educational objectives relating to their goals; write curricula that teaches each one of those objectives; then create tests that measure student mastery of each objective—the economic utility style reform we have come to label as the "standards movement."

Broad Support for Standards

Across the political spectrum, almost everyone from President George W. Bush to Senator Edward Kennedy supports the push for national standards and the testing necessary to support the standards. In a January 23, 2001 press release issued by the Republican National Committee, Governor Paul Cellucci of Massachusetts echoes the widespread support President Bush has garnered by making this a top priority in the early days of his administration: "President Bush's decision to tackle the difficult problems of education as the first initiative of his new Administration is good news for America's families. The President has made it clear that comprehensive education reform must start by insisting upon high standards and strengthening accountability for student performance."

In an article published in the Summer 1996 issue of *The Brooking Review,* educational historian and former Department of Education official Diane Ravitch joins the chorus of approval: ". . . standards are essential both for excellence and equal opportunity." Ravitch, President Bush, and many others recognize that national education standards are pointless without testing as an enforcement mechanism. If it isn't tested, it won't be taught. Consequently, Ravitch and other standards advocates call for either the expanded use of the federally-funded National Assessment of Educational Progress (NAEP) test or state tests aligned with and calibrated to the NAEP standards.

The new tests must be what are called **high-stakes tests** (you lose a lot if you fail to pass), otherwise the national standards won't have any influence. At present, states use a variety of tests. Some use the familiar standardized tests such as the Iowa Test of Basic Skills (ITBS) and the SAT 9. Many states have developed or are in the process of developing their own exams such as the Texas Assessment of Academic Skills and California's Golden State Exams. While the older standardized tests measure general academic knowledge and skills, the new tests are aligned directly with each state's standards or framework that measure whether or not students at each grade level have mastered very prescriptive lists of content and skills.

Problems arise because, thus far, the standards and tests created by various states are not identical. States differ in what they believe is important for students to learn, although not by much. The National Education Goals Panel, which was created by Goals 2000, set up Technical Planning Groups to work out the details of Goals 2000. As far back as November 15, 1993, in a publication called "Promises to Keep: Creating High Standards for American Students," one of these groups concluded, "There can logically be only one set of national education standards per subject area."

Standards Conflicts

Groups of subject matter experts have formed around the country to try to come up with a single set of national standards for each subject that will be accepted nationwide. However, many people began to realize how challenging, and perhaps impossible, this might be with the presentation of national history standards in 1994. The seemingly simple choice of what historical information to include or not to include was recognized to be a powerful determiner of attitudes and values for children. Fans of western civilization felt betrayed when European history and classic American heroes such as George Washington and Patrick Henry, whose lives clearly shaped American history, were demoted in favor of a more multicultural approach that allotted space to less influential heroes representative of minorities and other cultures.

The Kansas State School Board conflict was actually more important than most people realize because it demonstrated the hollowness of claims that the educational standards were merely voluntary guidelines that would not control the curriculum. Teachers were not forbidden to teach macroevolution, but that topic wouldn't be included in a standards-based test. Yet, many understood that what was on the tests is what would get taught in the classroom and vice versa. Pro-evolution forces marshaled their armies and waged a successful campaign to unseat conservative board members in February, 2001. New, pro-macroevolution board members promptly voted to revise the standards so they are now in alignment with the national standards from the National Academy of Sciences. The NAS standards are based upon five "unifying concepts" or "cornerstones of science"—one of which is "evolution and equilibrium."

The end result for Kansas is the same as the more peacefully achieved results in most other states. National standards for each subject are being used as the basis for state standards, resulting in a high degree of similarity in the curriculum from state to state. This is a highly desirable goal for backers of national standards and testing since one of their objectives is easy comparability from state to state.

High-Stakes Testing

Rewards and punishments play a crucial role in the push for national standards. To make sure school personnel understand the importance of teaching the new standards, many states have instituted "high-stakes tests" with rewards and punishments meted out to school personnel in relation to student scores. At present, 41 states already have high-stakes testing. Increasingly, states are tying improved test scores to cash bonuses (up to $25,000 per teacher in California) and positive job evaluations for both teachers and principals. As an important side note, cheating incidents among educators have risen dramatically with implementation of high-stakes testing. See for example the December 2000 issue of *AASA School Administrator* for an illuminating article entitled "When Educators Cheat."

Implementing high-stakes tests creates pressure for state standards, since these tests do not currently line up with the existing curriculum and standards. In the *Education Week* issue of February 21, 2001, Earl H. Wiman, principal of Alexander Elementary School in Jackson, Tennessee, echoes a typical complaint that "the test does not reflect the state's academic standards closely enough to help focus instruction. If we're going to hold schools accountable, we need to very clearly identify for teachers and schools what needs to be taught, and we need to very clearly identify for teachers how that's going to be tested."

Jeanne Allen, president of the Washington-based Center for Education Reform, has heard such complaints. In an *Education Week* interview of January 31, 2001, she comments, "The issue before was, how the heck do you make sure that state standards and state tests are good enough in order to make these rewards and impose these consequences?" She believes that

President Bush's education proposal has the answer. "Mr. Bush has proposed verifying state test-score gains by comparing them with NAEP results." If state exams results are substantiated by similar results on the NAEP, this would be a good indicator. However, the comparison cannot even be made in many states because they either do not participate in NAEP testing or too few schools participate to give representative scores for comparison. Thus, for Bush's plan to work, more states would have to participate in the NAEP.

Whether the Bush administration will choose to expand the NAEP or, instead, opt for NAEP-equivalent questions imbedded in states exams remains to be seen. If the "standards" trend continues, the result will be the same either way. Testing programs will expand, and the federal role will become much more significant. States that are not yet closely aligned with national standards and tests will be brought into alignment one way or another.

Clashing Worldviews

As the standards and tests are being implemented, it becomes increasingly clear that the standards will not easily accommodate those who would have their children learn a Christian worldview or any other worldview that does not align with the dominant secular materialist worldview reflected in the standards. Neutrality isn't an option. Education has an undeniable cultural/philosophic/religious aspect that is transmitted whether purposely or not.

In their 1940 book *The History and Philosophy of Education Ancient and Modern* (Prentice-Hall) historians F. Eby and C.F. Arrowood tell us, "Education is more than the acquisition of a certain body of knowledge; it comprehends the transmission to the younger generation of the entire culture of a people. Now the culture of a people involves an ideal of character and of religious faith, a system of behavior, together with some theory of the universe, however simple it may be."

In his book *The Philosophy of the Christian Curriculum* (Ross House Books, 1981) the late R.J. Rushdoony wrote even more explicitly: "Not only does education find its foundation in religion, but the educational curriculum expresses the religious standards and expectations of a culture." This holds true even if the religious foundations are nontheistic. For example, "statism" was the religion of the Soviet Union, so its educational system clearly reflected the state's beliefs, philosophy, historical interpretations, and goals. Under that system, professing Christians were typically shut out from college admissions, and hence from all but menial jobs, since they did not adhere to the state's philosophy and goals—its "standards."

Can We Work Around the Standards?

Some people suggest that private and home schools can work around the standards by first teaching the required content, then adding worldview-focused curricula to the mix. Others suggest ignoring the standards but providing students with a solid liberal arts education with the expectation that they will then be intelligent enough to "outsmart" the tests.

Unfortunately, neither solution is realistic. According to an *Education Week* article of February 2, 2002, teachers increasingly complain that school days are consumed with teaching to the standards and preparing for tests. The standards have become so extensive and detailed that teachers have no extra time to teach beyond them. Homeschoolers might be able to manage the time to do both, but I suspect that most parents would see the hypocrisy and waste in teaching material that supports conflicting worldviews.

Testing is likely to become more and more problematic. If private schools and homeschools try to ignore the standards and implement a classical liberal education (or any other alternative curricular agenda), their students might test poorly as tests become more and more narrowly focused on details dictated by the standards that would be unlikely parts of their educational program.

As the standards movement gathers steam, pressure will be exerted upon private schools and homeschools to adhere to the same standards and tests as government schools.

Exit exams (tests students must pass before graduating from high school) might well have the strongest impact. As of 2001, according to a January 24 *Education Week* article, 24 states have exit exams in place or in the planning process thus far. Students in government schools must pass these tests to earn a high school diploma.

Could "Standards" Be Forced on Homeschoolers?

Early in 2001, the Maine legislature introduced legislation (LD 405) requiring homeschoolers to take the state's Maine Educational Assessment exam. Although this legislative effort failed, it demonstrates that it is not a far-fetched concern for homeschoolers in general. Also, as colleges and universities explore linkage of college entry to student scores on standards-based tests and exit exams, it is likely that they will come to expect private and home school students to pass the same tests just as they now take the same SAT I, SAT II, and ACT exams as public school students for college entry exams.

Private and home schools that choose to teach a significantly different curriculum will be faced with choices of sacrificing their own agenda so their students can achieve high test scores, accepting the risk of low student scores, or fighting for alternative evaluation.

What We Must Do

We might be able to avoid these dismal alternatives if we can keep private and home education free from the standards movement. That means:

- Resisting or getting rid of state and/or federal laws that require home educators to take standards-based tests
- Encouraging colleges and universities to rely on evaluation tools other than standards-based test results
- Not enrolling our children in government-sponsored home-school programs (which will all use standards-based tests)
- Educating others about the dangers of the standards movement
- Clearly identifying our own educational goals and diligently working to accomplish them

Only if we resist government-imposed standards will we be free to develop our own standards of education that reflect God's purposes for our own families.

CHAPTER 42

Evaluating & Testing

Why do we test our kids?

- To find out what they know . . . or don't know
- Because they have to perform in the top 3 to 10 percent on a standardized test to qualify for the various regional Talent Search programs
- As good practice for later tests they will have to take, such as the SAT and ACT
- Because the state we live in requires it

Some of these reasons may be more compelling to you than others. Nonetheless, the vast majority of homeschooled kids will take some kind of nationally standardized test during their years at home.

Standardized tests are not all they could be. As famed activist Phyllis Schlafly notes,

The testing system has been corrupted. Not only do all students score "above average" (a marvel of statistical fakery), but many tests are peppered with questions that ask for non-objective responses about feelings, attitudes, or predictions, or which have a built-in bias toward political correctness.

Other critics have pointed out flaws in test design ranging from overly high "guessability" to questions geared to mainstream middle-class kids that other kids will get wrong through not being familiar with that environment. None of these are a huge problem as long as a number of competing tests are allowed to exist. That's why homeschoolers have always opposed any national testing standards, despite the fact that homeschooled kids have al-

What Good Are Standardized Tests?

I tend to view standardized tests the same way I do studio portraits: lovelier than a snap-shot but not always a realistic picture. It's usually been my experience that standardized tests don't tell me what I didn't already know in the first place.

So, am I saying that there's no place for testing homeschooled children? Absolutely not! Testing can be a wonderful tool to help us as teachers know whether or not we're doing our jobs well, or whether we need to work on an area or two. I'm all for comparing children to a standard and saying "How're we doing?" as opposed to comparing them to other children and saying "Where do we rank in the standings?"—*Renee Mathis*

Reading & Riting & Readiness for Tests

The public schools are actually pushed into being test-preparation organizations.
—*Robin Sampson, author of* What Your Child Needs to Know When

States That Require Standardized Testing

Most states do not require homeschooled students to take standardized tests. Here are the states that do require testing:

- Arkansas
- Colorado
- Florida
- Georgia
- Hawaii
- Minnesota
- Nevada
- New York
- North Carolina
- North Dakota
- Oregon
- Pennsylvania
- South Carolina
- South Dakota
- Tennessee
- Virginia

Many other states offer a choice of assessments, of which standardized testing is one, and some of the listed states have different options for homeschools operated as private schools or in other ways. See Appendix 2 for details.

The Four Steps of Evaluation

Teresa Moon, in her book *Evaluating for Excellence*, lays out a four-step evaluation process. First, you **diagnose** the child's current abilities and skill levels. A diagnostic test works well at this stage. Second, you set academic goals and create a **plan** for achieving those goals. Third, you **guide** the student to reach those goals. This step involves determining what *you* have to do to help the student succeed. Fourth, you **evaluate** how the student has done. This step may involve achievement testing. From the results of the achievement test, you form a new diagnosis and begin the four steps again.

ways scored higher on standardized tests than public-school kids; the power to dictate the test is the power to dictate what must be taught.

Why Bother with Testing?

As I said in an earlier book, **Schoolproof**, people are always confusing *teaching* (putting information out where the student can get it) and *feedback* (finding out what the student knows).

> "Teaching is telling or showing people what they don't know."

Asking students to show and tell you what they already know is feedback, not teaching!

You do have good reasons for wanting to know what your learner knows. For one thing, you can keep from wasting your time and his. I say this as a student who struggled through her entire academic career with schools that insisted I take courses on material I had already learned on my own. The excitement just leaks out of teaching and learning when the student already understands what you are trying to teach.

Another good reason for finding out what your learner knows is to locate gaps in his knowledge and understanding. Like little cracks in a house foundation, these are best found and mended before you build any further on them.

Finally, as many others have observed, showing what you know tends to reinforce your knowledge. The simple act of explaining or demonstrating knowledge to another cements it in your own mind. In this last sense, getting feedback from your learner tops off your teaching effort.

The Difference Between Diagnostic & Achievement Tests

Diagnostic tests are, in theory, a helpful tool to discover your student's grade level in the academic areas tested. In addition, some diagnostic tests pinpoint specific areas of weakness (e.g., punctuation skills, addition facts from 11-99, alphabetization) that need more work.

I said, "In theory," because today some "diagnostic" tests are actually probes designed to label as many children as possible. Tests of developmental readiness are particularly notorious in this respect.

At home, academic diagnostic tests are extremely helpful when you begin homeschooling, in order to determine your child's correct grade level in each subject.

Achievement tests show how well your child is performing in academic areas, as compared to other children in that grade. Typically, scores are expressed as percentiles. A score in the fifty-first percentile means your child did better than 51 percent of the children taking the test; a score in the ninety-ninth percentile (the highest possible) means he did better than 99 percent of test-takers.

State "Assessments"

Until recently, when states required homeschoolers to take tests, the tests required were nationally-standardized achievement tests. However, an increasing number of states now have their own state "assessments."

Typically these are given at grade 3 or 4, possibly grade 6 or 8, and (sometimes) as a high-school exit exam.

According to a *Phyllis Schlafly Report* of March, 2001:

> *Tests are now called assessments, which is a semantic clue to the large element of subjectivity that has invaded the questions and the scoring. The most commonly understood meaning of the word assessment is the tax-collector's assessment of our property, and we all know how subjective that can be. Some of the questions have no right or wrong answers and are scored by temporary workers rewarded for speed. More and more tests are burdened with the liberal/feminist dogmas called Political Correctness.*
>
> *One Michigan test required students to write an argument for or against sending women into military combat. That topic will inevitably be scored on attitudes and values rather than on composition, grammar or spelling.*
>
> *One National Assessment of Educational Progress (NAEP) test contains three questions that ascribe unworthy motives to the white settlers who came to America, three questions that measure the student's support of radical environmentalism, and a question instructing students to write a letter to their U.S. Senators telling them which government programs the student wants funded.*

Did you know that most state writing assessments use "prompts"—statements or unfinished sentences such as "I have experienced various things that have made me feel worthwhile, but I never felt better than when—" (this is an actual writing prompt from the SAT II)? And that these prompts usually require students to share their personal experiences, beliefs, or feelings?

According to a 1999 study by the Education Trust and National Association of System Heads entitled *Ticket to Nowhere*, reported in the *Education Advocate* of July/August 2001, the research revealed that:

> *Scoring personal essays is subjective; the writing assessment score is therefore invalid. "Because the response is personal reflection, the validity of the essay's content can't be judged objectively." Although essay organization and language usage and mechanics can be objectively scored, the personal opinions expressed by the student affect the scores. . . .*
>
> *The type or genre of writing being tested is wrong. "The writing needed in college and in work is not primarily concerned with personal feelings or ruminations, but with analysis, reporting, summary, argument, persuasion." Students who can writing adequate essays about their feelings and opinions are often unable to complete complex analytical or research-based assignments required in college or the workplace.*
>
> *In Ticket to Nowhere, researchers expose the mistaken belief that any large-scale assessment cannot assume a common body of knowledge [such as asking students to compare two literary works or to analyze an important historical event]. So writing prompts intentionally require as little content as possible. . . .*
>
> *Some critics claim that personal student responses provide a venue for profiling students—identifying students who are potentially dangerous or students who express politically incorrect opinions.*

Why Mushy Assessments?

In states where tests have been mandated by law, the first order of business of the teachers' unions has been to introduce as much mushy subjective material as possible into these tests, in order to prevent anyone from finding out how much—or how little—academic skills they are actually providing their students.

The more fundamental question is whether our educational establishment has even been trying to impart academic skills as a high priority goal. Over the past hundred years, American educators have been resisting the idea that schools exist to pass on to the next generation the basic mental skills that our culture has developed. They have said so in books, articles, speeches—and by their actions in the schools.

Since the rise of teachers' unions in the early 1960s—which coincided with the decline of student test scores—the education establishment has increasingly succeeded in de-emphasizing academic skills. In that sense, our schools have not failed, they have succeeded in changing the goals and priorities of education.

Despite all-out efforts by the education establishment to blame the declining educational standards in our schools on everything imaginable except the people who teach there—on parents, students, television or society—the cold fact is that today's students are often simply not taught enough academic material in the first place. Even if there were flawless parents, perfect students, no television and no problems in society, students could still not be expected to learn what they were never taught.

—*Thomas Sowell, "Teaching to the Test,"* Jewish World Review, *August 20, 2002*

When B+ Is the Average Grade

American educators are proud of the increasing number of students who receive high grades. Headlines in local newspapers boast of students' academic accomplishments:

- 70% of middle school students on honor roll
- 26 Valedictorians honored at graduation
- Over 30% of graduating class attains honors . . .

To many researchers, these headlines are clear evidence of grade inflation. Beginning in elementary school and continuing through the college level, many teachers and professors are giving students better grades than they deserve.

The College Board, the nonprofit group that administers the SAT and other standardized tests, is alert to grade inflation. Their statistics show that in 1987, 28% of test-takers had an A average. Twelve years later, that number grew to 39%. However, during this same twelve years the combined SAT verbal and math scores of the A students dropped 14 points.

Statistics from the Higher Education Research Institute at UCLA echo similar findings from their annual national survey of approximately 300,000 college freshmen. In 1969, 12.5% reported having an A average in high school, with 32.5% having a C average. By 1999, 34.1% of the college freshmen reported an A average and 12% a C. Yet, even with freshmen entering with higher GPA's, the number of remedial college classes is growing, another indication that grades often do not represent student achievement.

—Education Advocate, September/October 2000

And as the *Education Advocate* of May/June 2000 points out:

> *Controversial state assessment tests are the major trend in today's education. Researchers and state governments "are not willing to give up on the kind of leverage that high-stakes testing programs provide for school reform," according to Debra Viadero of Education Week (5/8/00). This "leverage refers to the reality that state standards often force schools to* revise *proven curricula while state assessment tests act as a compliance checklist for those changes." This "leverage" thereby takes away local control of curriculum and accountability.* [Emphasis theirs]

Maintaining parental control of "curriculum and accountability" is the whole point of homeschooling, so we should continue to resist having our kids take those state assessment tests. Standardized achievement tests have some value in helping us keep an objective view of our homeschool's progress. Considering that state assessments were only introduced as an attempt to correct *public* school failures, there is no reason why homeschoolers should be subjected to these politically correct, invasive attempts to force the use of certain curricula and certain attitudes.

Grade Inflation

The other testing issue you need to know about is grade inflation. This is a serious problem because your homeschooled student will be competing for college acceptance and scholarships with public-school kids who mostly have an A average.

According to a Fox News article of May 8, 2002,

> *In 2001, according to [the testing service] ACT, 44.1 percent of students reported having an A average—up from 23.2 percent of students in 1989. But ACT test scores have remained a constant.*

> *"Their level of achievement is really the same, but students think they're better prepared than they really are," [Kirk] Witzberger, [of the ACT's Office for the Enhancement of Educational Practices] said.*

The bottom line is that the *average* high school student today has a B+ average. And here we always thought that "C" was the "average" grade! When those who don't plan to go to college aren't included, you end up with close to *half* of all college aspirants with an A average.

Obviously, most of those kids don't deserve those grades. According to the *Education Advocate*, teachers are giving undeserved A's to:

> 1. *elevate a student's self-esteem*
> 2. *reduce drop-out rates*
> 3. *assist in securing a student's place in a good university*
> 4. *appease demanding parents*
> 5. *improve public opinion of the school district and its teachers*

Unfortunately, grade inflation is like an arms war. If School A raises its grades, then students from other schools look bad by comparison. So School B raises its grades, and so on.

While I am not advocating that you give your children automatic A's so they can compete, just be aware that especially harsh grading will make them look far worse by comparison than you can imagine. The best solution: Demand A work and have them redo anything that's not up to par.

A Parent's Guide to Standardized Tests in School

Parents. $14.95.
Educational Dept., LearningExpress, NY. (888) 551-5627, www.learnatest.com. Type the words "Parent's Guide" into the "Search" window of your Web browser.

Having trouble finding your way around the maze of nationally standardized tests? **A Parent's Guide to Standardized Tests in School** lays it all out for you. From a brief overview of the history of standardized testing, the book moves briskly to cover these topics:

*   Can you really prepare for a standardized test? The answer is yes, and the authors (both PhDs) tell you why.
*   Rundown of the most popular standardized tests
*   Sample questions, with answers, from popular standardized tests
*   How to interpret those impenetrable score sheets
*   Does your child qualify for test exemption or special testing conditions? How exactly is a "learning disability" diagnosis—which may allow such exemption or special testing conditions—implemented? What about special testing accommodations for a child with physical disabilities? Nitty-gritty answers here, that may or may not apply to your homeschooling situation, depending on whether your state requires school-administered standardized testing.
*   How schools use test scores, and what you should do about it if your child is in school

Some of the information isn't needed by homeschoolers, such as the chapters on working with your child's teacher and how schools use test scores. However, it's all interesting to know. This is the clearest, most parent-friendly introduction to the subject I have seen. Recommended.

More Books That Explain Testing

Written just for homeschoolers, **Evaluating for Excellence** breaks new ground. The oversized, 200-page book first presents a four-step approach—Diagnose, Plan, Guide, and Evaluate—then breaks each step down.

Mostly this consists of showing you how to use the 66 pages of reproducible checklists and forms for every academic subject found at the end of the book. Some forms are "student inventories"—the student evaluates his own progress in various subskills on a scale of 1 to 10 and describes his interests and goals in his own words. Some are diagnostic checklists, objectives lists, assignment sheets, critiques, evaluation forms, guidelines, and notes pages for the parents to fill out. Four pages of forms are designed to help you develop an IEP (Individualized Education Plan) for your child, which author Teresa Moon believes you should do whether your child has official "special needs" or not. The body of the book includes sample filled-out examples of each form, often with comments explaining how and why to use it.

The method of portfolio assessment and how to create a portfolio are also covered, again with samples of student work showing how you can evaluate progress using this method.

A "Putting It All Together" section shows how to begin using this method with three different grade-level groups: preK–3, 4–6, and 7–12. This section also includes the Sample Forms Use Guide, a chart showing which forms correspond to which of the four steps. For example, the "Book Projects" form can be used for the Guide and Evaluate steps, while the Educator's Diagnostic Survey can be used to Diagnose, Plan, and Evaluate. Information on teaching and evaluating critical thinking is also found in this section, which is followed by a glossary of terms referring to education and evaluation, taken from the 1828 Noah Webster's *American Dictionary of the English Language*.

Nowhere will you find a list of norms against which to compare your student. The book's philosophy is that you need to chart the student's *progress*—how he is doing now compared to how he was doing before.

Studying this book will give you a lot of food for thought. It is certainly packed with ideas! As to whether you will use each and every form, that de-

Evaluating for Excellence

Parents. $17.95 plus shipping.
Beautiful Feet Books, MA.
(800) 889-1978, www.bfbooks.com.

pends on how much time you want to spend getting comfortable with this level of grading, whether you have easy access to a photocopy machine, and just how "measurement-minded" you are. A folder of these filled-out forms certainly should impress school officials, relatives, and neighbors, but will be way more fun to produce if you are a Progress Person than if you are an Action Man, People Person, Puzzle Solver, or Performer. (If you don't know what these terms mean, see our chapter on Thinking Styles!)

Anything titled **Special Educator's Complete Guide to 109 Diagnostic Tests** can be expected to be huge, and it is. "Comprehensive" is just the word to describe this oversized 328-page book. It covers all the following:

Special Educator's Complete Guide to 109 Diagnostic Tests

Parents. $29.95
Jossey-Bass, a division of Wiley. Available through bookstores and online.

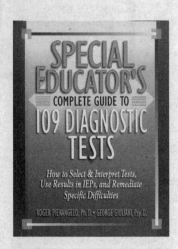

- Wechsler Scales of Intelligence. What you need to know about the three most commonly used IQ tests
- Intellectual Assessment Measures. Facts on nine different tests that measure such things as perception, mental processing speed, and long- and short-term memory, including the Stanford-Binet Intelligence Scale, Kaufman Assessment Battery for Children, and more
- Achievement Assessment Measures. 31 tests that evaluate math, reading, spelling, and writing achievement are covered
- Perceptual Measures. 14 tests designed to diagnose thinking styles and discovery channels are covered.
- Language, Psychological & Social, and Adaptive Measures. 25 tests that evaluate a child's development in the areas of language, emotional and social growth, and behavior.
- Early Childhood, Hearing Impaired, Occupation & Physical Therapy, and Bilingual Tests. 29 tests designed to check for potential disabilities are covered in this section.
- How to understand the stages of evaluation, test interpretation, how tests are used to diagnose and prescribe educational and therapy strategies, and more
- How to write and develop an IEP
- How to put remediation techniques into practice in a classroom situation

Each test has a one- or two-page description, including its author, the address/phone/fax of its publisher, its purpose, a brief description including administration time/type of test/who is allowed to administer it/appropriate grade levels, "subtest" information (what further details can be gleaned from test subscores), its strengths, and its weaknesses.

Appendixes provide contact information for the test publishers, test reference guides by category and name, glossary of terms, and glossary of special education abbreviations.

Although naturally we don't agree with all of the theories behind some of these tests, or the labels they are used to confer, this book can be a huge help towards understanding the system as it currently works, why and how your child was labeled, and what tests you might want to use yourself to explore puzzling areas of your child's educational development. I would say this book is a "must" for a well-stocked support-group library.

Formal and Informal Tests and Evaluations

BJ Testing and Evaluation (formerly the Bob Jones University Press Testing and Evaluation Service) is the largest and oldest of four organizations providing homeschool families access to standardized achievement tests. The Testing Service began offering the Iowa Tests of Basic Skills (for grades 1–8) and Tests of Achievement and Proficiency (for high schoolers) in 1984. In 1993 the Stanford Achievement Test series was added, as BJ Testing and Evaluation assumed the testing that the Home School Legal Defense Association had been providing for its members. Since that time, a full range of writing evaluations (grades 3–12) and a career assessment have been added to its growing list of evaluation tools. Most recently a writing club, exclusively for homeschooled students in grades 5–12, has been included in the available services.

Also available for grades 3–12 only is the Cognitive Abilities test, "a test to appraise reasoning ability that yields verbal, non-verbal, and quantitative evaluation scores."

In order to administer the test you must either be (1) currently certified as a teacher by a national or state organization, (2) a graduate of a four-year college program, or (3) a current teacher in an operating conventional school. These requirements were established in conjunction with the test provider.

For test security reasons, the tests can only be mailed to the qualified tester, and all testing materials including answer sheets must be returned within 60 days of receipt to BJUP for scoring and interpretation. You get back an analysis of the results in four to six weeks.

We have personally used Bob Jones testing for several years now and are quite pleased with the results. Since these are the same tests used in many public and private schools, with the same fill-in-the-boxes-with-number-two-pencil interface, our children are learning test-taking skills they might need later on. They are also being evaluated against a huge group of public-school children, so we have a good idea where they stand relative to this group. The returned scores break down the children's results into specific enough areas that we can see exactly what areas are weak or strong—e.g., capitalization, punctuation, map-reading.

Hints: Be sure to follow ordering instructions carefully to ensure you get the proper grade-level test for your child. Call Bob Jones University Press if you have questions about which test to order. You might also do better to plan on testing in the late spring and summer. During the months of April and August test scores returned will not only include grade placement and percentile rankings, but an "item analysis of test results" as well. This item analysis pinpoints your student's strong and weak areas and provides other useful information.

Covenant Home Curriculum sells self-test materials. They carry their own **C.H.A.T. Little Windows on Progress series** (Covenant Home Achievement Tests). These are meant to give you an accurate reading of your child's grade level equivalence in the two main academic areas of math and language. The tests are easy to administer, taking only 30 minutes for each of the two sections. Scoring by Covenant Home Curriculum staff is included.

The C.H.A.T. series is partially patterned after the sample SAT national standards and grade levels. Standards are also based on curriculum levels established in *Warriner's English Grammar and Composition*, a standard work.

This is as informal as testing gets! Unlike a typical trivia game, **The Game of Knowledge** mostly deals with actual education-related questions, and is designed so kids can compete on equal terms with adults. The enclosed 496 cards have two questions on each side of each card—one question for ages 10–15, and the other for ages 16 and up—for a total of 1,584 questions in all. Questions are worded in such a way that even if you are unfamiliar with the topic, you might be able to figure out the answer by drawing on your previous knowledge. Categories for questions are:

BJ Testing and Evaluation

Order by grade as per instructions on order form. Cognitive Abilities Tests, $23.50 each. Achievement Tests, $28 each. Test Set (combining the two), $39.50 each.
Bob Jones University Press Customer Service, Greenville, SC 29614-0062 (800) 845-5731
www.bju.edu/press/

The tests themselves take quite a long time. You will need to spend several hours reading the instructions carefully before giving the tests. Then you and your students need to set aside an hour or two a day for a week during which you will be giving the tests. This extra time investment, however, results in much more accurate results.

Covenant Home CHAT Tests

Grades K–12, $25 each grade. Indicate grade level just completed.
Covenant Home Curriculum, WI. (800) 578-2421,
www.covenanthome.com.

The Game of Knowledge

Grades 5–adult. Original game, $24.98. Travel edition, $10.98.
University Games, CA. (800) 347-4818 to find a story near you.
www.areyougame.com.

- Science—space, inventions, famous scientists, extinct animals, physics, biology, the human body, chemistry, and energy
- Sports—baseball, basketball, football, hockey, soccer, golf, fishing, tennis, car racing, and Olympic sports; most questions involve rules and facts related to each sport, although some do require knowledge about famous players and games
- Media—TV, movies, books and stories, music, comics
- Nature—plants, animals, land, oceans, weather, the environment, natural phenomena; a few questions are evolutionary
- Fame—entertainers and stars, US Presidents, world leaders, heroes, myths and legends, Biblical characters, fictional characters, artists, authors, composers, and royalty
- Our World—US history, world history, geography, politics, man-made structures, justice and the law, economics and currency, and food

Your aim, as one of the two to six competing players, is to collect one ring for each of these six topics. Gameboard play determines which topic questions you can be asked at any given move, adding an element of chance. My guess is that the travel version doesn't have a gameboard; the catalog says it does have 400 "all-new" questions.

The **Personalized Assessment Summary System (PASS)**, like other achievement tests, evaluates student achievement in reading, math, and language. Unlike the others, PASS was designed for you to give at home and takes into account the type of individualized curriculum your child may have been studying; it is also untimed.

PASS was "normed" (that is, calibrated for accuracy) using a standardized item bank. The difficulty of each question on the test was figured using a method developed by Danish mathematician Yorg Rasch. All items on any given test fall within a limited difficulty range, which presumably makes it easier to find gaps in learning.

The student taking the PASS first takes a placement test designed to find his or her approximate achievement level. The computer-scored results from the PASS test itself include suggestions for reaching goals in each subject area. You can also compare results with homeschool and national norms for that grade level.

Sycamore Tree offers a wide variety of diagnostic and achievement tests from other publishers.

The first nationally standardized test in their catalog, the **Comprehensive Test of Basic Skills**, is completed in your home. The CTBS is an achievement test covering reading, language arts, spelling, math, science, social studies, and reference skills. Twice a year batches of these tests are submitted by Sycamore Tree for machine scoring—on May 15 and August 15. At other times of the year, Sycamore Tree staff will hand-score the test for an extra $10. You need to provide your child's age and grade level when ordering the CTBS, and should allow six to eight weeks for test results to be returned to you.

Each of the **Achievement Tests** series (available for grades 1–7) is a 32-page booklet covering both math and language arts. These inexpensive tests are designed for use by parents and may be helpful for your own peace of mind, but aren't accepted by outside authorities such as Talent Searches and state authorities, as the nationally standardized tests above are.

As opposed to these achievement tests, diagnostic tests help you find a child's proper grade level in a subject. The **Diagnostic Prescriptive**

Hewitt Tests

Grades 3–8. PASS Test, $26 plus shipping.
Hewitt Homeschooling Resources, PO Box 9, Washougal, WA 98671
(800) 890-4097
www.hewitthomeschooling.com

Sycamore Tree Testing Services

Grades K–12. Comprehensive Test of Basic Skills, $50. Diagnostic Prescriptive Assessment, $28/grade. Achievement Tests, $4.98/grade. Total Language Diagnostic Assessment with Remedial Strategies and Answer Key, $40.
The Sycamore Tree Center for Home Education, 2179 Meyer Place, Costa Mesa, CA 92627
Orders: (800) 779-6750
Information: (949) 650-4466
www.sycamoretree.com

Assessment series, available for grades K–5, includes the test and an outline of material that should be learned at that grade level. It can be used as a yearly evaluation or as the basis of a portfolio or an Individual Education Plan (required in some states for special-needs students). Each 50-plus page test booklet is designed for use by parents. The "Prescriptive" part of the name means the booklet includes suggestions for dealing with problem areas uncovered by the test.

For an all-in-one language arts diagnosis you can use for grades K–5, the **Total Language Diagnostic Assessment with Remedial Strategies and Answer Key** is the real deal. This 101-page workbook covers all tested areas of reading and language, includes test items from criterion-referenced diagnostic tests, and includes 30 pages of strategies for remediating problem areas. All six grade levels are covered in the one fairly pricey product.

Sycamore Tree also carries test-prep materials. See the separate write-up later in this chapter.

Scope & Sequence

If you know what your child is supposed to know when, you can use your own preferred method to find out whether he or she *does* know it . . . and then fill in any gaps you find. That's the premise behind a "Scope & Sequence," a list of topics and skills arranged by grade level.

A number of books have been published that list such skills and facts, sometimes with instructional help included to teach the facts. Or you can simply request the Scope & Sequence from one of the major textbook publishers you'll find in the Quick Resource Guide section of this book.

Teaching Children: A Curriculum Guide to What Children Need to Know at Each Level Through Sixth Grade by Diane Lopez is the third in the Child Light series published by Crossway Books. The first two books in the series, *For the Children's Sake* by Susan Schaeffer Macaulay and *Books Children Love* by Elizabeth Wilson were both enthusiastically received. This naturally created a lot of anticipation for *Teaching Children*.

The basic premise of *Teaching Children* is sound—to present a "Scope and Sequence" for each subject area based on the Charlotte Mason style of education. The Scope and Sequence you do get, with a tremendous amount of suggested topics of study, most following the standard public-school curriculum. However, *Teaching Children*'s specifically Christian emphasis is not all I had hoped for. Apart from a brief rehash of the Charlotte Mason methodology and some Christian literature selections, the topics often sound quite secular—e.g., the study of Occupations, which the public schools use to thrust careerism on little girls. The way these topics are studied also is often secular. So under Substance Abuse Prevention (a topic most homeschoolers don't feel much need to meddle with), we find "Learn how to express feelings." Charlotte Mason never would have said that! Like the Bible, which says you conquer "drunkenness" (not "Substance Abuse"!) by being filled with the Holy Spirit, Charlotte Mason always stressed developing self-control, a love of the Lord, and habits of Christian character.

Those who expected the gentle approach of *For the Children's Sake* will be surprised at the tone of this book. Skills are rigidly divided into grade levels, parents and teachers are told to do this and do that, and we find the passive tense widely employed (e.g., "It is recommended that . . ."). Again, this is far from Charlotte Mason's own approach to education.

Teaching Children
Parents. $12.99.
Crossway Books, IL. (800) 635-7993, www.crosswaybooks.org.

Another weakness: The "Developing a Christian Mind and Worldview" chapter is limited to resources put out by L'Abri workers. Yes, I know the Child Light people are all products in some way of L'Abri, the Christian fellowship founded in the Swiss Alps by Dr. and Mrs. Francis Schaeffer, but *Teaching Children* would have been a much stronger book if the author had been aware of the excellent work others not connected with L'Abri are doing in the area of Christian thinking and education.

Typical Course of Study

Grades K–12. 99¢ plus shipping from Sycamore Tree (see listing on page 308), or available free online (downloadable version) at *www2.worldbook.com/parents/course_study_index.asp*.

The classic scope-and-sequence published for years by World Book, **Typical Course of Study** can probably be obtained most painlessly through homeschool cataloger Sycamore Tree, who actually answer their telephone. Based on studies of what topics are taught in each subject area in public schools around the country, *Typical Course of Study* should not be used as a slavish guide but as essential "comfort reading" that lets you know you're doing as much or more than the schools and a starting point to your own set of objectives. After all, if you wanted to teach exactly what the public schools do, you could just send your

kid to public school! Feel free to skip the transparently politically correct objectives, to forge ahead in math (kids don't need four years to work their way up to writing numbers in the millions, as just one example), and to rearrange the entire science curriculum. Should Life Science be taught before Earth Science, or vice versa? Who cares?

What Your 1st/2nd/3rd . . . Grader Needs to Know: The Core Knowledge Series

Grades K–6. $12.95 each.
Random House. Available in bookstores and online.

You probably know the **Core Knowledge Series** better by the names of its individual volumes. For instance, *What Your 1st Grader Needs to Know: Fundamentals of a Good First-Grade Education*. The titles for the other grade levels are similar: *What Your 2nd Grader Needs to Know, What Your 3rd Grader Needs to Know*, etc.

Edited by E.D. Hirsch, Jr., author of *Cultural Literacy*, these books were originally published by the Core Knowledge Foundation, whose mission is "improvement of education for all children." Consequently, this series is not just a list of what should be learned at what age, but contains actual reading selections and instructions for all major school subjects in each grade level covered.

For example, in the first-grade book, you get familiar nursery rhymes, classic children's stories, a number of Aesop's fables, explanations of famous sayings such as "If at first you don't succeed, try, try again," a quick tour of world geography, an introduction to world religions and civilizations, an introduction to American civilization that starts at the fabled crossing of the Bering strait, introductions to the fine arts, explanations of first-grade math concepts (math facts, geometry, time-telling, calendar, money, and more), and introductions to various sciences. The illustrations include classic engravings, photos, and maps.

The outlook behind these books is similar to that driving Bill Bennett's "virtue" books. Realizing that the public schools are failing to produce culturally and morally literate Americans, a number of people have taken it upon themselves to fill in what's missing. However, they are still operating from the same basic outlook as the schools: statist, evolutionary, multicultural, eco-socialist, and feminist, among other things. What these people want is, in Mr. Hirch's own words, to "create a *school-based* culture" (emphasis his) that is "fair and democratic." This means ignoring unpleasant realities, such as the fact that, while many Africans were captured for use as slaves, others were sold into slavery by their own greedy chieftains. It means that the only three scientists considered worthy of study in first grade are Nicholas Copernicus, Charles Drew (a black man who pioneered the use of blood plasma for transfusions), and the ecologist Rachel Carson. It means encouraging children to act out pagan religious ceremonies (e.g., a Chinese New Year celebration that "lets in the good spirits of the new year") and to consider all religions equally valid (except possibly the Aztecs, whose human sacrifices are correctly condemned). It means teaching a child to think of himself as "a very special animal," which though true from the point of view of physical anatomy, should have been balanced with some thoughts on people as spiritual beings.

The more I look at these books, the more frustrated I get. Such a good idea. Such a good design. So many useful facts. Presented as a conservative solution for America's academic ills, but larded throughout with politically correct bias. What a waste.

If you are contemplating the return of your child to a traditional classroom, you must read **What Every Parent Needs to Know**. If your plans include continued home education, you might glean some insights and ideas here.

Written by a trio of professional educators with a combined 70 years of educational experience, this 166-page book guides parents through appropriate teaching practices for each primary grade subject. It gives parents a list of what to look for to evaluate the effectiveness of a teacher's approach. Parents are then given suggestions for activities to do at home to support the child's work in the classroom.

A good science program, for example, encourages children to think like a scientist and to apply this thinking to active investigations of the subject matter. In this area, parents should look for a good mixture of hands-on experiments and book learning.

This book is helpful because it can serve as a basis to evaluate your child's classroom. For home educators, it can help the parent to look at the components of their home program to determine if they really fit the way children in this age group learn.

There is a very helpful section on assessment, which tells parents to look beyond their child's performance on standardized tests. A thoughtful evaluation of a child might include skills checklists, written observations of children at work, portfolios and student logs. This is a good reminder to all parents, whether homeschooling or not, to look at the whole picture of a

What Every Parent Needs to Know About 1st, 2nd & 3rd Grades, Second Edition
Parents. $12.95.
Sourcebooks, IL. (800)727-8866.
www.sourcebooks.com.

child's experience as we evaluate our programs and methods in the home,

The authors support the implementation of national standards and are unmistakably in favor of quality public education. If I were returning my child to the school system, I would consider this a must-read. As a die-hard homeschooler, it is of limited value. *Christine Field*

What Your Child Needs to Know When is really two books in one. The second half of the book includes:

- One Year Through God's Word, a study plan using *The Narrated Bible,* a narration based on the NIV and published by Harvest House Publishers. Instead of just Bible reading assignments, you get a week-by-week outline of the point each passage makes, plus check boxes to track your progress.
- An alphabetical list of positive character traits, from *appreciative* to *virtuous,* with definitions and Scripture references.
- The most popular part of the book—119 pages of "Evaluation Check Lists." These are arranged by subject: language arts, mathematics, science, social sciences, and state history. Each subject is further divided into grade levels, and inside the grade levels, into subtopics. For example, under Language Arts, the second-grade listing is subdivided into Language Mechanics and Expression, Spelling, Study Skills, and Listening and Comprehension. Check boxes to the right of each listed skill are provided for up to five children. You assign each column of check boxes to a particular child, and there are five columns of check boxes. A typical skill to check off might be, "Identify correct use of singular and plural nouns."

Unlike some other books of this type, each grade level's skills list in *What Your Child Needs to Know When* does *not* include every single skill already checked off in the lower grades. Rather, you get skills needed at *that* grade level.

Did I say "other books of this type"? Actually, aside from the checklists, there *are* no other books of this type.

The first half of this oversized 296-page paperback is devoted to exploring the differences between biblical-based education and secular education and the history of each, analyzing the pros and cons of standardized tests versus other feedback methods (such as evaluation checklists!), and introducing author Robin Sampson's own "Heart of Wisdom," or H.O.W., teaching approach.

The H.O.W. approach is an attempt to make the Bible the core of the curriculum by having students read through it in a year and create their own Bible portfolios. Along the way, they practice reading, handwriting, spelling, creative writing, critical thinking, phonics, grammar, vocabulary, map skills, and economics. This approach is based, as Robin tells us, on a combination of methods from the Judah Bible Curriculum, Ruth Beechick's books, Charlotte Mason's books, Marilyn Howshall's *Lifestyle of Learning,* David Mulligan's writings, and the write-to-learn philosophy of the Write Source books. History and science is added by reading aloud related books. For example, if your Bible reading for that day mentions the eye, you can read a library book about the eye. If it mentions a king of Persia, you can study Persia.

Robin's website offers oodles of prepared unit studies created using the H.O.W. method, so once you've figured out where your child is academically, if you're interested, be sure to check it out.

What Your Child Needs to Know When, New Expanded Edition

Parents: covers grades K–8. $24.95. E-book version available for download online, $29.95.
Heart of Wisdom Publishing, TN.
(800) BOOK LOG,
www.heartofwisdom.com.

Test Preparation

After a couple of months off of school I wished I could send my kids to math camp because they suddenly claimed they had developed a math block. **Math Camp** to the rescue! For 20 days your students can work on material that will improve their math skills year around.

I reviewed the materials for grades 3 and 5. These covered problem solving, geometry, algebra, measurement, and data analysis

Does that sound like a lot? It's not, because Math Camp has broken it down and applied it to real life situations.

For example, in the geometry section of Grade 5 the student will learn how to measure for tile, while in the algebra section he will learn how to measure for grams of fat and apply the information to a graph.

To begin, you may want to discover your child's strengths and weaknesses by assigning the pretest. The student text provides most of the teaching, while the teacher's manual provides the answer key and a few instructional hints. Many of the problems require the student to break down word problems step-by-step and use a variety of operations in order to solve the problem.

Math Camp will help you cover all the bases and be a great add-on to your existing math program. *Irene Buntyn*

Math Camp
Grades K–6. Each level: student booklet, $1.99; teacher's guide, $4.95.
Curriculum Associates, Inc., MA. (800) 225-0248 or (978) 667-8000, www.curriculumassociates.com.

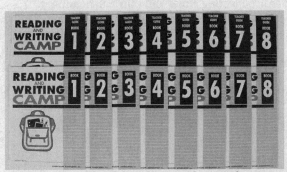

Give your children an extra academic boost during the summer months by providing them with a **Reading and Writing Camp.** Developed by Curriculum Associates, Reading and Writing Camp was created to supply students with a 20-day program that would improve their reading comprehension, critical thinking, and writing skills.

Each student booklet consists of 13 lessons, a pretest, and a posttest. To begin, the student takes a three-part pretest that evaluates his ability to read and write narrative, expository, and poetry pieces. The teacher's guide provides rubrics for grading writing that will help you to see where your child needs help.

After you have made your evaluation, you begin the lessons. Flip open the teacher's guide because it gives you excellent ideas for instructing the students on how to make inferences, interpreting words in context, and writing various types of paragraphs and poetry. Once you're done, the student will read a passage using the skill and then write his own piece in a similar format.

My favorite part of the program for the two grades I reviewed (3 and 5) is the poetry section, which allows the student to interpret poetry works by Tennyson, Longfellow, and Rossetti. Since this is an often-neglected part of my homeschool, I felt like this part alone was worth its weight in gold.

Reading and Writing Camp
Grades K–6. Each level: student booklet, $1.99; teacher's guide, $4.95.
Curriculum Associates, Inc., MA. (800) 225-0248 or (978) 667-8000, www.curriculumassociates.com.

This inexpensive program will enable you to evaluate your students and fill in the gaps. *Irene Buntyn*

Sycamore Tree Test Prep

Grades K–12. Scoring High series: student's editions, $3/grade except CTBS, $4/grade; teacher's manuals, $10/grade. Scoring High Test Prep software, grades 3–5 or 6–8, $19.95 each. Preparing Students to Raise Achievement Scores series, $10.95/workbook. Test Smart!, $29.95.
The Sycamore Tree Center for Home Education, 2179 Meyer Place, Costa Mesa, CA 92627
Orders: (800) 779-6750
Information: (949) 650-4466
www.sycamoretree.com

Sycamore Tree not only carries tests, but books, workbooks, and software designed to help your children ace their tests.

I've covered SAT and GED test preparation thoroughly in Volume 3. Sycamore Tree does offer a small selection of preparation helps geared to these high-school-level tests. What we're concentrating on right now is what they have that can help your K–8 student face and ace the diagnostic and achievement tests they may be asked or required to take.

The **Scoring High** series is for people who take nationally standardized tests seriously. Available in separate series for the California Achievement Test, Iowa Test of Basic Skills, Stanford Achievement Test, and Comprehensive Test of Basic Skills, each grade level for each test has its own student edition and teacher's manual, except for the CTBS, which is divided into K–1, 1–3, 3–5, and 5–8. Basically, your child will be taught how to take the test, trained in the skills and facts covered in the test, and provided with problems strongly resembling those on the actual test. You need the teacher's manual to score the practice tests and to figure out how to use the student books. Software is also available in this series for some grade levels.

A more generic series, **Preparing Students to Raise Achievement Scores**, prepares kids for any of the above standardized tests and more. These reproducible workbooks do not require or have separate teacher's manuals. Three workbooks are available for grades 1–2, 3–4, and 5–6.

Test Smart! Ready-to-Use Test-Taking Strategies and Activities for Grades 5–12 has over 100 worksheet activities to help students prepare for tests covering language arts and writing.

Test Ready series

Grade 2–8. Student workbooks, $6.95. Teacher guides, $3.50.
Curriculum Associates, P.O. Box 2001, North Billerica, MA 01862-0901
(800) 225-0248. Fax: (800) 366-1158
www.curriculumassociates.com

Does the idea of standardized testing stress you out? Curriculum Associates has a set of workbooks that prepare your child for testing. You can choose from a variety of test subjects in the **Test Ready** series, such as:

- OMNI Mathematics
- PLUS Reading
- Reading and Vocabulary
- PLUS Math
- Mathematics
- Language Arts
- Algebra I
- Social Studies
- Science
- Tips and Strategies

This program was designed to help ease test anxiety, identify skills and problem areas, familiarize students with test procedures, and indicate growth with a pretest and a posttest. Curriculum Associates guarantees if your child spends 14 days with Test Ready his score will increase. He will learn the strategies needed to be successful. Some of the subjects have writing exercises to help prepare your child for test that require more than fill-in-the-bubble answers. This is a comprehensive test preparation program, allowing you to buy only the workbooks for subjects that your child needs to practice. Of course, you can buy the whole set and be ready for anything! *Maryann Turner*

PART 9

Homeschooling Your Special-Needs Child

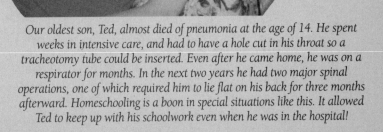

Our oldest son, Ted, almost died of pneumonia at the age of 14. He spent weeks in intensive care, and had to have a hole cut in his throat so a tracheotomy tube could be inserted. Even after he came home, he was on a respirator for months. In the next two years he had two major spinal operations, one of which required him to lie flat on his back for three months afterward. Homeschooling is a boon in special situations like this. It allowed Ted to keep up with his schoolwork even when he was in the hospital!

CHAPTER 43

Special-Needs Homeschooling: You Can Do It!

Teaching a child with special needs is a privilege—but it is also hard. It requires much sacrifice, patience, and unconditional love from the parents.

We cannot forget to consider what the child with special needs experiences as well. Living with a handicap such as blindness, cerebral palsy, a speech impediment, autism, retardation, a disease, or one of many types of learning disabilities is difficult. It is a daily struggle emotionally, mentally, and many times physically. The child's self-confidence is constantly put to the test. Some handicaps or learning disabilities can be overcome with consistent and focused effort. Other handicaps can only be managed and may never go away.

Living with multiple sclerosis these last few years has helped me appreciate the struggles of a physically handicapped person. Every day it is hard for me to simply walk, put my socks on, or stay in 80-degree weather for any length of time. The emotional drain is intense. The need to think and plan for logistics to achieve normal movement is a heavy burden. The quality of life from a human perspective is diminished. Hiking in the woods or camping is too hard, going to the beach is incapacitating, and participating in most sports that I love is out of the question.

Personal attention and love by my family is more important to me than ever before. I know a child with special needs truly needs this extra support and reassurance. Homeschooling your special-needs child makes that intense, loving support possible.

We have seven children, including a set of twins who were supposed to have died in the womb. Yet God answered our desperate prayers in a miraculous way. Amy, whose head was caved in, whose spine was twisted, and who was not hooked up right, completely recovered in the womb and was born alive at two pounds, thirteen ounces. Although Amy was miraculously delivered, she is mentally much slower than her twin sister, Charity.

Christopher J. Klicka, the author of this chapter, and the father of seven homeschooled children, is Senior Counsel of the Home School Legal Defense Association (HSLDA). Chris has successfully represented thousands of homeschool families—including those with special-needs children—threatened by prosecutors, social workers, and truant officers. He also works on drafting federal legislation and lobbying on Capitol Hill. Although personally afflicted with multiple sclerosis, Chris has accomplished all this while traveling widely and taking the time to write and update *The Right Choice: Home Schooling* and his new book *The Heart of Home Schooling*.

What the Research Shows

Two of the biggest differences between home and public school education classrooms are in the *physical arrangement of the room* and the *amount of academic responses.* Home schools had children and teachers sitting side-by-side or face-to-face 43 percent of the time, while special education classroom had such an arrangement only 6 percent of the time. This is an obvious educational advantage for home schools. Public school classrooms used a divided group approach most (67 percent) of the time, and only placed children with special needs in a full group setting 25 percent of the time. Home schools, by contrast, used the divided group approach only a fraction of the time (11 percent) and were much more likely to include the special child in a full group experience (43 percent). Home schools therefore provide special children with more one-on-one attention and more full participation than public school special education classrooms do. . . .

In conclusion, parents, even without special education training, provided powerful instructional environments at home that assisted students with learning disabilities to make significant improvements in their basic skills. . . :

The end-of-year academic results of homeschooled children were significantly higher than those of the children in public school special education classrooms.

Dr. Steven Duvall,
The Impact of Home Education
on Learning Disabled Children:
A Look at New Research

At six years old, Amy is not ready to read like her sister. She requires much more time, attention, and love. Sending her to an institutional school would devastate her fragile self-confidence. Teachers could not possibly give her the one-on-one attention and love she needs.

In light of these experiences, I am convinced that homeschooling children with special needs is the most effective way to successfully teach them, and your home is the ideal environment in which they will learn and thrive.

Parents Excel in Teaching Their Special-Needs Children

Objective studies demonstrate that parents provide a superior form of education for their special-needs children by teaching them at home. Contrary to the claims of the education elite, parents do not have to be specially certified or have special qualifications to teach their handicapped children at home.

In fact, in one of the most thorough studies performed thus far, Dr. Steven Duvall conducted a yearlong study involving eight elementary and two junior high students with learning disabilities. He compared one group of five students that received instruction at home with a group of five students who attended public schools. He was careful to match the public school students to the homeschool students according to grade level, sex, I.Q., and area of disability. Using a laptop computer, Dr. Duvall sat in on teaching sessions and took an observation every 20 seconds, creating tens of thousands of data points that were then fed into a statistical analysis package. Usually his research included a second observer who double-checked Dr. Duvall's readings. Dr. Duvall recorded and analyzed academically engaged time by students during instructional periods. He also administered standardized achievement tests to them to measure gains in reading, math, and written language. His results show that the home-school, special-needs students were academically engaged about two and one-half times as often as public school special-needs students! He found the children in the public school special education classrooms spent 74.9 percent of their time with no academic responses, while the homeschool children only spent 40.7 percent of their time with no academic responses. He also found that homeschools have children and teachers sitting side-by-side or face-to-face 43 percent of the time, while public education classrooms had such an arrangement for special needs children only 6 percent of the time. This was a tremendous advantage for the homeschoolers.

His study further demonstrated that the homeschool students averaged six months' gain in reading compared to only a one-half month gain by the special public school students. Furthermore, the homeschool special-needs students during the year gained eight months in written language skills compared to the public school counterparts, who gained only two and one-half months

In his report, *The Impact of Home Education on Learning Disabled Children: A Look at New Research,* Dr. Duvall summarized, "These results clearly indicate that parents, even though they are not certified teachers, can create instructional environments at home that assist students with learning disabilities to improve their academic skills. This study clearly shows that homeschooling is beneficial for special-needs students."

It is interesting to note that Thomas Edison was expelled from public school at age seven because he was considered "addled" by his public school teacher. He lasted only three months in formal schooling. Over the next three years, his mother taught him the basics at home, and as Edison himself stated, "She instilled in me the love and purpose of learning." Without any special qualifications, Mrs. Edison helped her son overcome his disabilities to be come a great inventor.

Once again we see homeschooling works for any child!

The Home Is the Ideal Environment for Special-Needs Children

All children need to know they are loved. For children with special needs it is even more important. Homeschooling gives special-needs children teachers (the parents) who truly love them and intimately know their weaknesses and strengths. This gives parents a tremendous advantage in delivering an effective education program to their children.

Homeschooling also gives the parents an opportunity to teach what really matters. Having a handicap, as I have said, is a daily struggle. A handicapped child is constantly aware of his weakness and inability, and this can often regularly lead to feelings of worthlessness and inadequacy. In homeschooling, parents can spend much time teaching their special-needs child that they were created in the image of God. They have worth and value because God loves them. Their struggles and difficulties have purpose in glorifying God and being conformed more into the image of His Son.

Weakness and disability remind us of our mortality and our great need for a Savior. The spiritual object lessons to be drawn from our children's handicaps are endless and of eternal value to them and the whole family. I can truly say my multiple sclerosis and Amy's limitations are blessings that are reaping tremendous spiritual growth. God is teaching us to walk by faith, not sight (II Corinthians 5:7).

What Are My Rights?

Since 1983, the Home School Legal Defense Association (HSLDA) has worked to win and protect all parents' rights to teach all their children at home, including special-needs children. When we started it was only clearly legal to homeschool in approximately five states. It is now legal in all 50 states. Even though homeschooled special-needs children are being taught well by their parents and it is legal, they are still faced with regular legal challenges.

When Israel left Egypt, the Amalekites attacked Israel. However, they would rarely attack armed forces or the main group of the Israelites. Instead they would pick off the stragglers, who were often made up of the sick or weak.

Some public school authorities, unfortunately, seem to have adopted the tactics of the Amalekites when they are dealing with handicapped children who are being homeschooled. When they find it difficult to pick on homeschoolers with average or above average students, they turn to harassing the handicapped or special-needs homeschool children. Going after handicapped children that are homeschooled is somewhat easier since it is harder for the family to prove educational progress. It is also easier to intimidate the families into thinking they are not qualified. Of course, the incentive is greater also, since special-needs children are worth nearly twice as much in state and federal tax dollars that will be sent to the local school district.

As a result, oftentimes, homeschool families with children with special needs or handicaps are harassed and restricted more than other homeschool families. As a result of this discriminatory treatment, many homeschoolers with special-needs children begin to think they have less parental rights than everyone else. Constitutionally, this could not be further from

STEPS HSLDA RECOMMENDS

If your child has special learning needs (as opposed to a simple physical handicap non-related to learning), Home School Legal Defense Association recommends that you "keep accurate records demonstrating how you are meeting these needs and how your child is progressing," taking special care to document "periodic evaluations of your child's educational progress." HSLDA will provide a sample evaluation form as part of its services to members with special-needs children.

HSLDA also recommends that you obtain assistance with your homeschool program if your child

- Has received special education services in this school year
- Has been enrolled in special education services for the coming school year
- Has been evaluated and diagnosed as having a special learning need
- Is functioning substantially below grade level
- Has a physical disability that significantly hinders his or her ability to learn
- Has significant educational difficulties that have been observed but not professionally diagnosed

This assistance can be from an educational consultant, preferably not related to your child, who has "either credentials or experience in the same area as your child's special need." HSLDA recommends this consultant be in personal contact (as opposed to mail or phone) "a minimum of four times during the school year to document your child's progress." To locate a consultant, they suggest you check with your friends, support groups, specialists, and local colleges and universities. Private educational programs are also a possibility. It's generally best to avoid public-school programs, as "many families have found themselves mired in legal difficulties as a result of their involvement in public school services."

Homeschooling a Child with Fetal Alcohol Syndrome
by Linda Heinen

I am homeschooling two special-needs kids. Some of my friends think that I am very silly to do that. Their advice is to send them off to school because kids need socialization.

I like my friends, but I do not think their advice is suitable for my situation.

My kids are suffering from Fetal Alcohol Syndrome. That means that during the birth mom's pregnancy, she frequently drank, and her baby was damaged. In fact, both kids have retardation due to the alcohol and are classified as having serious brain injury. This brain damage cannot be reversed!

Children with FAS can learn but often in a very different way than offered in the classroom. They must have a place where it is quiet and with very little activity. These kids tend to be ADHD as well, and are constantly minding everyone's business but their own.

Our son was happily attending an Independent Christian School until he was in the fourth grade. However, it became apparent that his good buddies were steadily outgrowing him and the gap in abilities was ever widening. Soon he became very unhappy as he realized that he was different and could not do the things that they were doing. So I began homeschooling him, and the lad became more cheerful.

Joe Heinen learns at home

That year I became his scribe and wrote out his oral answers. We even wrote out his stories, which were quite well told. However, the following year we had to go back to basics as he was not using phonics to read but had begun to guess at what he saw. He was also losing the ability to spell even the simple words he once knew. I used the A Beka program, and he began to improve.

Over the last few years I have used the pick-and-choose method for buying curriculum. I ask him what he is interested in, and search for workbooks and unit studies to match his interests. One year he was interested in knights and the folklore of that era. So we studied the Medieval Times and tied in a Medieval Christmas as well. Later, we studied Ancient Egypt, and he laughed when Mom got squeamish in the mummy informational part of that unit. He went to the local library and took out a National Geographic video on Ancient Egypt and enjoyed it so much.

Science this year is a unit study on the horse. Besides learning about horses we are reading real novels such as *King of the Wind, The Black Stallion,* and so on. Perhaps he will learn enough so that he will be able to train a pony and do it well enough to have a career with horses.

Math was a mystery for him years ago, and we will be happy if he learns how to buy food and clothing within his budget when he is older.

In Language Arts we are busy with basic spelling and writing sentences. We also read books relating to his interests. I try to expose him to a variety of materials including comprehension. He does quite well orally and not so well with the written word. Those with FAS are very forgetful, and a fact they knew for days will suddenly be forgotten. To relearn it causes great frustration for him and for me because we both know that it could be forgotten again in a short time.

Our son finds great joy in using the computer. He often puts in the World Book CD and looks up any interesting person or fact that was in his studies for the day. Last week we were studying Mozart's life and his works, and answering questions from the unit on Great Composers. Later I heard him on the computer checking out some of Mozart's musical works and then going on to other composers of yesteryear as well as those of today.

Social Studies this year consists of studying Canada. Soon we will be finished with that unit and will move on to Ancient Greece, which is what he chose to study this year.

Joe is not all that interested in art, but we do look at pictures done by the Great Masters and discuss them in a very simple way. As a little fellow he did not like to color, cut, or paste. It took too long to get the result he wanted, and he did it in a hurry.

There are times when he totally lacks the motivation to complete his work for the day. All studies are done on a one-on-one method, and I cannot leave the room as he will wander off to another area. So we limit each day to a three-hour school day. That suffices both of us.

Our little gal has FAS, but it affects her differently. She sees much of life as a joke. If I have to leave her side for a moment, she might stay and work independently, or she might wait for my return. Often she decides that now is the time for her to hide under the table or desk or else run off to her room. When she receives a consequence, she becomes very upset and just doesn't understand why I didn't appreciate her fun and games time.

She is able to understand her math and knows some of her facts. Sometimes she has to use her counting cubes or a number line because she has forgotten what she used to know. We are now on the money unit, and so far she is able to do it.

Social Studies consists of studying about "Our Community." We have completed the section on "The Policeman." We now have to visit the local police station. When we have completed "The Postman," we will see how the mail is sorted and stamped at the post office in our town. Next on the list are the Baker, the Fireman, and other people in the nearby town.

the truth. Parents with special-needs children are protected by the same Constitution as all other parents. Therefore, they too have the protection of the First and Fourteenth Amendments.

For example, one Home School Legal Defense Association (HSLDA) homeschool family in Colorado had their child in special-needs classes in the public school. After a while, their child basically stagnated as the classroom atmosphere became unbearable. They decided that they could do a better job themselves, so they notified the school district that they were going to homeschool. Although it was legal to homeschool in the state, the local school district would not disenroll the child. The district felt the child's Individual Education Plan (IEP) recommendation could not be fulfilled by a mere mother. It called the family nearly every week, trying to pressure them back in for more meetings and more conferences with the public school's specialists. The mother could barely stand the intimidation and began to doubt herself. I was called and was able to convince the school district to retreat and recognize her right to homeschool privately.

In Illinois, a family disenrolled their child from all special-needs programs except speech therapy. Over and over again the school district tried to pressure the family to come into various meetings in which the child would be evaluated and recommendations given. The school district believed the parents were not qualified. Finally, the school district initiated a due process proceeding, pursuant to the "Individuals with Disabilities Education Act" or "IDEA," since they believed the family was still under the jurisdiction of that act because the child was still receiving speech therapy. The family followed my advice and withdrew their child from speech therapy and provided a written statement to the school district breaking all ties. After we further negotiated with the school district, the family was finally left alone. In Indiana, a couple who educated nine adopted handicapped children was harassed repeatedly by school officials. Scores of other families were homeschooling in the area, but this family was singled out because all the children had special needs. The school district was losing a lot of money.

The personal experiences I have had with defending handicapped children who are harassed only because they are homeschooling could go on and on. In every instance, the situations were resolved by HSLDA attorneys, and in every instance, the parents were able to do a better job because they cared about their children and best understood their special needs.

We are using a simple unit on Science and have added a unit on Animals. She just loves all of God's creatures, big or small, tame or wild. As we live in the country, we have close-up encounters with deer, porcupines, skunks, coyotes, prairie dogs, and marmots.

We are focusing heavily on Phonics, and she is using two workbooks plus a book on comprehension and some phonics readers. She is reading, but it is not coming easily. A word that she could read yesterday suddenly becomes a struggle to sound out. We also use a unit study, Come Sit with Me, that uses real books.

If she could have her way, she would have art every day. She is forever cutting, pasting, and making things from paper. She also looks at works of the Great Masters when her brother does. She loves to paint and uses up a lot of it at one time, but we are pleased that she has a good imagination.

She has music at the same time as her brother, and listens to the tapes and to the information that we read about the composer. In fact, she often drifts in when I teach in the morning and listens in as we read a novel connected to the history or language unit we are studying on that day.

Our school day is about two hours long, and that is long enough for us at this time. We do read at bedtime, and sometimes read and do crafts in the late afternoon or early evening.

So you can see that special-needs kids can learn and enjoy their studies even if they have to be modified according to ability and not age. It is very important that they succeed at what they do and not be frustrated with what others think that they should be doing!

HSLDA SPECIAL-NEEDS SERVICES

HSLDA members who indicate on their application or renewal form that they are home schooling a special-needs child will be sent *HSLDA's Recommendations for Home Schooling Children with Special Needs,* which includes these forms along with instructions for filling them out.

In addition to legal representation if required, HSLDA provides:

- A special-needs coordinator who is available to assist members with their concerns about home schooling their special-needs child.
- Names of credentialed professionals who have experience with special-needs children.
- Lists of some resources useful for home schooling special-needs children.

Tests members may rent from HSLDA:

- The Woodcock-Johnson PsychoEducational Battery— Revised, Tests of Achievement: This individually administered test is useful for children who may not test well in a group setting. It must be administered by a special education teacher.
- Brigance Diagnostic Inventories: These are tests that parents or professionals may administer to determine what skills a child has or has not mastered. These tests are used routinely in public and private schools to develop an IEP.
- Inventory of Early Development (yellow)—birth through developmental age 7.
- Inventory of Basic Skills (blue) —grades K–6.
- Comprehensive Inventory of Basic Skills (green)—grades preK–9.
- Inventory of Essential Skills (red)—grade 6–adult.
    —*www.hslda.org/hs/specialneeds*

How Can I Get Help?

There are two basic options homeschoolers can choose to receive help: private special-needs resources or resources from the public schools through the federal IDEA program. Of course, some homeschoolers could do a combination of them both.

At this time, the US Department of Education's Office of Special Education Programs (OSEP) has interpreted that the IDEA special education resources only have to be made available to students in public schools or private schools. They specifically explain homeschool students cannot qualify. This policy letter from the OSEP, however, seems contrary to the purpose of IDEA "to assist States . . . to provide for the education of ALL children with disabilities" 20 USC section 1400(d)(C).

HSLDA has filed suit in federal court to end this discrimination, and we are working with the Bush Administration to issue a new policy letter from the OSEP to recognize all homeschoolers can qualify for special-needs services.

In the meantime, certain states have passed regulations allowing homeschoolers to participate. Also, if a homeschooler is in a state that recognizes homeschools as private schools, the homeschoolers can generally get the assistance.

However, parents should consider the possible side effect of loss of freedom when using government special-needs services. A common adage, that government *controls* nearly always follow government *money,* often rings true with homeschoolers who receive public school services for their special-needs children. Many times the controls are not immediately visible, but they usually surface as soon as the parents begin to disagree with the public school authorities' "recommendations" for new therapy or a different educational approach. At the very least, homeschoolers who receive public school services for their special-needs children place themselves under the jurisdiction of the federal IDEA and local state regulations which implement that act. The types of problems homeschoolers encounter are described above.

The intent of IDEA is to provide statutory guidelines for local public schools to make available a free public education to the handicapped. The act is not a compulsory attendance statute for handicapped children. It is clearly apparent, therefore, that parents who do not want to take advantage of a free public education for their handicapped child are not mandated to do so. Such a mandate would also violate the parents' fundamental right to direct the education of their children, as guaranteed under *Pierce vs. Society of Sisters.* In the 1925 *Pierce* case, the US Supreme Court declared parents have the right to choose a private educational program for their children, and, as a result, the Court struck down an Oregon law that mandated only public school attendance.

Parents of special-needs children are not required to use any public educational services. To privately educate their special-needs child is the parents' choice. By doing so, they avoid the state's controls pursuant to the IDEA.

Homeschooling special-needs students privately carries the least risk for government intervention. Be cautious if you choose to work with the public schools for the reasons discussed above. Homeschoolers should also carefully watch their legislatures in order to oppose any attempts to create excessive regulations for handicapped children being homeschooled. All homeschoolers need to stand together to protect special-needs homeschoolers from being separately and excessively regulated.

CHAPTER 44

How Real Are Learning Disabilities?

Eight million American children are labeled learning disabled. Over $1 billion annually flows to pharmaceutical companies for the stimulants and antidepressants prescribed for these labeled children. Over $1 billion yearly lines the pockets of mental health workers as a direct result of labeling those eight million children "learning disabled."

Clearly, labeling children is a growth industry with lots of profits for lots of players.

But are the labels deserved? Do they represent any kind of concrete reality? Are they even helpful? Do we even know what is being done to our children and what the words really mean?

Genetic Holocaust or Defective Theory?

Before the advent of psychoactive drugging of children, somehow classrooms managed to function, even with slow kids, late bloomers, tomboys, class clowns, daydreamers, and all the other old, non-medical labels we used to use.

Somehow the tough old teachers of my youth seemed to muddle along. So did the tough old teachers of my mother's and grandmother's youth. But now each generation of teachers gets worse results than the ones before it.

According to an article in *School Reform News* of April 2002, the number of students "deemed learning disabled grew from 3 percent to 6 percent of all students over the past two decades."

So are we in the midst of some huge genetic holocaust in which the gene pool has gradually turned murky, yielding massive crops of defective kids?

Or is it possible that there is something defective about the theory of "learning disabilities"?

Real vs. Unreal Learning Difficulties

I readily admit that some kids are harder to teach than others. Some kids are *much* harder to teach than others. There are a number of real learning difficulties:

> In this age of labels, when there is a government program for every label, parents have to be on guard against having their children pigeonholed. The stakes are just too high.
>
> —*Thomas Sowell*

Labeling Fads

In 1990, when NATHHAN first started, we got thousands of calls from parents whose children were diagnosed with ADHD. This all but ceased and was replaced with autism and Pervasive Developmental Disorder. Presently we are getting lots of calls from families frustrated at the educational and medical field's new "rage diagnoses" Bipolar and Oppositional Defiance Disorder. What will it be next?

These diagnoses cheapen the help children with real LD, ADHD, true autism, or PPD get. Parents whose children do have these problems are not faking it and really do need help.

These "quick diagnoses" are being handed out like candy by the public school system and some medical professionals. Families may not realize that these labels follow children through life.

Thousands of these parents are excited about homeschooling. They are not accepting the label and "help" that does not fit their child, in exchange for being a school district's money making decoy. Special-needs children bring in a school district anywhere from $10,000 to $19,000 and up, depending on the IEP signed by the parent.

—*Tom and Sherry Bushnell*
National Challenged Homeschooling
Associated Network (NATHHAN)

- **Organic damage (brain trauma and genetic brain defects) is real.** These types of problems are the only ones we *should* be calling learning disabilities, since there is an actual testable medical condition.
- **Allergies are real.** Kids who itch and twitch find it hard to concentrate. However, allergies can be detected and treated, as you'll see in the next chapter.
- **Emotional distress is real**, though hopefully temporary and fixable, and not exactly an inbuilt "disability."
- **Hunger is real.** Ever try to concentrate while your stomach was sounding off? Even if your stomach isn't growling, if your body is hungry for needed nutrients, that can really slow you down.
- **Undisciplined folly is real.** As a rule, kids will get away with whatever they can, and if you have trustingly fallen under the spell of "progressive" parenting methods, attitude and misbehavior are more to be expected than not.
- **Boredom is WAY real.** You know *you* doodle or snore when you're bored—why shouldn't your kids?

Now, here are some ways to cause learning difficulties that aren't "real" since the problem comes from *outside* the child:

- **Unrealistic academic and behavioral expectations** on the part of the parent and/or the school. Yes, homeschoolers can fall prey to this one, too!
- **Expecting every kid to have one and only one learning style: the Progress Person.** This is the same as expecting every adult to dream of someday becoming an accountant.
- **Expecting boys to be girls.** Drawings of planes dropping bombs doesn't mean the little guy is fated to be a terrorist, any more than playing "cops and robbers" means he'll grow up to star in *Die Hard 4*. Why is it OK for men to be "from Mars," but not for boys?

Diagnosis by Pocketbook

All the above reasons why kids might be inattentive or hyper, or why we might be mistaken when we are annoyed at their behavior, have one thing in common—**you don't need psychoactive drugs to treat them.**

As I pointed out at the beginning of this chapter, every year *billions* of dollars flow to pharmaceutical companies and to those who prescribe and monitor the use of psychoactive drugs on children. Ever since the public decided that it was OK to give mind-altering drugs to kids—as long as a doctor prescribed them—the use of such drugs has ballooned every year. And the key to getting more and more kids on such drugs—legally, that is—is to label more and more kids as having "disabilities" that "need" drug treatment.

The most insidious thing about all of this is the way our "watchdog" media are buying into the use of psychoactive drugs on children as normal and reasonable. But how much of a surprise should that be, once you realize how many millions of dollars pharmaceutical companies spend each year on radio, TV, and magazine ads? There's a certain loss of objectivity when your company's profit for the year depends on keeping the "Pharm Industry" happy.

A School Principal on Learning Disabilities as Alibis

I have observed that in the last several decades there have been three classic "learning disabilities" promulgated by the educational community—or more properly, by the educational establishment. Each one has served its purpose for that time—namely, to get the responsibility off the back of the (public) schools and on to the back of "disabilities," with which everyone sympathizes.

The first of these classic three "disabilities" was **dyslexia**. This was a popular cause given for the inability of children to learn to read in the late 50s and 60s, when the educational establishment was reaping the grim fruits of their new, popular "Look-Say" or "Sight" reading system. Now, dyslexia is indeed a valid physical impairment. It is a specific disorder of the visual system, causing images to be perceived upside down or reversed left to right. However, if one consults a reputable ophthalmologist, or a text book on the subject, he will find that the **incidence of dyslexia is about one in 10,000.**

In his 1970 book, *Classroom Countdown*, Dr. Max Rafferty addressed this "disability." Dr. Rafferty, who served as the Superintendent of Public Instruction of the state of California for many years, states on page 242:

> For any of you who are not of the Inner Sanctum of education, dyslexia is the tendency of certain children to see letters in reverse. Obviously, it would nicely explain inability to read, and equally obviously this makes it alluringly attractive to "look-say" reading teachers, who are compelled now and then to explain why their pupils can't read.

To ward off a Niagara of letters from parents of allegedly dyslexic children, let me hasten to state that I do indeed believe in dyslexia. During my thirty years in education, I have known precisely one case. But, of late, as reading difficulties have burgeoned despite our gloriously "modern" teaching methods, the learned estimate of persons affected by dyslexia has grown enormously, from practically none a few years back to as high as 30 percent of the population today!

> *Dyslexia neatly fits education's classic definition of the perfect alibi: It's scientific-sounding, it's mysterious, and it's something the teacher can't be expected to do much about.* (Emphasis added)

We may observe an interesting point here: If we substitute the term "Attention Deficit Disorder" for "dyslexia," the emphasized paragraph, now some 27 years old, makes perfect sense even today!

I will leave the subject of dyslexia with the final note that in my 15 years as school principal, during which time I interviewed every parent of children coming into the school, I found a high percentage of supposedly "dyslexic" children; the parents had been told that the reason for the child's difficulty in reading was some (mild?) form of dyslexia. **In no case was the "dyslexic" diagnosis accompanied by a note from a doctor;** it always seemed to be the "diagnosis" of someone connected with the school system, including the school psychologists. **But in every case, the child soon learned to read**, as we used a traditional, structured classroom and traditional teaching methods based largely on phonics.

The second of the three classic learning "disabilities" became popular in the early 70s; it was **Hyperactivity**. Again, neither the child nor the teacher was to blame. Just like dyslexia, or the now popular ADD, it was something that just happened to this particular child. The principal of one of the elementary public schools in a reasonably affluent section of the city of Columbus, Ohio, told me in 1973 that about 25 percent of the students there were on "Ritalin," which was then the drug of choice for "hyperactivity."

Again, as principal of the Christian school, I had parents bringing their children from the public school to ours and cautioning us that their child was "hyperactive." Needless to say, in a structured classroom, and with proper discipline for any "hyperactivity" that disrupted the classroom, these students soon settled down and learned to read. To my knowledge, only a very few continued with their Ritalin. When I retired from the school, now ten years ago, hyperactivity had pretty much subsided as a problem.

The third of the three classic learning "disabilities" has now replaced Hyperactivity. That is the currently rampant **Attention Deficit Disorder**, or **ADD**. I heard one man, who had taught for some 40 years from the early 50s to the early 90s, ask where ADD had been for all these years. He simply didn't believe such a thing could have existed for the 40 years of his teaching, and he had not ever observed it. And there are many like him.

I submit that though, like dyslexia, ADD is a real disorder for a very few children, it simply has become the educational establishment's latest scientific-sounding excuse for the failure of the students to learn. Please note that I did not say the "inability." After ADD has run its course, I wonder what the educational establishment will think of next to excuse its failure?

I would submit that, when it comes to these learning disabilities, it was not doctors but the psychologists and school administrators who "diagnosed" the condition. Again, in my 15 years as principal, though I consulted with doctors on many occasions, I never once heard a doctor say, "Little Johnny Jones is really hyperactive, and needs to be treated accordingly."

—*Jack E. Willer, Worthington, OH*

Labels Don't Help

ADD [and just about every other LD] is a description of behavior, not an explanation. It tries to describe symptoms rather than explain the causes of those symptoms. It tries to answer the question, "What is this child doing?" but not, "Why is this child doing it?" . . .

It would not be helpful if someone asked, "Why is your son always squirming in his chair?" If you responded, "Because he has ADD," that is really no different from saying, "He squirms in his chair because he fidgets." You are merely describing his behaviors with different vocabulary. . . .

Dr. Edward T. Welch, Journal of Biblical Counseling, *Winter 1996*

Diagnosis by Checklist

But surely all those children who are diagnosed *need* professional treatment and possibly drugs, right?

Not if the diagnosis itself is false or meaningless.

The typical medical outlook on diagnosing ADHD, the most frequently drugged LD, is shown in this quote from Marcia Zimmerman's book, *The ADD Nutrition Solution* (Henry Holt & Company, 1999):

> *A diagnosis for this disorder should be given only after a thorough evaluation by a team of professionals who specialize in AD/HD. First, you should see a pediatrician to rule out possible medical reasons for the disorder. AD/HD will not reveal itself through the usual battery of laboratory tests, although some abnormalities in brain function have been observed with the use of brain-imaging techniques such as magnetic resonance imaging (MRI) and positron emission tomography (PET) scans. "There is no laboratory test or set of tests that currently can be used to make a definitive diagnosis," according to Dennis Cantwell, M.D.,* Journal of the American Academy of Child and Adolescent Psychiatry, *August 1996.*

So the bottom line is:

- There is no *medical* test—blood, urine, DNA, X-ray, or otherwise—that can detect ADHD. As Dr. Peter Breggin fully documents in his book, *Talking Back to Ritalin*, "There are no objective diagnostic criteria for ADHD—no physical symptoms, no neurological signs, and no blood tests.
- However, "abnormalities in brain function have been observed" via MRI and PET scans

It's this last sentence that sells millions of parents on the idea that ADD and ADHD are somehow medically diagnosable diseases.

However, you need to take a closer look at those "abnormalities." Dr. Breggin states, "Despite claims to the contrary, there are no brain scan findings and no biochemical imbalances. No physical tests can be done to verify that a child has 'ADHD.'" He devotes large sections of his book to debunking what he calls the "Brain Scan Scam." Briefly, here are the facts:

- No practitioner can look at a brain scan and tell by the scan alone whether a child has ADHD or any other LD.
- The "abnormalities" found in scans, and reported widely as "physical proof that ADHD is a disease," were found in populations of children labeled ADHD *who had already been taking stimulant drugs such as Ritalin,* which have been shown to *cause* that kind of abnormality. As Breggin notes, "To the extent that brain scan studies do show abnormalities in these children, the scans are detecting damage and dysfunction caused by stimulants and other psychiatric drugs."

In other words, brain scans have shown that labeled kids *who have been taking prescribed drugs* do have some brain abnormalities.

Dr. Breggin really knows what he is talking about. He actually presented a paper at the NIH conference that drug advocates thought would give the "ADHD is a brain disease" theory a clean bill of health. However, things didn't work out exactly as they intended:

After hearing all the scientific presentations and discussions [at the recent National Institutes of Health (NIH) Consensus Development Conference on Attention Deficit Hyperactivity Disorder], the consensus conference panel concluded "there are no data to indicate that ADHD is due to a brain malfunction." The conclusion was so threatening to the establishment that the National Institute of Mental Health edited it out of the final version after the consensus panel had already disbanded and gone home. However, the failure of brain scans to show any distinct abnormality attributable to ADHD is reconfirmed by the American Academy of Pediatrics in its official 2000 report.

How Kids Actually Get Labeled

So, if you can't detect learning disabilities with blood tests, urine tests, neurological exams, or even brain scans, how *do* children get labeled as LD?

For what is now called "learning disorders," the main question is whether the child is performing up to grade level in reading, math, and writing. If not, he is presumed to have "Reading Disorder" (this used to be called *dyslexia*), "Mathematics Disorder," or "Disorder of Written Expression." As Breggin says, "The everyday concept of the 'underachiever' has been turned into a disorder."

For all other "learning disabilities," they use a checklist. A school worker or medical professional sits down with your child for somewhere between ten minutes and half an hour. They ask the child a number of questions. If the parents are present, they also ask the parents to rate the child on a number of criteria. Then, if the total score adds up to a certain number, the child is "diagnosed" with ADD, ADHD, autism, etc.

Autism by Checklist

Here is one typical example. I got this from the AGS Publishing website, intended to promote their "Childhood Autism Rating Scale (CARS)." It is described as "suitable for use with any child over 2 years of age," and explains that various "professionals" such as "special educators, school psychologists, speech pathologists, and audiologists" who have "had only minimal exposure to autism" can be "easily trained to use CARS." In other words, the "professionals" who will be administering the test *know nothing* about autism. The list could presumably just as well include janitors and bell hops. How can someone who *knows nothing* about autism determine if your child is autistic? Simple: "After the child has been rated on each of the 15 items, a total score is computed by summing the individual ratings." If your child scores above a certain number, he is "categorized as autistic."

So, this person who *knows nothing* about autism observes your child and "examin[es] relevant information from parent reports and other records" and "rates the child on each item" on a scale of 1 to 7. That's it! Instant diagnosis!

Actually, the CARS system is a model of scientific thoroughness compared to the way ADD and ADHD are diagnosed.

ADD and ADHD by Checklist

Here is the official definition of ADD from the American Psychiatric Association's DSM-IV (the Diagnostic Standards Manual, 4th edition). This

The Brain Scan Scam

The public continues to be bombarded with media misinformation about brain scans supposedly showing abnormalities in the brains of children diagnosed with ADHD. Indeed, several brain scan studies have claimed to demonstrate brain abnormalities associated with ADHD. Most of the studies have found relatively small brain abnormalities in frontal lobes and basal ganglia in children diagnosed with ADHD. (These areas are among those known to be damaged by stimulant drugs.) The differences were based on comparisons between groups of normal children and groups of children labeled ADHD. The findings were not detectable on a case-by-case basis and cannot be used for diagnostic purposes. There are no physical defects associated with the ADHD diagnosis.

The differences found between normal brains and those of children diagnosed with ADHD are almost certainly due to medication effects. For example, a typical study is entitled "Evaluation of Cerebellar Size in Attention-Deficit Hyperactivity Disorder." According to its summary, it finds that children with ADHD have abnormalities in the cerebellum, a lobe at the back of the brain.

However, in the text of the report, the following information is provided about the 12 children with ADHD: "Seven of the patients with ADHD had . . . . received methylphenidate in the past. One of these seven individuals had also received dextroamphetamine and pemoline. Another had received chlonidine." This is actually a study of drug-treated children diagnosed with ADHD and the failure to indicate this in the title or the abstract indicates a Brain Scan Scam. . . .

Peter R. Breggin, M.D., Talking Back to Ritalin, *revised edition (Perseus Publishing, 2001)*

is the official diagnosis "bible" of the psychiatric profession. It doesn't get any more official than this. And here it is, the official checklist for diagnosing ADD and ADHD:

A. Either (1) or (2):

(1) Six (or more) of the following symptoms of inattention have persisted for at least six months to a degree that is maladaptive and inconsistent with developmental level:

Inattention

(a) *Often makes careless mistakes in schoolwork, work, or other activities.*

(b) *Often has difficulty sustaining attention in tasks or play activities*

(c) *Often does not seem to listen when spoken to directly.*

(d) *Often does not follow through on instructions and fails to finish schoolwork, chores, or duties in the workplace (not due to oppositional behavior or failure to understand instructions).*

(e) *Often has difficulty organizing tasks and activities.*

(f) *Often avoids, dislikes, or is reluctant to engage in tasks that require sustained mental effort (such as schoolwork or homework).*

(g) *Often loses things necessary for tasks or activities (e.g., toys, school assignments, pencils, books, or tools).*

(h) *Is often easily distracted by extraneous stimuli.*

(i) *Is often forgetful in daily activities.*

(2) Six (or more) of the following symptoms of hyperactivity/impulsivity has persisted for at least six months to a degree that is maladaptive and inconsistent with developmental level:

Hyperactivity

(a) *Often fidgets with hands or feet or squirms in seat.*

(b) *Often leaves seat in classroom or in other situations in which remaining seated is expected.*

(c) *Often runs about or climbs excessively in situations in which it is inappropriate (in adolescents or adults, may be limited to subjective feelings of restlessness).*

(d) *Often has difficulty playing or engaging in leisure activities quietly.*

(e) *Is often "on the go" or often acts as if "driven by a motor."*

(f) *Often talks excessively.*

Impulsivity

(g) *Often blurts out answers before questions have been completed.*

(h) *Often has difficulty awaiting turn.*

(i) *Often interrupts or intrudes on others (e.g., butts into conversations or games).*

B. Some hyperactive-impulse or inattentive symptoms that caused impairment were present before age 7 years.

C. Some impairment from the symptoms is present in two or more settings (e.g., at school [or work] and at home).

D. There must be clear evidence of clinically significant impairment in school, academic, or occupational functioning.

Now let's break this down a little.

- We're looking at a *checklist.* Did you see anything on that list about brain scans, blood or urine tests, physical measurements, or any other *scientific* or *medical* evidence of a "condition"?
- We're looking at *subjective judgment.* The word "often," for example, occurs no less than 18 times on the DSM-IV checklist. But how often is "often"? Once a day? Once an hour? Once every three minutes?
- We're looking at the *attitude of the evaluator* more than the actual child himself or herself. "Impairment" and "maladaptivity" is mostly in the mind of the person in charge of the child. It's an indication of how much the *adult* is annoyed by the child, not that there is necessarily anything wrong with the child.
- The checklist includes "symptoms" that are *normal* for very smart children, kinesthetic/tactile children, and four out of five personality types.
- The "inattention" checklist is also a perfect list of behaviors for people who are bored silly. Yet the list does not include any indicators of whether the prospective ADD candidate was presented with tasks that any reasonable person would *not* consider worthless and boring. In other words, something could just as easily be wrong with the school as with the child.
- The "hyperactivity" checklist could just as easily be renamed a "high energy" checklist. Yet having a lot of energy is actually a sign of excellent health! The problem here seems to be that the child is disrupting the classroom or annoying the teacher. And are the folks who made this checklist aware that boys, who are much more frequently diagnosed hyperactive than girls, often have bony little rear ends which actually *hurt* when they have to sit long hours in an unpadded plastic school chair? (Some actual medical conditions, such as allergies or hypoglycemia, also cause kids to fidget and run around like crazy—we'll be talking about those later.)
- I find it almost incredible that anyone ever considered treating the "impulsivity" category with drugs. Here you have a child who actually *wants* to answer the teacher's questions and is eager to rush into every activity. So let's drug him or her?

I'm ADD, You're ADD . . . At Least on Certain Days

Most discussions about ADD assume that the list of descriptions is equivalent to establishing a medical diagnosis. The popular assumption is that there is an underlying biological cause for the behaviors, but the assumption is unfounded. Although there are dozens of biological theories to explain ADD, there are presently no physical markers for it; there are no medical tests that detect its presence. . . . At this point, we can't say that anyone has ADD in the way that someone has a virus. . . .

The ever-present "often" in the diagnostic criteria betrays the loose boundaries of ADD, and it explains why Americans use the diagnosis so frequently. Almost anyone can squeeze into the parameters—at least on certain days.

Dr. Edward T. Welch, Journal of Biblical Counseling, *Winter 1996*

I was fascinated to discover that my husband, Bill, who received both the Harvard Book and the Rensselaer Science medal in his high school, has a B.S. in Math from M.I.T. and both an M.A. in Missions and an M.Div. degree from Covenant Theological Seminary, is a classic ADD case! But he has nothing to boast about, because *I* turn out to be a classic ADHD (until I turned 40 and lost all my energy, that is!). This hurt my academic life so much that I wasn't able to graduate high school until age 16 and college until age 18. In fact, looking back on it, most of my fellow classmates at Rensselaer Polytechnic Institute, one of the nation's top engineering colleges, clearly manifested symptoms of at least one or two LDs. This LD stuff sure is powerful stuff—so powerful that we all graduated from top colleges without a speck of difficulty.

The Autism Dragnet

As you might have guessed from the autism checklist I mentioned on page 397, an all-out effort is underway to label more and more kids autistic.

Autism as the "Label du Jour"?

One of the leading authorities on autism, Dr. Bernard Rimland of the Autism Research Institute in San Diego, has said: "In recent years autism has become fashionable, and the term is vastly overused."

Thomas Sowell, "Mice, Giraffes and Autism," Jewish World Review, *Nov. 5, 1999*

According to an Autism Society of America press release of November 26, 2003, entitled "U.S. Gov't Releases 10-Year Autism Roadmap at Summit,"

> The federal government has for the first time mapped out a long-term plan for addressing the growing problem of autism in the United States. The 10-year Autism Research Roadmap was announced at the government's Autism Summit Conference held on November 19-20, 2003, in Washington, DC. . . .
>
> The roadmap was one of the many items addressed at the summit, which was organized by the U.S. Department of Health and Human Services and the U.S. Department of Education and focused on the federal government's role in biomedical autism research, early screening and diagnosis, and improving access to autism services. Autism experts, government researchers, Members of Congress, and ASA leaders presented on a range of issues, including the announcement of a new program on the importance of early diagnosis of autism. . .
>
> The seven-page roadmap overviews goals and activities for the next 10 years, which are broken down by time—short term (1-3 years), medium term (4-6 years), and long term (7-10 years)—and by level of risk—from low to high.. . .

Forced Screening of Your Kids?

Homeschoolers may be particularly interested in the "new initiative" announced at the summit by ASA President Beck—the National Early Childhood Developmental Screening Program. According to the press release,

> The goal of the new program is to develop "an ongoing, multi-stage, national, public awareness and education program to foster the earliest detection of developmental disabilities like autism in children to provide prompt appropriate interventions and services to those children and to lay the foundation for more meaningful and productive lives."
>
> More specifically, Beck said, the goals of the program, over the next decade, are to:
>
> 1) Screen all children in the U.S. for developmental disabilities, including autism, by age 3,
> 2) Reduce by 50 percent the number of undiagnosed children with autism by school age,
> 3) Increase access to treatment/services to children with developmental disabilities, such as autism, and
> 4) Reduce/free up national healthcare and education dollars through early diagnosis and intervention.

That sounds just yummy. Take *all* our children from our homes, plop them in front of people who have "had only minimal exposure to autism" in the words of the CARS promo blurb, and then label them at will. The point of all this, of course, will be to *enforce treatment* that the "professionals" consider your "autistic" child needs. I am expecting to hear any day now of a new wonder drug that is just the thing to treat all such children.

Real vs. Unreal Autism

There is such a thing as genuine autism—although again the label does not seem to help provide any cures. However, there is also such a thing as varying stages of development and kids who like to "spin" themselves. As one of my favorite writers, Thomas Sowell, said in his column "The Autism Dilemma" published in October, 2001:

There is no definitive word to this very moment as to whether Amanda [a Nevada girl whose parents sued to get copies of the evaluations that declared her autistic] is or is not autistic. This is not uncommon. Many parents report conflicting diagnoses as regards autism. As the 9th Circuit [Court of Appeals] decision [of September 25, 2001] says: "No single behavior is characteristic of autism and no single known cause is responsible. . . ."

There are lists of things that autistic children do, but many other children who are not autistic do those same things. Amanda, for example, liked to spin herself, as autistic children do— but so have many other children, including yours truly as a child.

Against this background of troubling uncertainties, there are nevertheless dogmatic certainties proclaimed by various zealots, bureaucrats and movements. One claim is that accurate diagnoses of autism can be made as early as age 2 by "professionals experienced in the diagnostic assessment of young children."

But what percentage of the people who actually diagnose children fall into that exemplary category, and how many inaccurate diagnoses are also made at that age—or at any other age? Such crucial questions are seldom asked, much less answered. Nor has there been much attention paid to the bad consequences of wrong diagnoses. . . .

It is also dogma that "early intervention" can only help. Yet Amanda improved after being removed from an early intervention program. So did a little boy in Nebraska who was diagnosed as autistic, but who was removed from an early intervention program after a legal challenge was made. He began to improve greatly, after having retrogressed while in the program. Other parents have reported similar experiences.

Uncertainties can be painful, but bogus certainties can be worse. . . .

Obviously, whatever can be done to help genuinely autistic children should be done. Indeed, concentrating resources on those who are in fact autistic makes more sense than spreading the label and the money to many others. More important than the financial costs are the human costs of pulling children into the autism dragnet who are in fact not autistic.

There is, in fact, mounting evidence that genuine autism is caused by reactions to the increasing load of vaccines forced on tiny babies and young toddlers. In particular, the mercury still found in some vaccines can cause the exact same symptoms labeled "autistic." In which case, you need to find someone who can perform chelation therapy on your child, to remove as much of the mercury as possible (try www.acam.org to locate a doctor who does chelation therapy). However, vaccines are another sacred cow

The Autism Dragnet

The U.S. Department of Education and the National Institutes of Health have launched a campaign to get a government program created to "identify" children with autism at age two and then subject them to "intensive" early intervention for 25 hours a week or more. . . .

Just who is to "identify" these children and by what criteria? A legal case in Nebraska shows the dangers in creating a government-mandated dragnet that can subject all sorts of children to hours of disagreeable, ineffective or even counterproductive treatment for something they do not have.

A four-year old boy, whom we can call Bryan, was diagnosed as "autistic" and put into a program in which he grew worse instead of better, despite the protests of his parents. Eventually, these parents sued the school district, calling in as their expert witness Professor Stephen Camarata of Vanderbilt University.

Professor Camarata examined Bryan and concluded that he was not autistic and should not be kept in the program that was not doing him any good. However, the hearing officer sided with the school district, for reasons that are a chilling example of what can happen when bureaucratic criteria prevail.

Many children have already been labeled "autistic" or "retarded" on the basis of evaluations that lasted less then ten minutes—and many of these evaluations have later been contradicted, either by more highly qualified specialists or by the course of events as the child developed. . . .

Parents of late-talking children have reported that they have been urged to allow their kids to be labeled "autistic" in order to get federal money that can be used for speech therapy. Maybe that has contributed to the "increase" in autism we hear about—which in turn has contributed to the stampede for a new federal program.

—*Thomas Sowell*

In a *Canadian Medical Association Journal* article of October, 2001, researchers found that among schoolchildren in Eastern Canada, about 15 percent of children who were prescribed stimulants reported giving the drugs to other children, and 7 percent said they had sold the drugs to others. The study also revealed that about 4 percent of the children said the drugs had been stolen from them, and 3 percent said other children had taken their drugs away by force. Keep in mind these are Canadian kids, who are well known to be far less violence prone than Americans. Yet we find 29 percent of them passing Ritalin to others, sometimes by theft and force.

THINK YOUR CHILD HAS ADHD? CHECK THIS OUT FIRST!

See the excellent "50 Conditions That Mimic ADHD" site at adhdparentssupportgroup.homestead.com/50conditionsmimicingADHD.html.

The site divides the 50 conditions that mimic ADHD into:

- Conditions most overlooked
- Other good possibilities to check for
- Definitely check if there is a family history of the condition
- General problems you can think about yourself and check if you see fit
- Rare conditions but still good to check for and know about

Some of the conditions it lists are potentially life-threatening. Others simply are matters of diet, exercise, toxins, etc. It is really worthwhile to go through this list first just to see how many things besides a nebulous "ADHD" label can explain your child's behavior.

that causes untold billions to flow to pharmaceutical companies, so once again the politicians and mass media have no interest in checking this connection out. But if *your* child has autistic symptoms, there's nothing stopping *you* from having him or her tested for heavy metal toxicity. At the worst, you have wasted a few hundred dollars. At best, you'll have found a genuine medical cause for your child's problems.

What Does It Hurt If Your Child Is Labeled?

Even if you're already homeschooling, it's important to know whose opinions about your child can be trusted and who has an agenda.

If you are only *thinking* about homeschooling, and maybe already have a child or two in school, it's even more vital that you fight to prevent them being unreasonably labeled as learning disabled, ADD, ADHD, autistic, OCD, dyslexic, and a host of other labels that are freely and wildly misapplied to perfectly normal children.

It matters because:

- Once your child is put on any psychoactive drugs, he is disqualified forever from serving in the military. Ironically, the very same high-energy boys who would do great in the Army, Navy, Air Force, or Coast Guard can't even get in if someone gave them a dose of Ritalin 15 years ago.
- Once your child is diagnosed LD, the school system can demand you accept their recommended therapy—*including* psychoactive drugs in most states—or face potential loss of custody for "medical neglect." This is very bad news if you happen to disagree with their diagnosis or treatment plan.
- Even an innocuous diagnosis such as "dyslexic" blames the child, not the teaching method, resulting in lowered self-confidence and less enthusiasm for schoolwork. Oddly enough, dyslexic children seem to lose their dyslexia when retrained with intensive phonics.
- Ritalin, today's most common prescription drug for LD, is now a street drug as well.
- *All* the drugs commonly prescribed for various learning and behavioral problems are addictive. Once on them, withdrawal is a tricky business, just as is the case when withdrawing from heroin or other "street" drugs.
- Kids today are not only taking Ritalin by mouth but also snorting it and mainlining it, which are far more dangerous. Once it is in your house, your child could theoretically abuse it in this way by just hiding for five minutes in the bathroom.
- "Learning disabilities" diagnoses don't actually tell you what is wrong or how to fix it. There could be a spiritual, physical, social/emotional, or other serious problem that is masked by the diagnosis. It's like only giving an aspirin when a patient complains of continuous severe migraines.

In the next few chapters, you'll learn surprising facts about the most commonly diagnosed learning disabilities. You'll also learn how to check your child, your home, and even your own expectations and teaching style to find and remove any *genuine* impediments to your child's learning. So before you submit to any label for your child, give homeschool a chance. You might just find the label no longer applies!

CHAPTER 45

Beating the Labeling Trap

To date, the homeschool movement has been ambivalent to the concept of learning disabilities. On the one hand, some homeschoolers believe there really is no such thing as a "learning disability." On the other hand, people credentialed by the education establishment as learning disabilities experts have been popping up with increasing frequency as featured speakers at homeschool conventions.

After years of studying this issue—and years of raising nine children, two of whom at least would qualify for a public-school "LD" label—I have reached the following conclusions:

- **There is no reason**, except for getting government grants, **for using the term "learning disability."** The term exists to shift responsibility for a child's scholastic failures from the school and parents to the child's DNA.
- **By definition, learning "disabilities" have no physical origin.** Real learning *problems* have actual medical names, such as "brain damage" or "Down's Syndrome."
- **What one person calls a "disability" could just as readily often be called a "gift."** Picture the difference between, "What an energetic little boy you have!" and, "Oh, that boy of yours is hyperactive." Or between, "Janie has Attention Deficit Disorder," and, "Janie is such a thinker!"
- **More important than labeling** is *what are you going to do about* your child's slowness or distractibility?
- **The first step toward solving a problem is getting a *correct* diagnosis**—as opposed to a responsibility-shifting "label." "Jimmy is disobedient" leads to entirely different parental responses than "Jimmy has ADHD." "Suzy has poor visual perception" requires a different line of treatment than "Suzy is an LD child."

Unreasonable Goals

. . . The National Education Goal . . . states that *all* children will start school prepared to learn. Unfortunately, because schools generally set things up so that only one type of learner [the Progress Person] can be recognized as "prepared to learn," this goal is basically impossible to meet. . . . Because the school traditionally decides *what* is supposed to be learned *when,* those kids who have natural abilities in those areas become the "gifted" ones and those who don't become the "learning disabled." Those who are unable to earn either of those distinctions are doomed to be "average," "below average," or "slow." . . .

If we continue to label students because their brains do not operate the way our educational system wants them to, we will continue to spread the idea that millions of brains are not as good as other brains, and perpetuate lifetime patterns of low self-worth, which affect future learning, career opportunities, and relationships.
—*Discover Your Child's Learning Style*

Do Drugs Substitute for Discipline?

There is a medical, educational, and legal controversy raging over the issue of the drug Ritalin in dealing with "problem" children, children described as "hyperactive" or "inattentive." From Massachusetts to California indignant parents have filed suits against school systems and doctors seeking redress against the quasi-mandatory use of this drug. Sweden has outlawed its use. From Canada come warnings of what the epidemic use of Ritalin may ultimately do to society.

The controversy has attracted relatively little attention in our news media, even though it is estimated that over a million children in this country are routinely being required to take a drug that is listed in the Drug Enforcement Agency's "Drugs of Abuse" as a "Schedule Two" drug, along with cocaine and opium.

Last June, the controversy over the use of Ritalin attracted the attention of ABC's "Nightline." In a program aired on June 10, Ted Koppel promised to examine Ritalin's "effectiveness in controlling hyperactivity in children and its occasional negative side effects." He went on to say, "Nearly a million American children suffering from what is know as A.D.D., an acronym standing for Attention Deficit Disorder, take Ritalin or some similar drug." Since then an article in the *Journal of the American Medical Association* revealed that in the public schools in Baltimore County, MD, six percent of the elementary school students, four percent of the middle school students, and 0.4 percent of the high school students were taking Ritalin. The Baltimore figures indicate that the use of this drug has been doubled every four to seven years. If extrapolated to the country as a whole, they suggest that 1.6 million children may now be taking Ritalin to "cure" their hyperactivity and inattentiveness.

What exactly is this Attention Deficit Disorder mentioned by Koppel? It has been recognized only in the last 25 to 30 years, and psychiatrists have yet to agree on its exact characteristics and even its name. The last changes in the diagnostic criteria took place as recently as 1987, when it was renamed Attention-Deficit Hyperactivity Disorder.

Exactly how powerful and addictive is the drug Ritalin (methylphenidate hydrochloride), so freely given to grade school age children to treat the new "disease"? How exactly is the decision arrived at to give a child the drug?

Despite his reputation as an interviewer who is persistent in seeking answers to tough questions, Ted Koppel failed to get good answers to the hard questions that need to be asked about Ritalin. Indeed, many of the questions weren't even asked.

Drugs in Lieu of Discipline

Showing a boy at play, ABC reporter Gail Harris commented, "Shooting baskets in his backyard, Casey Jesson seems like any other energetic 9-year-old." But then she pointed out that Casey had been diagnosed as "hyperactive" and treated with Ritalin. What exactly are the indications that Casey suffers from an illness requiring treatment with a potent drug? David Brown, Superintendent of Schools in Casey's home town of Derry, New Hampshire, explained: "Always doing something, humming, movement of furniture, looking for attention, outward bursts, verbal bursts, refusal to do all kinds of things." Superintendent Brown was supported by Dr. Betsy Busch of the New England Medical Center, who explained, "What Ritalin and other medications that are used for children who have attention-deficit seem to do is help children focus their attention."

No one pointed out that in other days, and even now in other countries, these are the kinds of problems that parents and teachers were expected to overcome with discipline. With the demise of discipline in our schools, a drug is becoming a disciplinary tool.

This may be easy for teachers, but it can be hard on children and families. Casey Jesson's mother, Valerie, strongly objected to the use of Ritalin to solve what the school thought was Casey's problem. She said, "The child right from the beginning [of medication] complained of headaches, stomach cramps, he couldn't wind down, he couldn't fall asleep, so therefore he didn't want to go to bed." She said that getting him to eat was even starting to be a real problem.

When Casey went off the drug these side effects disappeared, but the school authorities wanted him back on it. His parents refused. His father said, "The child was sick from the drug. Why are they trying to force us to put drugs down our son's throat . . . ?"

Nightline brushed these objections aside. Gail Harris reassuringly declared, "Despite the Jesson's experience, the evidence is that Ritalin helps most hyperactive children cope with their condition."

Whose Evidence?

The 1988 edition of the authoritative *Physician's Desk Reference* states, "Sufficient data on safety and efficacy of long-term use of Ritalin in children are not yet available." The entry goes on to mention reports of stunted growth with long-term use on children. Ritalin's manufacturer, Ciba-Geigy, has included this same warning about the lack of data on long-term use on children in a product information release on the drug.

"It can have side effects, including loss of appetite and loss of sleep," reporter Gail Harris acknowledged, but she stopped short of mentioning even more serious adverse reactions among the 28 side effects to Ritalin listed in the *Physician's Desk Reference*. One of them is Tourette's Syndrome, whose sufferers display uncontrollable facial tics and sometimes bark like a dog as their nervous systems are affected by the drug.

A 1982 article in the *Journal of the American Medical Association* on Tourette's Syndrome says researchers "reported the development of motor tic symptoms in 1.3 percent of children receiving methylphenidate hydrochloride [Ritalin] for their attention-deficit disorder. Tics were said to disappear when therapy was discontinued, except in one child out of 1,520 studied." The article states, "The continuing appearance of Tourette's Syndrome in children after periods of stimulant pharmacotherapy remains a cause of concern for clinicians."

No mention was made on Nightline of dangers during withdrawal from Ritalin, but the *Physician's Desk Reference* warns, "Careful supervision is required during drug withdrawal." *The Diagnostic and Statistical Manual of Mental Disorders* (third edition, revised), published in 1987, the book known as the "bible" of psychiatry, discusses "complications" during withdrawal from Ritalin and drugs in its class. "Suicide," it states, "is the major complication."

Oblivious to such dire warnings, Nightline's Gail Harris reported, "The vast majority of doctors and psychiatrists say that for every failure there are many more success stories." She did not, of course, say how many cases of less active behavior it would take to offset a child's suicide.

In a Class with Cocaine

Gail Harris assured Nightline viewers that Ritalin is "strictly regulated by the Drug Enforcement Administration," and said that "doctors say in proper dosage it is not addictive in children." This implies that all doctors agree on this, but they don't. The doctors and medical scientists who compiled the Drug Enforcement Administration's list of "Drugs of Abuse" classed Ritalin together with cocaine and opium as a "Schedule Two" drug. The DEA describes these "Schedule Two" drugs as having a "high potential for abuse" and "may lead to severe psychological or physical dependence."

Less than a decade ago cocaine was considered a nonaddictive drug. Today even laymen in the U.S. are familiar with the addictiveness of cocaine. In Canada, where cocaine is less readily available than in the U.S., Ritalin is used as one of the major street drugs, with addicts injecting it directly into their veins. In some areas in both Canada and the U.S., schools have been broken into by street drug addicts looking for Ritalin.

Nightline did not address the question of whether the U.S. is running the risk of making its already serious drug abuse problem worse by introducing millions of elementary school aged children to a Schedule Two drug like Ritalin. Apart from the imperfectly understood side effects, we have no way of knowing what the long-term effects of this will be in terms of influencing receptivity to the abuse of this and other Schedule Two drugs.

Schools Bullying Parents

Many parents object to being pressured by school authorities to put their children on Ritalin. Ted Koppel sided with the parents on this issue. When Superintendent Brown explained why his school system disagreed with Casey Jesson's parents and insisted that the boy go back on Ritalin, Koppel asked, "Doesn't the next stage belong to the parents to decide?" Brown said, "Not really." This prompted Koppel to ask, "Where does the school administration, or a superintendent, or a school board as a whole come off saying, 'Your child must take drugs?'" Brown retreated saying, "Well, indeed we didn't say that." Koppel persisted, "The decision has to be the parent's doesn't it?" Brown replied, "Uh, yes, it does."

But off camera, in conferences with parents called to discuss their "difficult" child, school authorities have tended to insist that unruly children be put on Ritalin, taking the attitude first expressed by Superintendent Brown, that this is "not really" a question for the parents to decide. A standard procedure is for school officials to gang up on a parent in a meeting with the teacher, the principal, the school counselor, a school nurse, or a psychologist. If the parent resists efforts to have the child placed on Ritalin, they threaten not to promote the child to the next grade. Two parents who fought school officials over Ritalin refused to be quoted for this article, saying they had endured enough trouble and didn't want to stir up any more for themselves and their child.

When confronted with lawsuits over Ritalin, school systems claim that they do not diagnose or directly suggest to parents that a child be given Ritalin. But the record shows otherwise.

Dr. Michael Levine, a San Antonio, Texas, psychiatrist and child development specialist, told the New York Times, "I know of instances in Texas where school districts specifically told parents that they thought their children needed Ritalin, and they gave them the names of physicians they knew would prescribe it."

Andrew Watry, executive director of the Composite State Board of Medical Examiners in Georgia, and head of a probe to determine the cause of a huge rise in the consumption of Ritalin in the state, found that teachers were pressuring parents to have their children placed on the drug. Watry commented, "The school systems are to blame if someone says, 'Your child needs Ritalin,' because they [the teachers] cannot make a medical judgment."

Commenting on the results of his probe, Watry said, "What we found was that there was a general notion that this drug was a panacea for a lot of behavior problems. People would seem to think it was a miracle drug and would suggest it for any kid who squirmed in his seat."

Diagnostic Difficulties

This brings up a basic question with regard to the use of Ritalin and the diagnosis of the conditions it is used to treat. What exactly are the criteria for determining that a child is suffering from A.D.D. or Attention-Deficit Hyperactivity Disorder, to use the name adopted in 1987? *The Diagnostic and Statistical Manual of Mental Disorders* (1987 edition) lists 14 indicators of this disorder, of which at least eight have to be present for at least six months. It cautions that each of the behavioral patterns listed must be "considerably more frequently than that of most people of the same mental age." Here are some of the indicators:

1. Fidgets or squirms in seat.
2. Talks excessively.
3. Has difficulty playing quietly.
4. Has difficulty waiting turn.
5. Shifts from one uncompleted activity to another.
6. Easily distracted by extraneous stimuli.
7. Fails to finish chores.
8. Loses things.

The ease with which the rules of diagnosis can be disregarded was shown on Nightline. Koppel introduced Dr. Jerry Wiener, president of the American Academy of Child and Adolescent Psychiatry and chairman of the Department of Psychiatry at George Washington University Medical Center. Speaking of Casey Jesson, seen earlier in the program, Dr. Wiener said, ". . . it is painful to see the film of that young boy, who is obviously even in the film so hyperactive and sort of so driven, and to hope that some effective treatment could be found."

Dr. Wiener made a diagnosis right on the air apparently based on the footage of Casey shown earlier in the program. He had seen the boy playing in his backyard, shooting a basket, doing gymnastic exercise while hanging on the basketball rim, and then playing inside, singing a song and yelling and laughing with his sister. ABC's Gail Harris had said that Casey "seems like any other energetic 9-year-old." But Dr. Wiener viewed his behavior as symptomatic of a disorder requiring drug therapy.

When Koppel asked if there weren't alternatives to Ritalin, Dr. Wiener immediately suggested another drug. When Koppel asked if there wasn't any other alternatives to the giving of drugs, Wiener replied that people do not object when certain other types of medication "they need" are prescribed for children. He said, "We don't have that reluctance after all with antibiotics . . ."

John Coale, attorney for several families suing school officials and physicians for damage to their children resulting from Ritalin, came on the program to criticize the criteria used to diagnose the disorder. He said, "These are little children—seven, eight-year-olds. Are we going to drug them because they don't behave, they don't stand in line?" Koppel asked Dr. Wiener, "Where is the line drawn? All children tend to fidget."

The question went to the heart of the controversy, but Dr. Wiener ducked it. He replied with an attack on Mr. Coale. The crucial question of precisely how the line is drawn between misbehavior that is so severe that it requires drugging the child and actions that should be handled in other ways went unanswered. Ted Koppel concluded his exploration of the Ritalin controversy saying, "I'm sure we'll be following this story in the months to come."

Teachers Play Doctor

In most cases the medical profession jealously guards its license to diagnose illness. Since the symptoms of Attention-Deficit Hyperactivity Disorder have to be observed for at least six months and often don't show up in a visit to the doctor, physicians are generally reduced to making diagnoses based on what teachers say. A child's being placed on Ritalin hinges on how a teacher chooses to interpret words such as "often" and "frequently."

Often the symptoms for which Ritalin is prescribed may be due to external circumstances including bad nutrition, problems at home or outside of school, boredom, or antagonism that may be caused by lack of skills on the part of the teacher. "Drugs should be the treatment of last resort," says child psychologist David Elkind of Tufts University. Yet the organization CHILD (Children with Hidden or Ignored Learning Disabilities) found that only two out of 102 children given Ritalin underwent the complete battery of tests that manufacturers recommend before a child is put on the drug.

While Ritalin definitely influences "social" behavior in the classroom, no study has ever shown that it improves academic achievement (such as reading skills or any other area). It is truly surprising to discover that much of the administration of drugs to young school children to deal with school problems is based on mere speculation, without any proven scientific basis.

Very Big Business

Another point not touched on the Nightline program is the question of how much money is being made on Ritalin. No exact figures are available from Ciba-Geigy, the drug's manufacturer, but in 1987 the Drug Enforcement Administration reported that a growing demand for the drug caused the agency to increase its proposed ceiling on Ritalin to twice the amount it had been two years earlier. "Its potency ranks right up there with cocaine," says the DEA's Gene Haislip. "I don't feel very comfortable about the production increases."

A state investigation took place in Utah, where the consumption of Ritalin was the highest in the country, four times the national norm. "The problem is, we really don't know why we use so much here," the New York Times quoted David E. Robinson, director of the State Division of Occupational and Professional Licensing. His division was trying to determine if the drug was being illegally diverted to street sales, or if Ritalin had become "trendy these days" because doctors were "over-diagnosing a problem."

A 1983 book put out by the American Academy of Child Psychiatry detailed ways of increasing business for psychiatrists through building up connections with school systems. The book, entitled Child Psychiatry: A Plan for the Coming Decades, lists Dr. Jerry Wiener as one of its contributors. At one point, the book suggests, "Service contracts can be developed between the schools and private child psychiatrists and with other groups such as medical centers" (page 67). Today Dr. Wiener is the most prominent and frequently quoted psychiatrist sponsoring use of Ritalin for school children.

Writing of the growing discussion developing over drug treatment for school children in an article appearing in the Journal of Applied Behavior Analysis back in 1980, K. Daniel O'Leary of State University of New York commented, "When the potential market for a medication is five percent of all elementary school children, that market is very big business."

Teachers asked about Ritalin often support its use, saying that it makes their daily job easier. There are many physicians who believe that when properly monitored, as any powerful drug should be, Ritalin can be of benefit to children who suffer learning disabilities that impair their ability to concentrate and perform assigned tasks. Many parents are also satisfied that the drug has helped improve the behavior of problem children, but many others are not only complaining but also suing because they were not informed about the possible side effects of the drug when they were urged to put their child on Ritalin.

For example, LaVerne Parker sued school officials and doctors in Georgia over harmful effects to her son resulting from taking Ritalin. Parker said teachers pressured her to put her son on Ritalin, insisting that he take it if he wanted to stay enrolled in public school. She says it stunted his growth, and he became violent and suicidal. Later she discovered that his original school difficulties stemmed from other problems than those which were earlier diagnosed and for which he was given Ritalin. As such suits go to trial, Ritalin controversy will become more visible in the news.

The news media may even be inspired to make an effort to alert the public to the dangers posed to our children by the excessive prescription of Ritalin. They showed how effectively they can do this kind of thing in publicizing charges that aspirin could cause Reyes Syndrome in children, sometimes with fatal results. This led to drug manufacturers being required to warn aspirin users of this possibility.

The *Journal of the American Medical Association* of October 21, 1988, acknowledged the possibility that Ritalin is being prescribed for children that don't need it. It said it was possible that the increased use of Ritalin reflects a "return to an antiquated simplistic approach that views all school and behavior problems as one." The Journal said, "In such a view, the diagnostic process is replaced by the reflex use of a particular treatment, in this case stimulants, prescribed for almost any child presenting with a behavioral or learning problem."

The *Journal* said this possibility should be of concern to physicians, educators, parents, and legislators interested in public policy. That amounted to a call for an investigation of the possible abuse of this potent drug. That is a call that the media have so far done little to amplify.

—Ann Steinberg

Just Say No to Drugs, Schools, and Labels

I am writing to comment on the recent article "Do Drugs Substitute for Discipline?" I read it with great interest . . . and a heavy heart.

We have been homeschooling four children (ages 16, 15, 13, and 7) for four years. It is a decision we have *never* regretted. They are a delight, and I cannot imagine spending my days alone with them in school.

However, we have five children. My oldest son is 21 and is currently in jail for parole violation after having spent four years incarcerated in a state prison. He began life as any other child, except he was very active. In 1982, when he was in the first grade, his teacher expressed concern that he may be hyperactive (ADD) and encouraged us to have him evaluated. We did. At that time we believed that teachers knew what our child needed better than us. The doctor felt that he may also be hyperactive and told us of a new drug being used with hyperactive children—Ritalin. Although admittedly stupid, we still didn't believe in "drugging" him, and we declined using Ritalin permanently. He struggled through school, and I sat up with him many nights to get him to finish schoolwork that he had not done that day at school. He hated it, and so did I.

When his impulsive behavior finally put him in the Juvenile Justice system at the age of 15, he was put on Ritalin, Lithium, Prozac, and who knows what else. He spent three weeks in a Psychiatric Unit for attempting suicide, and another six weeks at the Minirth Meyer Clinic in Chicago. When he was 16, he was finally kicked out of school for taking a .22 shell to school. I might also add that he was on Ritalin and under a counselor's care at the time he attempted suicide. This is the true story of a hyperactive child not disciplined correctly.

Our youngest child, Emily, displays many of the same symptoms of ADD. She has never been to school and has been taught to read at home by her "incompetent" mother. She currently reads at a fifth grade level. She did not learn until she was almost seven and had great difficulty sitting still and paying attention. She continues to blossom here at home, but I feel that she would quickly wither in a public school setting.

We had to go through some very deep waters before we were willing to let the Lord have his way. In looking back, I know that my son was not disciplined properly, and sometimes not at all. He was a constant source of irritation, and I frankly did not deal with him in a godly way. However, I do know that we are now on the right path. This child had put me into the depths of despair, but with that I have also reached a total commitment to the Lord.

I would not advise anyone to put their child on a drug. I would follow the suggestions given in the referred article and even more importantly, I would fall down on my face before the Lord. I would never, never send an ADD child into a public school setting. They must have a loving, godly home for shelter.

—PHS reader "S.M." from MI

Picture Learners & Dyslexia

Most people who are labeled dyslexic are Picture Learners. . . . Picture Learners are often mistakenly treated as Print Learners. I am convinced that this misconception is the cause of the majority of reading problems among our students.
—*Discover Your Child's Learning Style*

HOW TO GET YOUR CHILD OFF PSYCHOACTIVE DRUGS . . . SAFELY

According to *Talking Back to Ritalin,* "The longer the child has been exposed and the higher the doses, the more caution the parent must use, and the more need there is for gradual withdrawal and for experienced clinical supervision. The more troubled a child has been, the more cautious a parent needs to be during withdrawal. It is common for behavior to worsen temporarily."

To find out more about how to withdraw your child from psychoactive drugs, get Peter Breggin and David Cohen's book, *Your Drug May Be Your Problem: How and Why to Stop Taking Psychiatric Medications* (Perseus Publishing, 2000)

With all this in mind, we offer you the following diagnostic checklist designed to help you figure out what your child's problem, if any, really is, and what to do about it.

What to Do If Your Child Has Trouble Learning

If your child is having trouble with just one subject, try a fresh approach with that subject, or even leave it alone for a while in order to allow him to catch up to it developmentally.

But if your child doesn't seem able to do grade-level work on *any* subject, and you are not aware of any genuine physical problem, such as Tourette's Syndrome or head injuries, try the following:

- **Check your expectations.** Young parents and new homeschoolers often get carried away by the glowing success stories they read about, and expect genius-level behavior from their children. Just because *someone's* kid wins the Science Fair with a homemade particle beam generator doesn't mean *your* kid should be expected to do this! Also, just because an older sibling is gifted athletically or academically doesn't mean all the younger siblings will be equally gifted in those identical areas. Take a breath and relax!

Then if your expectations are in line with reality, and you still see a problem, start with checking *physical* reasons for that problem.

- **Check his eyesight.** This may seem almost too obvious to mention, but I personally, although blind as a bat, didn't get a single eye test until I was a teen, and didn't get contacts until I was 20 years old. If your child holds books close to his face or rubs his eyes a lot, a vision test should be a priority. Even if he doesn't show signs of poor vision, it's a good idea to have vision checked as soon as your child can tell left from right and up from down.
- **Check his visual perception.** This differs from a regular vision test in that you aren't looking at eye charts. Instead, you are checking such things as how evenly your child's eyes "track" from left to right. Again, red eyes and having trouble "seeing" the page are a sign of this problem. You may have to look around a bit to find someone in your area who does this kind of testing. However, if visual perception is the problem, eye exercises can make a huge difference in your child's ability to take in information visually.
- **Check your child's hearing.** If he's had a lot of ear infections, he very well may have trouble hearing, especially in a noisy environment.
- **Check his gross motor skills.** Children who are especially clumsy or delayed developmentally may have something physically wrong with them. This is not a learning *disability,* but an actual learning *problem* that needs remediation. Neurological patterning exercises, such as those offered by the National Academy for Child Development, can be helpful for children with neurological and other physical problems.
- **Check him for allergies.** As you'll see in the next chapter, undiagnosed allergies to specific foods or environmental factors (e.g., new carpet fumes) can make children lethargic,

hyper, confused, and/or highly irritable—all of which effectively prevent peaceful concentration on learning. If your child has pale skin, circles under the eyes, dry or cracked skin, unexplained rashes, ridged or spotted fingernails, dry or slow-growing hair, or cracked and peeling lips, grab one of Doris Rapp's books reviewed in the next chapter! Also consider allergies as a possibility if you see lots of chronic mucous and earaches (classic dairy allergy symptoms) and chronic constipation or diarrhea.

- **Check him for dietary deficiencies.** I know this is a tough one, as there is not a mom in the world who believes she is feeding her children a poor diet. However, if you find the following things creeping into your shopping bag—chips, sugary snacks, soda pop—and your child isn't getting protein at breakfast and five to seven servings of fruits and vegetables a day (fruit roll-ups don't count!), he may well be deficient in essential nutrients—just like most kids today. Luckily, you can fix this with a few nutritional supplements and protein shakes. See the *Crazy Makers* review in the next chapter for more details.

- **Check out his activity level.** Kids today get far less exercise than just a generation ago. They don't walk to school, and once home, they are cooped in the house for fear of criminals. Kids today are fatter than ever before—and lack of dopamine, which exercise releases in the blood, can make a kid either hyper or lethargic, depending on his basic constitution.

- **Consider checking him for heavy-metal toxicity, parasites, and yeast infections.** Any of these can cause physical irritations that manifest as highly distractible behavior and inability to focus. Try looking online at www.acam.org, the website of the American College for Advancement in Medicine; it's a good place to find doctors who are willing to check for allergies and toxins.

Obviously we couldn't cover every single situation with this checklist. But we hope this checklist, and the information that follows, will help make it clear that kids are never a set of walking "labels," but individuals with varying gifts and interests.

Furthermore, any "remediation" or "therapy" that doesn't actually *cure* the problem it addresses isn't worth our respect or attention. The public schools' "special education" doesn't produce kids who ultimately work at grade level. They don't even *pretend* to achieve these results. In fact, they make *more* money for each child who remains in special education. So why listen to them or use their failed methods?

Although homeschoolers are rightly wary of public education methods and philosophy, at this point we seem all too ready to let them in through the "back door" of special education. If we can be persuaded to label our kids, and call on a public-school-credentialed "expert" to tell us how to homeschool our labeled kids, we're right back in the public school's lap.

School Expectations

Traditionally, "prepared to learn" has meant that the child arrives at school ready and eager to:

- sit in a desk and work alone quietly for long periods of time
- follow the teacher's sequential directions
- focus and listen . . . even when there is the ongoing noise of construction outside
- do worksheets instead of playing with toys
- be quiet for long periods of time . . . [more examples follow]

The child who comes to school prepared to do the above is then labeled motivated, smart, eager to learn, and most probably, above average, maybe even gifted. Now let's look at some different children. These children arrive at school ready and eager to:

- play at recess
- draw or fingerpaint
- tell imaginative stories
- entertain the teacher and other students . . .
- tap on the desk with a pencil or any object, in the absence of musical instruments . . .
- play, act, and/or sing
- ask a lot of questions . . . [more examples follow]

Teachers become concerned about these students because they do not behave or perform according to school expectations. Many of these children are labeled slow, unmotivated, immature, distractible, disruptive, or lazy. If problems persist, someone usually suggests testing to find out if there is a learning disability.

—*Discover Your Child's Learning Style*

Perhaps kids are labeled because it is easier to attach the blame to a "learning problem" than to search for the teaching method, the setting, and the materials that fit each child. Many "learning problems" are actually created because an individual child's unique learning timetable is not taken into account. Who said they should all learn the alphabet in preschool, start reading in kindergarten and first grade, do fractions in third, and so on?
—*Discover Your Child's Learning Style*

If your own personality type and teaching style is different from your child's, that alone may be the source of your problems! An auditory child won't keep his eyes glued on you while you're talking, which miffs a visual mom—but he *will* hear and remember what you say! That's just one example of how your preferred "discovery channel" may clash with your child's. You also have to consider you and your child's "thinking styles": Puzzle Solver, People Person, Action Man, Progress Person, or Performer. See Chapters 14 and 15 for more help in this area.

You've looked at your expectations, diet, exercise, and obvious physical shortcomings that need addressing. Now it's time to consider academic, emotional, and spiritual reasons for your child's learning difficulties.

- **Check his vocabulary level.** A reduced vocabulary level can be a sign of genuine physical problems, or of unresolved emotional problems which are affecting his learning. Or he could just be a late bloomer who is slow to talk. See Thomas Sowell's book *The Einstein Syndrome* before you let anyone label your late-talking child as "autistic."

- **Check for interpersonal and environmental problems or trauma.** All these big words mean, "Has anyone betrayed, persecuted, or scared your child?" A divorce or the death of a relative or friend can cause a child to lose interest in learning. Or, if he has attended school in the past, he may well have emotional baggage left over from unpleasant school experiences. It's been said that a child needs as many years to *recover* from public school as he *spent* in public school. While that's not true in all cases, giving your child some "time off" after a rough emotional experience won't ruin him for homeschool, especially if you provide lots of library books and interesting outings! Gentle books such as *Winnie the Pooh* can help traumatized folks of all ages start to feel the world isn't wholly bleak and hopeless after all.

- **Check his attention span *when he's doing something that interests him.*** If your child just "can't sit still" even for activities he favors, he likely has a chemical imbalance or allergies. In these cases, talking to a doctor *qualified in these areas* can yield excellent results. Again, I suggest finding a practitioner through www.acam.org. Beware of practitioners who prescribe Ritalin at the drop of a hat. Also beware of labeling a child "distractible" who is only distractible when he's doing what *you* want!

- **If your child doesn't have any of the above problems**, but is always "zoning out" or daydreaming, consider the following options: (a) Pick more interesting and involving activities. (b) Check up on him frequently. (c) Encourage artistic, musical, and scientific pursuits. (d) Add more hands-on projects. Also consider that your child's "problem" may actually be a case of giftedness, in which case offering more demanding activities is the solution.

- **If none of the above applies**, you may just have a child who is a slow learner. Throughout the history of the world, some have always been faster and some have been slower. This is really no big deal in homeschool, since there is no class to "keep up" with or "fall behind." We can afford to let our children learn at their own rates. The worst thing you can do is to keep harping on a child's failure by repeatedly pushing tasks at him that he isn't ready to do. In this case, the answer is to lose some of that parental anxiety, scale back on your expectations, pick only resources that break tasks down into simple steps, review a lot, and remember that you have 13 school years to teach this kid to read, write, and do basic arithmetic. If you succeed at these minimal tasks, your "slow learner" will actually be more advanced by high-school graduation time than 99 percent of public school graduates!

What to Do If Your Child Doesn't Follow Your Instructions

If your child can see and hear just fine, has an OK vocabulary level and motor skills, has no allergies, is not suffering from any recent traumas, has an OK attention span when doing what he wants, is not a daydreamer, and *can* do the work "when he feels like it" (except that he rarely feels like it), what you likely have here is an old-fashioned case of disobedience. This is even more obvious in cases where the child explicitly refuses to do what you say or shows disrespect in other ways.

It happens all the time, and the solution is the same as it has always been: structure, consistent discipline, patience, more of your personal attention, and lots of prayer. Depending on the circumstances, discipline may mean a spanking, taking away distracting toys, or, "You don't eat supper until you finish your schoolwork."

The key here is not to get discouraged and give up prematurely. Contrary to what some child-training books make it sound like, rare is the child who responds with exemplary obedience to the very first time he is disciplined. Your job is to let him know that "school doesn't have to be fun, it just has to be done," in the deathless words of Luanne Shackelford (author of *A Survivor's Guide to Homeschooling*), and that he isn't going to get away with a thing. Once he is convinced of this, and you have *also* made sure that he realizes you are in sympathy with his aspirations and tribulations, most kids will settle down and (even if grudgingly) do the work.

Training in diligence is very helpful, since it's even rarer to find a rebellious child who isn't also lazy. Good old family chores are great for this training, which proves once again that it's always best to do chores *first*. It's also important for the parents to show a cheerful attitude about work. The lessons learned in chore time carry over to better work all through the homeschool day.

The one rare exception to the above is the case of a child who is so intensely focused on an interest that he keeps coming back to it in spite of all instructions to spend his time otherwise. In this case, you need to determine if the activity in question is bad—in which case you have a spiritual problem requiring even more prayer and discipline—or positive—in which

Structure, Discipline, & More

If you have a balky or defiant child, you might be interested in the free online book, *The Bible's Way to Victory over ADHD and Other Childhood Challenges*. Coming from an entirely different perspective than either the "take this drug" or "everything has a physical cause" schools of thought, it has some intriguing thoughts on how to "prevent and overcome behavioral, emotional and learning problems, including ADD (Attention Deficit Disorder), ADHD (Attention Deficit Hyperactivity Disorder), ODD (Oppositional Defiant Disorder), Conduct Disorder, and Tourette's Syndrome." Go to **www.audiblox2000.com/ onlinebook/index.htm** if you're interested

Square Pegs in Round Holes

Modern education generally does recognize that people are different. In fact, starting in preschool we get the "I am so special! I am wonderful!" treatment. Problem is, this encouraging litany does not mean what it says. It does not mean that children are unique human beings created in the image of God, each with his own personality, talents, and tendencies to sin. As we proceed through the grades we discover these same "special" and "wonderful" children forced into peer-group herds. The energetic are labeled "hyperactive" and sedated. The slow-and-steadies are labeled "learning disabled" and shunted into Special Ed. The mean and destructive are not told to shape up or ship out, but labeled "emotionally handicapped" and coddled. Solitary types who hate the group pressures and inanity of school schedules are labeled "school phobic" and granted no concessions to their sensitive natures.

The bottom line of all this, you will notice, is that children are forced to fit in to the school. Kids who don't fit in are forced in. Square pegs in round holes. Hard on the square pegs, and not too great on the round holes, either.

Could it be that highly critical people, and aggressive people, and slow methodical people, and humorous people all have a right to their own personalities? Can it be OK for students to be human not only in how they learn and are motivated, but in their different personalities as well? Could we perhaps get a nice big garbage can and place all those hundreds of little labels out on the curb for the trashman to take away?

—*Schoolproof*

case he may just be a genius who is following his vocation. Many famous musicians, scientists, and artists started this way!

Homeschool special education has the advantages of common sense, lots of time, one-on-one interaction, and a devotion to results. That is why it *gets* results. My "dyslexic" daughter now reads above grade level and her spelling has vastly improved. My "ADD" son was doing college work in ninth grade. Hundreds of other homeschool families have similar results. They are the true special education experts, not the guys with the Ed.D.'s and Ph.D.'s.

We don't need trendy buzzwords and theories, we need *results*. As long as we only listen to people who can demonstrate results, we'll be heading in the right direction—and special education at home will be *really* special.

More Reading

Everyone Is Able— Exploding the Myth of Learning Disabilities

Parents. $3.95.
Fun Books, MD. (888) 386-7020, www.fun-books.com.

If you would like to find out why intelligent people are questioning the whole premise of "learning disability," and why you should fiercely resist your child being branded with this label, this booklet from Holt Associates provides the ammo. In **Everyone Is Able** you hear from the "other experts"—parents of labeled children (or whose children would be labeled if the mainstream experts got their hands on them) and specialists within the schools who see what the LD label does to children and education. These are real-life stories. Many articles were written especially for this booklet. The quality of the writing as a whole is thoughtful, but not dispassionate. Must reading.

Learning In Spite of Labels

Parents. $9.95.
Greenleaf Press, TN. (800) 311-1508, www.greenleafpress.com.

Get out the clear Contac paper and cover this book right away! It's destined to be dog-eared, so be prepared. Joyce Herzog has written a book on teaching strategies that will encourage, instruct, inspire, and revive you. By the way, did I mention that **Learning In Spite of Labels** was written for parents of children with learning difficulties? Doesn't matter! Anyone with a heart for helping children learn in whatever way is best for them will benefit from this book. Chapters cover:

- What it feels like to be learning-disabled: what learning is, how it works, typical behavioral characteristics, and strengths common to most of these children
- 10 issues to consider (applies to all children): what Scripture has to say, where to school, discipline, success, priorities, goals, and more
- 25 Teaching Techniques that Work
- Teeny-tiny teaching tips: hints on specific subject areas, as well as structuring the environment for success
- How to begin, learning styles, legal issues to consider
- Famous historical figures, mini-biographies of those who overcame obstacles
- ADD, normal speech development, vision problems
- How to create an Individualized Education Plan
- Resource list to help anyone locate expert help when needed

After reading this book, you'll be firmly convinced that labels belong on clothing, not children. Highly recommended. *Renee Mathis*

CHAPTER 46

Help for Distractible Learners

First, let's all agree on this:

Some children are easily distractible.

Now that we have this out of the way, we can get to the *real* question:

How should we teach distractible learners?

We are not talking about "retarded" or brain-damaged children. The children in question *can* learn, but do not usually tackle their school studies with zest and success. Well, that's true of the average schooled child! But in this case, the teacher encounters additional difficulties. The child is just plain hard to teach.

This is not a new problem. What's new is the sheer *number* of children considered distractible today, and the number of labels invented to disguise the simple fact of what we're talking about, making it sound like a genuine disease.

Schools & Distractible Children

How do schools handle distractible children?

- **Drugs.** In the schools, the favored approach is to drug the child, usually with Ritalin.
- **Isolation.** Another favored school tactic is to place the distractible child in a cubicle where he is cut off from all stimulation from other children or the objects in the classroom.

Since you are reading this book, I assume you are looking for better ideas than these! Solitary confinement on drugs has got to be one of the most grotesque ways a supposedly civilized country has ever found to handle its young people. As Thomas Armstrong says in his book, *The Myth of the A.D.D. Child:*

Boring, Repetitive Tasks

The most interesting description of ADD I have ever read appeared in an ad for an organization that works with children. It reads, in part,

It [ADD] is is often present at birth, but may not be diagnosed until the elementary years because the symptoms go unnoticed at home. . . . But when sustained attention is required for boring, repetitive tasks in distracting settings like classrooms, the symptoms become easier to see. Sustained cartoon watching or video-game playing doesn't count. The behavioral symptoms are seen with boring, repetitive tasks in distracting settings.

It then goes on to describe the testing that is available and the treatment options, including medication.

I often think, Don't the people who read this ad see anything strange about it? In the first place, why would I want my child to spend most of the day in a place where she is required to do boring, repetitive tasks? And if that is what school is all about, why on earth would I medicate a child to ensure that he does those boring, repetitive tasks?

—*Discover Your Child's Learning Style*

Bouncing—That's What Tiggers Do Best!

My young daughter would surely be labeled ADD if she were in public school. She was the only child of my four who threw temper tantrums. She had no attention span and was always easily distracted. She was also very sickly.

I thank the Lord for a very perceptive pediatrician who had the foresight to pursue other avenues rather than slapping her with the "hyperactive" label. Because of her frequent illnesses, he suggested a blood test to see if something was wrong with her immune system. The test showed that her allergen count was abnormal. We took her to an allergist, where she was found to be allergic to wheat, corn, yeast, and other foods. Almost everything she ate had those three foods in them. Her immune system was so busy fighting the food allergies that there was nothing left to combat any virus or bacterial infection that entered her system.

We immediately changed her diet and cleansed her system of everything she was allergic to. We gradually introduced the various foods to her, and she has out-

Children who were once seen as "bundles of energy," "daydreamers," or "fireballs" are now considered "hyperactive," "distractible," and "impulsive": the three classic warning signs of attention deficit disorder. Kids who in times past might have needed to "blow off a little steam" or "kick up a little dust" now have their medication dosages carefully measured out and monitored to control dysfunctional behavior. . . . I wonder whether there aren't hundreds of thousands of kids out there who may be done a disservice by having their uniqueness reduced to a disorder and by having their creative spirit controlled by a drug.

There's plenty of relevant information throughout this chapter to hopefully convince you that the drug/disease/isolation model is *not* the way to go when teaching distractible children.

Help for Distractible Children

Let's attack this from another angle. When do *you* get distracted? When you're:

- Bored
- Hungry
- Worried
- Out of control (we adults call this "losing it")
- Overstimulated (too many decisions to make at once, too much to see)

"Bored" is a chronic state for schoolchildren, not for homeschooled kids. "Hungry" is again a state you can control at home by providing good food at regular intervals. "Worried"—there's a lot less to worry about at home. See Beverly Cleary's *Ramona* series for examples of how even nice suburban kids in a nice suburban school get emotionally overwrought about what their teachers and classmates think of them. How much more so in more dangerous school environments! "Out of control" is cured when the parents get *in* control

Drug It Down or Run It Out?

I propose we stop acting ashamed of little boys, and energetic little girls. There's nothing wrong with lots of energy and a desire to be the boss. Give it a place to go instead of stomping on it.

An example: We were looking at a house a while back. The owners, former foster parents, told us this story about two young fellows (call them John and Don) who came to live with them. The first two days, John and Don ran everywhere. Up the hill, down the hill, up the front steps, through the house, out the back, around the house. Nobody stopped them. The foster family was used to kids having strong reactions to a new placement. John and Don stopped running around wildly on the third day, and were subsequently enrolled in a local school.

Some time after this, the boys' caseworker came by to talk to the foster parents.

"Have you been giving John and Don their hyperactive medicine?" she inquired.

"Why, no," the foster mother replied. "Nobody told us they needed any medicine."

"Well, have you at least enrolled them in their Special Ed classes?"

"Special Ed? They're doing fine in regular classes!"

John and Don needed to run. They did not need counseling, Special Ed, or alligator tears of sympathy. Running made them feel better. When they felt better, they acted better and started learning.

Another example: our friend Jim helped found a private school. I asked him if he had ever had any trouble with "hyperactive" children. "Oh, you mean those wired-up boys?" he grinned. "Nope, never had any trouble. Whenever one of them started jumping around and acting wild, I took him out to the football field and had him run around it a couple of times. Settled 'em right down."

—Schoolproof

through simple, fair, consistent discipline (something you won't find in most schools, thanks to the Supreme Court). That leaves "overstimulated" as the last factor which can make *normal* kids hyper. Here, the answer is simple: dump the TV, eliminate sugar and caffeine, and get that kid some exercise!

Now that we've eliminated "false hyperactivity"—stuff that drives normal kids wild—let's take a look at some more productive approaches to educating *all* children, regardless of their averageness, slowness, genius, or distractibility.

- **I mentioned *exercise*.** This is a must. Cardiovascular exercise to the point of sweating, 20 minutes or more a time, three days a week, is necessary for general health. Highly energetic kids and couch potatoes both need *more*. Sometimes *much* more. See the box entitled "Drug it Down or Run it Out?" on the previous page for an example of how exercise alone instantly cured two foster kids of hyperactivity.
- **I also mentioned *good food*.** And let's stop kidding ourselves here: The mass-produced, packaged American diet does *not* include all the nutrients any of us need, especially growing children. Vitamins alone can't make the difference, so unless you grow your own food and grind your own grain, supplement drinks may be in order. See the *Crazy Makers* review later in this chapter for an example of how a once-a-day protein supplement noticeably improved mood, and slightly improved academics, in a reluctant group of teen testers.
- **Eliminating sources of allergies.** This is a big one. If exercise, good food, consistent and meaningful discipline for well-understood offenses, eliminating TV and video games, and interesting curriculum don't seem to make any difference, I suggest you have your child checked for allergies. Our chiropractor had a testing package we could send directly to the processing company for $75 per child. I found out my daughter had dairy and wheat allergies—not surprising, since dark circles under the eyes, pale skin, very fine hair that was lusterless and not growing, and unexplained rashes all are signs of allergies. Now she has beautiful hair, no dark circles, no rashes, and is *much* calmer. Thanks for asking!

grown all food allergies except for her allergy to wheat. When she eats wheat, she becomes hyperactive and does not concentrate well on her schoolwork. We call her our "bouncy Tigger" when she eats wheat. She knows that she "bounces" when she eats wheat, and is very responsible about eating only the special breads or cookies we have for her.

A friend of mine who is a teacher told me that my daughter would easily have been labeled ADD if she attended public school. Because we know how to "control" her, she is very "normal" in her behavior. I wonder how many children are being forced to take Ritalin, Prozac, Lithium, or other dangerous drugs to control their behavior, when it could be a simple food allergy. I have been able to share with friends whose children were very active and inattentive. Some were indeed allergic to certain foods: most commonly wheat, milk, or soy products.

I hope this letter may help some parents who may think that their children are "bouncy Tiggers." The Lord makes each child a unique individual, and who better to nurture and minister to that uniqueness than his/her parents?

—*Kathleen McC., Cool, CA*

Reading, Writing, and Ritalin

An estimated two million children (three times as many boys as girls, and four times as many as in 1990) have been labeled with Attention Deficit Disorder (ADD) or Attention Deficit Hyperactivity Disorder (ADHD). The most widely used drug to treat this condition is methylphenidate, known as Ritalin. A powerful stimulant, it juices up the central nervous system, takes effect in 30 minutes, and peters out in three to four hours. Ritalin is classified as a Schedule II controlled substance in the same category as cocaine, methadone, and methamphetamine.

In 1994, the U.S. Department of Education, Office of Special Education Programs, under contract HS92017001, gave the Chesapeake Institute of Washington, D.C., the funding to produce two slick videos: *Facing the Challenges of ADD* featuring actress Rita Moreno, and *One Child in Every Classroom* with Frank Sesno as moderator. Parts of the videos sound like an infomercial for Ritalin.

In a PBS documentary following eight months of investigation, a Department of Education spokesman was asked if he was aware that the parents who spoke so enthusiastically about Ritalin on the videos were board members of Children and Adults with Attention Deficit Disorder (CHADD), and if he knew that CHADD has received cash grants of $900,000 plus in-kind services from Ciba-Geigy, the manufacturer of Ritalin. Obviously embarrassed, the bureaucrat denied such knowledge. . . .

Parent of a child who is diagnosed, labeled, or treated by school-paid personnel would be well-advised to seek an independent, unbiased medical opinion.

—*Phyllis Schlafly Report*

Physicians often tell parents that the fear of addiction [to Ritalin and other amphetamines used to treat ADD/ADHD] is unfounded. Try the following exercise:

Call your family doctor's office and make an appointment for yourself. When the doctor comes in to examine you and asks what you are there for, tell him you want to lose some weight and you read that amphetamines are excellent drugs to reduce appetite (one of the side effects of amphetamines). Firmly insist that the doctor start you immediately on a prescription for any of the amphetamines, and be sure to state clearly that you want to stay on the medication for two, three, or even more years. Watch your doctor's reaction and response.

Your doctor will tell you that under no circumstances would he do such a thing. He will tell you that these are dangerous drugs that you shouldn't fool around with. He'll tell you about the side effects, such as insomnia, nervousness, irritable stomach, hypertension—perhaps even feelings of paranoia—and so forth. Then, I promise you, he will say, "Besides, these drugs are too easy to get addicted to, and it would be unethical to prescribe them in such a fashion, especially for so many years!"

Think about this. Doctors will not prescribe these drugs to you, a responsible adult, but they readily load your children down with them.

David B. Stein, Ph.D., Ritalin Is Not the Answer (John Wiley & Sons, 2001)

Joyce Herzog has been working with homeschoolers for almost 15 years. She is the author of the popular Scaredy-Cat Reading System, *Learning in Spite of Labels, Choosing & Using Curriculum: Including Special-Needs,* and more. Her company, Simplified Learning Products, can be reached at 800-745-8212 or www.joyceherzog.com.

The **Learning Style Model** developed by Mariaemma Willis and Victoria Kindle Hodson, and explained in their wonderful book *Discover Your Child's Learning Style,* reviewed in Chapter 15, provides a promising new approach. Instead of "labeling" and "remediating" children, they suggest the following. In their own words:

1. *All aspects of learning style are identified, including talents and interests.*
2. *A program is set up to work with those learning style needs.*
3. *The student's potential is seen as unlimited.*
4. *Excuses are replaced with problem solving and collaboration.*
5. *Strengths are used to overcome weak areas.*

In other words, students are seen as capable rather than disabled.

Here are some other thoughts to consider for your distractible child:

- **Training.** At the Catholic private school I attended for four years, the nuns made us sit quietly in study hall for one hour a week. Being slightly hyper myself (normal for a strongly kinesthetic kid), I at first found this hard to take. But eventually, the practice in sitting still taught me to calm down and just *think* for an hour without any distractions, even schoolwork. You might not want to start with a whole hour, but for a Wild Child, working up to it might help.
- **Have you thought of thanking God** for your child's high energy level and hyperacute senses?
- **Maybe your child should be outdoors more.** Former generations of kids spent most of their out-of-school time outdoors, and nobody complained about their energy levels then!

Now I'll turn over the floor to special-education expert Joyce Herzog, who has some more specific suggestions for you.

Joyce Herzog on How to Help

The following examples suggest that a child is poor at blocking out the variety of stimulus in his environment: He hears the curtains rustle, he sees the dust flecks floating, he feels the breeze lift the hairs on his arms. Many of these children who have been labeled hyperactive, hyperkinetic, ADD, or ADHD may not be able to shut out the overwhelming stimuli that confront their bodies and brains and, therefore, cannot concentrate on what is being said.

How Can I Help Him Listen?

- Allow him to hold and mold clay or Silly Putty as he listens.
- Save gum or hard candy as something he gets only when it is time to listen.
- Allow him to use crayons or markers with blank paper as he listens.
- As you read him a story, or in church, firmly rub his back.

How Can I Help Him Slow Down?

- Decrease the stimulus in his learning environment.
- Only ask for slow down when essential.

- Structure his learning time and always include something for his hands and/or mouth to be doing.
- He, above all children, needs to know what is expected, needs consistent discipline.
- Allow some kind of white background noise (ocean waves, very gentle and quiet classical music, even quiet static) when he is to concentrate.
- Start with very small times of concentration interspersed with periods of total body involvement such as running, stretching, or somersaults. Gradually increase concentration time.
- Keep him out of situations that you know will over-stimulate him (unstructured situations, large numbers of people, loud concerts, etc.).

Other Helpful Hints

- Teach him early to jog, run, swim, and play ball, and allow those activities as breaks between academics as often as possible. Start with two minutes of concentration followed by three minutes of controlled physical activity.
- Use a teaching style that allows him to get totally involved in a controlled way. This means body, mind, and spirit, not just see, say, and write.
- Separate behavior from the person: "That behavior will not be tolerated." "You are always welcome, but that behavior is not." "Go to your bedroom (or a time-out area) until that behavior is under control." "I love you so much, but that behavior is dangerous (disturbing me, distracting to others, etc.)." "We will have to leave . . . if you persist (until that is under control, until it stops, etc.)."
- As often as possible, he needs to understand the purpose of what he is doing and be motivated by his own agreement that it is important.
- It will be very important to keep the child from feeling worthless or inadequate. Praise him every **real** chance you get—not just for achievement, but for who he is or for trying his best. Believe in him and his potential to become a good person. Discover strengths and encourage their expression.
- Find something he is really interested in (cars, airplanes, horses, etc.) and try to associate anything you want him to learn with what he likes.
- He may rarely see a difficult project through to completion. Give him some very simple projects (one at a time) and see that they are finished. Then help him identify and enjoy the good feeling that comes from having finished the job.
- Encourage him to read aloud and use a marker to keep his place, but allow him not to if he becomes more distracted.
- Encourage him to make at least one good friend outside the family. This may be an older child who understands the need, an adult, or even a pet. He needs to have affirmation from someone other than Mom and Dad.
- The child will need to grow up and be involved in decisions about his learning as young as possible. He will succeed only with a great amount of effort on his own part, and he will be willing to put that forth only if he sees it is worth it.

What ADD and ADHD Really Stand For

In most instances, people who have been labeled "LD" are learning *deceived*—that is, they have grown up believing that they are deficient and their own natural abilities are not worth much. In my opinion, ADD more aptly refers to Attention to Dreams and Discoveries, and ADHD describes Alert to Daydreams and Humorous Diversions. . . . I will admit there is some truth to ADD standing for attention deficit disorder—there is a definite *deficit* in the kind of *attention* that our young learners receive; therefore the *disorder* is with those schools who are labeling our children!
—*Discover Your Child's Learning Style*

- Give him a timer with a gentle count-down. Have him concentrate for a designated period of time, continually increasing the increments. When the timer signals, he may take a designated break, in continually decreasing increments. At first, he will need a signal to get back to work as well. The timer's signal should be gentle and unobtrusive.
- Don't give options. **It must be done now**. Be sure he understands in a firm but gentle way.
- You must always remain firm but gentle. Know what you expect, know what the limits are, and communicate them to him in a way that he understands. Do not allow him to continually break the rules, causing you to become angry, yell, and strike out. Any disobedience must be stopped early and consistently and redirected.
- Find times and ways to enjoy your child and your relationship with him. He won't find acceptance in many places or from many people. It is **essential** that he knows that you love him (always) and enjoy him.

Diet, Environment, and Your Distractible Child

The A.D.D. and A.D.H.D. Diet!
Parents $9.95.
Safe Goods, CT. (800) 903-3837,
www.safegoodspub.com.

The A.D.D. and A.D.H.D. Diet! is a small, concise paperback book that shares information about possible causes of ADD and ADHD, and suggestions about changes in your child's diet and living environment that can have positive effects on his or her ADD and ADHD behaviors.

The following questions are addressed in the book:

- Is there a connection between chemical fumes and learning ability?
- Can poor digestion contribute to behavior problems?
- What is commonly misdiagnosed as ADD or ADHD?
- Can diet contribute to fatigue and depression?
- What really is ADD/ADHD?
- Is the problem hereditary?

Nutrition, recipes, detoxifying methods, supplements and non-dietary approaches to ADD/ADHD are topics included in the book. A resource directory and bibliography make it easy to find the products and resources that the authors are discussing. There is a wealth of information about how foods affect behavior and nutrients necessary for optimum control of ADD symptoms. *Maryann Turner*

The Crazy Makers
Parents. $14.95.
Jeremy P. Tarcher/Putnam, a member of Penguin Putnam Inc., NY.
(212) 366-2000,
www.penguinputnam.com or order through online catalogs and booksellers.

This book could save your homeschool... or even your child's life.

We're used to thinking in terms of individual children having food sensitivities or allergies. But the problem may be much more widespread. **The Crazy Makers: How the Food Industry is Destroying Our Brains and Harming Our Children** demonstrates that a huge number of children today are having their academic performance and emotional stability undermined by what passes for food in our society.

Based on new research and a formal study the author, nutritionist Carol Simontacchi, conducted of American school children's eating habits, *The Crazy Makers* makes a compelling case that American food manufacturers are eroding our mental and emotional functions, all in the name of profit. Consider this:

- Twenty percent of teens contemplate suicide each year—and the rate of actual teen suicide increased nearly 30 percent from 1980 to 1992.
- The rate of mental depression has been soaring since World War II, especially among young men.
- Up to 24 percent of adults experience a mental health crisis in any given year.
- Seven to 14 percent of children will experience an episode of major depression before the age of 15.

Now, we all know that modern life has its pressures and that the downfall of the church and family has dramatically affected society. But in past centuries, people withstood greater pressures—wars, serfdom and slavery, death of family members at a young age, wholesale loss of babies due to unhygienic living conditions—without going nuts. So what's up?

Food used to be complete fruits and vegetables, brown grains with the bran intact, *un*homogenized milk and other dairy products not subjected to temperatures that kill all the enzymes needed to digest them, meat from animals who had never tasted an antibiotic, and fish. Now, our food mostly comes in packages and boxes, "enhanced" by substances with names like allyl antharnilate, methyl delat-ionone, and FD&C Blue No. 1. Carol Simontacchi claims—and demonstrates from research—that the effects of this daily chemical onslaught includes hyperactivity, depression, fatigue, confusion, and aggressive, even violent behavior. When it comes to our children, the problem escalates, especially around puberty, when the body is subject to massive changes.

The typical teenager's diet is grossly inadequate in most vitamins and minerals, in particular the B complex vitamins. Simontacchi had children keep food diaries listing everything they ate, and found that "it is not uncommon to see a seven-day food diary containing 21 meals with almost no vegetables, no fruit, no protein, and no water." When she had one group of teens from a Christian high school drink a protein supplement shake before school every day, even though they had not wanted to be part of the study, even though they did not change any of their other eating habits, and even though some were uncooperative to the point of washing the nutritional drink down with soft drinks, a mood test showed significant improvement in these teens' emotional state, as compared to the control group who received no supplement.

Food affects mood. As the book puts it,

Take a child and deprive his brain of adequate nutrition through his entire life, dump him into a hostile, unstable social scene [she's referring to school], and pull away the pillars of his support network (his family—he pulls away from them).

Then load up his breakfast cereal with stimulants, feed him more stimulants at lunch, snack, and dinner, and at the same time, rob him of the very nutrients he needs to process the stimulants. Toxic chemicals from his food target his endocrine system and prevent his natural hormones from locking into place. Inject other toxic chemicals from his food into his nervous system that prevent neurotransmitters from relaying messages back and forth. This is a recipe guaranteed to make him or her crazy.

Contributing to the problem are our schools, who make deals with vending machine companies, fast-food franchises, and others to provide low-quality, high-profit food to 51 million children and young adults. Over $750 million is spent annually on vending machines in schools alone, not counting the less-than-wonderful products parading through the cafeteria kitchens. The most chilling part of the book, to my mind, is where the author chronicles how school nutritionist after school nutritionist, knowing better, sells out their students for a few thousands in profit for the school.

What this all means is that perfectly normal children with excellent parents can still go nuts if their diets are deficient—and bad, but tasty, food drives out the good.

- Iron deficiency is markedly associated with overaggression in young men; nearly twice as many incarcerated males are iron deficient as their nonincarcerated peers.
- Magnesium deficiency causes chronic fatigue, twitching, constipation, anger, depression, frustration, agitation, and panic attacks. Weepiness, clinging, or secluding oneself are symptoms.
- Zinc deficiency leads to fuzzy-mindedness, confusion, depression, headaches, and bread cravings. Copper-toxic, zinc-deficient people may become verbally abusive.

It gets more serious. As the book explains, "Twenty-five percent of all teenagers will engage in activities so severe that if they even survive adolescence, some form of permanent damage will haunt them the rest of their lives." We're talking about anorexia, bulimia, suicide fixation, self-mutilation, violence towards others, drug abuse, and drunkenness, to name a few.

Bottom line: The more pre-packaged and fast food your children eat, even supposedly "good" packaged food, and the less they eat fresh fruit and vegetables, exercise, and supplement with proper protein, vitamins, and minerals, the more likely you are to see mild-to-severe emotional disturbances and academic problems, especially in the teen and young adult years, even from children who never before gave you a day's trouble in their lives. Even good home-cooked meals might not be enough if you frequently cook the same things and they lack some essential nutrient. Conversely, if a child is experiencing emotional problems and is unhappy about it (e.g., not wilfully rebelling), following the author's advice and possibly following up with personalized nutritional therapy from a professional you can locate through her appendix could end the nightmare.

I hope we all know that evil behavior is sinful, not just an inevitable result of chemical programming, and that a major reason today's kids "act out" is that society sends them the message that even kids who commit major crimes don't get punished. Given this situation, a kid under stress does not have social taboos and peer pressure as bulwarks against bad behavior. Indeed, today our media are avidly *selling* bad behavior, and peer pressure is a major *cause* of bad behavior. This leaves the child with just his inner character and parental support to offset any overwhelming emotional impulses he may be experiencing. The Lord's Prayer includes the prayer to be preserved from temptation—stresses that make it easy to fall into bad behavior. And Micah 6:14 also makes it clear that, when God judges a nation, "Thou shalt eat, but not be satisfied," which in our day may well include a food supply geared more to tastiness than to fulfilling our nutritional needs. Protecting our children from unnecessary temptation—in the form of chemicalized food and nutritional deficiencies that make them irritable, displeased, or confused—may become an increasingly important part of our role as parents.

So, what are we going to do?

First step, read this book. Divided into chapters on how to nourish the unborn baby, babies and toddlers, young children, teens, and adults—each of which explains what can go wrong at each age as well as what is needed—*The Crazy Makers* can easily be used as an introductory nutrition course at the junior-high or high-school level, one much better than anything I've seen on the market. You will learn a ton about how food provides energy to your body, the ingredients of good and bad food, and food deficiencies, all far beyond the typical (and unhelpful) "food pyramid" taught in textbooks. The author is not into any form of food faddism, so you don't have to worry about her preaching that you should eat odd food, avoid all meat, etc. Meanwhile, you'll be getting an easy-reading education on the food industry, nutritional research, and why this all matters.

The Crazy Makers also includes recipes, a primer on how to create your own healthful menus, an appendix of resources, another appendix listing groups who can refer you to a trained nutritionist, and an index.

So now we have one more reason to homeschool—to protect our kids from the body-and-emotion-destroying school food.

The Feingold Association is a reputable organization that boasts of amazing results in helping parents of hyperactive children, with abundant proof to back up their claims. The material is easy to understand and well worth the money.

Starting from the premise that dietary allergies are a leading cause of hyperactivity, the Feingold diet was designed to eliminate the major dietary culprits. **Diet, Learning & Behavior** is a 13-page, spiral-bound introduction to the Feingold diet. It explains what membership in the Feingold Association provides. It lists symptoms of additive/salicylate sensitivity, and specifies the dangers of artificial colors, flavors, preservatives and environmental chemicals. Salicylates are defined, and research studies are provided.

Included in your membership package is a list of acceptable foods from a varied assortment of items available in your supermarket. The list includes over a thousand brand-name products that are free of unwanted additives. You also receive the Feingold Handbook, which provides the most current information on the use of diet to help you or your child. A list of additive-free medications is also included. Recipes and a two-week menu make planning your first few weeks easier. A one-year subscription to their newsletter, *Pure Facts,* accompanies your membership. A "Dear Grandma" letter is included that explains the program to relatives, friends, teachers, etc. Program Assistant List and FAUS Counseling Line, staffed by parents who are experienced in the Program, are available to answer your questions and give support. *Maryann Turner*

"There is a subset of children who appear to learn well and easily on one day, but not on another. They seem unable to function consistently well in school. They often act appropriately but suddenly, for no apparent reason, their behavior can exasperate the most patient teacher or parent. Other children appear unable to learn or behave most of the time. Some are too active; others are too tired . . . Many have recurrent headaches, leg aches, or digestive complaints."

Any of this sound familiar? It's a quote from *The Impossible Child,* Dr. Doris Rapp's first book on detecting and treating childhood allergies. Though that book is now out of print, it has been followed by several larger and more complete books (proving this is a woman after my own heart!)

Is This Your Child? starts right on the back cover showing you pictures of typical symptoms of potentially unrecognized allergies. The allergic nose rub . . . eye circles . . . red ears . . . red cheeks . . . eye wrinkles . . .

Diet, Learning & Behavior
Parents. Feingold Association membership & program materials, $77 plus shipping.
Feingold Association of the United States, 127 E. Main St. Riverhead, NY 11901
(800) 321-3287 or (631) 369-9340
www.feingold.org

Is This Your Child?
Is This Your Child's World?
Parents. Child, $15. World, $24.95
Child, published by Quill, division of HarperCollins. World, published by Bantam Books. Both available online and in bookstores.

aggression . . . lack of alertness . . . and mottled tongue are all displayed in rather gruesome color.

The purpose of this extremely thorough, well-indexed, 626-page paperback book is to show you how to detect if your youngster is experiencing an unsuspected allergic reaction, and what to do if he or she is. The book does not lay the blame for all bad behavior at the feet of allergies. It does, however, point out that some kids get high on some foods, or bummed out by molds and pollens, and that we all have a much harder time functioning properly under such circumstances.

This is not a superficial book, in spite of its easy-reading style. You are given specific facial or body clues to tip you off to a possible allergic reaction—including more in-depth descriptions inside the book. The book also includes numerous before-and-after examples of children's work and considerable detail about specific allergies and how to spot and treat them.

Is behavior modification therapy the solution to non-allergy-caused behavior problems? Author Doris Rapp says yes. I say no. This fairly major disagreement aside, I think this is a good book. We do owe it to our kids to find out if they suffer when exposed to chemicals, pollen, pets, or dairy products. However, in no way can the vast increase in kids' rotten behavior today be blamed on allergies. Allergies may indeed provide extra pressure, but even a splitting migraine does not have the power to force any of us to bite, spit, and swear unless we let it. All this granted, before you give up on a child who is not responding normally to character training, it's worthwhile checking out whether he is suffering extra pressure from undetected allergies—and this book can help with that.

Also available from the same author: **Is This Your Child's World: How You Can Fix the Schools and Homes That Are Making Your Children Sick**. This book examines *environmental* causes of toxic and allergic reactions, of which there are far more than you might suspect.

Nature's Ritalin for the Marathon Mind

Parents. $9.95.
Upper Access Books, VT. (802) 482-2988, www.upperaccess.com.

Need an alternative to Ritalin? Exercise just might be the answer. Ritalin is a relatively new drug to the market. What did families do before the 1970s? According to Stephen C. Putnam, author of **Nature's Ritalin for the Marathon Mind**, millions of children can reduce or eliminate their need for medication by exercising. Laboratory experiments have concluded that aerobic exercise causes a chemical effect in the brain very similar to that of Ritalin. Children who respond to medication also respond to the effects of exercise. Simple theory, yes… but not so simple to implement in our society of couch potatoes.

This book has motivational advice on starting an exercise program for your child. It also provides a method to determine the optimum amount of exercise needed to benefit your child. The improvement in the way your child feels acts as an impetus to motivate your child to continue. Not to mention, ADHD children like movement.
Maryann Turner

More Books with More Facts

There are dozens of books about alternatives to Ritalin. Here are what I consider the "cream of the crop."

A good, quick, inexpensive place to start your studies is with Dr. Mary Ann Block's little book **No More Ritalin: Treating ADHD Without Drugs**. Dr. Block passionately believes "you can't treat the problem until you identify the *underlying* causes of ADHD." Some common causes: "hypoglycemia, allergies, environmental factors, and hyperthyroidism." This handy-sized 144-page paperback gives oodles of tips and case histories, including the horror story of what happens when Dr. Block's own daughter Michelle got caught up in the medical meat grinder. An index is included.

In the five years since that first book came out, Dr. Block continued her researches and clinical practice at her clinic, The Block Center, yielding a larger, more detailed book, **No More ADHD: 10 Steps to Help Improve Your Child's Attention and Behavior Without Drugs**. This one starts off with a rather shocking chapter entitled "Step 1— Understand the Medical System." This chapter will blow the lid off any lingering belief you might still have that giving kids psychoactive drugs is a good idea. The other nine steps are: educate yourself on the school system (where you'll find *more* good reasons to homeschool!), dump the sugar, take your vitamins, attack the allergies, repair the gut, learn how to learn, clear the head with "OMT" (a special osteopathic manipulative treatment she explains in the book), stand up for your child, and consider other underlying causes. There's a lot of food for thought here!

The Caregivers' Skills Program is a unique method designed to help children who are labeled ADD and ADHD behave correctly, pay attention, function independently, and solve problems without medication. The author, David B. Stein, Ph.D., is a behaviorist who does not believe in the ADD/ADHD labels. Instead, he prefer IA/HM: Inattentive or Highly Misbehaving. Thus, his book does not deal with the physical aspects of treatment like Dr. Block's and Dr. Rapp's.

Ritalin Is Not the Answer details a drug-free program, designed and tested for over 25 years The dangers of Ritalin are discussed, and an alternative method of teaching your children to handle his problems is explained in detail.

The 203-page paperback book is divided into the following chapters:

- What Are We Doing to Our Children?
- Understanding the Myths of Attentional Disorders
- The Importance of Effective Parenting
- Beginning the Caregivers' Skills Program
- Improving Behaviors
- Punishment
- Beginning to Learn Discipline
- Using Time Out Correctly for the IA or HM Child
- Reinforcement Removal for Very Difficult Behaviors
- Improving School Performance
- Helping the IA or HM Child to Feel Better
- Ten Ways to Stop Creating an Attentional Disorder Child

Appendices, reference lists, and an index are also included.

By learning the techniques explained in this book, you can equip yourself with the necessary ammunition to help your child succeed. The tools

No More ADHD
No More Ritalin

Parents. ADHD, $12. Ritalin, $5.99.
Ritalin book published by Kensington Publishing Group, NY, www.kensingtonbooks.com. ADHD book published by The Block System, Inc, TX, www.blockcenter.com.

Ritalin Is Not the Answer

Parents. Book, $15. Action Guide, $19.95
Jossey-Bass, CA, a division of Wiley. (800) 956-7739, www.josseybass.com.

that Stein uses are ignoring, time-out, and reinforcement removal (taking away objects and activities that are most important to your child). He explains how to overcome the traps that can occur with these methods so that you are able to be more consistent. He also strongly suggests paying the child more attention, which often yields great results even with non-labeled kids!

The methods Stein suggests build your child's confidence and encourage him to think for himself. This book offers helpful advice and motivates you to seek appropriate discipline in order to bypass the use of Ritalin.

Also available from the same author: **Ritalin Is Not the Answer Action Guide**, a workbook for parents who are attempting to use his methods, and **Unraveling the ADD/ADHD Fiasco: Successful Parenting Without Drugs**, a book that first attacks the ADD/ADHD mythology and secondly introduces his program. This one is from a different publisher. I don't really see the point of this additional book, as long as you have his other two. *Maryann Turner*

Talking Back to Ritalin is the king. This is the book you *must* read if you want to truly understand the drug wars in our schools. I am referring, of course, to the compulsory drugging of schoolchildren in order to get them to stop annoying the teacher and their classmates.

Dr. Peter Breggin, the author of this book, is an internationally recognized expert on the marketing of stimulants to children. He is a psychiatrist in private practice, and also the director of the International Center for the Study of Psychiatry and Psychology. He knows whereof he speaks, and he has plenty to say.

This 428-page, fully indexed book is aptly subtitled "What Doctors Aren't Telling You About Stimulants and ADHD." Part One explains how these drugs really work and what they do and won't do for your child. Part Two explains what is wrong about the ADHD label. Part Three takes on the ADHD/Ritalin lobby, correcting their self-aggrandizing misinformation. Part Four gives helpful advice about how to find out what is *really* bothering your child (including a handy checklist of potential environmental stressors) and what to do about it.

Having appeared on hundreds of radio and TV shows, Dr. Breggin is well aware of all the questions and arguments parents and professionals might raise about what he has to say. What makes his book so helpful is that he brings these very questions and arguments up—before you even have to bother to ask them—and answers them with fully footnoted detail. Yet the book is very easy to read.

Highly recommended.

Talking Back to Ritalin

Parents. $16.50.
Perseus Publishing, MA.
(617) 242-5200,
www.perseuspublishing.com.

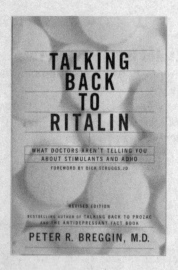

CHAPTER 47

Help for the Challenged

Families have many reasons for homeschooling. Perhaps one of the most compelling is that the school system either has already failed their child or does not offer the help they believe their child needs. This is often true in the case of children with challenges—among which we include both physical impediments and learning problems with an *organic* physical cause, such as a recognized birth defect or actual brain damage resulting from an accident.

True, today's schools have immense funding to help just such children, and laws compel them to do so. But often the results bear no resemblance to the amount of funding and good will invested. As with every other area of school operations, special education has its fads. The fad of the moment may involve lumping physically challenged kids with mentally challenged kids, or even with "emotionally challenged" kids—a euphemism that now includes the youthful assaulters, rapists, and murderers whom the courts require to be kept *in* school. Maybe it's a craze for teaching all deaf kids sign language—and nothing *but* sign language—so they can form a separate language group incapable of communicating with others and as such press for more government funding. (I'm not making this up. The anti-lip-reading lobby is large and loud.) Maybe your school district mainstreams all physically challenged kids, and you have reason to fear for your frail or disabled child's physical safety at the hands of the school bullies. Maybe you just think your child is capable of a whole lot more than the school will admit, and you're starting to believe you can do a better job yourself.

Or perhaps you feel homeschooling really is your only option. Maybe your child is housebound, confined to the vicinity of life-support machines, like my oldest son. Perhaps you simply believe in an educational philosophy or rehabilitative method unavailable in your local school.

Whatever the cause, you want to homeschool.

But can you homeschool a child with physical or mental challenges—even serious physical challenges?

Can you homeschool your children even if *you* are the one with the challenges?

The answer to both questions is yes!

And the good news is, you don't have to do this all on your own.

In this chapter, you will find organizations and products geared especially to help you in your homeschooling endeavor.

Lateblooming, Laziness, and Deficiency

Kids, of course, will try to sucker you into going easy on them. In this, they are exactly like adults. You will need to be able to distinguish between lateblooming, laziness, and deficiency.

- **Lateblooming** is when a child needs more time to learn.
- **Laziness** is when he won't even do what he knows how to do. (Very little kids forget things easily—keep this in mind).
- **Deficiency** is when the poor kid actually has something organic wrong with him. "Mental retardation" is not deficiency. It's what doctors say when they don't know what's wrong with you. On the other hand, identifiable birth defects may cause a child to be slower across the board than other children.

You need more patience for lateblooming and deficiency, less for laziness. Remembering that human beings are more than organic brain cells, I would be inclined to treat "deficient" kids as latebloomers who possess all the spiritual equipment of other human beings. This includes the ability to understand a story, make jokes, and resent being treated like a machine or animal.

—*Schoolproof*

Organizations That Can Help

Many groups whose titles suggest they help children and parents of children with disabilities are less than helpful. Some of these groups promote erroneous beliefs about human nature and education. Others seem to exist mainly to demand huge legal settlements and huge amounts of taxpayer money for their agenda. Yet others have some helpful resources, along with others that are less helpful or downright unhelpful.

We suggest that you steer clear of materials and "experts" who encourage you to obsess about your child's problems. Rather, ask these people and groups what successes they have had. Use these groups and resources to meet other families who are contending with the same challenges and to find out about breakthrough technologies and methods that are not covered in the mainstream press.

Remember, your fellow homeschoolers are a goldmine of information. With the notable exception of a few special-education "experts" who can be seen from time to time peddling the same old failed public-education strategies at homeschool conventions, your fellow parents have no axe to grind. They know what works for them and what doesn't.

ERIC Clearinghouse on Disabilities and Gifted Education
1110 North Glebe Road
Arlington, VA 22201-5704
(800) 328-0272
www.ericec.org
Database of information, curriculum, software, etc., for disabled and gifted

Foundation for Technology Access
2173 East Francisco Blvd., Suite L
San Rafael, CA 94901
(415) 455-4575
FTA works to provide assistive technologies to those who need it. If your child is physically disabled in some way (blind, deaf, paraplegic, etc.) these people can lead you to equipment that can help your child interact with a computer.

National Academy for Child Development
549 25th Street
Ogden, UT 84401-2422
(801) 621-8606
www.nacd.org
NACD has books, tapes, seminars, and in-person consultations at local chapters around the country. Helps for the physically and neurologically challenged, the slow learner, and the gifted. Very compatible with homeschool philosophy. NACD trains parents to do the therapy themselves. They were a big help with our son Ted.

NATHHAN
National Challenged Homeschoolers Associated Network
PO Box 39
Porthill, ID 83853
(208) 267-6246
nathanews@aol.com
www.nathhan.com
$25/year NATHHAN membership offers folks all of these services:
NATHHAN News, NATHHAN Family Directory, Lending Library, HSLDA

Group discount, and posting privileges on their online forum. If you are unable to afford the fee, families who really need encouragement may still contact NATHHAN for further information.

THE ORTON DYSLEXIA SOCIETY
Name recently changed to The International Dyslexia Association
Chester Building, Suite 382
8600 LaSalle Rd.
Baltimore, MD 21286-2044
(410) 296-0232
www.interdys.org
Pioneering organization studying dyslexia. Promotes phonics methods for dyslexia reversals.

An Organization for Challenged Homeschoolers

The NATional cHallenged Homeschoolers Associated Network (NATHHAN) is a "national and international support network for families with special needs, who home educate." The network began in March of 1990, when Kathy Salars telephoned a friend asking for help with her special-education homeschooling. Kathy's friend Diane, who was already writing to several families through a newsletter column titled "Dear Special Ed," decided to begin a network of parents helping one another. NATHHAN was born.

Since its humble beginning in 1990, the families in NATHHAN have received hundreds of letters and phone calls asking for resources, ideas, and encouragement. The exponential growth experienced by NATHHAN demanded the formation of a centralized office. In the fall of 1992, Tom Bushnell, his wife Sherry, and their children stepped into this rapidly growing ministry to write the newsletter and operate the support network. Tom came home to work in the NATHHAN office full-time in January of 1995.

NATHHAN has always invited families to participate in the sharing of experiences in order to help and encourage one another, most of all through prayer. NATHHAN's goals and purposes speak for themselves: "To be spiritually and financially equipped to help others with their needs in home educating their children. To speak and share with families personally. To act as a support network, uplifting families. To have this ministry and all of its activities be forthright and consistent in giving honor and glory to the Lord Jesus Christ."

NATHHAN currently has four specific services to offer homeschoolers:

- **NATHHAN Support Network** is made up of 12,600 families throughout the world. The network provides an abundance of resources, encouragement, and friends. The service is free and can be joined by sim-

ply sending a letter or postcard describing the challenge or questions that need to be addressed.

- **NATHHAN NEWS** is a 56-page quarterly newsletter. It includes features on resource reviews, adoption of special-needs children, and articles pertaining to raising and homeschooling a challenged child. It also includes a section devoted to finding help for individual families and many letters from challenged homeschooling families around the world.

- **NATHHAN Family Directory** is published once a year and includes families who graciously share encouragement and experiences with those in need. The trusting families who appear in this directory do so out of love and care, not monetary funds. "Only those who ask to be a part of this directory will receive their own to use. It is NATHHAN's sincere hope that many wonderful friendships will be formed."

- **NATHHAN Lending Library** is located at the NATHHAN office in Porthill, ID. However, it is available to all members through the mail. Postage is paid by the people who use it. Write NATHHAN for information on what books are available.

It is easy to feel confused and isolated when attempting to choose the right path. NATHHAN is full of love and enthusiasm for the task set out before us.

Presently disabilities represented in NATHHAN range all the way from children with dyslexia or learning disabilities to the multihandicapped, blind, cerebral palsy, and seizure-disordered children.

—*Tom and Sherry Bushnell, NATHHAN*
Tom and Sherry Bushnell live in Porthill, Idaho with their 9 children, 3 of whom are adopted and have special needs. Along with working in the office and writing the NATHHAN NEWS, the Bushnells give NATHHAN presentations to churches and attend a few homeschooling fairs.

Making Your Individualized Education Plan

An Individual Education Plan (IEP) may be required in your state, if your child has been labeled "special needs." Check with HSLDA for the law in your state. Below is the (as far as we know) only resource ever developed to help homeschool parents develop their own IEP.

IEP's made easy! This multi-grade level, **Individual Education Planning System for the Handicapped Student** is designed just for homeschoolers in an easy to use fill-in-the-blank format. You will create professional looking IEPs specific to the special needs of your home-educated student.

The fruit of author Deborah Mills' eight years of experience teaching workshops and creating IEPs for her disabled son, it is largely based on the use of a Functional Curriculum format. A Functional Curriculum is one that teaches skills through Daily Living Tasks. When using a non-traditional curriculum such as this, it is important to be able to document the learning process in a meaningful way. HSLDA recommends that a special-needs student have quarterly evaluations. The IEP forms included in the manual provide you a way to credibly demonstrate that your student is indeed learning and making progress, even if you have a severely retarded child who is only learning personal grooming skills and daily chores.

The Manual explains how to develop your own IEP specific to your child's special needs. Its planning sheets and Activities Listing serve as a springboard of ideas for IEP goals. Also included: articles of encouragement and examples from the author's personal experiences with her son. There is even a section that explains how a regularly educated sibling can receive high-school credit for a four-year Special Education Course!

Topics included in the manual are:

- What is an IEP?
- Functional Curriculum vs. Traditional Curriculum
- How to design an IEP for Home Education
- How to set goals
- How to implement the plan
- How to evaluate progress
- Lesson planning and documentation
- High-school planning
- The ITP (Individual Transition Plan)
- Graduation requirements
- Post-high-school services, programs, and options
- Resource listing

Reproducible Master IEP Forms come with permission to copy for personal, in-home, family use. These are:

- Individual Education Program (statistics)
- General Information Page
- Life Space Domain/Current Functioning Levels
- Basic Skill Infusion Grid
- Individual Education Plan (forms for each domain)
- Activity Evaluation Sheet
- Summary of Achievement (quarterly assignment)
- Daily Activity Worksheet, Grid
- Daily Lesson Plan, Grid
- IEP Planning Sheets, Target Activities (three pages)

Individual Education Planning System for the Handicapped Student

Parents. $35.
Deborah Mills, 8266 Leucadia Ave., San Diego, CA 92114. (619) 469-5822.

An updated version is out with journal notes of the author's experience in preparing an IEP. It also includes pictures.

The Chronological Age-Appropriate Activities Listing for students with severe handicaps offers a menu of ideas from which to draw when developing an IEP. You are encouraged to use this as a starting point for your own curriculum.

The curriculum information contained in this guide is organized according to four "life space domains"—*community, domestic, recreation/leisure,* and *vocational* domains. Each domain is addressed across six age groups: Ages 2–3, Preschool (ages 3–5), Elementary School/Primary (ages 6–8), Elementary School/Intermediate (ages 8–12), Middle School (ages 12–16), and High School (ages 16–18).

This 226-page manual comes 3-hole punched, ready to put into a binder for easy shelf reference.

How to Homeschool with Special Needs

Need help choosing material for your special-needs child? Joyce Herzog is the expert. This book is filled with Joyce's wisdom and down-to-earth advice. **Choosing & Using Curriculum for Your Special Child** includes hundreds of reviews for programs in math, reading, language arts, handwriting, geography, history, and science. In this oversized, 76-page paperback Joyce discusses the different curriculum types and evaluates the advantages and disadvantages of each. She pulls no punches when pointing out the disadvantages to some of the more popular programs. Throughout the book are tips for teaching each subject. She covers spiritual, religious, and Bible training in her product reviews. Included are chapters on testing, special-education resources, deaf-education resources, legal information, support groups, and magazines. Joyce is very matter-of-fact with her reviews, making this a very valuable tool when choosing curriculum for your special-needs child. *Maryann Turner*

Educational Care is based on the view that education should be "a system of care that provides for the specific needs of individual students." This 320-page textbook starts by identifying and describing 26 common behaviors that interfere with learning. These phenomena are grouped in chapters according to the following six themes: weak attention controls, reduced remembering, chronic misunderstanding, deficient output, delayed skill acquisition, and poor adaptation in school. Note that this list does *not* include dietary, emotional, or environmental problems—for that kind of help, check out the books we reviewed in the previous chapter. The book also includes information on "dysfunctions" such as ADD, gross-motor dysfunction, problems with short-term memory, and weak visual processing.

Following the analysis of each behavior are lists of suggestions about how to help students who are having difficulty with the particular area. In addition, these chapters provide ideas about how to help demystify disabilities by naming, explaining, and discussing them.

The author, Dr. Mel Levine, believes that many problems result from labeling and segregating impaired students. He states, "Without denying the existence of specific conditions, we will avoid the labels and explore in some depth the phenomenas."

The book concludes with descriptions of teaching methods, kinds of assessment, and bypass strategies. The book also discusses available medical

Choosing & Using Curriculum for Your Special Child
Parents. $9.95 plus shipping.
Greenleaf Press, TN. (800) 311-1508, www.greenleafpress.com.

A new edition, titled **Choosing & Using Curriculum: Including Special Needs**, is available for $14.95 from Simplified Learning Products, (800) 745-8212, www.joyceherzog.com.

Educational Care: A System for Understanding and Helping Children with Learning Problems at Home and in School
Parents. $32.75.
Educators Publishing Service, Inc., MA. (800) 225-5750, www.epsbooks.com.

treatments, all of which will be helpful in letting you see what kinds of approaches you can expect a school to subject your child to.

The appendixes contain a variety of handy forms. Some, such as the mathematics interview, can be used for diagnosis, while others, like the report and story organizers, help the student organize, carry out, and evaluate specific tasks. Numerous tables and graphs help the reader navigate and recognize important information.

Unfortunately, *Educational Care* asserts that children with learning problems should be educated through "collaborative management" of parents and teachers, and does not discuss home education.

My advice: Don't skip the book because it is not specifically targeted toward homeschoolers. When applying the doctor's suggestions, just remember, you are the teacher and your home is the school. *Brad Kovach*

Home Schooling Children with Special Needs

Parents. $12.95 plus shipping.
Noble Publishing Associates, OR.
(800) 225-5259,
www.noblepublishing.com.

Written to meet the questions and needs of the Christian homeschooler, and subtitled "Turning challenges into opportunities," **Home Schooling Children with Special Needs** is intended to be a framework to aid you in teaching your special child.

This 180-page manual is broken down into three easy-to-understand sections: Section 1—Getting the Facts, Section 2—Tackling the Issues, and Section 3—Planning Your Program. Each section is further divided into short, authoritative lessons about every facet and emotion involved with teaching a special learner. The author, Sharon Hensley (M.A. Special Education), speaks

from experience. She is a homeschooling mother of three, one of whom is autistic.

Section 1 identifies and analyzes numerous behaviors that can disrupt learning. These are grouped in six segments: learning mismatches, learning disabilities, slow learners, language/communication disorders, mental retardation, and autism. Some of the behaviors discussed include auditory system disorders, motor sensory disorders, and attention disorders. After discussion of each phenomena, the author provides a list of judging criteria, suggested therapies, and resources.

Section 2 tackles two important issues in the home education of special learners: emotions and expectations. The author discusses, from experience, feelings of inadequacy, grief, anger, acceptance, and discouragement and how to deal with their appearance. She provides a loose schedule of expectations and talks about balancing the education of siblings. The author also uses this portion of the book to face the moral and ethical reasoning behind home education of the special learner: public vs. home school, medication vs. behavior modification, etc.

Section 3 helps readers plan their homeschool program. Developing a consistent and individualized plan with set goals and testing is discussed in detail. The author explains the importance of choosing the correct teaching method and curriculum. Teaching methods such as computer-assisted learning, interest-directed learning, therapies, textbooks, and unit studies are defined and analyzed. Curriculums are similarly broken down and discussed. The author even reviews of large list of curricula and products designed for the special learner.

A final note promising the continuation of the book leaves the reader wanting more: more curricula, more resources, and more of the heart-felt writing. *Brad Kovach*

Special Education: A Biblical Approach is a practical handbook for pastors, parents, Christian school officials, home educators, or anyone needing to deal with the gamut of special education problems.

The publisher of this book, Hidden Treasure School in Greenville, SC, established by the Rev. John Vaughn after his own daughter had been severely burned, is a school for children with physical, mental, and learning disabilities. The folks at Hidden Treasure have built their philosophy of education firmly on the Bible. They believe that every child is born fully equipped to do the job God has planned for him. It is the parents' and teachers' role to guide the child in developing his gifts. They repeatedly emphasize that special education is individualized education (which concept homeschoolers are already very familiar with). They are also right that the church has in general failed miserably in ministering in any real way to the handicapped.

With these points established, they orient parents and teachers to special-ed concepts, major legislation, problems requiring special ed, and available resources. Then follow excellent chapters on physical disabilities, emotional disabilities, learning disabilities, educable mentally retarded and slow learners, and trainable and severely/profoundly mentally retarded.

The chapter on learning disabilities should be helpful even for those who object to that label. The chapter on emotional disabilities calls the church back to its role of counselor of troubled families, thus practically eliminating this area of special education.

The book's only real drawback is that it is too friendly toward the state. It is pro-state certification of teachers and not wary of state evaluations and testing of prospective special-ed students.

This book should be a great asset in aiding the Christian community in fulfilling its responsibility to the disabled among us. *Betty Burger*

Maneuvering the maze presented to parents of special-needs children can be frustrating. The challenges faced by your child can be further complicated by technical jargon and "expert" advice. **Strategies for Struggling Learners** by Joe Sutton, a professor of Special Education at Bob Jones University, helps you understand your options and offers unconventional methods to help your struggling learner. Practical advice is interspersed with professional explanations of the various testing available, individualized education plans, and techniques that may be implemented with your child.

Included are chapters titled:

- Formula for Success
- Learners with Limitations
- Essential Teaching Beliefs
- Scriptural Model for Teaching
- Testing and Evaluation
- Blueprint for Instruction
- Consultant Services
- Modifying Instruction
- Generic Teaching Techniques
- Techniques for Specific Subjects
- Educational Procedures
- Managing Student Behavior

The Suttons offer their sound advice in a manner that educates you, as a parent, on the resources available for your special child. They help you wade through the jargon and counsel you in all areas of special education.

Special Education: A Biblical Approach

Adult. $14.95.
Hidden Treasure Publications, SC.
(864) 235-6848,
www.hiddentreasure.org.

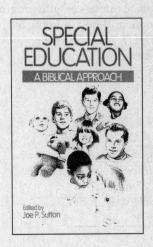

Strategies for Struggling Learners

Parents. $18 plus shipping.
Exceptional Diagnostics, SC.
(864) 967-4729, www.edtesting.com.

Miracles of Child Development

Parents. Six-hour cassette program with note outline, for home use, $50. *NACD, UT. (801) 621-8606, www.nacd.org.*

This 212-page, paperback book is a valuable resource filled with information and suggestions. *Maryann Turner*

Neurological Therapy at Home

Founded by Robert Doman, the National Association for Child Development specializes in home therapy programs for the really hard cases. Children who have suffered severe brain damage, or who have neurological problems, or fits, or physical handicaps, are thoroughly diagnosed by NACD's staff and then presented with a home program tailor-made for them. NACD is expensive (hundreds of dollars a year per child), and many of their methods are severely criticized by the medical establishment. They do have some spectacular success stories, however, and their philosophy of optimism at least keeps them trying to achieve results, whereas medical experts seem to be getting more and more pessimistic these days. We were members of NACD for a while, and Ted just loved his program (all except the knee bends).

NACD programs are a lot of work for the parents and are highly patterned. You do exercise A for two minutes three times a day and listen to tape B for three minutes twice a week, etc. NACD is also into the "dominance" theory of brain organization, whereby the goal is to be right-handed, right-footed, right-eyed, and right-eared, or conversely left-handed, -footed, -eyed, and -eared. Thus your child may end up wearing an eye patch or ear plug to assist him in "switching over" from right to left, or vice versa. NACD also believes strongly in the stages of development, and enrolled teenagers and even adults sometimes wind up crawling around like babies until they improve their coordination in that stage.

You can order NACD's introductory tape set, **The Miracles of Child Development**, for $50. The tapes are fascinating and inspirational, but take them with a grain of salt. Behavior modification is not the answer for *all* childhood discipline problems as Mr. Doman believes, though his suggestions for motivating children, and especially his stress on praise and encouragement, are well worth hearing.

Deal Me In

Ages 6 and up. Price $9.95. *Audio-Forum, division of Jeffrey Norton Publishers, Inc., CT. (800) 243-1234, www.audioforum.com.*

Social Skills

Deal Me In, subtitled *The Use of Playing Cards in Teaching and Learning*, is more than directions for a slew of card games. The author, Dr. Margie Golick, contends that playing cards are high-interest educational tools as well as a means of social entry for children who lack physical prowess or social skill. Some skills she claims card games can develop: rhythm, motor skills, sequencing, sense of direction, visual skills, number concepts, verbal skills, intellectual skills, and social skills.

After a lengthy introduction presenting her case for card games, she gets down to cases with more than five dozen games, plus card tricks and logic games. Every card game is summarized, learning skills enhanced by the game are summarized, and then you get the rules: rank of cards, basic overview of the game, bidding (if appropriate), object of the game, rules of play and scoring, comments, and necessary vocabulary for play.

The book includes several indexes to help you find the game you want, and some psychotherapeutic moralizing by the author. She approves of gambling and swearing, and although her comments on these subjects do not take up any significant part of the book, I didn't want you to buy it and then accuse me of not warning you! By and large a helpful resource that could use some light editing in the next edition.

Betty B. Osman's pioneering book **No One to Play With** deals frankly with the problem of the "living disabilities" which affect many children with so-called "learning disabilities." For youngsters who lack confidence both in the classroom and on the playground, life may not be easy in any area.

No One to Play With is excellent on diagnosis, but spotty on cures. Christian parents, for example, may not appreciate the suggestion that LD children "may require far more concrete and graphic presentations [of sex] than many local school boards deem appropriate." I also can't share the author's faith in behavior modification as the cure for poor behavior. Where this book shines is (1) in its realistic appraisal of a problem too many of us ignore, and (2) in the compelling case histories which, if nothing else, create empathy for the victims of living disabilities. You may recognize your child, or yourself, in the story of Freddy, the withdrawn TV-watcher who avoided other children, or in the saga of Susan, whose own brother and sister called her names at home. Distractible George; Jimmy, who was never included in games; Jeff, whose parents were divorced; ornery Danny, who always "had to" pick fights; and a host of other children pass before your eyes, along with the tale of what the author did to help each of them and why it worked. She also covers the situation of gifted kids with learning disabilities and LD adults.

No One to Play With— Revised: Social Problems of LD and ADD Children

Parents. $15 plus $3 shipping. *Academic Therapy Publications, CA.* (800) 422-7249, *www.academictherapy.com.*

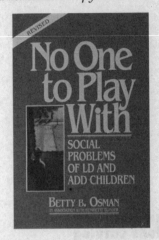

Speech Therapy at Home

I wish I had known about **Help Me Talk Right: How to Correct a Child's Lisp in 15 Easy Lessons** *before* spending several hundred dollars on speech therapy for my daughter. Author Mirla G. Raz has done parents a great service in providing them with the information allowing them to help their own children. A speech therapist herself, she doesn't discount the need for calling on a professional if necessary.

The book contains instructions for carrying out 15 therapy sessions, practice requirements, worksheets, and troubleshooting ideas for use when things aren't progressing. Children are motivated with a great deal of positive reinforcement, games, prizes, and contests. Directions are clearly and concisely spelled out. You won't need any additional materials other than some games and toys that you already have on hand.

Much of what I saw in this book we experienced personally with our speech therapist.

Helpful would have been some photographs or detailed illustrations of the correct and incorrect tongue placement, as well as a basic discussion of speech theory; the "why" to go along with the "how." *Renee Mathis*

It's a miwacle! Um, a miracle! At least that's what we hoped **Help Me Talk Right: How to Teach a Child to Say the "R" Sound in 15 Easy Lessons** would be.

Having a little one who can't say her "r"s was kind of cute. Until she passed age 6. And then when her little sisters imitated her. At one point we had *three* "wah wah" birds in the Pride family! It was time for help. Hence this book.

"Help Me Talk Right" series

Ages 5 and up. Help Me Talk Right: How to Correct a Child's Lisp, Help Me Talk Right—"L" Sound, Help Me Talk Right—"R" Sound, $32 each plus shipping. *Gersten Whitz Publishers, AZ. Credit card orders only: Thinking Publications, (800) 225-GROW. Also available through Amazon.com, Barnes and Noble, and Borders online. Other orders & inquiries: (480) 951-9707, www.speechbooks.com.*

You've seen Renee Mathis' glowing recommendation of Mirla G. Raz's earlier book above. Now I see why Renee was so excited. With the very clear lessons, from tongue positioning with the "jelly spot" to practicing initial and final r's in single words, phrases, and sentences, any parent can use this book. With the built-in games, worksheets, and activities, any child will be happy to go along.

Mirla Raz believes you should consult a speech pathologist several times during these lessons to make sure the child is in fact saying the "r" sound properly. She suggests that you request the free services of your local public-school speech pathologist. Having heard some horror stories about homeschooling parents whose encounter with the "free" therapists or pathologists at the school turned into intrusive attempts to force their child into the public school, I think you'd be smarter to go the "private practitioner" route, if you find it necessary.

Also available, but not reviewed by us in time for this edition, **Help Me Talk Right: How to Teach a Child to Say the "L" Sound in 15 Easy Lessons.** We also hear a book on preschool stuttering is in the works.

Special Equipment

Attainment Company Options Catalog

Free catalog.
Attainment Company, WI.
(800) 327-4269,
www.attainmentcompany.com.

Debra Evans, the author of several Crossway books on womanhood and mothering, sent me a very nice catalog called **Options**. It's "an exclusive selection of gifts for people with special needs," published by the Attainment Company. On the cover is an attractive picture of a young woman with Down's Syndrome sitting by a basket of apples. Inside are all sorts of products designed to help mentally-handicapped teens and adults gain independence in their shopping, cooking, eating out, grooming, housekeeping, and so on. Many of these products are also good for people who have trouble, for whatever reason, with communicating intelligibly. The catalog is uniformly respectful of the abilities and needs of those who can benefit from its products, and is targeted at their families and friends.

Computer and Web Resources for People with Disabilities, 3rd Edition

$20.95 paperback, $27.95 spiral bound, plus shipping.
Hunter House, Inc., Publishers, CA.
(800) 266-5592,
www.hunterhouse.com.

This 284-page book is an absolutely splendid resource! Inside **Computer and Web Resources for People with Disabilities**, which was produced by the Foundation for Technology Access (see their organization listing earlier in this chapter), you'll find all the information you need to locate hardware and software options for people with disabilities. Lists of support groups, publications, professional associations, and training institutions are included, as well as personal stories and product reviews by type of product. For example, if the book is talk-

ing about touch screens, it will tell you how they work, who they benefit, features to consider, cost, and list "common vendors," i.e., companies known to regularly carry this type of product. An "additional information" section gives an insider's view of how a touch screen hooks up, whether you'll need special software, and so on.

Why is this important? Because assistive devices make the difference between learning and not learning, working and not working, and communicating and not communicating, for many people. Legally blind? Try a Braille printer, or voice technology that lets the computer read to you. Physically impaired? Your choices range from voice entry, to special keyboards, to mouth sticks, and lots more. And the list goes on. Even carpal-tunnel sufferers can find help here!

The book is physically attractive and easy to use, packed with charts, graphs, lists, and photos.

As I said, school supply houses and firms that cater to preschoolers are good places to start, especially those that carry Montessori materials. For physical therapy, **Rifton Equipment** has the stuff. Exercise chairs, bolsters, wedges, play equipment, and so on—it's all here. Prices are acceptable for the quality, and it's possible that insurance may pay for some of it if you get a doctor's prescription. We've used similar equipment of our own manufacture, and it did Ted a lot of good.

Rifton: Equipment for the Handicapped
All ages.
Rifton Equipment, NY.
(800) 777-4244, www.rifton.com.

Resource Guides

Resources for People with Disabilities is over 1,000 pages big. That's a lot of resources! In its two volumes, you'll discover

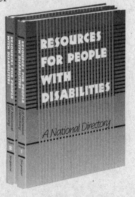

- Where to find 17 categories of assistive technology: communications devices, mobility and transportation, and a lot more
- Where people with disabilities can get scholarships, grants, and awards, with eligibility and deadline information
- Publications, publishers, and conferences devoted to the issues
- Organizations and associations for people with disabilities—14 categories, from legal assistance to independent living centers and government agencies

Resources for People with Disabilities
High school to adult. Set of two library-bound volumes, $89.95 plus shipping.
Ferguson Publishing Company,
c/o Facts on File, NY. (800) 322-8755,
www.fergpubco.com.

Introductory essays cover such topics as teaching students with learning disabilities and understanding the basics of assistive technology. The books have three indexes, making it possible for you to search for information by state, by type of disability, or by name of organization. Be aware that, thanks to political pressure, "disabled" now includes all kinds of behavioral and lifestyle choices, as well as physical handicaps.

PART 10

Homeschooling Your Gifted Child

While her peers were learning how to walk, Colleen K. Kilpatrick was also learning how to read. She knew the alphabet by age one, and now at two and a half years old, she can read second-grade-level books and write her name. She knows the capitals of all the states, can identify 30 countries on a globe, and can recognize most of the numbers from 1 to 100. Aside from counting in English, she can also count from 1 to 10 in three other languages: Spanish, French, and Tagalog (Philippines). Absolutely amazing!

If your child is athletically gifted, she will thrive on athletic competition. Homeschooler Kayla Bingham, age 8, from Lake George, CO, won first place in her age division for her Acro-dance solo, "Hot-Hot-Hot," at Star Power National Dance Competition, held in Las Vegas in July. Acro-dance is a combination of gymnastics and dance. Kayla also brought home four gold medals in group (team) dances in pom-pom, lyrical, and acro. Kayla represents Robin's Danceworks of Colorado Springs. Way to go, Kayla!

CHAPTER 48

Help for the Gifted

In one sense, every child is gifted. God has given each of us special abilities and talents, so that what is easy and obvious for one person may be difficult or impossible for another. It's also true that every organically normal child has the ability to *appear* gifted if he or she home-schools.

However, not every child is "gifted" in the *technical* sense of precocity and strong internal drive to master a given subject area (or "domain" to use the technical term). Not every gifted child is equally gifted. And yes, children who are "gifted" in the technical sense *do* have special needs.

Is your child gifted in the technical sense? If so, how much? What kind of education and home support do such children need? Can they get what they need in school? How can you have your child recognized as gifted by a Talent Search program, and what opportunities does that open up? Is acceleration at home a good idea?

This section will answer these questions.

Multiple Intelligences or Multiple Gifts?

Howard Gardner has gained much attention with his "multiple intelligences" theory. In his book *Frames of Mind: The Theory of Multiple Intelligences* he lists the following types of intelligence:

- Logical-Mathematical Intelligence
- Spatial Intelligence
- Musical Intelligence
- Bodily-Kinesthetic Intelligence
- Interpersonal Intelligence
- Intrapersonal Intelligence

Although these represent some of the natural forms of giftedness, I don't think it helps much to transmute the classic term "intelligence" to include all the above. "Intelligence" has traditionally meant "quickness in learning academic material." The term "giftedness" more accurately represents both the categories Gardner lists, and several more besides.

FOR THE GIFTED, HOMESCHOOLING IS A BLESSING

Although there are no statistics on how many gifted students are turning to home-schooling, educators who work with such kids say they believe the number is increasing. Financially beleaguered public schools across the country have cut gifted programs in recent years, figuring that bright kids will do fine in a regular classroom. But they don't. A recent Department of Education study found that smart kids desperately need work geared to their abilities. Students like Gabriel Willow, who live in rural areas, have the toughest time. They don't have many cultural institutions, like museums or colleges, for after-school stimulation. "Home-schooling is often their best choice," says Kathi Kearney, a specialist in gifted education at Columbia University who works with home-schoolers.

—*Barbara Kantrowitz with Debra Rosenberg, "In a Class of Their Own,"* Newsweek, January 10, 1994

True in 1994. Still true today.

Giftedness & IQ

"Giftedness" covers a wide range of ability levels as measured by IQ (Intelligence Quotient) tests. Here are some ways it is defined:

- **Moderately gifted.** IQ of 120–139. About 2 or 3 out of 100 children have IQs of 130 and up. A typical cutoff for entrance into gifted programs is an IQ of 130, although some Talent Search programs have now extended this downward to the 120 level.

- **Highly gifted.** IQ of 140–159. About one in 100 children has an IQ at this level.

- **Profoundly gifted.** IQ of 160 and up. About one in 10,000 to 30,000 has an IQ at this level.

- **IQ of 180 and up:** about one in a million. There is no special term for this level of giftedness, since the children exhibit the same characteristics as profoundly gifted children, and they are so rare as to be little studied.

- **Prodigy.** Regardless of IQ level, this is a child who can perform at an adult level in a given domain—e.g., Mozart.

High IQ, Low Support

To be honest, it appears to more acceptable today to be athletically gifted, musically gifted, artistically gifted, or even socially gifted than intellectually gifted. Even within the homeschooling community, there is a definite sense of isolation among the parents [of gifted children] with whom we've spoken.

—*Janice Baker, Kathleen Julicher, and Maggie Hogan, Gifted Children at Home*

What's more, as Ellen Winner's excellent book *Gifted Children: Myths and Realities* makes clear, an overview of the research on giftedness shows that, while children with the various gifts outlined below all share certain characteristics, they are *not* all equally good at schoolwork. So, while children who exhibit any of Gardner's "multiple intelligences" may be quick at learning the rules of their particular domain (music, socialization, sports, etc.) they are not necessarily quick at learning *in general*, as traditionally "intelligent" children are.

With that in mind, let's take a quick peek at some of the types of giftedness:

- **Academic giftedness.** This is normally called "intelligence" and is what IQ (Intelligence Quotient) tests are supposed to measure. Academic giftedness is usually divided into *mathematical* and *verbal* giftedness, with possibly the additional category, sometimes linked with mathematical giftedness, of *spatial* giftedness.
- **Artistic giftedness**
- **Musical giftedness**
- **Strategic giftedness** (e.g., chess and other strategy games)
- **Mechanical giftedness** (the ability to understand, fix, assemble, and invent items made of many parts)
- **Charismatic giftedness** (leadership and dramatic ability)
- **Emotional giftedness** (the ability to "read" people effortlessly and respond appropriately to their emotional needs)
- **Athletic giftedness**

Types of Academic Giftedness

In the sidebar you will see how levels of academic giftedness are defined by IQ scores. Now, we must consider two more categories of academic giftedness:

- **Global giftedness**—equal ability in both mathematical and verbal areas
- **Unbalanced giftedness**—the child scores high in verbal ability, but not in math, or vice versa. Such a child might even be labeled "learning disabled" in one area, while he is demonstrably gifted in the other.

Now here's an important point:

All these types of giftedness are normal.

As you go through the checklist below, you may find yourself shouting, "That's my kid!" Compared to the children around him, he may appear different. But compared to other gifted children, you'll see that he is "one of the gang."

Checklist for High Academic Giftedness

Wondering if your child is highly gifted? If so, Winner suggests you should have seen at least some of these signs before your child turned five:

- ☐ Recognizes and responds to you at a very early age
- ☐ Long attention span in infancy
- ☐ Easily bored, wants to see and do something new
- ☐ Early at crawling, rolling, and walking
- ☐ Early talker, often jumping right into sentences and complex vocabulary. My Hungarian mother was a great example of this. She was talking at six months, causing old ladies on the street to make the sign of the "evil eye" to protect themselves from this obviously strange child!
- ☐ Learns to read with very little help. Winner notes, "It is not unusual for such children to read at sixth-grade level in kindergarten."
- ☐ Oversensitive to noise, pain, and frustration

Is your child five years or older? Look for the following:
- ☐ Learns well with minimum instruction
- ☐ Persistently curious; asks tons of questions
- ☐ High concentration on topics that interest him
- ☐ High energy level that may come across as "hyperactivity" when he runs out of interesting things to do
- ☐ Highly aware of his own reasoning processes
- ☐ Obsessive interests, to the point of becoming an expert in one or more topics
- ☐ Loves to explore numbers and math topics—the kind of kid who considers a book of math puzzles a great gift
- ☐ Great memory
- ☐ Excels at logic and abstract thinking
- ☐ Prefers typing to handwriting—it's faster!
- ☐ Gets along better with older children and adults than with children her own age, mainly because age mates do not understand or share her interests
- ☐ Worries at a young age about the "big questions"—justice, world peace, the meaning of evil, the existence of God
- ☐ Has an excellent, sharp sense of humor that may manifest itself in annoying puns and practical jokes

Testing for Giftedness

To confirm your child's academic giftedness, you can

- **Have him take an intelligence test**, which usually must be administered by a licensed professional. Two such are the Stanford Binet Intelligence Test and the Wechsler Intelligence Scale for Children, now in its third revision referred to as the "Wechsler for Children III." Other tests for various forms of giftedness are the Goodenough-Harris Drawing Test (originally designed as an IQ test called the "Goodenough Draw-A-Person Test" and now mostly used to test for artistic giftedness), and the Ravens Progressive Matrices Test (this uses picture symbols only and tests for logical thinking and spatial ability).
- **Have him take a standardized test.** You can order several such tests from BJ Testing and Evaluation, Christian Liberty Academy, or Sycamore Tree, among other sources, and administer them yourself at home. See the write-up of these services in the Evaluation & Testing chapter for details. If your child scores in the top two percentiles, he will be eligible for all of the regional Talent Search programs. If he scores in the top five percentiles, he will be eligible for some of them.

Some Cautions

Bear in mind that IQ tests may be administered in such a way as to make the results less meaningful. I well remember being tested at the age of seven by a psychologist who made me wait the entire time prescribed for each section of the test, although I finished each in half the time. This exhausted me to no purpose (the entire process took over four hours of alternate intense anxiety and boredom, with nothing to eat or drink), and the final score did not reflect the fact that I was able to finish each section early. Test anxiety and "dumb errors," such as skipping a question and then forgetting to skip a line on the response form, or expecting a question to be more tricky than it was and answering it accordingly, can also lower scores.

In the long run, you will be able to determine where your child falls on the "giftedness" range quite accurately by his characteristic personality and behavior, and by his achievements, such as his scores on other tests and his performance in national contests.

Beware of the temptation to declare your child "profoundly gifted" if he is not. Remember, this giftedness level brings with it a host of social problems. If a child has that level of giftedness, he also has the fortitude to face the corresponding isolation from his age mates. But if he does not, persuading him that he is profoundly gifted may set negative social factors into play without any offsetting inner benefits.

What to Do If Your Child Is Academically Advanced

First, thank God for this special gift!

Second, **make plans to spend some time teaching your child basic social skills.**

Gifted kids tend to be "project"-focused rather than "people"-focused. That's what helps them advance so rapidly in intellectual matters. This type of child is unlikely to pick up appropriate social behavior by osmosis, the way other, less focused, children do. However, this type of child also responds well to social skills taught as a "school" subject.

Beside the usual mall manners, restaurant manners, and library manners, you may need to teach your gifted child not to interrupt . . . to listen courteously to others . . . to not share *everything* he knows on a given subject . . . cues that tell him it's time to leave . . . how to introduce himself at a gathering . . . and so forth.

Such children also tend to be hypercompetitive and hypercritical. Continually minimizing the achievements of others by bringing up your own superiority does not win friends or influence people. So time spent teaching your gifted child how to encourage others (*without* patronizing them) will be well spent.

These social skills will make the difference between raising a hyper-intelligent geek, who people tolerate but nobody likes, and raising a future leader, whose intellectual skills can be used to their maximum capacity and who has the respect of others.

Books to Answer Your Questions, or Not

Creative Home Schooling for Gifted Children

Parents. $28.95.
Great Potential Press, Inc., AZ. (602) 954-4200, www.giftedbooks.com.

Creative Home Schooling for Gifted Children by Lisa Rivera, mother of one gifted child whom she has homeschooled for a few years, reads like two books grafted together.

The first book, taking up the bulk of the 430 oversized pages, is yet another how-to homeschooling book. This is intentional. The publisher's data sheet proclaims, "For a comprehensive guide to home-based education that does not promote any particular curriculum or religious view, this is the one book parents should buy!" This would be fine, if so much of the material hadn't already been covered both earlier and better by other people. Chapters on making the decision to homeschool, learning styles, what a curriculum is, unschooling, classical homeschooling, unit studies, recordkeeping and testing, etc., etc. have been dealt with by at least a dozen other homeschool books and by authors with far more knowledge and experience, going right back to the first edition of my *Big Book of Home Learning* in 1987. To help with the angst of the secular homeschooling mom, an entire chapter on "The Full-Time Parent/Teacher" tackles such questions as "Will Home Schooling Swallow Up My Life?" There is also, no surprise, a resource list, with contact information provided for some of the resources.

The second, more interesting, and much smaller book actually deals with giftedness and the particular educational issues surrounding it. This includes the chapter on "Traits of Giftedness," the chapter on "Intellectual Needs," and several pages of the late-in-the-book "Special Topics" chapter.

To make it more personal, sprinkled throughout the book are many semi-anonymous comments by homeschooling parents and kids. Chapters also end with a "Key Points" summary. Most chapters also have "Questions for Reflection" and an "At Home with Home Schoolers [or Unschoolers or Home School Parents]," in which more folks identified only by their first names comment on the chapter's topics or give their answers to some of the reflection questions.

The book's overarching theme is "homeschooling for full potential . . . to 'educate for self-actualization' rather than to 'educate for success.'" This is to be accomplished through "four key aspects of home-based education," the first being "understanding and acceptance of self." This explains why you will find many quotes from psychologists dotted throughout the book. (The other three key aspects are "creative learning," "self-directed study," and "natural extension into the community," in case you wanted to know.) If this all sounds a little vague and not exclusively applicable to gifted kids, I can only say I agree.

In my opinion, the author hasn't made enough of an effort to make things easy for the reader. It often seemed every other page was telling me I should read this book or that book or watch this video or that video. This is not helpful. Tell me more about the book, or tell me the points it makes, or simply say something based on your own experience, but don't just throw a book title at me and suggest I "may want to" read it and dozens of others.

I wanted to like this book, but I really can't find a reason why it should take 430 oversized pages and cost $26. If you want information about giftedness, Ellen Winner's book is far better researched, better written, and much more helpful. If you want information about homeschooling, many other books treat those topics more effectively. If you want information about homeschooling gifted children, the authors of *Gifted Children at Home* have many more years of experience with many more gifted children, and they write about it better. The author has put a lot of effort into this book, but it's just too many words and too little help or originality.

Educating Your Gifted Child by Vicki Caruana was not written solely for homeschoolers. I feel obligated to mention this up front, because since Vicki's two other books from Crossway, *The ABC's of Homeschooling* and *The Organized Homeschooler*, have both been about homeschooling, readers may assume this book is intended for the same audience.

The book starts off by exploring the three educational options—public school, private school, and homeschooling—and continues to provide input for parents whose children are in all three environments throughout.

Like the author of another book reviewed in this chapter, Vicki has homeschooled one gifted child a few years. There the resemblance between the authors ends. For one thing, Vicki has a Master's degree in gifted education. For another, she taught gifted children in the public schools before deciding to homeschool. Written with the assistance of other parents of gifted kids and other experts on giftedness, her book has just one purpose: help the Christian parent deal with the nitty-gritty needs of his or her gifted child.

This 208-page book covers the "big issues" first. Aren't all children gifted? Should we label this child as gifted or not? What are gifts, talents, and intelligence, and what difference does it make which terms we use? Even in these preliminary chapters, you'll find frequent exhortations to keep your own spiritual house in order, acknowledging God as the giver of gifts and avoiding the sin of pride ("Look how smart MY kid is!") The next chapter, on "Mixed Blessings," shows the author knows what it's *really* like for gifted kids—the good *and* the bad. The "Big Fish in Little Ponds" chapter includes suggestions for challenging your gifted child to excel when it's so easy to get A's already without effort. Not much new info is in the chapter on "Matching Teaching and Learning Styles," but it at least is well presented. Three chapters then deal with academic needs, emotional needs, and social needs from a biblical and practical point of view. The "Great Expectations" chapter leads you to many opportunities (contests, organizations, and resources) where your child can develop or showcase his talents. Four

Educating Your Gifted Child
Parents. $13.99.
Crossway Books, IL. (800) 635-7993, www.crosswaybooks.org.

GIFTED KIDS BENEFIT, SAYS NEWSWEEK

Kids with special needs—gifted or learning disabled—are more likely than most to benefit from home schooling, researchers say, but only if their parents have the right training and resources. Ryan Abradi, a 10-year-old who lives in central Maine, started multiplying when he was just 2½, and even then understood the concept of negative numbers. "From the beginning, he seemed hard-wired for math, says his mother, Valerie, a mechanical engineer. When he reached school age, she checked out the local gifted program and could tell right away that Ryan was already well beyond it. "He had no patience," she says. "He was intolerant of the questions other kids would ask." Ryan is now happily at home, working his way through second-semester college calculus.

—Newsweek, *October 5, 1998*

chapters lead you through the preschool, elementary, middle school, and college-and-beyond years. "Finding Support" rates a chapter of its own. None of this is overwhelming, and resources for further study are neatly gathered at the end of each chapter rather than tossed here and there into the middle.

This book has a hefty number of appendixes:

- A list of suggested reading on giftedness (not annotated, unfortunately)
- Gifted & Talented Schools and Programs
- Groups and Organizations
- Journals and Magazines

It also features references, bibliography, and a helpful index.

This shouldn't be your one and only book on gifted education. You'll also need two books reviewed further on, *Gifted Children: Myths and Realities* and *Gifted Children at Home*. But if you're a Christian looking for an inexpensive, easy-reading introduction to the practical and spiritual sides of giftedness, pick this one up as well.

Gifted Children at Home, 2nd Edition

Parents. $24.95 plus $5 shipping.
Castle Heights Press, Inc., TX. (800) 763-7148, www.castleheightspress.com.

There are a multitude of resources to help parents who have children with learning difficulties. But the pickings can be pretty slim if you have a child (or children) who are academically gifted, and even slimmer if your gifted child also has learning or behavior disabilities.

The well-known homeschool authors of **Gifted Children at Home: A Practical Guide for Homeschooling Families** (Kathleen Julicher of Castle Heights Press, Maggie Hogan of Bright Ideas Press, and writer Janice Baker) all have years of experience in teaching their own gifted children. Janice's oldest, Seth, is finishing his MBA at University of Delaware at age 20. Kathleen's highly gifted children are all out of the house now and excelling in the Air Force, at work, and in college. Maggie's oldest son, JB, graduated at 15 and was a National Merit Finalist.

These homeschool moms want you to know that your gifted child is just that . . . a gift. These children come with their own unique set of challenges, both academic and emotional. This information-packed 152-page manual will offer you encouragement, tools, and lots of great ideas that will help you tailor your homeschool to meet the needs of your gifted child.

The book starts with a wonderful discussion about evaluation: What makes a child gifted? Though the usual litmus test is IQ, testing alone will not present a complete picture. *Gifted Children at Home* gives a brief but specific analysis of the testing process for those that choose that route or have been in public school, as well as a discussion of characteristics of the gifted. They strongly encourage home education as the best alternative for these children, not only for the usual spiritual and academic reasons, but because you can tailor an educational program plus outside activities to best meet the needs of your child.

This guide tells you not only why, but how. After the introductory chapters on giftedness and homeschooling, chapter topics include parenting the intellectually gifted learner, what to teach when, curriculum considerations, usable techniques, acceleration and grade skipping, activities for gifted kids, computers, apprenticeship, preparing for high school and college, record keeping, mentors for parents, and the perspective of a home-schooled gifted child looking back over his education. Tons of resources, including useful websites. The text is spiced with great first-person anecdotes, and fills a niche that is often overlooked in standard home education materials. Highly recommended! *Michelle Van Loon*

Gifted Children: Myths and Realities by Ellen Winner is the first book you should read about giftedness in children. This 450-page book will quickly bring you up to speed on all the current theories about giftedness, the history of gifted education, the ways schools and families try to deal with gifted children, and more. Chapter titles are:

- Nine Myths About Giftedness
- Globally Gifted: The Children Behind the Myth
- Unevenly Gifted, Even Learning Disabled
- Artistic and Musical Children
- The IQ Myth
- The Biology of Giftedness
- Giftedness and the Family
- So Different from Others: The Emotional Life of the Gifted Child
- Schools: How They Fail, How They Could Help
- What Happens to Gifted Children When They Grow Up?
- Sorting Myth from Reality

The author divides gifted children into two classes, the moderately gifted and the profoundly gifted. She points out that much that is written about gifted children—their superior social adjustment and leadership roles—only applies to the moderately gifted. The stereotype of the eccentric, socially isolated genius is still reality for many of the profoundly gifted—and this also applies just as much to those who are outstandingly gifted in the areas of athletics, art, and music.

Gifted Children is not just a stream of facts and figures. The author has thought about all this data and has plenty of opinions to share. She identifies and disproves these myths about giftedness:

- Global giftedness, the notion that "gifted children have a general intellectual power that allows them to be gifted 'across the board.' " As she says, "The child with a combination of academic strengths and weaknesses turns out to be the rule, not the exception. Children can even be gifted in one academic area and learning-disabled in another."
- The distinction between "talented" (referring to children who are exceptional in the arts, music, dance, or athletic areas) and "gifted" (referring to children who are exceptional in academic areas.) She says, "Both classes of children exhibit the three characteristics of giftedness"—precocity, marching to their own drummer, and a rage to master.
- The myth that children "talented" in the areas of art and music must have high IQs, even though IQ tests only measure "a narrow range of human abilities, primarily facility with language and number."
- The myth that either genetics or environment is *solely* responsible for giftedness.
- The myth that giftedness is produced by an overzealous, driving parent. As Winner says, "It is true that parents of gifted children are highly involved in the nurturance of their children's gifts. But such an unusual degree of investment and involvement is not a destructive force. It is a necessary one if a child's gift is to be developed."
- The myth that gifted children are "popular, well-adjusted, exceptionally moral, and glowing with psychological and physical health." Winner goes into some detail to demonstrate this

Gifted Children: Myths and Realities
Parents and gifted children searching for self-understanding. $21.
Basic Books, A Division of HarperCollins Publishers, Inc., PA.
(800) 386-5656, www.basicbooks.com.

applies only to the moderately gifted child; profoundly gifted children often are socially inept, physically awkward, and unhappy.
- The myth that all children are gifted.
- The myth that gifted children become eminent adults. Actually, a child's personality and character is much more reliable predictor of future success than his IQ.

If I may put it this way, Winner has really done her homework on the current research. Her far-ranging book takes you from case studies of individual gifted children, to the classic large-group studies, to studies of gifted autistic children and savants that reveal some fascinating glimpses of how some types of giftedness work. She does not confine herself to the academically gifted, but spends plenty of time on the musically, artistically, and athletically gifted as well, and appears to know every study that is or has ever been done with gifted kids in any country around the world.

If you are gifted, if you have a gifted child, or if you have ever known a gifted person, you'll catch yourself saying, "Aha!" and "She got that right!" at frequent intervals. For further study, you can revel in the excellent bibliography, footnotes, and index.

My one and only gripe: The author obviously knows very little about homeschooling or the life of most homeschooling families. She speaks against homeschooling in one place as being an extreme last resort because it cuts children off from other children their own age, which readers of this book know is not true. (Can we all spell Y-M-C-A, A-W-A-N-A, and S-c-o-u-t-i-n-g?) On the other hand she repeatedly mentions that homeschooling, sometimes with private tutors, had been the educational method of choice for gifted students until recently, and she tells about the excellent results, both emotionally and educationally, of one homeschooling mom. (She does mention how "lucky" the young student was to have a sister being taught with him, to provide the necessary socialization, I assume.)

Perhaps the best service this book provides is, paradoxically, to assure gifted children and their parents that they are normal. Different from other kids, yes, but with characteristics in common with *other* mildly, highly, or profoundly gifted children, depending on into which category the child falls. Winner excels in her analysis of what giftedness is, how it affects children, and what families can do to maximize the beneficial aspects of extreme giftedness while overcoming its social and emotional pitfalls. Very highly recommended.

The Gifted Kids Survival Guide series

Ages 5–10 (Survival Guide), 10 and up (Guide for Teens). Survival Guide, $10.95. Guide for Teens, $15.95.
Free Spirit Publishing, MN.
(800) 735-7323, www.freespirit.com.

Over the years I have come to rely on the enormously helpful, down-to-earth guides published by Free Spirit Publishing for parents, children, and teachers. Whether your child (or you?) are gifted, talented, highly creative, or just a square peg in a round hole, you are sure to find a book to help from the thoughtful folks at Free Spirit.

These two books are aimed at the gifted traditionally schooled child and written in an engaging style that invites the young reader to feel at home. Gifted kids are often puzzled by everyday life, so the authors of these guides provide sensitive and encouraging advice that can help such a child understand his strengths, and practical suggestions for overcoming weaknesses.

The Gifted Kids' Survival Guide, For Ages 10 & Under, is a slim volume that explains giftedness to children in terms that they can understand, alleviates fears adults may not realize they have ("Am I expected to be perfect just because I'm gifted?"), and guides them in responding to challenges they face at home and at school. Topics include The Six Great Gripes of Gifted Kids, Smart Ways to Make and Keep Good Friends, Coping with Teasing, Famous GTs Who Were First Pegged as Losers, and more. When You're Bored Silly would have helped my youngest child one Sunday when his teacher asked, "What are you thinking?" Surely, the advice in this book might have kept him from blurting out, "I'm so bored I could scream!"

The Gifted Kids Survival Guide, A Teen Handbook, disappeared into my teen daughter's room as soon as it arrived. She read it through that evening, and the next morning at breakfast she pronounced it, "Great!" Once again, giftedness is explained and topics of interest are covered in more detail, with references to other books and materials for the teen who wants more information. Teens face greater challenges than younger children, and gifted children are perhaps more at risk. Some have social skills or common sense that are seriously lagging; others find that they are more bored than ever in school or that their giftedness is offset by areas of profound weakness; while others seek risks and stimulation that are extremely dangerous. This book provides essential advice for teens, and it pulls no punches in warning them of dangers and folly. Many teens will find the authors understand them as few others do, and parents will find that the authors present advice that is 99 percent pure and only occasionally politically correct. Teens are encouraged to be proactive in their education and to create positive change in their schools.

If you and your children are looking for books that are easy to read and show a sensitive understanding of giftedness, you would be hard-pressed to find books better than these. *Kristin Hernberg*

Think You're Smart? Check It Out!

The International High IQ Society has teamed up with Brain.com and prominent psychologist Arthur Jensen to add two IQ tests to the Society's lineup. The International High IQ Society has expanded its free IQ tests to include a five-minute IQ test and a twelve-minute IQ test. . . .

The tests are part of the new automated sign up program the Society recently implemented. To become a member you simply visit the site, take one of the seven free IQ tests and, if you score 126 or higher, join online. The completely automated signup procedure has put the Society at the vanguard of the industry. It is the only high IQ organization that has successfully switched to an automated, online signup format, making it the first serious competition to Mensa. Their seven IQ tests are currently taken by over 4,000 people a day, making it one of the most popular destinations on the Internet for online testing.

The International High IQ Society was founded in 2001 to enable bright people from around the world to come together on the Internet. The Society is currently the second largest high IQ organization in the world with members in over 50 countries. . . .

Membership in the International High IQ Society is open to persons who score within the top five percent of the general population on one of our official admissions tests. There is no other qualification for membership. [So all ages are welcome!]

Once you finish the test, it will be graded automatically and your score will be displayed. If your score is 126 or higher [on *any* test—you don't have to take all seven], you will be taken to our membership application page and invited to join the society

There is a one-time, lifetime membership fee of $59.95. There are no annual fees.

As a member, you will have access to our chat rooms, discussion forums (both general and subject-specific), online game tournaments, puzzles, and the Society's publication, *IQ Magazine*. You will also have the opportunity to become a member of the International Research Institute, an online think tank which assists corporate, government, and non-profit entities in the search for solutions to complex problems.

—Press release and membership info page,
www.highiqsociety.org

Homeschooling My Gifted Child
by Elise Griffith

Shortly before his second birthday, as we were walking through the airport to pick up his dad from a business trip, Bobby pulled away from me and ran towards the ticket counter.

"Twaay! Twaay!" he shouted.

"I'm sorry, honey, I don't understand you." I scanned the area for clues.

"Twaay! Der! Twaay!"

He was beginning to get frustrated, and I didn't want to cause a scene in the middle of the airport. "Can you show Mommy?" I asked.

He ran over to a large cardboard sign. T-W-A. Twaay. My toddler had somehow taught himself to read.

Bobby had never been a "textbook child." He did things his own way, at his own pace. When he decided to walk, for example, he simply stood up and walked down the hallway to his nursery!

Lenore Francine was the senior pastor's wife at our church during this time. She had directed Challenger Preschool in San Jose, California for nearly 20 years. One Sunday morning, she spotted Bobby reading a bulletin board.

"You're dealing with an especially gifted child here," she told us. "You really ought to think about homeschooling him."

I was very hesitant to even consider homeschooling. I worried that I wouldn't be able to teach Bobby properly, and that he'd be socially and emotionally damaged for life. I enrolled him in a local "Mother's Day Out" program, and worked as a substitute so I could keep an eye on him.

At about this time, Bobby began to erupt into violent tantrums regularly. He'd break toys, hit other children, and carry on until he'd make himself throw up. Every week, I was asked by his MDO teachers to come and "control" him.

Steven and I tried everything that the popular child development books suggested, especially concentrating on the books by T. Berry Brazelton, M.D. and William Sears, M.D. Ignoring the tantrums, which one book suggested, escalated the problem. We had several long, grueling days of screaming and migraine headaches before giving up on that idea. Trying to diffuse or distract Bobby also failed. He would punch or kick us whenever we tried to console him during a tantrum. Spankings had no effect on him, and made me feel guilty. Bobby learned to manipulate me, carrying on as if mortally wounded when I spanked. Giving him a "time out" in his room (or on a chair in another room) seemed to have marginal success, though it was done more for me than for him.

When he was still "throwing fits" at age five, we consulted Dr. Shepherd, a Christian family practitioner and pediatrician in Lewisville, Texas. He and his wife have ten children. They homeschool all of them. One of their nine sons had problems similar to Bobby's. Dr. Shepherd advised us to teach Bobby at home.

"Bobby's a very bright little boy," he told me, "and very intense. A public school will immediately suspect ADD (attention deficit disorder), but this isn't Bobby's problem. He's gifted. And gifted kids have slower emotional development. Boys, especially, seem to exhibit frustration by becoming violent. You should homeschool him, and be sure to establish firm boundaries."

"Doesn't he need to learn socialization?" I asked.

"All children learn to socialize," he said. "Human beings are social creatures. Unless you isolate him, he'll develop at his own pace, in his own time."

Steven and I discussed our options. I still felt very inadequate, but reluctantly sent for sample curriculum and catalogs. Sifting through the incoming stacks of material, I felt overwhelmed. How would I be able to choose the right curriculum for Bobby? I checked out a few books from the library that dealt with gifted children, and another that explained the homeschooling process.

Bobby displayed several of the "gifted" traits described in *Smart Kids With School Problems* by Priscilla L. Vail (published by E.P. Dutton in 1987):

- Rapid grasp of concepts
- Awareness of patterns
- Energy
- Curiosity
- Exceptional concentration
- Exceptional memory
- Empathy
- Vulnerability
- Heightened perceptions
- Divergent thinking

He also seemed to fall within the visual learning style described by the author. Visual learners acquire knowledge by "seeing"—they have more of a photographic memory. Bobby knew the alphabet by sight at eleven months. He memorized letters and words by sight. Our options were narrowed by this information. The cassette programs dedicated to auditory learners (those who learn best by hearing the lesson) and project lessons for kinesthetic (tactile or "hands on") learners wouldn't be as appropriate for Bobby as they would be for another child.

We considered combination programs, where we'd have the option of choosing textbooks according to Bobby's specific level in each subject. A Beka curriculum can be purchased a book at a time. So can Rod & Staff. A.C.E. curriculum involves self-paced worktexts. Calvert School's home education program was very appealing because books, worktexts, paper, pencils, rulers, scissors, and every implement necessary for the course is shipped with the grade level package.

With Bobby's needs and our budget in mind, the first materials we purchased were coloring and activity books. They helped to get Bobby in the habit of doing lessons. The kindergarten materials from Rod & Staff (our choice) were wonderful in their progressive approach to learning, gradually incorporating phonics and mathematics concepts. They weren't colorful or high tech, but Bobby did quite well with them, proving that simple materials can work with gifted children.

When his baby brother, Zachary, was born in December of 1992, Bobby had completed his kindergarten materials and was beginning the first grade. His tantrums were becoming a faded memory as our schedule and home life gained structure. We'd purchased the first quarter, first grade materials from Rod & Staff.

Then, from April of 1992 until February of 1994, Bobby's education hit a snag. Major changes hurled us into a state of chaos. We'd chosen Bob Jones books and worktexts for the remainder of the first grade, because, as Bobby said, "they look more like real school books." He now had six subjects to cover, and this posed a problem. Each day started well. Bobby did excellent work on the first two subjects, but it always went downhill from there. He was regressing. The tantrums returned.

I was overwrought at this point. I'd just had a difficult pregnancy and delivery, Steven had changed jobs and we'd moved three times and 700 miles—all within ten months! I tried to be patient and understanding with Bobby's regression but usually ended up screaming and packing up the books for the day. As Bobby disappeared into his room, I'd collapse, sobbing, on the loveseat.

Family and friends began bombarding us with unsolicited advice, blaming Bobby's behavioral problems on homeschooling. Yet we knew that homeschooling had been the single "constant" during those long months of instability.

When weeks passed with little progress in his behavior, we consulted a Christian with a doctorate in psychotherapy. She repeated information that we'd heard in some form before.

"Often children with special abilities, like Bobby, will be behind in emotional development," she explained, adding that Bobby's outbursts and lack of interest in school were an unconscious response to his stress. "With so much brain activity spent on absorbing his environment, there isn't enough for all areas to develop at the same pace."

The therapist suggested we give Bobby time to adjust to his new environment, and enroll him in a school for gifted children. The advice seemed contradictory. Steven and I felt as if no one really understood our day-to-day life with Bobby. Most of the time, he was an amiable child. The outbursts were as difficult for him as they were for us. He began to perceive himself as "bad." This increased everyone's frustration.

I decided another trip to the library was necessary to find ways we could help Bobby move along in his emotional development.

In their book, *Managing the Social and Emotional Needs of the Gifted* (1985: Free Spirit Publishing), Connie C. Schmitz and Judy Galbraith contend that, while children with special abilities don't have a common collection of personality traits, they do share common problems. These problems include:

- Feeling insecure because they're "different"
- Feeling isolated and "weird"
- Feeling misunderstood
- Feeling overwhelmed by perceived expectations of perfection

Helping your gifted child understand that he's not alone in his feelings and struggles can produce remarkable results. We encouraged friendships with other gifted children, and showed Bobby the charts in the books.

On a whim one day, I purchased a pack of composition notebooks, water-based markers, and ballpoint pens. I explained to Bobby that they were tools to produce his own books. He could write whatever he wanted in his books, and didn't have to share the contents with us if he didn't want to. This enabled him to express his feelings safely.

Bobby's attitude improved, as did his school work. He began to show an interest in learning again. We moved our old computer into his bedroom and gave him basic word processing software and a few math and story games. Time on the computer was a reward for good school work. Often, computing time took the place of recess. To give me a much needed break, we enrolled Bobby at a local Homeschool Supplemental Program. Art, music, and P.E. are the core focus of this program, which meets two afternoons a week.

As Bobby has grown (he's seven now), we've been able to find more effective means of teaching him self-discipline. He's held responsible for his actions. If he breaks a toy in a fit of temper, for example, he won't get a replacement and will have to pay for the item from his allowance.

We have found that, while all children need a balanced education, gifted kids especially need a variety of outlets for their curiosity and creativity. We do our best to expose Bobby to the arts, culture, music, and physical activity. Often this translates to "nature walks" and "museum trips," but a simple trip to the printer can be a rich experience for the inquisitive child. Even staying home can sometimes be stimulating! I run a desktop-publishing business from home. Bobby already knows the basic typefaces, layout designs, and printing process. He helps me choose appropriate colors for newsletters and designs his own work on his computer.

Bobby now reads with comprehension at the fifth-grade level. His math skills are also well above his age level, using A Beka materials. Still, while he is two to three years ahead academically, he remains about one to two years behind in his emotional development. We've learned to adjust to this, and can see definite progress. After dealing with emotional outbursts and tantrums for years, I almost threw a party the day Bobby came to me and said, "Mom, I'm really frustrated with . . . "

Occasionally I am asked if I'd recommend home-schooling. My response is always the same. It depends on the child and the parents. We've discovered over the years that quick fixes and easy answers don't exist. If you're willing to work within the boundaries of your child's unique abilities and quirks, and can make the commitment to teach your child—no matter how rough the road gets—then I'd say, "Go for it!"

There have been a lot of rough days for us, but I have no regrets. We've provided Bobby with the best start he could have. With a solid, Christian foundation and parents who strive to meet his needs (while insisting on responsible behavior), the sky's the limit for Bobby.

Children who are homeschooled often reach for higher goals as adults. We praise God every day for our two little boys, and the opportunity He has given us to raise them!

CHAPTER 49

Talent Searches

Would you like a helping hand with getting your child into a top-notch college . . . preferably with a large merit scholarship? Does the chance to enroll in special summer, weekend, and online courses with other high-IQ children appeal? Or would you just like to know where your grade 3–10 child fits into the academic universe?

Then you might be interested in applying to a Talent Search program.

What Is a Talent Search?

These are really "IQ searches." Think of them as an academic competition in which you are competing mainly against the test. In other words, the performance of other Talent Search entrants won't affect your chances of being a finalist. That is determined by your score on the final standardized test. However, if scholarships are offered, these will be reserved for the entrants with the best overall scores.

Four sponsoring universities have divided the USA up by states, and one of them (CTY from Johns Hopkins) has added an International Talent Search for those outside the USA. Schoolchildren in a sponsoring Talent Search's state have the opportunity, if their standardized test scores qualify, to apply to that Talent Search. If the student's score on a follow-up test is high enough, he can now attempt to enroll in a panoply of advanced courses—summer courses, weekend courses, correspondence and online courses, and CD-ROM courses, depending on what is available through that particular Talent Search program.

As a homeschooler, your child won't be offered the Talent Search information through his school. So I have told you all about them, and how to apply, below.

The main advantages of qualifying for a Talent Search program are (1) the excellent advanced courses, (2) the social opportunity to meet kids who can compete at your child's level, and (3) the entrée these courses provide to top-tier colleges, which *love* Talent Search kids.

Search vs. Program

To avoid confusion, in this chapter I refer to a Talent Search as a "Talent Search competition," or a "TS competition." The *competition*—where they are "searching" for the "talent"—is not the same thing as the associated Talent Search *program*—courses and services offered to qualifying students.

The courses and most of the other benefits of Talent Search programs are available *both* to TS competition finalists *and* to those who never entered a TS competition, but whose grades on standardized tests put them within the qualifying top percentages to enroll in those programs.

To participate in a Talent Search program (classes and other activities), scores on a standardized test may suffice. To be recognized in the Talent Search itself (with a ceremony, certificate, and other honors), you must go through the entire Talent Search process, as described for each program.

Also please note there is an application fee for each program.

Contact the program(s) of your choice for their brochure and follow the guidelines. Good luck!

How to Apply for a Talent Search

You have never seen this written up before in a homeschool publication (except for the previous edition of this book)—at least not in any book or magazine that *I* have read! Here, after dozens of hours of phone calls and more dozens of hours spent poring through the literature from every Talent Search program in North America, are the steps you must follow to participate in a Talent Search if you are a homeschooler.

1. **Give your student a standardized test in the fall** (early fall is best). If he or she achieves a score in the top 90 percent, 95 percent, or 97 percent (depending on the Talent Search in question) you can proceed to the next step. Each program has a list of qualifying standardized tests. For homeschoolers, the simplest route is to sign up for BJ Testing and Evaluation Service, as described in the Evaluation & Testing chapter. Both of the major tests offered through BJUP—the Iowa Test of Basic Skills (ITBS) and Stanford Achievement Test—are accepted as preliminary standardized tests by every Talent Search I checked. Other commonly accepted tests: The California Achievement Test (CAT), Metropolitan Achievement Test, ERB Comprehensive Testing Program (offered through local private schools—maybe yours will let you take it), the Comprehensive Test of Basic Skills (CTBS), and the Cognitive Abilities test.

2. **Apply to the Talent Search for your state.** For your convenience, under each Talent Search listing in this chapter you'll find its associated states. In the past, students used to be able to apply to any Talent Search competition. But now Duke University's Talent Search website specifically lists residency in one of "their" states as an application requirement. I couldn't find any such requirement on CTD's site or the Rocky Mountain site. However, although the CTY's site disingenuously claims under the question, "Who is eligible?" that you don't have to attend school or homeschool in one of "their" states in order to "receive full Talent Search benefits," in practice their online application form's pulldown menu does not even include states other than "their" states. This means it's impossible to sign up online if you're from, say, Missouri. So play it safe and stick with your regional Talent Search.

3. **They will send you a test registration packet** with instructions on how to . . .

4. **Register your student with the SAT or the other follow-up test** your Talent Search requires. The follow-up test usually must be taken in January through March. If your student has the option to take it at a Sylvan Learning Center or Prometric Testing Center, be warned that Sylvan and Prometric will not sign your youngster up for the test without a referral from the Talent Search program, who of course you will list on your test form as one of those chosen to receive a copy of the results.

5. **If your student becomes a Talent Search Finalist, you will be sent a variety of mailings** outlining the available summer, online, and computerized courses available through your Talent Search. If you requested third-party mailings when you applied, your student also may be solicited by colleges and other learning venues.

6. **You can then apply for the courses you want your student to take**, but again be warned—there is a pecking order for who gets accepted. Returning students have the first crack, and Talent Search registrants beat out those who merely have a qualifying SAT score. So if you are serious about such courses, you're better off having your student enter the program as young as possible, rather than gambling that

he or she will be able to take their very first course in eighth grade. Again, sooner is better when applying, as summer courses have a cut-off sign-up date.

7. **If you do all this correctly at the right time of year**, your student may be awarded a certificate at the annual award ceremony. Then you can get a nice picture taken at the ceremony, write up your achievement, and send it in to *Practical Homeschooling*, where it may get printed on our "Show & Tell" page!

How to Pick a Talent Search Course

All the same warnings that apply to school gifted & talented courses also apply to Talent Search courses. Beware of political correctness, paganism, and values deprogramming. Some folks have the erroneous notion that gifted children should form the core of a new group of technocrats, managing the masses on behalf of elite leaders. The future these folks envision has nothing to do with Constitutional liberties or Christian families. While you are much more likely to encounter such courses through a Governor's School program or local G&T course, the possibility exists that whoever is in charge of a given Talent Search program or teaching a given course at the time your child is thinking of taking it might have bought in to this worldview. Hence, some sensible cautions are in order.

Courses that emphasize "open-ended thinking" and encourage children to reinvent the future typically are the most likely to mess with your child's values and beliefs. Math and science courses typically are just straight academics that will do your child's future academic career a lot of good, with the exception of highly evolutionary biology courses. History, foreign languages, and so forth can go either way, depending on the instructor. Ask for a syllabus or talk to the instructor if you're trying to figure out where a given course is coming from.

The EPGY CD-ROM math courses, available through many Talent Search programs, are widely reputed to be excellent. I hope to check them out for myself by the next edition of this book. I would expect the online writing courses to be wholesome, since parents can read the child's writings.

Talent Search Programs

Founded in 1972, the Johns Hopkins University-sponsored talent search is the oldest and most exclusive. **CTY** absorbed the previous University of Arizona Talent Search a few years ago, making it also the largest talent search. Students must place in the top 3 percent on the qualifying test to be admitted.

Three Talent Searches are offered through CTY: one for grades 2–4, one for grades 5–6, and one for grades 7–8.

In all three levels, students present a standardized test score when registering for the Talent Search. This must be in the 97th percentile or better on the math section *or* the verbal section *or* ideally on the composite of both. Provision is also made for parents to nominate a child who does not have an initial standardized test score.

Center for Talented Youth Johns Hopkins University

Application fee: grades 2–4, $25; grades 5–6, $33; grades 7–8, $33. Test fee: SCAT, $50; PLUS, $46; SAT, $28.50 for paper-based, $75 for computerized. Fee reduction available for low-income families (anyone who qualifies for free/reduced price school lunch).
3400 N Charles St
Baltimore, MD 21218
(800) 548-1180
www.cty.jhu.edu

States served:

Alaska	New Hampshire
Arizona	New Jersey
California	New York
Connecticut	Oregon
DC	Pennsylvania
Delaware	Rhode Island
Hawaii	Vermont
Maine	Virginia
Maryland	Washington
Massachusetts	West Virginia

Since 1981, CTY has offered an International Talent Search. This is identical to their grade 7–8 Talent Search, except that it is for students outside the USA. For an application and further details, go to **cty.jhu.edu/ts/internat.html.**

The follow-up test for grades 2–4 is the School and College Abilities Test (SCAT); for grades 5–6 it is the PLUS (developed by ETS for Johns Hopkins); for grades 7–8 it's the good old SAT 1.

The SCAT must be taken on a computer. The PLUS and SAT can be taken in either paper-based or computerized versions. Information will be included in your registration packet. The SAT can be taken when it is normally offered to high-school students; however, to fit into the TS schedule, you'd have to do it in January or earlier. Computerized versions of the SCAT, PLUS, and SCAT are offered nationally through Prometric Test Centers.

Johns Hopkins offers advanced courses in math (including the EPGY courses from Stanford) and writing online for all included grade levels, and summer courses on science, computer science, and the humanities as well. To qualify for summer programs, your grade 2–6 student's PLUS or SCAT score must be in the 98th percentile of his or her age mates, and your grade 7 and up student must score in the 99th percentile of those of the same age.

Additional benefits to Talent Search competition participants:

- Planning Guide for parents of gifted kids
- Suggested Reading List
- For grades 5 and up, Program Opportunities Guide
- For grades 5 and up, Talent Search Times newsletter

For Talent Search finalists in grades 5 and up:

- Awards ceremony
- Additional merit awards
- For top scorers in grades 7 and up: one-course scholarships to local colleges and universities

Whether you are a Talent Search whiz or not, you can also take advantage of the many CTY publications and their *Imagine* periodical of resources and learning adventures for students in grades 7–12. A free sample issue is available online.

Center for Talent Development
Northwestern University

Application fee: MTSY, $51 (includes EXPLORE test); MTS plus ACT, $55.50; MTS plus SAT, $58. Fee reduction available for low-income families (anyone who qualifies for free/reduced price school lunch).
617 Dartmouth Place
Evanston, Illinois 60208-4175
(847) 491-3782
www.ctd.northwestern.edu
States served:

Illinois   North Dakota
Indiana   Ohio
Michigan   South Dakota
Minnesota   Wisconsin

Students who wish to enter the **Center for Talent Development** competition of Northwestern University must have scored in the top 5 percent on national standardized tests. The Midwest Talent Search, for grades 7 and 8, uses the SAT or ACT for its follow-up test. The MTS for Young Students grades 3–6, lovingly called the MTSY, uses the paper-based EXPLORE test or (for students in grades 5–6 only) the computerized PLUS test.

Like CTY, CTD offers a "parent nomination" offer and fee waivers for lower-income students.

CTD Talent Search competition participants receive:

- Student Guide with test-taking and career planning suggestions

- Educational Program Guide to *all* summer, commuter, residential, and overseas programs available to MTS and MTSY participants, including those offered by universities who are not among the four Talent Search sponsors.
- MTSY Planning and Resource guide to coursework and extracurricular activities
- List of recommended readings
- Talent Development annual newsletter
- Statistical summary and interpretation report, to give you the skinny on overall student performance across the board on the MTS and MTSY
- Certificate of recognition for having participated
- They'll even put you on a mailing list for private high schools and colleges that are looking for very smart kids!

In addition, top scorers have the option of being honored in a daylong ceremony at Northwestern University. Very top students are also awarded scholarships.

Now, their program (as distinct from their Talent Search competition). As you'll recall, you do *not* have to participate in the Talent Search to be qualified for these program options. A 97th percentile score on a nationally normed standardized test will suffice. Qualified students can take their "Learning Links" (previously "LetterLinks") distance courses. Besides their own Northwestern-based courses, which include courses for younger children and an assortment of Honors and Advanced Placement courses for grades 6 and up, they offer the Education Program for Gifted Youth (EPGY) courses on CD-ROM, with teacher assistance via email or phone. A huge variety of summer courses, from debate to chemistry, from social theory to recombinant DNA, are also available.

Duke University's Talent Identification Program (TIP) now has an addition, the Motivation for Academic Performance (MAP) program, available to students in the fourth or fifth grades who have scored in the top 10 percent or better on national standardized tests. The TIP Talent Search competition is for students in grade 7 who have scored in the top 5 percent on a nationally normed standardized test. In case you wondered, the MAP program doesn't *test* in those grades, but learning experiences are provided for sixth graders. For follow-up tests, MAP uses the EXPLORE test, and TIP allows students to choose either the SAT or ACT. Benefits available to MAP and TIP entrants include:

- Educational Resources Handbook with tips and strategies for test-taking, working with schools, and college options
- Results summary comparing your student's results to the Talent Search competitors as a group
- Educational Opportunity Guide listing over 400 programs for academically gifted students, plus academic competitions, state associations of the gifted, etc.

Even if you never entered anyone's TS competition, for $15, you can obtain CTD's latest *Educational Program Guide* and see what options your very smart kid has.

Duke University Talent Identification Program

MAP application fee, $17. EXPLORE test is about $28, payable to ACT. TIP plus SAT, $48. TIP plus ACT, $47. Fee reduction available for low-income families (anyone who qualifies for free/reduced price school lunch).
*Box 90781 (for the MAP) or Box 90780 (for the TIP)
Durham, NC 27708-0747*
(919) 684-3847
www.tip.duke.edu/index.html

States served:
Alabama	Mississippi
Arkansas	Missouri
Florida	Nebraska
Georgia	North Carolina
Iowa	Oklahoma
Kansas	South Carolina
Kentucky	Tennessee
Louisiana	Texas

My old version of the very valuable Educational Opportunity Guide

- Subscription to their twice-yearly *Insights* newsletter
- College sampler magazine sent during tenth grade

Those achieving top scores in the Talent Search competition may:

- Attend a recognition ceremony in their state
- Receive a Certificate of Distinction
- Super-duper top scorers are invited to the Grand Recognition ceremony at Duke University
- Single-course tuition scholarships for top scorers to a participating university in your state

Again, you don't actually have to go through the MAP or TIP competitions to take advantage of the following educational opportunities. A satisfactory score on the tests and an accepted application entitle you to take many excellent advanced summer courses, including history, physical education, and even travel-related courses that involve trips to Europe. TIP also offers textbook-based correspondence courses in many subjects and EPGY computer-based math courses.

Rocky Mountain Talent Search

Application fee, $29. Test fees:
PLUS, $46; ACT, $25; SAT, $26.
University of Denver
1981 S. University Blvd.
Denver, CO 80208
(303) 871-2983
www.du.edu/education/ces/rmts.html

States served:

Colorado	New Mexico
Idaho	Utah
Montana	Wyoming
Nevada	

The **Rocky Mountain Talent Search (RMTS)** caters to students in grades 5–9. Your initial application requires a score in the top 10 percent on a national standardized test taken less than two years ago, or the parent can submit a recommendation letter. The list of standardized test possibilities is pretty liberal, including math, science, social studies, language arts, or math/verbal composite. A 90th percentile score in any of these areas will qualify your student to enter the competition. The Talent Search competition then requires the score in the 90th percentile on the PLUS (grade 5 and 6 applicants) or the SAT or the ACT (applicants in grades 7–9).

As far as I can tell, this old guide is the last version in print. The new one is on their website.

A good score on the tests, or failing that by some insignificant margin, a good portfolio demonstrating academic skills, means you'll be eligible for the Rocky Mountain Talent Search Summer Institutes. These are advanced courses in math, science, and the humanities, with titles covering such topics as robotics, genetics, chemistry, physics, geometry, creative writing, mock trial, acting, and more along the same lines. The course catalog, pictured here, is fairly small compared to the other talent programs' catalogs, shown above. There are no distance courses, not even the EPGY computer-based courses, *yet*. In order to take advantage of the RMTS courses, you must show up physically at the Denver University campus at the correct time. Of course, some would say showing up and spending time with the other gifted kids is the most important part of the experience . . .

Typical Talent Search Calendar

- Order standardized test in May–July
- Take standardized test in June–August
- If your child's test scores qualify, then request, fill out, and return Talent Search application in September or October
- Take follow-up test in November–January
- Talent Search results announced in March

CHAPTER 50

What About Acceleration?

I f you use a traditional textbook or worktext curriculum, it's possible to do *two* lessons each day and complete a regular 13 years of school (kindergarten through high school) in just six years. That is the method followed by former *Practical Homeschooling* columnist Joyce Swann. Each of her ten children completed high school at age 11, college at age 15, and received a Master's degree at age 16. All of their work was completed at home through correspondence schools and external degree programs offered by major Western universities.

An accelerated education program of this type would be a lot harder to construct using unit studies, difficult to complete via online courses, and completely antithetical to someone favoring the Charlotte Mason method. With textbooks and worktexts, however, it's easy to see just how much progress you need to make each day.

While few homeschoolers have the Swann family's level of drive, many families enter homeschooling with one or more children needing to "catch up." For these children, accelerated education is a wonderful way to quickly meet—and surpass—the level of work expected of them in school. And for the increasing number of families willing to clip a year or two off the school schedule, workbooks and textbooks make it easy.

Ways to Accelerate

There are four basic ways to accelerate a child's education.

Compacting. Your child learns all the material but skips unnecessary assignments. For example, you might assign every other question in the math book, or every other sentence in the Latin translation, instead of all of them. Every homeschool parent can apply this technique to some extent by merely writing "SKIP" next to every assignment that smacks of twaddle or that covers material the child has already demonstrated he knows. Profoundly gifted children can often move ahead amazingly fast using this method.

Telescoping. Your child completes all the normal school work but in a shorter time frame. The Swann family uses this method; they do every single Calvert assignment, but at the rate of two a day instead of one a day. As Joyce Swann stresses, special giftedness is not required in order to telescope successfully, but hard work is.

Some Curricula Suitable for Use with a Program of Accelerated Education

Grades K–8
- A.C.E. (worktext, easy)
- A Beka (worktexts, pretty easy except math)
- Calvert School (correspondence, courses, *not* easy)
- Teach Your Children Well (worktexts & readers, step-by-step, language arts only)

High School
- American School (correspondence, easy courses)
- Gateway Prep Academy (online program designed to teach accelerated learning techniques)
- Keystone National High School (correspondence, easy courses)
- University of Nebraska-Lincoln Independent Study High School (some courses online; all also available as correspondence courses; courses are *not* easy)

What Curriculum Did the Swanns Use?

Mrs. Swann chose the Calvert School curriculum for K–8; then, since Calvert has no high-school courses, she switched to American School for the high-school years. Her children then completed college through Brigham Young University, which only requires brief stays on campus, with most work completed at home. Mrs. Swann accompanied her still-quite-young children during their campus stays. Postgraduate work was via the external degree program of University of Southern California—Dominguez Hills.

EDITOR'S NOTE: *Joyce's children do move along more quickly than most—they have been "accelerated" up to a faster speed—but they are not "accelerating." Twice as fast is fast enough! :-D*

Skipping. Your child skips a grade entirely. Typically, skipping a grade or two works best for moderately gifted children. If your child can read, write, and cipher before age 6, skipping straight to second grade makes sense.

Lewis Terman, author of possibly the most famous long-term study on moderately gifted children, opined that students who enter grade 1 with a mental age of ten should be able to reach fourth-grade level by the end of that school year. This would mean a two-year skip, allowing the child to enter college at age 16. The junior-high years also work well for skipping, as they cover little that is not repeated in high school. If your older child is behind in school, once he does the work to catch up to the sixth grade level in basic writing, grammar, and math skills (via compacting), skipping seventh or eighth grade can work well. The prospect of finally being up to the proper grade level is often a great motivator for students of this age.

Radical Skipping. The child jumps three grade levels or more all at once. As Ellen Winner, author of *Gifted Children: Myths and Realities* points out, "No large-scale study of *radical* grade skipping has been conducted . . ." She did mention that the available case studies of profoundly gifted children who were only skipped a grade or two showed them still bored, frustrated, and socially isolated.

If your child has an IQ or 170 or above, and demonstrates the signs of profound giftedness outlined in Chapter 48, I'd say, "Go for it." If your six-year-old can do fifth-grade work, get her fifth-grade curriculum. If you have pulled your 11-year-old out of school, where he was bored out of his mind repeating work he had mastered four years ago, jump him straight to ninth grade. Bear in mind this advice applies only to *profoundly* gifted children, who will thank you for giving them a real challenge for once, and that once your child is working at the higher grade level, you may then choose to slow down once again and add more enrichment material. Five years of high-school level work leaves lots of time for sport, music, art, community service, and Advanced Placement courses; two years of middle school followed by three years of high school generally means a lot of unneeded repetition and much less opportunity for enrichment.

Joyce Swann on Accelerated Education

Webster defines "accelerate" as "to go faster; to make something go faster." From some of the letters I receive, I suspect there is an image among homeschoolers of me standing next to my children whispering, "Faster! Faster!" in their ears as they press forward to meet more and more demanding deadlines.

When John and I decided that I would teach our children at home, acceleration was never a consideration. We wanted what most homeschooling parents want for their children—a superior education delivered in a safe and moral environment. Our home, of course, provided what we considered to be the ideal environment, but it was the search for a superior educational experience that led to the early graduations.

In the true sense of the word, acceleration has never occurred in our homeschool. At no time have we gained speed as we move forward. In fact, I would describe us as faithful plodders who are able to accomplish quite a lot because we are *consistent*.

The key to our success is simple: When God told me to homeschool, I said yes. And then I committed myself to the task. Any homeschooling mother can do the same if she is willing to make a long-term commitment to a disciplined lifestyle that centers around an unwavering homeschool schedule.

The first thing I did after making the decision to homeschool was to decide on a teaching schedule. I planned from the beginning to have a

12-month school year so that I would not have to constantly re-teach lessons that were forgotten over summer vacation. I also decided that I would give the children **short holidays**: Memorial Day, the Fourth of July, Labor Day, one day for Thanksgiving, Christmas Day (I later allowed them to take off Christmas Eve as well), and New Year's Day. In addition they had off every Saturday and Sunday. I then scheduled **a three-hour school day** and worked everything else I had to do to care for my rapidly growing brood (I had ten children in twelve years with no multiple births) around those hours.

I carried that same philosophy of commitment into the classroom. We have undergone some scheduling changes over the years. For instance, when I had lots of preschoolers, I scheduled half of the school day in the morning and the other half in the afternoon during the preschoolers' naps. As my number of preschoolers diminished, however, I changed the schedule to one three-hour session from 8:30 to 11:30 A.M. The rules that had always governed our homeschool stayed in effect:

1. **No talking about anything not pertaining to lessons.** Given the opportunity, nearly all children will attempt to distract the teacher so that they can escape their assignments. Frequently, that effort will take the form of pretending to be interested in something that has little if anything to do with the subject at hand. A simple, "I would love to talk about that, but we will have to do it after school," works wonders. Nine times out of ten the child has no interest in the subject and does not want to discuss it later.

2. **No wasting time.** At times everyone is tempted to sit staring out the window or gazing into space. It is the teacher's responsibility to gently remind them to get their minds back on their work so that they will be free to act out those daydreams after school.

3. **No food or drinks.** Virtually anyone can go for three hours without eating. Students should get that drink of water *before* school.

4. **No breaks** unless a trip to the bathroom is absolutely essential. Students should also make it a habit to use the bathroom before school. It is then seldom necessary to interrupt for a bathroom break. All breaks should be avoided because they do exactly what their name implies—they *break up* the school day, *break apart* concentration, and *break down* order and discipline.

In a stable atmosphere there is really nothing to do *but* learn. I am always present in the classroom to answer questions and help with any difficulty a student may encounter.

Given the right reinforcement and encouragement, children are able to grasp a great many concepts that adults tend to think of as "too difficult" for youngsters—especially if no one tells them that they are difficult! I love discussing my student's assignments with them and helping them discover new insights into lessons in history, literature, philosophy, etc. For me, some of the most meaningful moments with my children have been spent in the quiet, undistracted atmosphere of that home classroom, and I feel that many of them would agree.

Now, the big question. Should *your* child be accelerated? And if so, how? Via "fast-and-steady" continual progress, as per Joyce Swann's insights in the sidebar, or would it ever be OK to skip a grade?

Unit Studies & Acceleration

Trying to accelerate while using a unit study program is not a good idea. Unit studies are almost the opposite of an accelerated approach. It's like the difference between going cross-country by plane or by bicycle. By plane, you get there much more quickly. By bicycle, you have much more time to savor the scenery.

If your child is extremely focused and either math/science-oriented or longing to get into a college program, acceleration might make sense. After all, you have the rest of your life to pursue any educational interests you whizzed over quickly the first time.

But if your child enjoys getting deeply into humanities topics, such as history, art, or literature, in a hands-on way, there's little to be gained by rushing.

In the spirit of considering every fun learning experience to be substandard educationally, college classes do not as a rule include or encourage hands-on studies. (The sole exception: science lab courses, which nobody ever accused of being fun.) So if you enjoy unit studies, forget acceleration. Now is the time to re-enact historical battles, dress up like major historical or literary figures, make your salt dough maps, cook ethnic cuisine from around the world, crawl through that oversized model ear, and do all the other fun projects you'll never have time for again . . . until you homeschool your own children!

Fast & Steady Wins the Race

Perhaps the whole topic of accelerated education can best be illustrated with a simple algebra problem.

Q: Car A leaves Smithtown traveling due south at 100 miles per hour. At the same time car B leaves Happyville traveling due north at 55 miles per hour. Smithtown and Happyville are 450 miles apart. How long will it take the cars to meet?

A: **The cars will never meet.** The car traveling at 100 miles per hour will crash and burn, and the police will have cleared away the dead bodies and debris long before car B approaches the site of the accident!

If you would like to see your children move ahead in their educational experience, forget everything you have ever heard about accelerated education. Do not even consider skipping grades. Banish all thoughts of eight-hour school days. Never concentrate on how you can get your children to "go faster." Instead, set a steady pace that can be maintained over your children's academic lifetimes, and put your homeschool on a course that will allow your children to move forward naturally, while reaping the full benefits of their educational experiences.

—*Joyce Swann*

Sue Richman on To Skip or Not to Skip

Maybe your child was a **late bloomer**, getting off to a nice relaxed start with reading at age nine (that is, a nice, relaxed start in retrospect; you were a nervous wreck until he finally caught on). So you decide to call him a first-grader (or perhaps "non-graded primary") for longer than usual, and gradually he does fine until he's now pushing 15 and only in seventh grade. Now he begins to complain about the lower grade placement—he wants to be up with his agemates, and you begin to realize just how old he will be when he graduates from high school at home. Will he stick it out? Can you now boost him ahead and skip a grade or two? Did you make a big mistake to hold him back?

Or possibly you have **two children close in age** and you teach them together, using the older one's textbooks. The younger one takes part easily in all studies and seems to be doing fine. Shouldn't he get credit for doing fifth-grade work like his sister? Shouldn't you call him a fifth-grader also? Maybe his test scores as a fifth-grader aren't so hot, and his handwriting is pretty atrocious, but, gee, he *is* doing that fifth-grade level work.

Or this: Your child is a **very bright student**, always has been. Learned to read early and effortlessly, catches on to new ideas readily and quickly, is an eager learner in many fields. But you don't want to appear to be saying that your kid is better than anyone else, so you have always just kept your child at her age level grade-wise. On top of that, your child's birthday is in early November, which means that she is actually one of the very oldest at her grade level. She has always aced achievement tests and has always been above grade level in the actual work being accomplished. Now that she's hit junior high you are wondering about skipping a grade. Can you? Should you? What about socialization questions, what about future chances of scholarships, what about other possibilities?

And then there is this variation: Through a combination of compacting, telescoping, and skipping, **you now have a 13-year-old ready to graduate next year**. So far, so good. Then perhaps doubts start arising. Your daughter isn't so eager for this after all. She may not *want* to be faced at the young age of 14 with the types of decisions kids need to make after graduation. She certainly doesn't want to leave home for college that early, and might not really be ready even for college-level correspondence work. She took the PSAT and earned only mediocre scores—are scholarships lost? Maybe this plan just won't work for you. You and your daughter realize there is still lots more to learn about, and after all she never was that hot in mathematics even though she'd always been a super reader. Can you slow down at this point without making your child feel she has been "failed?" And what will colleges think of a "fifth" or "sixth" year of high school?

Over the many years that I've been talking with and counseling homeschool parents, I've encountered all of these situations, and many other variations on the theme. I've also dealt with many of these questions in our own family, and made different decisions based on each child. Maybe I should start here, to give you all some perspective on where I'm coming from.

Some Examples

Slow Start, No Skipping. Jesse is now 23 and in grad school (married too, first baby due this coming winter). As a six-year-old first grader, he scored in the lowest 2 percent on a standardized test of reading ability. I actually thought to myself that if I were putting him in a regular school, I might have held him back a year, in part because he had a late birthday . . .

and that reading score. However, I realized that at home, grade-level distinctions didn't really make much difference, and I strongly felt he'd do fine as he went along. He did do fine, and I was very glad that I hadn't kept him back. But as strong a student as he was all through his homeschooling (once he got the hang of how to read!), I was never tempted to skip a grade with him.

By the end of high school he was clearly ready for college-level work, but instead of early admission we did a college correspondence course through Penn State University and also helped him prepare for taking four different Advanced Placement exams. He went into the University of Pittsburgh Honors College with 18 college credits. This cushion of extra credits enabled him to really broaden his studies in college—he was not eager to finish college early, just eager to try out as many fields as possible while he was there for four years. He ended up with a double major in history and political science, along with an honors degree for completing a major senior research project, and had time to travel around the world on the Semester at Sea program also.

Jacob, now 20 and heading into his junior year at Carnegie Mellon University studying computer science, also had a July birthday, and also got off to a bit of a slow start in reading. Again, I decided against holding him back, and again that panned out as a good decision. Jacob early on showed a marked ability in mathematics and computer programming, and by mid-fourth grade was working with his older brother Jesse on high-school algebra. He completed high-school-level geometry in seventh grade, then went right on to calculus in eighth and ninth grade. He was a very bright kid, but not necessarily in all areas. Again, I was never tempted to skip grades with Jacob, and again I'm pleased with this decision. Jacob had the time to really develop his strong interests, take part in many special accelerated academic programs in the summer and throughout the year, and build up his somewhat weaker areas. There really is a lot to be said for just plain growing a bit older. I felt he was ready to go on to college when he turned 18, and indeed he's done super. He also used the AP program to validate the college-level work he did in high school, and ended up taking a college-credit distance learning course in multi-variate calculus through Stanford University's EPGY program (Educational Program for Gifted Youth). And he also got to be my tech man in my online AP US History course, as well as a course participant—in short, there was plenty for him to do at home those last couple of years. I'm glad he had that time.

Early Start, Skipped a Grade. Molly, not quite 17, is another story. While riding in our car right before her fifth birthday (and she has an early August birthday, making her very young even for her proper grade level) she began reading aloud fluently from the loved book *Charlotte's Web*. She had started beginning reading very early and caught on very quickly. She also seemed socially very mature and competent. She also did reasonably well in math understandings. It just didn't seem quite correct to call her a kindergartner at that point. Early on we let our local school district know that because she was advanced overall, she was boosted ahead a grade. She did third grade testing (required in PA) as a very young seven-year-old, and did very well (math computation was average, but concepts were at the top of the chart, and she had a perfect score in reading). I've never regretted my decision of skipping a grade with her. This is a kid who read *Jane Eyre* for the first time when in sixth grade (and remember, that meant young fifth-grade age for her), who picked up Shakespeare plays to read independently for fun, and who took on major challenges like entering the "Written and Illustrated by . . ." competition two times. She's also a pretty good pianist, is an incredible artist, has now taken eight AP exams, is a National Merit

Radical Skipping at Home

Seth Baker, son of Janice Baker, one of the authors of *Gifted Children at Home*, had the chance to experience acceleration through **radical skipping**. His school history is as follows: homeschooled in preschool and kindergarten, first school in a Christian school, second grade at a new school (the family moved), starting to get bored in third and fourth grade, homeschooled from fifth grade on. In his own words:

We had a great time [homeschooling] through the sixth grade. Then I started to get bored again. I convinced Mom that I already knew virtually all the material in the seventh grade textbooks, and she got me eighth grade books. I really think that this was the turning point in my schooling career. At the same time that we realized I was getting pretty good at this "student" thing, we realized that we didn't actually have to follow any kind of traditional grade system. So I skipped seventh grade altogether. I was ecstatic.

In much the same fashion, as we continued the high school experience, I skipped the ninth and eleventh grades. Like I said before, I don't think this was because I was "smart" or gifted," I just caught on to this stuff and didn't have to go over it time and time again. I have a sneaking suspicion that a whole lot of kids in the world could breeze through school a lot faster (and with far fewer headaches) if they were just given the chance.

As a 12-year-old, Seth took his first class at the University of Delaware, and got an A. The next semester, he took pre-calculus, and discovered he was the highest scoring student in the class. He graduated high school at age 14 and was accepted at Delaware State University with a full scholarship, graduating *summa cum laude* with a B.S. in Business Administration at the age of 18. Like Alexandra Swann, he has no regrets about his early graduation.

Pick a Grade Level and Stick with It

Jacob and Jesse every now and then used to point out that they thought that it was a mistake to have boosted Molly ahead though—thinking mainly of the various academic competitions our family enjoys taking part in. Being a grade ahead meant she lost out on being in Math Olympiad for one more year, or the Geography Bee for one more year, or MathCounts for one more year, and more, as most of these competitions have grade-level guidelines.

I firmly believe that homeschoolers can't play it both ways—that is, can't be one grade for some purposes but another grade for other purposes, especially when it comes to academic competitions. If there is a grade-level designation, you need to be consistent with what you've decided your child is—you can't waffle around and try to have your proverbial cake while eating it too.

Molly and I actually discussed this whole issue together quite a few times, and realized that because she's been a grade level ahead, that's how we've viewed her—our expectations were raised because of it. If she'd been at the lower grade level, most likely we would never have encouraged work at the level she was actually very able to meet.

It's hard to even explain why I feel so comfortable with skipping Molly ahead a year, when I never considered it with either of the boys, or with Hannah, our youngest. But I've also never considered skipping any more grades with Molly—she was after all just barely a teenager when officially entering high school at home, and she had plenty of growing up to do before being thrown in with much older students at college. One year of skipping was plenty.

—*Susan Richman*

Finalist, went to France twice during her high-school years, and more and more. She's heading off to the University of Pittsburgh Honors College this fall with a full-ride academic scholarship—tuition plus room and board all paid for four years. Seems like the right decision for her to have skipped a grade—it's all worked out even better than we might have hoped.

Young for the Grade, No Skipping. Hannah is now 12, and properly just finished with seventh grade, although again with her very late summer birthday she is young for the grade. It seems perfect for her—she's excelling at this level, has plenty of fun challenges through her work with Mathcounts and the National French Exam and the Mythology Exam, but is not thrown in over her head. She's able to be a really nice bright seventh-grader. Skipping grades never entered my head with her.

Some More Options

So how can a family make these types of decisions regarding grade level? What questions do you need to ask yourself? What factors should be considered?

I think families need to look at this issue very carefully.

In many ways skipping a grade means very little in homeschooling, as we can always do whatever level of work we feel is appropriate for a given child, no matter what the grade level. A fourth-grader does not have to be stuck plodding through a fourth-grade reader when he's ready for meatier stuff.

At the far end of the scale, if a student does feel very ready for going on with college attendance early, but didn't skip a grade earlier on, he can still go to college ahead of time. He just goes right after 11th grade, using the college's early admission policy. If he can demonstrate a very strong record, strong SAT or ACT scores, and the maturity to handle college life, most colleges are more than happy to have a student who would otherwise be a senior in high school. Several students in the Pennsylvania Homeschoolers diploma program have done this with no problem. They then receive their diploma from PHAA after completing their freshman year in college, which is the standard procedure with most public or private high schools also.

Skip to Catch Up

In the scenario mentioned above, of the child who needed a longer starting-out time to gain basic academic abilities, though, I feel it's very reasonable and probably very desirable to skip the child ahead a grade at some point, even if the child would only be considered barely average according to test scores at the upper grade level. There is a wide variation found within any grade level, and sometimes it can be very motivating to a child to realize that now is the time to step on the gas and zoom ahead a bit to catch up with his agemates. Some kids can get very discouraged by realizing they have been held back and now are significantly behind grade-wise—they feel no reason to even try to do their best, because after all, they must be pretty stupid since they were once kept back a year or two. You might set very concrete goals with a student in this situation: If you can complete this level math work, read this many books, and write this many compositions next year, and take the eighth grade level test and do at least OK on it, we'll consider next year as covering both seventh and eighth grades, putting you where you should be age-wise. This generally gets a very positive response from the student, encouraging hard work and effort and real concrete gains. The parents then have a real goal to help their kids meet. Everybody wins.

Skip If the Student Is Superior at the Next Grade Level

It gets trickier for the me when I talk with families who want to skip ahead nice, normal bright kids. I often ask what the rush is; is there some specific plan ahead, some goal that requires double promotion? Test scores I think can be very useful here—if a kid takes an achievement test at the upper grade level and still scores in the superior range (that is, 90th percentile or above), I feel skipping a grade might be a good idea. If a student scores very well at the current grade level, but is only mildly above average when taking a test at the next grade level, I'd stop thinking about skipping grades, even if a child is officially using books from the upper grade level. There is frankly not that much difference between books at, say, the fourth- and the fifth-grade level—using the upper-level books does not really mean your child should be skipped. An elementary school principal once said to me, "What's the point in boosting a kid ahead to be average? Why not let him stay a nice bright kid at his grade level?" Even though some of us might be reluctant to admit that any school principal knows anything, I think the man made a good point here.

Skip If the Student Craves It

Then there are some parents who are faced with a child who really feels it's important to get things moving along faster. Often this is a junior-high student, and he may have realized that at least in some diploma programs he might not be allowed to skip a grade during the high-school years. If it's going to be done, the time is now. These kids have plans, they have goals, they are ready for upper level work and they know it. Test scores are superior, the child is strong overall in many subject areas, and everyone is just beginning to feel that the current grade level description just isn't even, well, honest. Often, though not necessarily, these are kids with birthdays that put them at the older end of their current grade level. They are the kids who I always thought were a grade ahead of what was listed on paper. The homeschooling families I know who have had a child skip a grade for reasons like this are generally very pleased. The kids usually rise to the occasion and really achieve strongly.

If You Have to, Slow Down in High School

What if you did accelerate, and now partway through high school at home you want to cool things down and call your child a lower grade level? What will colleges think? It is in general easiest to just rewrite a transcript to reflect the new, and lower, grade levels and not tack on a fifth or sixth year of high school—unless you are ready for doing some real justifying. Not that it can't be explained well—in fact I know a couple of terrific homeschooling families in PA that opted for naming this extra year a fifth year of high school, and all went just fine with college admissions.

It's Your Decision

So, to skip or not to skip? To accelerate or not to accelerate? It depends on the child's birth date, the child's ambition, the parent's energy level and commitment, whether the child needs to catch up, and the child's ability to do superior work at a higher grade level. This decision should always be a family one, and I hope people don't feel that they should accelerate just because some others find it works for them. The Swann family's example shows it *can* be done; your family's needs will determine whether, in your case, it *should* be done.

How to Graduate Early

1. **Prepare your students to take the Advanced Placement tests**. AP students are allowed to count their courses towards high-school credit, and depending on their AP test results, they can earn college credit as well. You can do the same with CLEP tests. See the chapters on AP and CLEP in my upcoming grades 7–12 volume.
2. **Design your high-school plans to reflect an accelerated curriculum.** For example, you could create a curriculum of your own that includes in one semester a French course (for 3 credits), American literature (your own choice of books and assignments, for 3 credits), algebra (3 credits), a social studies unit-study course incorporating history, geography, art, and philosophy (6 credits), physical science (3 credits), music theory (3 credits), physical education (1 credit), and home economics (as an elective, for 3 credits). This would give you a total of 25 credits for that semester, as opposed to the usual 15 credits, enabling your student to meet graduation requirements much more quickly.
3. **Do as the Swanns do and take a correspondence course,** which you complete according to an accelerated schedule.
4. **Pre-enroll in college.** One of our local Christian colleges has started recruiting 16-year-old homeschoolers to take some college science courses. Community colleges will often do this too. You take the course while in high school, and it is counted toward college credit upon receipt of proof of high-school graduation. Just make sure that the college of your choice will accept transfer credits from the institutions in question. *Mary Pride*

Ideas for What to Do After High School When They're Too Young for College

Of course, you're only "too young" for college if *you* say so. With that in mind, here are some answers to the question, "What will I do with myself if I graduate high school at age 12, 13, or 14?"

- **Get a job.** Our outmoded child labor laws still allow some minimal kinds of employment outside the home. You can work for your parents' business, or start your own business, or volunteer to help a nonprofit group. A year or more of full-time work, no matter how you can swing it, is a super preparation for college, and may even help you find the right major.

- **Travel.** If you're smart enough to graduate high school, you're smart enough to travel with a tour group. Most of us will never have the necessary free time to spend a month in Europe, or visit all the historic spots in the Old West, or spend a year living with a French family, or helping out with a cattle drive, or bike across the USA with a few good friends. If you look around, the world is full of great enrichment opportunities.

- **Have some adventures.** Go on an Outward Bound survival adventure, learn to sail via Hocking College's inexpensive (and college-credit-bearing) summer course (www.hocking. edu), go on safari.

- **Indulge your sports and arts ambitions.** Join a band, take all the martial arts courses you want to, get a part in the local community theater's production, spend days in the museum sketching famous paintings.

- **Get your lifesaving and CPR certification.** Useful to have, and easy to manage while you're not trying to juggle school courses.

- **Get a mission.** Short-term missions assignments are available for teens through several missions organizations. You may be on the young side, but as a high-school grad you should be able to talk your way into the group. Again, months spent serving others in the inner city or overseas, under the protective umbrella of the group, can give you a sense of purpose and competence while enabling you to perform useful service to others.

- **Study on your own.** My daughter Sarah took a year off after high school. During this time she completed three correspondence courses, completed the Body for Life challenge twice and got in really great shape, earned her black belt in Tae Kwon Do (her college doesn't offer martial arts), and advanced to Tech Sergeant in Civil Air Patrol. If you have a "Five Foot Wall" of great books your student never had time to read in high school . . . if there's a hobby that takes serious time to pursue (more than will be available while attending college) . . .

if you'd just like to take extra time for those "worldview" discussions that got crowded out by math and English . . . a year off can provide that time.

Ignore the myth that if you don't go straight from high school into college you'll lose your desire and ability to study and *never* complete college. That is the main reason people use to discourage teens from taking a year off after high school to pursue adventures they may never have again. If 40-year-old adults can go back to college to get a degree, a year off won't kill you.

Also ignore the myth that if you're "too young" for college, you're too young for any solo adventures or responsibility. The peer pressure and misbehavior on college campuses is generally not found to the same extent in the adult and professional world, unless you live in Hollywood!

Finally, be aware that most colleges will hold scholarships open a year for students who have a well-thought-out plan of work, travel, service, or enrichment for that year.

Many of the options I have listed above allow for adult supervision, while others can be done while living at home. Those that involve "going solo" can usually be done with friends (so now you need to talk some friends into graduating early, too!). When you're done, you'll be *more* mature and experienced than the typical college freshman . . . and more interesting to colleges as well.

—*Mary Pride*

PART 11

Homeschooling with a School or Group

These homeschooled children were all winners at the regional Awana Bible Quizzer competition in Albuquerque, NM. They're from the Awana club that meets at First Baptist Church in Santa Fe, NM. Left to right, bottom to top, we have Stephen Rodriguez, 2nd Place, Brave Rank; Olga Garcia, 2nd Place, Maiden Rank; Emily Oh, 1st Place, Maiden Rank; Whitney Jaramillo, 2nd Place, Maiden Rank; Ryan Olivas, 2nd Place, Brave Rank; Addela Bransford, 1st Place, Maiden Rank; Andrew Rice, 2nd Place, Explorer Rank; Arielei Bransford, 1st Place, Princess Rank; Erin Herrmann, 3rd Place, Anchor Rank; and Rebecca Birch, 3rd Place, Anchor Rank.

The Flagstaff Home Educators team, from Flagstaff, AZ, competed against 42 other teams from around the state and took first place in the statewide LifeSmarts competition. They won a savings bond each and went on to New York to compete in the national competition, where they were beaten by only one question and took third place nationwide. Every member of the team received a $150 savings bond and a duffel bag full of hats, shirts, gift certificates, and other souvenirs from contributing companies. LifeSmarts is sponsored by the National Coalition for Consumer Education and is run similar to a game show, with questions about consumer knowledge ranging from taxes and insurance to bike safety and health.

Back row, left to right: Sarah Zanone and coach Mark Mayrand. First row: Roslyn Bearchell, Meredith Mayrand, Kat Toenjes, and team captain Jeremy Young.

CHAPTER 51

Co-ops & Clubs

Are you a "team" player—the kind of person who enjoys group activities? Do you shudder at the thought of facing homeschool completely on your own? Are you sure you'll never be able to teach all the school subjects, especially the ones that threw you for a loop while you were in school?

Relax. Homeschooling doesn't have to be a solo endeavor. In this section, you'll see why homeschoolers laugh heartily when outsiders bring up the tired old socialization issue. You'll learn about the wide variety of homeschool co-ops, support groups, and clubs . . . including how to start your own. You'll learn about community clubs and groups your children can join. You'll see how some homeschool families take advantage of private and public school activities, and how the emerging "University Model School" model combines the best of private schooling with homeschooling. Finally, you'll see why charter schools are the *least* wise option for homeschool families, and how they differ from online academies and other distance-learning options.

Homeschool Co-ops

We begin our odyssey with the simplest group educational option: the co-op.

What is a homeschool co-op? Linda Koeser and Lori Marse, authors of *The Complete Guide to Successful Co-oping*, answer the question this way:

> **A homeschooling co-op is a group of families who have come together to provide their children with educational experiences that they would not ordinarily have the opportunity to participate in as individual families.**

Now, this definition could also apply to a support group that clubs together for planned outings, so they refine their definition a bit further:

Some Advantages of a Homeschool Co-op

1. Would you consider giving your children the opportunity to learn from someone in addition to yourself, someone who has planned and prepared exciting material and hands-on activities, someone whose gifts are in an area where perhaps you may rate a minus ten?
2. Would you like your child to take field trips and do projects that complement the learning experience?
3. Would your child benefit from learning to work in a small group of children being taught by someone you love and trust?
4. Would you like to have your children socializing with a group of children that you have personally hand picked?
5. Would you like support in your homeschooling effort; someone to laugh and pray with or a shoulder to cry on when needed?

—*Linda Koeser and Lori Marse, Complete Guide to Successful Co-oping*

Co-oping for Cowards Video & Instruction Guide

Parents. $29.95. Guide alone, $19.95. Video alone, $15.95. *DP&K Productions, TN, (423) 570-7172, www.co-oping4cowards.com.*

The **Co-Oping for Cowards Video & Instruction Guide** are your passport to the "Tag Team" style of co-oping.

Pat Wesolowski, author of the popular "Information Please!" research curriculum, has teamed up with fellow co-oper Karin Carpenter to create a model whose main emphases are on researching, writing, and speaking skills. They believe these are ideally motivated and practiced in a co-op.

Don't expect anything slick from the video—you'll see the authors as talking heads in front of a wall and "family cam" quality coverage.

The video begins with Karin Carpenter energetically presenting her view of the benefits of unit studies as an extended travel metaphor. From this point, you see the co-op in action, with voice-over narrative explaining what you're seeing.

In the accompanying guide you'll find cookbook instructions for this style of co-op, right down to a suggested schedule broken into 10- and 30-minute segments. The lengthy FAQ answers any questions you are likely to have about how to set up and run this type of co-op.

The combo set is the best deal. It includes a nice video binder.

> A co-op is a place where each parent uses his or her unique talents for the benefit of all.

In other words, the parents co-operate (hence the term "co-op") by sharing the teaching chores.

Legal Considerations

Since our outdated educational laws don't yet recognize that home-schooling is "parent-directed education" not merely "parent-taught education," a full co-op in which all the teaching is done "team" style by co-operating parents, without taking on the legal form of a private school, is not legal anywhere. To avoid any problem with this, savvy co-opers designate their co-op days as "supplementary" education, in the same category as field trips and other outside-the-home educational opportunities.

Many Ways to Co-op

There are two main models of homeschool co-ops now in print:

- A co-op where one parent handles a dropped-off group of kids, perhaps with assistance from another helping parent or older student
- A co-op where all the homeschooling parents hang around and take turns giving lessons to the entire group of kids

However, what looks like a choice between two menu options is not as simple as it seems. The models differ in their type of cooperative teaching . . . in the amount and style of cooperative learning . . . in the target audience for presentations . . . and that's just for starters!

In keeping with my lifelong mission of trying to make something that took me weeks to understand sound simple (it *has* to be simple before I can understand it well enough to explain it to anyone else!), let's first introduce the two current models and then break down your co-op options.

The Tag Team Co-op

The newest homeschool co-op model is that promoted by Pat Wesolowski and Karin Carpenter, authors of *Co-oping for Cowards,* a brand-new video and instructional guide with step-by-step instructions for setting up this kind of co-op.

I call this the "Tag Team" model because all the homeschool parents take turns one after another teaching a lesson or leading an activity. Those who do not wish to be "onstage" can provide refreshments or put together the newsletter.

Ideally, the teaching chores are divided up according to the participating parents' skills and interests. One mom will handle geography, while another supervises the crafts project, and another is in charge of the science segment, for instance.

Classes are run by the clock, for obvious reasons. Each mom (or perhaps dad) wants the full allotted time for her (or his) moment in the sun.

Another characteristic of the Wesolowski/Carpenter model is that every student gives a presentation every week. This is meant to provide motivation for research and study and to sharpen speaking and writing skills.

The One-Room Schoolhouse Co-op

More familiar to veteran homeschoolers is the type of co-op described in *The Complete Guide to Successful Co-oping.* This is what I call a "One-Room Schoolhouse Co-Op."

KONOS co-ops have been run like this for decades. Basically, one mom is responsible for all the dropped-off children. The typical co-op of this type runs one day per week, and each mom is the main teacher for one month per year.

As Linda Koeser and Lori Marse explain,

> *Our co-op schedule involves each parent selecting one month of the school year to teach one day a week [the co-op day]. This allows each participating parent one day a week off for four months.*

Where the group of children is small (maybe just three to six young kids) or older (well-behaved middlers and teens), just one parent can manage the entire group by herself. For larger groups of youngsters, or just for moral support, you may want to adopt Linda and Lori's suggestion of having a second parent come by part of the day to help out. Of course, the teaching mom's own older children make marvelous teaching assistants!

How Do the Parents Cooperate?

A "co-op" can involve many different types of co-operation. The first to come to mind is how the parents cooperate.

You can cooperate in the areas of *scheduling, preparation,* and *financing.*

Scheduling. All homeschool co-ops that I've ever heard of have the parents sharing teaching chores to some extent. But how can you do this?

Where friends know each other well and trust each other, the One-Room Schoolhouse is the simplest type of co-op. You just drop off your children of teaching age at the home of the teaching parent. Then, in another month or two, the kids are all dropped off at *your* house.

Since one mom is in charge, there's no need to break up the learning time into arbitrary timed segments, making it possible to get really "into" projects that can last all day or all month. That's one big reason this type of co-op has been popular for years with unit-study fans. If you've swapped babysitting with a few close pals, you are a likely candidate for this kind of co-op.

In the Tag Team model, scheduling is to the minute, not to the month. Parents split up the teaching chores into time segments, all done on the same day.

Resource Preparation. In both models, families can share the work of locating and shopping for resources. I'm talking about cloth and notions for costumes, ingredients for theme meals, art supplies, science supplies, etc. This is more obvious in the Tag Team model, but in practice, One-Room Schoolhouse co-ops can divvy up the resource prep chores among the moms who will *not* be teaching that month, so the "teaching mom of the month" won't have that to worry about as well as lesson preparation.

Financially. One benefit of either type of co-op is the ability to use resources that are just too expensive for one family alone. You can rent supplies, share field-trip expenses, or even invite an outside speaker. As Jessica Hulcy told me when I called her to discuss this chapter, "Last year I had fencing classes for 20 kids while we were studying KONOS History of the World II, the medieval period. I could never have afforded to hire a fencing tutor for just my kids. Plus, he came to my house!"

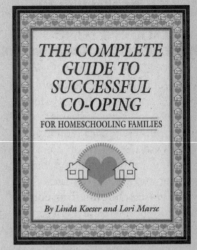

The Complete Guide to Successful Co-oping for Homeschool Families

Parents. $14.95 plus $2.50 shipping. *Lori Marse, 4117 Floral Dr., Boynton Beach, FL 33436. May also be available from some online catalogs.*

If you'd like to know why to co-op . . . how to pick compatible families for your co-op . . . how to plan and schedule a one-room schoolhouse-style co-op . . . where to find resources and field trips for your co-op . . . how to deal with record keeping . . . pitfalls to avoid and possibilities to embrace . . . here is a simple one-step plan.

Buy and read **The Complete Guide to Successful Co-oping for Homeschool Families.**

Veteran homeschoolers and co-opers Linda Koeser and Lori Marse answer all your questions in this oversized 79-page book, including those you haven't thought of yet!

Published in 1995, the slim Resource Appendix is somewhat out-of-date, but who cares, because up-to-date addresses and other info for the companies they recommend are in the book you're reading now.

CO-OPING SAVES TIME

Adding co-oping to "your already busy schedule" does more to relieve your workload than add to it.

Complete Guide to Successful Co-oping

If you'd like to be part of a one-room schoolhouse style co-op, but feel you need to *see* how it's done first, and to have it explained to you, you're in luck. Jessica Hulcy, the world's greatest expert on homeschool co-oping, has just come up with a website for you. On her site, **www.homeschoolmentor.com,** depending on what level of service you sign up and pay for, you will be able to:

- View actual co-op classes
- Receive teaching instruction from Jessica about the class you viewed
- Receive instruction in how to run a co-op (be the organizer, not just a teacher)

I also heartily recommend Jessica's *Creating the Balance* video series, available from KONOS, Inc. As we go to press, I am trying to persuade her to make the co-oping information from that series available as a separate, less-expensive, video. Check her other website, **www.konos.com**, for details.

Both the Tag Team co-op and the One-Room Schoolhouse co-op are "general academic co-ops," meant to cover a wide range of academic subjects.

But a Single Interest co-op is also possible.

See the end of this chapter for an outstanding example of a Single Interest co-op, solely devoted to music, which combines elements of both academic co-op models!

How Much Do the Kids Do?

"Never get a mom to do a kid's job" is my educational motto. If a kid *can* do what you're doing, you need to move over and let him or her practice.

So, how do the two co-op types we're examining stack up?

For both co-op types, pairing a younger child with an older child would work well, although with all those moms hanging around, it's not as likely to happen in the Tag Team model. The older child can help the younger stay on task and overcome obstacles. However, don't expect to pair a tenth-grader with a preschooler!

The Tag Team model ladies are missing a bet by not suggested that *kids* make the refreshments, give the geography lesson (and as many other lessons as are practicable), and put together the newsletter, to name three obvious possibilities that jumped out at me. If moms are doing these jobs just to have something they can contribute, maybe the idea that "all moms teach on the same day or help with something" needs rethinking.

Since the One-Room Schoolhouse moms are on their own, there's a built-in incentive to use all the help they can get. Unit study programs such as KONOS, which have been widely adopted by co-ops, encourage kids to do the cooking, sewing, and even some of the teaching, especially reading to younger children. However, this is not always explicitly stated, so you should keep the question, "Am *I* really the only one who can do this?" in the back of your mind when planning your co-op day.

Babies obviously can't do much at a co-op except play. Toddlers can have some simple activities (sandbox, water play). Non-readers from ages 4 to 6 can do some simple language activities and hands-on projects. Readers of all ages, up to and including preteens, can be taught as a group, while junior high and high schoolers can often work together on part of their activities. The older the children, the more useful it is for them to spend extra time outside co-op preparing for their next project, report, or presentation.

How Cooperative Is the Learning?

Unit studies, as you recall, integrate a number of subjects into one overlying theme. So instead of studying the Revolutionary War in a textbook, for example, the children will make colonial costumes, re-enact major battles with toy soldiers, create maps showing the troop movements and battles, make a colonial meal, study the science behind how a flintlock gun works, or similar hands-on projects.

Co-oping is probably the only way most of us will ever do such big, involved projects. Many kids working together can put together a stage set, prepare a very fancy theme meal, re-enact historical events, and much more.

Plus, there's a strong "performing" streak in many of these projects; they gain luster when shared with a group.

So, how much cooperation do your co-op's projects allow or require?

On the *Co-oping for Cowards* video, and in the first unit of their proposed curriculum, the projects were what I call "Sunday school style crafts," with each kid doing the same activity: potato prints, candle dipping, making your own little pontoon bridge, and the like. As with the kids' weekly presentations, competition seems to be encouraged.

Although in theory kids in the One-Room Schoolhouse co-op *could* each sit at a table with their own little kit of supplies doing the same activity, in *practice* co-ops of this type tend to favor activities where the group is working together on a large project. This is actually more entertaining and involving for most kids, and eliminates the stress of having your craft compared to everyone else's. Also, as my husband, Bill, pointed out, larger projects are less likely to be "throw-aways," unlike cheapo kid-portion crafts. Cooperative crafts can cost the same per kid as individual crafts, but the end result is usually more impressive and useful. When you've all made and decorated a wigwam you can actually fit in, you are not likely to pitch it in the trash (or leave it on a shelf collecting dust bunnies).

When you have all the moms present, as in the Tag Team model, there is no reason you couldn't spend more time on larger projects for which a lot of experienced hands would be helpful and less on other things. I'll watch with interest to see if future "Co-oping for Cowards" units include any such projects as an option.

Who Is the Intended Audience for Presentations?

One big benefit of co-ops is that you have a built-in audience for everything you do. The Tag Team style co-op has the bigger audience—all the moms and all their kids. The One-Room Schoolhouse's built-in audience is smaller, but still larger than just one family.

KONOS has always recommended inviting friends and family to the really *big* co-op events. KONOS units always end with a major theme meal, dramatization, or presentation. All the work that goes into these seems more worthwhile when shared with more friendly people.

In theory, you could plan your co-op around a climactic presentation (such as a play) of such quality you could invite the community. From a backyard festival to an actual play in an actual (rented) school auditorium, the sky's the limit! Of course, this is even easier when you've expanded beyond co-op size, to . . .

The Support Group

The next step up the scale when it comes to group size is the homeschool support group. Group activities typically involve meetings for the parents, at which tips and encouragement can be shared and activities planned, and a variety of group outings. Sometimes the group sponsors an ongoing activity, such as a homeschool band or basketball team.

Tutoring and **special classes** are also often available through your local support group. You may find people offering music lessons, dance lessons, math tutoring, and more in your state or local newsletter.

Check with your state group, or online in the "Groups" area of www.home-school.com, to locate support groups in your area.

The Family Club

Homeschoolers are often friendly sorts whose enthusiasm for a topic leads them to start their own clubs.

In its simplest form, this can be a **family club** started by one or more of the kids in your family. See the "Money Club" sidebar for an example of a family club my littlest daughters invented.

The impulse to have your own kid-run club seems to be universal, as witness the traditional "No Girls Allowed" treehouse or "No Boys Allowed" doll tea party. Inside the typical homeschool family, the girls are allowed in the treehouse (they might even have helped build it!) and the boys stop by to scarf the dolls' cookies. The main point is that the kids are in control.

An adult can mention casually, "I really loved my old treehouse when I was a kid," and when pressed, give some guidance and supervision throughout the building process, but it needs to be done with a light touch. Resist the temptation to take over and do it *right*. This is *their* club.

CO-OP RENEWS VETERAN HOMESCHOOLER'S ENERGY

After years of homeschooling, I was tired. . . .

Co-op was the answer. It divides the responsibility and work load for the teachers, while it multiplies the learning and fun for the kids. . . .

It's true that the month I teach involves many hours of studying and work. It takes research, shopping, prayer, and planning. But I only have to be dazzling for a month, then it's someone else's turn!

—*Co-op member "Karen," The Complete Guide to Successful Co-oping*

MORE ADVANTAGES OF A HOMESCHOOL CO-OP

Our kids have loved co-oping and have developed strong friendships. . . . The kids definitely did more projects than they would have done in our individual homeschooling programs. . . . The children received many benefits by being exposed to different teaching styles. . . . They seemed to work harder for other teachers, particularly if the project had to be demonstrated to the group as a whole. . . . There was greater learning as one [homeschool teacher] specialized in a certain area. . . .

The co-op provided many opportunities for our children to sharpen their public speaking skills. . . .

Complete Guide to Successful Co-oping

A Family Club Example: The Money Club

You know about unit studies. You know about contests. You know about field trips. These are all great ways to spice up your homeschool.

Now here's a new technique you can use to add interest to any subject area: **Start a family club!**

I know this is a great idea because my children invented it on their own. Over the years, they have put together the Spy Club (studying codes, hiding secret messages, and sneaking invisibly to meetings), the Adventurers Club (pretending they were sailing to distant ports in a variety of crafts, from overturned kitchen chairs to our jungle gym), and the one we are going to look at right now, the Money Club. All these were done without any adult input whatsoever.

Here's how a Money Club meeting works.

First, the members come to order. In this case, the club only has two officers: Lillian (the president) and Madeleine (the vice president).

Next, each club member gives a speech, using an invisible hand-held microphone. The latest round of speeches I heard were Madeleine's speech on "How and Why I Started the Money Club" and Lillie's speech welcoming everyone to the Money Club.

Now, the games! These were all inspired by some review samples from Learning Resources that I gave the girls to try out. The biggest hit was the electronic cash register, which comes with a good supply of play cash and coins.

Each Money Club meeting starts with the Pledge of Allegiance

- **Money Traps.** This is similar to Calvinball (for those of you who are fans of Calvin and Hobbes!) in that all the traps are imaginary and revealed just before each kid has to run the gauntlet. For example, "Here is some dynamite. You have two seconds to get past it without stepping on it." If a player makes it to the end of the course, she wins a toy money prize. In other words, this particular game has almost nothing to do with money or education. It's just for fun.
- **Hide the Quarters.** One child hides the quarters in plain sight, and the other one has to find them. If the searcher is very young or has trouble finding a quarter, the one who hid it gives "hot" and "cold" hints.
- **Toss the Dimes.** A necklace is placed on the floor in the shape of a circle. The players take turns trying to toss a dime into the circle.
- **Nickel Tic-Tac-Toe.** Heads are "o"s and tails are "x"s.
- **Penny Story.** A member tells a story using pen-

nies as the various characters. For example, if a fox is chasing a rabbit, the "fox" penny is moved along the table after the fleeing "rabbit" penny.

- **Making Change.** Although it's harder to "play store" today than when we were kids, thanks to the lack of visible product pricing on your typical supermarket can of beans, books still usually have their prices marked. So now they "play bookstore" with the electronic cash register.

Finally, a Money Club meeting ends with a stirring rendition of some song. A favorite is "The Star Spangled Banner."

I had no idea all this creativity was taking place, until I asked Madeleine if she enjoyed the play money and other goodies. She then told me about their Money Club, and I asked to see a meeting. I was very impressed by the way they were trying to run it like a real meeting, especially the speeches.

It seems to me that this "club" concept can be used both to jazz up school subjects and to teach kids a number of important social skills:

- **How to run a meeting.** This can start off very simply and gradually incorporate more rules until the members have learned all of *Robert's Rules of Order* (the standard work on parliamentary procedure, available in your local bookstore or library). Kids love learning these rules, which may seem odd to those of us who think kids prefer to be spontaneous at all times, but is not odd at all to those of us who have enjoyed reading about Calvin and Hobbes' G.R.O.S.S. (**G**et **R**id **o**f **S**limy girl**S**) Club, whose main point (besides providing little-boy annoyance to neighbor Suzy) seems to be thwarting each other with parliamentary maneuvers.
- **How to give a speech** or make a presentation. I can imagine no less threatening environment for the budding public speaker than giving a speech to a brother or sister, with Mom or Dad occasionally invited to listen in. This provides natural "teachable moments" for demonstrating proper platform technique and general poise. Introducing the next speaker, for example, is a natural chance to teach graciousness.
- **How to wait your turn.**
- **How to applaud others.**

As for the academic opportunities, the list seems endless. What about the Science Club (invent your own experiments!), the Nature Club (everybody brings some natural treasure to the meeting), the Math Club (give each other mental math problems), the Spelling Club (have a spelling bee), the Grammar Club (one person sings out sentence parts, the others use them to make up silly sentences), the Drama Club (write and put on a play). . . . The club format lends itself to any school subject, while the formal ritual (a "meeting") adds emphasis and importance to what otherwise might seem yet another mundane homeschool activity, without adding a lot of effort or time.

Of course, your child can always join a "real" club, such as 4-H, Awanas, or Royal Rangers. These provide opportunities to make friends outside the family, focus intensely on one particular skill area for a long period of time . . . and take quite a bit of effort. For that very reason, you don't want to flop about from real club to real club just to give a jolt to a particular subject area. It's a real commitment to join even one or two real clubs; joining too many is the quick

Giving a Money Club speech. Notice the invisible microphone!

road to burnout.

For a family club, on the other hand, only two members are needed: two kids, or a parent and a child. You don't have to get in the car or fit your meetings into anyone else's schedule. All you need is a little extra bit of enthusiasm and imagination—and the kids can even supply most of the imagination!

While you wouldn't want to come up with a family club for every school subject, a family club might be just the thing from time to time to add some extra zip to subjects that are beginning to lose their interest, or to introduce a new subject. A family club can meet sporadically and last only as long as the kids are enthusiastic about it. The best family clubs are those the kids run themselves, with proud parents invited to observe and be impressed from time to time, since there is no practical difference between a club rigidly organized and run by a parent and any other unit study, at least to the students. Getting to act like a grown-up, being an officer and a speechmaker, and being in control are what makes a family club fun for the kids.

The Special Interest Club

One step up from the family club is the **special interest club**. The Richman's writing club described on the next page falls into this category, as does her daughter Molly's Shakespeare Sleepover Society, whose description you'll also see when you turn the page.

Here, a homeschool kid, parent, or a few parents come up with a format to encourage interest and work in a school subject. It could be writing or Shakespeare, but it could also be geography, science, or rock climbing! Other families' kids are then invited to participate.

The interest club differs from the Drop-Them-Off co-op in that there is no required sharing of work. It is not expected that all the other parents share this same interest or have the same level of skill as the sponsoring parent. Typically, the incentive for one family to set up the club is to provide additional friends and motivation for their own children. An altruistic desire to share the fruits of one's studies is also likely involved.

The beauty of an interest club is that if you want one that doesn't exist, you can start it yourself! Just place a notice in your local support group newsletter and see who turns up.

Community Clubs

Community clubs come in a variety of flavors:

- **Community interest clubs** (science fiction, juggling, rockhounds, community theatre, etc.) sometimes are friendly to children and homeschoolers; sometimes not. The social environment might or might not be what you've been trying to avoid by homeschooling in the first place, so check it out carefully.
- **"Rank" based clubs** that allow children to progress through levels of instruction, which are recognized by merit badges, rankings, belt levels, awards, and the like are some of the most

Our Homeschool Writing Club

by Susan Richman

My dining room is filling up. After setting snacks out in the kitchen, kids are are hastily opening up folding chairs and setting them out, squeezing around our double tables pushed together, and scooting their typed essays toward me across the table for reading aloud. Lots of laughter and talking fill the room as we wait for a few more kids to arrive. I can already tell it's going to be another great two hours of Writing Club.

This diverse group has high school seniors all the way down to younger siblings who are just starting kindergarten at home. It's almost astonishing to look back and see how much being part of this group has helped these homeschool kids as they've developed into really fine young writers.

Why has it worked so well?

Create an Audience

You all know the old joke about real estate, that there are three main factors that are most important in finding the right house—location, location, location. Well, I think it's the same thing with writing. There are three main factors that are most important in motivating writers—audience, audience, audience. And writing clubs are one way to help kids find a real and lively audience.

We have been hosting a monthly writing club for years and years, and over time I can see that whatever else the group does that's positive for these kids, creating an audience is one of the most important things. All kids taking part realize that real homeschoolers they know and care about will be listening to their work as it's read aloud—and who would want to bring something boring or dull to a group of their friends? The kids instead inspire one another in a really positive way, as the strong and imaginative writers help encourage the others to reach for higher quality just by their example. The kids all clap enthusiastically after each piece is read, laugh aloud over funny parts, get hushed when someone writes something really touching, and spontaneously share similar experiences of their own when someone's story sparks a memory. We aim to be a positive audience—we are not an audience that is going to nitpick over spellings or an occasional awkward phrasing. We don't grade or evaluate. We really just encourage and enjoy—and this seems to make all the difference.

Open-Ended Assignments

The kids in our writing club also gain a real sense of direction for their writing by completing the various open-ended assignments I set for them. Where do I get ideas for these assignments? From books on writing, from writing my own kids are doing on their own, from other writing clubs I know. The kids have done memo-ry pieces, reflecting on an old favorite toy or piece of clothing. They've described a real person's personality by solely telling about where that person lives or works. They've remembered times when things didn't go as planned, written about how changes in weather affected or reflected a change in a character's outlook on life, and thought about times when they've learned something new or difficult. They've shared about funny dreams they've had, described people they've observed out in the larger world, and written about life from a pet's slant. They've imagined new twists on folktales told from another character's viewpoint, written spoof "application essays" for characters from well-known novels or stories, created letters to the editor for publications they've known or imagined, and more and more.

Such assignments keep the students thinking in fresh new ways about writing, giving them both guidelines and freedom. We are always happy when someone takes an assignment in a direction no one had anticipated, as when one student had a sweater tell the story of his not-very-responsible owner when kids were asked to write about a favorite old piece of clothing.

Sharing Examples

I often give the students short examples of other students' writings to illustrate an idea, sometimes found in my book *Writing from Home,* sometimes from publications such as *Stone Soup* or other magazines that publish student work, sometimes from family newsletters I receive, and sometimes from kids who've taken part in our writing club in earlier years. Assignments help the kids feel a full part of the group as they all tackle the same task, and they actually gain more appreciation for others work once they have grappled with the same idea.

I read all of these assignment pieces aloud, as I feel that kids deserve having their stories read sometimes by someone who will put real expression and liveliness into them—as well as reading loudly and clearly enough so that everyone can hear well. There's nothing worse than a wonderful piece read in a too-quiet voice or a monotone.

After a ten-minute break for snacks, we gather around the tables again, this time to hear everyone read their free-choice piece of writing, something they've written on their own at home. This encourages kids to realize that real writers need to think up their own ideas and find their own formats and ways of presenting them to others. And after hearing me read aloud, even the little kids get the idea that they are expected to read with bounce and spirit.

Just Bring Something

I let kids know that if they somehow don't have time to write something on their own, they are to bring something they've written a while back. One longtime participant recently brought a whole stack of her journals and diaries from when she was a little girl up through her senior year at home, and she then wrote a reflective personal essay sharing how her diary writing had grown and changed over time, sharing funny and touching excerpts from her early entries. This presentation encouraged my daughter Hannah to rededicate herself to her own journal writing, and she now keeps the light on late into the night jotting down her thoughts and observations on each day. Kids really do inspire one another.

I hope your own home will soon be full of expectant young writers, ready to share with one another and learn from one another. By starting a homeschool writing club you'll probably be doing your own children a greater favor than if you bought any new writing curriculum—or a new red pen for correcting their work. You'll help motivate your kids through creating a vibrant audience for their work, giving them new reasons for writing, and motivating them to do their best. May your home soon resound with the laughter and appreciation and excitement that a homeschooling writing club can create.

Howard and Susan Richman have four always-homeschooled children, two in college, and have written several books about homeschooling, including Three R's at Home. *You can visit their web site at www.pahomeschoolers.com. This article was originally published in* Practical Homeschooling *magazine.*

The Sleepover Shakespeare Society
by Susan Richman

It's late. Very late. But the happy noises are still wafting over to my bedroom where I'm trying to sleep.

"Hey, I know, we could have the soap opera version of Romeo and Juliet next . . . and then the pet version . . . and then the 90's version!"

"Is the camera working? Here, you do the sound for this scene."

"Anyone find some dress-up clothes that would work for the courtship version of Romeo and Juliet? How about some bandannas and overalls, and we'd make them be farm kids?"

The next morning I get to see the handiwork of the night's labors. It's the Sleepover Shakespeare Society's latest spoof of a play the group has discussed—seven new ways of looking at the famous balcony scene, ad-libbed by the cast of a half-dozen homeschooled girls. I've rarely laughed so hard, especially at the feminist version, where an outraged Juliet tosses a proffered flower back at a rather wimpy Romeo, who tries to assure her that he actually likes girls who are dominant.

The Sleepover Shakespeare Society was my daughter Molly's idea, and now that Molly's off at college, Hannah, heading into ninth grade, has taken over leadership. It's been a surprise path into the delightful world of creative dramatics for them all—a surprise partly because making their own spoofs of plays wasn't in the original game plan. The idea was to discuss a chosen play for about 45 minutes together after a potluck meal and then watch a movie version of the play, followed by maybe more discussion, followed eventually by heading to bed. The discussions, totally led by the students, were terrific, but some months we couldn't find a good movie to watch (and do not watch *Ten Things I Hate About You* as a substitute for *The Taming of the Shrew*—unless you want to know a few more reasons not to send your kids to public high school!). We did, however, have a video camera on hand, and the idea was born. There was something really charming about these teenage girls all diving into our old dress-up clothes trunk, creating on-the-spot wild outfits for *Macbeth, King Lear,* or *Hamlet* (well, actually that one was called *Omelet*). There were times when I'd think this was all just silliness—until I'd listen more closely to the talk surrounding their decision making. Then I'd realize how much the girls really had to understand about these plays in order to create these impromptu spoofs. They'd debate back and forth about what scenes would be most important to include, how to do each character, what they might say and why, and more. Plus they were feeling that wonderful sense of camaraderie that all involved in any play production feel! Many friendships were formed during those late night giggling drama times.

The girls also enjoyed reading through selected scenes together, and playing the lively game from Aristoplay called *The Play's the Thing: A Dramatic Introduction to Shakespeare,* where the kids answered questions about plays, performed very short dialogues, and worried about escaping from the Plague or challenging other actors to a duel. Lots of laughter during this game!

The group also moved into the real world of serious Shakespeare also. They attended live performances in our region—sometimes free productions given on college campuses, sometimes student matinees where we'd get the inexpensive school-group price. Many of them took part in the annual Shakespeare Monologue and Scene Competition offered by the Pittsburgh Public Theater, even taking advantage of free professional coaching offered by the staff at the theater. (I've heard of other cities doing similar monologue contests. A homeschool group outside of Philadelphia took part for years in a Shakespeare competition that eventually led one of their students to compete in New York City against winners from other regions.) When performing their own scenes on the main stage of the Pittsburgh Public Theater, the girls also got to see many other student performances. Often these would spark interest in reading new plays, just to find out what that one very funny or very touching scene was all about. Shakespeare was becoming more and more accessible through all of these many opportunities for active learning and doing.

At this year's Shakespeare Competition, the winner of the younger age group turned out to be a homeschooled boy—and his older brother, who had been homeschooled during his earlier years, was back in the finals also. Talking to their mother afterward, I found that homeschooling had enabled her older son to really take part actively in community theater for many years. Because he was homeschooled, his schedule was so much more flexible (read this to mean he could sleep in after a late-night rehearsal on a "school night") that he had the time to work on major roles when quite young. He was now planning on heading to college and majoring in drama. The younger brother seems to be following suit, and the whole family is really enjoying being part of the larger community through these drama activities. Shakespeare can lead you all sorts of places.

Other homeschool groups I know have actually put on major Shakespeare productions, sometimes over the summer when everyone had more free time, sometimes working as a co-op group during the whole school year.

You never know where creative dramatics may lead your homeschool group. A group in New York state is now in their fourth summer of Shakespeare, and all the kids and parents involved have really gained from the experience of really learning about these plays by doing them. They started out just reading through *A Midsummer Night's Dream* together very hesitantly, then gradually gained confidence, understanding, and insight into what they were doing, until they were ready to stage an actual public performance. One mother told me afterward that when the group had the chance to see a professional production of this first play, "We all went, even the six-year-olds, and all of us were riveted—none of us, I think, had ever appreciated a play, certainly not a play by Shakespeare, as much as we did after having acted in it ourselves."

So jump into the Bard's work, even in very informal ways that may seem just like . . . well, play. After all, the other word for drama is "play."

Howard and Susan Richman have four always-homeschooled children, two in college, and have written several books about homeschooling. You can visit their website at www.pahomeschoolers.com. Originally published in Practical Homeschooling.

popular extracurricular options for homeschoolers. These include such well-known options as 4-H, martial arts clubs and schools, AWANAS, Civil Air Patrol, Boy Scouts, and Royal Rangers. All these require much higher levels of discipline and decorum than most public schools or community activities.

- **Career clubs** such as Police Explorers (for high schoolers considering a law enforcement career), Future Farmers of America, Junior Achievement, and others offer opportunities for kids to "try out" career options.
- **Community mental sports:** bridge and chess clubs, for example. And how about Toastmasters, the public-speaking club?
- **Community physical sports clubs:** soccer, swimming, softball, golf, etc. These can be a great addition to your homeschool physical education program, and look wonderful on a college application.
- **Community general-purpose organizations** such as YMCA, YWCA, and the Jewish Community Center offer a wide variety of classes in all sorts of sports and activities. The worldview of the academic and leadership classes tends to be secular and public-school-friendly; however, the class structure is much less rigid and more homeschool friendly than the schools. Some of these organizations, such as our local YMCA,

have taken advantage of homeschoolers' more flexible hours by offering classes just for homeschoolers during the school day.

- **Community service organizations** may enjoy having one of your older children volunteer to help out for several hours a week. This list is almost endless: churches, food pantries, hospitals, animal shelters, vet clinics, museums of all kinds, nursing homes . . .

Whew! That was just a whirlwind tour of some of the options likely already available to homeschoolers in your community. Maybe that's why the average homeschooled child participates in *more* extracurricular activities than the average schooled child!

Now, as I promised, we'll close this chapter with the story of a homeschool co-op that shows us what can happen when parents who care about their children get together.

How to Start a Music Co-op
by Rhonda Barfield

It's a typical Thursday morning for our homeschooled family. At precisely 8:10 A.M., my four children and I are waiting in our minivan in an empty parking lot of a church in suburban St. Louis County, Missouri. Eric, 15, begins unloading his keyboard and synth module. Christian, 13, grabs a bag with *Math-U-See* and a notebook, and the girls, Lisa, 12, and Mary, 10, gather their violins and music folders. I am in charge of the choir accompanist's notebook and, equally important, a football and two basketballs.

Soon the church secretary unlocks the back door. Mothers with children of all ages straggle into the church. Within an hour, other families begin to arrive. Chatham Bible Church will soon house nearly 170 homeschooled students plus teachers, assistants, parents, and younger siblings.

For now, it's still relatively quiet. In one classroom, an orchestra is setting up chairs and tuning instruments. Eric goes to the church gym and assembles his keyboard gear. Christian shoots a few hoops with friends before settling into a comfortable corner of an upstairs lounge where he can work on math. Lisa and Mary, part of a beginning strings class, join six other children who are learning to play violin. I take a stroll to the main entrance and check out the bulletin board that features today's hand-written announcements.

It's another business-as-usual weekly meeting of the Northwest County Home School Music Cooperative.

Lessons for all your kids in strings, orchestra, keyboard, guitar, and choir, for $20 per kid per semester. And it only takes one day a week. How does the Northwest County Homeschool Music Co-op do it?

Four Good Reasons to Co-op

I've been involved with co-ops for ten years, but for our family, this particular one has provided the most satisfying experiences of them all. It is no ordinary cooperative, for at least four reasons.

First, as Terri Blackwell, director of the co-op, notes, "We've put God first. We decided in the beginning that we were going to serve Him, to pray about everything, and to search His will for what we do." The co-op's mission statement is summarized in Psalm 118:23: "The Lord has done this, and it is marvelous in our eyes."

Second, the co-op is staffed entirely by volunteers, including the director, teachers, and assistants, and no one receives direct pay. (This doesn't minimize the quality of instruction; it is surprisingly high.) All parents who enroll their children are expected to take an active role in helping out, from setting up chairs in classrooms to supervising toddlers to assisting teachers. Other jobs might include manning the information desk, singing along with the struggling tenors in choir, or helping to keep order in the beginning theory class.

Third, the co-op is designed to be very convenient to homeschoolers' schedules. Last year, I had checked out an excellent choir program in my suburb, but decided against it when I realized I would have had to drive 20 minutes one way to two separate weekly 90-minute practices for my four children. The Northwest County program, in contrast, offers classes for ages pre-K through high school simultaneously, all in one morning, plus babysitting. Homeschool parents can block out one three-hour period for all of their children, of all ages and abilities, and know that formal music instruction for the entire family is covered in a single day.

Finally, the co-op is hard to beat when it comes to cost. I was astonished to learn that a child can take up to four classes each Thursday for $20 total per semester. A few extra costs are involved, such as music books for some classes, a low church maintenance fee, and $10 per child for a 90-minute afternoon drama class. As an assistant teacher, I was charged half the going rate. Our family's total tab for the semester for four children's instruction, other fees, and the use of two violins, was $90 total.

Northwest County Homeschool Music Co-op has officially been in operation since the fall of 1994. That spring, several mothers made the decision to form their own band and choir rather than continue to participate in a homeschool group led by only two teachers. Terri Blackwell and friends envisioned a cooperative situation where several parents shared responsibilities. They also hoped to provide a ministry with costs held to an absolute minimum.

Over the course of seven years, the co-op has changed locations four times, now meeting and filling a majority of Chatham Bible Church's classrooms plus a gym, and, occasionally, the sanctuary. Each year, students produce two full-length concerts and two drama productions. The choirs, bands, and some individual players are involved in an annual, competitive, city-wide music contest. They also play and sing at a nearby nursing home twice a year.

Beginning Recorder class. All photos in this article are by Andrew Schmickley, age 16.

Schedule of Classes

The current schedule is arranged as follows:

8:30 Beginning Strings. Lisa and Mary learn violin in this class. God's Glory Orchestra, the most advanced orchestra of the four offered.

9:30 Beginning Orchestra. Intermediate Orchestra. Advanced Orchestra. (Eric plays keyboard in the orchestra class.) Beginning Guitar. Intermediate Guitar. Beginning Keyboard. I assist in this class of young beginners with their electronic keyboards. Beginning Recorder. Advanced Recorder. Beginning Theory. One teacher, with several helpers, leads a class of four- and

five-year-olds in lively games, songs and an introduction to music theory. Advanced Theory, including kindergartners and first graders, continues work on theory.

10:30 Devotional. All children break into two groups for a short age-appropriate devotional and prayer time. Older students produce their own highly creative presentations.

10:40 Beginning Choir. Intermediate Choir. (Mary is in this group.) Advanced Choir. Eric, Lisa and Christian sing while I accompany the choir of sixth through twelfth graders.

At **11:30**, some members of the co-op go home for the day, but many meet at a designated fast-food restaurant for burgers and fellowship. My boys, being very sports-minded, stay at the church gym and/or parking lot, where there are ongoing, informal basketball and touch football games. My girls, in another corner of the gym, play games of Foursquare, Red Light, and Piggyback with other girls and younger boys.

1:00 brings, as Lisa puts it, my favorite class . . . drama. Thirty-two children ranging from ages seven to seventeen are currently working on a series of 12 skits to be presented between music acts at the next concert.

At **2:30**, when drama class officially dismisses, there's more time in the gym for those who want it. All of us, though tired from the intensity of the day, still find it difficult to leave. Many mothers and kids linger for a last snatch of conversation or a hoop to shoot or a pass to catch.

Beginning Piano class

Prayer Helped Co-op Thrive

While some co-ops struggle to fully involve even a few interested parents and children, the Northwest County Music Cooperative has reached maximum capacity and maintains a waiting list of 30. Some members, such as Peggy Capps, a mother of five children ages newborn to 16, drive as much as an hour and fifteen minutes one way in order to participate; Peggy leaves home every Thursday at 6:45 A.M. "When we started with the co-op nearly seven years ago," Peggy recalls, "we had only 20-plus kids. There are probably groups out there with more credentialed talent. But we stuck with this group mainly because they had more praying people. Every time they've gotten bigger, they've prayed. They pray about every decision."

When Terri Blackwell was diagnosed with cancer a few years ago, co-op members not only prayed but also pitched in to clean her house and provide meals for the family. Peggy Capps experienced a similar outpouring when her youngest child, Samuel, was born with half a heart. "There were people from co-op showing up at the hospital," Peggy says, "people I never expected." Because of this closeness among participants, the co-op has thrived.

Advanced Orchestra class

Top Tips for Starting Your Own Music Co-op

Members also look for ways to help and improve the overall musical experience. "Music itself is a shared gift," says Julie Burgess, director of the advanced choir and teacher of the beginning keyboard class. "It's so important that kids learn to work together toward the goal of a good presentation. I also like the fact that there are so many personalities—and parents with different skills—involved, so kids can learn from different people instead of just one person's way all the time."

Through several years of in-the-trenches experience, organizers of the cooperative have learned what works for them. Here are their recommendations for other homeschoolers who might consider forming their own co-op [or in fact *any* co-op—*Mary*].

- **Designate a parent committee** as being in charge; avoid placing control in the hands of only one or two people. At this co-op, all parents are expected to be actively involved, fully in charge of their children, familiar with rules, and present at two parent meetings per semester.
- **Recognize and use the talent within the group.** One of the instructors in the co-op recently confided that she never earned a high school diploma. I would not have guessed, as she is an outstanding teacher. The co-op has encouraged such women's participation, based on dedication, willingness to try, and ability to work with children, rather than on degrees.
- **Know what you want to accomplish and make sure it's in writing.** Besides listing goals, the co-op has compiled a handbook to explain rules and procedures. In August, a meeting is held before school

starts to carefully review the handbook and give parents a chance to provide input.
- **Keep the hours limited.** The first music co-op's set-up, with only two instructors, made it necessary for some families to stay for an entire day while all their children waited for instruction. By using several teachers, all music classes at the Northwest County co-op are completed within three hours.
- **Communicate.** Besides the required parent meetings, announcements are written weekly on a large bulletin board next to the front entrance. Nearby is a large box of file folders, one per family, where mothers can check for memos and other important notices. A directory lists phone numbers and e-mail addresses, plus directions on whom to call, and when, if a question arises; one woman is designated as the person to contact when members don't know who else to call!

The volunteers at this music co-op say that, given the chance to do it again, they would have changed a few procedures and/or implemented others sooner. "We had five years with no handbook and no rules," Terri Blackwell says, "and it was chaos. We put that handbook into practice and things changed immediately. We started to grow by leaps and bounds as soon as we had guidelines established."

Debbie Goldsmith, treasurer and teacher of the percussion class, agrees. "We have also learned to shift more responsibility to parents," she says. A couple of years ago, some women involved in a Bible study complained about students running through the church's halls after morning classes ended. "We didn't want to jeopardize our opportunity to stay at the church," Debbie notes, "so we decided, after the final class of the morning, to have the parents go directly to their children's classroom and pick them up. It made a 180-degree improvement with crowd control and other problems."

The co-op continually improves and expands its scope. Typical homeschoolers, the mothers (and a few dads) are creative in recognizing needs and filling them. In our keyboard class, for example, volunteers constructed music stands made of cardboard. Moms also organized a free clothing and shoe exchange to help families meet the dress code requirements of white shirts, black pants and skirts, and black shoes for performances.

Beyond members' best efforts, there is a sense that another Presence is in control and rewarding their efforts. "I could tell you so many stories," Debbie Goldsmith says, smiling. "Once, we had made arrangements to buy a clarinet from a music store. The store was supposed to put aside a certain clarinet for us to look at, one that cost $200 to $250. Terri and her sister went to check it out and the clerk couldn't find it anywhere. Instead, the clerk went to a rack with other instruments, where she pulled out a $450 clarinet and said she'd sell it for $200. This kind of experience, of God blessing us, has happened to us over and over again."

On another occasion, a co-op member's church owned a tympani with a broken mechanism that wasn't being used. Terri and Debbie talked the church into letting them repair the tympani, then use it for the co-op's orchestra until the church needed it again. "Chatham Bible Church had just freed up a space under the stairway where a discarded trash can had previously been stored," Debbie remembers, "so we put the tympani there for safe keeping. It's been two years, and the other church still hasn't asked for it back."

These are just a few of many blessings that God has poured out on the Northwest County Homeschool Cooperative. In return, the co-op greatly blesses those who participate. Speaking from personal experience, these Thursday morning classes have revitalized and energized my family's homeschool, and my children work harder on their other assignments so they'll be ready for music and drama. For the first time, we have been able to afford both private and group music lessons outside the home. Best of all, the co-op has added a dimension of richness and intensity to our lives without requiring huge time commitments.

Perhaps a similar music cooperative is a possibility in your area, for your homeschooling community. I would highly recommend the experience.

Rhonda Barfield is the author of a new book called Real Life Homeschooling: Twenty-One Families Who Make It Work, *now available in bookstores, as well as the newly revised,* Feed Your Family for $12 a Day. *You can visit her online at www.lilacpublishing.com or via email at barfield@aol.com. This article was originally published in* Practical Homeschooling *magazine.*

CHAPTER 52

Private & Christian Schools

As a homeschooler, you may find yourself interacting with private and Christian schools in the following ways:

- **As a satellite school**. This has nothing to do with outer-space satellites! A "satellite school" is a small local operation of a larger, usually campus-based school. Typically, these have sprung up where the unenlightened state law does not recognize homeschools except as satellites of private or church schools, or where the law requires you to register and be accountable to public school officials *unless* you are affiliated with a private school. In Alabama, for instance, homeschools can either employ a tutor who has a teaching certificate or enroll in a church school. So some Alabama church schools allow homeschoolers to operate as "satellites" of their school. In Florida, you can choose to be accountable either to your public school (registering with them and being evaluated by them) *or* to a private school, which can be either a traditional private school or "a legally incorporated group of homeschool families," in HSLDA's words. The private-school option generally is preferred, since it provides a more supportive and less potentially hostile environment. When you're a satellite, the private or church school provides testing, keeps records and transcripts, and may provide any or all of the following: curriculum, parent instruction (how to teach), a homeschool support group, conferences, lending library, sports access, and more.
- **For special courses and activities.** You may find a local private or Christian school that lets homeschoolers sign up for single classes (art, music, and science are the most likely) or allows them to participate in some school activities, such as musical ensembles. Due to eligibility rules, which require players from a private school to be full-time students at that school, sports participation is unlikely.

PRIVATE MEANS <u>PRIVATE</u> IN TEXAS!

If you live in Texas, you are in the BEST state in the union for homeschooling! Just turn around three times, click your heels together, and say "My homeschool is a private school."

That's right! In Texas, homeschools are considered private schools. As such, they are not regulated in any way by the state! (Did you know that Texas private schools are completely unregulated? I'd bet some families spending a lot of money on private schools would be surprised to know that.)

Texas law basically states that as long as your school doesn't take state money, then the state cannot tell you what to do with your school.

—*Debbie Evans,*
"Texas Homeschooling Laws,"
www.texashomeschoolers.com/ texaslaws.htm

PRIVATE SCHOOL PREFERENCE

In 1985, the State of Florida made home education legal by adding a definition of home education to the statutes. . . . The law states that you must notify and register with the public school superintendent of the county in which you reside. Students are required to report attendance, submit a portfolio of work for evaluation at the end of each year, and be tested or evaluated by a certified teacher. Parents are free to choose curriculum. These children are considered public school students until the age of 16. However, they have none of the advantages of the public school such as credits and transcripts for high school students. In many instances there is a hostile environment for home educators within the public school system. . . .

Many families do not wish to register with the public school system. Such families may consider registering with a private school. You may hear such schools referred to as *617 or 623 schools*. . . . By enrolling in a private school you eliminate the need to inform the superintendent of your intent to homeschool.

Private schools are held to a higher standard and are held in greater esteem by their peers (other private schools and the public school system) than are home schools. Each child has a permanent file and full transcripts which follow him if and when he might be "mainstreamed" into a classroom environment.

Other advantages to private schools include accountability and support services, curriculum advisement, testing services, newsletters, support groups, field trips and many others.

—*From Beginning Homeschooling in Florida by Barbara Dunlop. Free copies, along with information on Tampa Educational Academy of Christian Heritage, Inc., are available to FL residents. Find it online at www.zipmall.com/teach/default.htm*

• **In your state, your homeschool might *be* a private school!** This is the case in Texas. Homeschools are considered private schools under the law. The laws regarding private schools vary by state. In Texas they're ideal: no state regulation whatsoever! In other states, you can declare yourself a homeschool *or* a private school. Various degrees of record keeping, attendance, and curriculum requirements may be imposed, depending on what you call yourself. In some states, the bureaucratic nightmare of building requirements, teacher requirements, and more mean that you absolutely do *not* want to be considered a private school, so check your state law carefully before invoking this option.

Much can be gained by closer links between homeschoolers and private and church schools. Maybe we don't want or can't afford their full program, but we still can support their basic work and want to be a part of *some* of it.

If your local private or religious school doesn't offer classes or activities to homeschoolers now, that doesn't mean they never will! Money talks, and if there's enough interest, enough families willing to pay for it, and the children are well-behaved, formerly recalcitrant administrators may end up singing a different tune.

Perhaps the ideal mix of private, Christian, and homeschooling is the University Model School method. See the next chapter on that option if you'd like your children to have *some* classes, but still want to be their main teacher (and save about half the price of regular private school!).

As more and more educational institutions go online, and videoconferencing becomes more common, it will hopefully soon become possible to take just about any K–8 class online, just as it now is possible to do your entire high school program online. With videoconferencing, even art and music classes can be online. The teacher can view or hear the home student's work, and the student can see what everyone in the classroom is doing. This will open up a host of options to homeschooling families. Some of us can continue to affiliate with an online school (which may or may not have an actual classroom campus). Others will just add a mix of local in-person and online classes to their home classes. The private schools that catch on to this technological revolution the fastest will be those that grow the largest and influence the most children.

Ideally, the day will come when parents will be free to sign up their children for individual classes at any educational institution that will accept them, and for which they are willing to pay. K–12 education will then look more like the YMCA and less like the lock-step grade-level public-school model. Your child will take the (relatively short) courses you want him or her to take and will repeat them as necessary without any stigma (who cares if a kid repeats the "Minnows" class at the Y swimming pool?). If a child is advanced in math and slow in reading, it won't make the slightest difference, since each course will be taken at the child's appropriate level regardless of his or her age. This will radically change the face of both private and church schools—for the better.

For more details on the ideal school system of the future, see my book *Schoolproof*. For the first steps towards this model, see the next chapter!

CHAPTER 53

University Model Schools

Art and music classes for little kids, with parents homeschooling most of the other subjects. Science, history, and more for middlers, each subject designed for a specific amount of parental supervision and/or teaching at home. A college prep high-school program, complete with sports and band, with parents and children still free to homeschool any subjects they choose.

If this sounds like the best-case deal you could work with your local Christian or private school, think again. Because University Model Schools (UMS) are far more than another private school offering homeschoolers access to some of its courses.

Grace Preparatory Academy in Arlington, TX, birthplace of University Model Schooling

Take a look at Grace Preparatory Academy in Arlington, Texas. The school that invented the UMS approach, Grace Prep's graduating class of 2001 proves there is indeed some proof in their pudding. Of the 45 graduates, three were National Merit Finalists and 70 percent earned college scholarships. The Class of 2001 calculus class earned second place in the Association of Christian Schools International math competition, and the Grace Prep basketball team were champions in the 3A division of the Texas Association of Private and Parochial Schools. All at about half the price of "regular" private school.

More than this, unlike most high-school graduates who find the transition to college life challenging, or even traumatic, Grace Prep graduates report that for them, college is "just like high school, only easier."

> University Model Schooling is not just academics, or activities, or preparation for college ... it's about giving parents more access to their children.
>
> —*UMS Update*

University Models Schools Around the Nation

The following schools were founded by individuals who attended the UMS seminars and understand the necessary components of a University-Model School. For more specific information regarding each school's program and their admission requirements, please contact each school directly.

Texas

Calvary Preparatory Academy,
 Denton, (grades 1–12),
 940-320-1944

Christian Life Preparatory School,
 Ft. Worth, (1–8), 817-832-1554

CrossPoint Preparatory Academy,
 Grapevine, (K–8), 817-488-2430

Faith Academy of Marble Falls
 (1–12), 830-798-1333

Grace Preparatory Academy,
 Arlington (1–12),
 817-557-3399

Kingdom Preparatory Academy,
 Lubbock, (3–6), 806-785-4843

Lucas Christian Academy, Lucas
 (K, 6–12), 972-429-4362

Waxahachie Preparatory Academy,
 Waxahachie, (K–6),
 972-937-0440

Wylie Preparatory Academy, Wylie,
 (1–6), 972-442-1388

Georgia

Heritage Academy, Gainesville
 (6–12), 770-536-6900

Missouri

Heritage Academy, Columbia
 (3–10), 573-449-2252

North Carolina

Grace Academy, Charlotte
 (K–12), 704-606-0163

Kansas

Christ Preparatory Academy,
 Kansas City (3–12),
 918-831-1345

—*UMS Update, July 2002*

For the latest listing of University Model Schools nationwide, plus news, seminars, materials, etc., visit **www.naums.net.**

What Is University Model Schooling?

Grace Preparatory Academy opened its doors in 1993, to an entering class of 183 students. When I interviewed founder Barbara van Wart in 2001, they had just under 600 students, and a large waiting list. Twelve more UMS schools were operating then or have started since: seven in Texas (Denton, Fort Worth, Grapevine, Lucas, Marble Falls, Waxahachie, and Wylie), one in Charlotte, NC, one in Gainesville, GA, one in Columbia, Missouri, and one in Kansas City, Kansas. Each of the sister schools was founded by families whose children had attended another UMS and then found they had to move out of the area.

Parents are involved every step of the way in a UMS. And we're talking a lot more than checking to see that homework is done and baking a cake for the bake sale. Every course requires a specific degree of parental participation, which is carefully spelled out in its catalog description, and on days that the children don't have school classes, the parents are expected to be teaching them at home.

The UMS Schedule

The UMS schedule is also unique. Just like college, it's set up so courses either run on Tuesday and Thursday or Monday-Wednesday-Friday. Typically, classes for younger children are Tuesday-Thursday only. Also, just as in college, high-school students complete most of their work at home. Having become used to the discipline of organizing a study schedule, UMS students find college life a breeze. Too, the scheduling of two different classes for the same classroom, since they use it on alternate days, also results in lowered facility and faculty costs. Finally, students sign up for individual courses, rather than entire grade levels—just as in college. So it's possible to take a tenth-grade English course and a twelfth-grade Math course in the same year, providing some of the academic freedom homeschoolers have always enjoyed.

Here's how it usually works. A younger child (grades 1 and 2) might have an enrichment class or two, while Mom and Dad teach the basics at home. As the child gets older, he or she might start taking some of the more time-consuming core subjects—e.g., literature and science—at school. To make the most of the classroom teaching time, parents do the drill work (spelling words, etc.), leaving the teacher free to engage young minds. By high school, usually the student is taking most courses at the school, while parents continue to supervise the assignments, which are researched and completed at home.

At all stages, the family chooses exactly which courses they want to take at the school and which to teach at home. Thanks to the amount of teaching the parents do, costs are kept much lower than at a typical private school.

The "Three Legs": Academics, Character, Activities

Proponents of UMS are quick to point out that it stands on three "legs." The academic program is only one of these legs. The character development program and student activities program make up the other two legs.

Obviously, children need a strong work ethic in order to succeed at an academic program that expects them to complete a good deal of work at home. So it's probably not an accident that all UMS schools to date are Christian schools, free to tell their students that God Himself expects certain attitudes and behaviors.

The UMS character curriculum is woven through the curriculum, especially the history classes and the sports/phys ed program. Parents receive a sheet of activities pertaining to that month's character trait, which is reinforced and drilled at school.

Barbara van Wart, who with her husband was one of the eight founding families, is now the chair of the GPA Ministries Outreach. She graciously answered my many questions about this unique approach to education. Discussing the UMS approach to character education, Barbara pointed out that 70 percent of churches have a membership of 100 or less. So Christian parents often have little opportunity to hear major Christian speakers who deal with children's issues. Grace Prep has been able to bring in such speakers and invite the parents to listen. They also have classes once a semester just for parents. Their most recent parent class, for example, was on helping your children sustain sound relationships with those in authority. Another class featured advice on how to help your children be good friends to others and make wise choices of friends.

The activities program is another UMS strength. "We try to offer something that everybody can plug into," says Barbara van Wart. "It may be Student Council; it may be athletics; it may be the band or the Praise & Worship Team . . . so that every student has a social glue that their parents can help support them in and that they can pursue friendships through. Again, this is just what they'll be doing at college, where you find friends through your preferred activities."

Grace Prep's sports now include volleyball, football, baseball, basketball, golf, track & field, cross-country and for girls, basketball and fastpitch softball.

Mrs. van Wart points out that, while most of their graduates who received scholarships received academic scholarships, a goodly number of scholarship recipients received sports or Christian character scholarships. Also, because of the UMS schedule, students are able to continue pursuing activities they may have followed when they were just homeschooling, or that they always wanted to do but couldn't because the parents' time was totally taken up with homeschooling.

Finally, the amount of teacher-to-parent communication in a UMS is far greater than in a typical private or Christian school. "We made a mistake in getting a low-end copier at first," laughed Mrs. van Wart. "We send home a *lot* of paper. Students don't take down assignments off the blackboard, like in a traditional school. Every teacher for every class sends home an informational sheet that says what went on that day, what the student needs to do at home, and what they need to bring back for their next school day. It's very clear to the parents exactly what's expected. Our copier wore out the first month! Now we have a super-duper copier, and we produce a syllabus for each course just like a university does."

Is University Model Schooling for You?

University Model Schools are not for everyone. The strong focus on college preparation isn't necessary for students who plan to go the apprenticeship route, and those fond of unit studies will find that University Model Schools do not provide unit-study or multi-grade-level courses, since all courses are geared to a single subject area and grade level, just as in the public schools. Some parents prefer to do all the homeschooling themselves, and others are quite comfortable relying for more complicated or Advanced Placement subjects on correspondence schools (such as Calvert School, Home Study International, and the University of Nebraska-Lincoln's Independent Study High School) and/or online academies (such as apexlearing.com, islas.org, and pahomeschoolers.com). Those who already have a full load of extracurricular activities, will not be especially en-

How to Start a University Model School

For information on how to start a UMS school:
NAUMS, PO Box 60154
Ft Worth, TX 76115
817-375-0800
tina@naums.net
www.naums.net

Onsite seminars are offered twice at year at Grace Preparatory Academy. Registration fee is a nominal $75. One-day seminar covers: overview, beginning a school—vital components and timeline, education the UMS way, continuing to promote your school, admissions: process and procedures, testing and evaluation of students, choosing staff and curriculum, parent/teacher communications, office management/equipment procurement, extracurricular program: purpose and function, Christian character education program, registration process, incorporation/tax exempt filing, and developing your board manual.

A manual containing all the forms, notes, sample bylaws, sample curriculum, schedules, and much more that you need to launch your school is available for $75 from NAUMS.

University Model Schools spokesperson Barbara van Wart at a Washington briefing on educational reform

ticed by a school activities program, and those families that consciously stress a strong faith and work ethic may not feel the need for outside support in this area, other than that they already get from their church.

However, for homeschool families that feel overwhelmed, or that wish to offer courses they are not prepared to teach, or that thrill to the idea of a well-organized social and academic outlet that is controlled by fellow homeschoolers, or who are looking for some serious help in completing high school and preparing for college, UMS could be the answer.

How to Get Started

The folks at Grace Preparatory Academy recommend the following steps.

1. Read *Character Driven College Preparation* by Dr. John William Turner, Jr. Mrs. van Wart says that the vast majority of questions they get from callers who want to know about UMS are answered in this book, and it will save both you and them lots of time if you read it first. You can order it for $12.95 plus $4 shipping from the book's publishers, Magnolia Publishing, at 1-800-856-8060, extension 128.

2. Allow an 18-month lead time to find the founding families, assign tasks, do research and marketing, locate a facility, hire faculty, etc.

3. Check with HSLDA to see how the laws in your state handle homeschoolers whose children attend private schools, and private schools that allow students to take courses at home under parental supervision. Your enterprise may affect the legal status of the families, who may not be considered homeschoolers if their children attend more than a certain percentage of out-of-the-home classes, and you also need to be aware of the legal regulations pertaining to private schools in your state.

4. You need a core group of about two to four families—a small enough number to make quick decisions without getting embroiled in committees. Two or more people from this group should plan to attend the annual summer Grace Preparatory Academy workshop on how to start a University Model School. An information packet and CD with the same facts and forms you would receive at the workshop is now available for $75—see sidebar on the previous page. You might also want to subscribe to the Grace Prep monthly newsletter, which covers trends in UMS and helps for those starting UMS schools. Suggested donation is $25, and the address is GPA Ministries, PO Box 60154, Ft Worth, TX 76115.

5. A large church that doesn't use its buildings during the week makes an ideal school location. It should have a large, open front office you can use, so parents can have a welcoming place to pick up assignments, ask questions, etc.

6. Be aware that enrollment might double your second semester, so don't underestimate your facility needs. Mrs. van Wart says a lot of families send a "scout child" to take just one or two courses to see how it works out. If they are happy with the results, you may end up with five more children from that family enrolled the second semester!

So, who needs government-run charter schools when we can have sports, Christian character training, academics, college scholarships *and* still homeschool? Bring it on, UMS!

CHAPTER 54

Public School Classes & Activities

Homeschoolers have come a long way. For almost 15 years, homeschoolers struggled to be free from the stifling control of the public schools. We at the Home School Legal Defense Association waged many of those battles in the courts, legislatures, school board hearings, and sometimes at the front door of the homeschool family. By God's grace, it is now legal to homeschool in all 50 states with minimal requirements.

As homeschoolers become more comfortable with their freedom, some are wondering if they can keep homeschooling and also participate in certain public school programs. Some of these programs include public school sports teams, band, clubs, and academic classes. The short answer is: "It depends."

You are probably thinking, "This is the kind of answer I expect from a lawyer!"

The reason the answer is vague is because **there is no fundamental right for any child to have access to the public schools** in the US Constitution or any state constitution. Equal access for homeschoolers to the public schools is a state-granted privilege, not a right. This means the state can give equal access to a homeschooler or take it away. The state or local public school determines the rules by which you must abide or have your privilege to participate in the public school service withdrawn.

This differs from parents' fundamental right to choose to educate their own children at home. This is a right guaranteed by the First and Fourteenth Amendments of the US Constitution. The right to homeschool is not a state-granted privilege.

Each state has a different approach to the equal access issue. In ten states, homeschoolers can participate in public school programs, since the state has enacted a specific law giving them a statutory right to do so. In the remaining states, the decision to allow equal access is left to the individual school districts or interscholastic athletic agencies.

Christopher J. Klicka, the author of this chapter, and the father of seven homeschooled children, is Senior Counsel of the Home School Legal Defense Association (HSLDA). For years Chris has represented homeschoolers in court and testified on our behalf before state legislatures. This chapter is based on an article he wrote for *Practical Homeschooling* magazine.

What You Could Get Through Equal Access

In the wake of lawsuits in many states by home-schooling parents, more communities are opening the doors to school libraries or computer rooms. Some districts have "part time" options that allow kids to sign up for a few courses or participate in extracurricular activities like the football team or the band. Oregon even allows students to register for courses at different schools, so that a teenager could take advanced biology at one high school and art at another. Almost every state now has a homeschooling coordinator, and some, such as Washington and Iowa, have established resource centers for parents—giving families a chance to get something in return for their taxes.

—Newsweek, *October 5, 1998*

What Do Schools Get?

A big part of the answer is economics. The number of home-schooled kids nationwide has risen to as many as 1.9 million from an estimated 345,000 in 1994, and school districts that get state and local dollars per child are beginning to suffer. In Maricopa County, which includes Mesa [where a public-school-sponsored enrichment program has been made available to homeschoolers], the number of home-schooled kids has more than doubled during that period to 7,526; at about $4,500 a child, that's nearly $34 million a year in lost revenue. And so school districts are getting entrepreneurial, offering homeschoolers classes in everything from building toy robots to art in an effort to bring children—and dollars— back into the fold. Most homeschoolers go to these classes once a week, so the districts get only partial reimbursement. But even that money is welcome.

—Newsweek, *November 6, 2000*

Equal Access States

Ten states currently force public schools to allow homeschoolers access to classes or sports part-time. These states are Arizona, Colorado, Florida, Idaho, Iowa, Maine, North Dakota, Oregon, Utah, and Washington. All of these states, except Utah, have passed equal access laws. Utah requires access through State Office of Education regulations rather than by statute. In both Arizona and Oregon, the law only requires school districts to allow access to homeschoolers for "interscholastic" activities.

Despite these laws, equal access is not offered without strings attached. Although specific requirements vary from state to state, homeschooled students can typically participate in public school programs only if the following requirements are met.

- First, the student must be in compliance with the state homeschool law.
- Second, the student must meet the same eligibility requirements as a public school student.
- Finally, the state requires the student to verify that he or she is passing his or her core subjects. Consequently, the homeschooler may be required to provide achievement test scores or periodic academic reports, even if the state's homeschool statute does not otherwise require them.

Also, Virginia allows schools to receive partial funding for homeschool students to whom they provide services. Massachusetts and Wyoming high-school athletic associations have passed bylaws that allow homeschoolers to play on public school sports teams.

And the Other 40 States?

In most of the 40 states without specific equal access laws, the decision of allowing homeschool students to participate in public school programs, activities, or sports is left up to each individual school district.

A homeschooler seeking to participate must contact his local superintendent for the privilege or make a presentation before his local school board for either a waiver or the adoption of an equal access policy. The school boards could rule either way.

If the homeschooler is seeking to play in public school sports, he will likely have to tangle with the interscholastic league in his state. Although athletic associations or leagues have a great deal of influence over public schools, they're typically private organizations. In many cases, schools and school districts who want to allow homeschoolers on teams have their hands tied. Most athletic organizations have what is commonly referred to as a "no pass, no play" rule. Students must show that they are passing a minimum number of classes, or they are not allowed to participate on sports teams. Thus, league rules are designed to prohibit schools from allowing students who are failing in school to play sports. This effort to keep below-average students and high-school drop-outs off sports teams also tends to categorically eliminate home-educated students as well. If a school violates these rules, the association can remove the school from the league or make the team forfeit its games.

Like most bureaucracies, interscholastic leagues are reluctant to change their rules. Especially since the majority of school district superintendents do not desire to be especially helpful to homeschoolers.

Don't Take It to Court

For home-educated students who reside in states that do not have an access law, the situation is extremely complicated. Virtually all the homeschoolers who have tried to force public schools, through court action, to give them access have lost. [It's possible, however, that the publicity from those court cases raised the consciousness of some districts that *weren't* sued. Such are the oddities of our mass society!—*Mary*]

For example, in 1996, a New York appellate court ruled against a homeschooler whose local school district denied him access to interscholastic sports. The court held that "Participation in interscholastic sports is merely an expectation and no fundamental right is involved . . ." *Bradstreet v. Sobol, 650 N.Y.S.2d 402, 403 (A.D.3 Dept 1996).*

Referring to other case precedent around the country, the Supreme Court of Montana decided that "participation in extracurricular activities was not a fundamental right" (*supra. 1316*). The court was unable to conclude "a private school student's interest in participating in public school extracurricular activities is more important than the school district's policy decision . . . that it needs to restrict participation to those students who are enrolled in the public school system" *Kaptein v. Conrad School District, 931 P.2nd 1311, 1317 (Mont 1997).*

No Strings Attached?

Many fear that pushing for access laws will only bring more government regulation on homeschoolers in general. Although to date no access law has directly affected any homeschoolers who have chosen not to receive services from public schools, this is a legitimate concern. Taking government money or services almost always invites government control.

In Utah, the state board of education passed regulations to allow private and homeschools access to public schools activities. However, Utah statutes or regulations had never previously defined a "private school." Problems then arose when the board of education introduced more regulations to define what a private school really was. With these new regulations, private schools had a new set of requirements to follow that were not issues before the access questions came up.

In 1996, some Georgia homeschoolers began a campaign for access to the state-funded college scholarships, which are given to public school students, and introduced two equal-access bills. The following year, the state legislature introduced a new, more intrusive homeschool law, which would have required parents to have a college degree, as well as testing and portfolio reviews for homeschooled students. The position of the legislators sponsoring the bill was, "If these homeschoolers want state money for education, we must make sure they are doing a good job teaching their children."

Pros and Cons

The issue of equal access is being debated even among the homeschooling community. Many homeschoolers oppose equal access for the following reasons:

- We should not trade our freedom for "freebies." We have fought so hard and have sacrificed so much to win the freedom to homeschool, we can't risk our liberty by pursuing free public school services. Government services never come without strings attached.

California Independent Study: Public School Supervision, Home Teaching

On October 5, 1998, *Newsweek* reported:

> In California—where the troubled public schools have pushed thousands of parents into home schooling—many families sign up for the independent study program at their local public schools to get books and other materials. A teacher monitors the child's progress, usually through monthly visits. Jon Shemitz, a computer-programming consultant, enrolled his son, Sam, 10, in independent study through his district near Santa Cruz. During the teacher's monthly visits, Shemitz says, she "fills out the paperwork, sits around and chats and allows us to participate in a few programs like field trips."

Do not confuse this type of public school supervised education with equal access. In equal access, you choose the activities and nobody is checking up on you as a parent or a teacher.

In today's climate, where professionals who work with children are taught to be suspicious of parents, anonymous reporting on child abuse hotlines is encouraged, and would-be teachers are taught it is their duty to rescue children from non-politically-correct worldviews, asking for such folks to monitor your home and your children's education is asking for trouble. By definition even the most politically correct homeschooler is outside the mainstream, and homeschooling itself is often seen as an implied criticism of these people's lifework.

Some amount of cooperation with public school officials is necessary, even in order to simply sign your child up for an Advanced Placement test. But coming under public school control, no matter how lightly wielded, is unwise and not recommended.

—Mary Pride

COOPERATION OR NOT

In some states, including California and Texas, school districts now allow home-schooled kids to sign up for such offerings as a physics class or the football team. A growing number of districts are opening resource centers where home schoolers come for class once or twice a week. In Orange County, Calif., two school districts have combined two reform ideas by opening charter schools that offer home-schooling programs.

This cooperation is largely motivated by self-interest—many schools can regain at least a percentage of their per-pupil funding by counting home schoolers, who get more options without being fully part of the system.

For their part, many home schoolers take the hard line of the movement's leading advocacy group, the Home School Legal Defense Association. It avoids representing home schoolers who are trying to get access to public school services that their taxes help fund. Many home schoolers feel that exposes the movement to too much government interference. "We are really afraid," says James Carper, an education historian at the University of South Carolina, who home schools. "When public schools extend the opportunity to become involved, it is inevitably going to compromise our independence."

—TIME, *August 27, 2001*

TAKING THE "HOME" OUT OF "HOMESCHOOLING"

Ernest Felty, head of Hardin County schools in southern Illinois, has 10 home-schooled pupils. That may not sound like much—except that he has a staff of 68, and at $4,500 a child, "that's probably a teacher's salary," Felty says. With the right robotics or art class, though, he could take the home out of home-schooling.

—Newsweek, *November 6, 2000*

- If states begin mandating that school districts open their doors to homeschoolers who want access, school officials and legislators will want to define and regulate all homeschoolers.
- Individuals who receive the services will become more and more dependent on the government and more likely to accept new regulation limiting their freedom.
- Private alternatives for homeschoolers will be less likely to arise if the government allows access.

Others assert it is unfair to keep homeschoolers out of public school programs. They support equal access because:

- Homeschool families are members of the community and pay the same taxes as families who send their children to public schools. These taxes fund public schools, too, whether homeschoolers elect to use them or not. It is unacceptable to exclude home-educated students from other public institutions such libraries, hospitals, or parks. Likewise, it should be unacceptable to keep them out of public education programs.
- A student is a student whether he attends public school, is homeschooled, or attends a private school. Specific economic and career advantages are available to public-school students. A home-educated student should not be denied the opportunity to take part in these advantages if he or she meets the qualifications.

Mary Pride Says:

Just as you can take a class at the YMCA without having to pledge eternal fealty to the Y (without having to diminish your right to take classes anywhere else you like), you should be free to enroll your children in any class or activity anywhere that you are willing to pay for, or have *already* paid for through taxes. Just as you are free to take your children to the tax-supported art museum without empowering state authorities to check on the quality of your child's art education, involvement in public school classes or activities doesn't *logically* require state snooping or restrictions on your educational program.

The very idea of having only one source for educational input—in other words, having to enroll in one, and only one, school option—is archaic in this day and age. The "a la carte" class concept is overdue—in fact, I predicted it as long ago as 1988 in my book *Schoolproof.*

However, we are not yet living in the ideal educational world. We should keep working for more educational freedom and flexibility, while rejecting all attempts to bring homeschooling under state control. Therefore, any public-school activity that involves them monitoring your homeschool or dictating curriculum is a step backward and should be rejected. Options that allow you to treat the public school as a community resource—in the same way you treat the YMCA—can be embraced, *provided* there is no sneaky attempt to saddle us with control simply because the community resource happens to be tax-funded.

Public school officials and state legislators: Either opt homeschoolers and private schoolers out of property taxes devoted to education, or start giving *all* parents back their right to pick and choose their children's education. Your call.

CHAPTER 55

What About Charter Schools?

I n the last chapter, we looked at whether homeschoolers can . . . or should . . . participate in individual public-school classes or extracurricular activities.

Now, let's take a look at the option many think of as "free homeschooling," but which actually turns out to be "public school at home," with all that that implies.

Chris Klicka on the Battle for the Soul of the Homeschool Movement

It seems everyone with school-aged children is talking about charter schools. Many are thinking, "This deal is too good to pass up: I can have my children educated outside of the public school system and have the government still pay the bill!" They believe it is the best of both worlds. Charter schools along with educational vouchers appear to be harmless since parents are only reacquiring their tax money.

Is it really that simple?

Let's look at charter schools and vouchers a little closer from the perspective of *freedom*—not from the perspective of what "freebies" we can receive from the government.

I am afraid the soul of the homeschooling movement is at stake. How we respond to charter schools and vouchers will determine the extent homeschooling remains free from government controls in the future.

To accurately understand this issue, we must first define the terms.

What Are Vouchers and Charter Schools?

Government educational **vouchers** constitute a legislatively specified amount of government money given to parents to spend on their child's education expenses. The money often can be used for public or private education. At present, there are only a handful of state government voucher programs for education in existence. Most of them have been struck down by the courts. No federal educational voucher program exists . . . yet.

Christopher J. Klicka, the author of the first part of this chapter, and the father of seven homeschooled children, is Senior Counsel of the Home School Legal Defense Association (HSLDA). For years Chris has represented homeschoolers in court and testified on our behalf before state legislatures. The first part of this chapter is based on an article he wrote for the September/October 2001 issue of *Practical Homeschooling* magazine.

Independent Public Schools

Typically, charter schools are defined as independent public schools of choice that operate with freedom from many of the regulations that apply to traditional public schools. They are, however, held accountable for student performance. Charter schools are federally and state funded, and state or local education agencies typically manage them....

Charter schools are expected to continue to grow now more than ever with the current favorable support of charter schools by the U.S. Department of Education.

"The State of the School Market," Summer 2003, a publication of the National School Supply and Equipment Association. Emphasis mine.

Supporters of government educational vouchers summarize the benefits this way. Vouchers create competition, giving private education programs an "even playing field" when competing with government-funded public schools. This, they say, will improve the quality of all education programs. Besides, it is the parents' money in the first place, and they are merely getting their tax dollars back.

A much more common educational program is the **charter school**. Charter schools are a type of public school. The school is established by a "charter" that lists the school's mission, educational program, and methods of assessment. Charter schools answer to the state or local school board for accessing the students and verifying academic progress. They are completely government funded.

Some charter schools operate as institutional schools, others as "online" schools or "cyber schools," and still others operate as homeschool programs.

Charter schools now exist in 37 states, the District of Columbia, and Puerto Rico. The Center for Education Reform estimates on its website that there are over 2,000 charter schools operating with more than 500,000 pupils enrolled in these schools. [*Another 750 or so schools have opened, and about another 200,000 students have enrolled in charter schools, since this article was written—Mary*]

Supporters of charter schools claim that creating competition in the educational market will result in more options and a higher quality of education. The idea is that if public charter schools draw enough students away from the regular public schools, the resulting lack of funds will force public schools to come up with creative alternatives to bring students (and the funding that comes with them) back into the system. Additionally, proponents claim that charter schools provide an innovative alternative of schooling that allows creative approaches to teaching, freed from the strict rules and regulation of the public school system. They point out that charter schools provide a protective environment like a smaller "private" school or home environment—where students can pursue their own styles of learning.

An increasing number of homeschoolers are examining the possibility of enrolling full-time or part-time in "cyber schools" or homeschool programs operated by these public charter schools or directly by regular public schools. Charter schools operate on taxpayer dollars, so there is virtually no cost for those enrolled. Other advantages cited by homeschoolers to participation in a charter school are the accredited high school diploma, free computer, Internet access, software, and support by certified teachers.

With government vouchers and public charter schools and public schools offering all of these benefits, we at the Home School Legal Defense Association often are asked why we would oppose such excellent educational options.

Freedom Is the Answer

Freedom is the answer. Freedom, I believe, is more important than "freebies."

Over the last 16 years, I have worked at the Home School Legal Defense Association helping to win the right of families to homeschool with minimal regulations. Many of these battles took place in the courts and legislatures throughout the country. I saw firsthand the tremendous sacrifices and risks parents took to follow God's leading to train their children at home. These families faced fines, jail, and even the threat of the state taking their children away. These families held on to their convictions, and God honored them in an incredible way. After 15 years of litigation and legislative battles, we won the right to homeschool in all 50 states.

Of course, the battle to maintain this freedom continues as school officials harass homeschool families with illegal requirements, and teacher's unions and other professional education organizations have legislation introduced to restrict homeschool freedoms. A survey of over 1000 public school executives by the *American School Board Journal* in February 1997 found 71 percent did not believe homeschoolers were regulated enough! Ninety-five percent of the superintendents and principals believed *anything* is better than homeschooling. The National Education Association passes a resolution each year condemning homeschooling and calling for legislation to require homeschools to be taught by certified teachers and have their curriculum approved by the state. The prejudices against homeschooling remain.

But our hard-fought freedom remains intact for now. Private homeschooling is thriving, with no help from the government. The studies all show homeschoolers are academically above average from the elementary level all the way through college. Homeschoolers have earned the right to be left alone.

All of this success has been achieved without the government's money. We have had tremendous success before the Congress and the state legislatures because we are not asking for a handout but simply to be left alone.

This liberty is at risk if homeschoolers begin crawling back to the government to drink from the public trough. This is the same government that once heavily restricted or prohibited homeschooling. We will become dependent on government money and as the controls are added, we will not be able to break free.

As homeschoolers "yoke" together with the public schools through charter school programs and cyber schools, the public schools and the state will once again dictate to us our curriculum, teacher qualifications, and methods.

This is not idle conjecture. It is already happening.

Government Homeschooling in Alaska

It is important to remember the old and true adage: "There is no such thing as a free government service." Government *money* always comes with government *strings*. Governments will demand accountability for funding. States want to be assured that no fraud is involved and that the monies are not used for an improper purpose. The types of regulations over parents who receive funding will depend on the type of government in power. The most common concern for the government is that the children learn certain concepts and progress academically.

Charter schools are accountable to the state or local school authorities. In addition to dictating the curriculum and teaching styles, they can impose requirements on the parents far beyond that which is required by state homeschool laws, in order to assure that the parents are teaching the children "appropriately."

The Alaskan government program is typical of many charter school homeschool programs.

On June 4, 1997, Alaska enacted the best homeschool law in the nation. Alaska's law has no teaching qualifications for parents, no regulation at any level of government, no notice to anyone of the parents' decision to conduct the home education, no registration with the state, no reporting to anyone of any information about the home education program, no testing of the children, no required subjects, and no evaluation of the program by anyone.

From Subsidy to Control

Each year, more homeschool families are accepting state reimbursement for the cost of certain textbooks and fees, or listing these costs as deductions on their yearly tax forms.

The danger is this: as a growing number of homeschool families participates in these reimbursement/tax deduction programs, state tax dollars are being used to subsidize an important part of homeschooling expenses. When the number of participating homeschool families reaches a sizable proportion, the state will be in a position legally to step in and *begin regulating homeschooling.* For the past several decades, both federal and state courts have ruled repeatedly that whatever the state subsidizes, it has the right to regulate.

But the danger does not stop here. As more participating homeschool families enroll in the various private and religious homeschool programs, these institutions and ministries, *in the eyes of the state,* will be seen as accepting state tax dollars for their curricula and services. Not only homeschoolers then, but educational ministries like Christian Liberty could come under state control.

From an open letter to "Friends of Home Education" by Christian Liberty Academy

Bribing Us Softly . . . with Our Own Money

Finding home education unbeatable in the courts, in the legislatures across the country, in the congress, now the enemy of the family turns its guns on the pocket books of homeschoolers . . .

With government money goes government controls. This is unavoidable. If you take their dollars today, you will accept their regulations tomorrow.

Their plans are certainly to control the test, the curriculum or the teacher certification (training) process.

You will bow to their teaching plan for your children or you will lose their money. The courts may even conclude that your acceptance of their money at some point in time could constitute a surrender of your rights to control the training of the child God has entrusted to you.

If you value your freedom and have a desire to control the education of the child for which you will give an account to God, do not accept their funds.

Why should we have a $1 taken from us to educate the children of the state and then surrender control of our home school for $.10?

Don't give me 10 cents on the dollar. Stop taking the dollar. You know that with the other 90 cents they are figuring out how to control your school and family.

Let's stop compulsory attendance. That's where the battle is.

For home, for liberty, to live as free people. It was for freedom that Christ set us free. Don't let us again take on a yoke of slavery.

Don't sell your heritage for a bowl of soup. Your children are your heritage.

Claiborne Thornton, President of the TN Home Education Association, quoted in an August, 2002, letter to homeschool leaders from HSLDA entitled "Virtual Charter School Troubles"

Despite having more freedom than any other state, a majority of homeschooling families are choosing to enroll their children in a public school program known as Interior Distance Education of Alaska (IDEA). Interestingly, this statewide program of correspondence study from the Galena School District was begun in June of 1997, just at the time that the new homeschool law was enacted. According to the information disseminated by Galena School District, the desire of the public school officials is "to provide educational, emotional, intellectual, and financial support to those who would like to work in partnership with a public school district."

Families who enroll their children in IDEA are provided curriculum materials, use of a computer with access to the Internet, and assistance from a certified teacher, among other services. However, public funds *may not* be used to purchase curriculum materials for teaching core subjects if the materials are distinctively religious in content. (Ironically, one of the reasons most often given by parents who have decided to teach their children at home is that they object to the atheistic content of public school curricula.)

I have talked to some parents who tell me the various ways they circumvent this but still use the state government's money to buy Christian textbooks. So already dependence on government money is encouraging people to lie!

Additionally, students in grades 4, 8, and 11 must take the standardized tests that Alaska uses for public school students at a test site designated by public school officials, and the tests must be administered by a certified teacher approved by the Galena School District. All IDEA students are required to take any assessment mandated by the Alaska State Department of Education of public school students in grades 5, 7, and 10. As a further evaluation of the student, each parent must report to Galena School District the progress of all students each semester. High school students are required to submit to a yearly interview with a representative from IDEA in order to establish a transcript.

The "freebies" are not so free after all. The price is actually too high. The price is a gradual but steady loss of freedom, control, and independence.

Homeschooling in Name Only

Despite all of the attractions for homeschoolers, charter schools are supporting homeschooling in name only. *Parents who enroll their children in charter schools are creating small public schools in their home.*

As seen in the Alaska example above, most charter schools will not allow funding to be used to purchase material that is religious in content. Thus, parents that would normally incorporate their faith into their teaching curriculum will only be able to do so at an extra expense to themselves.

Last week, I talked to a Christian lady who is a teacher in a large charter school program in Colorado. She said many Christian families are using the program and enrolling their children in the charter school. I asked her if the teachers can teach the Bible. She said, "No but we can teach virtues." I asked if she was allowed to teach the children about salvation and she said, "We are not supposed to." If you cannot teach the Bible and cannot teach your children about Jesus, what is the point of Christian education?

In Milwaukee, Wisconsin, an educational voucher program has been operating for several years. It has been touted as one of the best examples of a successful government educational program. What many do not realize is that *any Christian school that enrolls students who are using the government vouchers must comply with over 300 additional regulations.* Two of the requirements even prohibit the Christian school from mandating that these children with vouchers attend chapel or Bible class!

Is this compromise worth it? If we turn our back on Jesus Christ and His command to proclaim the gospel simply for government money, how much longer will God withhold His judgment?

Homeschool parents originally fought to be separate from the public schools in order to have the right to choose the curriculum that they believe would be best for their child. Parents removed their children from the public school system because of the non-Christian curriculum. So why would they want to go back to the same humanistic material? But this is happening with homeschoolers who enroll in charter schools or public school programs for homeschooling.

With little power in choosing the curriculum, parents in charter schools also face limited ability to incorporate creative teaching methods. The specific curriculum requires parents to "stick to the schedule" dictated by the public school, rather than use creativity in complimenting their child's learning style.

HSLDA members who have participated in charter school complain of this very thing. As one California homeschooler shared:

"Having been in a car accident and having been limited in my physical capabilities, I found myself not able to get my kids out as much as I felt they needed. Home educating independently for three years, I was reluctant to try a charter school, but I thought, 'How bad could it be? I'd have access to educational materials, and my children would have an opportunity to meet other home educated children.' At first it was exciting, though enrolling was very institutional. Then it came time to meeting with a teacher. We sat and talked, and I stated that I had been home educating independently for three years and was not interested in meeting weekly and that I would bring their work in monthly as they are required to turn in work at least monthly. That worked out great the first month. The next month,

The danger of government home school programs is clearly apparent in this letter from Carol Simpson, the Alaska Deptartment of Education Coordinator of their home school program, IDEA.

This is a letter to a Christian speaker and author who was scheduled to sell books and speak at five IDEA meetings throughout Alaska. At that last minute, it was determined her books were "Christian" and could not be sold or promoted at the IDEA conferences. Nor could home schoolers get reimbursed if they purchased these "Christian" books for their home school programs. Alaska is essentially creating an approved list of secular home school books. (Notice how gradual the changes have been. At first, Christian home school textbooks were paid for.) Over 75 percent of home schoolers in Alaska are dependent on the government funds now.

—Chris Klicka
Open letter to homeschool leaders

Charter Schools Are Not Homeschools

The Wichita Area Homeschool Athletics Association (WAHAA) has already begun to receive inquiries concerning the eligibility of students enrolled in the various charter/virtual schools currently available to home-schoolers in Kansas (Basehor/Linwood Virtual Charter School, Moundridge Mid-Kansas Independent Academy, Wichita eSchool, etc.). The number of students participating in such programs is obviously growing. (In fact, enrollment has grown so much over the Summer that BJU Press called recently to inquire why a public school in Moundridge, Ks. was placing such a large order for their materials!)

In light of this growth, and upon encouragement by TPA President Jim Farthing, WAHAA Coordinator Kenny Collins has researched the details of these programs as presented in their official literature. He also spoke at length with Shawn Morris, Director of the Wichita eSchool, at the recent TPA Conference. He did so in order to determine how (or whether) students enrolled in such programs could participate in WAHAA activities. . . .

Based on our reading of the requirements for enrollment and participation in the charter/virtual schools

noted above, it is clear that students in these programs are subject to the authority of the administering schools in such things as curriculum choice, teacher oversight, grading, testing, promotion and graduation.

1) To receive public school credit for the classes, students must follow the school's prescribed format, use their curriculum, submit to school and state testing, etc.

2) Upon entering the high school level, the public school teacher assigned to oversee the student is in charge of assignments, testing, grading and evaluation,

3) Students enrolled in the full program are considered full-time public school students. This is the basis for the school's claim to full state funding for such students.

Accordingly, students enrolled in these programs are clearly public school students subject to public school authority regardless of the fact that the educational program takes place in the home.

—Jim Farthing
President of Teaching Parents Association (Kansas)
C.H.E.C.K. News, August 2001

ever, the teacher wanted to plan out what we'd be doing for the following month. After being independent I was not interested in being told what my kids would be learning, so we agreed we'd do the work we wanted and would write up the plans retrospectively. This was not ideal but do-able since the kids enjoyed the Monday co-op classes and field trips.

"The next time we met, I took the kids' work but left the children behind. I never read or signed anything stating that my children had to be present. To me, turning in the work was the requirement. It soon became apparent that the teachers were required to talk to the children at these visits and assess them not only on their academics, but also on their physical appearance . . . looking for signs of abuse and/or neglect at their discretion. I had gotten so used to living my own life and had forgotten just how involved the government is in the lives of families enrolled in public schools.

"Make no doubt about it, a charter school is a public school . . . it's homeschooling in technical terms only. Enrolling in a charter school will give you more freedom than the traditional public schools, but still strips you of the independent responsibility of educating our own children. It is still an institution, that believes we need interference from trained government agents and that we are incapable of educating our own children.

"The principal was very eager to work with me, bending the many rules. I appreciated her efforts greatly. However, I found that we were . . . forced to learn in the 'one size fits all' methods of the schools, which I desperately avoid. It's my opinion also that charter schools try very hard to embrace all philosophies of home education; however, they are still run by government agents paid to spy on us and to dictate our parenting and educational skills. They still work under the framework of the 'one size fits all' mind-set, and some teachers forcefully dictate (assign) the work. We found ourselves so consumed in getting the work done that my children were not retaining any of the subjects. It was simply a race to get it done and turned in, stereotypical of schools. To me, academic work should be savored to allow them to retain it and enjoy it.

"In a charter school we found that the kids are still categorized by age; they maintained their institutional mind-set. 'You're this age, in this grade, you should be doing this or that.' 'You're in fifth grade, oh, you need to be studying American history, ancient history's next year.' I found this train of thought to be very limiting. Charter schools are still public schools, which are basically training kids to do well on standardized tests. Their first priority is their precious ADA; they want their $4,000 per child. Secondly, they still program the children for taking standardized tests to get good results, typical of schools."

This member went on to share that when she finally tried to remove her children from the charter school program, *she was contacted repeatedly by Child Welfare Services demanding that she place her children in school.*

Is government money worth it? Are not these the type of controls we cast off with much sacrifice and risk? Are we willing forge new chains to limit our liberty?

Homeschool parents want to be free to educate their children without this kind of government oversight.

Top Education Officials Have Warned Against Vouchers

Although we differ from the philosophy of many of the former Federal Secretaries of Education, their statements are valuable since they demonstrate the intent behind government funding of private education. Lamar Alexander, former Secretary of Education under George Bush, explained the transformation of private education that was publicly funded when he said: "A public school would become any school that receives students who brought with them public monies . . ."

Former US Secretary of Education, Richard Riley, had strong reservations about vouchers and government funding of private education. No doubt, his reason for opposing government funding of private education was mainly to protect the current public school system, but he has some interesting warnings for private schools:

> *You have to be accountable with public tax dollars . . . when it comes to taking federal tax dollars and giving those to parents and then having the absence of accountability as far as their children's education . . . If you have accountability, then you lose the private and parochial nature of those schools . . . It's bad, we think, for private schools and parochial schools. It takes away from them the private and parochial strength, which is being totally free from any federal regulations . . .*
>
> *[Vouchers] threaten the very nature of private and parochial schools. It makes them less private and less parochial.*

Chester Finn Jr., former Assistant Secretary of Education under Ronald Reagan, declared how government controls were inevitable: "There is no doubt in my mind that there will be some new regulations with voucher plans."

If the highest public school bureaucrats in the nation recognize that government-funded private education means loss of freedom, how can we deny it?

How to Eliminate Independent Homeschools

The sheer number of homeschoolers represents a distinct threat to the hegemony of the government school monopoly. Qualitatively, the academic success of homeschoolers, measured by standardized test scores and recruitment by colleges, debunks the myth that parents need to hire credentialed experts to force children to learn.

Homeschooling also refutes the "more money equals better education" mantra of the teachers unions. The average homeschooling family spends approximately ten percent of the per-pupil costs associated with government schools in achieving those academic results.

Besides challenging the legitimacy of government schools, homeschoolers also pose a more direct economic threat. Funding for government schools is based on attendance, with a national average of almost $6,000 per student. Homeschooled children represent over $7 billion out of reach of local government schools, and, at its current growth rate, each year over $1 billion more slips away. . . .

To combat those threats, defenders of the status quo are fighting back with all the legislative and economic weapons at their disposal. The most insidious of these tactics is the systematic undermining and co-opting of the homeschool movement by establishing government homeschooling programs. Those programs set seductive lures before families by providing "free" resources, teachers, extracurricular activities, facilities, and even cash reimbursement. When enough families have voluntarily returned to the government system, it will be a relatively straightforward matter to recapture the rest by imposing mandatory homeschooling oversight regulations. Will this seduction succeed in eliminating independent homeschoolers and derailing the growing free market in education? . . .

Having established a viable government alternative to the private sector and independent homeschooling, the government's next step is logical—outlaw or regulate independent homeschooling out of existence. Not only is it logical, it follows historical precedent.

This is the same pattern used in the 1800s to virtually eliminate the large private-education system that predominated at the time. First, fund it with compulsory taxes, though attendance [or in the case of charter schools, participation] is voluntary. Once private-sector competition is driven largely out of the market, make attendance [or in this case, participation in state-run charter "homeschool" programs] compulsory as well.

Chris Cardiff, "The Seduction of Homeschooling Families," The Freeman, March 1998

The Experience of Other Nations

Other nations have experienced the effects of government funding. Private education has almost completely disappeared.

For example, in Australia, over ten years, private school and Christian schools took more and more government funds. The regulations gradually increased until the difference between public schools and private schools is nonexistent. Homeschooling in Australia is the last bastion of educational freedom.

In South Africa, in 1996 their new National Education Act was passed that officially transformed all publically funded private schools into public schools.

In Alberta, Canadian homeschoolers enjoyed more liberty than almost all of the other provinces. Then several years ago, legislation was passed giving homeschoolers $500 per child in government funds. The very next year, one of the most regulatory legislative bills was passed, implementing restrictions on homeschoolers. When asked why, the Minister of Education stated that if they were giving money to homeschoolers they had to know who they are and have certain standards. These regulations apply to all homeschoolers—not only those who receive the government funding.

Many European countries have experienced similar scenarios.

Charter Schools Increase Government Spending

Charter school proponents claim that the resulting competition between educational providers will drive education costs down while increasing the quality of education offered.

Charter schools do not charge tuition, but are funded according to their enrollment. Charter school students may be eligible for state and federal funding. There are over 5.5 million children who do not attend public schools in this country. If these children suddenly began using money from the state's treasury for their schooling, taxes would have to be raised to generate the additional revenue.

It is highly unlikely that public schools would reduce their budgets in order to provide funds for private schools.

Today, non-public school parents are being double taxed—they pay tuition for both public school children and their own children. With vouchers, these parents would be *triple* taxed. In addition to footing the bill for their own children's tuition, they would pay for the public school students *and* the students participating in charter schools.

Alaska's IDEA program serves as a good example of the increase in government spending. According to Eddy Jeans, Finance Director at the Alaska Department of Education, Galena School District received $15,020,053 in state funds for fiscal year 2000. Of this amount, $14,093,136, or $4,104 per pupil, was received for the 3,434 students in IDEA. The balance of the funds in the amount of $926,917 was intended for the 226 students who receive classroom instruction as regular on-site students.

Each student enrolled in IDEA receives an annual allotment averaging $1,600 to cover curriculum and related expenses. Considering the $4,104 per pupil received from the state, Galena School District enjoys a gross profit of over $2,500 per pupil in IDEA for a total of $8,585,000 for fiscal year 2000. What amount of this profit is reduced by IDEA administrative expenses is unknown, but there is no question that this is a moneymaking enterprise for Galena School District.

Let's Choose Freedom

Government schools are failing everywhere. They are not providing students with the moral training necessary in any society, and students continue to fall short of academic standards. Why would homeschool parents wish to support this system by accepting funding to participate in it?

In spite of the enticements offered by charter schools, parents should realize that charter school programs are simply creating little public schools in our homes. The teaching may take place in private homes, but the government is pulling the strings.

The soul of homeschooling has its foundation built on the incredible sacrifices of many parents who risked all in order to win the right to be free from suffocating government control. To be free to teach their children according to God's ways and in obedience to His commands. God honors those who honor Him and who trust in His sovereign love and power. We do not need the government's "free" money. The price is too high.

Mary Schofield on Why Charter Schools Won't Work for Christians

You've seen the reasons why getting a "free" education means you won't really end up homeschooling . . . and you could unwittingly end up undermining your very right to homeschool.

But there are spiritual questions involved too.

Below, the leading homeschool expert on charter schools, Mary Schofield, explains "Why Charter Schools Won't Work for Christians." This is taken from her copyrighted brochure of the same name, and is used with permission.

What Is a Charter School?

According to the California Department of Education, "A charter school is a public school and may provide instruction in any of grades K-12. A charter school is usually created or organized by a group of teachers, parents and community leaders or a community-based organization, and is usually sponsored by an existing local public school board or county board of education. Specific goals and operating procedures for the charter school are detailed in an agreement (or "charter") between the sponsoring board and charter organizers."

The majority of charter schools nationwide are classroom-based, with children going to a school site each school day. We will focus on charter schools which enroll homeschoolers. These programs use a variety of titles: homeschooling; independent study; distance learning; virtual, on-line, cyber, or computer-based schools; co-op teaching; correspondence; work study; or home study. What these "non-classroom based" charter schools have in common is that the student completes most of his schooling without attending a classroom.

Christian Children Need Christian Education

Just as the Christian life cannot be lived only on Sundays while ignoring God the rest of the week, so Christian education cannot occur in a void apart from the other school subjects. God is the God of science, history, literature, arts, mathematics, and all other subjects. Instruction in *all* of these areas must point to Him and to His precepts. This cannot happen in a charter school.

Mary Schofield is a Christian homeschool leader in California who has studied and reported on the charter school movement since 1992. If you need a more in-depth analysis of charter schools than you find in this chapter, please order her booklet *Charter Schools* from CHEA, 800-564-243, www.cheaofcar.org.

For what shall it profit a man, if he shall gain the whole world, and lose his own soul? Or what shall a man give in exchange for his soul? (Mark 8:36-37)

In his "Preface to the Holy Bible," Noah Webster wrote, "The scriptures were intended by God to be the guide of human reason." Biblical teaching is not merely supplemental, rather, it is essential and foundational. Such open recognition of this primary position of Scripture cannot happen in a charter school.

Charter Schools Cannot Offer a Christian Education

The law clearly prohibits religious instruction in *all* public schools, including charter schools: no "sectarian or denominational doctrine [shall] be taught, or instruction thereon be permitted, directly or indirectly" in public schools. (California Constitution, Article IX, Section 8)

Some charter school administrators claim that parents may teach their own children religious doctrine whether they are in a charter school or not. This is true only in the sense that it is true for parents of any public school student—they may pray with him each morning before sending him off to school, they may teach Bible before or after school, and they may take him to church each Sunday. However, they may not teach him any subject from a biblical perspective during school.

Non-Christian Philosophy and Goals

Trying to give children a Christian education within a system which does not function from a biblical perspective requires a continual shifting of perspectives, from secular to biblical and back again. This creates a double-minded man, who attempts to deal with life sometimes from a biblical perspective and sometimes from a humanist perspective.

If the goal of education is to bring children to a saving knowledge of Jesus Christ, to raise them to glorify God and love the Lord their God with *all* their heart, mind, soul, and strength . . . If the goal is to raise children who know God's Word and are able to apply God's wisdom to every situation they encounter throughout their lives, then an education program is needed which openly declares Christ as Savior and King. This cannot happen within a charter school.

Non-Christian Influences

There is no guarantee that children in charter schools will be assigned a Christian teacher. Charter schools cannot lawfully consider religious affiliation when hiring teachers or other staff. And since charter schools cannot consider religious affiliation when enrolling students, there is also no way of knowing whether the other students participating in various school activities are Christians.

Privately homeschooling parents can ensure that only professing Christians influence their children. They can also maintain full authority over all activities which provide opportunities for others to develop relationships with their children. This cannot happen in a charter school.

Non-Christian Curriculum

Charter schools are prohibited by law from purchasing religious materials, and they are prohibited from allowing religious materials to be used in their programs *even if* those materials are purchased by parents or others. Parents of *any* public school student may *supplement* their children's education with Christian materials, but this must be done outside of regular school time.

Non-Christian Tests

Beginning with the graduating class of 2004, all public school students (including those in charter schools) must pass the California High School Exit Exam (HSEE) in order to get a high school diploma. The content of the HSEE is dictated by the California State Board of Education and is aligned with the secular content standards for each subject area: "The content standards also serve as the basis for the curriculum frameworks, and all adopted instructional materials and state tests are aligned with them." (California Department of Education. California High School Exit Examination (CAHSEE).) The only way to opt out of having government bureaucrats dictate what your student will learn is to opt out of the government tests entirely. But this is not an option in the charter schools.

Non-Christian Control of Your Child's Education

The discerning parent will note that there is a difference between parental *involvement*, and parental *control*. God has not ordained that parents should have a government facilitator, specialist, guide, teacher, advisor, or assessor for the training of their children to His glory.

It is important for parents to recognize that the God-ordained family order is subtly undermined in government schools. Parents are the ones who are responsible to God for educating their children—not civil government. Roy Hanson, private and homeschool legislative consultant, stated it well in his Jan/Feb 2002 article "Charter Schools," published in HSLDA's *Court Report*:

"When we choose not to look to the government, but rather to take full personal responsibility for our children's education, we acknowledge the authority of God and His Word in our lives. We teach our children to honor God, His Word, and his ordained jurisdictions of authority and responsibility. We also teach them to be content with what God provides through our faith and diligent obedient labors."

Children in charter schools are *public school* students. Charter schools are funded by taxpayer monies and, according to the California Constitution, all publicly funded schools must be under the "exclusive control of the officers of the public schools." The very heart of homeschooling is the return of that control to the parents. This cannot happen within a charter school.

Non-Christian Yoking

Charter schools offering independent study require the parents to enter into a contract with the government school:

"Each written agreement shall be signed, prior to the commencement of independent study, by the pupil, the pupil's parent, legal guardian, or caregiver, if the pupil is less than 18 years of age, the certificated employee who has been designated as having responsibility for the general supervision of independent study, and all persons who have direct responsibility for providing assistance to the pupil." (California Education Code § 51747 (c)(8))

Non-Christian Funding Methods

Some parents have looked at charter schools as an opportunity to "get back" some of the hard-earned money they pay in taxes to support public schools. The truth is that when private school students switch to charter schools, it creates an additional tax burden. The best way for families to get the benefit of more of their own money is to work toward *reducing* government spending.

Parents pay the same amount of taxes whether their children are in a public school, private school, homeschool, or stay home with a hired tutor. The difference is whether parents *add* to the tax burden by insisting that

---

EXIT EXAM DICTATES CONTENT
How can schools best prepare students for the HSEE? It will be important that students take classes that include instruction in state content standards for English/language arts and math. Students will need to use their knowledge of the content identified for the test.
California high school exit Examination: Q & A for Teachers

CHRISTIAN HOME EDUCATION DEFINED:
- The parents have 100 percent responsibility
- The parents have 100 percent authority
- The parents have 100 percent control

Do not be unequally yoked together with unbelievers. For what fellowship has righteousness with lawlessness? And what communion has light with darkness? (2 Corinthians 6:14)

they get a piece of the tax fund pie. And when parents consider the incredible spiritual cost to their children's real education by subjecting them to godless government schooling, it's easy to see why it's worth the extra cost of paying for your own children's education.

Destruction of Christian Freedom

The charter school movement is a serious threat to true family freedom for several reasons. First, when families participate in charter schools, they support the assumption among many "professionals" that parents are incapable of raising their children without government supervision. Second, as larger numbers of families leave private education in favor of charter schools, it weakens the private education movement by reducing their numbers. Third, as charter school members increasingly earn the reputation of wanting their "share" of taxpayer funds, they become just another special interest group trying to get money—at least in the eyes of the Legislature.

Conclusion

The charter school option may look good to many Christian parents—at first glance. The financial cost of private home education may seem high when compared with the "free" benefits offered by the charter schools. But when parents consider the cost of their children's future—their Christian discipleship—then the truth becomes clear. The financial cost of keeping children away from a system that cannot openly proclaim Christ and His Word is a small price to pay. The Christian education that is necessary to raise children to the glory of God simply cannot be found in a charter school.

YES, OTHERS WOULD BE SUBSIDIZING YOUR CHARTER SCHOOL TUITION; IT'S MORE THAN YOU PAY IN TAXES

To pay enough taxes to cover the ADA funding for two elementary-age children, parents in California must fit the following example every year:

- Own a home that is assessed for property taxes at a value of $1,500,000, or more *and*
- Spend over $68,000 per year on items which are charged sales tax, *and*
- Have a taxable income of over $90,000 per year.

"I Want My Money Back." The Parent Educator. (*Christian Home Educators Press: April/May 2000*)

Mary Pride Says:

Do you want to sign up for a program, such as K12, that is also used in charter schools?

If you value your homeschool freedom, then choose to spend your own money on it.

If you can't afford this kind of program, government charter schools aren't the only option.

Try buying used curriculum, or swapping for it. (We have a popular forum just for this on our website!) Wear out your library card. Go on nature walks and visit free attractions, such as the zoo. You can still give your child a great education, and it sure beats having government "change agents" inspecting your children and wondering if they should hotline you every time you and they disagree about how your children should be taught or raised.

PART 12

Homeschooling Away from Home

Homeschooling doesn't have to mean just sitting at home! Your child can attend a worldview training week or NASA Space Camp. Your teen might head off to a juggling convention or a summer program in England. Mountain climbing, caving, camping, rappelling, scuba diving, and more can all be part of your homeschool program. Remember, it's not just a homeschool . . . it's an adventure!

Photo by Randy Levensaler. Provided courtesy of Summit Adventure.

Start homeschooling and see . . . Russia? Here we see the Clarkson and Custer homeschool families in costume for the musical-drama, The Promise, at the Kremlin Palace Theater in Moscow, Russia. "The response of the Russian people to the production was overwhelmingly positive. During one of the seven performances, the upper tier of the 6,000-seat facility was opened for the first time in the history of the theater," reported former Practical Homeschooling *columnist Clay Clarkson. The Moscow production also was filmed by TBN and was dubbed in Russian for broadcast to millions of Russian viewers.*

CHAPTER 56

Field Trips

Field Trips! They are something every homeschooling family winds up scheduling sooner or later. Unless you are living in the isolated back country, chances are your community is packed with learning opportunities for the home-teaching family. And all just for the asking.

Would the idea of digging for human bones alongside a real archeologist absolutely enthrall your adventure lover? Would the prospect of dipping mosquito larvae out of a swamp fascinate your science whiz? Would your teen like to spend a little time with a bank president, brain surgeon, attorney, or the mayor? Is Dad looking for an excuse to take a behind-the-scenes peek at that new state-of-the-art forensic lab, astronomy lab, or SCUBA shop? How about the Blue Angels air show next weekend? Uh . . . with the children, of course!

Over the course of a few weeks, I discovered that our community was absolutely teeming with over 300 teaching tours and tempting trips. Every time I thought there could be nothing else a homeschooler could ever want to see or do, I would think of (another) new idea, spot a new source, or stumble across an activity—while not even looking!

If all these learning opportunities are available in and around our town of 50,000, what kinds of possibilities are there in *your* town?

Just Ask

The secret to finding the best field trips in town, lies in . . . just asking. Chances are your community is packed with a variety of fantastic hands-on learning opportunities, educational guided tours, and career-shadowing possibilities. Even that new swim park with the killer slides will probably let you in for half price, as long as you book using group rates and have enough children at the gate.

If you share the results of your research with your local support group, or are willing to place a copy of your finished product in the public library, you will want to use the actual numbers of homeschooled students in your area, instead of asking about a single-family tour. This not only adds credibility to your survey, it makes it easier on each business, which might be willing to host three field trips per year for 20 students at a time, as opposed to 20 field trips (or none) for three students at a time. It also lets

The author of this chapter, **Mardy Freeman**, has been homeschooling her seven children with the help of her husband, Bill, for 16 years. She is a regular contributor to the *FPEA Almanac,* the magazine of the Florida Parent Educators Association, and a popular conference speaker. She is also the author of *Children of Character,* a practical handbook for parents on how to raise children with good character, available from her site at **www.afn.org/~afn18300/** or from **www.rocksolidinc.com**. Her free newsletter, *A Mary Heart* (based on Luke 10), can be requested through her website or by emailing *amaryheart-subscribe@associate.com.*

> I think one of the best things about being home-schooled is the chance to get into my community. I've been behind the scenes at many local businesses, and I enjoy knowing how my community works. I'm sure you'll enjoy it too!
>
> —*Online columnist Leslie Goyer is the ten-year-old daughter of Practical Homeschooling reviewer Tricia Goyer.*

you know who is offering group rates. And it helps out your fellow home-schoolers.

What to Ask

Here is what to say: "I am putting together a simple (or comprehensive) guide to educational opportunities for X number of homeschooling students in our area. I have a few questions for your organization." Stay clear and to the point. Remember, you are using their time. Then ask appropriate questions. It should take no more than a few minutes.

1. Do you offer any type of group tour/guided tour/educational tour/school tour/career-shadowing opportunities, etc.?
2. What is the minimum number of students for which you would schedule? The maximum?
3. How much advance notice would you prefer?
4. How long do you estimate a tour would last?
5. What kind of things will a student observe?
6. Are there any special restrictions? (No preschoolers? Age- or interest-grouped? Materials to study before arriving?)
7. If there is an entrance fee, what are the restrictions and prices for group rates?
8. Would you like us to schedule with you, or is there someone else who should take the reservation? If so, what is this person's name and number?
9. Where are you located, and what is your mailing address? (So you can send a thank-you note later.)

Sometimes your contact has never been asked these types of questions and will falter for answers or ask you what you want out of a tour. Think about these things before you call.

They Usually Just Say Yes!

Whom to ask is just as simple. Anyone. Everyone. Does your daughter dream about one day being an actress? Ask your local playhouse or theater if they would be open to a behind-the-scenes tour, and invite other students. Or offer to have you and your daughter usher one night in exchange for viewing a play.

Do you have a future Dr. Doolittle? "I always have room in the truck for one more," was the response of the horse and cow vet I found in the Yellow Pages, adding, "Long as they don't mind gettin' a little dirty, and walkin' round a bit, they can watch me all day long!"

Out of approximately 300 sources I checked, only two said they could not accommodate some number of students during the year. And in both of those cases, it was due to limited space or time, and never to unwilling-ness to participate.

Our infamous "Mosquito Trip" was the result of calling the city mosqui-to-control program. "Students will learn the lifecycle of the mosquito, re-lease mosquito fish, use a dipper to collect mosquito larvae, distribute bri-quettes used to keep larvae from becoming adult mosquitoes, and more," said my contact. "We'll spend a good two hours in a nasty swamp," she promised. My kids can't wait.

The archeological dig was "unearthed" by calling a firm in the Yellow Pages, listed under "archeology." "We *love* getting high-schoolers to volun-teer on a dig," chuckled the manager. "By the end of the day, they have worked off any illusions that real archeology is even close to the Indy Jones variety. But," she emphasizes, "for those who are kindling a genuine spark of interest, a dig will often fuel that flame, whether we find what we were looking for or not. Those are the kind we talk their ears off. And they keep coming back."

A Taste of the Country . . . and City

I found the following opportunities for our support group of about 135 families just by calling City, County, and State Listings in the Government section of the phone book:

- **City/County Commission Meetings.** Students can arrive early, personally meet each commissioner, and then be recognized during this public meeting.
- **Courtroom.** Students can attend First Appearances, Traffic Court, Court, and more. They may stay to meet the judge and ask questions, depending on previous arrangements with the judge's schedule.
- **Fire Station.** The fire engine will even come to your group for a tour, if requested!
- **Fire Safety.** Smokey Bear Presentation for K–3 includes fire safety, use of matches, how wildfires start, a short video, and a visit from Smokey Bear.
- **Grocery Stores.** From receiving to bakery to the registers, covers every aspect of the store and finishes off with free coloring books and a bakery treat.
- **Jail.** Walk through the entire incarceration process from booking to release, observing the prisoners, laundry area, commissary, and living quarters.
- **Landfill.** Observe a leachate treatment plant, methane gas processing, class one and three waste, and more.
- **Library.** A preschool story hour, elementary-age-level instruction on library layout, and computerized card catalogs. High school tours offering instruction on specialized resource tools, such as microfiche and indexes. Free basic and advanced Internet classes for all ages.
- **Mosquito Control.** "Wear casual clothes. Bring pencils and paper. We'll provide the mosquito dippers!"
- **Nuclear Power Plant.** Includes a free museum filled with hands-on exhibits and scientific principles and history of energy sources.
- **Police Station.** Students will see and learn about the inside of a police car, communications, records, detective division, fingerprint technician, and forensic lab.
- **Post Office.** "The smaller the group, the more fun we have!" this contact teased. She asks students to bring a stamped letter to themselves or to each other in the same group to mail. They can then follow their letter through each machine and receive it the next morning in their own mailbox, having observed and understood the coded markings on the envelope.
- **Recycling Center.** Observe various recycling opportunities, and learn ways in which you can help.
- **State Legislature.** A Page/Messenger program is available upon acceptance. Students 12 and up are paid to work one week for their Representative during the regular legislative session.

PLACES TO LOOK FOR FIELD TRIP IDEAS
- Cultural and historical societies
- Elected officials
- Friends and family
- Government administration
- Grandparents/seniors
- Homeschoolers
- Newspapers
- Internet
- Outlying communities
- Professionals in your church, social life and neighborhood
- Universities and colleges
- Yellow Pages

The A to Z Guide to Home School Field Trips

Parents. $21.95.
Noble Publishing Associates, WA, (800)
225-5259, www.noblepublishing.com.

The A to Z Guide to Home School Field Trips, edited by Gregg Harris, is a wonderful resource for planning field trips or just gathering field trip ideas. The field trips include everything from "A"—a trip to an advertising agency—to "Z", a trip to the zoo. Fun idea for field trips include visiting a beekeeper, the city government, garbage disposal site or junk yard, a midwife, and a real estate broker. Most any place in your community can be turned into a field trip using this handbook!

In the "contents" section, field trips are listed in alphabetical order. Then under each entry, you get background information to use to research before your trip. You'll also find a list of possible questions to ask while on your field trip, a vocabulary list to study, and "Tips from Barnabus" sidebars with biblical perspectives on that topic. There's also a small space to write down the name of the place you are visiting, the contact person's name, telephone number, address and best time to visit, allowing you to use the book as a permanent record of your field trips.

The variety of topics covered and the well-organized layout make this book a very useful tool to plan and document extra activities for your homeschool. *Maryann Turner*

- **State Parks.** In my area, these sell an annual family pass that allows free entrance into all state parks for up to eight immediate family members. I found 15 state parks, many of them with hiking trails, swimming areas, canoe-rental, ranger-led hikes (arranged in advance), camping, and free educational nature talks, all within 40 miles.
- **Waste Water Management.** Follow the process of waste water from start (raw sewage) to finish (effluent). Learn about sludge, and biological and chemical treatment tanks. Tour includes 15 minute video. At the drinking water plant, students will observe the lime-softening process, chlorination, fluoridation, filtration and infiltration. Learn how water begins in the environment and ends up in your home.

By posting a "Field Trip Ideas" question onto some Internet homeschooling newsgroups, and asking other homeschooling families, I found these opportunities:

- **Airport.** Complete tour of the airport, including boarding the private UF Gator football team's plane and other commercial planes when available.
- **Animal Retirement Center.** See retired zoo animals in a close-up environment with guided tours.
- **Architect.** A tour and explanation of the many facets of designing and building various types of architecture.
- **Astronomy Lab and Observatory.** A free guided tour, including star-gazing through powerful telescopes.
- **Bakeries and donut shops.** Local bakeries were fairly limited due to early baking hours small working space. Large name-brand bread bakeries are easier to get into.
- **Fire Engines.** We have a plant where children can observe fire engines being assembled!
- **4-H.** Free career-mentoring programs for members. One does not have to participate in a club, but may be a "home-study" member.
- **Horse Farm Tours.** Area Thoroughbred racing farms give these free.
- **K-9 Demonstration.** Sheriff's Office offers two-hour demonstrations with dogs trained to do tracking, bomb detection, aggressive protection, article and narcotics searches. Students will handle animals.
- **Museums/Art Galleries.** At least five, all with different themes, four of them right in town.
- **Pizza Huts.** From the Internet, I learned that all Pizza Huts offer tours in which students tour the kitchen and then create and eat their own personal pan pizza before store hours, just for the cost of the pizza.
- **Radio Stations.** Not one turned down my request for a tour. One station allowed our children to stay during a live two-hour "Old Time Radio" broadcast.
- **Reptiles.** A slide presentation, plus live snakes and baby alligators that every student can handle during the presentation. Teaches students how to identify poisonous snakes and what to do. Free.
- **Science Center.** Observatory, planetarium, plus hands-on science exhibits, with discounted field trip rates. Another is pri-

vately owned and offers two-hour workshops on a scientific principle, or an overnight scientific excursion with group rates.

- **Ship.** School tours offered aboard Navy ships in port.
- **Television Station.** Students tour the entire station, including general offices, newsroom, studio, and control room.
- **Tourist/Vacation/Fun Spots.** For us Florida residents, substantial discounts on field-trip rates for spots such as EPCOT, Florida Sports Hall of Fame, Kennedy Space Center, Marineland, Sea World, Silver Springs, and Wild Waters.
- **Veterinarians.** Every clinic and hospital asked to be posted for school tours.
- **Wildlife Sanctuary.** See endangered animals, threatened and rare cougars, wolves, cats, deer, hawks, owl, prairie dogs. Group rates for school tours.
- **Wildlife Museums and Zoos.** Two in our area are free; two have group rates for school tours.

Where to Find More Great Field Trips

By asking our local Cultural and Historical Societies I learned of a permanent Picasso exhibit, an original 1800s plantation, a historical tour that allows students to try on period costumes, and countless local, state and national historical landmarks, such as forts, burial mounds, Civil War re-enactments, and famous explorer trails. There were usually plenty of free maps and teaching material available.

In looking for fun individual and group sporting-type activities, I received a newcomer's guide to our city published by the Junior Women's League, and I also called City Hall and checked the Yellow Pages. I found archery and rifle ranges, bicycling tours, and hiking trails, all free. I also located a list of all the public parks and playgrounds that showed which ones had baseball diamonds, basketball courts, tennis and racquetball courts, picnic tables, grills, playground equipment, restrooms, and swimming pools. And finally, group rates at bowling alleys, mini-golf centers, and ice- and roller-skating rinks are available . . . just for the asking.

From the newspaper, the events section in the phone book, and by asking the city administration and local homeschooling families, I also discovered annual local events such as a Civil War battle re-enactment, a medieval fair, a sailboat race, a free professionally-done Passion Play, a free walk through a recreated Bethlehem, the Nutcracker Ballet with special field trip rates, and a student Walk Through the Orchestra in which students actually "walk through" an orchestra during a performance. I found arts and folk festivals, historical and holiday parades and festivities, sugarcane boiling demonstrations, State Legislature in session, air shows with skydivers, stunt planes, military jets and ultralights, and last but not least, county-, youth-, historical-, engineering-, and career-oriented fairs.

Do you have a college nearby? Many state universities give mini school tours in the various colleges of interest. Ours sponsors four science symposia a year in which homeschoolers may participate. Additionally, the Colleges of Agriculture, Astronomy, Entomology, Journalism, Law, Medicine, and Veterinary Science all offer individual field trips. There is also a free natural history museum with changing exhibits.

Have you checked what's happening in your surrounding communities? Christmas and Independence Day parades and festivities are often "downhomier" and packed full of old-fashioned activities in smaller towns. Annual events that commemorate a town's origins often have activities that

Carschooling

Parents. $16.95.
Prima Publishing, CA. (800) 733-3000, www.primapublishing.com.

Spending way too much time in the car on your way to and from vital locations such as the homeschool co-op, field trips, grocery shopping . . .? Feeling guilty because your kids are missing out on precious educational time while trapped in the car?

"Carschooling" may be the answer! The new book by Diane Flynn Keith, **Carschooling: Over 500 Entertaining Games & Activities to Turn Travel Time into Learning Time**, seeks to provide an entire curriculum for everything from preschool through high school—all made up of games and audio resources you can use in your car. Not content merely to cover all the standard school subjects (which she does, one chapter to each), the very complete table of contents even tackles such unexpected topics as "Carschooling Visual & Performing Arts." I've seen a sample of this curriculum, and it is well adapted to the mobile homeschool.

By the way, "Carschooling" is now a registered trademark. Beware, idea poachers!

—*Mary Pride*

are very educational and fun. What about grandparents, or seniors in your church or neighborhood? Do you have a retired rocket scientist, narcotics agent, or business owner?

Career Shadowing

To discover what types of high-school opportunities were available, I added one more question to my list.

> **"If one or more high-school students were considering a career in your field, would you allow a more technical career-shadowing or career-mentoring opportunity?"**

An incredible amount of organizations said, "Yes!" Each offered a different scenario, but all of them were tempting. Airports, architectural firms, banks, fire stations, hospitals, veterinarians, SCUBA shops, radio and television stations, along with the library, newspaper, nuclear power plant, police station, and waste water facility all expressed a fairly high degree of enthusiasm about sponsoring high-school-only tours or career days. I even called our city commissioners, who agreed to begin a "Spend the Day with a Commissioner" Day for homeschooled high schoolers! If your community sponsors any kind of career-shadowing program for high-school students, chances are homeschoolers can take part. It is just a matter of learning the requirements.

Don't forget to survey other homeschooling parents to see if they would be willing to sponsor a tour at their place of business. One homeschooling father who programs for an insurance company had already been giving high-school tours of the data-processing department from operations to main-frame programming. He quickly agreed to be listed for the entire support group.

I then had the idea of asking other business men and women if they would be willing to participate in a career-mentoring day for area homeschooled high schoolers. Of the 30 people I spoke with—a bank president, a brain surgeon, three attorneys, a pediatrician, developers, engineers, scientists, and therapists—all granted permission for high schoolers to shadow them for a day. Most of them were eager to discuss career options to the level of the student's knowledge and interest.

Our local Police Department explained that students 14 to 18 with good grades and high recommendations need not be in Boy Scouts to apply for the free Boy Scout-sponsored "Explorer Program," though acceptance makes one an automatic Boy Scout member. The program includes a free uniform and shoes, and summer academy training. Student activities include patrolling with an officer, assisting with special events, election returns, etc.

For the Truly Motivated . . .

Nothing interest you yet? Don't forget ideas like father/son campouts and hikes, and moms-only slumber parties (this mom's all-time favorite field trip!). Or how about a Couples-Only Sweetheart Dinner created by one of our moms?

Have you called and discovered that some of these programs are not available in your community? Offer to help start some! To start the career-shadowing program with our city commission took only one phone call and then posting the information to our group. Many times it only takes a few calls to connect the right people.

If all of this seems too close to home, you could always get a group of families together and tour our nation's capitol for a week. In the spring and fall, the weather is nicer, the crowds are fewer, and all the Smithsonians are free. If you are going on vacation, be sure to call ahead to the Chamber of Commerce or City Hall in the areas you plan to stay. Ask them to forward a newcomer's packet, and ask what is available for visitors. Chances are there are many free educational tours available just for the asking. Vacations tend to be one big field trip anyway. And if you can plan to meet other families at some of your favorite fun spots, you can probably qualify for some type of group rate or discount. All you have to do . . . is ask.

CHAPTER 57

Family Educational Travel

Are you an Action Mom or Dad? Do you like to get in the car and go, go, go to see new places? Looking for more excitement than you can find in field trips around your town? Then this chapter is for you! Books introduce a subject. Videos present it visually. But taking a trip to actually see and experience what you've read about and watched on the screen makes a particular subject "personal."

Visiting educational sites away from home gives my children the opportunity to look forward to the variety of ways a subject can be illustrated. Of course, while I (as the teacher) perceive these excursions as an opportunity to learn, my children view them as fun adventures.

Many Kinds of Museums

When it comes to places to visit, museums are at the top of my list, mainly because they provide an excellent method of teaching many subjects. You do, however, need to be aware that there are general guidelines for visiting all museums and some that vary from one place to another.

If you plan to visit a museum, make certain you call beforehand. Exhibits change throughout the year, and viewing times vary depending on the season. Also, keep in mind that most museums are closed on Mondays.

Since many school groups schedule their outings during the morning, the best time to attend a museum is afternoon. Naturally, during this less crowded period of time, the curators are available to answer questions, and the exhibits and displays are much more accessible.

Overall, we enjoy a wide variety of activities. Below, I've included some examples of the experiences that have greatly enhanced my homeschooling curriculum.

For supplementing the lesson plans I teach, I find that **historical museums** are an excellent visual source. Generally, they are categorized by theme such as local history, famous person, or cultural group. To help reinforce the subject, many historical museums provide interactive videos, questions and answer games, large storyboards, and dioramas. And since educational handouts and lesson plans are distributed throughout the museums to supplement their exhibits, we usually take these so we can work on them during the drive back home.

The author of this chapter, **Leila Randle**, graduated from Indiana University in 1988 with an MBA in Management Information Systems. She also worked as a Systems Analyst at major corporations in the Indianapolis, Indiana area for ten years. Currently, she is homeschooling her ten-year-old son, Dee Jay, and two-year-old daughter, Lindsey. Her most recent endeavor includes traveling around the country and writing a series of guides entitled *Soul Family Travels,* which reference regional historic and cultural activities throughout the US. If you'd like to experience all the adventures firsthand, make certain you visit her website at **www.soulfamilytravels.com**.

OLDER KIDS CAN TRAVEL ON THEIR OWN

Educational travel is not just for families. Our older children have traveled on their own to:

- International Jugglers Association conventions in Quebec, Nevada, and Pennsylvania
- Summit Adventures outdoor camp
- Worldview Academy camps in western Missouri and Texas
- Texas A&M Sea Camp in Galveston, TX
- Cambridge University Summer Program in Cambridge, England!

Generally, our younger teens got their first travel experience with us, then with an older sibling, and then went solo.

These are some of the most memorable educational experiences our children have had.

Bonus: University admissions officials love to see this kind of proof that homeschooled kids are not home*bound* kids tied to their mom's apron strings!

—*Mary Pride*

Living museums bring to life a period of time in the past. Docents walk around in full dress, talking and performing tasks that reflect the specific time period. Within these communities you'll find shops so you can actually purchase a piece of history. Overall, visiting these museums gives me the opportunity to teach how living off of the land was not a cliché but rather a way of life. To reinforce this concept of daily living that was presented by one of the museums, I even purchased a handloom so we could learn the fine art of weaving.

Art museums are an excellent choice, providing the ability to visualize the variety of ways individuals can express themselves. Not only are works displayed in time periods, types of art, and by culture, brochures and post cards capturing these creations are dispersed throughout the museum. We make a point of collecting these in order to compare and contrast the different artists and time periods. A great example of comparing artistic forms was experienced during our visit to the Columbus Art Museum, where you can take a snapshot of yourself and then view it as impressionist, expressionist, pop, or cubist art.

Science museums provide the ability to put theory and hypothesis studied in books into actual testing and practical applications. In general, these museums are defined by age appropriateness as well as subject area. Demonstrations and hands-on experiments are arranged to involve children, at their learning level. Also, many areas are designed to build items in order to learn specific concepts. For example, my two-year-old daughter built cars with plastic hammers while my ten-year-old son was able to build his own car with wood, a jig saw, and sandpaper. Plus, we were able to take these creations home and display them on our shelves as visual reminders of the experience.

History on the Road

Historical sites not only immortalize individuals and events that changed the course of history, they emphasize the significance of the contribution. We always make a point of driving to these locations during the day so we can take pictures for our history book.

If you'd like to actively participate in a specific period of time, **historical re-enactments** provide the perfect opportunity. Make certain, however, that you check how appropriate it is with regard to certain age groups. We attended an Underground Railroad journey re-enactment in which audience participation was not optional and felt it was much too intense for our children. On the other hand, having attended an Elijah McCoy characterization where the actor brought the story of this inventor to life, we found the performance engaging, entertaining, and very enlightening. He was the real McCoy!

Designated to a specific sport, a **Hall of Fame** is generally organized by their audience, for example, professional, collegian, or local. When a high achiever of the sport is inducted into the museum, their plaque is displayed in a shrine area. Many of these museums have running videos that depict both famous moments in time as well as the accomplishments of the honored player. Also, you'll find trivia games throughout the museum that allow you to test your knowledge about the specific sport. Personally, we have begun collecting pendants from all the different sports museums we've visited and then displaying them on the walls of my son's bedroom.

Renaissance faires are held all around the country, mostly during the summer and early fall. These fairs seek to re-enact the Middle Ages through costumed performers, artisans, jousting tournaments, and the like. If you don't live near a town with its own Renaissance Faire, you might want to include such a stopover in your travel plans.

Expos, Fairs, & Festivals

Expos are an excellent means of seeing the variety of business opportunities that are available. During the week, workshops are given, and weekends are filled with entertainment. To make the most of our own expo adventures, we purposely attend the vendor exhibition during the same time a free concert is given. This allows us the opportunity to visit vendor booths without all the crowd congestion. A lot of people feel the best time to attend an expo is on closing day because you can get a good "deal," but that just isn't the case. By then, the crowds have picked over the vendors' items, which means you don't have a good selection to choose from. Plus, the vendors are tired and busy packing their things. They're basically ready to move on to the next expo at that point and are not really interested in liquidating their inventory.

State fairs, **rodeos**, and **country fairs** are a great way to get up close and personal with farm animals, machinery, produce, and people. The biggest and best are in the Midwest, so if you plan to vacation there, you might be able to take in a fair!

Speciality fairs, such as the annual Airshow in Oshkosh, WI, can either spark an interest or nourish an interest your family already has. Look for fairs, such as the Airshow, that offer lots of booths and activities for the kids to participate in.

Local festivals, which provide a good way to experience different cultures, are celebrated every weekend throughout the summer in most towns. Generally, we attend these festivals on Friday for dinner. That way, we not only experience "authentic" cuisine of the culture, we get entertained in the process as well.

Education via Entertainment

Theme parks are a great way to visually explain nature. For example, at Sea World, we were able to experience aquatic animals in their natural habitat. All through the day, shows were given, helping to explain what life would be like for these animals. There were also opportunities available throughout the park to feed the animals, which definitely made it a great experience for the kids.

When it comes to exposing kids to farm animals, you just can't beat a good old-fashioned **petting zoo**. After all, feeding and petting animals is definitely the best way to get to know them firsthand. On one occasion, we even had the opportunity to see the birth of piglets.

A **circus** provides entertainment that makes you believe you can achieve anything if you just work hard. We attend the matinee shows, primarily because the prices are more reasonable, and since school groups pick them up, we always purchase our tickets when they first go on sale. Overall, the money we save on ticket prices allows us to purchase a booklet to remember our experience there.

Attending **traveling carnivals** is a fun way to take a break from the homeschooling routine. We always go during weekdays and purchase the all-you-can-ride armbands. By doing so, we not only save money but avoid the evening and weekend crowds.

Sporting events not only demonstrate team play, they have become our family picnics and free entertainment events during summer months. There are even areas designated in our baseball arena for families to picnic and to get into the game for free.

Roadside attractions have sparked some of our most memorable family conversations. To remember these moments, we visit during the day and take lots of pictures.

SCIENCE MUSEUM FREAKS, READ THIS!

My final advice? Purchase an ASTC (Association of Science-Technology Centers) membership. Their membership can be purchased at any science museum in their affiliation or online through their website, **www.astc.org**. This alone will provide your family the ability to get into more than 250 science museums throughout the country. Plus, a homeschooling family rate is available, and since we personally like visiting science museums, the ASTC membership has saved us a good deal of money.

—*Leila Randle*

Field Trips to Someone Else's Town

Factories are a good way to see how products are manufactured from beginning to end. Some famous factories, such as the Hershey's plant in Hershey, Pennsylvania, regularly welcome out-of-town families on their tours. Generally, though, I rely on library videos for viewing this type of activity. Also, the Food Network has special shows that depict the production of various types of food. We simply tape these shows and then discuss them.

Specialty Shops are a great source for locating unique items. It's a good idea to phone ahead to find out what they're selling and the hours the shop is open. And since most of these places are found in out-of-the-way areas, you might want to ask for directions as well. One of the largest distributors of foreign, classic, cult, art, and hard-to-find videos is Facets Multi-Media. They even allow you to rent from more than 40,000 videos by mail, which really helps when I'm trying to decide which videos I would like to keep in my collection.

Well, there you have it. All the activities I use to enhance the homeschooling curriculum. Wherever you travel this year—across the country, across the state, or across town—take your homeschool with you. You'll be making memories as a family and learning about life.

And that's what homeschooling is all about!

CHAPTER 58

Conferences, Retreats, & Homeschool Days for the Whole Family

I n the last two chapters we looked at how you could use your imagination and creativity to turn "going places with the kids" into an educational experience. In the Field Trips chapter, you learned how to turn your entire community into a real-world learning laboratory. In the Educational Travel chapter, you learned how to switch hats from "tourist" to "teacher" while on the road.

In both cases, the places you and your kids were visiting were not set up for the convenience of homeschool families. Some of the best field-trip locations in your town may never have been visited by a homeschool family before. And, since the number of students in public and private schools outnumber homeschoolers 100 to 2, you're more likely to encounter large groups of schoolkids at a museum or zoo than you are to run into your local homeschool group.

While there is some value in rubbing shoulders with a mixture of people, including those who don't share your beliefs or behavior, it is not always the most relaxing experience. There is also much to be said for the opportunity to get together with others of like mind.

In this chapter, we'll be looking at educational events and experiences specifically designed for homeschool families, plus a few that, although they aren't restricted to homeschoolers, are outstandingly "homeschool friendly." Some of these events are more specifically for *Christian* homeschool families, although you don't have to be a Christian to attend. Others are just for homeschoolers in general. These are places you can take your whole family for a day, weekend, or week together with fellow homeschoolers.

Take a family hike at Glorieta Conference Center . . . ride a roller coaster at Homeschool Day . . . cruise the ocean . . . or more, at special events and excursions just for you!

Homeschool Retreats

For a few days or a full week, a homeschool conference is a wonderful chance to recharge your batteries as a family and enjoy some time seeing new sights and meeting new people.

Glorieta Home School Retreat

Glorieta Conference Center
PO Box 8
Glorieta, NM 87535
(800) 797-4222
www.lifeway.com/glorieta

Glorieta Conference Center in Glorieta, New Mexico, holds an annual homeschooling conference. The conference center has many recreational activities—everything from horseback riding (pictured on the left), hiking, playing mini-golf, and boating, to just sitting back and taking in the wonders of God's creation in the Sangre de Cristo mountains.

I went there once as a speaker with my older kids, and they liked it so much they went back again on their own.

My son Joseph says, "The woods are fun to explore, the mini-golf course is challenging yet beatable, the air is fresh, and the trees are good to climb!" He should know—this is where he and his sister Sarah went on their first "snipe hunt"!

Each year special homeschool speakers are featured, and there are lots of workshops as well. Special activities vary from year to year, but have been known to include ballet, gymnastics, and a special lineup of activities for teens.

The package for a family of four, which includes food, lodging, recreation, and attendance at all conference activities for the entire five days, comes to under $900. You can get a good price on an extra room as well.

There are a number of lodging options, with prices ranging down to $279 for a tent site. If you bring a camper, this can be quite an affordable vacation!

TRAVELER'S TIP: Being high in the Rocky Mountains, the air at Glorieta is somewhat thinner than at sea-level. So you may find yourself short of breath before your lungs adjust to the thinner air. If you plan on visiting Glorieta, or any other mountain retreat, go and enjoy the view; but don't push yourself too hard if you're not used to the altitude.

Sandy Cove Homeschool Conference

Sandy Cove Ministries
60 Sandy Cove Road
North East, MD 21901-0257
(800) 234-2683
www.sandycove.org

A few thousand miles east, and a few thousand feet closer to sea level, you might try the annual **Sandy Cove Family Homeschool Conference**. The Sandy Cove conference center is located on the beautiful shores of the Chesapeake Bay in Maryland. This week-long homeschool conference is filled with all kinds of educational and fun activities, including well-known homeschool speakers. For instance, for several years, *Practical Homeschooling* columnist Kathy von Duyke was a featured speaker along with her husband, Tim, the owner of "Tim's Great Stuff" bagging service for homeschool conferences.

For lodging, you can splurge with a suite or pitch a tent on the campground. Take the whole family! Try out boats and waterskiing, hiking, minigolf, field trips, and more! This conference is focused more on Christian family life than homeschool per se, but it will have a curriculum fair, some homeschool workshops, and enough activities to make it worthwhile.

Get cool in the Sandy Cove pool!

The annual **HELP Conference**, sponsored by Bob Jones University Press, provides a chance for many homeschool parents to meet, receive encouragement, learn useful skills and techniques from others who've been there, and look at many kinds of curriculum in their Exhibit Hall, including of course the famous Bob Jones University Press line of materials. I've spoken there myself. Speakers in 2001 included Congressman Lindsey Graham, Janet Pershall (host of a national conservative talk show), Rev. Louis Sheldon (American Liberties Institute), and Bob Jones IV (Washington-based editor for *World* magazine). The convention is hosted at "The World's Most Unusual University," Bob Jones University in beautiful South Carolina, and is mostly targeted towards adults, though BJUP does allow you to bring the kids. The cost includes day care.

BJU requires conference attendees to agree to some behavior and attire restrictions, which are spelled out in the pre-conference registration kit. Basically, these involve their idea of modest dress for all family members, and sober and edifying behavior.

Home Education Leadership Program (HELP)

Bob Jones University Press
Greenville, SC 29614-0062
(864) 242-5100
www.bjup.com

TRAVELER'S TIP: Be sure to put aside some time to tour the campus. Don't miss their Art Museum, which houses an amazingly impressive number of paintings by famous artists!

EdVenture Tour

Go Classy Tours
Palm Harbor Executive Center
2676 West Lake Road
Palm Harbor, FL 34684
(888) 825-2779 or (813) 781-1405
www.goclassy.com/homeschool
/details.htm

Home Schooler's "Paradise" Cruise

AABA Cruise & Vacation Superstore
98 Powers Ferry Rd
Marietta, GA 30067
(770) 509-2500
www.cruisesale.com

For more information about the Carnival Paradise ship, including lots of photos of the various rooms on the ship, go to **www.cruiseweb. com/CARNIVAL-PARADISE.HTM**.

Windjammers Barefoot Cruises

Windjammers
1759 Bay Road
Miami Beach, FL 33139-1413
(800) 327-2601
www.windjammer.com

Homeschool Family Sun & Sea Adventures

Get into sea activities while sleeping ashore with the **annual EdVenture** by **Go Classy Tours.** This homeschool vacation opportunity has been available for three years in a row now, so it seems likely to continue. Spend an off-season week (sometime from late August to late September) at the Franklyn D. Resort in Jamaica! If you can afford a reasonably-priced resort vacation, you should check out the EdVenture. It's designed especially with the homeschooler in mind.

All week the FDR staff will host educational field trips and studies on the wildlife, geography, history, and culture around you in sunny Jamaica. Many of the courses will be taught by graduate students from the University of the West Indies Discovery Bay Marine Laboratory. I understand you get to explore the Marine Lab itself as well. You can check in on Saturday, go to church Sunday morning and spend the day relaxing, or maybe learning to sail, then during the week go SCUBA diving, take a glass bottom boat tour, learn about fish in Jamaican waters, or even hang out in the fully-equipped computer lab (though a Jamaica vacation seems a trifle too interesting to waste using computers). Every family will be assigned a "Vacation Nanny," who will make sure your stay is pleasant, and even help out with the kids if needed. The website has tons of details about the educational and fun options, plus everything you need to know about price options, so be sure to check it out.

Caribbean cruise vacation just for homeschoolers? The first one ran in 2001. Hosted by Dick Warren Worldwide Travel, a Christian-run company, the **Home Schooler's "Paradise" Cruise** for several years has visited Grand Cayman and Cozumel, and sailed up the Mississippi River Delta to New Orleans. Like  other "just for homeschoolers" events, this cruise has taken advantage of the fact that homeschoolers can take the whole family away from home in the "off season." Prices are lower because this cruise is in November.

One of the Carnival cruise line's ships will be both your home and your transportation on this week-long cruise. Your luxury liner will have a beauty salon; a number of on-board restaurants; and a gym, spa, pools, and jogging track. (A week of lounging doesn't have to kill your exercise program!) There are also lounges, a children's playroom, and a number of other attractions on this huge ship.

Here's where the education comes in. You can, of course, go ashore at any of the ports and explore, but you can also take tours priced from $16 up to $99. The tours are cultural (San Juan City and Shopping Tour), entertaining (Juan Carlos and His Flamenco Rumba Show), scientific (Bioluminescence Bay Kayak Tour), or simply unique (Glass Bottom Boat or Submarine tours).

For those who prefer a more hands-on sea adventure, **Windjammer Barefoot Cruises**, "the largest operator of tall ships in the world," is offering 6- and 13-day Caribbean sailing expeditions, targeted toward any able-bodied youngster with a spirit of adventure. There's a new expedition starting every Monday throughout June, July, and August. You can choose between two tall ships, the Flying Cloud and the Legacy, and learn skills such as trimming the sails, manning the helm, celestial navigation, tying knots, and other sailing skills. You can listen to sailor stories, enjoy music and dancing, and go on island excursions, including water sports and shoreside exploration. There's music and dancing onboard the ships, and when you're done with the whole experience you are awarded a cadet sailing certificate. You receive personal attention from counselors and water sports counselors. All the above is included in the Cadet Program, for ages 13–17.

Cadets need to bring along at least one parent or responsible adult (who pays the adult rate). Junior Jammers (age 6–12) get 50 percent off if one parent is along or can come along free if both parents are coming. Parents are not necessarily expected to hang around while the kids are doing their thing during the day.

Bear in mind that Windjammers also offers gay and singles cruises, and their family and teen activities are *not* specifically designed for homeschoolers. So you won't likely find as protected an environment as with the other "sea" options. Still, this is the only "ships with sails" activity for the whole family I've been able to locate thus far.

You can get this cool "wallpaper" for your computer desktop from the Windjammers website, plus about a dozen more!

Homeschool Family Camps & Safaris

Explore the last remaining frontierland on earth! Any kid who enjoys the Walt Morey books should love this trip. While not exclusively targeted at homeschoolers, "It is intended for active parents and grandparents who want to experience virtually every moment of their vacation with their children or grandchildren." In this era of "family" vacations where the kids spend all day with planned activities apart from their parents, I'd have to say that homeschoolers are probably the most logical group to whom this kind of vacation will appeal.

Lasting eight days and seven nights, the **Alaska Family Safari** includes everything from dinner on day one to fees, tickets, permits, lodging, transportation, guided events, and more. Beginning in Fairbanks, AK, the Safari takes you by way of the historic Alaska Railroad to Denali National Park, then to Talkeetna and Kenai Fjords. There you can take a small ship cruise and watch the glaciers and the wildlife. Mountain bikes are available for exploration. You can explore on your own, gold-pan, try grail fishing, take guided hikes led by trained naturalists, and enjoy naturalist programs in the evenings. For example, see wildlife photographers give slide shows and stories of their explorations, or wildflower experts and mountain climbers present their Alaska adventures. Very educational for anybody who wants to come back and explore on his own. Several of these Family Safaris are available in June, July, and August.

Here are a few of the activities you can participate in on the Alaska Family Safari. You could take a tour of the Alaska Sea Life Center, a research and showing facility, which recently unveiled a new marine wildlife and marine habitat exhibit. You can visit the new Alaska Native Heritage Center, where you learn about the history and culture of Alaska's native peoples. You can try more adventuresome activities, like kayaking, scenic rafting (no rapids, just a splendid view), or a one-day small-ship cruise to Kenai Fjords National Park, where you can see puffins, whales, otters, sea lions, eagles, mountain goats, and of course bears. The cruise rides by the glaciers, where you sometimes get to watch icebergs calve off.

The cost per person, even the kids, is about $3,000—about twice the cost of a dude ranch vacation and about 20 times the cost per person of the next (admittedly less scenic) family vacation option. So this would probably be a "once in a lifetime" trip, and you'd want to check it carefully in advance. Happily, the excellent website has more than enough information, photos, maps, and everything else you need to decide if this "homeschool of the rich and famous" type trip is for you!

Alaska Family Safari
Alaska Wildland Adventures
PO Box 389
Girdwood, AK 99587
(800) 334-8730 or (907) 783-2928
www.alaskawildland.com

Alpha Omega Institute

PO Box 4343
Grand Junction, CO 81502
(970) 523-9943
www.discovercreation.org

Aptly termed a "learning adventure," Alpha Omega's **Creation Mountain Adventure** offers inexpensive summer vacation packages in Colorado for the whole family.

There are plenty of opportunities for hiking, fishing, horseback riding, four-wheel drive trips, rock climbing, and rappelling at **Camp Redcloud**. This is the camp for "challenge" activities. If you'd like a slightly scaled-down version of what you might find at an Outward Bound expedition, you should attend the Red Cloud camp.

For more "laid-back" activities, you would attend the **Twin Peaks camp**, where you can try outdoorsy activities such as archery, fishing, hiking, and fossil hunting. A creation vs. evolution seminar is included, as well as activities for the kiddies. Find out why you can believe the Bible literally and still be a reputable scientist.

Remember, this is a family affair—the parents come as well.

Answers in Genesis Family Camps

PO Box 6330
Florence, KY 41022
(800) 350-3232
www.answersingenesis.org

Answersingenesis.org is the coolest Creation Science site on the Web. Visit it and prepare to be amazed at what they never told you in school!

Answers in Genesis (AiG), known for its unwavering position on the literal truth of a six-day-creation, as per the Bible, offers a variety of exciting **summer family camps and adventure trips.** The AiG Summer Retreats are for anyone who wants to know how science supports the Bible, what the Bible actually says about creation, and why it matters to us today. Seminar speakers include former *Practical Homeschooling* columnist and AiG founder and executive director Ken Ham, dinosaur sculptor Buddy Davis, Geoff Stevens, Dr. David Menton, Carl Kerby, Bill Jack from Worldview Academy, and others besides.

The **AiG Schroon Lake Family Retreat** is a relaxing weekend event held Mother's Day weekend in upstate New York, with Ken Ham and meteorologist Michael Oard. Good food, great accommodations, and creation science instruction.

The **AiG Grand Canyon Raft Trip** in June features talks by Dr. Gary Parker, author of many creation-science books for younger people, presumably *not* given while floating down the river!

Check their website's "Events" listing for other family camps and conferences, as these change from year to year.

Family Adventure Magazine

Opportunity Knocks, Inc., NY.
(845) 679-9321,
www.familyadventuretravel.com or
www.familyadventure.net

For a large number of alphabetical listings describing family adventure vacation providers and articles about many, many more family adventure vacations, **Family Adventure Magazine** is a great source.

I got my issue free in the mail and could not find a cover price or subscription price on it. By diligently scrutinizing their website, I found out you can order the current issue for $5 US or $7.50 Canadian.

At least visit their website. It lets you pick an activity and a region, then brings up vacations in that vicinity. You also can check on weather forecast, government travel advisories, currency exchange rate, and immunizations needed for out-of-country travel to any country.

Also available on the site are quite a few articles highlighting various types of adventures and "Howie's Bookshelf" of recommended family adventure travel books. The latter are available through links to amazon.com.

To be added to their mailing list (which may include getting the magazine, but who can tell from the way they have it set up?), select the "Send an Email" feature and check off the appropriate box.

Theme Parks

Finally, for homeschooling family fun with a more kinetic flavor, take a look at your regional theme park. If you have been reluctant to bring your family during one of the regular days because of the mass of rowdy teens that typically flock to these parks during the summer, attending a homeschool day can give you the best of both worlds—a friendly environment with a lot of good fun.

Six Flags theme parks, in cooperation with Harvest Home Educators, have been offering special homeschool family days for over five years now. The normal crowds are absent, so you actually have a chance to get at the rides. In addition to the regular attractions, parents can also browse the onsite curriculum fair, with a variety of vendors displaying their homeschool-friendly products. Or take a break to hear some words of encouragement and inspiration from a special speaker.

One year the special speaker was me! I couldn't believe anyone would tear themselves away from the face-painting and roller coasters to come to the theater to hear an overweight middle-aged mom in a red suit natter about homeschooling, but it happened, so go figure.

You should also drop by the exhibit hall, if only to keep the poor sweating exhibitors from feeling totally unloved and unwanted.

You'll be handed a goodie bag on your way in. My suggestion: March right back out to the car and sling that heavy sucker into the backseat. You won't want to lug it around with you all day, but you'll enjoy having it to sift through later for special deals and great catalogs.

The first ever Home School Day at **Sea World in Orlando, Florida,** was also arranged by Harvest Home Educators in 2002. The 2003 event was held on October 15, and future years' events probably will again be around this off-season time. They plan to make this an annual event, so check the Harvest Home Educators site!

Silver Dollar City, in Branson, MO, also offers a homeschool weekend. Theirs is in the fall, when school families are stuck near the classroom, but when homeschool families often are free to roam! You get about a third off the entrance fee, though you have to reserve your tickets by phone, as opposed to buying them at the front gate.

Silver Dollar City is an interesting mix of amusement park and history and culture exhibit, with fast, scary rides that involve getting the passengers very wet. The homeschool weekend will be held during the "Festival of American Craftsmanship," featuring American foods from coast to coast, native American artists, craftsmen, and storytellers, Civil War artifacts and

Six Flags Homeschool Days
For a current listing of homeschool days, visit the Harvest Home Educators website at *www.harvesthomeeducators.com*

Sea World Homeschool Day
For a current listing of homeschool days, visit the Harvest Home Educators website at *www.harvesthomeeducators.com*

Silver Dollar City Homeschool Day
Branson, MO
(800) 475-9370, ask for homeschool offer
www.silverdollarcity.com

experts, re-enactors, the Will Rogers Exhibit, and more besides. And when you get tired of immersing yourself in the culture of this grand nation, try the enormous loopy new roller-coaster, "Wildfire." Learn a little about colonial history while facing your fears on the ride's first startling drop. What could be more fun?

Probably so as not to upset the general public, who might feel miffed about being excluded from the day on Homeschool Day, there's nothing about this day on the website. You have to call the telephone number we provided to find out about it and make your reservation.

Dollywood Homeschool Day

Pigeon Forge, TN.
(865) 428-9488, (865) 428-9890 for groups, www.dollywood.com.

Finally, meet your last homeschool theme park hostess . . . Dolly Parton. No kidding! Her **Dollywood theme park,** located in the Great Smoky Mountains in Tennessee, is more than just an amusement park. Dollywood is about music, crafts, entertainment, education, and atmosphere.

As a sample of what Dollywood has to offer, students who attended the fourth annual homeschool day on Friday, September 21, 2001, received a lesson plan notebook, which they filled in during the day. In addition to the regular attractions, the rides, the music, and the workshops by Dollywood's Master Craftspeople, students enjoyed a theme park with no lines . . . on a Friday, everybody but homeschoolers is in a classroom!

CHAPTER 59

Specialty Camps for Kids

Homeschooling away from home doesn't always have to involve the whole family. Though we looked at field trips, educational travel, and family adventures first in this section, it's now time to move on to solo activities.

There are some powerful reasons for considering sending your homeschooled students away from home for a while.

- **You don't know everything.** Camps can offer specialized training in areas you are not expert in and don't want to take the time to become expert in.
- **You can't be everywhere at once.** Camps can provide intensive instruction that you simply don't have the time, location, or resources to offer in your home.
- **Your child has to grow up sometime.** You don't want his or her first time away from home to be freshman orientation at college! Carefully supervised away-from-home activities, offered by people you have checked out and feel comfortable with, provide a great stepping-stone to independence.

Remember, homeschooling isn't about being at home. It's real-world learning controlled by the parents. This can include experiences away from the parents.

Medieval Exchange Programs

In olden times, people used to send their children away from home, sometime between ages 10 and 13, to live with another family and learn a trade. The children of aristocrats served as pages in other aristocrats' households. The children of less privileged families worked as apprentices. Often this was accomplished by "swapping" kids. Family A would take in Family B's kid, and vice versa. It was felt that a father would be too easy on his own son, and that children could only acquire social graces and adult traits under the tutelage of a less involved adult.

In today's overregulated world, this kind of "kid exchange" usually isn't possible. It's actually easier to send your high-school student overseas for a

Most of the camp reviews in this chapter were written by my son **Joseph Pride**, now a cadet in the United States Coast Guard Academy, while he was working as our magazine editor. Joseph began traveling on his own, or with his younger sister Sarah, to camps and conferences in his mid-teens. These away-from-home activities were a valuable part of his college application resumé, which helped him achieve the rank of National Merit Finalist and got him accepted at a number of top universities.

year as an exchange student than it is to swap kids within this country. There is no legal provision at all for homeschool families to teach each others' kids, and in fact in most places this is explicitly *not* allowed.

You can still do "kid swaps" in the summertime, when school isn't in session. But the people you know probably have lives similar to yours and live in your neighborhood. So the only way most of us can provide special away-from-home experiences is through . . . summer camps.

Sue Richman on Summer Academic Programs

I've sometimes thought it's a bit ironic that I like summer academic programs so much. After all, I don't send my kids to the school five miles down the road for five hours a day, but I will send them off across the country to attend a two-week camp in French, or to learn about international studies at the University of Pittsburgh, or to study computer science at the University of Wisconsin.

In all the ways that matter, these summer academic programs are different from public school. There is no compulsory attendance law forcing children to attend them, for one thing! For another, they are focused on a specific academic area, and expected to show results. Parents wouldn't pay to send their kids to an academic camp otherwise. (Even if the camp is free, travel to the camp is not!) Academic camps also tend to be a lot more fun than "real" school, because otherwise kids would fight to not attend. Finally, most academic camps have no delusions of grandeur. They do not try to educate the "whole child" via a barrage of unwanted social services and political indoctrination. (Exception: Those run by government agencies may have some of this, especially those aimed at "gifted" kids. Be sure to check out their proposed teaching content and worldview first.)

My kids and many other homeschool teens I know have really benefited from these unique opportunities. Now is the time to start planning ahead for your own kids to jump off on their own in a summer academic program.

Now, don't get me wrong—I'm not really an advocate of "year-round homeschooling". . . at least not if that involves doing the same type of thing all year. Summer is different—the weather makes everyone want to get out, go traveling, do something new and untried. My kids are very reluctant to imagine July doing typical daily math lessons, inside at home! But to take part in a special summer program involving new people, a new place, living off on a college campus or in the wilderness . . . they are very ready for that!

Prepares Them for College

Summer programs have a special plus for homeschool kids aiming for college. My three older kids all felt much more ready to jump into college life after being away from home for a while in the summer. And with each program they attended, they were able to meet professors and teachers who were very willing to write positive letters of recommendation to help them move to their next step in life. Jacob used a letter of recommendation from a summer math program at Rose-Hulman Institute of Technology to apply for next year's program at Kutztown University, and met a professor there (who just happened to be a homeschool dad) who wrote him a letter to help him get into the PA Governor's School for Sciences. And then his teachers from the Governor's School helped him get into Carnegie Mellon University's very selective School of Computer Science, where he's now a senior.

Howard and Susan Richman have four always-homeschooled children, two in college, and have written several books about homeschooling, including *Three R's at Home.*

You can visit their website at **www.pahomeschoolers.com**.

Sue Richman's comments in this chapter were originally published in *Practical Homeschooling* magazine.

Mary Says: If your kids are terrified at the thought of flying off somewhere strange and new, try father-son or mother-daughter activities, father-son camps, or father-son expeditions. However, if they're more independent-minded, it may be more of a growing-up experience for them to go it alone. Keep this in mind before you book little Jimmy into a stay-over camp for the first time in his life or before you book yourself into little Johnny's camp.

Jacob also got the chance to see what college life was like—including eating food service meals (made him appreciate home cooking for sure!), getting to figure out dorm life (and how to do his own laundry), meeting a wider range of people than he would have run into through our home-school network, and having challenging profs and advanced technical equipment. All of my kids had plenty of times for active fun at all their programs too. Even the most intense and organized programs planned in "mandatory fun" for everyone—square dances, mixers, trips to local movie theaters, informal frisbee games or juggling bouts, mock Olympics, talent shows, and more.

When applying for some summer programs, my kids had to write personal essays, fill out extensive applications, and pull together lists of special honors and awards and interests—especially for selective (and free!) programs like the Pennsylvania Governors Schools. This made college applications go much easier—they already had experience in it all, and they weren't starting out "from scratch" in their senior year wondering where to start in drafting an engaging essay about themselves.

Finding Summer Academic Programs

So how do you find out about the thousands of terrific summer academic programs out there? First, you need to be resourceful and keep your eyes open. You might see info in your city newspaper, your favorite homeschool magazine, in the college mail that starts poring into your home once your kids take the PSAT, or on a bulletin board at a college campus when you're attending a lecture with your kids. You can call up area colleges and see if they offer anything in the summers for kids. You may be surprised at what is available very nearby. Probably most helpful today is to learn to use the Internet. Turn the page for some general websites that can help you connect into a range of different types of summer programs. Happy hunting!

Sue Richman Recommends...

Governor's Schools. Almost all states now offer summer Governor's Schools programs, and most have dealt with homeschool applicants. Usually these publicly funded programs are free to accepted students—that's one of the reasons we've liked them! How to find out if your state has a Governor's School program? Check out **ncogs.org**. This is the site for the National Conference of Governor's Schools, and you'll find direct links to each program. And if you find that your state's Governor School does not yet allow homeschool students to apply, then you know you have your lobbying work cut out for you!

Summer Math Programs. Here is a site with terrific links to all the major math summer programs— **www.ams.org/employment/mathcamps.html** Although set up by the American Mathematical Society to help their members find summer work teaching at math camps, you can use it to find where your kids might want to go for a real "upgrade" of their math thinking. Direct links to summer math programs all over the US. At least one homeschool grad is now teaching at the Ross Math Program held each summer at Ohio State University, one of the programs listed on this comprehensive site. Noah Snyder of York, PA, first took part at Ross when he was in high school at home, and I don't think he's missed a year since. He's now a senior at Harvard and helping to write the problems for the summer courses. A really intriguing sounding math camp I found on this list is the one-week All Girls/All Math program held at the University of Nebraska-Lincoln, where girls are taught by women math professors and grad students, and work in a cooperative atmosphere on challenging work in codes and mathematical chaos. And the **www.mathcamps.org** website from this list has a neat and challenging application quiz. Even if your kids don't want to even think of applying, I encourage you to check out this quiz and see what real problem-solving fun is all about!

American Camping Association

5000 State Road 67 North
Martinsville, IN 46151
(765) 342-8456
www.acacamps.org

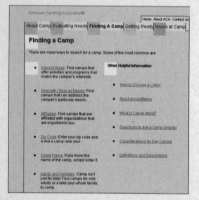

To locate a camp many different ways, go to find.acacamps.org

Where to Find Many, but Not All, Camps

The traditional, time-honored American camp experience is a great way to make a more rounded individual out of a kid. Traveling somewhere, meeting people, enjoying the outdoors, and having an experience beats hanging around the house. The **American Camping Association** publishes a half-inch-thick directory of accredited camps, certified to be kid-safe, as well as lots of practical advice, aimed at parents, on what to bring, how to prepare your kids for a stay-over camp, and much more. If you're looking for a special-interest camp, like a Jewish or YMCA camp, you may be able to find one in this directory. If your kids want to attend the kind of camp you'll find in the start of *The Parent Trap,* that's what this directory is full of, from cover to cover. It sells for $10.95, but it could conceivably save you a lot more in research and planning.

You can also find a free searchable directory on their website, which you can sort by a number of criteria, including featured activities, from academics and aerobics/exercise to baseball, from caving to clowning, from fencing to horseback riding, and lots more. See the list of special interests available on the facing page.

Religious studies is mostly cute fun Christian camps—far from the kind of intensive application found at Summit or Worldview Academy, both of which are written up in Chapter 61 of this book—with the descriptions full of "loving, caring, supportive, joyful, self-esteem building," et cetera. There are also a few Jewish camps. I suggest you try to sort out the science programs, animal encounters, entrepreneurship training, and foreign language lessons from the therapeutic camps . . . In a therapeutic camp, you can expect fellow campers who . . . need therapy.

Also be aware of what kinds of camps *won't* be included; you won't find serious worldview camps, and you won't find hunting/hunter safety camps, such as Ted Nugent's Kamp 4 Kids or the NRA Youth Hunter Education Challenge.

Still, in general, if you want to seek out a kind of camp that we haven't written up in this chapter, you should look in the ACA list. Though hardly a comprehensive list of all camps, it's certainly a good start.

Summer Opportunity Websites

www.summercamps.com This well-organized site helps you find all different sorts of summer camps, with handy categories that help you zero in on academic camps or special interest camps. Gives basic info (price per week, camp location, and focus of the program) and a website link to the camp. Includes study-abroad high-school options.

www.petersons.com/summerop/ Great database on summer programs of all sorts for kids and high-school students. Petersons also publishes several excellent guidebooks to summer opportunities—you can find them with a simple click on this site.

www.concordialanguagevillages.org This is the place to look for summer language camps. Concordia College in Minnesota hosts camps for all ages in almost every language you'd want. Besides the typical French, Spanish, and German, you'll also find Japanese,

Norwegian, Korean, Chinese, Russian, Finnish, and more, with each language meeting at a different camp location. Our daughter Hannah has attended the French camp for two summers and loves it. A total immersion, fun-filled program, with emphasis on using spoken language all through the day while learning about the cultures where the target language is used.

www.eskimo.com/~user/kids.html This is the site for the Gifted Resource Page. It has links to all the major regional talent search programs in the country. Many of these talent search programs offer special summer opportunities for bright kids. Usually these programs require qualification through standardized testing. For more information about Talent Searches, including exact program requirements and how these apply to homeschoolers, see the Talents Searches chapter in this book.

—*Susan Richman*

INTERESTS YOU CAN PURSUE AT A SPECIALTY CAMP

The following list was taken from the "Areas of Interest" pull-down menu on the American Camping Association site at **find.aca.org**. You can look for camps with many criteria, including cultural focus ("Christian" and "Jewish" turn out to be cultural in this respect, as are "African-American" and "Hispanic"), day or residential camp, single-sex or coed, state/regional preference, cost per week, and preferred length of session. The camp database is also searchable by special needs and accommodations, group affiliation (e.g., YMCA, Future Farmers of America, etc.), zip code, name, and camps that also accommodate parents and entire families.

- Academics
- Aerobics/Exercise
- Aquatics
- Archery
- Arts/Crafts
- Aviation
- Backpacking
- Baseball/Softball
- Basketball
- Bicycling
- Boating
- Camping Skills/Outdoor Living
- Canoeing/Caving
- Ceramics/Pottery
- Challenges/Rope Courses
- Climbing/Rappelling
- Clowning
- Community Service
- Computer
- Counselor Training
- Dance
- Drama
- Drawing/Painting
- Farming/Ranching/ Gardening
- Fencing
- Field Trips
- Fishing
- Football
- Golf
- Gymnastics
- Hiking
- Hockey
- Horseback Riding: English
- Horseback Riding: Western
- International Exchange
- Kayaking
- Language Studies
- Leadership Development
- Martial Arts
- Model Rocketry
- Music
- Nature/Environmental Studies
- Performing Arts
- Photography
- Radio/TV/Video
- Rafting
- Religious Study
- Riflery
- Sailing
- SCUBA
- Skating
- Soccer
- Sports: Field & Team
- Snow Sports
- Swimming: Instructional
- Swimming: Recreational
- Team Building
- Tennis
- Travel/Tour
- Waterskiing
- Wilderness Trips
- Windsurfing

This is it. *The* book for those who are looking for "safe, fun, and enriching summer programs." It's **Peterson's Summer Opportunities for Kids and Teenagers.** This annually updated guide provides complete information on more than 3,000 summer camps, art programs, sports clinics, academic courses, travel tours, wilderness adventures, and volunteer opportunities throughout the US and abroad. It's much more than just specialty camps. Outdoors adventures and pre-college camps (which I introduce in two chapters of this book) are also included in this huge guide.

Don't expect a lot of objectivity. The program descriptions are written by people who work for the programs. You get a lot of information—directors and staff members, background and philosophy, activities and facilities, medical and safety information, a typical day's schedule, application procedures and deadlines, costs, and contact information—but not a lot of insight into pros and cons of a given program, or its worldview

The 2003 edition is 1,588 pages thick. That's a lot of material to look through. There are several ways you can plumb the book's offerings. Sixty pages of "FastFacts" tables at the front let you scan for on-site programs by state and by country, and for travel programs inside and outside the USA. Once you've picked your category, check the table to pick programs by sex (boy only, girl only, coed), residence (day or overnight), age level, and program type (academic, sports, arts, wilderness/outdoors, special interest), whether jobs or financial aid are available.

The bulk of the book is concise program descriptions. In-depth descriptions "written by program directors exclusively for this guide" are provided for over 300 summer programs. Finally, there are several indexes to help you locate programs by primary activity, travel, religious affiliation, special needs, or sponsor, as well as by program name. Or you can go to Peterson's Summer Opportunities website and troll it for similar information.

Summer Opportunities for Kids and Teenagers

Parents and kids. $29.95.
Peterson's. Available in bookstores.
www.petersons.com/summerop/.

A Camp Sampler

I'm now going to provide a short list of camps that either sound especially interesting, that are notably homeschool-friendly, or that my family members have attended. Though this list obviously is not comprehensive, it will give you a taste of the kinds of experiences your children can get away from home at camp.

Outdoorsy Christian camps abound. I picked **Camp Sandy Cove** because it's in some way related to the Sandy Cove Conference Center, which hosts an annual homeschool conference.

Located in the Pocono Mountains of Pennsylvania, this camp offers a lot of physical activity and ongoing Bible study. Weeklong camps you could attend include canoeing, backpacking, Adirondack Mountains camping, and leadership training. These activities are aimed toward two age groups: "Scouts and Maidens," age 7–11, and "Warriors and Squaws," age 11–14. (In my opinion, the warriors got the better end of that deal . . .) The counselors are referred to as "chiefs," following the cowboys-and-Indians naming convention. Any kid who's got the will and the strength is welcome, "regardless of race, religion, or national origin." And, yes, the camp is ACA-accredited. The LIT (Leaders in Training) course, involving Bible study and a three-week out-of-camp expedition, is the sort of thing I'd have loved to do when I was young enough to try it. *Joseph Pride*

Looking for a summer camp that's a bit like boot camp? They exist, and here's an example.

The **Citadel Summer Camp** is run out of the Citadel, the Military College of South Carolina, in Charleston. Its purpose is to grow strong patriotic young citizens. The major focus of this camp is sports and athletic development. The boys and girls aged 10 to 15 who attend this camp should be enthusiastic about lots of healthy exercise, because that's what they'll be doing! Students will be drilled in formations, will be expected to wear uniform, and will have daily room inspections. You can expect them to come back not only stronger, but sharper. Fun activities include tennis, softball, football, team handball, soccer, basketball, volleyball, swimming, racquetball, wrestling, air rifle marksmanship, boy or girl scout projects, drum & bugle corps, SCUBA, beach trips, optional hunter safety programs, dances each weekend, and a lot more. Your kids will be in good hands; the Citadel staff have been training athletes, soldiers, and leaders for over a century. *Joseph Pride*

Computer camps are pretty much the direct opposite of the type of camp above. No military formations, no gung-ho physicality. Just the opportunity to take in-depth short-term programs in Web design, programming, robotics, digital arts, and/or game design. That's what **Cybercamps** offers. Programs take place on college campuses, with both day and residential options available. Register early for a hefty discount.

Experimental Aircraft Association Flight Academy. The name may not inspire parental confidence, but actually there's nothing "experimental" about this summer aviation camp in beautiful Oshkosh, Wisconsin. This is an excellent example of a "learn by doing" camp that teaches a specialized skill area. Twelve- and thirteen-year-olds learn about "basic aeronautics and flight concepts in a fast paced, hands-on, summer fun program." Fourteen- and fifteen-year-olds get to work on "aeromodeling, gliders, ultralight planes, powered parachutes, skydiving and hot air ballooning" plus "other

Camp Sandy Cove

Camp Sandy Cove
60 Sandy Cove Rd.
North East, MD 21901
(800) 234-2683
www.sandycove.org

Citadel Summer Camp

171 Moultire St. or
MSC 53/The Citadel
Charleston, SC 29409
(843) 953-7120
www.citadel.edu/summercamp

Cybercamps

Giant Campus, Inc., WA.
(888) 904-2267,
www.giantcampus.com

EAA Flight Academy

Young Eagles Program
EAA Aviation Foundation
P.O. Box 3086
Oshkosh, WI 54903-3086
(920) 426-4800
www.youngeagles.org

fascinating aspects of aviation through classroom and media presentations, hands-on laboratories, and demonstrations of air sports based on availability and weather." During some of the summer sessions, kids in this group even get to restore, build, and fly full-scale aircraft. But the "Top Gun" slots are reserved for 16- to 18-year-olds, who get actual pilot training via "ground instruction and introductory recreational flight experiences" plus ground instruction in skydiving and a demonstration of same—everything up to but *not* including getting to skydive yourself. All this, plus "hands-on instruction in homebuilt and antique aircraft, aeromodeling, gliders, ultra-light planes, powered parachutes, and hot-air ballooning." Don't forget to check out the new flight simulation lab while you're at it. Finally, for those who can't wait to leave the ground behind, First Flights Academy camps help you "accomplish the FAA Private Pilot Ground School written examination" and provide up to eight hours of dual flight instruction. All from the folks who bring you America's Big Air Show each summer.

A second type of science camps is one that presents a lot of history and simulations. **Space Camp** won't send you to the moon yet (give them time!) but it *will* get you into the Space Shuttle simulator, the monstrous IMAX theater, astronaut training simulators, classes on space exploration, rocket building and launches, the actual rockets that brought men to the moon, NASA research labs, space station construction software, technology museum, and maybe the spectator seating for an actual shuttle launch! I don't know about you, but for me there's something delightful about seeing an enormous Saturn rocket on display. If you have a kid who wants to be a rocket scientist some day, check out this camp! Parent/child weekends are also available.

And if you would like to save some money, we've provided contact information for you to attend as a part of "4-H in Space." This is open to all, not just 4-H members.

According to the director of the program, who e-mailed me asking me to share this information with homeschoolers:

> *4-H and the U.S. Space & Rocket Center, home of U.S. SPACE CAMP, introduced the 4-H MISSIONS IN SPACE program nation wide in 1990. Since that beginning, more than 8,000 youth, extension staff, and volunteer adult leaders from more than 45 states and territories have participated in various program offerings. We now offer "Pathfinder," "AstroTrek," and other opportunities.*

Travel camps may seem like a contradiction in terms. Yet travel programs are a huge part of what's available for your child. You'll find some examples of wilderness and outdoorsy programs in my chapter on that topic. Meanwhile, here's an example of a program intended to broaden children's cultural awareness.

Teen Missions offers a variety of missionary experiences to a wide range of countries, from Australia to Britain to Egypt or even America. Kids signed up for these courses will receive "boot camp" training. The emphasis will not be largely on fun, but on the work in question. That work may be personal ministry; it may be helping out with a hospital; it may be building facilities somewhere. In any case, while there may be some recreation time, shopping and exploring will have to be cut short in favor of the trip's main purpose. Students who enter these camps may be traveling to the other side of the world under adult supervision, likely doing physically challenging work. A great opportunity to gain experience, try out missionary work at a young age, and get a feeling for the field.

Space Camp
www.spacecamp.com
4-H in Space
Special discounted group rate of $265 per person for the Pathfinder program and $105 & $139 per person for the AstroTrek program. *Make arrangements for your group by contacting 4-H locally at the Cooperative Extension Office or through Space Camp, 4-H Group Coordinator 214 Duncan Hall Auburn University, AL 36849-5620 (334) 844-2233 jacook@aces.edu*

Teen Missions International
885 East Hall Rd.
Merritt Island, FL 32953
(321) 453-0350
www.teenmissions.org

Texas A&M Sea Camp

Ages 10–18.
Texas A&M University at Galveston
PO Box 1675
Galveston, TX 77553
(409) 740-4525
www.tamug.edu/seacamp

Visual Manna Art Camp

PO Box 553
Salem, MO 65560
(888) 275-7309
www.visualmanna.com

YMCA

www.ymca.net. You can use this site to locate a Y near you.

Texas A&M University at Galveston offers an example of the third type of science camps: camps that feature field work. Galveston has a large maritime and engineering campus, and their one-week summer camps are, accordingly, all related to the ocean. Ten camps are available: Ecology/Marine Biology, a second week of the above, Fish Camp, Marine Mammal Workshop, Coastal Camping, Study in Belize, Ecotourism Adventure—Quintana Roo Peninsula in Mexico, Ocean Careers Awareness, Coastal Photography, and Introduction to Marine Geological, Chemical, and Physical Oceanography. All camps include instruction from professional researchers and opportunities for the students to research on their own.

The Visual Manna Art Camp is actually three art camps at which homeschoolers are especially welcome. Held in Salem, MO, the first of their three five-day camps features fishing, swimming, hiking, biking, and of course all manner of artwork. Students spend the morning learning about the science of flight and the afternoon building flying machines and sculpting birds . . . and if they can stay through the evening, they can participate in other fun activities, including caving. Every day, guest presenters will teach a variety of hands-on activities. The second art camp is for talented artists and will bring in guest professional artists daily, including the well-known watercolor artist David Plank, to teach techniques to students. The camp features a variety of media, from watercolors to computer artwork, and the staff will help students produce portfolios of their best work. Finally, the last camp features a combination of horses, artwork, and ballet. This camp is located near Bixby, in small-town Missouri, out where they keep all the scenery . . . So while you're learning the technical skills of artwork, you'll have plenty of subjects to paint! Visual Manna teaches actual art skills, not "activities." Students use high-quality art equipment of many kinds. Enthusiastic artists, take note!

If your budget is somewhat more limited, you could try your local **YMCA**. Ours offers a good number of summer camps, from theater, dance, and art to gymnastics, circus, and in-line skating. Prices range from $25 to $205, depending on options and member status.

In any case, check out the camp beforehand. Make sure the operators share your expectations about worldview and behavior. Be aware that even the most pious and serious camp operators do not have total control over the types of children who attend. So don't say I didn't warn you:

> If you're not prepared to have your child exposed to a few R-rated words or some public-school attitudes about matters ranging from dating and sex to snide attitudes toward authority, you'd better wait until they are more mature.

Homeschoolers are often accused of sheltering our children too much from the real world. Camp is a way to expose them for a short time to a structured portion of the real world, in which the administration hopefully agrees with most of our academic and religious goals and values, and where they can learn and practice some skills they are not likely to pick up around the house. Finally, it is also an excellent way to show college admissions officials that your child can survive and thrive outside your home. For all these reasons, I think camp is an option every homeschool family should consider . . . and with the hundreds of camps available, you're sure to find one that's just right for you!

CHAPTER 60

Outdoor Adventures for Kids

Do you have a son who tries to spend his whole day in front of a computer screen or a video game? Is your daughter a "couch potato" who would rather read books all day than ever go outside?

If so, you're not alone. Today's kids are getting fatter, more sluggish, and have far less real-world skills than kids had even a generation ago.

It would be interesting to discuss what is causing this retreat from the real world. But right now, I think we can agree that one of the reasons we're homeschooling is to give our kids more real-world experiences . . . which in turn means they need some adventures away from home.

Father Bret Dalton and son Dan Dalton together at Summit Adventure

Great for College Applications

Having taken two kids (so far) successfully through the college application and scholarship process, I can tell you that admissions officials love it when homeschoolers can show educational adventures on their transcripts. In their minds, this proves two things: (1) the kids in question are not "hothouse flowers" who will go screaming back to Mommy out of homesickness, and (2) they can hold their own in the real world. Plus, the trips themselves add interest to the application.

Later on in this chapter, you'll see an actual college application essay based on one such trip, that garnered its author admission to one of the top universities in the country.

Toughens 'Em Up

I suppose you could send your little darling off to military school, but that would rather defeat the purpose of homeschooling. An outdoor challenge tests body, soul, and character in a way that's unlikely to occur around the home hacienda.

Summit 2004 Schedule

Name	Dates	Length in days	Price (Tuition only: airfare and shuttle not included)
Adventures in Fatherhood:			
AIF	Jun 16–20	5	$1,153 per pair
AIF	Jul 28–Aug 1	5	$1,153 per pair
AIF	Aug 4–8	5	$1,153 per pair
Adventures in Motherhood:			
AIM	Jul 26–30	5	$1,049 per pair
Alpine Mountaineering:			
21 Day	Jun 27–Jul 17	21	$1,853 (ages 16+)
14 Day	Jul 25–Aug 7	14	$1,136 (13–15)
10 Day	Jul 29–Aug 7	10	$885 (16+)

15% Tuition Discount for early prepayment available on all courses

Also available: Adult Course, Disabled Courses, and Instruction/Training

For more information contact
Summit Adventure
PO Box 498 • Bass Lake, CA 93604
(559) 642-3899 • www.summitadventure.com

Summit Adventure photo by Randy Levensaler

Gets 'Em Away from the Computer

This is the one that got my vote! It's not my kids fault that they get the "techie" gene from both sides (both Bill and I attended engineering schools). But in our suburb there just isn't all that much fascinating to do outdoors most of the year, let alone anything that presents a challenge or learning adventure.

All this led me to start thinking about sending one or more of the kids to Outward Bound. I had second thoughts, though, when I heard from an acquaintance that her son encountered not a few drug users and otherwise uncool lifestyle choices on an OB adventure. She strongly recommended a Christian alternative, one that her son and husband had attended.

Benefits of Christian Outdoor Adventure

That's how I first heard about Summit Adventure. Based in the Sierra Nevada mountains of California, they offer a variety of one-, two-, and three-week outings for homeschoolers, fathers and sons, and moms and daughters.

Thirty years ago, Summit Expedition, predecessor to Summit Adventure, was born when author and speaker, Tim Hansel, was teaching a classroom full of apathetic students. He couldn't escape the contrast he saw between the students in the classroom and the group of youngsters he'd just spent three weeks with in the back country. This contrast sent him in pursuit of a more effective way to teach. The result has been over 30 years of exciting wilderness ministry.

As former Summit Director of Development (and homeschool dad) Dave Kelly says, "If backpacking or recreation was the essence of what we do here at Summit, anyone could pack up a sleeping bag and some dehydrated food, set off down the trail, and expect to experience the same thing. But it's not just about physical activity, or even great scenery. . . . Summit Adventure is about life-changing adventure that has a lasting impact on participants, their faith, their relationships, and their families."

I asked Dave to list several key components that catapult a Summit Adventure well beyond an ordinary backpacking trip. Here they are:

- **A New Point of View**. Climbing a mountain literally provides a new vantage point on life. Students step outside of everyday life with the purpose of looking at who they are in Christ, how they're living their lives, and how that fits with what God has called them to. In Summit's family programs, the goal is to step out of daily routines to really focus on strengthening specific relationships. Their homeschooling course focuses on discovering the world around us.
- **Opportunities to Change.** The second critical component to what Summit does is that participants come seeking change and are aware that change is important in their lives and faith. As Dave says, "It's difficult for our staff to facilitate growth in someone who doesn't want to change or doesn't think they need to change. A Summit course offers far more than new, interesting information to think about."
- **Hands-On Learning.** Another key element that makes Summit Adventure effective is that the lessons being learned are experienced. Teens don't just hear about leadership, they don't just read about leadership, they lead! They don't talk about working as a team; they must work as a team or dinner

doesn't get fixed. They are engaged in the learning process. For example, the spiritual and personal lessons discussed around the campfire in the evening are discussions of what happened that very day during sweaty-palmed rock climbs and trust-demanding rope belays.

- **Growth Through Challenge.** Much of what drives today's world is comfort-based. But spiritual, mental, emotional, and physical growth results from challenging situations, not comfortable ones. The axiom "no pain, no gain" is easy to see as it relates to sports and our bodies. The same is true for our spiritual and interpersonal health and growth. Summit Adventure provides opportunities for growth in faith and in lives—growth through challenge, not comfort.
- **Small Groups.** Summit Adventure maximizes the benefits of small groups. Small groups actually impact how we learn by providing the encouragement, support, and accountability needed for lasting change.
- **Trained Staff.** Summit tries to hire only those who have a heart for ministry and for people. Once staff members are hired, they go through 32 days of training in both "soft skills" (the spiritual and interpersonal skills needed) and the "hard skills" (the back country and first aid skills required for the job). After the team goes through the initial training, they are continually being trained and mentored by peers and lead staff.
- **Fits the Homeschool Life.** Dave Kelly says, "I believe that a Summit Adventure course is a natural component in the homeschooling experience. On a personal note, our commitment to homeschooling and the great creativity that affords our family, has been a natural outgrowth of our years in this experience-based program. Learning by doing is a central value in our family's homeschool 'style.'"
- **God Uses the Wilderness to Teach Lessons.** Throughout the Bible, God uses the literal wilderness in the lives of those He loves. Moses, Elijah, and Jesus all put in serious time out in the wilderness. The things they learned and the fellowship they experienced with God Almighty couldn't have happened in the lush regions of Egypt or the comforts of ancient Jerusalem. In the wilderness they met God Himself. He called them out there; in the wilderness, He prepared and equipped them for the special ministry He had planned for each of them. To quote Tim Hansel, 30 years ago, "The wilderness is not the only environment for [learning]—it is simply one of the best. It is still the finest place to train servant leaders because it is a non-neutral learning environment which demands change, fosters community, trust, and interdependence. The wilderness encourages wholeness, reminds us of what is true and real and affords us an opportunity like no other to encounter God as He is without distraction. A new adventure explodes into being every time a person listens to God and faithfully obeys Him."

According to Mr. Kelly again, "That's why the physical, spiritual, and emotional challenges are just tools that Summit uses in order to bring about the ultimate goal . . . that a student would deepen his or her relationship with Christ by the end of the adventure."

AAVE Teen Adventures

Grades 6–12. Tuition, from $2288 to $4700, plus airfare.
2245 Stonecrop Way
Golden, CO 80401
(800) 222-3595
www.aave.com.

If your goal is simply to provide travel adventure for your children, and you don't care about Bible lessons, here's one company you should know about.

AAVE Teen Adventures provides a large variety of two-, three-, four-, and six-week trips from June through August. Programs are coeducational, with groups separated by age. Each group includes 13 teens and two adults. They have year-round bases in Colorado and Belgium. Trips include adventure camping in Colorado, Utah, Arizona, Alaska, Washington, California, Hawaii, Costa Rica, New Zealand, Australia, Thailand, Canada, and Europe. French and Spanish immersion programs are also available.

Here are a couple of their offerings I found particularly intriguing:

- *"Boot•Saddle•Paddle (28 days, Colorado, Utah, and Arizona)* Boot•Saddle•Paddle is set in the southwestern United States and includes three backpacking trips, including the southern rim of the Grand Canyon, a horseback riding adventure in Colorado, Native American intercultural experiences and community service projects, and an incredible class III-IV whitewater rafting trip."
- *"Sail Greece (21 days, Greece)* Sail Greece includes all the water activities you can imagine in the friendly, adventure-filled, and spectacular Mediterranean Sea area. No experience is needed. Team spirit, discipline, culture, action, and sheer fun make this a lifetime adventure."

If you send your teen, be sure to ask him or her to keep a diary and take lots of pictures!

Outward Bound

www.outwardbound.com

North Carolina Outward Bound offers physical challenges, and some mountain hiking and wilderness training, all in the Appalachians. There's some cliff climbing, whitewater paddling, mountain biking, wilderness hiking, leave-no-trace camping techniques, and of course classes in gourmet camp cooking. Other Outward Bound programs based in different locations offer similar activities.

In all, there are five Outward Bound schools, based in Raleigh, NC; Hurricane Island, ME; Golden, CO; Ely, MN; and Portland, OR. There are also two urban centers, international affiliates, and international expeditions.

Outward Bound prefers not to be known as a "survival camp" per se; they'll air-drop food and supplies at certain spots, and you're supposed to have enough provisions to make it without trouble. You don't have to go out picking mushrooms and hunting wild squirrel. Students will camp with groups, and solo at one point. They will be trained in wilderness skills and gradually given more initiative and less direction by counselors.

Outward Bound was originally designed by the British Navy, when they noticed that the older sailors would actually survive longer than the younger, stronger ones when a ship went down. They concluded that it was because the younger sailors didn't have the same will to live as the older ones, so they invented Outward Bound to build confidence, and foster a stronger will and instinct for survival.

When you attend an Outward Bound camp, you'll be learning how to explore the wild without spoiling it for anybody else, how to navigate in the wilderness, and of course many other outdoor skills such as water navigation, mountain climbing, and mountain biking. You'll also hopefully learn a modicum of teamwork, confidence, and discipline.

We Check It Out

Wow! That all sounded pretty good! So I arranged for my 14-year-old son, Frank, to go on a two-week adventure and report on what it was really like.

Before Frank even left, we discovered that, unlike my old college days when two pairs of jeans, a parka, a backpack, and a tent were all we thought we needed to hike the Appalachian Trail, Summit had an extensive list of required supplies. Since we haven't done any camping for 25 years (because our oldest son, Ted, has medical needs that can't be left unattended), we had none of this on hand. The total tab came to over $1,100 at our local outdoor store. On the plus side, Frank now has all the high-quality socks, hiking shoes, water-wicking shirts, and rain gear he'll likely need for the next 20 years (assuming he's not going to grow any more!)

Air fare from Missouri wasn't cheap, either—you guys who live close to an outdoor mecca definitely have an advantage here!

We messed up the flight schedule, but in spite of Frank's late arrival, a Summit helper made the drive to the airport just to ferry him to camp.

Frank's main memories of his two weeks at Summit are as follows:

- No toilet paper or other toiletries allowed, thanks to the "Leave No Trace" policy of the national park in question. Exception: if you feel inclined to pack it out after use in a ziploc baggie. (Nobody chose to do this!)
- Heavy exercise. It pays to get in shape before you go!
- Learning not to sleep with your head downhill—instant headache on arising!
- The public-school kids on the trip trying to increase Frank's vocabulary, if you know what I mean. (This diminished over time, as the counselors discouraged it.)
- Gorgeous scenery
- Swimming in mountain lakes
- Rock climbing and hiking
- Rappelling
- A lot of emphasis on building character through these activities
- Every morning, devotions, prayers, and Bible study with discussion questions, narration, and journaling
- Making friends with a fellow computer geek who happened to also have been homeschooled
- Going down is scarier than going up!
- Everyone pitching in to do all the work of cooking, dish washing, distributing supplies, and so forth
- The counselors were good role models: staunch Bible believers and very skilled at outdoor life
- The solo adventure. Spending a whole day alone on the side of a mountain overlooking a valley, out of touch with all the others
- Bring extra money to pay for any equipment lost or broken. Water bottles were the most common lost items.
- Delicious meal back at the base before the shuttle ride

Frank says his Summit adventure was extremely educational, built up great work habits, provided great exercise, and was highly inspirational.

Keep in mind that Frank attended the "generic" adventure. Summit Adventure also offers courses for dads and their kids, moms and daughters, adults, students with disabilities, families, an annual Homeschool Discovery Course in March, and courses for a wide variety of groups, including Focus on the Family, National Center for Fathering, California universities, and local churches. Obviously, the composition of the group you go with will affect your likelihood of encountering any unseemly behavior, But even with wild-'n-wooly public schoolers, having Christian counselors makes a lot of difference.

For example, my daughter Magda attended Texas A&M's Sea Camp last summer. Just like Frank at Summit, she had roommates who used bad language, had worldly habits, and pressured her to do likewise. However, the Sea Camp counselors used bad language, too, so Magda had to handle it on her own. (Which my little Civil Air Patrol sergeant did just fine!)

There's an important point here.

When your children leave home to attend camp, you lose some control of their environment.

If the people running the camp or educational experience share your beliefs and practices, they will try to preserve an uplifting environment. But as long as there are no "entrance requirements" for who may attend, your kids are bound to encounter some of the same things you've been protecting them from at home. Conversely, if you choose your venue carefully, the rough edges can be minimized. For example, just by virtue of Summit Adventure's ministry, Frank could expect uplifting behavior from his counselors and zero tolerance for drugs and alcohol (not that either were an issue with his group). You could further trim down the rough edges by selecting a fathers-and-sons or mothers-and-daughters outing, or the annual Homeschool Discovery Course.

In any case, be sure to consider the student's age and maturity level—especially his or her sensitivity to peer pressure—before assuming none of this will be encountered in a supervised environment.

Randy Levensaler

A Winning College Application Essay

Finally, I thought it would be inspiring to close this chapter with a true-life example of how an outdoor adventure helped at least one student get into a top university. So, without any further ado, here is the essay that helped John Eldon get into Stanford University.

NRA Shooting Sports Camps

National Rifle Association Hunter Services Dept, VA. (703) 267-1500, www.nrahq.org/education/ shootingcamp.asp.

Here's the opposite of the vegetarianism found at many outdoors camps, mixed with a good dose of old-time conservationism (what ecology used to be called before it became a political force).

The National Rifle Association hosts a large number of **NRA Shooting Sports Camps,** to teach at all different levels, from gun safety and basic operation to hunting or marksmanship. If you're a parent who wants his kids to know what guns can do and how to be safe around them, or if your kids are fond of their Second Amendment rights and you'd like to see them better educated, or if you'd like to learn about the art of hunting, most likely you can find a camp to help.

Conquering the Golden Toad
A Winning College Application Essay by John Eldon

From my perch atop the Golden Toad, I had a breathtaking view of towering Mt. Ritter and the Minarets stepping down to meet California's Sierra Nevada, with the San Joaquin thundering out of the mountains' base and winding westward in the valley below. I had only one remaining challenge before I could call this experience, which at one time had been in great jeopardy, a success. With a nod from an instructor, I began the rappel down the ground floor 210 feet below.

This large rock outcropping, which turns gold in the last of the sun's fading rays, was the final stop on a 21-day wilderness course I participated in this past summer. By reaching this point, I proved to myself that not only could I stride through the mountains with a pack weighing more than 70 pounds, but also, the sudden injury before my departure had not been enough to stop, or even slow me down. This trip gave me the understanding that high aspirations are still achievable under difficult situations, and a determined attitude will often fulfill them.

Two nights before embarking, I broke my pinky, ring, and middle fingers on my left hand in a freak Ultimate Frisbee collision. I distinctly remember the discussion I had the next evening with the expedition staff once I discovered the seriousness of the injury. The previous year, I was forced to postpone the trip when, after running and wrestling on school teams all year to get in shape, I received a debilitating back injury. This was still fresh in my mind and I feared another delay, but their response was indecisive and left the decision of participation entirely up to me. I had a pair of hiking boots, well broken in as a result of my conditioning, sitting in front of me as I contemplated missing the opportunity again—possibly for good. After several hours of deliberation that night, I opted to catch the plane the next morning, and overcome whatever challenges this course could throw me.

With this attitude, I couldn't allow the broken hand to hinder me. Once I accepted the blunt club I had for an appendage, seven working fingers were perfectly sufficient and I gave it no more thought. During periods of rock climbing, I became so adept at using my elbow as a prop and the thumb and pointer for balance that I outdid many of my companions both in number of routes and in speed.

Sitting on the Toad, watching as one by one my companions hooked into the line and descended over the edge, I felt nervous but not scared. In this way, I spent more than an hour on top in the cold, whipping wind, hardly moving or saying a word, just thinking back on the experience and how it had improved my self-esteem and determination. Although I have no great fear of heights, I couldn't help but feel queasy when it was my turn to walk backward over the precipice. The first fifteen feet of my descent was the only uncomfortable section as I tried to get a feel for the movement and control my body's actions. After this point, the face cut in and I was left suspended without even the superficial reassurance of my feet on the rock. I sat in this position for several minutes, looking out at the snow-capped peaks I had visited, then down to the hawk's nest at my feet, and at my comrades far below. This moment for contemplation and reflection calmed every nerve in my body and I completed the remainder surrounded by the butterflies that had escaped from my stomach.

After the conclusion of this trip, but before I had admitted to myself that it was over and left base camp, my parents asked an instructor if my broken hand had been a handicap. His reply was, "Once he decided not to see it as one, it wasn't." Although it was only a hand and not necessary for travel, had I allowed, it could have quickly become something that limited my participation.

Sir Martin Conway once said, "A man does not climb a mountain without bringing some of it away with him and leaving something of himself upon it." I feel that I left personal insecurities and doubt on that mountaintop in California. What I found was the capacity to view troubling, or demanding tasks not as problems, but as opportunities to prove to myself my ability and resolve. This insight was not easily found, but since discovered, has become an integral part of my outlook.

CHAPTER 61

Worldview & Leadership Training for Teens

Do you want your kids to change the world . . . or to be changed *by* the world into young adults who find your beliefs old-fashioned and your morality irrelevant?

Since the number one reason most parents homeschool is to provide their kids with lasting morals and beliefs, I would have to guess you'd be in favor of raising kids who will change the world, rather than the other way around.

If so, you're facing an uphill struggle. Everything from TV commercials, to the evening news, to agencies of the government, to schools, to major corporations, is pushing a worldview they want your kids to buy into. While your kids are young, you can avoid this worldview pressure by homeschooling and having no TV. But when they get older, your kids are going to make a choice. They are either going to make this choice *consciously*, aware of the differing worldviews and what they profess, or *unconsciously*, victims of the incessant propaganda from all directions.

College, Where Everything Is Relative?

Today, most college students don't know right from wrong. In fact, most college students—and their professors—are convinced there is no such thing as "right" and "wrong." Without even realizing it, they have become captives of the philosophy known as "relativism."

Public schools have been teaching relativism for years, formally in classes on "critical thinking" and "values clarification," and informally through the premises of most school drug education and sex education programs. Entire generations of kids have grown up believing that nobody has the right to tell them how to behave in their *personal* lives, while simultaneously being taught explicitly how to behave and believe in their *political* lives.

Yes, oddly enough, **relativism is the kissing cousin of political correctness.** That's because nature abhors a vacuum, and relativism isn't so much a worldview as a *lack* of worldview. Nobody can seriously believe everything is relative except psychopaths and those who believe that existence itself is a delusion. The minute you admit that you find *some* behavior to be outrageous, you are no longer a relativist.

> "We want to teach our teens to be leaders."
> Everyone says it.
> Now here's how thousands of homeschool parents are doing it.

Human beings are hardwired to believe in good and evil. But instead of learning the Ten Commandments, today's kids are being taught to define "good" as whatever the *New York Times* says is "good" and "evil" as whatever Dan Rather says is evil. "Informed public opinion" becomes God. Which is to say, "public opinion created and manipulated by the handful of wealthy people who own our media and purchase our politicians." Whoever disagrees with the word from Madison Avenue is vilified as being a fringe element, suspect, and likely dangerous. All without any need to actually respond to the dissenting opinion.

In short, **relativism is a dandy way to manipulate people and to shut dissenters up.** But relativism is powerful only so long as its assumptions aren't recognized or challenged.

That's where worldview training comes in.

Recognizing that kids who head off to college, and Christian kids in particular, are in for the philosophical fight of their lives from professors and peers who regard any deviation from relativism as worthy of harassment and perhaps even expulsion, a number of ministries and programs have sprung up to teach kids to recognize and resist the spirit of relativism.

Generally, such ministries also present a positive Christian view on major social and ethical issues, so the soon-to-be freshmen will at least know where the church has always stood and where they should take a stand.

Some programs have also developed to take teens a step farther—from recognizing and resisting relativism and all the "isms" that hang on to its coattails, to learning how to actively promote a Christian point of view in the public square.

I am very happy and pleased that such programs exist—and only wonder why more families don't take advantage of them.

Because, after all, what's the point of homeschooling your children for 12 years only to have them end up living and working contrary to the beliefs you did your best to instill into them?

Patrick Henry College Teen Leadership Camps

Ages 14–18. $425 per camp except debate camp, $995. Price includes housing, meals, classroom materials, field trips, and transportation to and from Washington Dulles International Airport (if needed). A non-refundable deposit of $150 is required upon initial registration, with full payment due by the first day of camp. Early registration discount available.
P.O. Box 1776, Purcellville, VA 20134
(540) 338-1776
www.phc.edu/teencamps

The Rockford Institute Summer School

Teens and up. Tuition, $195. Lodging and meals additional.
928 North Main Street
Rockford, IL   61103
(815) 964-5053
www.chroniclesmagazine.org/TRI/TRIMain.htm.

Worldview & Leadership Training Opportunities

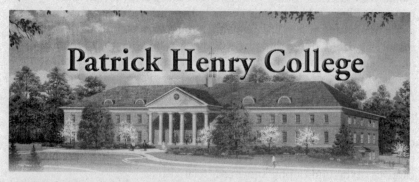

Patrick Henry College (PHC) offers week-long camps on Constitutional History, Constitutional Law, Journalism, American History, and Political Activism, and a two-week Debate camp, all from a Christian perspective, with an eye towards improving culture. Activities include visits to historical attractions and centers of government, and lectures taught by Michael Farris and the Patrick Henry College staff.

There couldn't be a more homeschooler-friendly environment than PHC, since it's the first college founded primarily to serve homeschoolers.

The Rockford Institute's Annual Summer School tackles a different worldview theme every year. Though designed originally for adults, savvy teen homeschoolers with a literary and historical bent should find the weekend fascinating. Familiarity with *Chronicles* magazine and the faculty's published work would be helpful.

Registration is priced pretty reasonably, and accommodations for out-of-town students are on riverfront property (Cliffbreakers Suites). Transportation is provided to and from Cliffbreakers every day, as well as to dinner. The Rockford Institute's Summer School is meant for future statesmen, educators, and citizens, plus of course their parents, with mature and educated enough minds to appreciate the material.

Another opportunity for worldview training is the **Summer Christian Leadership Seminar** sponsored by **Summit Ministries**. Young adults (16 and up) can choose from eight different two-week sessions in Manitou Springs, Colorado, and a session at Bryan College in Tennessee.

Plenty of recreational opportunities are available, but the heart of The Summit is teaching how to use God's word in life, in society, and in response to many of the problems that face the world today. Originally designed to prepare Christian youths for the many challenges of the college environment, Summit intends to give you a sound foundation in Christianity, and to bolster your faith by showing how the Bible relates to the real world.

In an excellent article by Dr. Gene Veith entitled "Summit Ministries: Four Worldviews and the Battle of Ideas," which he wrote in October 1997 for the *Compassion & Culture* newsletter of Capitol Research Center (find them online at www.capitalresearch.org/publications), he traces their history:

> Summit Ministries had its beginnings when David Noebel went to graduate school in philosophy at the University of Wisconsin in 1959. He faced intense intellectual opposition to his faith, and became convinced of the importance of both engaging secular thought and defending Christian truths. . . . "I had a great education there, but I very nearly lost my Christian bearings," he recalls. "My own experience is a perfect example of why we need to have this ministry."

> In 1962 [the year the Supreme Court outlawed prayer in public schools], Dr. Noebel, founded Summit Ministries in Manitou Springs, Colorado, to focus on reaching teenagers. Its purpose, in the words of its mission statement, is "helping Christian parents prepare their teenagers to withstand the non-Christian and even anti-Christian humanistic onslaught in the schools and throughout society. Teens equipped by Summit Ministries not only can weather anti-Christian attacks; they are capable of working to reclaim culture for Christ.". . .

> As the "culture wars" heated up, Summit grew. In 1989, Christian family expert Dr. James Dobson recommended the ministry to his thousands of radio listeners. In his book Children at Risk, co-written with pro-family activist Gary Bauer, Dr. Dobson laid out the importance of teaching children how to face today's moral, social, and religious issues: . . . "Those who would capture the hearts and minds of your kids certainly have a plan to get across what they want them to know. What countermeasures have you taken? Can we afford to prepare more haphazardly than they? . . . One of the best programs for teaching the concepts I've described is called Summit Ministries, located in Manitou Springs, Colorado."

Summit's program revolves around comparing four worldviews: Biblical Christianity, Secular Humanism, Marxism/Leninism, and Cosmic Humanism (this encompasses traditional Eastern religion and modern New

Summit Ministries

Ages 16–21. Program cost, including housing, meals, tuition, lectures, guest speakers, insurance, most outings, and class picture, $625. Non-refundable $75 deposit.
PO Box 207
Manitou Springs, CO 80829
(719) 685-9103
info@summit.org, www.summit.org

To find out about Bryan College credit for your Summit course, visit **www.bryan.edu/worldview/ summit/credit.pdf**

"What I Learned at TeenPact"
by Laura Hinely

Florida Governor Jeb Bush shook my hand in February of this year. In October of 2000, I visited the Mongolian Embassy to the United Nations in New York. I've traveled to Washington, D.C., to learn about campaigning, and spent a week in Alabama with over a hundred other Christian students who care about making a difference in today's government.

TeenPact is the nonprofit organization that enabled me to travel to these places as a high-school student. TeenPact has been one of my favorite parts of home-schooling.

All students begin at the same place in TeenPact—attending a four-day class at their state capital. Most of these classes take place from January to May. North Carolina and Massachusetts are presently the only states with summer classes. TeenPact is currently in 33 states, from Hawaii to New York, and their goal is to be in all 50. At a state class the goal is to get students involved in everything and let them experience the political process firsthand. Students coming to TeenPact do not just read a book about how a bill becomes a law; they write their own bill and pass it in a mock legislature using parliamentary procedure!

I attended my first TeenPact class only because some of my friends were going. First, I completed the preliminary homework—writing a bill, memorizing verses, setting up meetings with our legislators, reading the state of the state address, and writing a paper on "Leaders in the Bible." Then I packed my clothes and drove with three other friends to Tallahassee.

The excitement hit us when we realized we were in the very place that laws were passed and important people made decisions every day! I still remember the friendly smiles of the well-dressed staff greeting me when I arrived at the capital in Tallahassee for my first TeenPact class four years ago—they looked me in the eye and shook my hand. The week had so many surprises in store for my friends and me. Various elected officials gave motivating speeches. We watched anxiously and prayed as the senate debated a partial-birth abortion bill. I met my senator and Lieutenant Governor Frank Brogan. I learned the basics of parliamentary procedure and visited the Supreme Court. I couldn't wait to go home and tell my parents everything I had learned.

I know what you're thinking: "But my son or daughter doesn't want to be a politician! Why should they go to TeenPact?" I don't want to be the first female President of the United States either; I want to get married and be a mother. But I also want to be a good citizen. I want to know how to make a difference, understand legislation, and be aware of current events. TeenPact provides a way that someone as young as 13 can spend four days at their capital to begin to learn and be excited about being involved in government! Tuition is quite affordable: only $169 for all four days (meals not included). Even kids between the ages of 8 and 12 can attend the one-day class at their state capital, for just $29.

What better place to learn about the political system than TeenPact, with other Christian young people who hold high moral standards? TeenPact is extremely educational, yet it is also the spiritual aspect that inspires the students. The TeenPact staff begins each four-day class in prayer for all the students. Every day starts out with singing praises to God and a devotion led by one of the staff.

With this spiritual bond and a desire to be responsible citizens, TeenPact students find they have many things in common. I have been staffing TeenPact classes for the last three years and like many other TeenPact students, I've made lifelong friends. Most state classes provide a camp for students to spend the night at during the week, and after a long day at the capital, we have fun together!

TeenPact's motto is "Changing Lives To Change America." My life is one of the many that has been changed by TeenPact, spiritually and politically. Now I am always reading up on current events and bills that are on the floor. I've volunteered to help out my local Republican Party and met my congressman. Spiritually, I am more focused. I have had so much encouragement from TeenPact to honor my parents, to be modest, to serve others. I want to pass on the encouragement that the TeenPact leaders gave me, the encouragement and wisdom that has helped me grow as a Christian.

TeenPact plants the seed of desire in students to be leaders, a desire to serve others, and a desire to make a difference. Americans should have a passion for citizenship! TeenPact provides a positive environment that instills these values in families. I encourage all students and their parents who hold these same ideals to attend TeenPact.

If the alumni summer and fall events look good to you, then start planning to attend your next state TeenPact class in January through May of this year or the next!

Laura Hinely graduated May of 2002 after homeschooling for eleven years. She has written for the Orlando Sentinel *and plans to continue writing after attending Florida College.*

Age religion). Experts in various fields address students about the underlying worldviews behind hot-topic modern issues. In between classes, teens engage in outdoor and camplike activities.

Having seen Summit's *Understanding the Times* video curriculum and book (both reviewed in my guide to homeschooling grades 7–12), I wish they'd add one more: Psychology as "Science" and Religion. After all, psychology is the only fully established state religion of our day. Consider: when have you ever heard a lawyer call a humanist or a Marxist to the stand to give "expert" testimony about the culpability or credibility of a witness, or required a culprit to attend mandated New Age or Bible-reading sessions? Yet we don't blink when psychologists and psychiatrists are called as expert witnesses (although no two psychological theories agree!), or when courts mandate psychological "therapy" (even though study after study shows it doesn't work).

But in spite of Summit's oddly uncritical acceptance of extrabiblical psychological thinking, this program has taken tens of thousands of Christian teens farther than they ever have been before on the journey to confident Christian thinking.

Founded in 1994 by Tim Echols to show young Christians how government works, **TeenPact** has expanded to offer annual classes in two-thirds of the states. For more details, see Laura Hinely's article on the left!

Levels of participation in TeenPact vary. Some students may chose to only attend the four-day state class, while others may go on to staff future classes. After attending the four-day state class, students may chose to go to TeenPact alumni events. These events are only open to alumni of the state classes, so start planning to attend your state class next year if any of these interest you! Bear in mind that all the alumni class prices include room and board as well as tuition.

- For people who love the great outdoors, there is TeenPact Survival. This was one of Laura Hinely's favorite alumni events. "We had a whole day in the woods where each team cooked their own lunch, built a shelter and a compass," she explains. "I learned a lot about teamwork skills, and dependence on God." In 2003 it was available in three locations: Virginia, New Mexico, and Georgia.
- TeenPact University is an apologetics class. The 2003 TPU was from July 26–31 in Dallas, TX.
- Anyone who wants to be an Attorney or Judge should attend TeenPact Judicial (recently renamed "Take Back the Courts Pre-Law Training"). Attorneys give advice about what a Christian should do as an Attorney or Judge. The 2003 class was July 16–21 at Regent Law School in Virginia Beach, VA.
- TeenPact Challenge is for young men only! Set in the rural Alabama backwoods, it provides both physical and spiritual training for those who want to be mature Christian men, husbands, and fathers. Includes some "para-military training," including learning the safe use of firearms.

The National Convention is the most widely attended annual TeenPact event. Students come from all over the United States to listen to excellent speakers, such as Bill Jack from Worldview Academy, and attend various workshops. In 2002 the TeenPact National Convention was held in May on St. Simon's Island, Georgia. *Laura Hinely and Mary Pride*

TeenPact

Ages 13–19. Ages 8–12 can attend the one-day class. 1-day state class, $29. Four-day state class, $169. TeenPact Survival, $199. TeenPact University, $249. Take Back the Courts, $499. TeenPact Challenge, $199. National Convention, $299.
PO Box 9
Jefferson, GA 30549
(888) 343-1776
www.teenpact.com

TEENPACT STATE CLASSES ARE AVAILABLE IN:

AL, AZ, AR, CO, FL, GA, HI, IA, ID, IL, IN, KY, LA, MA, ME, MO, MS, NC, ND, NH, NM, NY, OH, OK, OR, RI, SC, TX, VA, WA, and WY. Over 1,000 students attended TeenPact state classes in 2003.

Worldview Academy

Ages 13–17. $545 for first year
student. $495 for alumni.
PO Box 310106
New Braunfels, TX 78131
(830) 620-5203
www.worldview.org

2004 Worldview Academy Camp Schedule

- Flagstaff, AZ June 13–18
- Oakland, CA June 27–July 2
- San Diego, CA June 20–25
- Mount Berry, GA July 18-23
- St. Paul, MN June 20–25
- Liberty, MO June 13–18
- Winston-Salem, NC July 11–16
- Oxford, OH June 27–July 2
- McMinnville, OR July 4–9
- Reading, PA July 4–9
- Waco, TX June 6–11
- New Braunfels, TX Oct 3–8
- Seattle, WA July 11–16 & 18–23

Worldview Academy Leadership Camps offer young adults intensive training in Worldview, Leadership, and Christian Apologetics. Camps are offered mostly during June and July at college campuses throughout the United States. The sole exception: The October camp at a ranch in Texas. That one is a particularly good camp at which to meet homeschoolers, since who else can take a week off in the middle of October?

My two oldest sisters and I attended the Missouri leadership camp a couple of years ago. Sarah and Frank attended the Sky Ranch camp in Van, TX, last year, and Magda attended the Liberty, MO, camp. These camps involve a lot of "classroom" time, and a lot of right-to-the-point educational lectures on how Christianity affects your perspective on the world, and on what other common worldviews you will face as a Christian. Since then, several of us have returned as alumni at our own request (and using our own money to pay for the camps!), which pretty much shows how we felt about the WVA experience.

When we visited the Liberty, MO, camp a couple of years ago, we toured an art museum, listened to commentary on the religious background of the art, and participated in frustrating debates with the WVA staff's "evil twins," who embody various anti-Christian worldviews and refuse to get caught by anything in debate. We adhered to a strict schedule, met some great folks, and had a "joyful" time. That "joyful" in quotes is a WVA inside joke. Go to WVA and find out what it means! *Joseph Pride*

My Week at Worldview Academy
by Sarah Pride

A "worldview camp." What on earth is that? That was my unspoken question the day my mom told my older brother and me that we were going to a camp for learning worldview. I didn't want to go anywhere I wouldn't know what to expect. Why would I need a "worldview" camp? My worldview was fine! But off to the camp—nervous, shy, and scared—I went with my older brother Joe and my younger sister Magda.

"WHAT'S YOUR NAME?!?" It was the first day of WorldView Academy camp, and all the kids were gathered around in a circle. The counselors had announced we would be split into three teams for camp-long fun competition. And now one of them had come within three inches of a male camper and screamed in his face. "A-adam," the camper replied, a little timidly. "LOUDER!" came the returning bellow. "ADAM!!!" he screamed, blowing back the counselor's hair. The counselor turned, red in the face and beaming, "Good. Now that's what you all have to do." He counted down to three, and each counselor was off like a shot! As soon as each new person screamed his or her name, he or she grabbed the shoulders of the counselor and ran behind him to another person. That person would grab the first one's shoulders, and so on, until there were huge snakes rushing around everywhere and everyone was picked.

That was obviously the icebreaker, and it worked, for nobody felt even a trace of shyness after acting like an idiot and watching everyone else do the same thing.

That was the beginning of a totally fun experience that left me feeling a certain companionship with every teacher and counselor, and with every student. It was like a little week away from the world, yet training us to live better in the world. Most of the time, even until 10:00 at night, we spent in intriguing lectures by such people as Jeff Baldwin, Bill Jack (a natural comedian), and Randy Sims. We studied several different types of religions and several particular worldviews such as atheism and Marxism. We held question-and-answer sessions where our instructors turned into their "evil twins," who played the part of an abortion advocate, an evolutionist, a New Ager, or a homosexual (as non-offensively as possible) to test our debate skill with these types of people. One day, we went out on the streets of Kansas City and surveyed people on the Ten Commandments as a step-off to discussing religion. Another, we walked to the Mormon tabernacle where Joseph Smith had stayed and politely discussed religion with the Mormons there.

Mentally, and spiritually too, the feeling of the camp was like one big body with all the little parts liking each other and working together—the body of Christ.

CHAPTER 62

Homeschooling Around the World

As I close this book, I thought you'd enjoy a look at the future of homeschooling as a worldwide movement. Homeschooling has grown amazingly in the USA, is picking up speed in Canada, and is well on its way in most other English-speaking countries. But will it end there? Or is the first *real* educational reform movement in over a century now posed to sweep worldwide?

The rest of this chapter, written by Home School Legal Defense Senior Counsel Christopher Klicka, and excerpted from two articles originally published in *Practical Homeschooling* magazine, gives you a glimpse of the future.

Homeschooling Around the World: A Special Report by Chris Klicka

When I began working at the Home School Legal Defense Association in 1985, it was only clearly legal to homeschool in about five states. It was essentially open season on homeschoolers everywhere as the Holy Spirit was moving on parents to remove their children from public school and to teach them at home. The battles were fierce from school district to school district and from state to state across the country. We at HSLDA spent much time in the courts and legislatures across the country to win the right for parents to choose homeschooling.

Now, I am pleased to report that homeschooling is legal in all 50 states. But the work is not over, as many officials try to misapply law, and state legislatures try to bring back the old restrictions and regulations.

The rest of the world has been watching us. HSLDA receives regular communications from around the world. Since God has blessed HSLDA's work, we are excited about sharing the strategies that have been successful to legalize homeschooling in the United States. We also, on a regular basis, share our research on the success of homeschooling.

As I have had the opportunity to travel around the world to many countries, I realize that homeschooling is no longer a United States phenomena. Homeschooling is gradually but steadily spreading across the world as the moral decay in public schools everywhere continues.

Homeschooling is spreading like wildfire! Join a globetrotting HSLDA attorney as he helps set up homeschool groups in other lands.

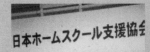

Practicacl Homeschooling columnist and Home School Legal Defense Association Senior Counsel Chris Klicka as keynote speaker, Hosa conference, Tokyo, Japan

The Internet is playing a major role in bringing the world closer together. Parents in foreign countries are able to learn much about homeschooling and as a result are looking to HSLDA to help them make it legal.

HSLDA legal staff work regularly with homeschool leaders and homeschool associations in various countries. The assistance includes recommending legal and political strategies, sending homeschool studies and materials, corresponding and sometimes meeting with members of Parliament and various government officials, organizing letter writing campaigns to various foreign embassies, talking to foreign press, visiting and speaking in the country, and helping establish national legal defense associations for homeschoolers.

HSLDA also has provided seed money to start legal defense associations, purchase printing equipment, and buy other needed resources to homeschool leaders in various countries.

We urge you to catch the vision of being a homeschool "missionary" to help homeschooling, and inevitably the Gospel, spread around the world. Our website, www.hslda.org, has a international section, which we update regularly of the news and developments in over 20 countries. I will try to give you just a small taste of the homeschooling work going on around the world.

Germany: Homeschoolers Still Face Difficulties

Schulunterricht zu Hause (Schooling At Home)
info@german-homeschool.de
www.german-homeschool.de

I have traveled to Germany three times, helping the fledgling homeschool movement by working to establish a legal defense organization for homeschoolers called School Instruction At Home. Presently it has over 40 member families and the main attorney, Gabrielle Eckermann, has been doing a tremendous job. He won several cases in the courts, convincing the judges that education is taking place and to simply leave the families alone, although German laws do not specifically allow for homeschooling.

German homeschool leaders Richard and Ingrid Guenther and their children

One of the legal defense organization's cases, called the Conrad case, is going before the high court in Germany and is being handled by Ronald Richert, a Christian constitutional lawyer with extensive experience in the courts. We are also working together with the European Center for Law and Justice to bring at least one case before the human rights court in the European Union. Approximately two years ago, we sent out an alert on behalf of the Harder family in Germany, who had their house ransacked by the police and were facing a two-year prison sentence. Within three weeks of sending out the alert, and having thousands of families contact the German embassy in the United States and around the world, the case was dropped and the family has continued to homeschool.

National Czech Home School Association
m.semin@volny.cz or semin@gts.cz

Czech Republic

Over 300 families homeschool in the Czech Republic. The Czech Home School Association is run very efficiently by Michal Semin, who has successfully lobbied the Parliament to win the right to homeschool until the fifth grade. Approximately a year ago, I visited the Czech Republic and discovered that they were facing legislation that would virtually outlaw homeschooling. Michal Semin asked for our help, and HSLDA sent out an alert to have homeschoolers contact the Czech Parliament. Within 24 hours the Czech Parliament server was shut down because of the volume of emails. The bill that would have negatively affected homeschoolers died.

Although they had a breather, the Czech Republic is facing new legislation again that we are prepared to help them with.

Australia: Things Are Looking Up Down Under

Australian Terry Harding and family

Australia has one of the oldest homeschool movements after the United States. They have waged many legal battles over the years to win and maintain the right to homeschool. All homeschoolers (estimated at 35,000 families) homeschool under fairly reasonable laws. The state of Queensland, however, continues to try to implement restrictive teacher qualification legislation. Terry Harding, who runs the Australian Christian Academy, estimates that he has over 1,500 families who are part of his homeschool program. He works hard to lobby before their Parliament and conducts research on the success of homeschooling.

Australian Christian Academy
terryharding@
australianchristianacademy.org

Mexico: Discipleship Time

Mike Richardson, an American missionary, has lived in Mexico for over a decade. He has established the *El Hogar Educador*, a free homeschool newsletter which is now distributed to over 19 Spanish-speaking nations. He also organizes two annual homeschool conferences near Monterrey and Mexico City. Thousands of

Mexican homeschool conference shoppers

Mexicans attend his conferences each year. He has translated some American books into Spanish and provides free copies of the tapes of the speakers at his conferences to any family who asks for them. Without clear compulsory attendance laws, homeschooling is flourishing and legal. Quality education is hard to come by in Mexico, and many families are poor. Homeschooling is providing an answer to this educational dilemma. It is enabling families to provide a good and affordable education.

El Hogar Educador
vnm@characterlink.net
www.elhogareducador.org

Hungary: Homeschooling Is Just Beginning

Sandra Lovelace in Hungary

Homeschooling is growing largely through the Christian church in Hungary. The law allows for private schools. Homeschoolers can easily qualify as private schoolers in Hungary and

Hungarian Home Schooling Association (HHSA)
kgtmi@axelero.hu

therefore can legally operate. At my urging, Imre Scszokoe established the Hungarian Home School Association. Over 25 families have joined and the ranks are growing daily.

Sandra with Hungarian children

The Hungarian Home School Association has held a homeschool convention at least twice a year for the last two years. Many of the Hungarians speak English and can use English textbooks. They are hoping to have many eventually translated into the Hungarian language. The Hungarian Home School Association is working through young pastors throughout the country to educate the congregations on the benefits of homeschooling.

Romanian Homeschool Association
curcubetg@nextra.ro

Romania: Homeschooling Is Close to Becoming Legal

Romanian Gabriel Curcubet and family

In Romania the homeschool movement is very small because the laws are not clear. Homeschooling is considered by many to be illegal. At my urging, Gabriel Curcubet established the Romanian Home School Association and is regularly lobbying Parliament to encourage them to pass a law legalizing homeschooling.

I have supplied him with resolutions from the US Congress recognizing the many benefits of homeschooling along with a letter from President Bush and Congressman Jim Ryun. These letters have been passed on to the Vice-Chairman of the Education Committee in the Romanian Parliament, who is now completely convinced of the need to legalize homeschooling. Earlier this year we sent out an email alert urging people to contact the Education Committee of the Romanian Parliament and to ask the Committee to officially recognize homeschooling. We will continue to work with Gabriel to strategize and provide support for drafting new language this spring that we hope will be passed so that home-schooling will be officially legal in Romania.

Curcubet children at work

Pestalozzi Trust
defensor@pestalozzi.org, pestalozzi.org

South Africa: Homeschooling Is Organized

We have worked with South Africa since 1995 to help homeschooling to become legal. In 1996, a national law was passed allowing for homeschooling throughout the provinces. However, the trouble is in the details. Each province is free to determine how they will regulate homeschooling.

Realizing this made legal battles likely, I traveled in 1997 to South Africa and helped them establish the Pestalozzi Trust Legal Defense Fund for Home Education. Leendert von Oostrum is president, and the Legal

Defense Fund has nearly 800 members across the country. The Pestalozzi Trust is keeping homeschooling free in South Africa. However, the battle is becoming more intense as the Minister of Education has declared war on Christianity and homeschooling in South Africa.

Japan: Homeschooling Is Catching On

Homeschooling father Hiro Inaba started the Christian Home Education Association of Japan a few years ago. I have been working with Hiro to help promote home-schooling in Japan through various means. Two years ago I traveled to Tokyo and spoke to hundreds of interested parents, urging them to homeschool. The business community strongly supports homeschooling and sees it as a solution to the 300,000 dropouts from high school each year. As a result, the business community has funded the establishment of another national group called HOSA. Although homeschooling is not technically recognized in Japanese law, the authorities are "looking the other way" as they leave families alone who homeschool.

Hiro Inaba family

Hiro Inaba, who is definitely a pioneer in the homeschool movement, is working to translate many homeschool curricula into Japanese.

In 2002 I was invited by the Atmark Corporation to come to Japan to speak at the first-ever national homeschool conference. I had urged the businessmen to hold a conference and to create a national homeschool association. The plan was to launch this national homeschool association, HOSA, at the time of the conference. I encouraged them to hold a press conference and to set up a meeting with the Ministry of Education.

When my wife and I arrived in Japan, the Tokyo Broadcasting Service (TBS) was waiting at the gate and filmed us as we walked down the corridors to customs. After going through customs, the TBS reporters whisked my wife and me away in separate vehicles to take us to the hotel. During the trip to the hotel, a cameraman in the front seat filmed me while I was interviewed in the back seat.

CHEA of Japan
HiroInaba@cheajapan.com
HOSA
adachi8@email.msn.com

Japanese homeschooleres have their own magazine!

Tokyo newspaper article about homeschooling

Over the next several days, I had nonstop interviews with the Japanese press and spoke at a large press conference with all the major networks and newspapers in attendance. Some of the newspapers that carried excellent stories on homeschooling were the *Daily Yomiuri*, the *Nikkei* (the *Wall Street Journal* of Japan), the *Tokyo Shimbun* (the largest paper in Tokyo), Japan Today.com, and many others. The newly established homeschool association, HOSA, had been endorsed by the president of Microsoft of Japan and other major business leaders. The university community also endorsed HOSA. In fact, the president of HOSA, Shigeru Narita, is an education professor at Hyogo University. Akio Hata, a professor at the Saitama Institute of Technology, also serves on the board of HOSA. The vice-chairman of HOSA, Kozo Hino, is the president of Atmark. He and his advisor, Jun Adachi, were the main organizers of HOSA and were instrumental in involving the press. HOSA now even has their own homeschool magazine!

The business leaders arranged for me to meet with a high-level official in the Ministry of Education who, upon understanding the homeschool concept, highly endorsed the idea. Because Japan's compulsory attendance law is at the federal level, the Ministry of Education's decisions and opinions are very important to local school authorities. We are hoping to get the Minister of Education to sign a letter publicly endorsing the homeschooling concept.

TBS and NHK have come out to our offices in the United States for a second time to do additional programs. The last program aired by TBS resulted in well over 300 phone calls to HOSA of interested persons. As a result, dozens of new homeschool families have joined the HOSA organization. My wife and I were utterly amazed at the professionalism of the HOSA organization and the 100 percent support of the Japanese media. In the meantime, the Christian Home Educators Association of Japan (CHEA of Japan) has started with Hiro Inaba as president. I was able to network CHEA and HOSA and encourage them to work together as partners. CHEA of Japan mainly represents the small Christian community of parents interested in homeschooling in Japan.

HOSA and the homeschoolers of Japan are now looking for curricular materials to translate into Japanese and are also working with the Christian homeschoolers to develop Japanese curricula.

Home School Legal Defense Association of Canada
www.hsldacanada.org

Canada: Homeschooling Is Well-Established

Canada is another country where homeschooling flourishes. We helped the Canadians form the Home School Legal Defense Association of Canada, which presently has 2,500 member families. The homeschool movement is proving very popular throughout the provinces of Canada. One nationwide study showed that homeschoolers in Canada are scoring above average on the standardized tests, and another study is in the works. The Legal Defense Association stays busy, however, like HSLDA in the United States, with many school officials throughout the provinces exceeding the law. Similar to the US, Canada's greatest problem is social workers. HSLDA of Canada stands up to the social workers to protect the privacy rights of homeschool families and have enjoyed much success through the negotiations and in court.

Russian Evangelistic Ministries
okhotin@hotmail.com

Ukraine: Homeschool Persecution Ceases

Earlier this year in the Odessa region of Ukraine, five homeschool families were prosecuted for teaching their children at home. HSLDA worked through Andrew Okhotin with the Russian Evangelistic Ministries to open up communication with these five families. We also issued an email alert urging people to contact the Ukrainian embassy. Within weeks of the Ukraine embassy being deluged with calls, letters, and emails, the federal government of Ukraine wrote a letter to the five families stating that it was legal for them to homeschool. Local authorities have since backed off. The homeschool movement is very small and not yet organized.

Home Service
info@home-service.org

England: Homeschooling Is Growing by Leaps & Bounds

In England, Roger and Ruth Slack of the Home Service organization have done much work to help homeschooling grow. It is estimated that as many as 100,000 children are being homeschooled in Great Britain. It is legal to homeschool, and all the American curricula are available to the English homeschoolers. The legal problems are almost non-existent as the homeschool ranks swell.

How You Can Help

Homeschooling is growing throughout the world. The task of helping other countries legalize homeschooling is daunting. The curriculum needs are great. We at HSLDA can't do everything, but we can do something. What we can do, we ought to do, to help the least of these who are desperate for our support. Here are some suggestions on what you can do to help.

- **Adopt a country.** Learn all you can about the homeschool movement there by checking the HSLDA website at www.hslda.org. For each country, we summarize the laws, the homeschool population, the latest news, and we also give a short history of the development of the homeschool movement in that country and a description of the Christian homeschool associations. Use this ministry as an opportunity to instruct your children and do a unit study on the country. Have your children explore its history, culture, traditions, and geography. Consider developing pen pals by directly contacting the organizations listed on HSLDA's website.
- **Pray regularly for homeschoolers around the world.** There is power in prayer. We have seen the miracles God has done on behalf of homeschoolers in the United States. If we do not pray for homeschoolers, who will?
- **Join HSLDA** to support our efforts to assist other countries in helping homeschooling to be legalized. You can join HSLDA by calling (540) 338-5600 or visiting our website at www.hslda.org. We could not assist homeschoolers in other countries without membership support.
- **Respond to HSLDA alerts** by writing or calling foreign embassies, encouraging them to inform their governments that parents need to be allowed to homeschool. Though these alerts and our work with governments in other countries, we've had great success. This has resulted in legalizing homeschooling in South Africa and freeing a family in prison, causing a case to be dismissed in Germany and establishing the legal defense fund, stopping cold legislation in Ireland that would have required homeschoolers to submit to home visits, derailing legislation that would have outlawed homeschooling in the Czech Republic, furthering the cause of homeschooling in Japan and Romania, ending prosecution of homeschoolers in Ukraine, and much more.
- **Donate** money, used books, and other homeschool products to help the fledgling homeschool organizations succeed.
- **Convince your homeschool support group to do a fundraiser** to help a particular country or foreign Christian homeschool association.

There are many other ideas, but these will give you a good beginning. Praise God for His work around the world!

CURRICULUM

Quick Resource Guide

In the next pages, you'll find a collection of resources almost as big as this brother and sister's collection of trophies! Wallingford, CT, homeschoolers Gabriel and Gabriella Bradley each began studying Shotokan Karate when they were 3 years old, under the instruction of Sensei Robert DeLeon, owner of DeLeon's American Shotokan Karate, located in their hometown. Gabriel (6 years old) and Gabriella (4 years old) together have won more than 40 trophies and medals in various competitions in the past two years, including 20 first-place awards. Gabriel holds the rank of High Green Belt and will soon test for his Purple Belt, while Gabriella has achieved the rank of Yellow Belt and is in preparation for her Green Belt test. Both kids are members of the school's elite Demonstration Team, and hold the distinction of being the youngest students ever to study with Sensei DeLeon. Their interest in and enthusiasm for martial arts make Gabriel and Gabriella kids to watch out for!

Quick Resource Guide

Most homeschool books include dozens of pages of lists of homeschool resources. These lists are often not as helpful as they look because many of them fall into one or more of these categories:

- **They are out of date.** For example, I have seen my own company listed with the wrong state, telephone number, and web address—all in the same book's listing! I can easily spot when an author's "resource list" is actually snaffled from other people's books by which telltale addresses are conspicuously out of date. Since my own company hasn't moved or changed its phone number or web address for many years, in order for someone to get any (let alone *all*) of these wrong, they are cribbing from someone's *very* old list. Or perhaps, to be charitable, it is their *own* list—which they haven't bothered to check or update for ten years.
- **They don't tell you enough to *use* them.** This is by far the most common failing. If you had time to personally check out hundreds of curriculum companies, you wouldn't be buying a book to help you with this in the first place.
- **They are slanted to favor a particular homeschool philosophy and exclude all others.** So while you think you're getting a complete overview of what's available, you're actually getting only contact information for products whose teaching method the author favors.
- **They leave out Christian publishers, organizations, and/or websites.** Since most homeschoolers are Christians, and most of the curriculum produced for homeschooling comes from Christian companies, this is a severe shortcoming. It is *not* "more balanced" to leave out $5/6$ of what's available.
- **They provide "laundry lists" of resources.** You could spend an afternoon at the library and another one online and come up with huge unannotated lists of books and websites yourself. So what kind of help is this?

What you *really* need is a large book or two that reviews all the most important curriculum, subject by subject, not a "Yellow Pages" style list that forces you to do all the work.

Start with Resource Books

In short, what you really need is a homeschool resource book.

You'll find lots of homeschool books in the stores these days. But only a handful are by authors who have been reviewing curriculum since the 1980s.

You can trust the reviews in the following books to be professional, helpful, and based on personal experience with the products. These books are all about resources with some how-tos mixed in, not the other way around.

Just what the doctor ordered, before you start spending hundreds of dollars on curriculum!

Christian Home Educator's Curriculum Manual: Elementary Grades (Fifth Edition)

Parents. $22.95.
Grove Publishing, CA. (714) 841-1220. www.grovepublishing.com

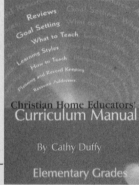

The latest edition at the time I'm writing this (January 2004) is the "2000" edition. Still, the vast majority of information in it is still current enough to be useful. Author Cathy Duffy started reviewing homeschool curriculum about the same time I did, which means you're looking at close to two decades of experience here.

The book is over 500 pages. The first 56 pages are devoted to "how to

homeschool" and the rest is reviews interspersed with some how-tos. Cathy reviews not just products from major curriculum publishers (although they of course are covered), but also software, parent helps, educational games and videos, etc. What you won't find: laundry lists of library books and websites. What you will find: products actually popular with homeschoolers. As she says, "Mary [Pride] and I differ in our opinions on many products," so if you want a second opinion, this is the book to get!

Cathy includes a section on what your child should know at each grade level (a mini "scope and sequence" followed by the California standards by grade level). She explains how to choose curriculum and how learning styles work. Other topics, such as testing, and how to teach worldviews, are also touched on.

Cathy's children are more "hands-on" learners than mine, so many of her reviews take special note of how well a product will work with this type of learner.

Solidly Christian throughout, as the name implies.

Christian Home Educator's Curriculum Manual: Junior/Senior Grades (Fifth Edition)

Parents. $22.95.
Grove Publishing, CA. (714) 841-1220. www.grovepublishing.com

Again, the latest edition at time of writing came out in 2000. Cathy Duffy has lots of very practical advice for parents of homeschooled teens. The first part of the book takes you step-by-step through developing a pre-college or

pre-career plan for your teen. Her reviews of curriculum are very meticulous, and you'll find over 300 pages of them in this 496-page book!

The Home School Source Book, 3rd Edition

Parents. $29.95.
Brook Farm Books, ME, or Box 101, Glassville NB E7L 4T4, Canada. Orders: (877) 375-4680 or (506) 375-4680. For free brochure and information or answers to questions email jean@brookfarmbooks.com. Website at www.brookfarmbooks.com under construction at the time of writing.

The first edition of this book was one of the very first homeschool books, and it still has some of that "excitement of unschooling" feel to it. The newest edition, published in 2001, is not just 480 pages of reviews, as you'll find many comments and small essays about various topics interspersed with over 3,000 product listings and reviews.

Some of the reviews are extremely short, while others are more detailed. It's not all curriculum, either. Though all the reviewed items are educational, quite a few reflect "out of the box" thinking about what exactly education means!

Many items can be purchased directly from Brook Farm Books, which is still being run by Jean Reed after the unexpected death of her husband and coauthor, Donn Reed.

Unlike the other resource books mentioned, this has a secular outlook.

Mary Pride's Complete Guide to Homeschooling from Birth to Grade 6

Parents. $26.99.
*Harvest House Publishers, OR. (888) 501-6991.
www.harvesthousepublishers.com.*

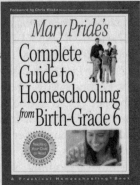

Due out in mid-2004, God willing, this will be a 600+ page book with complete, detailed reviews of products for every age level and school subject.

The most common comment I received from readers of the previous four editions of this book was, "It made me feel like an expert." That's the whole idea, folks!

Mary Pride's Complete Guide to Homeschooling Grades 7–12

Parents. $26.99.
Harvest House Publishers, OR.
(888) 501-6991.
www.harvesthousepublishers.com

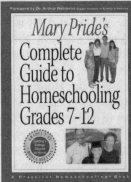

Due out somewhat later in 2004, this will be the most detailed, helpful book ever on how to find exactly the right curriculum and courses and how to prepare your teenager for college or career. At least, that's my goal!

It's the fifth edition of my resource book for this age level, and includes all the practical wisdom of dozens of *Practical Homeschooling* reviewers and contributors as well.

Traditional K–12 Curriculum

Here you'll find workbooks, textbooks, worktexts. Sometimes available as correspondence courses, sometimes a la carte.

The best use of this section, and those following, is to help you decide whose catalogs to send away for and whose websites to check out. Remember, most first-time homeschoolers do best when using a "packaged" curriculum (all from one publisher) for the first year. It gives you security, completeness, and a place to start your own journey as a teacher.

A Beka Correspondence School and A Beka Video Home School

A Beka School Services, Box 18000, Pensacola, FL 32523-9160.
(800) 874-3592. www.abeka.com

Correspondence courses and video courses using A Beka Book materials. Videos and (now) DVDs are only rented and must be returned. Creationist, Christian, patriotic.

A Beka Book Curriculum

A Beka Book, Box 19100, Pensacola, FL 32523-9160. (800) 874-2352.
www.abeka.com

The "a la carte" version. You can purchase books and other supplies directly. Lots of drill and testing. Colorful softbound books from one of the largest Christian school publishers.

Accelerated Christian Education

Accelerated Christian Education, PO Box 299000, Lewisville, TX 75029-9000. (800) 925-7777,
www.aceministries.com.

Just to make my life more interesting, this company seems to change its name every time I'm trying to put together a new book edition! Formerly School of Tomorrow, and before *that* known as Accelerated Christian Education, it's ACE again.

Started in the 1980s, its goal was to provide a curriculum so easy to teach that parents could start their own Christian schools. Result: very easy to use worktexts with less intel-

lectual depth than Alpha Omega's and others. They also offer some very nice video- and worktext-based high-school science courses.

Patriotic and creationist Christian content. Inexpensive. Many courses also available in Spanish.

Alpha Omega Publications

Alpha Omega Publications 300 N. McKemy Ave., Chandler, AZ 85226. (800) 622-3070, www.aop.com.

Publisher of "LIFEPAC Gold" and "Horizons" worktexts widely used in Christian schools and homeschools. Also publishes "Switched-on Schoolhouse" grade-level software. Christian. Not as conservative as some others; some secular thinking on "overpopulation" and ecological issues, among others.

Bob Jones University Press

Bob Jones University Press, Greenville, SC 29614. (800) 845-5731. www.bjup.com

Nothing racist or strange about the excellent, professionally-produced materials from this publisher. Whatever impression the media may have given you about Bob Jones University (fables abound), their curriculum materials are highly popular among Christian homeschoolers for a reason. Many hardbound texts, many teacher's helps, many courses rewritten especially for homeschoolers. Creationist, patriotic.

Calvert School

Calvert School, 105 Tuscany Rd., Baltimore, MD 21210. (410) 785-3400. www.calvertschool.org.

Founded in 1897, Calvert School has been providing a superior, state-accredited, college-prep education from K–8 for about that long. They offer a wide range of both courses and supplemental material. You can purchase entire grade levels as correspondence courses or a la carte. Some course segments are also available a la carte, as are many enrichment courses. Their learning-to-read programs are not intensive phonics, though they do contain some phonetic elements. Nicest feature: lesson plans that not only tell you what to do, but anticipate and head off possible learning problems before they occur.

The Teacher's Manuals for each course are only leased from Calvert and must be destroyed or returned when the course is done.

Because their program is state-accredited, Calvert is forced to use contemporary secular texts and workbooks in subjects for which they have not published their own materials. Until recently, they were always careful to choose the most propaganda-free materials.

Calvert raised some eyebrows in 2001 when they replaced their sixth- and seventh-grade history textbooks with the infamous *A Message of Ancient Days* and *Across the Centuries*. These accompanying workbooks to these textbooks (which Calvert does *not* use) require public-school children to role-play "jihad games," role-play Muslim warriors, and memorize verses from the Koran. The textbooks themselves betray a similar bias, and add to it politically-correct redefinitions of "family" (what is this doing in a *history* book?), reinvention of Attila the Hun as a nice guy (who are they kidding?), and other foolishness, plus blatant put-downs of Christianity and Judaism as compared to Islam throughout the two books.

For details see the various critiques of these books published online at www.blessedcause.org. Be sure to read both the actual textbook excerpts, the publisher Houghton Mifflin's claims about these books, and the site's responses to those claims. It turns out that "the Council on Islamic Education (CIE) helped write the textbook (originally denied by the publisher, Houghton Mifflin, "until their Editorial Director was caught bragging about it in print").

These textbooks are so bad that I found I could not use the course with my own children, forcing me to swallow over $1,000 of curriculum

expenses (since you can't return a Calvert course once you've started writing in the books).

Calvert told me they would work with parents who objected to the history text, but they also told me that practically nobody has complained.

It's true that you need to be able to detect textbook bias and have a pretty good understanding of history to be fully aware of what is going on with these books, so perhaps many parents have no idea what's going on. All the more reason to totally avoid any course based on these books, in my opinion.

Calvert also told me they intend to substitute different books at some point in time, but that it would take years to rewrite the courses. Since there was no actual date given, and this was just a private reassurance, I can't tell you when and if the changes are actually being made.

The last time I saw them (a couple of years ago), Calvert's kindergarten programs were still the best available. Their writing instruction is great throughout the curriculum, and kids who complete Calvert eighth grade should actually know as much as public-school high-school graduates. But if you're a Christian or Jewish parent, or just don't want your kids indoctrinated with Islamic beliefs, I'd avoid their sixth grade and seventh grade complete courses until those books are changed to something more acceptable.

Christian Liberty Academy Satellite Schools

Christian Liberty Press, 502 West Euclid Ave., Arlington Heights, IL 60004-5495. Free information packet: (800) 348-0899. www.homeschools.org.

The CLASS program includes many of their own worktexts and books, plus books from other (mostly Christian) publishers. This started out as a correspondence program, but you can now purchase their materials separately. Solidly Christian, conservative, creationist, patriotic.

Christian Light Education

Christian Light Education, PO Box 1212, Harrisonburg, VA 22803-1212. Orders: (800) 776-0478. To request catalog: (540) 434-0768. www.clp.org.

Very conservative Mennonite publisher. All art in book depicts Mennonite styles of hair and dress: women with hair under coverings, girls in pigtails, men with beards, very modest clothing. Serious, pacifist, creationist, unworldly. Some materials available in Spanish.

Covenant Home Curriculum

Covenant Home Curriculum, N 63 W 23421 Main St, Sussex, WI 53089. (800) 578-242, www.covenanthome.com.

Covenant Home Curriculum wants you to consider them as "the Christian alternative to Calvert." Developed over a 15-year period in a K–12 Christian day school in suburban Milwaukee, this eclectic curriculum strongly emphasizes a Reformed Protestant worldview, classical literature, writing and speaking skills, a reverently scientific and creationist outlook on life, and in-depth biblical knowledge. The curriculum includes the Covenant Home Preceptor, a manual for parents that explains how to administer the program; study guides especially prepared for homeschoolers; simple diagnostic tests; and study helps, such as Covenant's own Guide to Writing Book Reports, and Day-By-Day Scheduling, a calendar/lesson planner for each grade that tells what to do and when to do it. All texts and workbooks include answer keys and teaching guides.

Covenant publishes some of their own materials, and obtains the rest from a variety of (mostly Christian) publishers.

Home Study International

Home Study International, PO Box 4437, Silver Spring, MD 20914-4437. (800) 782-4769. www.hsi.edu.

Established originally in 1909 as "Fireside Correspondence School," a service to Seventh-day Adventists (SDA). Still available as correspondence program, approved by a number of organizations, including the Distance Education and Training Council, the International Council for Distance Education, and the Maryland State Department of Education.

Some of their own materials used, plus some SDA texts from other publishers, some Christian texts, and some from public-school publishers.

HSI's own materials are conservative and pro-family. Some of the public school texts HSI uses are less so.

Religiously, HSI is creationist and evangelistic.

Landmark's Freedom Baptist Curriculum

Landmark's Freedom Baptist Curriculum, 2222 E. Hinson Ave., Haines City, FL 33844. (800) 700-LFBC. www.landmarkbaptistchurch.org/lfbc.

Rather unattractive, simply laid out, spiral-bound worktexts. Definite "back to basics" feel. Christian, creationist, patriotic, and of course, conservative Baptist in outlook. Heavier on the Christian doctrine and lighter on the secular academics than other Christian publishers.

Rod and Staff Publishers

Rod and Staff Publishers, Box 3, Hwy 172, Crockett, KY 41413-0003. (606) 522-4348. Unofficial site (not theirs) where you can buy R&S material: www.anabaptists.org/ras/. Another unofficial site: www.rodstaff.com/.

Large, serious publisher of Mennonite books. Very inexpensive materials, many hardbound. Mennonite standards of hair, dress, and behavior depicted. Bible integrated as much as possible into all subjects. Curriculum only goes through grade 8, when some Amish and Mennonite children graduate school for good. Unworldly, pacifist, creationist.

Catholic Curriculum

Kolbe Academy

Kolbe Academy Home School, 2501 Oak Street, Napa, CA 94559. (707) 255-6499, www.kolbe.org.

A classical education program from an orthodox Catholic "Ignatian" point of view. Very serious implementation of the trivium. Short and sweet teacher materials. *Not a* correspondence program; parents do all the grading. Kolbe has been around since 1980, but only began making a splash in the homeschool community in the past five years.

Our Lady of the Rosary School

Our Lady of the Rosary School, 116-1/2 North 3rd Street, Bardstown, KY 40004. (502) 348-1338. www.olrs.com.

Hyper-Catholic program, more activity-oriented and less intellectual than the others. Uses classic Catholic schooltexts from years gone by whenever possible. Since 1983.

Our Lady of Victory School

Our Lady of Victory School, 421 S. Lochsa, Post Falls, ID 83854. (208) 773-7265. www.olvs.org.

Correspondence program with parents totally accountable to OLV, including the requirement of a dress code at home. Classical Catholic curriculum materials, including many they reprint themselves. Since 1977.

Seton Home Study School

Seton Home Study School, 1350 Progress Drive, Front Royal, VA 22630, (540) 636-9990, www.setonhome.org.

Textbook-oriented with some classical elements, flexibly structured, full-service correspondence program. Seton now publishes its own "For Young Catholics" textbooks for most school subjects. These are written for *home*, not classroom, use. Lesson manuals must be returned when you are done with the course. Since 1980.

Classical Curriculum

Great Books Academy

Great Books Academy, P.O. Box 11379, Bainbridge Island, WA 98110. Fax: (206) 855-1239, greatbooksacademy.org. They do not wish to receive phone calls or emails; either fax them or look at the FAQ on the website.

Classical education program based on the philosophy of the late Dr. Mortimer Adler, who spearheaded the renaissance of classical education in America. In grades nursery–8 the courses are built around the "Good Books" from the list of great children's classics created by the famed classicist, the late Dr. John Senior. In grades 9–12, they study the "Great Books of the Western World." Correspondence program includes 12 subjects: art, cartography (the study of maps), foreign languages, geography, history, language arts, literature, math, music, philosophy, science, and optional Great Books online discussion class for grade 3 and up (run according to the Socratic dialogue method). Services include placement tests, daily lesson plans, quarterly tests and grading. Students are provided online password-protected access to Britannica Encyclopaedia Online (of which Dr. Adler was the editor), Britannica's Annals of American History Online, The Oxford English Dictionary Online, Oxford Research Online, and *Classical Homeschooling* magazine.

Kolbe Academy

Classical education from a Catholic point of view. See listing under "Catholic Curriculum."

Veritas Press

Veritas Press, 1250 Belle Meade Dr., Lancaster, PA 17601. (800) 922-5082. Inquiries: (717) 519-1974. www.veritaspress.com.

Classical Christian approach, including Latin and world history for younger children. Their curriculum uses both their own materials and those from other publishers. Lots of buzz for this publisher, whose catalog has grown like Topsy.

Unit Study Grade-Level Curriculum

Most units last a few weeks. But some companies have put enough units together to make an entire curriculum. Here are the most popular:

Ancient History: Adam to Messiah

www.heartofwisdom.com

Ancient History: Adam to Messiah is a set of seven chronological unit studies you can purchase individually or in one huge binder. By Robin Sampson, co-creator of the original Far Above Rubies.

Far Above Rubies

In His Steps, 1618 Kendolph, Denton, TX 76205. (800) 583-1336 or (940) 566-6123, inhissteps@juno.com.

High-school unit study for girls that concentrates on preparing them to be Christian wives and mothers.

Five In A Row

Five In A Row, P.O. Box 707, Grandview, MO 64030-0707 . (816) 246-9252, www.fiveinarow.com.

Read the same picture book for 5 days. Each day choose a different activity that highlights a different part of the story and focuses on a different academic area. *Before Five In A Row* (for ages 2–4) covers 24 short picture books. The three volumes of *Five In A Row* (ages 4–8) cover 19, 21, and 15 titles respectively. Two fiction and two nonfiction chapter books are used in each volume of *Beyond Five In A Row* (ages 8–12). Unit studies are secular. Separate Christian supplement available.

KONOS Character Curriculum

KONOS, Inc., PO Box 250, Anna, TX 75409. (972) 924-2712, www.konos.com.

The original, much imitated, homeschool unit-study curriculum. KONOS Classic is three huge volumes of unit studies based on character traits. The handy Index makes it usable as an activity source for your own units. The various units of KONOS-In-A-Box and KONOS-In-A-Bag are "packaged" unit studies, with all the materials needed for the activities and reading included. Timelines with cutout historical figures, "History's Heroes" curriculum, and KONOS History of the World high-school curriculum also available. Christian, patriotic. Winner of numerous *Practical Homeschooling Reader Awards.*

Life in America

Life in America, Inc, 347 Rush Lake Rd., Pinckney, MI 48169. lifeameric@aol.com, www.lifeinamerica.com.

Christian unit-study program based on chronological history from 1000 A.D. to the present. Uses books and CD-ROMs (mostly multimedia tutorials) as source material. All books and software needed can be purchased in packages along with the curriculum manuals.

Presently available: *Life in a New World, Life in the Colonies, Life Establishing a Nation, Life in a Nation Divided,* and *Life on the Frontier.* Not yet available: *Life in a Victorian Age* and *Life in a World at War.*

Many specialty curriculum helps are included in the packages, and also available separately: *Learn Along Phonics, Picturesque Writing, Hands on Grammar,* and *Scrapbook of Virtues.*

TRISMS

TRISMS, 1203 S. Delaware Pl., Tulsa, OK 74104. (918) 585-2778, www.trisms.com.

TRISMS Volume I is the only homeschool curriculum developed just for the junior-high years. TRISMS Volumes II and III continue through high school. TRISMS stands for "Time Related Integrated Studies for Mastering Skills." Yes, this is a historical (chronological) and geographical unit study. Sketchier lesson plans than some others, but all the material you actually need is here. Has won the *Practical Homeschooling Reader Award.*

Weaver

Alpha Omega Publications, 300 N. McKemy Ave., Chandler, AZ 85226. (800) 622-3070, www.aop.com.

Alpha Omega bought this popular unit-study program several years ago. The whole enchilada, plus five new volumes of review questions to accompany the original five Weaver volumes, are now available.

The five Weaver volumes are unit studies based on Bible portions. The "prequel" for younger kids, the Interlock, covers Genesis 1–10. Volume 1 of Weaver then picks up at Genesis 11 and continues through the end of Genesis. Volume 2 covers Exodus and the Books of Law. Volume 3: Joshua, Judges, Ruth. Volume 4: Old Testament period of kings and people. Volume 5: Life of Christ. Each is a year of K–6 study in Bible, language arts, history, geography, and science. You can purchase a grades 7–12 supplement for each volume to extend it through those grade levels as well.

Also available: *Day by Day* daily lesson planning book, *Teacher's Friend* (how to get started with homeschooling and Weaver), *1-2-3-Read* beginning reading program, plus unique Weaver resources for spelling, penmanship, grammar, etc.

A World of Adventure

Learning Adventures, 1146 Kensington Court, Seymour, IN 47274. (812) 523-0999 www.learning-adventures.org.

A World of Adventure is the first of five books planned for the Learning Adventures series, a "history" themed unit study curriculum presented in chronological order. It covers Ancient Egypt through the Age of Exploration (from about 2300 B.C. to 1600 A.D.). The second book, *A New*

World of Adventure, covers from 1600–1800. The remaining three books, which aren't available at time of writing, will complete the series to the current day. Winner of the *Practical Homeschooling* Reader Award for unit studies in 2002 and 2003.

Literature Units

BJU BookLinks

Bob Jones University Press, Greenville, SC 29614. (800) 845-5731. From other countries: Call (864) 242-5100, x3349, www.bjup.com

Unit studies for grades 2–6 based on children's fiction published by Bob Jones University Press.

Calvert School

Calvert School, 105 Tuscany Rd., Baltimore, MD 21210. Orders: (888) 487-4652. Inquiries: (410) 785-3400. www.calvertschool.org.

Literature units based on classic (not classical) children's fiction: the Beatrix Potter books, the Robert McCloskey books, *Little House on the Prairie, Little Women, The Giver, Anne Frank: the Diary of a Young Girl, Drifter, Bridge to Terabithia, A Midsummer Night's Dream, Lorna Doone, Anne of Green Gables, Julie of the Wolves, Call of the Wild,* and *Lyddie.*

Covenant Home Curriculum Reader's Guides

Covenant Home Curriculum, N 63 W 23421 Main St, Sussex, WI 53089. (800) 578-242, www.covenanthome.com.

Insightful study guides based on classic children's fiction. Reformed Christian viewpoint. Currently available are Reader's Guides for: *The Adventures of Huckleberry Finn, Call of the Wild, Captains Courageous, Crime and Punishment, Great Expectations, Jane Eyre, Julius Caesar, King Arthur, Moby Dick, The Odyssey, The Red Badge of Courage, Robinson Crusoe, A Tale of Two Cities,* and *Wuthering Heights.* Mostly written and discussion activities. Add some KONOS activities to

make these real unit studies.

Prairie Primer

Cadron Creek Christian Curriculum, NM. (505) 534-1496. www.cadroncreek.com.

Very complete unit study based on Laura Ingalls Wilder's "Little House" books.

Progeny Press Bible Based Study Guides

Progeny Press, PO Box 100, Fall Creek, WI 54742. (877) 776-4369, www.progenypress.com.

Huge selection of study guides to children's literature. Christian viewpoint. Mostly written and discussion activities. Add some KONOS activities to make these real "unit studies."

Other Unit Studies

Amanda Bennett Unit Study Adventure Series

Amanda Bennett, RR. 1 Box 457A Dunlap, TN 37327. (423) 554-3381, www.unitstudy.com

"Adventure series" units currently available: *Baseball, Gardens, Olympics, Pioneers, Computers, Elections, Homes, Oceans, Thanksgiving,* and *Christmas.* Now available on CD-ROM.

Heart of Wisdom

www.heartofwisdom.com

Heart of Wisdom unit study series by Robin Sampson includes: *Creation, Electricity, Energy, Light, Matter, Motion,* and *Wisdom.* Some are currently available; some are due out later in 2004. These are "Internet-linked," with lots of sites you can check out for further study. Units on celebrating the biblical holidays are also available.

Kym Wright's Unit Studies

AlWright! Publishing, P.O. Box 81124-W , Conyers, GA 30013, www.openarmsmagazine.com.

"Learn and Do" units from the publisher of *Open Arms* magazine. Units

available are: *Color, Library, Turtles, Microscope Adventure, Volunteer, Botany, Photography, Spider, Arachnids, Flower Arranging & Wreaths, Bird, Goat, Sheep, Poultry,* and *Victorian Sewing & Quilting. Color* and *Turtles* units include CD-ROM.

Media Angels Creation Science Unit Studies

Media Angels, 15720 Pebble Lane S., Fort Myers, FL 33912-2341, www.mediaangels.com.

Creation-based unit studies: *Creation Science, Creation Geology, Creation Astronomy,* and *Creation Anatomy.* Completely revised from the first edition, these four units now include complete lesson plans for all school subjects except phonics and math. Also available: science fair success book that tells you what the judges are looking for, activity kits, and several creation-based novel series with accompanying literature guides.

One-Week-Off Unit Studies

Castle Heights Press, 2549 Temerity Way, Bulverde, TX 78163, (800) 763-7148, www.castleheightspress.com.

High-interest unit studies designed to take a week. *Aviation, Horses, Cats & Kittens, Dogs & Puppies, Like a Shepherd, Space Exploration,* and *Cars.* Company is also a source for their own homeschool science courses and materials.

Very Different Curriculum

Advanced Training Institute International

The Advanced Training Institute International, Box One, Oak Brook, IL 60522-3001. 630-323-2842, www.ati.iblp.org

Very conservative Christian curriculum based on the principles and Bible study methods taught in Bill Gothard's Institute on Basic Youth Conflicts. Parents must attend two seminars and an on-site training week, plus agree to various behavior and clothing strictures, in order to be allowed to participate in this program. Very beautiful, high-quality materials. Strong emphasis on authority. The whole family studies together.

BJ HomeSAT

BJ HomeSat, 1700 Wade Hampton Blvd., Greenville, SC 29614. (800) 739-8199, www.homesat.com.

Live video courses beamed by satellite (hence the "SAT" in the name), using Bob Jones University Press curriculum. You have the right to tape the courses for later playback. Pretty nice TV-style courses. Elementary grades spice it up with puppets, little video clips, experiments, vivacious teachers, etc. The high-school courses allow school students to interact with the teachers, but you can't do this at home. Your yearly fee allows you access to all courses, plus it also offers "programs of special interest to home educators, including workshops about teaching and parenting, seminars on Christian living, and programs providing both cultural enrichment and wholesome entertainment." Courses start in September, and you need to buy your equipment (satellite dish, antenna, cables, and receiver) a month prior to that.

Clonlara School

Clonlara School, 1289 Jewett, Ann Arbor, MI 48104. (734) 769-4515, www.clonlara.org.

One of the first homeschool programs. School founded in 1967. Progressive correspondence program with a relaxed "unschool friendly" feel. Clonlara has been serving homeschoolers for two decades now. They give as much or little guidance as you wish. Their curriculum listing tells you what subjects to study and provides objectives for each area. You can customize it to suit your own situation. Standard support services available. "Compuhigh" online high-school program also available.

Hewitt Homeschooling Resources

Hewitt Homeschooling Resources, P.O. Box 9, Washougal, WA 98671-0009. (800) 890-4097. www.hewitthomeschooling.com.

Correspondence program that promotes delayed formal learning in the early years. Unit studies in grades K–2. Individualized curriculum for grades 3–8 chosen from hundreds of educational products, plus teaching suggestions and standard support options (testing, record keeping, transcripts, counseling). College-prep high-school program that encourages exploration, creativity, and community involvement. Special Needs Program option will help you develop an IEP (required by some states) and monitor progress.

Oak Meadow School

Oak Meadow School, PO Box 740, Putney, VT 05346. (802) 387-2021. www.oakmeadow.com.

Waldorf-style "unfoldment" educational philosophy. Correspondence program for K–12; online program available for grades 5–8. Fairy tales, handcrafts, and respect for the earth in the early grades; emphasis on hands-on learning and community involvement plus regular college prep courses in upper grades. Since 1975.

The Robinson Curriculum

Oregon Institute of Science and Medicine, 2251 Dick George Rd., Cave Junction, OR 97523. (541) 592-4142. www.oism.org.

Program designed for children to teach themselves. You have to add math and phonics. Curriculum is on CD-ROM, but it isn't software, strictly speaking, as you aren't getting interactive programs. The CD-ROMs contain mostly "real" books and classics scanned as graphics. Some supplementary materials also available (e.g., vocabulary workbooks keyed to the books on the CDs). Learning plan included. Christian, conservative, patriotic. See chapter 30 for details.

Sonlight Curriculum

Sonlight Curriculum, 8042 South Grant Way, Littleton, CO 80122-2705. Inquiries only, no orders: (303) 730-6292. www.sonlight.com.

"Literature-based curriculum with an international perspective." Christian, missions-oriented, multi-cultural. Very complete Instructor's Guides with full lesson plans for all subjects. Uses mostly library books and "real" books—and *lots* of them—rather than textbooks. Science courses include optional materials packets. Several ways to customize your curriculum. "Regular readers" and "advanced readers" versions for early grades. Choice of math programs and handwriting methods. Online forums for parents. All books and materials can be purchased individually.

Sycamore Academy

Sycamore Tree, 2179 Meyer Place, Costa Mesa, CA 92627. Orders: (800) 779-6750. Inquiries: (949) 650-4466. www.sycamoretree.com.

Similar to Hewitt in that an individualized curriculum is chosen for you from among thousands of educational products. Standard grade-level curriculum packages also available. Sycamore Academy Online School, their online academy, uses Switched-On Schoolhouse software for the lesson material. Sycamore Tree also allows you to combine online courses with traditional courses. Christian tone, run by Seventh-Day Adventist family. Since 1981.

Tapestry of Grace

Lampstand Press, PO Box 5798, Rockville, MD 20855. (800) 705-7487, www.tapestryofgrace.com.

A relative newcomer. Four large expensive volumes, subdivided into "units" (that are not actually unit studies, but refer to a chunk of material), cover world and US history in chronological order. *World Book Encyclopedia* extracts in margins, other resources used in units must be obtained via purchase or from library. Each lesson is divided into Lower Grammar, Upper Grammar, Dialectic, and Rhetoric sections which correspond to those levels in the trivium (a classical education scope and sequence). Is currently undergoing revision, so not all parts of the curriculum are available. Extremely complete lesson plans that take a while to master. Christian.

Principle Approach Curriculum

Judah Bible Curriculum
Judah Bible Curriculum, PO Box 122, Urbana, IL 61801. (217) 344-5672. www.judahbible.com.

Bible study using the Notebook Method. Available in print version with audiocassettes or downloadable version.

Noah Plan
F.A.C.E., P.O. Box 9588, Chesapeake, VA 23321-9588. (800) 352-3223. www.face.net.

F.A.C.E. stands for the Foundation for American Christian Education. These are the people who invented the Principle Approach. The Noah Plan is a full Principle Approach curriculum, with note-books, curriculum guides, teacher instructions (including the "The Noah Plan Self-directed Seminar," which explains how to teach using the Principle Approach), and many other reference and ancillary materials. Definitely a curriculum for thinkers. Extremely patriotic and Christian.

Easy High School

American School
American School, 2200 E. 170th St., Lansing, IL 60438-1002. 24 hour info line: (800) 531-9268. 9 A.M. to 3 P.M.: (708) 418-2800. www.americanschoolofcorr.com.

"The School of the Second Chance," founded in 1897 to provide courses to high-school dropouts. Inexpensive, accredited

high-school courses. Joyce Swann of "Accelerated Education" fame (see chapter 50) used American School for all her children. Secular. Psychology is a required course, and the one they usually recommend you start with.

Keystone National High School
Keystone National High School, School House Station, 420 West 5th St., Bloomsburg, PA 17815. (800) 255-4937. www.keystonehighschool.com.

Founded in 1974 to provide students who had failed courses with a way to take them over again with greater success, Keystone National High School was once called the "Home Study Summer School." Accredited correspondence program that is somewhat tougher intellectually than American School (but not all *that* much). Exceptionally clear and helpful Learning Guides for each course. Secular.

State-University-Based High School

Indiana University Office of Academic Programs High School Course
Indiana University, Office of Academic Programs, Owen Hall, 790 E. Kirkwood Ave., Bloomington, IN 47405-7101. (800) 334-1011. scs.indiana.edu.

Over 100 fully accredited distance education courses, including dual-credit courses (that can be applied to both high school and college credit). Some courses offered online; some feature electronic learning guides. Diploma option. College courses also available.

North Dakota State Department of Public Instruction, Division of Independent Study
North Dakota State Dept. of Public Instruction, Division of Independent Study, PO Box 5036, 1510 12th Ave

N, Fargo, ND 58105-5036. (701) 231-6000. www.ndisonline.org.

Elementary, middle, and high-school distance learning. Proctor required. Accredited diploma program available. Many nifty electives and nice online newsletter (view it at the website). Easier courses than UN-L.

Texas Tech University Extended Studies
Extended Studies, Texas Tech University, Box 42191, Lubbock, TX 79409-2191. (800) MY-COURS. www.dce.ttu.edu.

Elementary, middle, and high-school distance learning. Proctor required. Accredited diploma program. Credit by examination option. Dual-credit courses. Some accredited college diploma programs and courses also available. More conservative course material than others in this section.

University of Nebraska-Lincoln Independent Study High School
Independent Study High School, P.O. Box 888400 Lincoln, NE 68588-8400. (402) 472-2175. dcs.unl.edu/ishs.

High-school diploma program. Courses and materials available separately. Proctor required. Most courses now available through excellent "Way Cool" (that's its name) online management system. Real "lab science" courses available with all materials included. See sidebar description on page 214.

High School with a Difference

KONOS History of the World
KONOS, Inc., PO Box 250, Anna, TX 75409. (972) 924-2712, www.konos.com.

Multi-year, multi-volume unit-study high-school curriculum. Great projects and activities, lots of background information, lots of training in writing and researching. You only need to provide separate math and science courses for a full program.

TRISMS Volumes II and III

TRISMS, 1203 S. Delaware Pl., Tulsa, OK 74104. (918) 585-2778, www.trisms.com.

Emphasis switches from history to humanities in these high-school curriculum volumes. Civilizations that were briefly surveyed in TRISMS Volume I are now studied in depth, with assignments growing out of interaction with source documents and the art, architecture, science, music, and literature of each culture. Literature excerpts from ancient manuscripts provided within the curriculum manual. Week-at-a-glance lesson plans.

World Views of the Western World

Cornerstone Curriculum Project, 2006 Flat Creek, Richardson, TX 75080. (972) 235-5149.

www.cornerstonecurriculum.com.

Worldview-oriented Christian curriculum based on philosophy and theology of Dr. Francis Schaeffer. Many books to read, cassettes to listen to, and videos to watch. Very serious course good for abstract thinkers.

Online Academies for Homeschoolers

Some of the curriculum providers mentioned earlier in the Quick Resource Guide offer some or all of their courses online. See Clonlara, Oak Meadow, and Sycamore Academy.

3DLearn Interactive Academy

(610) 736-3332. Fax: (215) 754-4356. www.3dlearn.com//inteact.

The one and only online learning program for grades 7–12 homeschoolers that uses 3-D learning environments. Willoway Cyberschool merged with this program and seems to be providing most of the content. Students travel through an online 3-D environment to access lessons, visit with classmates, and keep up with their schedules. Much time is spent online following links assigned for research: about 2 hours a day. About 40 minutes per day is spent talking and collaborating with peers, and 40 minutes in an online classroom. Projects may require some programming and graphics ability. Great option for highly computer-oriented kids who resist workbooks and textbooks. Secular, semester-based.

Alpha Omega Academy

Alpha Omega Academy, 300 North McKemy, Chandler, AZ 85226. 800-682-7396, www.aop.com.

Online academy, for grades 3–12, using Alpha Omega's Switched-On Schoolhouse educational software as course material.

Apex Learning Advanced Placement Courses

Apex Learning, 110 - 110th Ave NE, Suite 210, Bellevue, WA 98004. (800) 453-1454. www.apexlearning.com.

Company started by Microsoft co-founder Paul Allen. Well-designed online Advanced Placement courses, plus online French and Spanish courses and some "general" high-school courses as well. Most course content available on CD-ROM, so you don't have to connect to do all your lessons, only to take quizzes, see grades, email teacher, etc. Helpful AP exam review option lets kids who have taken AP courses elsewhere get extra "prep" time for the exam, with instant online grading of their answers to see if they are truly understanding what they need to know. See write-up on pages 212–214.

ClassicalFree Virtual Academy

ClassicalFree Virtual Academy, P.O. Box 497, Clackamas, OR 97015. (503) 658-1755. www.classicalfree.org.

Extremely conservative Christian classical approach based on the Trivium. Forty percent of their grade 7–12 courses are free. This includes the initial "grammar level" introductory course, in every subject sequence. "Dialectic" and "rhetoric" level courses are not free (generally, $99 each). Courses are self-paced and self-taught. Online exercises and automatically graded quizzes are provided. Preference for medieval classics over the Greek and Roman classics. Most courses can be started any time, but some are semester-based.

Eagle Christian High School

Eagle Christian School, 2526 Sunset Lane, Missoula, MT 59804. (888) 324-5348. www.eaglechristian.org.

Online courses for grades 7–12. Eagle has its own proprietary math curriculum, with audio and video lectures and online assignments and worked-out examples. All school subjects are offered. Diploma option. Eagle operates on a semester schedule. Its parent school, Valley Christian High, is accredited by the state. Eagle is accredited by the Montana Federation of Independent Schools.

Escondido Tutorial Service

Escondido Tutorial Service, 2634 Bernardo Ave., Escondido, CA 92029. www.gbt.org.

Home of the famous "Great Books Tutorial" by St. John's graduate Fritz Hinrichs, plus additional videoconferenced courses in Euclidean Geometry, Saxon Algebra, and Electronics. Portal for not only Fritz's courses, but also a wide variety of classical and college-prep courses offered through Oxford Tutorial Service, Alexandria Tutorials, SCHOLA Classical Tutorial Service, Talisker Tutorial Service, and Victory Tutorial Service. Read about our family's experiences with Escondido Tutorial Service on page 212.

K12

K12, 8000 Westpark Drive, Suite 500, McLean, VA 22102. (888) 968-7512. www.k12.com.

Extremely thorough, secular, multicultural program with a strong online component. Curriculum is based on E.D. Hirsch's "Core

Knowledge" scope and sequence. (See review of *What Your 1st/2nd/3rd Grader Needs to Know* on page 380.) Each grade level includes a huge package of books and supplies. Sign up for individual courses or an entire grade level.

Laurel Springs School

Laurel Springs School, P.O. Box 1440, Ojai, CA 93024-1440 (800) 377-5890 or (805) 646-2473. www.laurelsprings.com.

Innovative secular program offering web-based curriculum for grades 4–12. Other correspondence school options also available for grades preK–12. In its lessons Laurel Springs takes the student's learning styles into account; it is an official "Learning Style Model School" accredited by the authors of *Discover Your Child's Learning Style!*

NorthStar Academy

NorthStar Academy, 2808 Airport Rd., Kalispell MT 59901. (888) 464-6280. www.northstar-academy.org

Take your choice of US-, Canadian-, or UK-style online programs with a Christian emphasis! Attention, American kids who would like to attend school overseas: the NorthStar UK program follows European standards, which are much higher than American standards. You can actually study for GCSE and "A" level exams through this program! Although individual US students aren't generally allowed to take UK exams, all NorthStar UK program students will be able to sit for these exams at Trinity Christian School in Manchester, England. Uses FirstClass conferencing software.

Pennsylvania Homeschoolers Online AP Courses

Pennsylvania Homeschoolers, R. D. 2, Box 117, Kittanning, PA 16201-9311. (724) 783-6512. www.pahomeschoolers.com.

Advanced Placement courses offered online for homeschoolers. Semester-based. Some textbooks are available "used" for less cost. See my kids' comments about PA Homeschoolers on page 212.

The Potter's School

The Potter's School, c/o Janna Gilbert, 8279 Raindrop Way, Springfield, VA 22153. (703) 690-3516. www.pottersschool.com.

Online courses for grades 7–12. Kids do most of the work on their own offline, but also attend live instructor-led videoconferences. Like Escondido Tutorial Service, The Potter's School is a pioneer in Internet videoconferencing. Initially they were known for their popular online math courses, "Mrs. G's Math Tutorials," which feature direct instruction with live audio, an integrated whiteboard, and video. Almost three dozen other teachers have joined this "online cooperative." Some are well known to homeschoolers, such as Jay Wile of Apologia Educational Ministries and Sharon Jeffus of Visual Manna. Semester-based, Christian. Maximum of 15 students per class, so check this out well ahead of time if you're interested.

Scholar's Online Academy

Scholar's Online Academy, 9755 E McAndrew Ct, Tucson, AZ 85748. (520) 751-1942. www.islas.org.

Online classical, college-prep program for high school and adult, which also offers a few junior-high programs. Weekly or bi-weekly classes include live videoconferencing with teacher and other students, although most work can be done offline. Sister academies with a Catholic bent are Agnus Dei (for ages 10–13) and Regina Coeli (for high school to adult). Umbrella program for all these schools is called the Institute for the Study of the Liberal Arts and Sciences (ISLAS). See what my children have to say about these courses on pages 210–211. Semester-based schedule.

Willoway Cyberschool

See entry for 3DLearn Interactive Academy.

Want More?

Remember, this is not all the curriculum available by a long shot. This is a *Quick* Resource Guide, intended to give you enough information to get going. Hundreds of individual products, not published by any of the companies above, are available that teach art, music, Bible, foreign and classical languages, science, history, geography, economics, and more. The resource books at the beginning of this section will tell you all about them.

EXTRA INFO

Appendixes

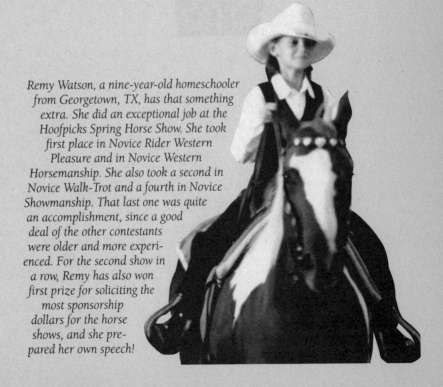

Remy Watson, a nine-year-old homeschooler from Georgetown, TX, has that something extra. She did an exceptional job at the Hoofpicks Spring Horse Show. She took first place in Novice Rider Western Pleasure and in Novice Western Horsemanship. She also took a second in Novice Walk-Trot and a fourth in Novice Showmanship. That last one was quite an accomplishment, since a good deal of the other contestants were older and more experienced. For the second show in a row, Remy has also won first prize for soliciting the most sponsorship dollars for the horse shows, and she prepared her own speech!

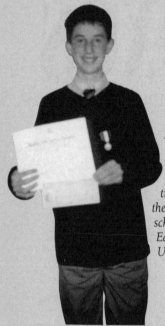

Fritz Nuffer, a homeschooler from Cincinnati, OH, won the DAR essay contest for his region in seventh grade. The contest ("write an obituary for George Washington") goes all the way up to national level, including grades 5, 6, 7, and 8. Out of the four winners from this region, three were homeschooled, and one won at the state level (6th grade). Each winner at the regional level received a $50 U.S. Savings Bond.

What the Research Shows About Homeschooling

D o you need hard facts to convince others—or even yourself—that homeschooling works?

Then you've come to the right place.

The following pages illustrate that homeschooling works for all races, both sexes, and parents of every educational and economic level. They also demonstrate convincingly that increased government regulation is of no help in improving homeschool results.

You can purchase a separate report, *Homeschooling on the Threshold*, reviewed in the sidebar, if you need an inexpensive handout to give others. But the information in this appendix can help you right now.

Aside from the growing numbers of children involved (now close to two million, up from 1.23 million), the rest of the data in this appendix has not changed much in the past five years. If anything, it has been more fully corroborated by additional studies. Go ahead, read . . . and be impressed!

For the latest information on homeschool research, you need to contact Dr. Brian Ray, the foremost homeschooling researcher in the world. Dr. Ray has published about 30 research reports, a video, and audiotapes. He also publishes a newsletter, *The Home School Researcher,* which collects and comments on research having to do with homeschoolers. It costs $25/year for 4 issues. For more information contact: The National Home Education Research Institute.

Homeschooling on the Threshold

Parents. $4.99. Quantity discounts. *National Home Education Research Institute, OR. (503) 364-1490, www.nheri.org.*

If you'd like a full-color, beautifully illustrated, 24-page booklet with the latest home education research summa-

rized for you, suitable for handing to friends, relatives and neighbors, get **Homeschooling on the Threshold.** More portable and easier to give away than this book, it covers the current research from a slightly different angle than this appendix.

Why are so many parents choosing to home school? Because it works.

A 1997 study by Dr. Brian Ray of the National Home Education Research Institute (NHERI) found that home educated students excelled on nationally-normed standardized achievement exams. On average, home schoolers outperformed their public school peers by 30 to 37 percentile points across all subjects *(Figure 1.0)*.

Figure 1.0 — How Do Home School Students Score?

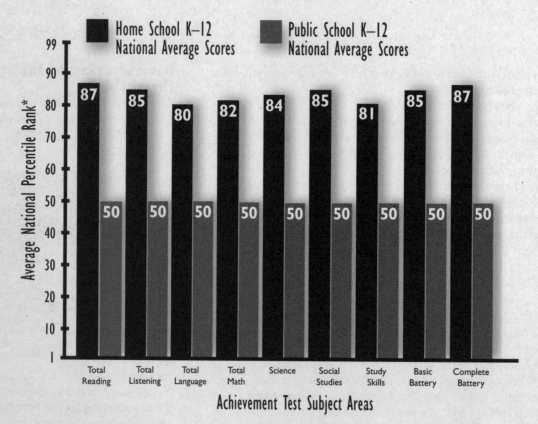

Footnote: (Ray, 1997) Data collected for standardized academic achievement tests for the 1994–95 academic year.

*For more detail about the non-equal-interval nature of a simple percentile scale which has distortion especially near the ends of the scale, see the complete study by Brian D. Ray, *Strengths of Their Own—Home Schoolers Across America: Academic Achievement, Family Characteristics, and Longitudinal Traits*, 1997, Salem, OR: National Home Education Research Institute, www.nheri.org.

How Do Minorities Fare in Home Education?

Figure 2.0 — Race Relationship to Reading and Math Test Scores

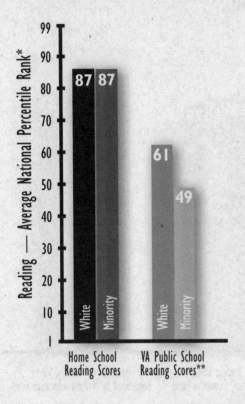

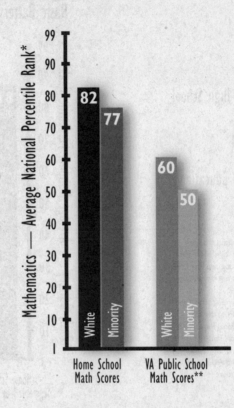

Footnotes: (Ray, 1997) *See study for more detail about the non-equal-interval nature of a simple percentile scale which has distortion especially near the ends of the scale.

**Public school achievement data are based on 8th grade scores from Table 4 of *The Virginia Assessment Program: Results for the 1995–1996 School Year* (1996, July). Richmond, VA: Virginia Department of Education.

The Virginia minority scores were weighted according to the proportions of minorities in this study of home schoolers to arrive at the numbers in this figure. The minority groups were American Indian/Alaskan Native, Asian/Pacific Islander, black, and Hispanic. Of home school minority students tested in this study, about 63% were black or Hispanic.

Public school achievement data are similar for the U.S. in general but the same detail of data was not available for all public schools. See U.S. Department of Education, Office of Educational Research & Improvement, National Center for Education Statistics (1996, November). *National Assessment of Educational Progress (NAEP) trends in academic progress* [trends report and appendices]. Washington, DC: U.S. Department of Education.

Home school data are for grades K–12.

What About the Gender Gap in Academics?

Figure 3.0 — Gender Relationship to Reading and Math Test Scores

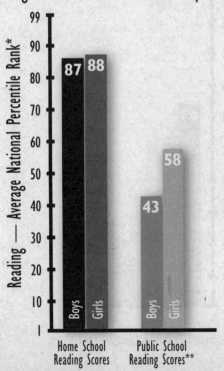

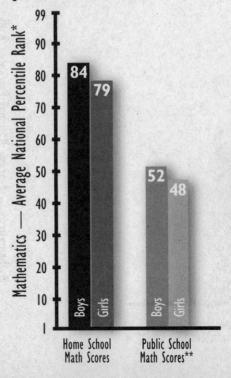

Footnotes: (Ray, 1997) *See study for more detail about the non-equal-interval nature of a simple percentile scale which has distortion especially near the ends of the scale.

**Public school achievement data are for 8th grade based on tables from the U.S. Department of Education, Office of Educational Research & Improvement, National Center for Education Statistics (1996, November). *National Assessment of Educational Progress (NAEP) trends in academic progress* [trends report and appendices]. Washington, DC: U.S. Department of Education.

Home school data are for grades K–12.

Does Parent Education Level Predict Student Achievement?

Key for Figures 4.1–4.3: Parents' Highest Education Level Attained

■ Graduated College

■ Some Education after High School

■ Graduated High School

■ Less than High School Education

Footnotes: (Ray, 1997) *For more detail about the non-equal-interval nature of a simple percentile scale which has distortion especially near the ends of the scale, see Ray 1997.

**Basic battery achievement test scores not available for public school students.

***Public school data are for 8th grade writing scores and 13-year-olds' math scores based on tables from the U.S. Department of Education, Office of Educational Research & Improvement, National Center for Education Statistics (1996, November). *National Assessment of Educational Progress (NAEP) trends in academic progress* [trends report and appendices]. Washington, DC: U.S. Department of Education.

Home school data are for grades K–12.

Figure 4.1 — Home School Achievement — Basic Battery Test

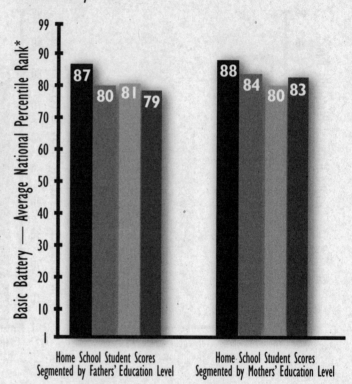

Figure 4.2 — Public School Achievement — Writing Test**

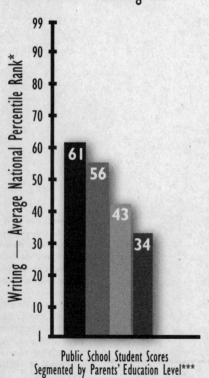

Figure 4.3 — Public School Achievement — Math Test**

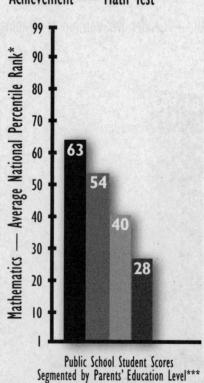

Figure 5.0 — Home School Percentile Rankings Based on Parent Certification

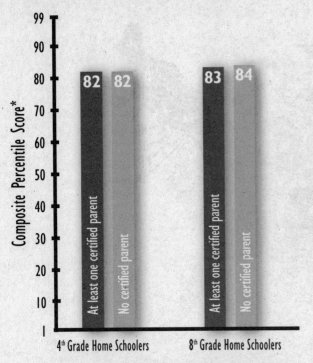

Footnote: (Rudner, 1999) *Composite Percentile Score refers to the percentile corresponding to the mean composite scaled score.

Figure 6.0 — Home School Percentile Scores Based on the Money Spent on Education per Child

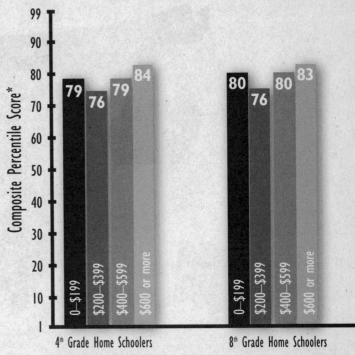

Footnote: (Rudner, 1999) *Composite Percentile Score refers to the percentile corresponding to the mean composite scaled score.

Is Government Regulation Necessary for High Achievement?

Key for Figures 7.1 & 7.2

Low Regulation
No state requirement for parents to initiate any contact with the state.

Moderate Regulation
State requires parents to send notification, test scores, and/or professional evaluation of student progress.

High Regulation
State requires parents to send notification or achievement test scores and/or professional evaluation, plus other requirements (e.g., curriculum approval by the state, teacher qualifications of parents, or home visits by state officials).

Figure 7.1 — State Regulation: No Impact on Home School Achievement

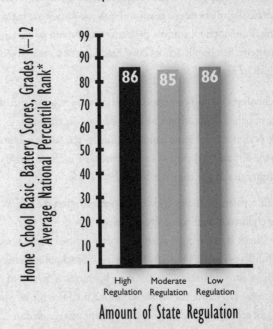

Footnote: (Ray, 1997) *See study for more detail about the non-equal-interval nature of a simple percentile scale which has distortion especially near the ends of the scale.

Figure 7.2 — Breakdown of States by Regulatory Policy
(Ray, 1997)

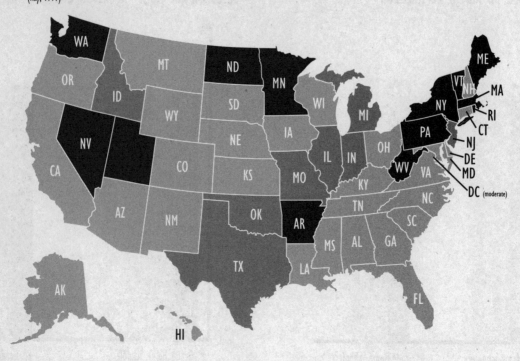

Traditionally, gender and race have been consistent predictors of student performance. But home schooling is breaking down those barriers. Math and reading scores for minority home school students show no significant difference when compared to whites. A similar comparison for public schools students, however, demonstrates a substantial disparity *(Figures 2.0)*.

When segmented by gender, test scores for home schoolers reveal that boys are slightly better in math and girls are somewhat better in reading. Public school student performance in math follows a similar pattern, but public school boys' reading scores are markedly behind girls' *(Figure 3.0)*.

Home schooling's one-on-one tutorial method seemed to equalize the influence of parents' educational background on their children's academic performance. Home educated students' test scores remained between the 80th and 90th percentiles, whether their mothers had a college degree or did not complete high school *(Figure 4.1)*.

In contrast, a parent's education level did appear to affect the performance of children in traditional school settings *(Figures 4.2, 4.3)*. Students taught at home by mothers who never finished high school scored a full 55 percentile points higher than public school students from families of comparable educational backgrounds. Similarly, in his 1999 study, Dr. Lawrence M. Rudner found no difference in achievement according to whether or not a parent was certified to teach *(Figure 5.0)*. For those who would argue that only certified

teachers should be allowed to instruct their children at home, these findings suggest that such a requirement would not meaningfully affect student achievement.

Rudner also found that the median amount of money spent in 1997 on educational materials for home school students was $400. Considering this relatively small expenditure in light of the high scholastic achievement of most home school students, it is reasonable to conclude that it does not require a great deal of money to home school successfully *(Figure 6.0)*.

According to Ray, the degree of governmental regulation had no significant effect on the academic performance of home schoolers *(Figure 7.1, 7.2)*. Whether a state imposed a high degree of regulation, low regulation, or no regulation, home school student test score averages were nearly identical. Such regulations may be legitimately questioned since there is no apparent benefit to student learning.

The first question the general public asks whenever home schooling is mentioned is, "What about socialization?" Data on home school students' activities and community involvement reveal that, on average, these children are engaged in 5.2 activities outside the home *(Figure 8.0)*.

Home schooling is an effective educational alternative chosen by dedicated and loving parents for their children. Not only is it working, it is working very well!

What about Socialization?

Figure 8.0 — Home Schoolers' Activities and Community Involvement

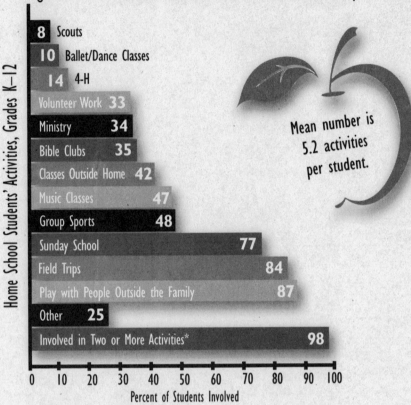

Mean number is 5.2 activities per student.

Home School Students' Activities, Grades K–12

Activity	Percent
Scouts	8
Ballet/Dance Classes	10
4-H	14
Volunteer Work	33
Ministry	34
Bible Clubs	35
Classes Outside Home	42
Music Classes	47
Group Sports	48
Sunday School	77
Field Trips	84
Play with People Outside the Family	87
Other	25
Involved in Two or More Activities*	98

Percent of Students Involved

Footnote: (Ray, 1997) *Participation in two or more of the 12 activities does not include "other activities." See Table 8 in study.

About the Research

Strengths of Their Own—Home Schoolers Across America: Academic Achievement, Family Characteristics, and Longitudinal Traits, Brian D. Ray, 1997 (book).

Dr. Brian D. Ray collected data on 5,402 home school students from 1,657 families for the 1994–95 and 1995–96 academic years. Nearly 6,000 surveys were sent to home school families. Some surveys were mailed directly to families (those randomly selected from numerous mailing lists and longitudinal participants from a 1990 study). Others were blindly forwarded to families through the leadership of independent home school support groups and networks in every state. This was the largest and most comprehensive study on home schooling to that point.

Brian D. Ray, Ph.D., is president of the National Home Education Research Institute. He holds a Ph.D. in science education from Oregon State University, has an M.S. in zoology (1979), and has been a professor and classroom teacher. NHERI conducts basic data gathering research; serves as a clearinghouse of information for researchers, home educators, attorneys, legislators, policy makers, and the public at large; and provides speaker services. NHERI also publishes research reports and the unique, academic, refereed journal *Home School Researcher.*

The full study is available from NHERI for $8.95, plus $2 shipping.

National Home Education Research Institute
P.O. Box 13939 • Salem, Oregon 97309
phone: 503-364-1490 *web:* www.nheri.org

The Scholastic Achievement and Demographic Characteristics of Home School Students in 1998, Lawrence M. Rudner, 1999.

Conducted by Dr. Lawrence M. Rudner and commissioned by HSLDA, this study involved seven times as many families as any previous study of its kind: 20,760 students in 11,930 U.S. families.

Unlike any previous study, families chose to participate before they knew their children's test scores, minimizing the possibility of selective reporting. All participants took the same tests: the Iowa Test of Basic Skills for grades K–8 and the Tests of Achievement and Proficiency for grades 9–12, both published by the Riverside Publishing Company.

Lawrence M. Rudner, Ph.D., is with the College of Library and Information Services, University of Maryland in College Park. He has been involved in quantitative analysis for over 30 years, having served as a university professor, a branch chief in the U.S. Department of Education, and a classroom teacher. For the past 14 years, he has been the director of the ERIC Clearinghouse on Assessment and Evaluation. Dr. Rudner holds a Ph.D. in Educational Psychology (1977), an MBA in Finance (1991), and lifetime teaching certificates from two states. His two children attend public school.

For a copy of the full report, see *Education Policy Analysis Archives* at http://epaa.asu.edu/epaa/v7n8/

Homeschool Laws by State & Territory

This section should quell the fears of relatives and friends! As you can clearly see, homeschooling is legal everywhere in the US, including its territories. The laws regarding homeschooling do vary quite a bit from state to state, though.

The listing below is a snapshot summary of the laws at one point in time—October 25, 2001. State laws change, so for the most recent listing for your state, visit www.hslda.org/central/states/.

The information below does not constitute the giving of legal advice. It is for your benefit in getting a broad picture of the laws nationwide, and as a starting point for your own study of the actual laws.

Also please note that while some states *require* a notice of intent to homeschool, others only *allow* for it. Where the chart says you "may" file a notice of intent to homeschool, generally state homeschooling groups advise against this. Contact your local state group for detailed information on how to comply with the homeschool law in your state.

The chart in this appendix is ©2004, HSLDA all rights reserved. Used by the gracious permission of the Home School Legal Defense Association, P.O. Box 3000, Purcellville, Virginia 20134, (540) 338-5600, www.hslda.org.

State or Territory	Compulsory School Age	Legal Options to Home School	Attendance Required	Subjects Required	Teacher Credentials	Notice Required	Record Keeping Required	Testing Required
Alabama	Between the ages of 7 and 16	Establish and/or enroll in a church school	None specified (175 days required for the public schools)	None	None	File a notice of enrollment and attendance with the local superintendent on a provided form (not required annually)	Maintain a daily attendance register to be kept by the principal teacher of the church school	None
		Use a private tutor	140 days per year, 3 hours per day between the hours of 8 A.M. and 4 P.M.	Reading, spelling, writing, arithmetic, English, geography, history of the United States, science, health, physical education, and Alabama history	Teacher certification	File a statement showing children to be instructed, the subjects taught and the period of instruction with the local superintendent	Maintain a register of the child's work showing daily attendance and make such reports as the State Board of Education may require	None
Alaska	Between 7 and 16	Establish and operate a home school	None	None	None	None	None	None
		Use a private tutor	180 days per year	Comparable to those offered in the public schools	Teacher certification	None	None	None
		Enroll in a state department of education approved full-time correspondence program	180 days per year	Comparable to those offered in the public schools	None	None	None	None
		Request school board approval to provide an equal alternate educational experience	180 days per year	Comparable to those offered in the public schools	None	None	None	None

State or Territory	Compulsory School Age	Legal Options to Home School	Attendance Required	Subjects Required	Teacher Credentials	Notice Required	Record Keeping Required	Testing Required
Alaska (cont.)		Qualify as a religious or other private school	180 days per year	None, but standardized testing must cover English grammar, reading, spelling, and math	None	File a "Private School Enrollment Reporting Form" with the local superintendent by the first day of public school; also file a "Private and Denominational Schools Enrollment Report" and a "School Calendar" with the state department of education by October 15 each year	Maintain monthly attendance records; also maintain records on immunization, courses, standardized testing, academic achievement, and physical exams	Administer a standardized test in grades 4, 6, and 8
American Samoa	Between 6 and 18 years of age inclusive, or from grade one through grade twelve	Request department of education authorization to operate a private school	Same as the public schools	A curriculum that is approved as being in the interest of good citizenship by the director of education	Teacher certification	A de facto part of the authorization process	Maintain permanent report cards; submit monthly enrollment reports and an annual report to the department of education	None
Arizona	Between 6 and 16; by noting so in affidavit (see Notice Required), instruction in a home school setting may be delayed until 8 years of age	Establish and operate a home school	None	Reading, grammar, math, social studies and science	None	File an affidavit of intent with the local superintendent within 30 days of the start (even if instruction will be delayed until age 8) or end of home schooling	None	None
Arkansas	5 through 17 on or before September 15 of that year; a child under age 6 on September 15 may be waived from kindergarten with submission of a state-provided form	Establish and operate a home school	None	None	None	File written notice of intent with the local superintendent by August 15 (for those starting in fall semester), December 15 (for those starting in spring semester), or 14 days prior to withdrawing child mid-semester from public school; re-file annually thereafter at beginning of school year	None	Participate in same state-mandated norm-referenced tests given to public school students (in grades 5, 7, and 10); no cost to parent unless alternate testing procedures are approved
California	Between the ages of 6 by December 2 and under 18 years of age	Qualify as a private school	None	Same as the public schools and in the English language	Must be capable of teaching	File an annual affidavit with the local superintendent between October 1 and 15	Maintain an attendance register	None
		Use a private tutor	175 days per year, 3 hours per day	Same as the public schools and in the English language	Teacher certification	None	None	None
		Enroll in an independent study program through the public school	As prescribed by the program	As prescribed by the program	None	A de facto part of the enrollment process	As prescribed by the program	As prescribed by the program
		Enroll in a private school satellite program, taking independent study	As prescribed by the program	As prescribed by the program	Must be capable of teaching	None	As prescribed by the program	As prescribed by the program
Colorado	7 and under the age of 16. Also appl[ies] to a six-year-old child who has been enrolled in a public school in the first [or higher] grade, unless the parent or legal guardian chooses to withdraw such child.	Establish and operate a home school	172 days per year, averaging four hours per day	Constitution of the United States, reading, writing, speaking, math, history, civics, literature, and science	None	File notice of intent with the local superintendent 14 days prior to start of home school and annually thereafter	Maintain attendance records, test and evaluation results, and immunization records	Administer a standardized test for grades 3, 5, 7, 9, and 11 or have the child evaluated by a qualified person selected by parent
		Enroll in a private school that allows home instruction	None	As prescribed by the program	None	None	None	None
		Use a private tutor	None	Constitution of the United States, reading, writing, speaking, math, history, civics, literature, and science	Teacher certification	None	None	None
Connecticut	Five years of age and over and under sixteen years of age; five- or six-year-olds can opt out when the parent goes to the school district and signs an option form	Establish and operate a home school	Generally, 180 days per year	Reading, writing, spelling, English, grammar, geography, arithmetic, United States history, and citizenship, including a study of the town, state and federal governments	None	None, but parents may voluntarily comply with State Dept. of Education guidelines by filing a Notice of Intent form with the local superintendent within 10 days of the start of home school	The guidelines require that parents maintain a portfolio indicating that instruction in the required courses has been given	None

State or Territory	Compulsory School Age	Legal Options to Home School	Attendance Required	Subjects Required	Teacher Credentials	Notice Required	Record Keeping Required	Testing Required
Delaware	Between 5 years of age and 16 years of age; can delay start (if in best interests of the child) with school authorization	Establish and/or enroll in a home school association or organization	180 days per year	Same as the public schools	None	Association or organization must register with the Department of Education; report enrollment, student ages, and attendance to Department of Education on or before July 31 each year; also submit annual statement of enrollment as of last school day in September in form prescribed by Department of Education	None	None
		Establish and operate a home school providing regular and thorough instruction to the satisfaction of the local superintendent and the state board of education	180 days per year	Same as the public schools	None	Report enrollment, student ages, and attendance to Department of Education on or before July 31 each year; also submit annual statement of enrollment as of last school day in September in form prescribed by Department of Education	None	Administer a written examination as prescribed during the approval process
District of Columbia	Age of 5 years by December 31 of current school year until minor reaches the age of 18	Provide private instruction not affiliated with an educational institution	During the period that the public schools are in session	None	None	None, unless the child is being removed from the public school	An accurate daily record of the attendance . . . shall be kept by every teacher who gives instruction privately	None
Florida	Attained the age of 6 years by February 1, but have not attained the age of 16 years	Establish and operate a home school	None specified	None	None	File notice of intent with the local superintendent within 30 days of establishment for home school (not required annually)	Maintain a portfolio of records and materials (log of texts and sample work sheets)	Annually, either: 1) administer any standardized test or a state student assessment test; must be given by a qualified teacher, 2) have child evaluated by a certified teacher, or 3) be evaluated by a licensed psychologist, or 4) have child evaluated by another valid tool that is mutually agreed upon
		Qualify and operate as part of a private school corporation (a legally incorporated group of home school families)	180 days	None	None	None	None	None
Georgia	Between 6th and 16th birthdays; A child under 7 who has attended public school for more than 20 days is also subject to the compulsory attendance laws	Establish and conduct a home study program	180 days per year, 4½ hours per day	Reading, language arts, math, social studies, and science	High school diploma or GED for a teaching parent; baccalaureate degree for any private tutor used	File a declaration of intent with the local superintendent within 30 days of commencing the home study program and by September 1 annually thereafter	Maintain attendance records and submit monthly to the superintendent; write and retain an annual progress report	Administer and retain the results of a standardized test every 3 years beginning at the end of the 3rd grade
Guam	Between the ages of 5 and 16 years	Private instruction by a private tutor or other person	170 days per year	Same as the public schools and in the English language	None	None	None	None
Hawaii	Have arrived at the age of at least 6 years and not at the age of 18 years by January 1 of any school year	Establish and operate a home school	None	Curriculum must be structured and based on educational objectives as well as the needs of the child, be cumulative and sequential, provide a range of up-to-date knowledge and needed skills, and take into account the interests, needs, and abilities of the child	None	File a notice of intent with the principal of the public school the child would otherwise be required to attend before starting to home school (not required annually); notify this same principal within 5 days after ending home school	Maintain a record of the planned curriculum	Administer standardized achievement test of parent's choice in grades 3, 5, 8, and 10; Submit annual report of child's progress to local principal comprised of either: 1) standardized test results, or 2) written evaluation by certified teacher, or 3) written evaluation by parent
		Enroll in a superintendent-approved appropriate alternative educational program	As prescribed during the approval process (about 3 hrs per day)	As prescribed during the approval process	Baccalaureate degree	None	None	Participate in statewide testing program at the public schools

State or Territory	Compulsory School Age	Legal Options to Home School	Attendance Required	Subjects Required	Teacher Credentials	Notice Required	Record Keeping Required	Testing Required
Idaho	Attained the age of 7 years, but not the age of 16 years	Provide an alternate educational experience for the child that is otherwise comparably instructed	Same as the public schools	Same as the public schools	None	None	None	None
Illinois	Between the ages of 7 and 16 years	Operate a home school as a private school	Generally, 176 days per year, but not mandated for private or home schools	Language arts, biological and physical science, math, social sciences, fine arts, health and physical development	None	None	None	None
Indiana	Earlier of the date the child officially enrolls in a school or reaches the age of 7 until his 18th birthday	Operate a home school as a private school	Same as the public schools; Generally, 180 days per year	None	None	None, unless specifically requested by the state superintendent of education	Maintain attendance records	None
Iowa	Age 6 by September 15 until age 16	Operate a home school	148 days per year (37 days each quarter)	None	None	Complete an annual Competent Private Instruction Report Form; file 2 copies with the local school district by 1st day of school or within 14 days of withdrawal from school	None	Complete by May 1 and submit to the local school district by June 30: 1) test results from an acceptably administered standardized test, or 2) a portfolio for review
		Operate a home school that is supervised by a licensed teacher	Same as above	None	None for teaching parent; license for the supervising teacher	Same as above	None	None; however, must meet with supervising teacher twice per quarter (one may be conducted by telephone)
Kansas	Reached the age of 7 and under the age of 18 years	Operate a home school as a non-accredited private school	Substantially equivalent to public school: 186 days per year or 1116 hrs per year; 1086 hrs for 12th grade	None	Must be a competent teacher (however, local school board has no authority to define or evaluate competence of private school teachers)	Register name and address of school with the state board of education (not subject to approval)	None	None
		Operate a home school as a satellite of an accredited private school	Same as above	As prescribed by the supervising private school		None	As prescribed by the supervising private school	As prescribed by the supervising private school
		Qualify for a state board of education approved religious exemption in the high school grades	As prescribed during the approval process	As prescribed in the approval process	As prescribed during the approval process	As prescribed in the approval process	As prescribed in the approval process	As prescribed during the approval process
Kentucky	Has reached the 6th birthday and has not passed the 16th birthday	Qualify a home school as a private school	185 days per year	Reading, writing, spelling, grammar, history, mathematics, and civics	None	Notify the local board of education of those students in attendance within two weeks of start of school year	Maintain an attendance register and scholarship reports	None
Louisiana	From the child's 7th birthday until his 17th birthday	Operate a home school as approved by the board of education	180 days per year	At least equal to the quality of that in the public schools including the Declaration of Independence and the Federalist Papers	None	File an application and a copy of the child's birth certificate with board of education within 15 days after start of home school and annually thereafter	Whatever form(s) of documentation is(are) planned to satisfy the testing requirement	Submit with renewal application documents showing satisfactory evidence that the program is at least equal to that offered by the public schools
		Operate a home school as a private school	180 days per year	Same as above	None	Submit notification to the state department of education within the first 30 days of the school year	None	None
Maine	7 years of age or older and under 17 years	Operate a home school	175 days per year	English, language arts, math, science, social studies, physical and health education, library skills, fine arts, Maine studies (in one grade between grade 6 and 12), and computer proficiency (in one grade between grade 7 and 12)	None	Keep copies of all material filed until homeschool program concludes	None	Annually, either: 1) administer a standardized test, or 2) take a local test, or 3) have child's progress reviewed by a certified teacher, a superintendent-selected local advisory board, or a home school support group that includes a certified teacher
		Operate a home school as a non-approved private school that teaches at least 2 unrelated students	175 days per year	English, math, science, health, fine arts, U.S. history, Maine history, geography, government, and citizenship	Competent as approved by the non-approved private school	None	None	Must give parents four progress reports annually

State or Territory	Compulsory School Age	Legal Options to Home School	Attendance Required	Subjects Required	Teacher Credentials	Notice Required	Record Keeping Required	Testing Required
Maryland	5 years old or older and under 16 with one-year exemption available for 5 year-olds	Operate a qualified home school	Must be of sufficient duration to implement the instructional program	Must provide regular, thorough instruction in the same subjects as the public schools including English, math, science, social studies, art, music, health, and physical education	None	File a one-time notice of intent with the state department of education at least 15 days before the start of home school. Verify to superintendant annually thereafter whether homeschool program will continue or not, and notify if status changes.	Maintain a portfolio of relevant materials, reviewable by the local superintendent up to 3 times per year	None
		Provide home instruction under the supervision of a church institution or school that complies with regulations	As prescribed by the supervising program	As prescribed by the supervising program	None	File a one-time notice of intent with the state department of education at least 15 days before the start of home school. Verify continuation to supervising program annually and notify of any status change.	As prescribed by the supervising program	As prescribed by the supervising program
Massachusetts	6 to 16 years of age (by December 31 of that year)	Establish and operate a home school as approved in advance by the local school committee or superintendent	None specified, though 900 hours at elementary level and 990 hours at secondary level are expected	Reading, writing, English language and grammar, geography, arithmetic, drawing, music, history, and constitution of United States, duties of citizenship, health (including CPR), physical education, and good behavior	None	A de facto part of the approval process	None	Not required by state law, but may be a negotiated condition for approval.
Michigan	Age of 6 to the child's 16th birthday	Establish and operate a home education program	None	Reading, spelling, mathematics, science, history, civics, literature, writing, and English grammar	None	None	None	None
		Operate a home school as a nonpublic school	None	Must be comparable to those taught in the public schools	Teacher certification (unless claiming a religious exemption)	Submit, to the department of education and local superintendent, at start of each school year a statement of enrollment	Maintain records of enrollment, courses of study, and qualifications of teachers (must be submitted to the Department of Education upon request)	None
Minnesota	Between 7 and 16 years of age	Establish and operate a qualified home school	None	Reading, writing, literature, fine arts, math, science, history, geography, government, health, and physical education	None	File a Non-Public Education Compulsory Instruction Report with the local superintendent by October 1 of each school year	If only teaching qualification is to be child's parent, submit a quarterly report to the local superintendent showing the achievement of each child in the required subjects	Administer an annual standardized test as agreed to by the local superintendent
Mississippi	Age of 6 on or before September 1 and has not attained the age of 17 on or before September 1	Establish and operate a home school	Whatever number of days that each [home] school shall require for promotion from grade to grade	None	None	File a certificate of enrollment by September 15 of each school year to the district's attendance officer	None	None
Missouri	Between the ages of 7 and 16 years	Establish and operate a home school	1,000 hours per year; at least 600 hours in the five required subjects; 400 of these 600 hrs must occur at the regular home school location	Reading, math, social studies, language arts, and science	None	None required	Maintain records of subjects taught, activities engaged in, samples of the child's academic work and evaluations or a credible equivalent, and a written log showing the hours required under "attendance"	None
Montana	7 years of age or older prior to the first day of school and the later of the following dates: the child's 16th birthday; the day of completion of the work of the 8th grade	Establish and operate a home school	180 days per year, 4 hours per day for grades 1–3 and 6 hours per day for grades 4–12	Same basic instructional program as the public schools	None	File annual notice of intent with the county superintendent	Maintain attendance and immunization records; must be available for inspection by county superintendent upon request	None
Nebraska	Not less than 7 nor more than 16 years of age	Establish and operate a home school as a private school	1,032 hours per year for elementary grades, 1,080 hours per year for high school grades	Language arts, math, science, social studies, and health	None, unless the teacher is employed by the family	File an annual notice of intent with the state commissioner of education by August 1 (or 30 days prior to the start of home school)	None	None

State or Territory	Compulsory School Age	Legal Options to Home School	Attendance Required	Subjects Required	Teacher Credentials	Notice Required	Record Keeping Required	Testing Required
Nevada	Between the ages of 7 and 17 years	Establish and operate a home school	Equivalent of 180 days of instruction	Parents must provide the local school board with satisfactory written evidence that the child is receiving at home . . . equivalent instruction of the kind and amount approved by the state board of education, including U.S. and Nevada constitutions	Either: 1) possess a Nevada teaching certificate for grade level taught, or 2) consult with a licensed teacher or 3-year home school veteran, or 3) use an approved correspondence course, or 4) possess or qualify for a teaching certificate in any state or have at least 1 year experience homeschooling in the U.S.	File, with the local school board, annual satisfactory written evidence that the child is receiving at home...equivalent instruction of the kind and amount approved by the state board of education	None	None
New Hampshire	At least 6 years of age [on September 30] and under 16 years of age	Operate a home school	None	Science, mathematics, language, government, history, health, reading, writing, spelling, U.S. and New Hampshire constitutional history, and art and music appreciation	None	Within 30 days of withdrawing from public school or moving into the school district, file a notice of intent with a private school principal, the state commissioner of education, or the local superintendent. See detailed analysis at hslda.org	Maintain a portfolio of records and materials including a log of reading materials used, samples of writings, worksheets, workbooks or creative materials used or developed by the child	By July 1, file either: 1) results from a standardized test, or 2) results from a state student assessment test used by the local school district, or 3) a written evaluation by a certified teacher, or 4) results of another measure agreeable to the local school board
New Jersey	Between the ages of six and 16 years	Operate a home school	None specified (180 days required for the public schools)	Must provide instruction academically equivalent to that in public schools	None	None	None	None
New Mexico	At least five years of age prior to 12:01 A.M. on September 1 of the school year to the age of majority unless the person has graduated from high school; children under eight can be excused	Establish and operate a home school	Same school year length as public schools	Reading, language arts, mathematics, social studies, and science	High school diploma or equivalent	File notice of intent with the state superintendent within 30 days of establishing the home school and by April 1 of each subsequent year	Maintain immunization records	None
New York	A minor who becomes six years of age on or before the first of December in any school year . . . until the last day of session in the school year in which the minor becomes sixteen years of age or completes high school	Establish and operate a home school	Substantial equivalent of 180 days per year; 900 hours per year for grades 1–6; 990 hours per year for grades 7–12	Grades K–12: patriotism and citizenship, substance abuse, traffic safety, fire safety; Grades 1–6: arithmetic, reading, spelling, writing, English, geography, U.S. history, science, health, music, visual arts, and physical education; Grades 7–8: English, history and geography, science, mathematics, physical education, health, art, music, practical arts, and library skills; At least once in grades 1–8: U.S. and New York history and constitutions; Grades 9–12: English, social studies—including American history, participation in government, and economics, math, science, art or music, health, physical education, and electives	"Competent"—A person is deemed to be competent if they follow the regulations	File annual notice of intent with the local superintendent by July 1 or within 14 days if starting home schooling mid-year; complete and submit an Individualized Home Instruction Plan (form provided by district)	Maintain attendance records (must make available for inspection upon request of the local superintendent); file, with the local superintendent, quarterly reports listing the number of hours of instruction during quarter, description of material covered in each subject, and a grade or narrative evaluation in each subject	File, with the local superintendent, an annual assessment by June 30; must be from a standardized test every other year in grades 4-8, and every year in grades 9-12; the child should score above the 33rd percentile or their home instruction program could be placed on probation; other years can be satisfied by either another standardized test or a written narrative evaluation prepared by a certified teacher, a home instruction peer review panel, or other person chosen by the parent with the consent of the superintendent
North Carolina	Between the ages of seven and 16 years	Establish and operate a home school	At least nine calendar months per year, excluding reasonable holidays and vacations	None, but annual standardized tests must cover English grammar, reading, spelling, and mathematics	High school diploma or GED	File notice of intent with the state division of non-public education upon starting home school	Maintain attendance and immunization records and results of standardized tests	Administer an annual standardized test measuring achievement in English grammar, reading, spelling, and mathematics, the results of which must be available for inspection

State or Territory	Compulsory School Age	Legal Options to Home School	Attendance Required	Subjects Required	Teacher Credentials	Notice Required	Record Keeping Required	Testing Required
North Dakota	A child between the ages of seven and sixteen years	Establish and operate a home school	175 days per year, four hours per day	English language arts, including reading, composition, creative writing, English grammar, and spelling, mathematics, social studies, including the United States Constitution, and United States history, geography, and government, science, including agriculture, physical education, health, including physiology, hygiene, disease control, and the nature and effects of alcohol, tobacco, and narcotics.	Possess either: 1) a teaching certificate, or 2) a baccalaureate degree, 3) a high school diploma or GED and be monitored by a certified teacher during first two years of home instruction; monitoring must continue thereafter if child scores below the 50th percentile on required standardized achievement test, or 4) proof of meeting or exceeding the cut-off score of the national teacher exam	File annual notice of intent with the local superintendent 14 days prior to the start of the home school or within 14 days of establishing residency inside the district. *For Autistic Children:* In addition to above, file a copy of the child's diagnosis from a licensed psychologist along with an individualized education program developed and followed by the child's school district and parent or by a team selected and compensated by the parent.	Maintain an annual record of courses and each child's academic progress assessments, including standardized achievement test results. *For Autistic Children:* Also file with the local superintendent progress reports from an individualized education program team selected by the parent on or before November 1, February 1, and May 1 of each school year	Take a standardized achievement test in grades 4, 6, 8 and 10; must be administered by a certified teacher; results must be provided to the local superintendent; a composite score below the 30th percentile requires a professional assessment for learning problems and submission of a plan of remediation to the local superintendent
		Operate a home school as a county- and state-approved private school	Same as the public schools	Same as above	Teacher certification	A de facto part of the approval process	None	None
Northern Mariana Islands	Between the ages of six and sixteen	Seek approval to operate a home school	180 days per year with at least 300 minutes of secular instruction daily	Same as the public schools	None	Submit a waiver application to the commissioner at least 60 days prior to start of school year	Submit to the commissioner monthly, quarterly, and annual reports on program progress	None
		Seek approval to operate a home school as an chartered non-public school	Same as above	As prescribed by the board in issuing a charter	None	Submit to the board of education an application for a charter	As prescribed by the board in issuing a charter	None
Ohio	Between six and eighteen years of age	Establish and operate a home school	900 hours per year	Language arts, geography, U.S. and Ohio history, government, math, health, physical education, fine arts, first aid and science	High school diploma, GED, test scores showing high school equivalence, or work under a person with a baccalaureate degree until child's test scores show proficiency or parent earns diploma or GED	Submit an annual notice of intent to the local superintendent	None	Submit with renewal notification either: 1) standardized test scores, or 2) a written narrative showing satisfactory academic progress, or 3) an approved alternative assessment
		Establish a Non-Chartered School ("08 School")	182 days per year for at least 5 hours each day, excluding recess	Language arts, geography, U.S. and Ohio history, government, math, science, health, physical education, fine arts (including music), first aid, safety, and fire prevention	Bachelor's Degree or equivalent form a recognized college or university	File annual "report" with Ohio Department of Education by September 30, and with treasurer of local board of education within first two weeks of school	None	None
Oklahoma	Over age of five (5) years and under the age of eighteen (18) years	Operate a home school as an other means of education expressed in the state constitution	180 days	Reading, writing, math, science, citizenship, U.S. constitution, health, safety, physical education, conservation	None	None	None	None
Oregon	Between the ages of 7 and 18 years who have not completed the twelfth grade	Establish and operate a home school	None	None	None	Notify education service district in writing when child starts being taught at home; when moving, notify new district in same manner	None	Participate in an approved comprehensive test in grades 3, 5, 8, and 10 administered by a qualified neutral person; if child was withdrawn from public school, the first test must be administered at least 18 months after child was withdrawn; children with disabilities are to be evaluated as per their individualized education plan

State or Territory	Compulsory School Age	Legal Options to Home School	Attendance Required	Subjects Required	Teacher Credentials	Notice Required	Record Keeping Required	Testing Required
Pennsylvania	From time the child enters school, which shall not be later than the age of eight (8) years, until the age of seventeen (17) years	Establish and operate a home education program	180 days per year or 900 hours at the elementary level or 990 hours at the secondary level	*Elementary level:* English spelling, reading, writing, arithmetic, U.S. and Pennsylvania history, civics, health and physiology, physical education, music, art, geography, science, safety and fire prevention. *Secondary level:* English language, literature, speech and composition, science, geography, civics, world, U.S., and Pennsylvania history, algebra and geometry, art, music, physical education, health, safety, and fire prevention	High school diploma or equivalent	File a notarized affidavit with the local superintendent prior to start of home school and annually by August 1st thereafter	Maintain a portfolio of materials used, work done, standardized test results in grades 3, 5, and 8, and a written evaluation completed by June 30 of each year	Administer standardized tests in grades 3, 5, and 8; submit results as part of portfolio
		Use a private tutor who: 1) is teaching one or more children who are members of a single family, 2) provides the majority of instruction, and 3) is receiving a fee or other consideration for the instruction	Same as above	*Elementary level:* Same as above. *Secondary level:* Same as above plus biology, chemistry, social studies, economics, a foreign language, general mathematics and statistics; and health and physiology instead of health	Teacher certification	File copy of certification and criminal history record with the local superintendent	None	None
		Establish and/or operate a home school as an extension or satellite of a day school operated by a church or other religious body	Same as above		None	School principal must file a notarized affidavit with the department of education	None	None
Puerto Rico	Between six and eighteen years of age	Establish and operate a home school as a non-governmental school	Same as the public schools	Same as the public schools	None	None	None	None
Rhode Island	Completed six (6) years of life on or before December 31 of any school year and not completed sixteen (16) years of life	Operate a home school as approved by the local school board	Substantially equal to that of the public schools	Reading, writing, English, geography, arithmetic, U.S. History, Rhode Island history (in fourth grade), Rhode Island government (fourth grade and high school), Rhode Island constitution (high school), U.S. government and constitution (high school), health and physical education (grades one through 12, to average 20 minutes per school day)	None	A de facto part of the approval process	Keep attendance record and submit to school committee if requested	Annual assessment may be required. Preference of parent as to type of assessment must be honored
South Carolina	5 years of age before September 1st until 17th birthday or graduation from high school; 5-year-olds may be excused from kindergarten with submission of written notice to the school district	Establish and operate a home school as approved by the local school board	180 days per year, 4½ hours per day	Reading, writing, math, science, and social studies; also composition and literature in grades 7–12	High school diploma or GED or a baccalaureate degree	None	Maintain evidence of regular instruction including a record of subjects taught, activities in which the student and parent engage, a portfolio of the child's work, and a record of academic evaluations, with a semiannual progress report	Participate in the annual statewide testing program and the Basic Skills Assessment Program
		Establish and operate a home school under the membership auspices of the South Carolina Association of Independent Home Schools (SCAIHS)	180 days per year	Same as above	High school diploma or GED	None	None required by statute; SCAIHS requires some recordkeeping	None required by statute; SCAIHS has certain testing requirements
		Establish and operate a home school under the membership auspices of an association for home schools with no fewer than fifty members	180 days per year	Same as above	High school diploma or GED	None	Maintain evidence of regular instruction including a record of subjects taught, activities in which the student and parent engage, and a portfolio of the child's work, with a semiannual progress report	None

State or Territory	Compulsory School Age	Legal Options to Home School	Attendance Required	Subjects Required	Teacher Credentials	Notice Required	Record Keeping Required	Testing Required
South Dakota	Six years old by the first day of September and who has not exceeded the age of sixteen (16) years; children under age 7 can be excused	Operate a home school	Equivalent to that of the public schools; generally a "nine-month regular term"	Language arts and math	None	Submit a notarized application to the local superintendent using the form provided by state department of education. If submitting an application for first time, include certified copy of child's birth certificate or affidavit notarized or witnessed by two or more witnesses, swearing that the child identified on the request for excuse is the same person appearing on the child's birth certificate.	Must keep copy of child's birth certificate on file at home.	Administer a standardized test to children in grades 2, 4, 8, and 11. Results must show satisfactory progress.
Tennessee	Between the ages of six (6) and seventeen (17) years, both inclusive; also applicable to children under age 6 who have enrolled in any public, private, or parochial school for more than six weeks; a parent of a six-year-old may make application for a one-semester or one-year deferral with the principal of the public school in which the child would be required to attend	Establish and operate a home school	180 days per year, 4 hours per day	*For grades K-8:* None *For grades 9-12:* Either college preparatory courses—those required for admission to state-operated four-year colleges, OR general studies courses—those required by the state board of education for high school graduation.	*For grades K-8:* High school diploma or GED *For grades 9-12:* College degree (or an exemption granted by the commissioner of education)	Submit a notice of intent to the local superintendent by August 1 of each school year	Maintain attendance records; must be kept available for inspection and submitted to the local superintendent at the end of the school year	Administer a standardized test in grades 5, 7, and 9; must be given by commissioner of education, his designee, or a professional testing service approved by the local school district
		Establish and operate a home school in association with a church-related school	As prescribed by the church-related school	As prescribed by the church-related school	*For grades K-8:* None *For grades 9-12:* High school diploma or GED	*For grades K-8:* None *For grades 9-12:* Register with the local school district each year	None	Administer the same annual standardized achievement test or Sanders Model assessment used by the local school district for grades 9-12
		Operate as a satellite campus of a church-related school	As prescribed by the church-related school	As prescribed by the church-related school	None	None	None	As prescribed by the church-related school
Texas	A child who is at least six years of age, or who is younger than six years of age and has previously been enrolled in first grade, and who has not yet reached the child's 18th birthday	Establish and operate a home school as a private school	None	Reading, spelling, grammar, math, good citizenship	None	None	None	None
Utah	A child who has reached the age of six years but has not reached the age of eighteen years	Establish and operate a home school as approved by the local school board	Same as the public schools	Language arts, math, science, social studies, arts, health, computer literacy, and vocational education	None specified; however, the local school board can consider the basic educative ability of the teacher	A de facto part of the approval process	None	None
		Establish a group of home school families as a regular private school	None	None	None	None	None	None
Vermont	Between the ages of six and 16 years; children attending a post-secondary school (approved or accredited by Vermont or another state) are exempt	Establish and operate a home school	None. 175 days per year required for public schools	Reading, writing, math, citizenship, history, U.S. and Vermont government, physical education, health, English, American and other literature, science, and fine arts	None	File a written notice of enrollment with the commissioner of education any time after March 1 for the subsequent year	None	Submit an annual assessment from: 1) a certified (or approved Vermont independent school) teacher, or 2) a report from a commercial curriculum publisher together with a portfolio, or 3) results of an acceptably administered standardized test

State or Territory	Compulsory School Age	Legal Options to Home School	Attendance Required	Subjects Required	Teacher Credentials	Notice Required	Record Keeping Required	Testing Required
Virgin Islands	Beginning of the school year nearest [child's] 5th birthday until the expiration of the school year nearest [child's] 16th birthday, except those who graduate from high school earlier	Seek commissioner of education approval to establish and operate a home school	As prescribed during the approval process	As prescribed during the approval process	As prescribed during the approval process	A de facto part of the approval process	As prescribed during the approval process	As prescribed during the approval process
		Apply for accreditation to operate a home school as a private school	As prescribed during the accreditation process	As prescribed during the accreditation process	As prescribed during the accreditation process	A de facto part of the accreditation process	As prescribed during the accreditation process	As prescribed during the accreditation process
Virginia	Has reached the 5th birthday on or before September 30, and has not passed the 18th birthday; 5-year-olds can be excused	Operate a home school	None	If operating under teacher qualification #4, math and language arts; for all others, none	Either: 1) possess a baccalaureate degree, or 2) be a certified teacher, or 3) use an approved correspondence course, or 4) submit evidence parent can teach and use curriculum that includes state objectives for language arts and math	File an annual notice of intent with local Superintendent by August 15; if starting or moving into the state after school year has begun, file notice as soon as practicable and comply with applicable requirements within 30 days of such notice	None	Administer a standardized test or have child otherwise evaluated every year (for those six years or older on September 30 of the school year); submit results to local superintendent by August 1
		Operate a home school under the religious exemption statute	None	None	None	File request to acknowledge religious exemption with the local school board chairman	None	None
		Use a private tutor	None	None	Teacher certification	Send letter to local superintendant asking him to recognize that parent (tutor) has the qualifications prescribed by the state Board of Education (i.e., teacher certificate)	None	None
Washington	Eight years of age and under eighteen years of age	Establish and operate a home school	180 days or in grades 1-12 an annual average total instructional hour offering of one thousand hours.	Occupational education, science, math, language, social studies, history, health, reading, writing, spelling, music and art appreciation	Either: 1) be supervised by a certified teacher, or 2) have 45 college quarter credit hours or completed a course in home education, or 3) be deemed qualified by the local superintendent	File an annual notice of intent with the local (or applicable nonresident) superintendent by September 15 or within two weeks of the start of any public school quarter	Maintain standardized test scores, academic progress assessments, and immunization records	Annually, administer and retain a state approved standardized test by a qualified person or have the child evaluated by a certified teacher currently working in the field of education
		Operate under extension program of an approved private school designed for parents to teach their children at home	Same as above	Same as above	Must be under the supervision of a certified teacher employed by the approved private school	None	None	Progress must be evaluated by a certified teacher employed by the approved private school
West Virginia	Compulsory school attendance shall begin with the school year in which the 6th birthday is reached prior to the 1st day of September of such year or upon enrolling in a publicly supported kindergarten program and continue to the 16th birthday	Seek local school board approval to operate a home school	Same as the public schools; generally 180 days per year	As required by board	Be deemed qualified to teach by the local superintendent and school board	A de facto part of the approval process	As prescribed during the approval process	As prescribed during the approval process
		Operate a home school	None	None, but must be assessed in areas of reading, language, mathematics, science and social studies	High school diploma	File a notice of intent with the local superintendent two weeks prior to starting to home school	None	Annually, either: 1) administer a standardized test, or 2) have certified teacher evaluate portfolio of work, 3) assess progress by other means agreeable to superintendent, or 4) participate in state testing program.
Wisconsin	Between the ages of 6 [by September 1] and 18 years	Establish and operate a home-based private educational program	Must provide at least 875 hours of instruction each year	Must provide a sequentially progressive curriculum of fundamental instruction in reading, language arts, math, social studies, science, and health; such curriculum need not conflict with the program's religious doctrines	None	File a statement of enrollment with the state department of education by October 15 each year	None	None

State or Territory	Compulsory School Age	Legal Options to Home School	Attendance Required	Subjects Required	Teacher Credentials	Notice Required	Record Keeping Required	Testing Required
Wyoming	Whose 7th birthday falls before September 15 of any year and who has not yet attained his 16h birthday or completed the 10th grade	Establish and operate a home school	175 days per year	A basic academic educational program that provides a sequentially progressive curriculum of fundamental instruction in reading, writing, math, civics, history, literature, and science	None	Annually submit to the local school board a curriculum showing that a basic academic educational program is being provided	None	None

Canadian Laws

To view information on the laws in each province, go to the "Laws" section of HSLDA of Canada at
www.hsldacanada.org/school/hslaws.asp

Homeschool Groups by State, Province, & Country

I don't know what other books and websites do to create their lists of homeschool groups. In our case, the list below is the "tip of the iceberg" of our ever-growing list of state, regional, international, and (available online only) local homeschool groups. We began compiling this list in 1985, and since then it has taken thousands of hours to keep it updated.

Picture my amazement when, not long after we first put our list online in 1993, a very well-known competitive website posted it on their site as "their" list! Due to some oddities in the way we formatted our data, it was clear this was our list. They never did respond to the emails I sent, but years later they did end up taking out a couple of large ads in my magazine, which made me feel better.

Right now, the most up-to-date and complete listing I know of is on our website, www.home-school.com. My son Ted, the webmaster, spends hours every week updating it. So . . .

- If you want your group listed, go online and follow the directions.
- If you need your listing updated, just email Ted at hsorgs@home-school.com using your official email address (one with your group's domain name after the "@" sign) and he'll take care of it.
- If you're putting together a homeschool website, feel free to link to our list, but not to copy it onto your own site or to pretend in some way it's "your" list.
- If you're writing a homeschool book and find our list helpful, please have the courtesy to mention where you found your data. And for goodness sake, don't just copy this list right out of my book. This is not only cheesy, but stupid. The most up-to-date info will always be found on our constantly updated website.

This list includes state groups; city groups for large cities; and large independent groups (covering a region of a state). We couldn't include local support groups because, (1) there are too many of them, and (2) they change much too frequently.

Finding and keeping up with this data is difficult, so we apologize if we left your large state, city, or regional group out. Visit the "Groups" area of www.home-school.com and fill out the online form to have your group added to our next listing and our website.

For the most recent listing of groups, and a listing of events by state and date, visit **www.home-school.com** and click on "Groups" and "Events"

United States: States & Territories

Alabama

Christian Home Education Fellowship of Alabama, Inc. (CHEF-AL)
P.O. Box 20208
Mongomery, AL 36120-0208
(334) 288-7229
www.chefofalabama.org

Alaska

Alaska Private and Home Educators Association (APHEA)
P.O. Box 141764
Anchorage, AK 99514
(907) 566-3450
www.aphea.org

Arizona

Arizona Families for Home Education (AFHE)
P.O. Box 2035
Chandler, AZ 85244-2035
(602) 235-2673 or (800) 929-3927
www.afhe.org

Arkansas

Home Educators of Arkansas
P.O. Box 192455
Little Rock, AR 72219
www.geocities.com/heartland/
garden/4555/hear.html

The Education Alliance
414 S. Pulaski St. Ste. 2
Little Rock, AR 72201
(501) 375-7000
www.familycouncil.org/eahms.htm

California

California Homeschool Network
P.O. Box 55485
Hayward, CA 94545
(800) 327-5339
www.californiahomeschool.net

Christian Home Educators Association of California (CHEA-CA)
P.O. Box 2009
Norwalk, CA 90651-2009
(800) 564-2432
www.cheaofca.org

Homeschool Association of California (HSC)
P.O. Box 77873
Corona, CA 92877-0128
(888) HSC-4440
www.hsc.org

Colorado

Christian Home Educators of Colorado (CHEC)
10431 South Parker Rd.
Parker, CO 80134
(720) 842-4852
www.chec.org

Concerned Parents of Colorado
PO Box 547
Florissant, CO 80816
(719) 748-8360
members.aol.com/treonelain/

Connecticut

The Education Association of Christian Homeschoolers (TEACH)
363 Carriage Dr.
Southburg, CT 08488
(890) 793-9968
www.teachct.org

Delaware

Delaware Home Education Association
PO Box 268
Hartly, DE 19953
(302) 337-0990
www.dheaonline.org

Florida

Christian Home Educators of Florida (CHEF)
P.O. Box 5393
Clearwater, FL 33758-5393
www.christianhomeeducatorsofflorida.com

Florida Coalition of Christian Private Schools Association, Inc. (FCCPSA)
P.O. Box 13227
Fort Pierce, FL 34979-3227
(561) 344-2929
www.flhomeschooling.com

Florida Parent-Educators Association (FPEA)
9951 Atlantic Blvd, Suite 102
Jacksonville, FL 32225
1-877-ASK-FPEA
www.fpea.com

Georgia

Georgia Home Education Association
141 Massengale Rd.
Brooks, GA 30205
(770) 461-3657
www.ghea.org

North Georgia Home Education Association
PO Box 5545
Fort Oglethorpe, GA 30742
(706) 861-1795
drwddrennan@juno.com

Georgians for Freedom in Education
209 Cobb St.
Palmetto, GA 30268
(770) 463-1563

Hawaii

Christian Homeschoolers of Hawaii
c/o 92-739 Makakilo Dr. #18
Kapolei, HI 96707
(808) 689-6398
www.christianhomeschoolersofhawaii.org

Idaho

Christian Homeschoolers of Idaho State
PO Box 45062
Boise, ID 83711-5062
(208) 424-6685
www.chois.org

Idaho Coalition of Home Educators
PO Box 878
Eagle, ID 83616
www.iche-idaho.org

Illinois

Christian Home Educators Coalition (CHEC) of Illinois
PO Box 47322
Chicago, IL 60647-0322
(773) 278-0673
www.chec.cc

Illinois Christian Home Educators
P.O. Box 775
Harvard, IL 60033
(815) 943-7882
www.iche.org

Indiana

Indiana Association of Home Educators (IAHE)
8106 Madison Ave.
Indianapolis, IN 46227
(317) 859-1202
ttp://www.inhomeeducators.org

Iowa

Network of Iowa Christian Home Educators (NICHE)
P.O. Box 158
Dexter, IA 50070
(515) 830-1614 or (800) 723-0438
www.the-niche.org

Kansas

Christian Home Educators Confederation of Kansas (CHECK)
PO Box 1332
Topeka, KS 66601
(785) 272-6655
www.kansashomeschool.org

Kentucky

Christian Home Educators of Kentucky (CHEK)
691 Howardstown Rd.
Hodgenville, Ky. 42748
(270) 358-9270
www.chek.org

Kentucky Home Education Association
P.O. Box 51591
Bowling Green, KY 42102-5891
(270) 779-6574
www.khea.8k.com

Louisiana

Christian Home Educators Fellowship of Louisiana
P.O. Box 74292
Baton Rouge, LA 70874-4292
(888) 876-2433
www.chefofla.org

Maine

Homeschoolers of Maine (HOME)
40 Curtis Rd.
Freeport, ME 04032
(207) 763-4251
www.homeschoolersofmaine.org

Maine Home Education Association
19 Willowdale Dr.
Gorham, Maine 04038
www.geocities.com/mainehomeed/

Maryland

Christian Home Educators Network, Inc. (CHEN)
P.O. Box 2010
Ellicott City, MD 21043
(301) 474-9055
www.chenmd.org

Maryland Association of Christian Home Educators
P.O. Box 417
Clarksburg, MD 20871-0417
(301) 607-4284
www.machemd.org

Massachusetts

Massachusetts Homeschool Organization of Parent Educators (MassHOPE)
46 South Rd.
Holden, MA 01520
(508) 755-4467
www.masshope.org

Michigan

Information Network for Christian Homes (INCH)
4934 Cannonsburg Rd.
Belmont, MI 49306
(616) 874-5656
www.inch.org

Minnesota

Minnesota Association of Christian Home Educators (MACHE)
P.O. Box 32308
Fridley. MN 55432-0308
(763) 717-9070 or (866) 717-9070
www.mache.org

Mississippi

Mississippi Home Educators Association (MHEA)
1535 Steens-Vernon Road
Steens, MS 39766
(662) 578-6432
www.mhea.net

Missouri

Christian Home Educators Fellowship
(314) 521-8487
www.chef-missouri.com

Families for Home Education (FHE)
P.O. Box 742
Grandview, MO 64030
(816) 767-9825
www.fhe-mo.org

Missouri Association of Teaching Christian Homes (MATCH)
2203 Rhonda Dr.
West Plains, MO 65775-1615
(815) 550-8641
www.match-inc.org

Montana

Montana Coalition of Home Educators (MCHE)
P.O. Box 43
Gallatin Gateway, MT 59730
(406) 587-6163
www.mtche.org

Nebraska

Nebraska Christian Home Educators Association
P.O. Box 57041
Lincoln, NE 68505-7041
(402) 423-4297
www.nchea.org

Nevada

Home School United—Vegas Valley
PO Box 93564
Las Vegas, NV 89193
(702) 870-9566
homeschool8.tripod.com

Northern Nevada Home Schools, Inc.
P.O. Box 21323
Reno, NV 89515
(702) 852-NNHS
www.nnhs.org

New Hampshire

Christian Home Educators of New Hampshire
P.O. Box 961
Manchester, NH 03105
(603) 569-2343
www.chenh.org

New Hampshire Home Schooling Coalition
P.O. Box 2224
Concord, NH 03301
(603) 539-7233
www.nhhomeschooling.org

New Jersey

Education Network of Christian Home Schoolers
P.O. Box 308
Atlantic Highlands, NJ 07716
(732) 291-7800
www.enochnj.org

New Mexico

Christian Association of Parent Educators - New Mexico (CAPE-NM)
P.O. Box 25046
Albuquerque, NM 87125
(505) 898-8548
www.cape-nm.org

New York

New York State Loving Education at Home (LEAH-NYS)
P.O. Box 438
Fayetteville, NY 13066-0438
(315) 637-4525
www.leah.org

North Carolina

North Carolinians for Home Education (NCHE)
4326 Bland Rd.
Raleigh, NC 27609
(919) 790-1100
www.nche.com

North Dakota

North Dakota Home School Association
P.O. Box 7400
Bismark, ND 58507-7400
(701) 223-4080

Ohio

Christian Home Educators of Ohio (CHEO)
117 W. Main St. Ste. 103
Lancaster, OH 43130
(740) 654-3331
www.cheohome.org

Oklahoma

Christian Home Educators Fellowship (CHEF) of Oklahoma
P. O. Box 471363
Tulsa, OK 74147-1363
(918) 583-7323
www.chefok.org

Oklahoma Christian Home Educators Consociation, Inc. (OCHEC)
3801 Northwest 63rd St, Building 3, #236
Oklahoma City, OK 73116
(405) 810-0386
www.ochec.com

Home Educator's Resource Organization (HERO) of Oklahoma
302 N. Coolidge
Enid, OK 73703-3819
www.oklahomahomeschooling.org

Oregon

Oregon Christian Home Education Association Network (OCEAN)
17985 Falls City Rd.
Dallas, OR 97338
(503) 288-1285
www.oceanetwork.org

Oregon Home Education Network (OHEN)
P.O. Box 218
Beaverton, OR 97075-0218
(503) 321-5166
www.ohen.org

Pennsylvania

Christian Homeschool Association of Pennsylvania (CHAP)
P.O. Box 115
Mount Joy, PA 17552-0115
(717) 661-2428
www.chapboard.org

Pennsylvania Homeschoolers
RR 2, Box 117
Kittanning, PA 16201
www.pahomeschoolers.com

Puerto Rico

Christian Home Educators Association of Puerto Rico
P.O. Box 867
Boqueron, PR 00622
www.tchers.net

Rhode Island

Rhode Island Guild of Home Teachers (RIGHT)
P.O. Box 11
Hope, RI 02831
(401) 821-7700
www.rihomeschool.com

South Carolina

South Carolina Association of Independent Home Schools (SCAIHS)
930 Knox Abbott Dr.
Cayce, SC 29033
(803) 454-0427
www.scaihs.org

South Carolina Home Educators Association (SCHEA)
P.O. Box 3231
Columbia, SC 29230-3231
(803) 772-2330
www.schomeeducatorsassociation.org

South Dakota

South Dakota Christian Home Educators
P.O. Box 9571
Rapid City, SD 57709-9571
(605) 348-2001
www.sdche.org

South Dakota Home School Association (SDHSA)
P.O. Box 882
Sioux Falls, SD 57101
www.southdakotahomeschool.com

Tennessee

Mideast Tennessee Home Education Association
261 County Rd #757
Riceville, TN 37370
(423) 336-5800
JerichoBelles@aol.com

Memphis Home Education Association
P.O. Box 171134
Memphis, TN 38187-1134
(901) 362-2620
www.memphishomeed.org

Middle Tennessee Home Education Association
P.O. Box 147
Old Hickory, TN 37138
(615) 794-3259
www.mthea.org

Northeast Tennessee Home Education Association
476 Hwy 70 South
Rogersville, TN 37857
phunnypharm@bellsouth.net
(423) 272-4529

Southeast Tennessee Home Education Association
PO Box 23374
Chattanooga, TN 37422
(423) 266-4663
www.csthea.org

Tennessee Home Education Association
P.O. Box 681652
Franklin, TN 37068
(858) 623-7899
www.tnhea.org

West Tennessee Home Education Association
P.O. Box 10013
Jackson, TN 38308-0100
(731) 559-4848

Texas

Christian Home Education Association of Central Texas (CHEACT)
P.O. Box 141998
Austin, TX 78714-1998
(512) 450-0070
www.cheact.org

Family Educators Alliance of South Texas (FEAST)
25 Burwood
San Antonio, TX 78216
(210) 342-4674
www.homeschoolfeast.com

Home School Texas (HOST)
PO Box 29307
Dallas, TX 75229
(214) 358-5723
www.homeschooltexas.com

North Texas Home Educators Network (NTHEN)
801 E. Main St, Suite G
Allen, TX 75002
(214) 495-9600
www.nthen.org

Southeast Texas Home School Association (SETHSA)
PMB 297, 4950 FM 1960 W, #A-7
Houston, Texas 77069
(281) 370-8787
www.sethsa.org

Supporting Home Educators of Lower Texas Educational Region (SHELTER)
2424 Holden Rd.
Aransas Pass, TX 78336
(512) 758-2777
www.intcomm.net/~shelter/

Texas Home School Coalition
P.O. Box 6747
Lubbock, TX 79493
(806) 744-4441
www.thsc.org

Utah

Utah Christian Home School Association (UTCH)
P.O. Box 3942
Salt Lake City, UT 84110-3942
(801) 296-7198
www.utch.org

Utah Home Education Association
P.O. Box 737
Farmington, UT 84025
(801) 254-4882
www.uhea.org

Vermont

Christian Home Educators of Vermont (CHEV)
PO Box 255
Woodbury, VT 05681
(802) 472-5491
www.sover.net/~kelrobin/chev

Vermont Association of Home Educators
c/o Tim Terhune
1646 E. Albany Road
Barton, VT 05822
(802) 525-4758
www.vermonthomeschool.org

Virginia

Home Educators Association of Virginia (HEAV)
1900 Byrd Avenue, Suite 201
Richmond, VA 23230-0745
(804) 288-1608
www.heav.org

Washington

Family Learning Organization
P.O. Box 7247
Spokane, WA 99207-0247
(509) 467-2552
www.familylearning.org

Washington Association of Teaching Christian Homes (WATCH)
1026 224th Ave. NE
Sammamish, WA 98074
(206) 729-4804
www.watchhome.org

Washington Homeschool Organization (WHO)
6632 S. 191st Place, Suite E100
Kent, WA 98032-2117
(425) 251-0439
www.washhomeschool.org

West Virginia

Christian Home Educators of West Virginia
P. O. Box 8770, S.
Charleston, WV 25303-0770
(304) 776-4664
www.chewv.org

Wisconsin

Wisconsin Christian Home Educators Association (WCHEA)
2307 Carmel Avenue
Racine, WI 53405
(262) 637-5127
www.wisconsinchea.com

Wisconsin Parents Association (WPA)
P.O. Box 2502
Madison, WI 53701-2502
(608) 283-3131
www.homeschooling-wpa.org

Wyoming

Homeschoolers of Wyoming
4859 Palmer Canyon Rd.
Wheatland, WY 82201
(307) 322-3539
www.homeschoolersofwy.org

Canada

Home School Legal Defence Association of Canada
2 - 3295 Dunmore Road SE
Medicine Hat, Alberta T1B 3R2
(403) 528-2704
www.hsldacanada.org

Alberta

Wisdom Home Schooling
Box 78
Derwent, Alberta T0B 1C0
(780) 741-2113
www.wisdomhomeschooling.com

Alberta Home Education Association
Box 84
Hughenden, Alberta T0B 2E0
(403) 236-1176
www.aheaonline.com

British Columbia

British Columbia Home Learners' Association (BCHLA)
c/o #8-4800 Island Hwy N
Nanaimo, British Columbia V9T 1W6
604-466-3098
www.bchla.bc.ca

British Columbia Home School Association
6225-C 136 St.
Surrey, British Columbia V3X 1H3
(604) 572-7817
bchomeschool.org/default.htm

Manitoba

Manitoba Association for Schooling at Home
c/o 185 Rossmere Cres.
Winnipeg Manitoba R2K 0G1
(204) 284-8183
www.theworldismyschool.com

Manitoba Association of Christian Home Schoolers (MACHS)
MACHS
Box 283, St. Vital Postal Station
Winnipeg, Manitoba R2N 3X9
www.machs.mb.ca

New Brunswick

Bluenose Natural Home School
P.O. Box 243
Newcastle, New Brunswick E1B 3M3

Home Educators of New Brunswick
c/o 44 Marks St.
St. Stephen's, New Brunswick E3L 2B3
(506) 472-6452
www.henb.org

Newfoundland

Peter & Pamela Hynes
52 Cottinwood Cres
St. John's, Newfoundland A1H 1A1
(709) 747-2041

Nova Scotia

Nova Scotia Home Educators Association
c/o Melanie Feltmate
1012 Club Crescent
New Minas, Nova Scotia B0S 1A0
902-681-0341
nshea1.tripod.com

Ontario

Catholic Home Schoolers Association
P. O. Box 9071, Stn. T
Ottawa, ON K1G 3T8

Ontario Christian Home Educators Connection
Box 2
Iona Station, Ontario N0L 1P0
905-689-7762
www.ochec.org

Quebec

Association of Christian Home Educators of Quebec (ACHEQ)
C.P. 1
Laurier-Station, Quebec G0S 1N0
(418) 796-2243
www.acpeq.org

Saskatchewan

Saskatchewan Home-Based Educators
403 22nd St. W Box 13
Saskatoon, Saskatchewan S7M 5T3
(306) 931-2910
www.shbe.info

Foreign Countries

Australia

Australian Christian Academy
PO Box 5677
Brendale, Queensland 4500
Australia
(07) 3205 7444
www.australianchristianacademy.org

Christian Academy of Life Ltd.
P.O. Box 7257
Toowoomba, Qld. 4352
(07) 4615 2076
www.swcs.com.au/caol/

Home Education Association (HEA) of Australia
4 Bruce Street,
Stanmore NSW 2048
(02) 9500 7664
www.hea.asn.au

Czech Republic

National Czech Home School Association
m.sermin@volny.cz

England/United Kingdom

Education Otherwise
P.O. Box 7420
London N9 9SG
0870 7300074
www.education-otherwise.org

Home Education Advisory Service
P.O. Box 98
Welwyn Garden City, Herts. AL8 6AN
+44 (0) 1707 371854
www.heas.org.uk

Home Service
48 Heaton Moor Rd.
Heaton Moor, Stockport SK4 4NX
161-432-3782
www.home-service.org

Learning In a Family Environment
PSC 37 Box 1215
APO AE 09459
01638-669864
www.geocities.com/lifehsgroup/

Germany

HEART for Germany (Home Educators are Real Teachers)
ICOAC4, Messtetten Unit 30405
APO AE 09131
7579-921873
wagnerwn@swol.de

Schulunterricht zu Hause e.V.
Buchwaldstr. 16
D-63303 Dreieich
+49-(0)1805-SCHUZH (724894)
www.german-homeschool.de

Hungary

Hungarian Home Schooling Association (HHSA)
kgtmi@axelero.hu

Japan

CHEA of Japan
03-5155-9212
www.cheajapan.com

HOSA
adachi8@email.msn.com

Kanto Plain Home Schoolers
PSC 473 Box 184
FPO AP 96349-5555
msbunny@surf-line.or.jp

Mexico/ Central America

El Hogar Educador
APDO 17
Arteaga Coahuila 25350
018-483-0377
www.elhogareducador.org

The Netherlands

Netherlands Association for Home Education
Postbus 761
1180 AT Amstelveen
020-6404690
www.nvvto.nl

New Zealand

Christian Home Schoolers of New Zealand
4 Tawa St.
Palmerston North 5301
06-357-4399
www.homeeducationfoundation.org.nz

Homeschooling Federation of New Zealand.
PO. Box 41 226
St Lukes Auckland New Zealand
(09) 376 6225
www.homeschooling.org.nz

Learning as Families
35A Primrose St.
Hamilton
07 847-8248
Email: salpow@ihug.co.nz

Romania

Romanian Homeschool Association
curcubetg@nextra.ro

South Africa

Pestalozzi Trust
Posbus 12332
Queenswood 0121
+27 12 330 1337
www.pestalozzi.org

Spain

Association for Freedom in Education (ALE)
Asociación para la Libre Educación
Apartado de Correos 68, 08880
Cubelles. Barcelona, Spain
www.educacionlibre.org

Contests Homeschoolers Can Enter

Art Contests

American Morgan Horse Art Contest

All ages. $5 fee per entry.
AMHA, 122 Bostwick Road, PO Box 960, Shelburne, VT 05482. (802) 985-4944. www.morganhorse.com/general/ gen_art.html

Draw, paint, sculpt, carve, or embroider a beautiful Morgan horse and you might a prize of money and AMHA merchandise. Deadline: October.

Arbor Day National Poster Contest

Grade 5 only. No fee.
The National Arbor Day Foundation, Poster Contest Coordinator, PO Box 85784, Lincoln, NE 68501-5784, www.arborday.org/programs/ postercontest/.

Each year the National Arbor Day Foundation hosts a poster contest. They estimate that more than 70,000 fifth-grade classrooms across America will participate. Homeschoolers are welcome. One year's winner was homeschooled!

National contest is judged in April, but the state contests are judged earlier. The exact date varies by state. Since the planting date for the northern states is later, the deadline is later.

The national winner, one parent, and the winner's teacher, will receive an expense-paid trip to Nebraska City, Nebraska, birthplace of Arbor Day, where they will participate in the National Arbor Day Awards ceremony. Winner also receives a $1,000 savings bond and lifetime membership in The National Arbor Day Foundation. The winning teacher also receives $200 for classroom materials. Second and third place winners and their teachers get smaller savings bonds and money awards.

Dick Blick Linoleum Block Print Contest

Grades 4–12.
Dick Blick, 3166 N. Lincoln Ave., Suite 405, Chicago, IL 60657. (800) 828-4548, www.dickblick.com.

Most of the contest listings in this appendix originally were compiled by Laurie Bluedorn of Trivium Pursuit and were taken in part from "Trivium Pursuit's List of National Contests Open to Homeschoolers." You can obtain the entire Trivium Pursuit list free by writing: Trivium Pursuit, 139 Colorado Street, Suite 168, Muscatine, IA 52761.

The other main contributors to our contest listings are Susan and Howard Richman, founders of Pennsylvania Homeschoolers. Over the years, their children have won more contests than any other children I know, and their state newsletter always is packed with announcements of other winning Pennsylvania homeschoolers. Remaining listings were compiled by Mary Pride.

Franklin Pride researched and updated all listings as of January 2004, making this list more up-to-date than that available in the current crop of "Contests" books. All contests listed welcome homeschoolers.

Annual contest for kids, focusing on linoleum block printing (no wood cuts, styrofoam, or other types of prints accepted), a technology that is easy enough for the homeschool. Prizes include art supplies. Three divisions, by grade level. Deadline: March.

International Children's Art Exhibition

Grades K–9. No fee.
ICAE, Pentel of America, Ltd., 2805 Columbia St., Torrance, CA 90509. (800) 421-1419.
www.pentel.com/1child.html

Original 2D artwork, any theme. I know of at least one homeschooled student who won a prize in this competition.

National Rifle Association Youth Wildlife Art Contest

Grades 1–12. No fee.
www.nrahq.org/youth/wildlife.asp

Contest entries are grouped into four categories according to school grade level: Grades one to three, four to six, seven to nine, and 10 to 12. Contestants submit drawings of animals that may be legally hunted or trapped in North America. The first place winner in each category receives a $200 cash prize. Second place winners receive $100. Third place wins $50.

Winning art may be viewed online at the web page listed above. That is also the page to visit for information about each year's Youth Wildlife Art Contest. Autumn deadline.

Practical Homeschooling Art & Photo Contests

Envelope Gallery contest open to all homeschool students. Photo contest open to all members of homeschooling families. Must be subscriber to enter. No fees.
Home Life, Inc., PO Box 1190, Fenton, MO 63026. news@home-school.com. Entries may be submitted via mail or email.

Envelope Gallery Draw, color, or paint a picture on an envelope and send it in. You may get your envelope published in *Practical Homeschooling*.

Annual Photo Contest Send in your best family photo. Honorable mentions get published inside the magazine. Winners get published on the cover and receive a $100 gift certificate from the Home Life catalog.

Essay & Fiction Contests

Ayn Rand Essay Contest

Grades 9–12. No fee.
Ayn Rand Essay Contest, 2121 Alton Pkwy., Suite 250, Irvine, CA 92606. www.aynrand.org/contests.

Essay contests with a libertarian twist. Essays written on certain Ayn Rand books. Grades 9–10 write about *Anthem*. Grades 11–12 write about *The Fountainhead*. Prizes up to $2,000 for 9–10; up to $10,000 for 11–12. Competition with prizes for college students, too. Deadlines in spring.

Concord Review

Grades 9–12. $40 submission fee.
The Concord Review, PO Box 661, Concord, MA 01742. (800) 331-5007. www.tcr.org.

Not exactly a competition in the usual sense, the *Concord Review* is a scholarly journal that publishes high-school students' history research essays. Excellent guidelines on their website, including a full range of past-published essays. Looking for in-depth papers on any aspect of world or US history, in the 4000–6000 word range. Homeschoolers welcome. You get four issues of *Concord Review* just for entering.

DuPont Challenge Science Essay Awards Program

Grades 7–12.
DuPont Challenge, General Learning Communications, 900 Skokie Blvd, #200, Northbrook, IL 60062-4028. (847) 205-3000.
www.glcomm.com/dupont.

Open-ended, 700–1000 word science essay competition in two divisions (junior and senior high). Student can choose topic of current interest. Poster available giving details, along with last year's winning essays to give students a feel for the quality being

sought. Deadline: January. Prizes $50–$1,500.

Kids Speak Out Contest

Ages 6–14.
World Almanac Books, World Almanac for Kids, "Kids Speak Out!" Contest, 512 Seventh Ave, 22nd Floor, New York, NY 10018.
www.worldalmanacforkids.com/fun-games/contest.html

Write an essay to answer a question. The question for 2004 was "Who are the three most important people in the world today and why?" Entries are judged for originality of content and descriptiveness.

The first prize winner receives an all expense paid trip for four to Washington, DC. 750 runners-up receive a limited edition World Almanac for Kids T-shirt. February deadline.

Letters About Literature

Grades 4–7 (level I). Grades 8–12 (level II).
LAL 2004 - Level I (or II), King's College, c/o The Graduate Reading Program, PO Box 609, Dallas, PA 18612. (203) 705-3500.
www.weeklyreader.com

Annual competition sponsored by Weekly Reader and The Center for the Book in the Library of Congress. Students are asked to write a letter to the author of a book that has had a great impact on them, sharing how the book affected them. They are not looking for the typical book report (the directions point out that the author already knows the plot of the book!)—students are instead urged to reflect on what impact the book made on their lives, how it made them act differently, see issues in a new light, etc. Kids in the Richman's writing club have won honorable mentions many times in this competition, and their daughter Molly was once a national finalist for her letter to Anne Frank. Cash awards, certificates. December 1 deadline. Weekly Reader also sponsors several other writing contests in poetry, fiction, and personal essays—check out their website regularly to see what's coming up.

National History Day

Grades 6–12. Entry fee.
University of MD, 0119 Cecil Hall, College Park, MD 20742. (301) 314-9739. www.nationalhistoryday.org.

This annual competition for junior high and senior high students has both project, presentation, and essay categories. Students first compete at regional, then state and national competitions. Many homeschoolers have qualified for state level competitions, and at least one homeschooler has been a national winner. Each year a broad theme is chosen. For 2004 it's *Exploration, Encounter, Exchange in History,* which students can examine through any era in history, local to worldwide. Use of primary documents is a must. Exemplary guidelines and handbook are available right online, helping you to design a whole curriculum with History Day at the core. Scholarship awards.

National Peace Essay Contest

Grades 9–12.
National Peace Essay Contest, 1200 17th St. NW, Suite 200, Washington, DC 20036-3011. (202) 429-3854, www.usip.org/ed/Programs/npec/npec.html.

This is a serious foreign policy essay contest, sponsored by the US Institute for Peace. Excellent and rigorous guidelines on website, including sample winning essays from previous years. Jesse Richman won second and third place in PA state competition when he was in high school at home, and his homeschool friend Brandon Geist won first place from PA, earning a trip to Washington, DC, for a special weeklong program on foreign policy. College scholarship awards for all state and national winners.

Optimists International Essay Contest

All high school students 19 and under.
(800) 500-8130 x235, www.optimist.org. Click "What do optimists do?"

A civics essay competition, with students responding in year 2004 to the topic "Being the Best I Can Be" in a 400–500-word essay. Students enter at local club level (contacts listed on website), then on to district level, and winners earn an all-expenses-paid weeklong trip to Valley Forge Freedoms Foundation 4-day workshop. Deadline for club level is end of February, districts mid-April.

Practical Homeschooling Story Contest

Ages: 10 and under and 11 and up. Must be subscriber to enter. No fees.
Home Life, Inc., PO Box 1190, Fenton, MO 63026. www.home-school.com.

Practical Homeschooling magazine gives you a story starter and you write the ending. Winners receive some desirable educational toy or book.

Scholastic Writing Awards

Grades 7–12. $5 per submission.
Scholastic Books, 557 Broadway, New York, NY 10012. (212) 343-6493. www.scholastic.com/artandwriting/

This very prestigious annual competition, sponsored by Scholastic Books, encourages a wide range of writing; there are categories for personal essays, short stories, plays, poetry, journalistic writing, even science fiction. Some special options for high school seniors who may submit a full portfolio of writing. Excellent guidelines. Cash awards. Due date: mid January.

Sons of the American Revolution Essay Contest

Grades 11–12.
Chairman, NSSAR Knight Essay Contest, Larry Perkins, 101 Curtis Ln, St. Clairsville, OH 43590-1154. www.sar.org/youth/knightrl.htm.

Now called the *George S. and Stella M. Knight Essay Contest,* this annual competition asks students to examine any aspect of the Revolutionary War, the Declaration of Independence, or the US Constitution, in a 750- to 1,000-word essay. Enter through your local chapter of NSSAR. You can find a list of chapters at their website, or write to the address above. Local competitions lead to state and national competitions. Cash awards and publication.

USA Weekend Student Fiction Contest

Grades 9–12.
USA WEEKEND Student Fiction Contest, PO Box 4252, Blair, NE 68009-4252. www.usaweekend.com/classroom

Sponsored by *USA Weekend,* the insert that goes in many Sunday newspapers across the country, students are asked to write an original short story of no more than 1500 words, that takes place at least partially in summer in the 1990's. A homeschooler from Pennsylvania, Dillon Wright-Fitzgerald, was one of the 5 national finalists in this competition in 1999, earning a gift certificate, and publication on the *USA Weekend* website, plus a great full-page newspaper article in her hometown paper. The guidelines on their website are quite helpful, including many intriguing ways to use a newspaper to help you gain ideas for stories. Homeschoolers are specifically welcomed. Mid-February deadline.

Young Naturalist Awards

Grades 7–12. $3 entry fee.
Young Naturalist Awards Administrator; National Center for Science Literacy, Education, and Technology; American Museum of Natural History; Central Park West at 79th Street, New York, NY 10024-5192. (212) 533-0222. www.amnh.org/youngnaturalistawards.

Sponsored by the American Museum of Natural History in NYC, this annual competition encourages wide ranging science research and thinking. Students write essays related to the selected theme for the year. For 2004, they want you to "conduct your own scientific expedition, one which will provide original data, questions, and observations on a topic in the natural sciences." Sample winning student essays are on their website. Scholarship awards at each grade level. Deadline: January. Next year's contest will start in June.

Computer Science Contests

USA Computing Olympiad
Grades 9–12.
usaco.uwp.edu

Computer programming competition for high-school students. Each year four students are chosen to represent the USA in international competition in programming using the C++ language. Alex Schwendner, a home schooler from Austin, TX, was on the USA International Olympiad in Informatics team in both 2003 and 2004. There are five "challenges" from November through March as well as the US Open competition in April. Students compete as individuals.

ThinkQuest
See listing under "Team Contests."

Math Contests for Individuals

American Statistical Association's Competitions
Grades K–12. No fee.
American Statistical Association, 1429 Duke St., Alexandria VA 22314-3402. (402) 472-2257.
www.amstat.org/education/poster1.html.

How about a competition where you develop an original statistics project or poster? Try the website for full details on both contests, registration info, sample winning posters, and much more. Also, if you live in Pennsylvania, check out the special web page for the PA Statistics Poster Competition at renoir.vill.edu/~short/posters/. You'll get to see lots of fun samples of winning posters from recent years (even some really cute ones by kindergartners!), helping you get your ideas together for your own project. You'll realize here that doing work with statistics does indeed involve the real world. No fee to enter.

The Mandelbrot Competition
www.mandelbrot.org

Started by several friends who'd all enjoyed various math competitions while growing up, this is both an individual and team competition, with three or four rounds of problems. Costs are very reasonable: $40 to $50 a year per team of four students (and more students can take part as individuals). There are two high-school-level divisions, plus a middle-school competition, and there are both individual and team components. Billed as "the competition that teaches as much as it tests"—and I can see it does just that. No calculators. Registration begins in May.

The Math Forum Problem of the Week
www.mathforum.org

This site has been going for about five years, and includes weekly math challenges for all levels. What's unique here? Students are expected to write out full solutions to problems, describing their solution strategy and thinking process. Recognition for correct solutions, and special notice for outstanding written explanations. The Math Forum also takes suggestions for original math problems to use on the site, and welcomes new people (even students!) to serve as mentors and readers of student solutions. There's also a full archive of past problems, along with many other resources for both students and teachers. Many students from all around the world take part. For all levels, elementary on up—and it's free!

Solve-It
www.udel.edu/educ/solveit

Want to try a summer distance math contest with a big emphasis on fun and parent involvement? Try Solve-It, sponsored by the University of Delaware, for a great program for 4th- to 8th-graders. Cost is $50 per student, and you can choose between two difficulty levels (you get to choose whichever would better match your child's current abilities—grade level is not crucial here). You'll receive problem sets in the mail, along with follow-up mailings and solutions, and prizes and awards for completing the program. Involves students writing out full solutions and telling how they went about working on the problem, rather than just giving the correct answer.

USA Math Talent Search
www.nsa.gov/programs/mepp (then go to link for USAMTS).

Tired of multiple-choice exams or speed tests? Want to take your time to really think and ponder and develop your mathematical ideas carefully? Then the USAMTS may be for you. This unique program was started by a professor at Rose Hulman Institute of Technology, based on the math competitions he'd remembered from his younger days in Hungary where speed was not the main goal, but rather well-reasoned and thoughtful work. This is an individual distance competition, where students have 4 weeks to solve a very challenging set of five math problems, developing full written solutions, proofs, or explanations, not just an answer. You are even allowed to research any topic to gain more background and information—you just can't discuss the problems with other people. Top students receive special recognition for each of the four sets of problems, and many prizes are awarded at the end of the year (Jacob Richman received a set of great math books one year). This program is free to students, and problems and full info are now up on the Internet. Although there is not a team or social aspect to this competition, all the students keep in touch through a newsletter. Excellent student solutions are published to help others see ways to develop their proofs. The emphasis is on encouraging students to only compete against themselves, learning to set high goals, work hard at very difficult tasks, and learn to achieve a higher level of competence than at the start of the program. Taking part and doing very well is another route to being chosen for the AIME mentioned above.

Science and Engineering Contests

Duracell/ NSTA Scholarship Competition
Grades 6–12.
Duracell, 1840 Wilson Blvd, Arlington, VA 22201. (888) 255-4242. www.nsta.org/programs

NSTA has two award programs for students. The Craftsman/NSTA Young Inventors Awards Program challenges students, working independently, to "use creativity and imagination along with science, technology, and mechanical ability to invent or modify a tool."

ExploraVision is a competition for US or Canadian students "to combine their imaginations with the tools of science to create and explore a vision of a future technology."

Intel Science Talent Search
Grade 12.
Science Service, 1719 N Street, NW, Washington DC 20036. 202-785-2255. sciedu@sciserv.org. www.intel.com/education/sts. Entry forms are available on the Science Service website at www.sciserv.org.

Formerly Westinghouse Science Talent Search, one of the most prestigious science awards for high school seniors, involving presentation of a major research project in any of the sciences (life sciences, behavioral and social sciences, engineering, math and physical sciences, etc.) done under supervision of a scientist (not necessarily a teacher).

In 1999 a homeschooler won the competition! Intel awards $1.2 million in prizes: $1,000 to each of the 300 semi-finalists and $1,000 per semi-finalist to their schools. The 40 finalists receive awards ranging from a $5,000 scholarship to a $100,000 4-year scholarship. Deadline for entries is early in December.

The information packet includes the rules (of which there are many), the guidelines for what the judges would like to see, and the process for entering the competition (quite convoluted and involving several officials

outside your family). This science competition is probably the most difficult a high-school student can enter.

Invent America!
Grades K–8. Enrollment kit: $17 online; $21 by fax/mail.
Invent America!, PO Box 26065, Alexandria, VA 22313. 703-942-7121. www.inventamerica.org.

Student invention contest. Schools and homeschools may submit one invention per grade. One $1,000, one $500, and one $250 savings bond are awarded at each grade. Deadline: June.

Junior Engineering Technical Society
Grades 9–12.
Junior Engineering Technical Society 1420 King Street, Suite 405, Alexandria, VA 22314. (703) 548-5387. www.jets.org.

Engineering examination and other engineering competitions.

NASA SIP Program
Grades 3–12.
NASA/Space Science Student Involvement Program, 1840 Wilson Boulevard, Arlington, VA 22201. (703) 243-7100. www.nsta.org/programs.

Five different space science contests. Win trips to NASA centers, internships with NASA scientists, Space Camp scholarships, medals, ribbons, certificates, and recognition. Deadline January.

Siemens Westinghouse Competition in Math, Science & Technology
Grades 9–12.
Siemens Foundation, 170 Wood Ave South, Isellin, NJ 08330. (877) 822-5233. www.siemens-foundation.org.

If Peter Parker had entered this competition, he wouldn't have had to rely on taking photos for cranky J. Jonah Jameson to get him through college.

Talented high-school science students who are capable of doing impressive research projects are who this competition is targeted to find. If you get

past the first round, you are invited to give an oral and poster presentation at one of six regional events. These take place at universities who have "partner" status with the competition. An individual and team Regional Winner is selected and given scholarships and a chance to compete in the National Competition in Washington, D.C., where top research scientists in the relevant field will judge each project. The first-place individual and team winners receive scholarships of $100,000, in addition to the scholarships already won at the regional level. Runners up receive scholarships from $10,000 to $50,000. This is also a recruiting tool: "successful competition participants may apply for valuable internships at Siemens operating companies."

More homeschoolers need to find out about the great big scholarships they can get through this competition. I couldn't find a single homeschooled Regional Finalist in 2003. However, in 2002, homeschooler Bethany Kindiger was part of a Regional Finalist team.

Languages & Mythology

Exploring Latin Exam
Grades 3–6.
www.etclassics.org/ele.htm.

Have a young Latin scholar? Want to see him strut his stuff? This is a very safe competition to enter, ego-wise. All participants receive certificates, and the highest achievers receive both certificates and ribbons.

The exam consists of 30 multiple-choice questions focusing on these vocabulary categories: Animals, Art/Architecture, Body Parts, Colors, Derivatives, Entertainment, Family Members, Geography/History, Housing/Life, Mottoes/Expressions, Mythology, Nature, Number Names, Oral/Classroom, Roman Numerals, and Translation.

While grammatical forms will not be tested, students should be able to recognize vocabulary in grammatical context.

This exam may be administered any time from October through mid-April.

Teachers must return completed exams within one week of administering them.

The website has all the info you need, including an exam syllabus and sample exam questions.

Medusa Mythology Exam

Students of Latin and Greek in grades 9–12. Fees: $2/student plus a $15 school fee.

Medusa Mythology Exam, PO Box 1032, Gainesville, VA 20156. (800) 896-4671. www.medusaexam.org.

Too old for the National Mythology Exam (see its listing in this category)? Try this one! Top achievers win certificates and medals and can apply for several cash prizes. Registration through March 1, exam is given in April. Registration packets can be downloaded from the website.

National French Contest

Grades 1–12. Small fee for each child entered.

Le Grand Concours, PO Box 32030, Sarasota, FL 34239. www.frenchteachers.org/concours.

There are exams (listening, oral, and reading) at all levels, for beginners to very advanced, with good outlines showing exactly what is expected at each stage. Regional and national recognition. Submission deadlines: Grades 1–6, late February to early March; Grades 7–12, early to mid-March. Must order tests at some point before then.

National German Examination

Grades 9–12. $4 per student.

American Association of Teachers of German, 112 Haddontowne Court No. 104, Cherry Hill, NJ 08034. (856) 795-5553. www.aatg.org/testing.htm.

Year 2004 is the 33rd year for this exam. Test is administered from early December to late January. Over 25,000 participants in 2003. Winners must be in 90th or higher percentile and may not be German. Prize is a month-long trip to Germany. Various cash, book, T-shirt, and other prizes.

National Greek Examination

Grades 9–college. $3 per student.

The American Classical League, Miami University, 422 Wells Mill Drive, Oxford, Ohio 45056. (978) 749-9446. nge.aclclassics.org

High school and college students taking elementary, intermediate, or advanced Attic or Homeric Greek are eligible to take the National Greek Examination sponsored by the American Classical League and the National Junior Classical League. Exam is administered in March. Applications need to be submitted in January.

The usual sequence of exams is Beginning Attic (for high school students only), Intermediate Attic, Attic Prose (which you can take two years in succession), and Attic Tragedy. Review the syllabi to determine which exam to take.

Winners receive ribbons. High school seniors winning purple or blue ribbons can apply for a $1,000 scholarship.

To request copies of previous exams, syllabi, or an application, call (513) 529-7741.

National Latin Examination

All grades. $3 per student.

National Latin Exam, Mary Washington College, 1301 College Ave., Fredericksburg, VA 22401. (800) 459-9847. www.nle.org.

Written Latin exam. Sign-up deadline mid-January. The exam is given the second week in March. Twenty $1,000 scholarships are awarded for seniors who earn gold medals in Latin III or higher exams. Others get gold or silver medals and/or certificates. Exams offered: Intro to Latin, Latin I, Latin II, Latin III-IV Prose, Latin III-IV Poetry, and Latin V-VI.

National Mythology Exam

Grades 3–9. Modest fee per student.

The American Classical League, Miami University, Oxford, OH 45056-1694. (513) 529-7741. www.etclassics.org.

This exam focuses mostly on Greek myths (using the wonderfully illustrated D'Aulaires books of Greek Myths for most of the required readings),

with additional sets of questions for grades 6 to 9 on specific chapters of the Iliad, Odyssey, Aeneid, and a selection of African myths and American Indian myths. This group also sponsors the National Latin Exam. Can be done individually at home or (more fun!) as a homeschool group (how about having everyone come dressed up as a favorite character from a myth?).

Other Individual Contests

The American Legion Oratorical Contest

Grades 9–12.

The American Legion, Box 1055, Indianapolis, IN 46206. (317) 630-1200. www.legion.org. Select "Programs and Events."

National oratorical contest. Local contests sometime between January 1 and March 12. Orations must be about the US Constitution.

Discover Card Tribute Award Program

Grade 11.

American Association of School Administrators, 801 N Quincy St., Suite 700, Arlington, VA 22203-1730. (703) 875-0708. www.aasa.org/discover.htm.

A scholarship award program, based on special talents, leadership, obstacles overcome, unique endeavors, and community service. State and national level scholarship awards. Deadline for applications: mid January. Applications for 2005 will be available March 1.

International Jugglers Association

All ages. Fee to attend the convention, no additional fee for competing.

International Jugglers' Association, PO Box 112550, Carrollton TX 75011-2550. 415-596-3307. www.juggle.org.

Hosts a regular "Juggling Festival," with many competitive events like combat juggling, joggling, 3-Ball Simon Says, and more, plus world-renowned competitions for overall performance. Small prizes, but lots of fun.

International Whistlers Convention

All ages. No fee.
International Whistlers Convention, Box 758, Louisburg , NC 27549. (919) 496-4771. www.whistlingiwc.com.

Whistling contests at convention. Always in Louisburg, NC, in April.

National Chess Competitions

All grades.
United States Chess Federation, 3054 U.S. Route 9W, New Windsor, NY 12553. (845) 562-8350. www.uschess.org.

Rise through well-defined ranks of chess mastery by competing in local, state, national and international competitions.

National Horticultural Contests

Ages 22 and below.
National Junior Horticultural Association, 1424 North Eighth Street, Durant, OK 74701. www.njha.org.

Numerous contests for lovers of plants and flowers.

National Model Rocketry Contest

All grades.
National Association of Rocketry, Box 177, Altoona, WI 54720. (800) 262-4872. www.nar.org.

Model rocketry contests. Must join NAR to compete. Signup is generally in July or August.

Team Competitions

In this context, "team" may mean either that you compete as a team, or that you must assemble a group to hold your own first-rung local competition, from which winners will be chosen to compete at higher levels.

American Mathematics Competitions

Grades 7–12. Registration fee, $35.
MAA American Mathematics Competitions, Attn: AMC 8 Registration, P.O. Box 81606, Lincoln, NE 68501-1606. (800) 527-3690. www.unl.edu/amc.

Homeschool groups are welcome to register for these challenging annual multiple-choice test competitions. Junior high and senior levels, state and national recognition.

American Statistical Association Competition

Grades K–12. No fee.
American Statistical Association, 1429 Duke St., Alexandria VA 22314-3402. (402) 472-2257. www.amstat.org/education/poster1.html.

The team version of this competition. (See listing under "Math Contests for Individuals on page 600.) Create an original statistical research project or poster. The project must involve two to six students. Deadline April.

FIRST LEGO League

Ages 9–14. Average cost for a new team to compete is $600. Average cost for returning team is $340. Most goes to robotic building supplies.
FIRST LEGO League, 200 Bedford St., Manchester, NH 03101. (800) 871-8326. www.firstlegoleague.org.

"Sports for the mind." Each fall, FLL announces its yearly challenge. This is a topic related to "a current scientific or technological problem facing the world." Your team of 7 to 10 children with one or two adult coaches has eight weeks to build, program, and test your robot to make sure it can complete the challenge mission. Local and state tournaments. Registration opens in May. Challenge announced in September. Local and state tournaments in December.

MathCounts Math Competition

Grades 7 and 8. $80 per team.
MathCounts Registration, PO Box 441, Annapolis Junction, MD 20701. (703) 684-2828. mathcounts.org.

Junior high level math competition, involving full-year coaching program plus regional, state and national competitions. A team is four students chosen from your school or homeschool group. Great coaching materials available. MathCounts is also sponsoring an ongoing project of encouraging students (both junior high and MathCounts alumni) to send in original math word problems for possible inclusion in future books of sample problems for their excellent coaching program. Registration date differs by state. The program starts at the beginning of the school year.

Mathematical Olympiads for Elementary & Middle Schools

Grades 4–6 and 7–8. Registration fee, $85 per team.
Math Olympiads, 2154 Bellmore Avenue, Bellmore, NY 11710-5645. (866)781-2411 www.moems.org.

A broadening yearlong program introducing kids to non-routine problems that really make kids think. Homeschoolers very welcome. Contest begins at the beginning of each school year. Two divisions: grades 4–6 and 7–8.

National Geographic Society Geography Bee

Grades 4–8. Fee: $50/school.
National Geographic Society, 1145 17th ST NW, Washington DC 20036-4688. (202) 828-6659. www.nationalgeographic.com/ geographybee.

Follow links to get to the Geo Bee—sample questions for kids online!

An oral bee that tests a wide range of geography and current events knowledge—way beyond dreary states and capitals. Cost: $50 per "school"—and for homeschoolers this means a *minimum* of six students from grades four through eight taking part together at your local bee. Local winner takes written test to see about qualifying for one of the 100 spots at the state level bee. State winner advances to nationals, and homeschoolers have made it to these levels. Homeschoolers have won three times in the last five years—David Biehl in 1999, Calvin McCarter in 2002, and James Williams in 2003!

The 10 top finalists get $500 apiece, and the top three divide $50,000 in scholarship money. Finals are televised and webcast, with *Jeopardy!* host Alex Trebek moderating. Registration deadline for your homeschool group is usually mid-October.

National History Day Competition

Grades 6–12. Fees at each level.
University of MD, 0119 Cecil Hall, College Park, MD 20742. (301) 314-9739. www.nationalhistoryday.org.

History project competition. Student research projects, papers, or performances related to a yearly broad history theme (students are very free to pick whatever specific topic they want, as long as they can show how it relates to the broad theme). Students are encouraged to use primary resource materials wherever possible. Excellent student guide book available. Regional competition that advances to state and national levels. Starts at the beginning of each school year. Can be done as team project. Fees vary with region.

National High School Mock Trial Championship

Grades 9–12.
www.nationalmocktrial.org.

Pretend you are lawyers and try a case according to courtroom rules of evidence. That's a "mock trial."

In 2002 a homeschool team won the National High School Mock Trial Championship. That year teams from 42 states and two US territories competed. The same homeschool repeated their win in 2003.

What becomes of kids who do well in mock trial competition? A law career may beckon. One homeschooled winner is now an associate with a law firm. HSLDA also informs us that one of their former interns, Nathaniel Goggans, who has now completed law school, was a member in the past of a mock trial team.

National Homeschool Speech and Debate League

Ages 12 to 18.
National Christian Forensics and Communications Association, NCF-CA Corporate Office, P.O. Box 212, Mountlake Terrace, WA 98043 – 0212 (615) 498-6596, www.ncfca.org. CLick on local contact, then email your local director to find league nearest you.

Speech and debate competitions just for homeschoolers. Formerly run by HSLDA, now by this group.

National LifeSmarts Competition

Grades 9–12. No fee.
LifeSmarts, c/o National Consumers League, 1701 K Street NW, Washington, DC 20006. (202) 835-3323. www.lifesmarts.org

The National LifeSmarts competition, started by the Coalition for Consumer Education in 1994, is designed to educate students about consumer rights relating to health and safety, environment, government, economics, personal finance, and technology. Competition is based on answering questions on those topics. Winning teams can advance from district, to state, to regional, to national competitions. A homeschool team took third place nationally in 2002. According to the website, "the regional and national competitions are generally held in April in a major city." In-person competition not available in every state. Internet-based competition available for all states.

National Reading Incentive Program

Grades K–6. No fee.
National Reading Incentive Program, (800) 4-BOOK-IT. PO Box 2999, Wichita, KS 67201. www.bookitprogram.com.

An easy-to-organize group activity. Each family sets individual goals for reading each month, and kids win coupons for free pizzas. If everyone in your group meets their goals, you can have a group pizza party at the end of the year. Great geography and reading resource booklet. Mid-June registration date each year.

Odyssey of the Mind

Grades K–college. $135 signup for entire homeschool group.
Odyssey of the Mind, c/o Creative Competitions, 1325 Rt. 130 S., Suite F, Gloucester City, NJ 08030. (856) 456-7776. www.odysseyofthemind.com.

Odyssey of the Mind is in its 25th year. Problem-solving contests. Seven members per team. Solve five problems in the time before the contest and present the results at the contest. Finals are held on a college campus. Fall deadline.

Rockets for Schools Contest

Grades 6–12. Level 1 team fee, $400. Level 2, $530.
Great Lakes Space Port Education Foundation, Inc., Rockets for Schools, PO Box 684, Sheboygan, WI 53082-0684, (920)458-6299. www.rockets4schools.org.

Build your own rocket! Team of 10 or less students and an adult advisor builds a rocket to launch at the competition, where an actual astronaut will appear. No previously flown rockets are allowed. "Awards are given to Student Rocket Teams for fit and finish, payload, displays, presentations and team spirit." A homeschool team won this in 2002. February application deadline, May competition.

Scripps Howard National Spelling Bee

Grades 1–8.
Scripps Howard National Spelling Bee, 312 Walnut St., 28th Floor, Cincinnati, OH 45202. (800) 672-9673. www.spellingbee.com.

Have a local spelling bee, then send your top three kids to regionals sponsored by large city newspapers, and maybe make it to the state or national level. Contact your local homeschool group in July or August to set up your bee. Homeschooler Rebecca Sealfon won the Bee in 1998; homeschoolers swept all three top places in 2000! First prize is $10,000 plus a cornucopia of smaller prizes.

Space Day

Grades 4–6 and 7–8.
SPACE DAY, 6801 Rockledge Drive, Mailpoint 178, Bethesda, MD 20817. (301) 897-6282. www.spaceday.com.

Challenger Center for Space Science Education provides Space Day with its annual Design Challenges for for teams made up of kids in grades 4–6 and 7–8. Challenges are based on national science standards, and involve solving problems such as astronauts may face.

Even if you don't plan to enter the contest, be aware that online lesson plans, innovative classroom activities and resources are available on the Space Day site. These tools are designed to inspire students about the wonders of the universe while underscoring the importance of math, science, and technology.

The deadline for submitting Space Day Design Challenge solutions is March. The earlier you form your team and register, the longer you'll have to work on your design challenge!

ThinkQuest

Ages 12–19. No fee.
Advanced Network and Services, 200 Business Park Drive, Suite 307, Armonk, NY 10504. (914) 765-1100. www.thinkquest.org.

Website-building contest with a team of 2–3 people. Start working on your project anytime and finish by the submission deadline (February 29 in 2004). One to three finalists and their coach in each of five categories will re-

ceive cash awards/scholarships from $5,000–$25,000. Scuttlebutt says "technical" sites (e.g., "how to program" and other geek topics) never win. Wish we'd known that before our daughter Sarah spent all her spare time for a year on this competition, only to earn Honorable Mention. Registration opens in October.

Individual Awards

These aren't really "contests," but they do provide a great way to challenge yourself and possibly to earn brownie points on your college application.

Congressional Awards

Ages 14 to 23.
The Congressional Award Foundation, PO Box 77440, Washington, DC 20013. (202)226-0130. To request a brochure, call 1-888-80-AWARD. information@congressionalaward.org. www.congressionalaward.org/congress. Click on the map to find your contact person.

Did you know your child could win a bronze, silver, or gold medal, personally presented by your congressman? These are the *only* medals civilians can win from Congress, actually!

When considering who to admit and who to shower with scholarship money, colleges love to see these awards on transcripts.

To earn the award, your student must have set and achieved goals in these four areas: expedition/exploration (this means a one-time trip that demonstrates certain character goals), personal development, voluntary public service, and physical fitness. Goals are achieved by putting in a certain number of hours in all four areas, doing activities consistent with

the guidelines of the program. Hours earned at one level (e.g., bronze) can carry over toward the next level. "Advisors" and "validators" are required to make sure everything is kosher. The student sends a Record Book in to the program, showing what was accomplished and signed by the validator(s).

President's Physical Fitness Challenge

Ages 6–17.
The President's Challenge Physical Activity and Fitness Awards Program, 400 E. Seventh St., Bloomington, IN 47405. (800) 258-8146. www.presidentschallenge.org.

Join over 65 million kids who have won patches and medals through this program since 1966. Depending on in what fitness percentile your child scores on various fitness tests, he or she could earn the Presidential Physical Fitness Award, the National Physical Fitness Award, the Participant Physical Fitness Award, or the Health Fitness Award.

Also available through this site: the President's Sports Fitness Awards. You log a specified amount of time in any of the included activities, mail in your log, and get a patch or certificate.

Mom and Dad, although you're too old for the Challenge, you can still go for awards via the Presidential Adult Active Lifestyle Award. It requires 30 minutes or more of fitness activities per day, and it doesn't all have to be done in one spurt. You can use a pedometer to measure 10,000 steps per day, if this works better for you. The kids' version of this one is the Presidential Active Lifestyle Award, which requires 60 minutes of fitness activities per day, which can be met via pedometer use.

What to Do If There's a Social Worker at Your Door

More and more frequently, homeschoolers are turned in on child abuse hotlines to social service agencies. Families who do not like homeschoolers can make an anonymous phone call to the child abuse hotline and fabricate abuse stories about homeschoolers. The social worker then has an obligation to investigate. Each state has a different policy for social workers, but generally they want to come into the family's home and speak with the children separately. To allow either of these to occur involves great risk to the family.

The homeschool parent should be very cautious when an individual identifies himself as a social worker. In fact, there are several tips that a family should follow:

Always get the business card of the social worker. This way, when you call the Home School Legal Defense Association, the HSLDA attorney will be able to contact the social worker on your behalf. If the situation is hostile, immediately call HSLDA and hand the phone out the door so an HSLDA lawyer can talk to the social worker. We have a 24-hour emergency number.

Find out the allegations. Do not fall for the frequently used tactic of the social worker who tells the unsuspecting victim that they can only give you the allegations after they have come into your home and spoken to your child separately. You generally have the right to know the allegations without allowing them in your home.

Never let the social worker in your house without a warrant or court order. All the cases that you have heard about where children are snatched from the home usually involve families waiving their Fourth Amendment right to be free from such searches and seizures by agreeing to

This appendix was originally written for *Practical Homeschooling* by HSLDA Senior Counsel Chris Klicka, who has successfully represented thousands of homeschool families threatened by prosecutors, social workers, and truant officers.

For further information on how to deal with social workers, we recommend Chris's book, *Home Schooling: The Right Choice,* which was written with the intention of informing homeschool parents of their rights in order to prevent them from becoming a statistic. Federal statistics have shown that up to 60 percent of children removed from homes, upon later review, should never have been removed. See the review on page 88.

THE RIGHT CHOICE
THE INCREDIBLE FAILURE OF PUBLIC EDUCATION AND THE RISING HOPE OF
HOME SCHOOLING
BY
CHRISTOPHER J. KLICKA

allow the social worker to come inside the home. A warrant requires "probable cause," which does not include an anonymous tip or a mere suspicion. This is guaranteed under the Fourth Amendment of the U.S. Constitution as interpreted by the courts. (In extremely rare situations, police may enter a home without a warrant if there are exigent circumstances, i.e., police are aware of immediate danger or harm to the child.)

However, in some instances, social workers or police threaten to use force to come into a home. If you encounter a situation which escalates to this level, record the conversation if at all possible, but be sure to inform the police officer or social worker that you are doing this. If entry is going to be made under duress you should say and do the following: "I am closing my front door, but it is unlocked. I will not physically prevent you from entering, and I will not physically resist you in any way. But you do not have my permission to enter. If you open my door and enter, you do so without my consent, and I will seek legal action for an illegal entry."

Never let the social worker talk to your children alone without a court order. On nearly every other incident, HSLDA has been able to keep the social worker away from the children. On a few occasions, social workers have been allowed to talk with children, particularly where severe allegations are involved. In these instances, an attorney, chosen by the parent, has been present. At other times, HSLDA had children stand by the door and greet the social worker, but not be subject to any questioning.

Tell the official that you will call back after you speak with your attorney. Call your attorney or HSLDA, if you are a member.

Ignore intimidations. Normally, social workers are trained to bluff. They will routinely threaten to acquire a court order, knowing full well that there is no evidence on which to secure an order. In 98 percent of the contacts that HSLDA handles, the threats turn out to be bluffs. However, it is always important to secure an attorney or HSLDA in these matters, since there are occasions where social workers are able to obtain a court order with flimsy evidence.

Offer to give the officials the following supporting evidence:

- A statement from your doctor, after he has examined your children, if the allegations involve some type of physical abuse.
- References from individuals who can vouch for your being good parents.
- Evidence of the legality of your homeschool program. If your homeschool is an issue, HSLDA attorneys routinely convince social workers of this aspect of an investigation.

Bring a tape recorder and/or witnesses to any subsequent meeting. Often times HSLDA will arrange a meeting between the social worker and the parents after preparing the parents on what to discuss and what not to discuss. The discussion at the meeting should be limited to the specific allegations, and you should avoid telling them about past events beyond what they know. Usually, anonymous tips are all they have to go on, which is not sufficient to take someone to court. What you give them can and will be used against you.

Inform your church, and put the investigation on your prayer chain. Over and over again, HSLDA has seen God deliver homeschoolers from this scary scenario.

Avoid potential situations that could lead to a child welfare investigation.

- Conduct public relations with your immediate neighbors and acquaintances regarding the legality and success of homeschooling.
- Do not spank children in public.
- Do not spank someone else's child unless they are close Christian friends.
- Avoid leaving young children at home alone.

In order for a social worker to get a warrant to come and enter a home and interview children separately, he is normally required, by both statute and the US Constitution, to prove that there is some "cause." This is a term that is synonymous with the term "probable cause." "Probable cause" or cause shown is reliable evidence that must be corroborated by other evidence if the tip is anonymous. In other words, an anonymous tip alone and mere suspicion is not enough for a social worker to obtain a warrant.

There have been some homeschooled families who have been faced with a warrant even though there was not probable cause. HSLDA has been able to overturn these in court so that the order to enter the home was never carried out. Home School Legal Defense Association is committed to guarantee legal defense for every member homeschooler who is being investigated by social workers, provided the allegations involve homeschooling. In instances when the allegations have nothing to do with homeschooling, HSLDA will routinely counsel most families on how to meet with the social worker and will talk to the social worker to try to resolve the situation. If it cannot be resolved, which it normally can be in most instances by HSLDA's involvement, the family is responsible for hiring their own attorney.

LATEST UPDATE: HSLDA is beginning to work with both the federal government and the states to reform the child welfare laws to guarantee more freedom for parents and better protection for their parental rights. Success was had in getting Congress to pass two critically needed child abuse welfare reform amendments in 2003. These require (1) that social workers tell the allegations at the first incident of contact with the family and (2) that all social workers be specifically trained in protecting the statutory and Constitutional rights of those they are investigating. However, if the implementation of this is left to the social worker bureaucracy in each state, the effectiveness of implementation is in doubt. HSLDA will be sending out Alerts to its members in various states where such legislation is drafted and submitted as a bill.

Meet the Reviewers

Irene Buntyn has been homeschooling her three children for nine years. She has an associate's degree in Sign Language interpreting and is currently working toward her bachelor's in Christian Education degree through Oral Roberts University. She conducts homeschooling workshops on curriculum, study skills, and language arts.

Charles & Betty Burger are homeschool parents from the Berkshire Hills of rural western Massachusetts. For many years, they reviewed homeschool books for Conservative Book Club. They are now Senior Editors for *Homeschooling Today*. The Burgers have homeschooled their eight children for 16 years.

Tammy Campbell is a homeschool mother of five children, four of whom are now grown. Tammy is a registered nurse who works in an emergency room. She is very active in her church and now also with the local deaf community.

 **Sharon Fooshe** attended Middle Tennessee State University. She is active in her church, where she started a tri-

level, weekly youth instruction program and a card program for shut-ins. She also plans and coordinates the church's youth summer camp. Shari has been homeschooling her three children for seven years. She and her husband, Michael, have been married 15 years and recently completed building their home in the woods of Tennessee.

 **Kristin Hernberg** began homeschooling in 1986. Each of her kids also attended school outside the home for a short time, so she's seen education "from both sides now." Two of her children are now in college and two more will enter shortly. Kristin has also helped lead a homeschool support group, and taught children from the slow to the gifted. She is currently enrolled in the Rochester Institute of Technology Physician Assistant Program.

Brad Kovach is a graduate of Indiana State University and a former copy editor for *Practical Homeschooling* and *Homeschool PC*. When we last heard from him, he was working as a news editor and photographer for the Topics Newspapers in Indianapolis, IN.

Renee Mathis has been homeschooling for 16 years. Her five children include two high school graduates. She teaches co-op classes in language arts, logic, and study skills; works part time at The Homeschool Store in Houston; and is a member and past leader of West Houston Home Educators. She and her family are members of Christ Church (PCA) in Katy, TX.

Kim O'Hara homeschooled her three kids, now aged 15, 19, and 24, for 12 years until they were ready to take over their own education. While homeschooling, she managed a homeschool bookstore in her home for two years and spent five years as the Articles Editor for *Home Education Magazine*. Currently, she is a freelance writer and editor, and teaches writing and math part-time at a Christian high school in Lacey, WA.

 **Marla Perry** lives with her husband and two teen boys in northern California. At the time she was writing for us, she said that homeschooling for the past nine years had been the best education; her history degree trailed in second place.

Bill Pride has been a homeschool dad for 24 years and did most of the layout on this book. He earned his B.S. in Mathematics from M.I.T. and his M.A. in Missions and M.Div. from Covenant Theological Seminary. For many years he has been the General Manager of Home Life, Inc., which publishes *Practical Homeschooling* magazine and the Homeschool World website. If there's anything scientific or mathematical Bill doesn't know, Mary has never discovered it.

 Joseph Pride, a National Merit Finalist, was a homeschooled student since he was born and has seen it all, from workbook work to many kinds of online academies. He helped out in the family business, Home Life, Inc., since he was five, doing everything from triple-folding piles of paper to editing *Practical Homeschooling* magazine and working for years on the book you're holding. Joseph is now in his third year at the United States Coast Guard Academy.

 Mary Pride is the mother of nine totally home-schooled children, ages 10 to 24, the publisher of *Practical Homeschooling* magazine, and the author of seven other books, not counting editions of the *Big Book of Home Learning*. Mary holds a BS in Electrical Engineering and a M.Eng. in Computer Systems Engineering from Rensselaer Polytechnic Institute, and has worked with every kind of computer systems from the days of punched cards to the present.

 Sarah Pride, our family's second National Merit Finalist and an international math champion, was home-schooled from birth through the end of high school, and has seen just as many flavors of homeschool as Joseph has. Sarah also helps out in the family business, doing any job that needs to be done, from janitor duty to helping fact-check this book. She currently attends Patrick Henry College.

 Michele Schindler is a homeschool mom of five children, ages 7 to 18. She has homeschooled since her oldest child was a toddler. She is also currently pursuing a degree in chemical engineering.

 Teresa Schultz-Jones attended Marymount College and Boston University where she earned a BS in Math and Computer Science. She grew up in New York, North Carolina, Belgium, Georgia, and France. She worked as an engineer for 20 years while homeschooling until homeschooling became her full-time job. She has three children. One is a full-time college student; one attends college part-time and is homeschooled part-time, and the youngest is homeschooled. Teresa currently teaches two classes at her local homeschool co-op.

 Judy Scott is a home-schooling mom of two boys and one girl, ages 14, 11, and 13. She has reviewed software products for *Practical Homeschooling* for several years. Judy has homeschooled for eight years and is active in Christian music ministry in her home town and surrounding area.

Jo Dee Soles is a mother of four totally homeschooled children between the ages of 2 and 13. She is the owner of the EntrustedToUs.com website, which offers articles, a discussion board, and other information for homeschoolers.

 **Christopher Thorne** served for two years as editor of *Practical Homeschooling*. Holding a bachelor's degree in physics, a minor's in astronomy, and earning a master's in systems engineering, he currently programs flight simulators for Boeing, which proves it *does* take a rocket scientist to edit our magazine!

 MaryAnn Turner is a former *Practical Homeschooling* columnist. She stays busy organizing homeschool sports, doing adoption advocacy, and changing diapers. She has 11 children and two grandbabies with another one due any day. Maryann has homeschooled for 21 years.

 Michelle Van Loon, mother of three homeschool graduates, has a wide variety of freelance writing work to her credit including plays, magazine articles, and numerous short stories for children. Michelle is the author of *From Heart to Page: Journaling Through the Year for Young Writers,* available through Wordsmiths at www.jsgrammar.com. She continues to serve the homeschool community through her writing tutorial business, offering skill building and writing coaching for students in grades 5–12. Email her at mishvl@yahoo.com for more information about her course offerings.

Melissa Worcester is the mother of two boys and has homeschooled for five years. After a three-year sabbatical called "private Christian school" she is now homeschooling again. Melissa occasionally dabbles in editing and proofreading as well as web page design and has served as the newsletter editor and webmaster of a local chapter of the New York state homeschool group LEAH.

Find It Fast

Index

Speaking of fast . . . homeschooler Stephen Dickerson (9) of New Woodstock, NY, collected three medals in his first season of running in 5 km and 8 km road races. He placed first in his age group in the "Human Race," held in Syracuse, NY, and placed second in his age group in two of the regional races, the DeRuyter Tromp Town Run and the Madison Hall run. He shows remarkable speed and endurance for his age, regularly besting many adults (including his out-of-breath father!).

General Index

YOUR ADVOCATES FOR FAMILY & FREEDOM

IN THE COURT ROOM

Every parent has the right to home school. HSLDA is committed to advocating the two fundamental principles of this liberty: parental rights and religious freedom. Since 1983, we have represented our member families every step of the way—from consultation to correspondence and negotiation with local officials, and in court proceedings all the way through the appellate courts. HSLDA pays all litigation costs for home school cases it undertakes.

HSLDA is committed to advocating the fundamental right to home school.

ON CAPITOL HILL

HSLDA monitors federal legislation and maintains relationships with key Senate and House offices as well as with other family-friendly organizations through the National Center for Home Education. Founded by HSLDA's board of directors in 1990, the National Center for Home Education also directs the Congressional Action Program (CAP). A two-pronged effort, CAP trains DC-area home school families to lobby our federal representatives on issues affecting home educators and disseminates emergency legislative alerts to volunteers nationwide by fax and e-mail.

IN THE STATE LEGISLATURES

HSLDA helps state leaders by tracking state legislation, alerting them to bills which may affect home educators, and fighting harmful legislation. At the invitation of state home school organizations, HSLDA assists with drafting statutes to improve their home school legal environment.

IN THE MEDIA

HSLDA strives to present an engaging, informative, and dynamic picture of the home schooling community by providing the media with articulate and knowledgeable spokesmen on the subject of home schooling. Our press releases alert the media to significant court decisions, research findings, or achievements by home schooled students, and articles authored by HSLDA staff are published in newspapers and magazines across the country.

The media have many questions about home schooling—from the why and how of teaching to the political issues that motivate our grassroots activism.

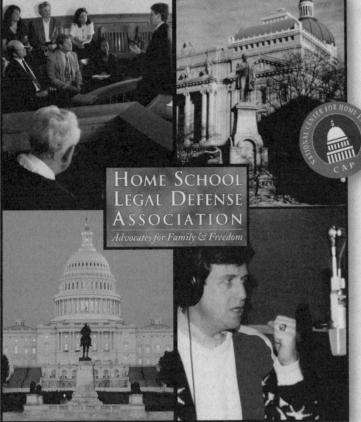

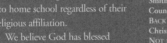

HOME SCHOOL LEGAL DEFENSE ASSOCIATION
Advocates for Family & Freedom

WHO ARE WE?

HSLDA is over 69,000 families, supported by more than 60 dedicated staff members, who have banded together to ensure that our rights are respected and our freedoms are protected.

Each of our eight lawyers has a demonstrated commitment to home education—seven are home schooling fathers; one is a home school graduate. We are committed to home education, not only as a legal right, but also as an educational opportunity and spiritual blessing. We are a Christian organization that advocates the right of all families to home school regardless of their religious affiliation.

We believe God has blessed HSLDA's efforts on behalf of the home schooling community. Our mission remains the same today as at our founding in 1983—to defend and advance the constitutional rights of parents to direct the education of their children and protect family freedoms.

HSLDA attorneys (L to R) FRONT ROW: Scott Woodruff; President J. Michael Smith; Chairman of the Board and General Counsel Michael P. Farris; Dewitt Black; BACK ROW: Darren Jones; Scott Somerville; Christopher Klicka NOT PICTURED: Jim Mason

Our national headquarters is in Purcellville, VA, about one hour west of Washington, DC.

HOW TO JOIN

For the low cost of $100 per year, your family may become part of HSLDA. Fill out the attached membership application form and return it to us with payment. Membership is effective upon date of approval.

If you are not currently home schooling, contact us to find out how you can still join the fight for families and freedom through our Friends of Home Schooling program.

MEMBER DISCOUNTS

■ *Group Discounts*—Members of organized groups participating in our group discount program may receive a $15 discount on their annual membership fee. Contact your local or state home school organization to see if it is a participating discount group.

■ *Special Discounts*—A $15 discount is also available to full-time pastors and missionaries, as well as active and retired military personnel. Contact our office for information on how to receive one of these special discounts.

HOME SCHOOL WITH CONFIDENCE!

WE'RE HERE FOR YOUR FAMILY

When you've got a problem that needs immediate attention, we're just a phone call away—24 hours a day. HSLDA enables our members to home school their children in peace and freedom.

WHAT KINDS OF CASES DO WE TAKE?

If a government official challenges your right to home school, HSLDA is there as your advocate, fully representing you at every stage of your legal proceedings.

Each year, thousands of member families receive legal consultation by letter and telephone, hundreds more are represented though negotiations with local officials, and dozens are represented in court proceedings. HSLDA also takes the offensive, filing actions to protect members against government intrusion and to establish legal precedent.

In child abuse and neglect investigations, we will provide members with initial consultation and full representation for the home schooling portion of the case. Once the home schooling issues are resolved, however, we do not guarantee representation.

In third-party custody cases (brought by a grandparent or other relative) HSLDA will provide members with defense for the portion of the case relating to home schooling. Although we do not take divorce or custody cases, we do provide a helpful packet of legal information and will, when there is an opportunity to set precedent, file an amicus brief on behalf of the home schooling parent.

HSLDA will take non-member cases for free if, in our sole judgment, the case could potentially affect the rights of all home schoolers.

YOUR INFORMATION SOURCE

- *Home School Court Report*—Our bimonthly newsletter updates you on what is going on in your state and around the nation, reporting on trends, issues, and items of general interest to home educators.
- www.hslda.org— Our website puts helpful resources, news, and information at your fingertips 24 hours a day.

- E-lerts—These timely messages keep state group leaders and members current on "hot" legislative issues that need their attention.
- Conference Speakers—Our attorneys and staff offer vision, encouragement, and helpful how-to-home-school information at state, national, and international conferences.
- Special Needs Coordinator—Counseling and helpful materials are available to members whose children face special challenges.

THE WISDOM OF EXPERIENCE

Nobody sets out to get into a legal battle, but it happens all the time—often because of what someone did not know about state requirements. Our membership coordinators, legal staff, and special needs coordinator can assist you in carefully planning and establishing your home school. We also offer an array of informative publications to help you.

ENCOURAGING HELP FOR HOME SCHOOL LEADERS

The National Center for Home Education, in addition to monitoring legislation, offers support to state and local support groups by providing information, regional and national leadership seminars, and networking.

A NEIGHBOR TO YOUR HOME SCHOOLING "NEIGHBOR"

Scripture says that we are to "love our neighbors as ourselves." Even if your family never needs to call HSLDA, your membership helps other home schooling families who desperately need us! Each year, thousands of families are able to confidently step into the "unknown" of home schooling because they know they've got friends—like you—standing beside them.

INTERNATIONAL HOME SCHOOLING

- Home Schooling in the Military— HSLDA is able to provide a complete range of services to American home schooling members in the military worldwide.
- American Citizens Residing in Other Countries—Although we cannot represent American families in foreign courts of law, we do offer assistance to American home schooling families living in other countries by advocating changes in public policy and writing letters on their behalf.